Lecture Notes in Computer Science 14904

The series Lecture Notes in Computer Science (LNCS), including its subseries Lecture Notes in Artificial Intelligence (LNAI) and Lecture Notes in Bioinformatics (LNBI), has established itself as a medium for the publication of new developments in computer science and information technology research, teaching, and education.

LNCS enjoys close cooperation with the computer science R & D community, the series counts many renowned academics among its volume editors and paper authors, and collaborates with prestigious societies. Its mission is to serve this international community by providing an invaluable service, mainly focused on the publication of conference and workshop proceedings and postproceedings. LNCS commenced publication in 1973.

Joseph K. Liu · Liqun Chen · Shi-Feng Sun ·
Xiaoning Liu
Editors

Provable and Practical Security

18th International Conference, ProvSec 2024
Gold Coast, QLD, Australia, September 25–27, 2024
Proceedings, Part II

Springer

Editors
Joseph K. Liu
Monash University
Clayton, VIC, Australia

Liqun Chen
University of Surrey
Guildford, Surrey, UK

Shi-Feng Sun
Shanghai Jiao Tong University
Shanghai, China

Xiaoning Liu
RMIT University
Melbourne, VIC, Australia

ISSN 0302-9743 ISSN 1611-3349 (electronic)
Lecture Notes in Computer Science
ISBN 978-981-96-0956-7 ISBN 978-981-96-0957-4 (eBook)
https://doi.org/10.1007/978-981-96-0957-4

This Springer imprint is published by the registered company Springer Nature Singapore Pte Ltd.
The registered company address is: 152 Beach Road, #21-01/04 Gateway East, Singapore 189721, Singapore

Preface

This volume contains the papers presented at ProvSec 2024: The 18th International Conference on Provable and Practical Security held on September 25–27, 2024 in Gold Coast, Australia.

ProvSec is an international conference on provable security in cryptography and practical security for information systems. ProvSec is designed to be a forum for theoreticians, system and application designers, protocol developers, and practitioners to discuss and express their views on current trends, challenges, and state-of-the-art solutions related to various issues in provable and practical security. Topics of interest include but are not limited to provable security for asymmetric cryptography, provable security for symmetric cryptography, provable security for physical attacks, privacy and anonymity technologies, secure cryptographic protocols and applications, security notions, approaches, and paradigms, leakage resilient cryptography, lattice-based cryptography and post-quantum cryptography, blockchain and cryptocurrency, IoT security, cloud security, and access control.

There were 79 submissions to ProvSec 2024. The committee decided to accept 26 full papers and 8 short papers. There were two keynote speakers: Man Ho Au from Hong Kong Polytechnic University and Kazue Sako from Waseda University.

We thank the Program Committee members and the external reviewers for their hard work reviewing the submissions. We thank the Organizing Committee, in particular, our General Co-Chairs, Leo Zhang, Guangdong Bai, and Xingliang Yuan, and all volunteers for their time and effort dedicated to arranging the conference.

September 2024

Joseph K. Liu
Liqun Chen

Organization

Program Chairs

Joseph K. Liu	Monash University, Australia
Liqun Chen	University of Surrey, UK

General Chairs

Leo Zhang	Griffith University, Australia
Guangdong Bai	University of Queensland, Australia
Xingliang Yuan	University of Melbourne, Australia

Program Committee

Elena Andreeva	TU Wien, Austria
Man Ho Au	Hong Kong Polytechnic University, China
Shi Bai	Florida Atlantic University, USA
Liqun Chen	University of Surrey, UK
Jie Chen	East China Normal University, China
Yu Chen	Shandong University, China
Cheng-Kang Chu	Huawei, Singapore
Hui Cui	Monash University, Australia
Nada El Kassem	University of Surrey, UK
Keita Emura	Kanazawa University, Japan
Junqing Gong	East China Normal University, China
Guang Gong	University of Waterloo, Canada
Jinguang Han	Southeast University, China
Xinyi Huang	Hong Kong University of Science and Technology, China
Sabyasachi Karati	Indian Statistical Institute, India
Shabnam Kasra Kermanshahi	UNSW Canberra, Australia
Yang Li	University of Electro-Communications, Japan
Fagen Li	University of Electronic Science and Technology of China, China
Yannan Li	University of Wollongong, Australia
Joseph K. Liu	Monash University, Australia

Xiaoning Liu	RMIT University, Australia
Dongxi Liu	Data 61, Australia
Zhen Liu	Shanghai Jiao Tong University, China
Xingye Lu	Hong Kong Polytechnic University, China
Xianhui Lu	Chinese Academy of Sciences, China
Kirill Morozov	University of North Texas, USA
Khoa Nguyen	University of Wollongong, Australia
Baodong Qin	Xi'an University of Posts and Telecommunications, China
Olivier Sanders	Orange Labs, France
Daniel Slamanig	Universität der Bundeswehr München, Germany
Shi-Feng Sun	Shanghai Jiao Tong University, China
Willy Susilo	University of Wollongong, Australia
Koutarou Suzuki	Toyohashi University of Technology, Japan
Atsushi Takayasu	University of Tokyo, Japan
Yangguang Tian	University of Surrey, UK
Yuntao Wang	University of Electro-Communications, Japan
Lei Wang	Shanghai Jiao Tong University, China
Zhe Xia	Wuhan University of Technology, China
Peng Xu	Huazhong University of Science and Technology, China
Haiyang Xue	Hong Kong Polytechnic University, China
Guomin Yang	Singapore Management University, Singapore
Zuoxia Yu	University of Wollongong, Australia
Fangguo Zhang	Sun Yat-sen University, China
Mingwu Zhang	Hubei University of Technology, China
Lei Zhang	East China Normal University, China
Liang Zhao	Sichuan University, China

Publication Co-chairs

Shi-Feng Sun	Shanghai Jiao Tong University, China
Xiaoning Liu	RMIT University, Australia

Publicity Co-chairs

Cong Zuo	Beijing Institute of Technology, China
Shujie Cui	Monash University, Australia

Web Chair

Xiangwen Yang Monash University, Australia

Contents – Part II

Contents – Part I

Signature

Tight Security

Efficient Variants of TNT with BBB Security

Ritam Bhaumik[1(✉)], Wonseok Choi[2,3], Avijit Dutta[4,5], Cuauhtemoc Mancillas López[6], Hrithik Nandi[4,7], and Yaobin Shen[8]

[1] CRC, TII, Abu Dhabi, United Arab Emirates
bhaumik.ritam@gmail.com
[2] Purdue University, West Lafayette, IN, USA
choi935@purdue.edu
[3] Georgia Institute of Technology, Atlanta, GA, USA
[4] Institute for Advancing Intelligence (IAI), TCG CREST, Kolkata, India
[5] Academy of Scientific and Innovative Research (AcSIR), Ghaziabad, India
[6] CINVESTAV-IPN, Mexico City, Mexico
[7] Ramakrishna Mission Vivekananda Educational and Research Institute, Belur, India
[8] Xiamen University, Xiamen, China

Abstract. At EUROCRYPT'20, Bao et al. have shown that three-round cascading of LRW1 construction, which they dubbed as TNT, is a strong tweakable pseudorandom permutation that provably achieves $2n/3$-bit security bound. Jha et al. showed a birthday bound distinguishing attack on TNT and invalidated the proven security bound and proved a tight birthday bound security on the TNT construction in EUROCRYPT'24.

In a recent work, Datta et al. have shown that four round cascading of the LRW1 construction, which they dubbed as $\mathsf{CLRW1}^4$ is a strong tweakable pseudorandom permutation that provably achieves $3n/4$-bit security. In this paper, we propose a variant of the TNT construction, called b-TNT1, and proved its security up to $2^{3n/4}$ queries. However, unlike $\mathsf{CLRW1}^4$, b-TNT1 requires three block cipher calls along with a field multiplication. Besides, we also propose another variant of the TNT construction, called b-TNT2 and showed a similar security bound. Compared to b-TNT1, b-TNT2 requires four block cipher calls. Nevertheless, its execution of block cipher calls can be pipelined which makes it efficient over $\mathsf{CLRW1}^4$. We have also experimentally verified that both b-TNT1 and b-TNT2 outperform $\mathsf{CLRW1}^4$.

Keywords: Tweakable Block Cipher · Tweak-aNd-Tweak · Cascaded LRW1 · Beyond Birthday Bound Security · Mirror Theory · Expectation Method

1 Introduction

A tweakable block cipher is a rich cryptographic primitive that serves to introduce variability within the cipher's structure. A tweakable block cipher is defined

J. K. Liu et al. (Eds.): ProvSec 2024, LNCS 14904, pp. 3–22, 2025.
https://doi.org/10.1007/978-981-96-0957-4_1

as a family of permutations $\widetilde{\mathsf{E}} : \mathcal{K} \times \mathcal{T} \times \{0,1\}^n \to \{0,1\}^n$ indexed by secret key $k \in \mathcal{K}$ and public tweak $t \in \mathcal{T}$. A prototypical design of a tweakable block cipher originally appeared in the Hasty Pudding Cipher [43], where an extra input, known as "spice" served the role of a tweak besides the key and the plaintext, to a block cipher. The actual intention of spice is to introduce randomization in the choice of the permutation family. Later in [32,33], Liskov, Rivest, and Wagner formalized the design and referred to the primitive as a tweakable block cipher.

Tweakable block ciphers have received significant acceptance as a fundamental cryptographic object. Over the years, TBCs have found diverse applications, in designing of AE schemes, e.g., Deoxys [27], Romulus [36], and several other candidates of AE schemes [1,4,5,8,15,20,38,41]. TBC has also been extensively used in designing many AE candidates for NIST and CÆSAR competitions, including [16,22,25–27,44]. Besides, TBCs have also been used in designing wide block encryption modes [6,39], message authentication codes [8,9,11,24,35,37], hash functions [14,18,21], and pseudorandom functions [10].

LRW1 and LRW2, proposed by Liskov et al. [32], are the first examples of tweakable block ciphers, which are built from block ciphers assuming their strong pseudorandom permutation security. Over the years, a few variants of the LRW2 construction have been proposed in [7,34,42] which have been shown to be secure up to the birthday bound of the query complexity. Landecker et al. [31] showed that cascading two independent LRW2 constructions, called CLRW2, achieves security up to $2^{2n/3}$ queries. Subsequent works [29] have improved the bound of Landecker et al. [31] from $2n/3$ bits to $3n/4$ bits. Lampe and Seurin [30] generalized CLRW2 construction to the cascading of $r \geq 1$ LRW2 construction and proved that it achieves security up to $2^{rn/(r+2)}$ queries for even r. Although the bound approaches the optimal security with increasing r, it comes at the cost of increasing the number of block cipher keys and primitive calls linearly with r. Bao et al. [2] showed that the three-round cascading of the LRW1 construction, called TNT (an abbreviation of *"The Tweak-aNd-Tweak"*) achieves CCA security up to $2^{2n/3}$ queries.

$$\mathsf{TNT}_{K_1,K_2,K_3}[\mathsf{E}](T,M) \triangleq \mathsf{E}_{K_3}(T \oplus \mathsf{E}_{K_2}(T \oplus \mathsf{E}_{K_1}(M))).$$

Guo et al. [17] showed a tight $3n/4$-bit CPA security bound of the construction. Zhang et al. [45] studied the security analysis of the generalized r-round cascading of the LRW1 construction, called $\mathsf{CLRW1}^r$ and showed that it achieves CCA security up to $2^{(r-2)n/r}$ queries, with $r \geq 2$. Furthermore, when r is odd, the construction attains enhanced security for up to $2^{(r-1)n/(r+1)}$ queries.

Jha et al. [28] showed a birthday bound CCA distinguishing attack on TNT, invalidated the previously asserted security claim of the construction, and proved a tight birthday bound security of the TNT construction. Recently, Datta et al. [13] showed that four round cascading of the LRW1 construction, called $\mathsf{CLRW1}^4$, achieves CCA security up to $2^{3n/4}$ queries. In fact, this result is the first one that provably shows the minimal number of rounds required for cascading LRW1 construction to ensure beyond-birthday-bound security against all

CCA adversaries. We would like to mention that a parallel work of [13] also established a similar security bound of the construction [28].

1.1 Our Contribution

Birthday bound security of the TNT construction has rendered the designer to include one extra block cipher call in $\mathsf{CLRW1}^4$ construction to achieve beyond-birthday-bound security. However, this additional invocation of the block cipher comes at the cost of evaluating it for every query. Moreover, to accommodate the decryption query, one needs to invoke the decryption circuit of the extra block cipher for every distinct ciphertext. Besides, we cannot execute the additional block cipher call in parallel to the execution of the TNT construction, i.e., to evaluate E_{K_4}, one needs to wait for the output of TNT to become available.

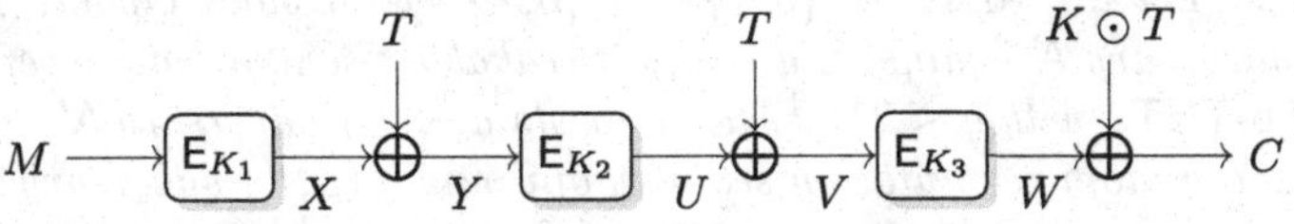

Fig. 1. b-TNT1 construction based on three block cipher calls and a field multiplication.

To address the above issues, we propose a simple fix to the TNT construction that does not require any extra block cipher call. In particular, we blind the output of the TNT construction by multiplying an n-bit secret key with the tweak and call the resulting construction b-TNT1. A pictorial description of the construction is shown in Fig. 1. Since the field multiplication is less costly than evaluating a block cipher, our proposed construction outperforms $\mathsf{CLRW1}^4$ in terms of throughput while retaining a similar level of security bound. Although b-TNT1 is better than $\mathsf{CLRW1}^4$ in terms of throughput, it incurs a larger hardware area compared to $\mathsf{CLRW1}^4$ due to the involvement of two different operations on the cipher. As a result, we propose b-TNT2, an another variant of the TNT construction, where we blind the output of the TNT construction with an encryption of the tweak. A pictorial description of the construction is shown in Fig. 2. Unlike $\mathsf{CLRW1}^4$, the last block cipher call of TNT can be executed parallel to that of the TNT construction. One can also pre-computes the last block cipher which becomes advantageous while making queries with same tweak.

In this paper, we have shown that both b-TNT1 and b-TNT2 provide security up to $2^{3n/4}$ queries. In particular, we have the following security results, the proofs of which are deferred to Sect. 3.

Theorem 1. *Let* $\mathsf{E} : \{0,1\}^\kappa \times \{0,1\}^n \to \{0,1\}^n$ *be a block cipher. Then, for any* (q,t) *adversary* A[1] *against the strong tweakable pseudorandom permutation*

[1] A (q,t) adversary A is one that makes a total of q queries to the oracle with running time of at most t steps.

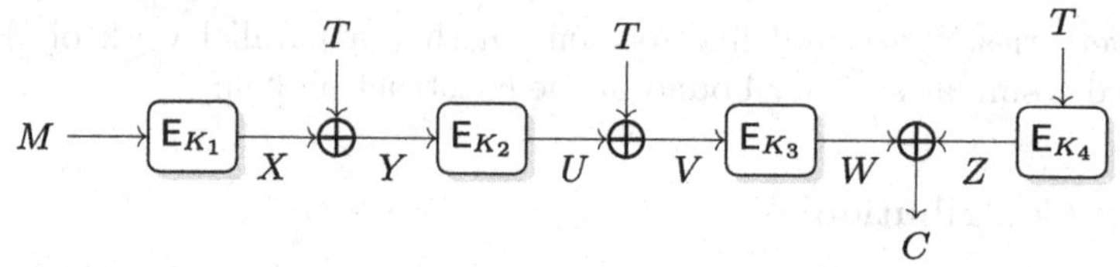

Fig. 2. b-TNT2 construcion based on four block cipher calls.

security of b-TNT1 *with* $q \leq 2^{3n/4}$, *there exists a* (q, t') *adversary* A′ *against the strong pseudorandom permutation security of* E, *where* $t' = t$, *such that*

$$\mathbf{Adv}_{\mathsf{b\text{-}TNT1}}^{\mathrm{STPRP}}(\mathsf{A}) \leq 3\mathbf{Adv}_{\mathsf{E}}^{\mathrm{SPRP}}(\mathsf{A}') + \frac{3q^2}{2^{2n}} + \frac{5q^{4/3}}{2^n} + \frac{45q^4}{2^{3n}} + \frac{1}{2^n}.$$

Theorem 2. *Let* $\mathsf{E} : \{0,1\}^\kappa \times \{0,1\}^n \to \{0,1\}^n$ *be a block cipher. Then, for any* (q, t) *adversary* A *against the strong tweakable pseudorandom permutation security of* b-TNT2 *with* $q \leq 2^{3n/4}$, *there exists a* (q, t') *adversary* A′ *against the strong pseudorandom permutation security of* E *and a* (μ, t') *adversary* B *against the pseudorandom permutation security of* E, *where* μ *denotes the number of distinct tweaks queried and* $t' = t$, *such that*

$$\mathbf{Adv}_{\mathsf{b\text{-}TNT2}}^{\mathrm{STPRP}}(\mathsf{A}) \leq 3\mathbf{Adv}_{\mathsf{E}}^{\mathrm{SPRP}}(\mathsf{A}') + \mathbf{Adv}_{\mathsf{E}}^{\mathrm{PRP}}(\mathsf{B}) + \frac{4q^2}{2^{2n}} + \frac{6q^{4/3}}{2^n} + \frac{53q^4}{2^{3n}}.$$

We have experimentally verified that both b-TNT1 and b-TNT2 perform better than the CLRW1[4] in terms of throughput while achieving a similar level of security bound.

2 Preliminaries

Notation. For $q \in \mathbb{N}$, we write $[q]$ to denote the set $\{1, \ldots, q\}$. For two natural numbers a and b such that $a \leq b$, we write $[a, b]$ to denote the set $\{a, a+1, \ldots, b\}$. For a natural number n, $\{0,1\}^n$ denotes the set of all binary strings of length n, and $\{0,1\}^*$ denotes the set of all binary strings of arbitrary length. For a natural number n and q, we write x^q to denote a q-tuple $(x_1, x_2, \ldots, x_q)$ where each $x_i \in \{0,1\}^n$. We write $\widehat{x^q}$ to denote the set $\{x_i : i \in [q]\}$. By an abuse of notation, we also write x^q to denote the multiset $\{x_i : i \in [q]\}$ and $\mu(x^q, x)$ denotes the multiplicity of $x \in x^q$. We also write μ_x to denote the multiplicity of $x \in x^q$, when the multiset x^q is understood from the context. For a set $\mathcal{I} \subseteq [q]$ and a q-tuple x^q, we write $x^{\mathcal{I}}$ to denote the sub-tuple $(x_i)_{i \in \mathcal{I}}$. We write a 2-ary tuple (x^q, y^q) to denote the q tuple $((x_1, y_1), (x_2, y_2), \ldots, (x_q, y_q))$, where each $x_i, y_i \in \{0,1\}^n$. We write $x \leftarrow y$ to denote the assignment of the variable y to x.

For a random variable X, $\mathsf{X} \leftarrow\!\!\$\ \{0,1\}^n$ denotes that X is sampled uniformly at random from $\{0,1\}^n$. For a tuple of random variables $(X_1, \ldots, X_q)$, we write $(X_1, \ldots, X_q) \leftarrow\!\!\$\ \{0,1\}^n$ to denote that each X_i is sampled uniformly from $\{0,1\}^n$

and independent to all other previously sampled random variables. We write $(X_1, \ldots, X_q) \xleftarrow{\text{wor}} \{0,1\}^n$ to denote that each X_i is sampled uniformly from $\{0,1\}^n \backslash \{X_1, \ldots, X_{i-1}\}$. The set of all permutations over $\{0,1\}^n$ is denoted as $\mathsf{Perm}(n)$. We say that a 2-ary tuple (x^q, y^q) is *permutation compatible*, denoted as $x^q \leftrightsquigarrow y^q$, if there exists at least one permutation $\mathsf{P} \in \mathsf{Perm}(n)$ such that for all $i \in [q]$, $x_i = x_j \Leftrightarrow y_i = y_j, i \neq j \in [q]$. Moreover, if (x^q, y^q) is not permutation compatible, then we denote it as $x^q \overset{\times}{\leftrightsquigarrow} y^q$. For three tuples $x^q = (x_1, x_2, \ldots, x_q)$, $y^q = (y_1, y_2, \ldots, y_q)$, and $\lambda^q = (\lambda_1, \lambda_2, \ldots, \lambda_q)$ of q n-bit elements, we write $x^q \oplus y^q = \lambda^q$, if for all $i \in [q]$, it holds that $x_i \oplus y_i = \lambda_i$. For integers $1 \le b \le a$, we write $(a)_b$ to denote $a(a-1)\ldots(a-b+1)$, where $(a)_0 = 1$ by convention.

2.1 (Tweakable) Block Cipher

Let $n, \kappa, t \in \mathbb{N}$ be three natural numbers. A *block cipher* $\mathsf{E} : \{0,1\}^\kappa \times \{0,1\}^n \to \{0,1\}^n$ is a function that takes as input a key $k \in \{0,1\}^\kappa$ and an n-bit string $x \in \{0,1\}^n$ and outputs an element $y \in \{0,1\}^n$ such that for each $k \in \{0,1\}^\kappa$, $\mathsf{E}(k, \cdot)$ is a bijective function from $\{0,1\}^n$ to $\{0,1\}^n$. A *tweakable block cipher* (TBC) is a mapping $\widetilde{\mathsf{E}} : \{0,1\}^\kappa \times \{0,1\}^t \times \{0,1\}^n \to \{0,1\}^n$, such that for all key $k \in \{0,1\}^\kappa$ and for all tweak $T \in \{0,1\}^t$, $\widetilde{\mathsf{E}}(k, T, \cdot)$ is a permutation over $\{0,1\}^n$. A *tweakable permutation* with tweak space $\{0,1\}^t$ and domain $\{0,1\}^n$ is a mapping $\widetilde{\mathsf{P}} : \{0,1\}^t \times \{0,1\}^n \to \{0,1\}^n$ such that for all tweak $T \in \{0,1\}^t$, $\widetilde{\mathsf{P}}(T, \cdot)$ is a permutation over $\{0,1\}^n$. We write $\mathsf{TP}(\{0,1\}^t, n)$ to denote the set of all tweakable permutations with tweak space $\{0,1\}^t$ and n-bit messages. We fix positive even integers n, κ (resp. t) to denote the *block size*, *key size* (resp. tweak size) of the block cipher (resp. tweakable block cipher) respectively in terms of number of bits.

2.2 Security Definition of (Tweakable) Block Cipher

Let $\widetilde{\mathsf{E}}$ be a tweakable block cipher and A be a non-trivial $(q, \mathtt{t})$ adaptive adversary with oracle access to a tweakable permutation and its inverse with tweak space $\{0,1\}^t$ and domain $\{0,1\}^n$. The advantage of A in breaking the strong tweakable pseudorandom permutation (STPRP) security of $\widetilde{\mathsf{E}}$ is defined as

$$\mathbf{Adv}_{\widetilde{\mathsf{E}}}^{\mathrm{STPRP}}(\mathsf{A}) \triangleq |\Pr[\mathsf{A}^{\widetilde{\mathsf{E}}_K(\cdot,\cdot), \widetilde{\mathsf{E}}_K^{-1}(\cdot,\cdot)} = 1] - \Pr[\mathsf{A}^{\widetilde{\mathsf{P}}(\cdot,\cdot), \widetilde{\mathsf{P}}^{-1}(\cdot,\cdot)} = 1]|, \qquad (1)$$

where the first probability is calculated over the randomness of $K \leftarrow\$ \{0,1\}^\kappa$ and the second probability is calculated over the randomness of $\widetilde{\mathsf{P}} \leftarrow\$ \mathsf{TP}(\{0,1\}^t, n)$. When the adversary is given access only to the tweakable permutation and not its inverse, then we say the tweakable pseudorandom permutation (TPRP) advantage of A against $\widetilde{\mathsf{E}}$. We say that $\widetilde{\mathsf{E}}$ is $(q, \mathtt{t}, \epsilon)$ secure if the maximum strong tweakable pseudorandom permutation advantage of $\widetilde{\mathsf{E}}$ is ϵ where the maximum is taken over all distinguishers A that makes a total of q queries to its oracle and runs for time at most $\mathtt{t}$. We assume throughout the paper the tweak size t

of the tweakable block cipher is equal to its block size n. When the tweak set is empty, then the notion of STPRP (resp. TPRP) boils down to the SPRP (resp. PRP) security.

2.3 Mirror Theory For Tweakable Random Permutations

Mirror theory fundamentally works for bounding the pseudorandomness of the sum-of-permutations [3,12,19,40] based constructions with respect to a random function. However, its traditional setup is not suited for bounding the pseudorandomness of tweakable block ciphers with respect to tweakable random permutation. Jha and Nandi [29] developed a variant of mirror theory result tailored for tweakable tweakable random permutations. We revisit their result below.

For a given system of linear equations $\mathcal{L}$, we associate an edge-labeled bipartite graph $\mathcal{L}(G) = (\mathcal{X} \cup \mathcal{Y}, \mathcal{E})$ with the labeling function L, an edge (x, y) with label λ is called an *isolated-edge* if the degree of both x and y is 1. We say that a component $\mathcal{C}$ is a *star* if $\xi_{\mathcal{C}} \geq 3$, where $\xi_{\mathcal{C}}$ denotes the number of vertices in component $\mathcal{C}$, and there exists an unique vertex, called *center vertex*, with degree $\xi_{\mathcal{C}} - 1$ and all the other vertices have degree exactly 1. A component $\mathcal{C}$ is called $\mathcal{X}$-type (resp. $\mathcal{Y}$-type) if the center vertex of the component $\mathcal{C}$ lies in $\mathcal{X}$ (resp. $\mathcal{Y}$).

For a given system of linear equations $\mathcal{L}$ and its corresponding associated equation graph $\mathcal{L}(G)$, we write α (resp. β, γ) to denote the number of isolated edges (resp. number of components of $\mathcal{X}$-type and number of components of $\mathcal{Y}$-type). Similarly, q_1 denotes the number of equations such that none of its variables have collided with any other variables. q_2 denotes the number of equations of $\mathcal{X}$-type and q_3 denotes the number of equations of $\mathcal{Y}$-type. Note that $\alpha = q_1$. Following result from [29] has given a lower bound on the number of solutions for a given system of linear equations $\mathcal{L}$ such that X_i' values are pairwise distinct and Y_i' values are pairwise distinct.

Theorem 3. *Let $\mathcal{L}$ be a system of the linear equation as defined above with $q \leq 2^{n-2}$ and any component of $\mathcal{L}(G)$ have at most 2^{n-1} edge. Then the number of tuple of solution $(x_1, x_2, \ldots, x_{q_X}, y_1, y_2, \ldots, y_{q_Y})$ of $\mathcal{L}$, denoted by $h(q)$, where $x_i \neq x_j$ and $y_i \neq y_j$, for all $i \neq j$, satisfies*

$$h(q) \geq \left(1 - \frac{13q^4}{2^{3n}} - \frac{2q^2}{2^{2n}} - \left(\sum_{i=\alpha+1}^{\beta+\gamma} \zeta_i^2\right) \frac{4q^2}{2^{2n}}\right) \times \frac{(2^n)_{q_1+\beta+q_3} \times (2^n)_{q_1+q_2+\gamma}}{\prod_{\lambda \in \lambda^q} (2^n)_{\mu_\lambda}} \quad (2)$$

where ζ_i denote the number of edge in i-th component $\forall i \in [\alpha + \beta + \gamma]$.

3 Proof of Theorem 1 and Theorem 2

This section is devoted to establishing the security bound as demonstrated in Theorem 1 and Theorem 2. Due to the structural similarity of the proofs of Theorem 1 and Theorem 2, we present a combined proof of both the results.

However, we will explicitly highlight the differences between the proofs of the two constructions.

From now onwards we use the notation b-TNTd, where d = 1 stands for the construction b-TNT1 and d = 2 denotes the construction b-TNT2. Initially, we replace the three independently keyed block ciphers, $\mathsf{E}_{K_1}, \mathsf{E}_{K_2}$ and E_{K_3}, used in the constructions with three independently sampled n-bit random permutations, $\mathsf{P}_1, \mathsf{P}_2$ and P_3 (for b-TNT2 fourth block cipher E_{K_4} will be replaced by another independently sampled n-bit random permutation P_4). This substitution comes at the cost of the strong pseudorandom permutation advantage of the underlying block cipher (replacement of E_{K_4} comes at the cost of pseudorandom permutation advantage). We denote the resulting construction as b-TNTd*. Therefore, we have

$$\mathbf{Adv}^{\mathrm{STPRP}}_{\text{b-TNTd}}(\mathsf{A}) \leq \begin{cases} 3\mathbf{Adv}^{\mathrm{SPRP}}_{\mathsf{E}}(\mathsf{A}') + \overbrace{\mathbf{Adv}^{\mathrm{STPRP}}_{\text{b-TNTd*}}(\mathsf{A})}^{\delta^*}, & \text{for d} = 1 \\ 3\mathbf{Adv}^{\mathrm{SPRP}}_{\mathsf{E}}(\mathsf{A}') + \mathbf{Adv}^{\mathrm{PRP}}_{\mathsf{E}}(\mathsf{B}) + \underbrace{\mathbf{Adv}^{\mathrm{STPRP}}_{\text{b-TNTd*}}(\mathsf{A})}_{\delta^*}, & \text{for d} = 2 \end{cases}$$

where A' is a (q, t') adversary such that $t' = t$. Our goal is now to upper bound δ^*. Note that, we have

$$\delta^* \leq \max_{\mathsf{A}} \left| \Pr[\mathsf{A}^{\text{b-TNTd*},(\text{b-TNTd*})^{-1}} = 1] - \Pr[\mathsf{A}^{\widetilde{\mathsf{P}},\widetilde{\mathsf{P}}^{-1}} = 1] \right|,$$

where $\widetilde{\mathsf{P}} \leftarrow\!\!\$\ \mathsf{TP}(\{0,1\}^n, n)$. This formulation of the problem now allows us to use the Expectation Method [23].

3.1 Description of the Ideal World

The ideal world consists of two stages: in the first stage, which we call the *online stage*, the ideal world simulates a random tweakable permutation $\widetilde{P}$, i.e., for each encryption query (M, T), it returns $\widetilde{\mathsf{P}}(M, T)$. Similarly, for each decryption query (C, T), it returns $\widetilde{\mathsf{P}}^{-1}(C, T)$. Since the real world releases some additional information, the ideal world must generate these values as well. The ideal transcript random variable X_{id} is a 9-ary q-tuple

$$(M^q, T^q, C^q, X^q, Y^q, U^q, V^q, W^q, K(\text{for d} = 1)/Z^q(\text{for d} = 2))$$

defined below. However, the probability distribution of these additional random variables would be determined from their definitions. The initial transcript consists of (M^q, T^q, C^q), where for all $i \in [q]$, T_i is the i-th tweak value, M_i is the i-th plaintext value, and C_i is the i-th ciphertext value. Once the query-response phase is over, the next stage of the ideal world begins, which we call the *offline stage*. In the offline stage, the ideal world samples the intermediate random variables as follows: let us define the set

$$\mathbb{M}(M^q) = \{x : x = M_i, i \in [q]\}.$$

Let us assume that $m := |\mathbb{M}(M^q)|$ be the number of distinct plaintexts. Then, it samples

$$X_{x_1}, X_{x_2}, \ldots, X_{x_m} \xleftarrow{\text{wor}} \{0,1\}^n,$$

where $(x_1, x_2, \ldots, x_m)$ is an arbitrary ordering of the set $\mathbb{M}(M^q)$. For $\mathsf{d} = 1$ the ideal world samples a key $K \leftarrow\!\$ \{0,1\}^n$ independent over X_{x_i} and for $\mathsf{d} = 2$ it samples the intermediate random variables Z^q,

$$Z_{z_1}, Z_{z_2}, \ldots, Z_{z_t} \xleftarrow{\text{wor}} \{0,1\}^n,$$

where $(z_1, z_2, \ldots, z_t)$ is an arbitrary ordering of the set, $\mathbb{T}(T^q) = \{z : z = T_i, i \in [q]\}$. Let us assume that $t := |\mathbb{T}(T^q)|$ is the distinct number of tweaks. Moreover, Z_{z_j} is independently sampled with X_{x_i}. From these sampled random variables $(X_{x_1}, X_{x_2}, \ldots, X_{x_m})$, we define q-tuple X^q as follows: $X^q = (X_1, X_2, \ldots, X_q)$ such that $X_i = X_{M_i}$ and $Z^q = (Z_1, Z_2, \ldots, Z_q)$ such that $Z_i = Z_{T_i}$. Having defined q-tuple of random variables X^q, we define two q-tuples (Y^q, W^q) as follows: for each $i \in [q]$,

$$Y_i = X_i \oplus T_i, \; W_i = \begin{cases} C_i \oplus (K \odot T_i), & \text{for } \mathsf{d} = 1, \\ Z_i \oplus C_i, & \text{for } \mathsf{d} = 2. \end{cases}$$

Given this partial transcript, $\mathsf{X}'_{\text{id}} = (M^q, T^q, C^q, X^q, Y^q, W^q, K \text{ or } Z^q)$, we wish to define whether the sampled value X^q and (K or Z^q) is good or bad. We say that a tuple $(X^q, K \text{ or } Z^q)$ is **bad** if one of the following predicates hold:

1. $\mathtt{Bad}_K$: $K = 0^n$ (This condition is only for $\mathsf{d} = 1$).
2. $\mathtt{Bad}_1$ (cycle of length 2): $\exists i, j \in [q]$ such that the following holds: $Y_i = Y_j, W_i = W_j$.
3. $\mathtt{Bad}_2$: $|\{(i,j) \in [q]^2 : i \neq j, Y_i = Y_j\}| \geq q^{2/3}$.
4. $\mathtt{Bad}_3$: $|\{(i,j) \in [q]^2 : i \neq j, W_i = W_j\}| \geq q^{2/3}$.
5. $\mathtt{Bad}_4$ (Y-W-Y path of length 4): $\exists i, j, k, l \in [q]$ such that the following holds: $Y_i = Y_j, W_j = W_k, Y_k = Y_l$.
6. $\mathtt{Bad}_5$ (W-Y-W path of length 4): $\exists i, j, k, l \in [q]$ such that the following holds: $W_i = W_j, Y_j = Y_k, W_k = W_l$.

If the sampled tuple $(X^q, K \text{ or } Z^q)$ is bad, then U^q and V^q values are sampled degenerately, i.e., $U_i = V_i = 0$ for all $i \in [q]$. That is, we sample without maintaining any specific conditions, which may lead to inconsistencies. However, if the sampled tuple $(X^q, K \text{ or } Z^q)$ is good, then we study a graph associated with (Y^q, W^q). In particular, we consider the random transcript graph $\mathcal{G}(Y^q, W^q)$ defined as follows: the set of vertices of the graph is $Y^q \sqcup W^q$. Moreover, we put a labeled edge between Y_i and W_i with label T_i. For two distinct indices $i \neq j$, if $Y_i = Y_j$, then we merge the corresponding vertices. Similarly, for two distinct indices, if $W_i = W_j$, then we merge the corresponding vertices. Therefore, the random transcript graph $\mathcal{G}(Y^q, W^q)$ is a labeled bipartite graph. Now, we have the following lemma which asserts that the random transcript graph $\mathcal{G}(Y^q, W^q)$ is **nice** if $(X^q, K \text{ or } Z^q)$ is good.

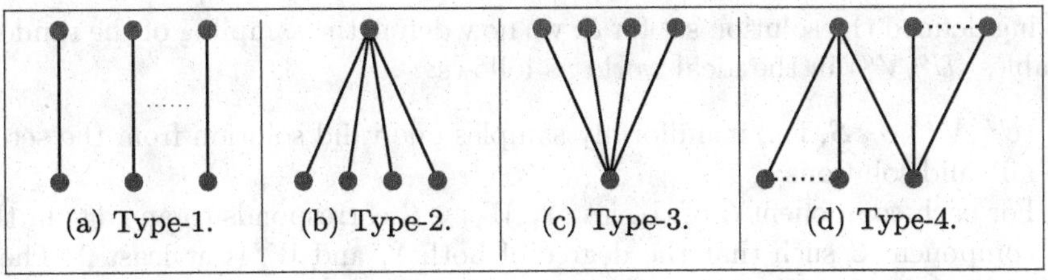

Fig. 3. Type-1 is a graph of isolated edges, and the maximum path length of a Type-1 graph is one. Type-2 is a star graph with Y being the centered vertex, and Type-3 is also a star graph with W being the centered vertex. The maximum path length of Type-2 and Type-3 graphs is two. Type-4 is a connected graph that is not an isolated edge or a star. It can have degree 2 vertices in both Y and W. The maximum path length of the Type-4 graph is three.

Lemma 1. *The transcript graph $\mathcal{G} := \mathcal{G}(Y^q, W^q)$ generated by a good tuple $(X^q, K$ or $Z^q)$ is nice, i.e., it satisfies the following properties:*

- *$\mathcal{G}$ is simple, acyclic, and has no isolated vertices with no adjacent edges such that their labels are equal.*
- *maximum component size of $\mathcal{G}$ is $2q^{2/3}$ and every component of G is either a star graph, isolated edges, or contains a path of length 3.*

Proof of this lemma is included in the the full version of this paper. We depict the type of subgraphs generated from a good tuple $(X^q, K$ or $Z^q)$ in Fig. 3. After describing the potential structure of random transcript graphs, we define the sampling of (U^q, V^q) when $(X^q, K$ or $Z^q)$ is good. Referring to Fig. 3, we observe four types of possible random transcript graphs for a good tuple $(X^q, K$ or $Z^q)$, denoted as $\mathcal{G}_1, \mathcal{G}_2, \mathcal{G}_3$, and $\mathcal{G}_4$ respectively, where $\mathcal{G}_i$ is a Type-i graph, for $i \in [4]$.

- $\mathcal{G}_1$ is the union of isolated edges.
- $\mathcal{G}_2$ is the union of star components containing Y as centered vertex.
- $\mathcal{G}_3$ is the union of star components containing W as centered vertex.
- $\mathcal{G}_4$ is the union of components containing at least one path of length three.

Therefore, we define for each $b \in [4]$,

$$\mathcal{I}_b = \{i \in [q] : (Y_i, W_i) \in \mathcal{G}_b\}.$$

Since, the collection of sets $\mathcal{I}_b$ are disjoint, we have $[q] = \mathcal{I}_1 \sqcup \mathcal{I}_2 \sqcup \mathcal{I}_3 \sqcup \mathcal{I}_4$. We define $\mathcal{I} = \mathcal{I}_1 \sqcup \mathcal{I}_2 \sqcup \mathcal{I}_3$. Now, we consider the following system of equations

$$\mathcal{E} = \{U_i \oplus V_i = T_i : i \in \mathcal{I}\},$$

where $U_i = U_j$ if and only if $Y_i = Y_j$. Similarly, $V_i = V_j$ if and only of $W_i = W_j$ for all $i \neq j \in [q]$. Thus, the solution set of $\mathcal{E}$ is

$$\mathcal{S} = \{(u^{\mathcal{I}}, v^{\mathcal{I}}) : u^{\mathcal{I}} \leftrightsquigarrow Y^{\mathcal{I}}, v^{\mathcal{I}} \leftrightsquigarrow W^{\mathcal{I}}, u^{\mathcal{I}} \oplus v^{\mathcal{I}} = T^{\mathcal{I}}\}.$$

Having defined the solution set for $\mathcal{E}$, we now define the sampling of the random variables (U^q, V^q) in the ideal world as follows:

(i) $(U^{\mathcal{I}}, V^{\mathcal{I}}) \leftarrow\!\$\, \mathcal{S}$, i.e., it uniformly samples one valid solution from the set of all valid solutions;
(ii) For each component $\mathcal{C}$ of $\mathcal{G}_4$, let $(Y_i, W_i) \in \mathcal{C}$ corresponds to an edge in the component $\mathcal{C}$ such that the degree of both Y_i and W_i is at least 2. Then, we sample $U_i \leftarrow\!\$\, \{0,1\}^n$ and set $V_i = U_i \oplus T_i$;
(iii) The final possibility is that for each edge $(Y_i, W_i) \in \mathcal{C}$ such that $(Y_i, W_i) \neq (Y_j, W_j)$, where $(Y_j, W_j) \in \mathcal{C}$. Suppose, $Y_i = Y_j$, then $U_i = U_j$ and $V_i = U_i \oplus T_i$. Similarly, if $W_i = W_j$, then $V_i = V_j$ and $U_i = V_i \oplus T_i$.

Therefore, we completely define the random variable represents the ideal world transcript as follows:

$$\mathsf{X}_{\mathsf{id}} = (M^q, T^q, C^q, X^q, Y^q, U^q, V^q, W^q, K(\text{for } \mathsf{d}=1)/Z^q(\text{for } \mathsf{d}=2)).$$

In this way, we achieve both the consistency of the equations in the form $\{U_i \oplus V_i = T_i\}$ and the permutation compatibility within each component of the graph $\mathcal{G}$ when the tuple $(X^q, K \text{ or } Z^q)$ is good. However, we need to anticipate collisions among U values or V values across different components of the random transcript graph $\mathcal{G}$, which we will discuss in detail in the next section.

3.2 Definition and Probability of Bad Transcripts

Given the description of the transcript random variable in the ideal world, we define the set of all attainable transcripts Ω as the set of all q tuples

$$\tau = (M^q, T^q, C^q, X^q, Y^q, U^q, V^q, W^q, K \text{ or } Z^q),$$

where $M^q, T^q, C^q, X^q, Y^q, U^q, V^q, W^q, Z^q \in (\{0,1\}^n)^q$, $K \in \{0,1\}^n$, $Y^q = X^q \oplus T^q$, $W^q = C^q \oplus (K \odot T^q)$ (for $\mathsf{d}=1$) or $W^q = Z^q \oplus C^q$ (for $\mathsf{d}=2$) and (M^q, T^q) is *tweakable permutation compatible* with (C^q, T^q). Now, we will discuss what specific events constitute a bad condition.

- Consider the event $Y^{\mathcal{I}} \overset{\times}{\leftrightsquigarrow} U^{\mathcal{I}}$ or $W^{\mathcal{I}} \overset{\times}{\leftrightsquigarrow} V^{\mathcal{I}}$ that occurs while sampling $(U^{\mathcal{I}}, V^{\mathcal{I}})$, where $\mathcal{I}$ encodes the edges that belongs to either Type-1 or Type-2 or Type-3 graphs. However, this condition cannot arise as we sample a valid solution from the set of all valid solutions $\mathcal{S}$;
- Due to the sampling of (U^q, V^q), it may so happen that $Y^q \overset{\times}{\leftrightsquigarrow} U^q$ or $W^q \overset{\times}{\leftrightsquigarrow} V^q$.

We define transcripts to be bad depending upon the characterization of the pair of q-tuples $(X^q, K \text{ or } Z^q)$. Following the ideal world description, we say that a pair of q-tuples $(X^q, K \text{ or } Z^q)$ is bad if and only if the following predicate is true:

$$\mathtt{Bad}_K \vee \mathtt{Bad}_1 \vee \mathtt{Bad}_2 \vee \mathtt{Bad}_3 \vee \mathtt{Bad}_4 \vee \mathtt{Bad}_5 \ (\mathtt{Bad}_K \text{ is only for } \mathsf{d}=1).$$

We say that a transcript τ is *tuple-induced* bad transcript if $(X^q, K \text{ or } Z^q)$ is bad, which we denote as

$$\mathsf{Bad} := \mathtt{Bad}_K \vee \mathtt{Bad}_1 \vee \mathtt{Bad}_2 \vee \mathtt{Bad}_3 \vee \mathtt{Bad}_4 \vee \mathtt{Bad}_5 \text{ } (\mathtt{Bad}_K \text{ is only for } \mathsf{d} = 1).$$

The other type of event that we need to discard, arises due to the bad sampling of (U^q, V^q) which causes permutation incompatibility, i.e., $Y^q \overset{\times}{\leftrightsquigarrow} U^q$ or $W^q \overset{\times}{\leftrightsquigarrow} V^q$. To bound such bad events, we need to enumerate all the conditions that results to the above inconsistencies. Note that, when the tuple $(X^q, K \text{ or } Z^q)$ is bad, then the transcript is trivially inconsistent as we sample (U^q, V^q) degenerately. Therefore, for a good tuple $(X^q, K \text{ or } Z^q)$, if $Y_i = Y_j$ or $W_i = W_j$, then we always have $U_i = U_j$ or $V_i = V_j$ respectively and hence in that case permutation inconsistencies won't arise. Therefore, we say that a transcript τ is *sampling induced* bad transcript if one of the following conditions hold: for $\alpha \in [4]$ and $\beta \in [\alpha, 4]$,

- $\mathtt{Ucoll}_{\alpha\beta}$: $\exists i \in \mathcal{I}_\alpha, j \in \mathcal{I}_\beta$ such that $Y_i \neq Y_j$ and $U_i = U_j$;
- $\mathtt{Vcoll}_{\alpha\beta}$: $\exists i \in \mathcal{I}_\alpha, j \in \mathcal{I}_\beta$ such that $W_i \neq W_j$ and $V_i = V_j$.

Note that, by varying α and β over all possible choices, we would have obtained 20 conditions, but due to the sampling mechanism of (U^q, V^q), some of them could be immediately thrown out. For example, $\mathtt{Ucoll}_{11}$, $\mathtt{Ucoll}_{12}$, $\mathtt{Ucoll}_{13}, \mathtt{Ucoll}_{22}, \mathtt{Ucoll}_{23}, \mathtt{Ucoll}_{33}$ does not get satisfied. Similarly, for $\mathtt{Vcoll}_{\alpha\beta}$, where $\alpha \in [3]$ and $\beta \in [\alpha, 3]$. For the sake of completeness, we listed out all the 20 conditions and combine them into a single event as follows:

$$\mathsf{Bad\text{-}samp} := \bigcup_{\substack{\alpha \in [4] \\ \beta \in [\alpha, 4]}} (\mathtt{Ucoll}_{\alpha,\beta} \cup \mathtt{Vcoll}_{\alpha,\beta}). \tag{3}$$

Finally, we consider a transcript $\tau \in \Omega_{\text{bad}}$ if τ is either *tuple-induced* bad or it is *sampling-induced* bad. All other transcripts $\tau \in \Omega_{\text{good}} := \Omega \setminus \Omega_{\text{bad}}$ are good and it is easy to see that all good transcripts are attainable one.

3.2.1 Bad Transcript Analysis Now, we analyze the probability of realizing a bad transcript in the ideal world. Based on the preceding discussion, it is evident that analyzing the probability of realizing a bad transcript is only possible if either of the following two conditions, Bad or Bad-samp, occur. Therefore, we have

$$\epsilon_{\text{bad}} = \Pr[\mathsf{X}_{\text{id}} \in \Omega_{\text{bad}}] = \Pr[\mathsf{Bad} \vee \mathsf{Bad\text{-}samp}] \leq \Pr[\mathsf{Bad}] + \Pr[\mathsf{Bad\text{-}samp}], \tag{4}$$

where these two probabilities are calculated using the ideal world distribution of the random variables. The following two lemmas establish an upper bound on the probability of the event Bad and Bad-samp under the ideal world distribution.

Lemma 2. *Let* X_{id} *and the event* Bad *be defined as above. Then, for any integer* q *such that* $q \leq 2^{n-2}$*, one has*

$$\Pr[\mathsf{Bad}] \leq \begin{cases} \frac{q^2}{2^{2n}} + \frac{5q^{4/3}}{2^n} + \frac{1}{2^n}, \text{ for } \mathsf{d} = 1, \\ \frac{2q^2}{2^{2n}} + \frac{6q^{4/3}}{2^n}, \text{ for } \mathsf{d} = 2. \end{cases}$$

Lemma 3. *Let* X_{id} *and the event* Bad-samp *be defined as above. Then, for any integer* q *such that* $q \leq 2^{n-2}$*, one has*

$$\Pr[\mathsf{Bad\text{-}samp}] \leq \frac{8q^4}{2^{3n}}.$$

Following Lemma 2, Lemma 3 and Eq. (4), we obtain the probability of bad transcripts as

$$\Pr[\mathsf{X}_{\mathsf{id}} \in \Omega_{\mathsf{bad}}] \leq \begin{cases} \frac{q^2}{2^{2n}} + \frac{5q^{4/3}}{2^n} + \frac{8q^4}{2^{3n}} + \frac{1}{2^n}, \text{ for } \mathsf{d} = 1, \\ \frac{2q^2}{2^{2n}} + \frac{6q^{4/3}}{2^n} + \frac{8q^4}{2^{3n}}, \text{ for } \mathsf{d} = 2. \end{cases} \tag{5}$$

3.2.2 Proof of Lemma 2 Recall that Bad $=\mathsf{Bad}_K \cup \mathsf{Bad}_1 \cup \mathsf{Bad}_2 \cup \mathsf{Bad}_3 \cup \mathsf{Bad}_4 \cup \mathsf{Bad}_5$ (the condition Bad_K is only for d $= 1$). In this section, we bound the probability of the individual events, and then by virtue of the union bound, we sum up the individual bounds to obtain the overall bound of the probability of the event Bad.

□ **Bounding** Bad_K. Since K is sampled uniformly at random after the query response phase is over, the probability that it becomes equal to all zero string is exactly 2^{-n}. Therefore, we have

$$\Pr[\mathsf{Bad}_K] = \frac{1}{2^n}. \tag{6}$$

□ **Bounding** Bad_1. Here we need to consider only the case when $T_i \neq T_j$. Note that if $T_i = T_j$ then $M_i \neq M_j$ and $C_i \neq C_j$, and hence the probability of the event is 0. Now, when $T_i \neq T_j$, using the randomness of X_i and K(or Z_i), the probability of the above event can be bounded by $1/((2^n - m) \cdot 2^n)$ (or $1/(2^n - m)(2^n - t)$). Therefore, by varying over all possible choices of indices, and by assuming $q \leq 2^{n-1}$, we have

$$\Pr[\mathsf{Bad}_1] \leq \begin{cases} q^2/2^{2n}, \text{ for } \mathsf{d} = 1, \\ 2q^2/2^{2n}, \text{ for } \mathsf{d} = 2. \end{cases} \tag{7}$$

□ **Bounding** Bad_2. We first bound the probability of the event Bad_2. For a fixed choice of indices, we define an indicator random variable $\mathbb{I}_{i,j}$ which takes the value 1 if $Y_i = Y_j$, and 0 otherwise. Let $\mathbb{I} = \sum_{i \neq j} \mathbb{I}_{i,j}$. By linearity of expectation,

$$\mathbf{E}[\mathbb{I}] = \sum_{i \neq j} \mathbf{E}[\mathbb{I}_{i,j}] = \sum_{i \neq j} \Pr[Y_i = Y_j] \leq \frac{q^2}{2^n}.$$

Applying Markov's inequality, we have

$$\Pr[\mathtt{Bad}_2] = \Pr[|\{(i,j) \in [q]^2 : Y_i = Y_j\}| \geq q^{2/3}] \leq \frac{q^2}{2^n} \times \frac{1}{q^{2/3}} = \frac{q^{4/3}}{2^n}. \tag{8}$$

□ **Bounding** $\mathtt{Bad}_3$**.** Using a similar argument as used in bounding $\mathtt{Bad}_2$, we have

$$\Pr[\mathtt{Bad}_3] \leq \frac{q^{4/3}}{2^n}. \tag{9}$$

□ **Bounding** $(\mathtt{Bad}_4 \mid \overline{\mathtt{Bad}_2})$**.** Let us consider the event $(\mathtt{Bad}_4 \mid \overline{\mathtt{Bad}_2})$. Due to $\overline{\mathtt{Bad}_2}$, the number of $(i,j),(k,l)$ pairs such that $Y_i = Y_j$ and $Y_k = Y_l$ holds is at most $q^{4/3}$. For each such choices of i,j,k,l, the probability of the event $W_j = W_k$, i.e., $K \odot (T_j \oplus T_k) = C_j \oplus C_k$ (for $\mathsf{d} = 1$) or $Z_j \oplus Z_k = C_j \oplus C_k$ (for $\mathsf{d} = 2$) holds with at most $1/2^n$ (for $\mathsf{d} = 1$) or $1/(2^n - t)$ (for $\mathsf{d} = 2$). This is due to the randomness of K or Z values. Therefore,

$$\Pr[\mathtt{Bad}_4 \mid \overline{\mathtt{Bad}_2}] \leq \begin{cases} q^{4/3}/2^n, & \text{for } \mathsf{d} = 1, \\ 2q^{4/3}/2^n, & \text{for } \mathsf{d} = 2. \end{cases} \tag{10}$$

□ **Bounding** $(\mathtt{Bad}_5 \mid \overline{\mathtt{Bad}_3})$**.** Using a similar argument as used above and using the randomness of X values, we can obtain

$$\Pr[\mathtt{Bad}_5 \mid \overline{\mathtt{Bad}_3}] \leq \frac{2q^{4/3}}{2^n}. \tag{11}$$

Finally, by combining Eq. (6), Eq. (7), Eq. (8), Eq. (9), Eq. (10) and Eq. (11), we obtain the result.

3.2.3 Proof of Lemma 3 Recall that from Eq. (3) we have

$$\Pr[\textsf{Bad-Samp}] \leq \Pr\left[\bigcup_{\substack{\alpha \in [4] \\ \beta \in [\alpha,4]}} (\mathtt{Ucoll}_{\alpha,\beta} \cup \mathtt{Vcoll}_{\alpha,\beta})\right]$$
$$\leq \sum_{\alpha \in [4]} \sum_{\beta \in \{\alpha,\ldots,4\}} \Pr[\mathtt{Ucoll}_{\alpha,\beta} \cup \mathtt{Vcoll}_{\alpha,\beta}]. \tag{12}$$

Now we will bound the probability for different values of (α, β) as follows:
□ Case 1: $\alpha \in [3], \beta \in [\alpha, 3]$: In the ideal world we have done all the sampling of U and V consistently for all three $\mathcal{I}_1, \mathcal{I}_2$ and $\mathcal{I}_3$. Recall that, $\mathcal{I} = \mathcal{I}_1 \cup \mathcal{I}_2 \cup \mathcal{I}_3$. Now for any $\alpha \in [3], \beta \in [\alpha, 3]$, we have

$$\sum_{\alpha \in [3]} \sum_{\beta \in [\alpha,3]} \Pr[\mathtt{Ucoll}_{\alpha,\beta} \cup \mathtt{Vcoll}_{\alpha,\beta}] = 0. \tag{13}$$

□ Case 2: $\alpha \in [3], \beta = 4$: For this case we will analyze the probability for $\alpha = 1 \wedge \beta = 4$ and other five cases will attain the same bound by the same approach as bounding the probability of $\texttt{Vcoll}_{\alpha,\beta}$ is similar to bounding that of $\texttt{Ucoll}_{\alpha,\beta}$. Hence we have to bound only $\texttt{Ucoll}_{1,4}$. Example 1 in Fig. 4 illustrates the event $\texttt{Ucoll}_{1,4}$. Recall that

$$\texttt{Ucoll}_{1,4} := \exists i \in \mathcal{I}_1,\ j \in \mathcal{I}_4, \text{ such that } Y_i \neq Y_j \text{ and } U_i = U_j.$$

Since $j \in \mathcal{I}_4$, so $Y_j - W_j$ is an edge in some component of $\mathcal{I}_4$ say C. This C is a connected component having a path of length 3. Hence, at least one of these Y_j and W_j have degree ≥ 2. Let us consider following conditions:

(i) $\mathsf{deg}(Y_j) \geq 2$ and $\mathsf{deg}(W_j) \geq 2$: These two vertices of degree-2 clearly implies that there exist $k, l \neq j$ such that $W_k - (Y_k = Y_j) - (W_j = W_l) - Y_l$ forms a path of length 3 in C. To satisfy this case, we need $\mathtt{E}_1 := (Y_k = Y_j \wedge W_j = W_l)$.

(ii) $\mathsf{deg}(Y_j) \geq 2$ and $\mathsf{deg}(W_j) = 1$: In this case having a 3-length path implies that there exists $k, l \neq j$ such that $Y_l - (W_l = W_k) - (Y_k = Y_j) - W_j$ path exists in C. Hence, we need $\mathtt{E}_2 := (Y_j = Y_k \wedge W_k = W_l)$.

(iii) $\mathsf{deg}(Y_j) = 1$ and $\mathsf{deg}(W_j) \geq 2$: In this case having a 3-length path implies existence of $k, l \neq j$ such that $W_l - (Y_l = Y_k) - (W_k = W_j) - Y_j$ is path in C. Hence, we need $\mathtt{E}_3 := (Y_l = Y_k \wedge W_k = W_j)$.

Clearly from random sampling of X's and K we have

$$\forall a, b, c \in [q],\ \Pr[Y_a = Y_b \wedge W_b = W_c] \leq \frac{2}{2^{2n}}.$$

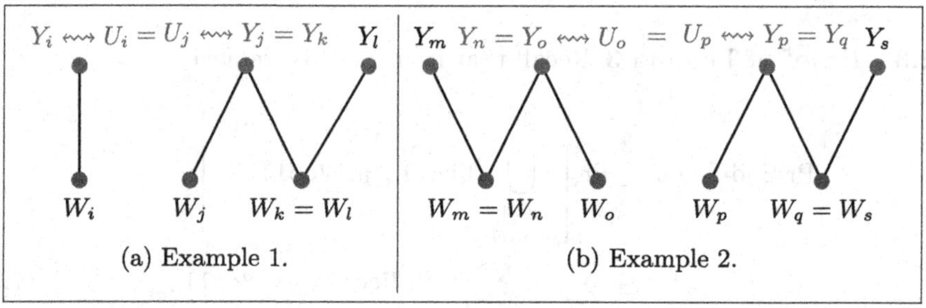

Fig. 4. These are two events where Bad-samp occurs. Example 1 indicates the event $\texttt{Ucoll}_{1,4}$ i.e. $\exists\, i \in \mathcal{I}_1,\ j \in \mathcal{I}_4$, such that $Y_i \neq Y_j$ and $U_i = U_j$. Example 2 indicates the event $\texttt{Ucoll}_{4,4}$ i.e. $\exists\, o\ \&\ p \in \mathcal{I}_4$, such that $Y_o \neq Y_p$ and $U_o = U_p$.

Now clearly from the definition of $\texttt{Ucoll}_{1,4}$ we have

$$\begin{aligned}\Pr[\texttt{Ucoll}_{1,4}] &= \Pr[\exists i \in \mathcal{I}_1, \exists j,k,l \in \mathcal{I}_4 : \ U_i = U_j \wedge (\mathtt{E}_1 \vee \mathtt{E}_2 \vee \mathtt{E}_3)] \\ &\leq \sum_{i \in \mathcal{I}_1} \sum_{j \neq k \neq l \in \mathcal{I}_4} \Pr[U_i = U_j] \times \Pr[\mathtt{E}_1 \vee \mathtt{E}_2 \vee \mathtt{E}_3] \\ &\leq q \times \binom{q}{3} \times \frac{1}{2^n} \times \frac{6}{2^{2n}} \leq \frac{q^4}{2^{3n}}. \end{aligned} \tag{14}$$

As stated before following a similar approach we can achieve the same bound for other five cases $\texttt{Ucoll}_{2,4}, \texttt{Ucoll}_{3,4}, \texttt{Vcoll}_{\alpha,4}$, where $\alpha \in [3]$. Hence

$$\sum_{\alpha \in [3]} \sum_{\beta=4} \Pr[\texttt{Ucoll}_{\alpha,\beta} \cup \texttt{Vcoll}_{\alpha,\beta}] \leq \frac{6q^4}{2^{3n}}. \tag{15}$$

☐ Case 3: $\alpha = 4, \beta = 4$: For this case we will follow the similar approach as the previous case. Here we will bound the probability of $\texttt{Ucoll}_{4,4}$ and other case will attain the same bound by a similar approach as bounding the probability of $\texttt{Vcoll}_{4,4}$ is similar to that of bounding $\texttt{Ucoll}_{4,4}$. Hence, we have to bound only $\texttt{Ucoll}_{4,4}$. Example 2 in Fig. 4 illustrates the event $\texttt{Ucoll}_{4,4}$. Recall that

$$\texttt{Ucoll}_{4,4} := \exists i \& j \in \mathcal{I}_4, \text{ such that } Y_i \neq Y_j \text{ and } U_i = U_j.$$

Since $j \in \mathcal{I}_4$, so $Y_j - W_j$ is an edge in some component of $\mathcal{I}_4$ say C. This C is a connected component having a path of length three. Hence at least one of these Y_j and W_j have degree ≥ 2. Now, following the same approach as the previous case, we will have same $\mathtt{E}_1, \mathtt{E}_2, \mathtt{E}_3$ for some $j \neq k \neq l \in \mathcal{I}_4$. Then we will have the same final bound

$$\Pr[\texttt{Ucoll}_{4,4}] \leq \frac{q^4}{2^{3n}}.$$

Moreover, we will have same bound for other case $\texttt{Vcoll}_{4,4}$. Hence, we have

$$\Pr[\texttt{Ucoll}_{4,4} \cup \texttt{Vcoll}_{4,4}] \leq \frac{2q^4}{2^{3n}}. \tag{16}$$

The result follows by combining Eq. (13), Eq. (15), and Eq. (16).

3.3 Analysis of Good Transcripts

We fix a good transcript $\tau = (M^q, T^q, C^q, X^q, Y^q, U^q, V^q, W^q, K \text{ or } Z^q)$ and we have to lower bound the real interpolation probability and upper bound the ideal interpolation probability.

Lemma 4. *Let* X_{re} *(resp.* X_{id}*) be the transcript random variable induced by the interaction of adversary* A *with the real (resp. ideal) world. For any good transcript* τ *and with the notations defined above, we have*

$$\frac{\Pr[\mathsf{X}_{\mathrm{re}} = \tau]}{\Pr[\mathsf{X}_{\mathrm{id}} = \tau]} \geq \left(1 - \frac{13q^4}{2^{3n}} - \frac{2q^2}{2^{2n}} - \left(\sum_{i=e_1+1}^{\xi_2+\xi_3} \zeta_i^2\right)\frac{4q^2}{2^{2n}}\right). \tag{17}$$

Using Eq. (5), Lemma 4 and the Expectation Method, both theorems follow. The proof of the above lemma and the subsequent analysis can be found in the the full version of this paper.

4 Experimental Results

We have implemented $\mathsf{CLRW1}^4$, b-TNT1, and b-TNT2 using AES-NI instructions and school book multiplication with instruction PCLMULQDQ. The target processor is an Intel Core i9-9960X at 3.10 GHz. The results in cycles per byte are shown in Table 1. The source code was compiled with GCC 10.2.1 with 03 optimization. In the target processor, one AES round takes four clock cycles as it has a skylake architecture.

If the proposed construction would be implemented in hardware, b-TNT1 would be the biggest one because it needs an additional multiplier besides one AES core. A sequential AES hardware implementation takes eleven clock cycles, while a multiplication can take two or four clock cycles, depending on the desirable speed. The best option for hardware implementation is to compute the round keys on the fly; this saves registers. So, for hardware implementation, b-TNT1 is not the best option as the throughput per area is less than for the other constructions based only on a block cipher.

Table 1. Cycles and cycles per byte for proposed constructions, constructions labeled with * also include the key schedule cost.

Construction	Cycles	Cycles per byte
$\mathsf{CLRW1}^4$	184	11.5
b-TNT1	150	9.37
b-TNT2	164	10.25
$\mathsf{CLRW1}^4$*	1719	107.44
b-TNT1*	1240	77.5
b-TNT2*	1645	102.81

Table 1 shows that reducing one permutation key has a notable impact as the key schedule is very costly; this is achieved for b-TNT1 construction. Both proposed constructions improve $\mathsf{CLRW1}^4$ as they need fewer clock cycles. It is important to note that all the AES calls are executed sequentially in all constructions. $\mathsf{CLRW1}^4$* and b-TNT2* use four key schedules, but b-TNT2* has two AES calls that can be performed in parallel or pipelined. It requires fewer clock cycles than $\mathsf{CLRW1}^4$*. The best performance is for b-TNT1, as it changes one block cipher call for one multiplication.

5 Conclusion

In this paper, we have proposed b-TNT1 and b-TNT2 and have shown that both of them provably achieve $3n/4$-bit strong tweakable permutation security. We have experimentally verified that the throughput of b-TNT1 is better than $\mathsf{CLRW1}^4$ in tens order of magnitude. We have also experimentally validated the fact that the evaluation of the last block cipher call for b-TNT2 can be made parallel to the execution of the TNT evaluation, whereas $\mathsf{CLRW1}^4$ enforces the evaluation of the last block cipher until the output of the TNT is available. This phenomenon allows b-TNT2 to achieve a better throughput than $\mathsf{CLRW1}^4$.

Acknowledgements. This research problem originated in a research discussion at the workshop ASK 2023 in Guangzhou, China. Part of the work was done when Ritam Bhaumik was affiliated with EPFL, Lausanne. Wonseok Choi was supported in part by the National Research Foundation of Korea (NRF) grant funded by the Korea government (MSIT) (No. RS-2023-00239620), by AnalytiXIN and by Sunday Group. Yaobin Shen was supported in part by Ant Research, Ant Group.

References

1. Andreeva, E., Bogdanov, A., Luykx, A., Mennink, B., Tischhauser, E., Yasuda, K.: Parallelizable and authenticated online ciphers. In: Sako, K., Sarkar, P. (eds.) ASIACRYPT 2013. LNCS, vol. 8269, pp. 424–443. Springer, Heidelberg (2013). https://doi.org/10.1007/978-3-642-42033-7_22
2. Bao, Z., Guo, C., Guo, J., Song, L.: TNT: how to tweak a block cipher. In: Canteaut, A., Ishai, Y. (eds.) EUROCRYPT 2020. LNCS, vol. 12106, pp. 641–673. Springer, Cham (2020). https://doi.org/10.1007/978-3-030-45724-2_22
3. Bellare, M., Impagliazzo, R.: A tool for obtaining tighter security analyses of pseudorandom function based constructions, with applications to PRP to PRF conversion. Cryptology ePrint Archive, Paper 1999/024 (1999). https://eprint.iacr.org/1999/024
4. Bellizia, D., et al.: Spook: sponge-based leakage-resistant authenticated encryption with a masked tweakable block cipher. IACR Trans. Symmetric Cryptol. **2020**(S1), 295–349 (2020)
5. Bhattacharjee, A., Bhaumik, R., Nandi, M.: Offset-based BBB-secure tweakable block-ciphers with updatable caches. In: Isobe, T., Sarkar, S. (eds.) Progress in Cryptology - INDOCRYPT 2022 - 23rd International Conference on Cryptology in India, Kolkata, India, 11–14 December 2022, Proceedings. LNCS, vol. 13774, pp. 171–194. Springer (2022)
6. Bhaumik, R., List, E., Nandi, M.: ZCZ - achieving n-bit SPRP security with a minimal number of tweakable-block-cipher calls, pp. 336–366. Springer (2018)
7. Chakraborty, D., Sarkar, P.: A general construction of tweakable block ciphers and different modes of operations. In: Lipmaa, H., Yung, M., Lin, D. (eds.) Inscrypt 2006. LNCS, vol. 4318, pp. 88–102. Springer, Heidelberg (2006). https://doi.org/10.1007/11937807_8
8. Chakraborty, D., Sarkar, P.: A general construction of tweakable block ciphers and different modes of operations. IEEE Trans. Inf. Theory **54**(5), 1991–2006 (2008)
9. Choi, W., et al.: Highly secure nonce-based macs from the sum of tweakable block ciphers. IACR Trans. Symmetric Cryptol. **2020**(4), 39–70 (2020)

10. Choi, W., Lee, J., Lee, Y.: Building PRFs from TPRPs: beyond the block and the tweak length bounds. IACR Cryptology ePrint Archive, p. 918 (2022)
11. Cogliati, B., Lee, J., Seurin, Y.: New constructions of MACs from (tweakable) block ciphers. IACR Trans. Symmetric Cryptol. **2017**(2), 27–58 (2017)
12. Dai, W., Hoang, V.T., Tessaro, S.: Information-theoretic indistinguishability via the chi-squared method. In: Katz, J., Shacham, H. (eds.) CRYPTO 2017. LNCS, vol. 10403, pp. 497–523. Springer, Cham (2017). https://doi.org/10.1007/978-3-319-63697-9_17
13. Datta, N., Dey, S., Dutta, A., Mandal, S.: Cascading four round LRW1 is beyond birthday bound secure. IACR Trans. Symmetric Cryptol. **2023**(4), 365–390 (2023)
14. Ferguson, N., et al.: Skein. SHA-3 submission to NIST (2006 –2012)
15. Granger, R., Jovanovic, P., Mennink, B., Neves, S.: Improved masking for tweakable blockciphers with applications to authenticated encryption. In: Fischlin, M., Coron, J.-S. (eds.) EUROCRYPT 2016. LNCS, vol. 9665, pp. 263–293. Springer, Heidelberg (2016). https://doi.org/10.1007/978-3-662-49890-3_11
16. Grosso, V., et al.: Scream. Submission to CAESAR Competition (2013–2019). https://competitions.cr.yp.to/round2/screamv3.pdf
17. Guo, C., Guo, J., List, E., Song, L.: Towards closing the security gap of Tweak-aNd-Tweak (TNT). In: Moriai, S., Wang, H. (eds.) ASIACRYPT 2020. LNCS, vol. 12491, pp. 567–597. Springer, Cham (2020). https://doi.org/10.1007/978-3-030-64837-4_19
18. Guo, C., Iwata, T., Khairallah, M., Minematsu, K., Peyrin, T.: Romulus v1.3. Submission to NIST Lightweight Cryptography Standardization Process (2018–2023). https://csrc.nist.gov/CSRC/media/Projects/lightweight-cryptography/documents/finalist-round/updated-spec-doc/romulus-spec-final.pdf
19. Hall, C., Wagner, D., Kelsey, J., Schneier, B.: Building PRFs from PRPs. In: Krawczyk, H. (ed.) Advances in Cryptology—CRYPTO '98, pp. 370–389. Springer, Heidelberg (1998)
20. Hirose, S.: Compactly committing authenticated encryption using tweakable block cipher. In: Kutylowski, M., Zhang, J., Chen, C. (eds.) Network and System Security - 14th International Conference, NSS 2020, Melbourne, VIC, Australia, 25–27 November 2020, Proceedings. LNCS, vol. 12570, pp. 187–206. Springer (2020)
21. Hirose, S.: Collision-resistant and pseudorandom hash function using tweakable block cipher. In: You, I., Youn, T.-Y. (eds.) Information Security Applications - 23rd International Conference, WISA 2022, Jeju Island, South Korea, 24–26 August 2022, Revised Selected Papers. LNCS, vol. 13720, pp. 3–15. Springer (2022)
22. Hoang, V.T., Krovetz, T., Rogaway, P.: Robust authenticated-encryption AEZ and the problem that it solves. In: Oswald, E., Fischlin, M. (eds.) EUROCRYPT 2015. LNCS, vol. 9056, pp. 15–44. Springer, Heidelberg (2015). https://doi.org/10.1007/978-3-662-46800-5_2
23. Hoang, V.T., Tessaro, S.: Key-alternating ciphers and key-length extension: exact bounds and multi-user security. In: Robshaw, M., Katz, J. (eds.) CRYPTO 2016. LNCS, vol. 9814, pp. 3–32. Springer, Heidelberg (2016). https://doi.org/10.1007/978-3-662-53018-4_1
24. Iwata, T., Minematsu, K., Peyrin, T., Seurin, Y.: ZMAC: a fast tweakable block cipher mode for highly secure message authentication. In: Katz, J., Shacham, H. (eds.) CRYPTO 2017. LNCS, vol. 10403, pp. 34–65. Springer, Cham (2017). https://doi.org/10.1007/978-3-319-63697-9_2
25. Jean, J., Nikolic, I., Peyrin, T.: Joltik v1.3. Submission to CAESAR Competition (2013–2019). https://competitions.cr.yp.to/round2/joltikv13.pdf

26. Jean, J., Nikolic, I., Peyrin, T.: Kiasu v1. Submission to CAESAR Competition (2013–2019). https://competitions.cr.yp.to/round1/kiasuv1.pdf
27. Jean, J., Nikolic, I., Peyrin, T., Seurin, Y.: The deoxys AEAD family. J. Cryptol. **34**(3), 31 (2021)
28. Jha, A., Khairallah, M., Nandi, M., Saha, A.: Tight security of TNT and beyond - attacks, proofs and possibilities for the cascaded LRW paradigm. In: Joye, M., Leander, G. (eds.) Advances in Cryptology - EUROCRYPT 2024 - 43rd Annual International Conference on the Theory and Applications of Cryptographic Techniques, Zurich, Switzerland, 26–30 May 2024, Proceedings, Part I. LNCS, vol. 14651, pp. 249–279. Springer (2024)
29. Jha, A., Nandi, M.: Tight security of cascaded LRW2. J. Cryptol. **33**(3), 1272–1317 (2020)
30. Lampe, R., Seurin, Y.: Tweakable blockciphers with asymptotically optimal security. In: Moriai, S. (ed.) Fast Software Encryption - 20th International Workshop, FSE 2013, Singapore, 11–13 March 2013. Revised Selected Papers. LNCS, vol. 8424, pp. 133–151. Springer (2013)
31. Landecker, W., Shrimpton, T., Terashima, R.S.: Tweakable blockciphers with beyond birthday-bound security. In: Safavi-Naini, R., Canetti, R. (eds.) CRYPTO 2012. LNCS, vol. 7417, pp. 14–30. Springer, Heidelberg (2012). https://doi.org/10.1007/978-3-642-32009-5_2
32. Liskov, M., Rivest, R.L., Wagner, D.: Tweakable block ciphers. In: Yung, M. (ed.) CRYPTO 2002. LNCS, vol. 2442, pp. 31–46. Springer, Heidelberg (2002). https://doi.org/10.1007/3-540-45708-9_3
33. Liskov, M.D., Rivest, R.L., Wagner, D.A.: Tweakable block ciphers. J. Cryptol. **24**(3), 588–613 (2011)
34. Minematsu, K.: Improved security analysis of XEX and LRW modes. In: Biham, E., Youssef, A.M. (eds.) Selected Areas in Cryptography, 13th International Workshop, SAC 2006, Montreal, Canada, 17–18 August 2006 Revised Selected Papers. LNCS, vol. 4356, pp. 96–113. Springer (2006)
35. Naito, Y.: Full PRF-secure message authentication code based on tweakable block cipher. In: Au, M.-H., Miyaji, A. (eds.) ProvSec 2015. LNCS, vol. 9451, pp. 167–182. Springer, Cham (2015). https://doi.org/10.1007/978-3-319-26059-4_9
36. Naito, Y.: Tweakable blockciphers for efficient authenticated encryptions with beyond the birthday-bound security. IACR Trans. Symmetric Cryptol. **2017**(2), 1–26 (2017)
37. Naito, Y.: A highly secure MAC from tweakable blockciphers with support for short tweaks. In: Jang-Jaccard, J., Guo, F. (eds.) ACISP 2019. LNCS, vol. 11547, pp. 588–606. Springer, Cham (2019). https://doi.org/10.1007/978-3-030-21548-4_32
38. Naito, Y., Sugawara, T.: Lightweight authenticated encryption mode of operation for tweakable block ciphers. IACR Trans. Cryptogr. Hardw. Embed. Syst. **2020**(1), 66–94 (2020)
39. Nakaya, K., Iwata, T.: Generalized feistel structures based on tweakable block ciphers. IACR Trans. Symmetric Cryptol. **2022**(4), 24–91 (2022)
40. Patarin, J.: Introduction to mirror theory: analysis of systems of linear equalities and linear non equalities for cryptography. IACR Cryptology ePrint Archive 2010/287 (2010)
41. Peyrin, T., Seurin, Y.: Counter-in-tweak: authenticated encryption modes for tweakable block ciphers. In: Robshaw, M., Katz, J. (eds.) CRYPTO 2016. LNCS, vol. 9814, pp. 33–63. Springer, Heidelberg (2016). https://doi.org/10.1007/978-3-662-53018-4_2

42. Rogaway, P.: Efficient instantiations of tweakable blockciphers and refinements to modes OCB and PMAC. In: Lee, P.J. (ed.) ASIACRYPT 2004. LNCS, vol. 3329, pp. 16–31. Springer, Heidelberg (2004). https://doi.org/10.1007/978-3-540-30539-2_2
43. Schroeppel, R.: Hasty pudding cipher specification. In: First AES Candidate Workshop (1998)
44. Wang, L.: Shell v2.0. Submission to CAESAR Competition (2013–2019). https://competitions.cr.yp.to/round2/shellv20.pdf
45. Zhang, Z., Qin, Z., Guo, C.: Just tweak! Asymptotically optimal security for the cascaded LRW1 tweakable blockcipher. Des. Codes Cryptogr. **91**(3), 1035–1052 (2022)

ROM Reduction Failures: Reasons and Solutions

Ziyi Li[1,2], Xianhui Lu[1,2(✉)], and Yao Cheng[1,2]

[1] Key Laboratory of Cyberspace Security Defense, Institute of Information Engineering, CAS, Beijing 100049, China
{liziyi,luxianhui,chengyao}@iie.ac.cn

[2] School of Cyber Security, University of Chinese Academy of Sciences, Beijing 100049, China

Abstract. The Random Oracle Model (ROM), proposed by Bellare and Rogaway (CCS 93), is a crucial tool for providing heuristic security of well-performing cryptographic schemes utilizing hash functions. Several generic transformations, such as Encrypt-with-Hash, OAEP, and FDH, suffer from a class of ROM failures. These failures expose flaws in the existing security proofs for these generic transformations in the ROM. This paper focuses on analyzing these ROM reduction failures. To understand and address these failures, we introduce a tool named Hierarchical ROM (HROM). In this model, Random Oracles (ROs) are classified into two types: RO used in generic transformations and RO used in underlying primitives. Existing ROM reduction proofs overlook the existence of the latter ROs. When the former RO depends on the latter, the (re)programming of ROs by reductions is constrained, causing failures of existing reductions. We refine reductions in the HROM and provide a generic framework for addressing the ROM reduction failures of generic transformations.

Keywords: Random Oracle Model · Reduction Failure · Generic Transformation · Hierarchical ROM

1 Introduction

1.1 Background

The Random Oracle Model (ROM), proposed by Bellare and Rogaway [4], is a crucial tool for balancing the security and efficiency of cryptographic schemes. In this model, the hash function is idealized as a Random Oracle (RO), behaving like a true random function and accessible in a black-box manner. Many well-performing cryptographic schemes that use hash functions may lack standard security proofs but can be proven secure in the ROM. Examples of such schemes include Optimal Asymmetric Encryption Padding (OAEP) [5], Fujisaki-Okamoto (FO) [13], Full-Domain Hash (FDH) [6], and Fiat-Shamir (FS) [11].

J. K. Liu et al. (Eds.): ProvSec 2024, LNCS 14904, pp. 23–42, 2025.
https://doi.org/10.1007/978-981-96-0957-4_2

The idealized nature of the RO is the core reason these schemes can be proven secure in the ROM. Specifically, several widely used techniques for proving security in the ROM, such as efficient simulation, adaptive programming, and preimage awareness [9], rely on the advantageous properties of the RO. This capability allows the reduction to simulate the security game for the adversary effectively. Many existing security proofs apply the above techniques, especially for generic transformation in the ROM.

However, the use of these techniques poses some problems. In 2021, Bernstein [8] pointed out that when the underlying scheme also uses an RO, the One-Wayness under Chosen-Plaintext Attacks (OW-CPA) security of the T transformation[1] [2,15] in the ROM cannot be tightly reduced to the OW-CPA security of the underlying PKE scheme. The work only considered scenarios in which the RO used in the underlying PKE is independent of the RO used in the transformation. Unlike Bernstein's work, we analyze the transformation T in more general scenarios. We find that the security reduction in the ROM of T fails[2] when the RO used in the underlying PKE is not independent of the RO used in the transformation.

Indeed, Zhandry [17], in proposing the Augmented Random Oracle Model (AROM), emphasized that a secure generic transformation in the ROM should consider scenarios where the underlying primitive also utilizes the RO. This naturally encompasses cases where the RO employed by the underlying primitive is the same as the RO used by the transformation. In such scenarios, the reduction failure of the T transformation is not unique; similar failures arise with transformations like OAEP, among others. In this paper, we investigate these failures and propose solutions.

1.2 Our Contribution

Considering scenarios in which the underlying primitives also utilize the RO, existing proofs of generic transformations in the ROM may no longer be applicable. Consequently, some generic transformations proven secure in the ROM fail to convert such primitives into secure target schemes. This paper examines several well-known generic transformations in the ROM, such as T [15], OAEP [5], and FDH [6], to illustrate the failures of ROM reductions. We introduce a novel tool called the Hierarchical ROM (HROM) to address these issues. HROM

[1] Let $\Pi := (\mathsf{Gen}, \mathsf{Enc}, \mathsf{Dec})$ be a Public Key Encryption (PKE) scheme and O be an RO. The transformation T converts Π into a Deterministic PKE (DPKE) scheme through de-randomization. Furthermore, the encryption algorithm of the resulting DPKE scheme $\mathrm{T}^{\Pi,O}$ is denoted as $\mathsf{Enc_1}^O(pk, m) := \mathsf{Enc}(pk, m; O(m))$. The transformation was proven OW-CPA in the ROM, i.e., it converts an OW-CPA secure PKE scheme into an OW-CPA secure DPKE scheme in the ROM.

[2] We illustrate the failure by constructing the following counterexample. Modify any OW-CPA secure PKE $\Pi := (\mathsf{Gen}, \mathsf{Enc}, \mathsf{Dec})$ into a PKE scheme $\overline{\Pi} := (\overline{\mathsf{Gen}}, \overline{\mathsf{Enc}}, \overline{\mathsf{Dec}})$. If $r = O(m)$, $\overline{\mathsf{Enc}}(pk, m; r) = m$. Otherwise, $\overline{\mathsf{Enc}}(pk, m; r) = \mathsf{Enc}(pk, m; r)$. It is easy to demonstrate that $\overline{\Pi}$ is also OW-CPA secure in the ROM. However, $\mathrm{T}^{\overline{\Pi},O}$ is not OW-CPA secure in the ROM.

offers an approach to handling ROs by classifying them into distinct types based on their roles. Based on the model, we capture these ROM reduction failures and provide a framework for refining existing transformations to ensure their security.

1.3 Technique Overview

A generic transformation can convert an underlying primitive into a secure target scheme in a black-box manner, relying solely on the input/output behavior of the primitive. Therefore, the security of a generic transformation could be independent of the specific construction of the underlying primitives. However, as previously mentioned, many generic transformations in the ROM are not secure when the underlying primitive relies on the RO. This fact is inconsistent with the strict definition of a secure generic transformation in the ROM [17]: it converts any underlying primitive in the ROM that meets the security requirements, including those primitives that rely on ROs, into a secure target scheme in the ROM. Furthermore, existing security proofs for generic transformations in the ROM do not work under the definition.

We introduce a new tool, the HROM, to provide more reliable security proofs in the ROM. This model covers scenarios where the underlying primitive utilizes ROs and distinguishes between the ROs employed in the underlying primitive and those used in the transformation. The crux of this distinction lies in that, in security proofs, a reduction acting as an adversary against the underlying primitive is unlikely to program the ROs used by the underlying primitive. In contrast, it can program the ROs used by the transformation.

Definition 1.1. *In the HROM, for any oracle-aided transformation T^{O_1} and oracle-aided underlying scheme Π^{O_2}, we have the resulting scheme $\Pi_1^{O_1,\overline{O_2}} := T^{O_1,\Pi^{\overline{O_2}}}$. Here, O_1 is an RO publicly accessed by any parties, and $\overline{O_2}$ means that O_2 can only be publicly accessible by Π and the adversary against Π^{O_2}.*

Additionally, we define reduction within the HROM. Specifically, drawing from the framework proposed by Fischlin et al. [12], we introduce three types of HROM reductions: non-programmed, randomly-programmed, and fully-program-med, based on the level of programming of ROs in the transformation. When the same RO is used by both the underlying primitive and the transformation, the adversary's queries to the RO may involve information from both. As a result, the HROM reduction capabilities are constrained compared to previously defined reductions. This constraint causes existing reductions to fail in the HROM. Consequently, HROM effectively captures the reduction failures mentioned earlier and serves as a tool to refine and improve existing transformations.

Many generic transformations proven secure in the ROM are not secure in the HROM. Fortunately, they can be made secure in the HROM through simple modifications. One approach is to impose an additional restriction on the transformation: the RO used by the transformation must differ from the RO used by the underlying scheme. Another approach is to refine the transformation using domain separation techniques [3,7]. In the modified transformation, the RO value $O(x)$ is replaced with $O(s,x)$, where s is a randomness generated during the key generation phase. Therefore, the RO used by the transformation is independent of the RO used by the underlying scheme with overwhelming probability. As a result, the new transformation can avoid the failure. We demonstrate that for any generic transformation in the ROM, if it has a reduction meeting the definition defined in [12], then the new transformation has a valid HROM reduction. Therefore, even if the original transformation fails in the HROM, the modified version can be proven secure in the HROM.

1.4 Related Work

The idea that a secure generic transformation should convert underlying primitives using ROs into a secure target scheme has been discussed by Zhandry [17]. From ROM uninstantiable results, Zhandry [17] analyzed ROM failures and proposed the Augmented ROM (AROM). This model differs from HROM in that it is designed to capture a wide range of ROM uninstantiable results rather than focusing solely on ROM reduction failures. Additionally, the domain separation technique, formalized by Bellare et al. [3] in 2020, is commonly employed in the ROM to convert one RO into multiple ROs [7][3].

2 Preliminaries

2.1 Cryptographic Primitives

We recall the formal definitions of several cryptographic primitives in Appendix A.2, including Trapdoor Function (Permutation) (TDF(P)), (Deterministic) Public Key Encryption ((D)PKE), and Signature (SIG).

2.2 Security Properties in the ROM

Security Properties. A security property of cryptographic schemes is denoted as a (game, probability) pair (G, p), where G takes a security parameter 1^λ as input and outputs a bit $b \in \{0, 1\}$, and p takes a security parameter 1^λ as input and outputs a real number in the range $[0, 1]$. Let Π be a (G, p)-candidate and $\mathcal{A}$ be an adversary. The advantage of $\mathcal{A}$ in attacking (G, p) security of Π is a function of λ defined as $\mathsf{Adv}^{G}_{\Pi,\mathcal{A}}(1^\lambda) := \Pr[1 \leftarrow (\mathcal{A} \leftrightarrow G^{\Pi})(1^\lambda)] - p(\lambda)$, where $(\mathcal{A} \leftrightarrow G^{\Pi})(1^\lambda)$ denotes the interaction between $\mathcal{A}$ and Π as defined by G. In addition, G indicates whether adversaries are computationally bounded or unbounded.

[3] In practice, ROs are instantiated as hash functions. In some specific constructions, domain separation [3] is often used to ensure that the hash used by different schemes is different. However, our investigation still holds theoretical significance for refining the ROM and security proofs within it.

Definition 2.1 **((G, p)-Secure Scheme).** *A cryptographic scheme Π securely implements (G, p) if, for any adversary $\mathcal{A}$, there exists a negligible function $negl(\cdot)$ such that $\mathsf{Adv}^{G}_{\Pi,\mathcal{A}}(1^\lambda) \leq negl(\lambda)$.*

Definition 2.2 **($(G, p_G) \to (H, p_H)$-Secure Transformation).** *A transformation T from (G, p_G) to (H, p_H) is secure if, for any (G, p_G)-secure cryptographic scheme Π, the resulting scheme $\Pi_1 := T^{\Pi}$ securely implements (H, p_H).*

Remark 1. In this paper, we focus on black-box transformations or constructions that utilize primitives in a black-box manner. This approach solely considers the input/output behavior of the primitive.

Security Properties in the ROM. Bellare and Rogaway [4] introduced the ROM in which a hash function is idealized as a truly random function that can only be accessed via a black-box way for any parties.

Definition 2.3 **((G, p)-Secure Scheme in the ROM).** *An oracle-aided cryptographic scheme Π^O securely implements (G, p) in the ROM if, for any oracle-aided adversary $\mathcal{A}^O$, there exists a negligible function $negl(\cdot)$ s.t. $\mathsf{Adv}^{G}_{\Pi^O,\mathcal{A}^O}(1^\lambda) \leq negl(\lambda)$.*

Remark 2. For certain oracle-free constructions, the oracle O can be omitted.

Definition 2.4 **($(G, p_G) \to (H, p_H)$-Secure Transformation in the ROM, [17]).** *An oracle-aided transformation T^{O_1} from (G, p_G) to (H, p_H) is secure in the ROM if, for any oracle-aided cryptographic primitive Π^{O_2} which securely implement (G, p_G) in the ROM, the resulting scheme $\Pi_1^{O_1,O_2} := T^{O_1,\Pi^{O_2}}$ securely implements (H, p_H) in the ROM.*

Remark 3. Compared to previous definitions, there is an emphasis on the fact that the underlying primitives may be constructed with the RO.

2.3 Black-Box Reduction in the ROM

Reductions in cryptography are commonly used to prove security. They transform adversaries against a target scheme into adversaries against the underlying primitive. This paper focuses on Fully Black-Box (FBB) reductions [16], which only access the underlying primitive and the adversary in a black-box way. FBB reductions are essential for schemes in the ROM that aim to achieve desirable efficiency.

Definition 2.5 **(FBB Reduction for Transformation, [16]).** *A $((H, p_H) \to (G, p_G), \delta, t, q_{\mathcal{A}})$-FBB reduction for transformation T is a machine $\mathcal{B}$ with the property that for any adversary $\mathcal{A}$ and any (G, p_G)-candidate Π, if*

$$\mathsf{Adv}^{H}_{T^{\Pi},\mathcal{A}}(1^\lambda) > \epsilon(\lambda)$$

for $\epsilon \geq 0$, *then*

$$\mathsf{Adv}^{G}_{\Pi,\mathcal{B}^{\mathcal{A}}}(1^{\lambda}) > \delta(\epsilon, t, q_{\mathcal{A}}),$$

where $\mathcal{B}$ *runs in time* t *and runs* $q_{\mathcal{A}}$ *instantiations of* $\mathcal{A}$. *These two quantities also are functions of* λ. *Furthermore,* $\delta(\epsilon, t, q_{\mathcal{A}})$ *is non-negligible when* ϵ *is non-negligible.*

In the ROM, Fischlin et al. [12] introduced a framework to provide a more detailed classification of FBB ROM reductions based on their ability to program the RO. This framework defines three levels of programming: none, random, and full.

Definition 2.6 ([12]). *A* $((H, p_H) \to (G, p_G), \delta, t, q_O, q_{\mathcal{A}})$*-FBB non/randomly/fully-programming reduction in the ROM for an oracle-aided* T^O *is an oracle-aided machine* $\mathcal{B}^{(\cdot)}$ *with the property that for any* (H, p_H)*-adversary* $\mathcal{A}$ *and any* (G, p_G)*-candidate* Π*, if*

$$\mathsf{Adv}^{H}_{T^O,\Pi,\mathcal{A}^O}(1^{\lambda}) > \epsilon(\lambda)$$

for an RO O *and* $\epsilon \geq 0$*, then*

$$\mathsf{Adv}^{G}_{\Pi,\mathcal{B}^{\mathcal{O}_1},\mathcal{A}^{\mathcal{O}_2}}(1^{\lambda}) > \delta(\epsilon, t, q_O, q_{\mathcal{A}}),$$

where $\mathcal{B}$ *runs in time* t*, makes* q_O *queries to given oracle* $\mathcal{O}_1$ *and runs* $q_{\mathcal{A}}$ *instantiations of* $\mathcal{A}$*. These three quantities are functions of* λ*. Furthermore,* $\delta(\epsilon, t, q_O, q_{\mathcal{A}})$ *is non-negligible when* ϵ *is non-negligible. Moreover,* $\mathcal{B}^{(\cdot)}$ *is*

- *a non-programming reduction in the ROM, then* $\mathcal{O}_1 = O$ *and* $\mathcal{O}_2 = O$*. In this case,* x *is forwarded to* $\mathcal{B}$ *when* $\mathcal{A}$ *queries* x *to* O*. Then* $\mathcal{B}$ *queries* x *to* O *and forward* $O(x)$ *to* $\mathcal{A}$*.* $\mathcal{B}$ *cannot influence the responses in this process.*
- *a randomly-programming reduction, then* $\mathcal{O}_1 = (O, O_{Evl}, O_{Prg}, O_{Rnd})$ *and* $\mathcal{O}_2 = O_{Evl}$*. Here,* $O' = (O_{Evl}, O_{Prg}, O_{Rnd})$ *is a Randomly-Programming RO (RPRO)*[4] *defined in [12]. In this case,* x *is forwarded to* $\mathcal{B}$ *when* $\mathcal{A}$ *queries* x *to the RO. Mainly,* $\mathcal{B}$ *performs a number of* O_{rnd} *queries followed by a suitable* O_{prg} *query to obtain a desirable response* $O_{Evl}(x)$ *and forward* $O_{Evl}(x)$ *to* $\mathcal{A}$*. In this process,* $\mathcal{B}$ *cannot fully determine* $O_{Evl}(x)$ *obtained by* $\mathcal{A}$*.*
- *a fully-programming reduction, then* $\mathcal{O}_1 = O$ *and* $\mathcal{O}_2 = (\cdot)$*.* $\mathcal{A}^{(\cdot)}$ *means that the RO queried by* $\mathcal{A}$ *is simulated by* $\mathcal{B}$*. In this case,* x *is forwarded to* $\mathcal{B}$ *when* $\mathcal{A}$ *queries* x *to the RO.* $\mathcal{B}$ *can choose any suitable strategy to program* O *to obtain the corresponding response* y *Then,* $\mathcal{B}$ *forward* y *as* $O(x)$ *to* $\mathcal{A}$*.*

2.4 Security Properties

Definition 2.7 (One-Wayness). *A TDF* $F := (\mathsf{G}, \mathsf{F.Evl}, \mathsf{F.Inv})$ *with domain* X *is One-Way (OW) if for any PPT adversary* $\mathcal{A}$*, there exists a negligible function* $negl(\cdot)$ *such that*

$$\mathsf{Adv}^{\mathsf{OW}}_{F,\mathcal{A}}(1^{\lambda}) := \Pr_{(e,t)\leftarrow \mathsf{G}(1^{\lambda}), x \xleftarrow{\$} X}[\mathcal{A}(e, \mathsf{F.Evl}(e, x)) = x] \leq negl(\lambda).$$

[4] We give a detailed description of the RPRO in Appendix A.3.

Definition 2.8 (Partial-Domain OW). *A TDF* $F := (\mathsf{G}, \mathsf{F.Evl}, \mathsf{F.Inv})$ *with domain* $X = X_1 \times X_2$ *is partial-domain OW if for any PPT adversary* $\mathcal{A}$, *there exists a negligible function* $negl(\cdot)$ *such that*

$$\mathsf{Adv}_{F,\mathcal{A}}^{\mathsf{PD\text{-}OW}}(1^\lambda) := \Pr_{(e,t) \leftarrow \mathsf{G}(1^\lambda), x_1 \| x_2 \xleftarrow{\$} X} [\mathcal{A}(e, \mathsf{F.Evl}(e, x)) = x_1] \leq negl(\lambda),$$

where $x_1 \in X_1$ *and* $x_1 \in X_2$.

$\mathsf{GAME}_{\mathsf{PKE},\mathcal{A}}^{\mathsf{OW\text{-}CPA}}(1^\lambda)$	$\mathsf{GAME}_{\mathsf{PKE},\mathcal{A}}^{\mathsf{IND\text{-}CPA}}(1^\lambda)$
1: $(pk, sk) \leftarrow \mathsf{Gen}(1^\lambda)$	1: $(pk^*, sk^*) \leftarrow \mathsf{Gen}(1^\lambda)$
2: $m^* \xleftarrow{\$} M$	2: $(m_0, m_1) \leftarrow \mathcal{A}(pk)$
3: $c^* \leftarrow \mathsf{Enc}(pk, m^*)$	3: $b \xleftarrow{\$} \{0,1\}$
4: $m \leftarrow \mathcal{A}(pk, c^*)$	4: $c^* \leftarrow \mathsf{Enc}(pk, m_b)$
5: **return** $\|m = m^*\|$	5: $b' \leftarrow \mathcal{A}(pk, c^*)$
	6: **return** $\|b' = b\|$

Fig. 1. OW-CPA and IND-CPA security games for PKE

Definition 2.9 (OW-CPA). *A PKE scheme* $\mathsf{PKE} = (\mathsf{Gen}, \mathsf{Enc}, \mathsf{Dec})$ *with a message space* M *is One-Way under Chosen-Plaintext Attacks (OW-CPA) if for any PPT adversary* $\mathcal{A}$, *there exists a negligible function* $negl(\cdot)$ *such that*

$$\mathsf{Adv}_{\mathsf{PKE},\mathcal{A}}^{\mathsf{OW\text{-}CPA}}(1^\lambda) := \Pr[\mathsf{GAME}_{\mathsf{PKE},\mathcal{A}}^{\mathsf{OW\text{-}CPA}}(1^\lambda) \rightarrow 1] \leq negl(\lambda),$$

where $\mathsf{GAME}_{\mathsf{PKE},\mathcal{A}}^{\mathsf{OW\text{-}CPA}}(1^\lambda)$ *is the game described as in Fig. 1.*

Definition 2.10 (IND-CPA). *A PKE scheme* $\mathsf{PKE} = (\mathsf{Gen}, \mathsf{Enc}, \mathsf{Dec})$ *is Indistinguishable under Chosen-Plaintext Attacks (IND-CPA) if for any PPT adversary* $\mathcal{A}$, *there exists a negligible function* $negl(\cdot)$ *such that*

$$\mathsf{Adv}_{\mathsf{PKE},\mathcal{A}}^{\mathsf{IND\text{-}CPA}}(1^\lambda) := |\Pr[\mathsf{GAME}_{\mathsf{PKE},\mathcal{A}}^{\mathsf{IND\text{-}CPA}}(1^\lambda) \rightarrow 1] - \frac{1}{2}| \leq negl(\lambda),$$

where $\mathsf{GAME}_{\mathsf{PKE},\mathcal{A}}^{\mathsf{IND\text{-}CPA}}(1^\lambda)$ *is the game described as in Fig. 1.*

Definition 2.11 (EUF-CMA). *A SIG scheme* $\mathsf{SIG} = (\mathsf{Gen}, \mathsf{Sig}, \mathsf{Ver})$ *is Existentially Unforgeable against Adaptive Chosen-Message Attacks (EUF-CMA), if for any PPT adversary* $\mathcal{A}$, *there exists a negligible function* $negl(\cdot)$ *such that*

$$\mathsf{Adv}_{\mathsf{SIG},\mathcal{A}}^{\mathsf{EUF\text{-}CMA}}(1^\lambda) := \Pr[\mathsf{GAME}_{\mathsf{SIG},\mathcal{A}}^{\mathsf{EUF\text{-}CMA}}(1^\lambda) \rightarrow 1] \leq negl(\lambda),$$

where $\mathsf{GAME}_{\mathsf{SIG},\mathcal{A}}^{\mathsf{EUF\text{-}CMA}}(1^\lambda)$ *is described as in Fig. 2.*

$\mathsf{GAME}^{\mathsf{EUF\text{-}CMA}}_{\mathsf{SIG},\mathcal{A}}(1^\lambda)$	$O_{sig}(m)$
$L_m \leftarrow \emptyset, (pk, sk) \leftarrow \mathsf{Gen}(1^\lambda)$	$\mathsf{Sig}(sk, m) \rightarrow \sigma$
$(m^*, \sigma^*) \leftarrow \mathcal{A}^{O_{sig}(\cdot)}(pk)$	$L_m \leftarrow L_m \cup \{m\}$
if $m^* \in L_m$; **return** 0	**return** σ
$b \leftarrow \mathsf{Ver}(pk, m^*, \sigma^*)$	
return b	

Fig. 2. EUF-CMA game of SIG

2.5 Generic Transformations in the ROM

T Transformation. The transformation T converts a PKE scheme into a DPKE scheme. Let $\Pi = (\mathsf{Gen}, \mathsf{Enc}, \mathsf{Dec})$ be a PKE scheme and O be a RO, then the resulting DPKE scheme $\Pi_1^O := T^{O,\Pi} = (\mathsf{Gen_1}^O, \mathsf{Enc_1}^O, \mathsf{Dec_1}^O)$ can be described as follows:

- $\mathsf{Gen}_1^O(1^\lambda)$: Run $(pk, sk) \leftarrow \mathsf{Gen}(1^\lambda)$, then output (pk, sk).
- $\mathsf{Enc}_1^O(pk, m)$: Compute $r := O(m)$ and $c := \mathsf{Enc}(pk, m; r)$, then output c.
- $\mathsf{Dec}_1^O(sk, c)$: Compute $m := \mathsf{Dec}(sk, c)$, then output m.

Lemma 1 ([15]). *Let Π be an OW-CPA secure PKE scheme and O be a RO, then the DPKE scheme Π_1^O is OW-CPA secure in the ROM.*

FDH Transformation. FDH transformation [4] can be used to construct EUF-CMA secure SIG scheme in the ROM. Let O be a RO and $F := (\mathsf{G}, \mathsf{F.Evl}, \mathsf{F.Inv})$ be a TDP, then the resulting SIG scheme $\Pi^O := \mathrm{FDH}^{O,F} = (\mathsf{Gen}^O, \mathsf{Sig}^O, \mathsf{Ver}^O)$ can be described as follows:

- $\mathsf{Gen}^O(1^\lambda)$: Run $(e, t) \leftarrow \mathsf{G}(1^\lambda)$. Let $pk := e$ and $sk := t$, then output (pk, sk).
- $\mathsf{Sig}^O(sk, m)$: Compute $r := O(m)$ and $\sigma := \mathsf{F.Inv}(sk, r)$. Then output σ.
- $\mathsf{Ver}^O(pk, m, \sigma)$: Compute $r := O(m)$. If $\mathsf{F.Evl}(pk, \sigma) = r$, output 0. Otherwise, output 1.

Lemma 2 ([4]). *Let $\mathcal{F}$ be OW secure TDP and O be RO, then the SIG scheme Π^O is UF-CMA secure in the ROM.*

OAEP Transformation. OAEP transformation [5] is widely used to construct PKE scheme in the ROM. Specially, RSA-OAEP [14] is IND-CCA security in the ROM. Let O_1, O_2 be different ROs and $F := (\mathsf{G}, \mathsf{F.Evl}, \mathsf{F.Inv})$ be a TDP, then the resulting PKE scheme $\Pi^{O_1,O_2} := \mathrm{OAEP}^{O_1,O_2,F} = (\mathsf{Gen}^{O_1,O_2}, \mathsf{Enc}^{O_1,O_2}, \mathsf{Dec}^{O_1,O_2})$ can be described as follows:

- $\mathsf{Gen}^{O_1,O_2}(1^\lambda)$: $(e, t) \leftarrow \mathsf{G}(1^\lambda)$.Output $pk := e$ and $sk := t$.

- $\mathsf{Enc}^{O_1,O_2}(pk,m)$: Sample $r \xleftarrow{\$} \{0,1\}^{l_r}$ and compute $c_L := m\|0^l \oplus O_1(r)$ and $c_R := r \oplus O_2(c_L)$. Output $c := \mathsf{F.Evl}(pk, c_L\|c_R)$.
- $\mathsf{Dec}^{O_1,O_2}(sk,c)$: Run $\mathsf{F.Inv}(sk,c) \to (c'_L, c'_R)$ and $s = O_1(c'_R \oplus O_2(c'_L))$ compute $m' = c'_L \oplus s$. If $[m']_l \neq 0^l$, output $\bot$. Otherwise, output $m := [m']^{l_m}$.

Remark 4. $[x]_l$ denote the last l-bits of x and $[x]^l$ denote the first l-bits.

Lemma 3. *Let $\mathcal{F}$ be partial-domain OW secure TDP and O_1 and O_2 be different ROs, then the PKE scheme Π^{O_1,O_2} is IND-CPA secure in the ROM.*

3 ROM Failures

This section illustrates some ROM failures of several well-known generic transformations. These examples show that such failures are not accidental but rather common issues in the ROM.

3.1 Failure of the T Transformation

The T transformation is a typical example of de-randomization by the RO and has been proven to maintain OW-CPA security in the ROM. However, the transformation fails when the underlying PKE relies on the RO.

OW-CPA security implies that the adversary's probability of recovering the message m from a corresponding ciphertext c is negligible. For PKE schemes, this probability depends on the randomness used for encryption. In existing proofs of the transformation T, $O(m)$ is deemed to retain enough randomness for encryption due to the inherent randomness of RO. Consequently, the transformation T was proven OW-CPA security in the ROM.

However, for some OW-CPA secure underlying PKE schemes in the ROM, $O(m)$ may be pre-marked, making m easily recoverable from the ciphertext encrypted with $O(m)$. The transformation T cannot convert such schemes into OW-CPA secure DPKE schemes in the ROM. We illustrate this with a specific construction as follows.

Construction 1. *Let $\Pi = (\mathsf{Gen}, \mathsf{Enc}, \mathsf{Dec})$ be a PKE scheme with the randomness space R and O be a RO. We can construct an oracle-aided PKE scheme $\overline{\Pi}^O = (\overline{\mathsf{Gen}}^O, \overline{\mathsf{Enc}}^O, \overline{\mathsf{Dec}}^O)$ as follows:*

- $\overline{\mathsf{Gen}}^O(1^\lambda) \to (pk, sk)$: *Run* $\mathsf{Gen}(1^\lambda) \to (pk, sk)$ *and output* (pk, sk).
- $\overline{\mathsf{Enc}}^O(pk, m) \to c$: *Pick* $r \xleftarrow{\$} R$ *and set* $c' := \mathsf{Enc}(pk, m; r)$. *Let* $r' = O(m)$. *If* $r = r'$, *output* $c = m\|c'$. *Otherwise, output* $c = 0^{l_m}\|\mathsf{Enc}(pk, m; r)$, *where* l_m *is the bit-length of* m.
- $\overline{\mathsf{Dec}}^O(sk, c) \to m/\bot$: *Parse* c *into* c_1 *and* c_2. *If* $c_2 \neq \mathsf{Enc}(pk, c_1; O(c_1))$ *and* $c_1 \neq 0^{l_m}$, *output* $\bot$. *Otherwise, run* $\mathsf{Dec}(sk, c_2) \to m$ *and output* m.

Proposition 1. *For any OW-CPA secure PKE scheme Π, $\overline{\Pi}^O$ is OW-CPA secure in the ROM. However, $\Pi_1^O := \mathrm{T}^{O,\overline{\Pi}^O}$ is not OW-CPA secure in the ROM.*

Proof. Firstly, we state that the PKE scheme $\overline{\Pi}$ is OW-CPA secure. The main difference between Π and $\overline{\Pi}^O$ is that the message m is exposed in the ciphertext $c := \overline{\mathsf{Enc}}(pk, m; O(m))$. Because r is chosen uniformly at random from R, the probability $\Pr[r = O(m)]$ is negligible. Therefore, $\overline{\Pi}^O$ is also OW-CPA secure in the ROM. Formally, we can construct a reduction $\mathcal{B}^O$. For any OW-CPA adversary $\mathcal{A}^O$ against $\overline{\Pi}^O$, $\mathcal{B}^O$ attacks Π as follows:

- The OW-CPA challenger of Π runs $\mathsf{Gen}(1^\lambda) \rightarrow (pk, sk)$ and sends pk to $\mathcal{B}^O$. $\mathcal{B}^O$ then invokes $\mathcal{A}^O$ and provides it with the public key pk.
- The OW-CPA challenger chooses $r^* \xleftarrow{\$} R$, $m^* \xleftarrow{\$} M$, and calculates $c'^* := \mathsf{Enc}(pk, m^*; r^*)$. It sends c'^* to $\mathcal{B}^O$, which constructs $c^* := 0^l \| c'^*$ and forwards it to $\mathcal{A}^O$.
- For any query x from $\mathcal{A}^O$ to O, $\mathcal{B}^O$ queries O and returns $O(x)$.
- When $\mathcal{A}^O$ outputs m, $\mathcal{B}^O$ outputs m.

According to definition of OW-CPA security, we have

$$\mathsf{Adv}^{\mathsf{OW\text{-}CPA}}_{\Pi,\mathcal{B}^O}(1^\lambda) = \Pr[m = m^*, r^* = O(m^*)] + \Pr[m = m^*, r^* \neq O(m^*)].$$

Because r is chosen uniformly at random from R,

$$\begin{aligned}\mathsf{Adv}^{\mathsf{OW\text{-}CPA}}_{\overline{\Pi},\mathcal{A}^O}(1^\lambda) &\leq \Pr[r = O(m^*)] + \Pr[m = m^*, r^* \neq O(m^*)] \\ &\leq \frac{1}{|R|} + \Pr[m = m^*, r^* \neq O(m^*)].\end{aligned}$$

Thus,

$$\mathsf{Adv}^{\mathsf{OW\text{-}CPA}}_{\overline{\Pi},\mathcal{A}^O}(1^\lambda) \leq \mathsf{Adv}^{\mathsf{OW\text{-}CPA}}_{\Pi,\mathcal{B}^O}(1^\lambda) + \frac{1}{|R|}.$$

As a result, $\overline{\Pi}^O$ is OW-CPA secure in the ROM if Π is OW-CPA secure.

Additionally, it is obviously that the resulting PKE scheme $\Pi_1^O := \mathrm{T}^{O,\overline{\Pi}^O}$ derived from $\overline{\Pi}^O$ is not OW-CPA secure in the ROM. This indicates the transformation T fails in the ROM.

3.2 Failure of the FDH Transformation

The FDH transformation has been proven to be EUF-CMA secure in the ROM. However, when considering an oracle-aided TDP, we encounter the failure of FDH. Specifically, we can construct a special OW-secure TDP in the ROM. The transformation FDH fails to convert it into an EUF-CMA secure SIG scheme.

The transformation FDH generates a signature for a message m by providing the preimage of $O(m)$ i.e., $\mathsf{F.Inv}(sk, O(m))$. Furthermore, RO is introduced to preform randomization on m. Since the underlying TDP is OW secure, it is hard to forger a signature for m without the secret key sk when $O(m)$ is random. Thus, FDH is considered secure in the ROM.

However, in our construction of the TDP, a particular RO value is pre-marked, and the TDP is easily invertible at this value. Consequently, an adversary can forge the signature corresponding to the pre-marked RO value. As a result, the resulting SIG scheme is not EUF-CMA secure even in the ROM.

Construction 2. *Let $F = (\mathsf{G}, \mathsf{F.Evl}, \mathsf{F.Inv})$ be a TDP with output length l, and let O be a RO with output length l. We construct an oracle-aided TDP $\overline{F}^O = (\overline{\mathsf{G}}^O, \overline{\mathsf{F.Evl}}^O, \overline{\mathsf{F.Inv}}^O)$ as follows:*

- $\overline{\mathsf{G}}^O(1^\lambda) \to (e,t)$: *Run* $\mathsf{G}(1^\lambda) \to (e,t)$ *and output* (e,t).
- $\overline{\mathsf{F.Evl}}^O(e,x) \to y$: *Compute* $y' := \mathsf{F.Evl}(e,x)$. *If* $y' = O(0^l)$, *output* $y := 0^l$. *If* $y' = 0^l$, *output* $y := O(0^l)$. *Otherwise, output* $y := y'$.
- $\overline{\mathsf{F.Inv}}^O(t,y) \to x$: *If* $y = O(0^l)$, *output* $x := 0^l$. *If* $y = 0^l$, *output* $x := \mathsf{F.Inv}(t, O(0^l))$. *Otherwise, output* $x := \mathsf{F.Inv}(t,y)$.

Proposition 2. *For any OW secure TDP F, $\overline{F}^O$ is OW secure in the ROM. However, $\Pi^O := FDH^{O,\overline{F}^O}$ is not UF-CMA secure in the ROM.*

Proof. Obviously, $\overline{F}^O$ is also a TDP. To demonstrate the OW security of $\overline{F}^O$ in the ROM, we construct a reduction $\mathcal{B}^O$. For any OW adversary $\mathcal{A}^O$ against $\overline{F}^O$, $\mathcal{B}^O$ attacks F as follows:

- The OW challenger of F generates (e,t) using $\mathsf{G}(1^\lambda)$ and sends e to $\mathcal{B}^O$. $\mathcal{B}^O$ calls $\mathcal{A}^O$ and provides it with the public key e.
- For any query to O made by $\mathcal{A}^O$, $\mathcal{B}^O$ forwards the query to O and returns the response.
- The challenger selects $x^* \xleftarrow{\$} \{0,1\}^l$ and computes $y^* := \mathsf{F.Evl}(e, x^*)$, then sends y^* to $\mathcal{B}^O$ as the challenge.
- $\mathcal{B}^O$ forwards y^* to $\mathcal{A}^O$ and outputs x when $\mathcal{A}^O$ outputs x.

It follows that:

$$\mathsf{Adv}^{\mathsf{OW}}_{F,\mathcal{B}^O}(1^\lambda) + \Pr[y^* = 0^l] + \Pr[y^* = O(0^l)] \geq \mathsf{Adv}^{\mathsf{OW}}_{\overline{F}^O,\mathcal{A}^O}(1^\lambda).$$

Since x^* is chosen uniformly at random:

$$\Pr[y^* = 0^l] + \Pr[y^* = O(0^l)] = \frac{2}{2^l}.$$

Thus,

$$\mathsf{Adv}^{\mathsf{OW}}_{\overline{F}^O,\mathcal{A}^O}(1^\lambda) \leq \mathsf{Adv}^{\mathsf{OW}}_{F,\mathcal{B}^O}(1^\lambda) + \frac{2}{2^l}.$$

Therefore, $\overline{F}^O$ is OW secure in the ROM when F is OW secure.

However, the resulting SIG scheme Π^O is not secure in the ROM. An adversary can easily generate a valid signature $\sigma = 0^l$ for the message 0^l without the secret key t. This indicates FDH fails in the ROM.

3.3 Failure of the OAEP Transformation

The transformation OAEP converts a TDP into a PKE scheme using a two-round Feistel structure [10]. The resulting PKE scheme has been proven IND-CPA secure in the ROM when the TDP is partial-domain OW secure. However, OAEP also fails in the ROM. We construct a special TDP to illustrate the fact.

The TDP first checks if the input x satisfies a specific structure. If the input meets this structure, the TDP directly leaks x. For all other inputs, it remains hard to invert. The detailed construction of this TDP is as follows:

Construction 3. *Let O_1 and O_2 be different ROs and $F := (\mathsf{G}, \mathsf{F.Evl}, \mathsf{F.Inv})$ be a TDP, where $\mathsf{F.Evl}(pk, \cdot) : \{0,1\}^{l_m+l} \times \{0,1\}^{l_r} \to \{0,1\}^{l_m+l} \times \{0,1\}^{l_r}$. We can construction an oracle-aided TDP $\overline{F}^{O_1,O_2} := (\overline{\mathsf{G}}^{O_1,O_2}, \overline{\mathsf{F.Evl}}^{O_1,O_2}, \overline{\mathsf{F.Inv}}^{O_1,O_2})$ as follows:*

- $\overline{\mathsf{G}}^{O_1,O_2}(1^\lambda) \to (e,t)$: *Run $\mathsf{G}(1^\lambda) \to (e,t)$ and output (e,t).*
- $\overline{\mathsf{F.Evl}}^{O_1,O_2}(x) \to y$:
  - *Parse x into x_1 and x_2, where $x_1 \in \{0,1\}^{l_m+l}$ and $x_2 \in \{0,1\}^{l_r}$.*
  - *If $[O_1(x_2 \oplus O_2(x_1)) \oplus x_1]_l = 0^l$, output $y := x_1 \| x_2$.*
  - *Calculate $y' := \mathsf{F.Evl}(e,x)$ and parse y' into y_1 and y_2.*
  - *If $[O_1(y_2 \oplus O_2(y_1)) \oplus y_1]_l = 0^l$, output $y := x_1 \| x_2$.*
  - *Otherwise, output $y := \mathsf{F.Evl}(e,x)$.*
- $\overline{\mathsf{F.Inv}}^{O_1,O_2}(t,y) \to x$:
  - *Parse y into y_1 and y_2.*
  - *If $[O_1(y_2 \oplus O_2(y_1)) \oplus y_1]_l = 0^l$, output $x := y_1 \| y_2$.*
  - *Otherwise, output $x := \mathsf{F.Inv}(t,y)$.*

Proposition 3. *For any partial-domain OW secure TDP F, $\overline{F}^{O_1,O_2}$ is partial-domain OW secure TDP in the ROM. However, $\Pi^{O_1,O_2} := OAEP^{O_1,O_2,\overline{F}^{O_1,O_2}}$ is not IND-CPA secure in the ROM.*

Proof. It is straightforward to verify that $\overline{F}^{O_1,O_2}$ is also a TDP. We can prove its OW security in the ROM by constructing a reduction $\mathcal{B}^{O_1,O_2}$. For any OW adversary $\mathcal{A}^{O_1,O_2}$ against $\mathcal{F}^{O_1,O_2}$, we define the OW adversary $\mathcal{B}^{O_1,O_2}$ against $\overline{F}$ as follows:

- The OW challenger of F runs $\mathsf{G}(1^\lambda) \to (e,t)$ and sends s to $\mathcal{B}^{O_1,O_2}$. Subsequently, $\mathcal{B}^{O_1,O_2}$ invokes $\mathcal{A}^{O_1,O_2}$ and provides it with e.
- The OW challenger picks $x_1^* \| x_2^* \xleftarrow{\$} \{0,1\}^{l_m+l} \times \{0,1\}^{l_r}$ and calculates $y^* := \mathsf{F.Evl}(e, x_1^* \| x_2^*)$. This resulting y^* is transmitted to $\mathcal{B}^{O_1,O_2}$, which then relays it to $\mathcal{A}^{O_1,O_2}$.
- For any query from $\mathcal{A}^{O_1,O_2}$ to O_1 or O_2, $\mathcal{B}^{O_1,O_2}$ queries O_1 or O_2 and returns the result to $\mathcal{A}^{O_1,O_2}$.
- When $\mathcal{A}^{O_1,O_2}$ outputs x_1, $\mathcal{B}^{O_1,O_2}$ outputs x_1.

Parse y^* into y_1^* and y_2^*. According to definition of partial-domain OW security,

$$\mathsf{Adv}^{\mathsf{OW}}_{\overline{F},\mathcal{A}^{O_1,O_2}}(1^\lambda) \leq \mathsf{Adv}^{\mathsf{OW}}_{F,\mathcal{B}^{O_1,O_2}}(1^\lambda) + \Pr[[O_1(x_2^* \oplus O_2(x_1^*)) \oplus x_1^*]_l = 0^l] + \Pr[[O_1(y_2^* \oplus O_2(y_1^*)) \oplus y_1^*]_l = 0^l].$$

Due to the randomness of O_1 and O_2,

$$\Pr[[O_1(x_2^* \oplus O_2(x_1^*)) \oplus x_1^*]_l = 0^l] = \Pr[[O_1(y_2^* \oplus O_2(y_1^*)) \oplus y_1^*]_l = 0^l] = \frac{1}{2^l}.$$

Thus,

$$\mathsf{Adv}^{\mathsf{OW}}_{\overline{F},\mathcal{A}^{O_1,O_2}}(1^\lambda) \leq \mathsf{Adv}^{\mathsf{OW}}_{F,\mathcal{B}^{O_1,O_2}}(1^\lambda) + \frac{2}{2^l}.$$

Consequently, $\overline{F}^{O_1,O_2}$ is partial-domain OW secure in the ROM if F is partial-domain OW secure.

For any $m \in \{0,1\}^{l_m}$, the ciphertext $c = (c_1, c_2)$ encrypted by $\Pi_1^{O_1,O_2}$ satisfies $c_1 := m\|0^l \oplus O_1(r)$ and $c_2 := r \oplus O_2(c_1)$, where r is the randomness used during encryption. It's trivial to obtain m from c. Hence, $\Pi_1^{O_1,O_2} := \mathsf{OAEP}^{O_1,O_2,\overline{F}^{O_1,O_2}}$ is not IND-CCA secure in the ROM.

4 Hierarchical ROM

The above failures suggest potential flaws in existing security poofs of these generic transformations in the ROM. This section introduces an ideal model called Hierarchical ROM (HROM) to understand and fix these reduction failures.

4.1 HROM

Considering the following two facts, we introduce the HROM by hierarchically organizing all ROs in the resulting cryptographic scheme after a generic transformation:

- For generic transformations in the ROM, the underlying schemes may also use ROs.
- In the security proofs for generic transformations in the ROM, the reduction can observe and program the RO [1] used in these transformations for the adversary. However, when the reduction acts as an adversary attacking the underlying scheme, it cannot observe and program the RO used in the underlying primitive.

In the HROM, the RO used by the transformation remains globally publicly accessible, just as the normal RO defined in the ROM. However, the RO used by the underlying primitive is restricted to be accessible only by the scheme and the adversary attacking the scheme. This restriction prevents the reduction from observing and programming the RO in the underlying primitive. The formal definition is stated as follows:

Definition 4.1 (HROM). *In the HROM, for any oracle-aided transformation T^{O_1} and oracle-aided underlying scheme Π^{O_2}, we have the resulting scheme $\Pi_1^{O_1,\overline{O_2}} := T^{O_1,\Pi^{\overline{O_2}}}$. Here, O_1 is an RO publicly accessed by any parties, and $\overline{O_2}$ means that the RO O_2 can only be publicly accessible by Π and the adversary attacking Π^{O_2}.*

Furthermore, when O_1 and O_2 are the same RO, the information generated by the underlying primitive may involve the RO, and this information can be forwarded to the adversary attacking $T^{O_1,\Pi^{\overline{O_2}}}$. Thus, in the process of the adversary's attack, the information about the RO interacted between the adversary and the resulting scheme $T^{O_1,\Pi^{\overline{O_2}}}$ may be generated by the transformation or underlying primitive. However, a reasonable reduction can only simulate the information generated by the transformation and not affect the corresponding information generated by the underlying primitive. Thus, reductions in the HROM are naturally constrained compared to the previous reductions.

4.2 Reductions in the HROM

These reductions, as defined in Definition 2.6, are essential tools for proving the security of cryptographic schemes in the ROM. However, they overlook that the underlying scheme may be constructed using ROs. Intuitively, when $O_1 = O_2$, the reduction's capabilities in the HROM are more constrained compared to the reductions in [12]. Therefore, we formally define reductions in the HROM as follows.

Definition 4.2. *A $((H, p_H) \to (G, p_G), \delta, t, q_O, q_{\mathcal{A}})$-FBB non-programming HR-OM reduction for $T^{O_1,\cdot}$ is a machine $\mathcal{B}^{O_1,\cdot}$ with the property that for any (H, p_H)-adversary $\mathcal{A}$ and any (G, p_G)-candidate Π^{O_2} in the ROM, if*

$$\mathsf{Adv}^{H}_{T^{O_1,\Pi^{\overline{O_2}}},\mathcal{A}^{O_1}}(1^\lambda) > \epsilon(\lambda)$$

for ROs O_1, O_2 and $\epsilon \geq 0$, then

$$\mathsf{Adv}^{G}_{\Pi^{\overline{O_2}},\mathcal{B}^{O_1,\overline{O_2}},\mathcal{A}^{O_1}}(1^\lambda) > \delta(\epsilon, t, q_O, q_{\mathcal{A}}),$$

where $\mathcal{B}$ runs in time t, q_O is the total number of $\mathcal{B}$'s queries to given ROs O_1 and $\overline{O_2}$ and $\mathcal{B}$ runs $q_{\mathcal{A}}$ instantiations of $\mathcal{A}$. These quantities are functions of λ. Furthermore, $\delta(\epsilon, t, q_O, q_{\mathcal{A}})$ is non-negligible when ϵ is non-negligible.

Remark 5. If no RO is utilized in the (H, p_H)-candidate Π, then O_2 is null. If the RO used by Π^{O_2} is identical to the RO used in transformation T^{O_1}, then O_1 equals O_2.

Definition 4.3. *A $((H, p_H) \to (G, p_G), \delta, t, q_O, q_{\mathcal{A}})$-FBB randomly-programming HROM reduction for $T^{O_1,\cdot}$ is a machine $\mathcal{B}^{O_1,\cdot}$ with the property that for any (G, p_G)-adversary $\mathcal{A}$ and any (H, p_H)-candidate Π^{O_2} in the ROM, if*

$$\mathsf{Adv}^{H}_{T^{O_1,\Pi^{\overline{O_2}}},\mathcal{A}^{O_1}}(1^\lambda) > \epsilon(\lambda)$$

for ROs O_1, O_2 *and* $\epsilon \geq 0$, *then*

$$\mathsf{Adv}^G_{\Pi^{\overline{O_2}}, \mathcal{B}^{O_1, \overline{O_2}, (O_{Evl}, O_{Prg}, O_{Rnd})}, \mathcal{A}^{O_{Evl}}}(1^\lambda) > \delta(\epsilon, t, q_O, q_\mathcal{A}),$$

where $\mathcal{B}$ *runs in time* t, q_O *is the total number of* $\mathcal{B}$*'s queries to given ROs* O_1, $\overline{O_2}$, O_{Evl}, O_{Prg} *and* O_{Rnd}, *and* $\mathcal{B}$ *runs* $q_\mathcal{A}$ *instantiations of* $\mathcal{A}$. $(O_{Evl}, O_{Prg}, O_{Rnd})$ *is the RPRO defined in* [12]. *These three quantities are functions of* λ. *Furthermore,* $\delta(\epsilon, t, q_O, q_\mathcal{A})$ *is non-negligible when* ϵ *is non-negligible.*

Definition 4.4. *A* $((H, p_H) \to (G, p_G), \delta, t, q_O, q_\mathcal{A})$*-FBB fully-programming HROM reduction for* $T^{O_1,\cdot}$ *is a machine* $\mathcal{B}^{O_1,\cdot}$ *with the property that for any* (G, p_G)*-adversary* $\mathcal{A}$ *and any* (H, p_H)*-candidate* Π^{O_2} *in the ROM, if*

$$\mathsf{Adv}^H_{T^{O_1, \Pi^{\overline{O_2}}}, \mathcal{A}^{O_1}}(1^\lambda) > \epsilon(\lambda)$$

for ROs O_1, O_2 *and* $\epsilon \geq 0$, *then*

$$\mathsf{Adv}^G_{\Pi^{\overline{O_2}}, \mathcal{B}^{O_1, \overline{O_2}, \mathcal{A}^{(\cdot)}}}(1^\lambda) > \delta(\epsilon, t, q_O, q_\mathcal{A}),$$

where $\mathcal{B}$ *runs in time* t, q_O *is the total number of* $\mathcal{B}$*'s queries to given ROs* O_1 *and* $\overline{O_2}$, *and* $\mathcal{B}$ *runs* $q_\mathcal{A}$ *instantiations of* $\mathcal{A}$. *These quantities are functions of* λ. *Furthermore,* $\delta(\epsilon, t, q_O, q_\mathcal{A})$ *is non-negligible when* ϵ *is non-negligible.*

We compare the above three kinds of reduction and draw the following results.

Proposition 4. *A* $((H, p_H) \to (G, p_G), \delta, t, q_O, q_\mathcal{A})$*-FBB non-programming HROM reduction for* T^{O_1} *implies a* $((H, p_H) \to (G, p_G), \delta, t, q'_O, q_\mathcal{A})$*-FBB randomly-programming HROM reduction for* T^{O_1}, *where* $q'_O = q_O$.

Proof. The result is easily to prove, we omit the proof.

Proposition 5. *A* $((H, p_H) \to (G, p_G), \delta, t, q_O, q_\mathcal{A})$*-FBB randomly-programming HROM reduction for* T^{O_1} *implies a* $((H, p_H) \to (G, p_G), \delta, t', q'_O, q_\mathcal{A})$*-FBB fully-programming HROM reduction for* T^{O_1}, *where* $t' \approx \Theta(t)$ *and* $q'_O \leq q_O$.

Proof. The result is easily to prove, we omit the proof.

4.3 Secure Transformations in the HROM

The existing security reductions of many generic transformations in the ROM do not satisfy our definitions of HROM reduction. Furthermore, when the RO used in these transformations is identical to that used in the underlying primitive, we can demonstrate that these transformations are insecure by constructing counterexamples. Therefore, it is necessary to refine these transformations to be secure in the HROM. To avoid the issue, we propose two approaches to lift existing "secure" generic transformations in the ROM to secure transformations in the HROM.

One approach is to directly restrict the RO used by the underlying primitive to be different from the RO used by the transformation.

Definition 4.5 (Constrained Transformation). *The constrained T^O is an oracle-aided transformation with an additional restriction: the RO O used in the transformation differs from the RO used in the underlying primitive.*

Theorem 1. *If there exists a $((H, p_H) \to (G, p_G), \delta, t, q_O, q_\mathcal{A})$-FBB reduction as defined in Definition 2.6 for T^{O_1}, constrained T^{O_1} is $(G, p_G) \to (H, p_H)$-secure in the HROM.*

Proof. Obviously, a $((H, p_H) \to (G, p_G), \delta, t, q_O, q_\mathcal{A})$-FBB reduction as defined in Definition 2.6 for T^{O_1} implies a $((H, p_H) \to (G, p_G), \delta, t, q_O, q_\mathcal{A})$-FBB HROM reduction for constrained T^{O_1}. When $O_2 \neq O_1$, we can construct an HROM reduction similar to the existing reduction for T^{O_1}.

The other lift approach uses the domain separation technique of RO. Let T^{O_1} be a generic transformation in the ROM; we can modify it to obtain a new transformation T'^{O_1}. For any candidate underlying scheme Π^{O_2}, the resulting scheme $\Pi_1^{O_1,O_2} := T'^{O_1,\Pi^{O_2}}$ can be described as follows:

- At the setup, T'^{O_1} picks $s \xleftarrow{\$} \{0,1\}^{l(\lambda)}$ and takes s as a public parameter, where $\frac{1}{2^{l(\lambda)}}$ is negligible.
- The rest of the construction is the same as $T^{O_1,\Pi^{O_2}}$, except that the $O_1(\cdot)$ used in $T^{O_1,\Pi^{O_2}}$ is replaced by $O_1(s, \cdot)$.

The randomness s is introduced to partition the RO. Based on the randomness of RO, even if $O_1 = O_2$, the actual RO $(O(s, c))$ used by the new transformation is mutually independent of the RO used by the underlying scheme with an overwhelming probability. Therefore, the new transformation avoids the failures mentioned earlier.

Theorem 2. *If there exists a $((H, p_H) \to (G, p_G), \delta, t, q_O, q_\mathcal{A})$-FBB reduction as defined in Definition 2.6 for T^{O_1}, the transformation T'^{O_1} is $(G, p_G) \to (H, p_H)$-secure in the HROM.*

Proof. We demonstrate the security of T'^{O_1} in the HROM by constructing a $((H, p_H) \to (G, p_G), \delta, t, q'_O, q_\mathcal{A})$-FBB HROM reduction for T'^{O_1}, where $q'_O = q_O$. Let the oracle-aided machine $\mathcal{B}$ be the $((H, p_H) \to (G, p_G), \delta, t, q_O, q_\mathcal{A})$-FBB reduction as defined in Definition 2.6 for T^{O_1}. According to the Definition 2.6, for any (H, p_H)-adversary $\mathcal{A}$ and any (G, p_G)-candidate Π, if

$$\mathsf{Adv}^H_{T^{O_1,\Pi},\mathcal{A}^{O_1}}(1^\lambda) > \epsilon(\lambda)$$

for the RO O_1 and $\epsilon \geq 0$, then

$$\mathsf{Adv}^G_{\Pi,\mathcal{B}^{O_1,\mathcal{A}^{O_2}}}(1^\lambda) > \delta(\epsilon, t, q_O, q_\mathcal{A}),$$

where $\mathcal{O}_1$ and $\mathcal{O}_2$ are defined as in Definition 2.6. For any (H, p_H)-adversary $\mathcal{A}'$ and (G, p_G)-candidate Π'^{O_2} in the ROM, we can construct $\mathcal{B}'$ as follows:

- $\mathcal{B}'$ interacts with Π'^{O_2} as defined by G. In this process, it runs $\mathcal{B}$ to invoke $\mathcal{A}'$.
- $\mathcal{B}'$ simulates the interactive environment $\mathcal{B}$ need.
  - $\mathcal{B}'$ simulates the security game for $\mathcal{B}$ by forwarding all information received during the interaction with Π'^{O_2}, and returns $\mathcal{B}$'s corresponding responses to Π'^{O_2}. Since s is chosen uniformly at random, $\mathcal{B}$ can distinguish the $\mathcal{B}'$ simulation with probability at most $\frac{1}{2^l}$.
  - $\mathcal{B}'$ forwards the information output by $\mathcal{A}'$ to $\mathcal{B}$ and returns corresponding responses to $\mathcal{A}'$. Specially, when $\mathcal{A}'$ queries $s\|x$ to $\mathcal{O}_2$, $\mathcal{B}'$ queries $\mathcal{B}$ on x and forwards the response to $\mathcal{A}$.
- $\mathcal{B}'s$ simulates the ROs queried by $\mathcal{B}$.
  - When $\mathcal{B}$ queries $O_1(x)$, $\mathcal{B}'$ queries $O_1(s, x)$ and forwards the response to $\mathcal{B}$.
  - If $\mathcal{B}$ is a FBB randomly-programming reduction: when $\mathcal{B}$ queries x to O_{Evl} of the RPRO $(O_{Evl}, O_{Prg}, O_{Rnd})$, $\mathcal{B}'$ queries $s\|x$ to O_{Evl} and forwards the response to $\mathcal{B}$. When $\mathcal{B}$ queries (x, y) to O_{Prg}, $\mathcal{B}'$ queries $(s\|x, y)$ to O_{Prg} nd forwards the response to $\mathcal{B}$. When $\mathcal{B}$ queries y to O_{Rnd}, $\mathcal{B}'$ also queries y to O_{Rnd} and forwards the response to $\mathcal{B}$.
- $\mathcal{B}'$ outputs and aborts when $\mathcal{B}$ outputs and aborts.

Since $\mathcal{A}'$ does not queries O_2 and G is the same for both oracle-free Π and oracle-aided Π'^{O_2}, we have

$$\mathsf{Adv}^{G}_{\Pi^{\overline{O_2}},\mathcal{B}'^{\overline{O_2}, O_1},\mathcal{A}'^{O_2}}(1^\lambda) > (1-\frac{1}{2^l})\cdot\mathsf{Adv}^{G}_{\Pi^{O_2},\mathcal{B}^{O_1},\mathcal{A}'^{O_2}}(1^\lambda) > (1-\frac{1}{2^l})\cdot\delta(\epsilon, t, q_O, q_{\mathcal{A}'}).$$

As a result, the oracle-aided machine $\mathcal{B}'$ is the $((H, p_H) \to (G, p_G), \delta', t, q_O, q_{\mathcal{A}})$-FBB HROM reduction for T'^{O_1}, where $\delta' = (1 - \frac{1}{2^l})\delta$ and $q_{\mathcal{A}'} = q_{\mathcal{A}}$.

A Appendix

A.1 Notation

We denote security parameter by λ and a set of negligible functions by $\mathsf{negl}(\lambda)$ where a function $f(\lambda)$ is negligible if $f(\lambda) = \lambda^{-\omega(1)}$. We denote the Boolean value $\|B\|$ that is 1 if the Boolean statement B is true, and 0 otherwise. Probabilistic polynomial time is represented as PPT.

For a finite set S, the cardinality of S is denoted by $|S|$, and $x \xleftarrow{\$} S$ means that x is uniformly random sampled from S. For two sets S_1 and S_2, $S_1 \times S_2$ means the Cartesian product of them. For an algorithm $\mathcal{A}$, if inp is a string, $\mathsf{out} \leftarrow \mathcal{A}(\mathsf{inp})$ or $\mathcal{A}(\mathsf{inp}) \to \mathsf{out}$ means that out is the output of $\mathcal{A}$ when $\mathcal{A}$ runs on input inp. If $\mathcal{A}$ is deterministic, the out is fixed denoted by $\mathsf{out} := \mathcal{A}(\mathsf{inp})$. We also use the notation $\mathsf{out} := \mathcal{A}(\mathsf{inp}; r)$ to make the randomness r explicit for a probabilistic algorithm $\mathcal{A}$. We denote an algorithm $\mathcal{A}$ with access to an oracle O by $\mathcal{A}^O$.

A.2 Cryptographic Primitives

We recall the formal definitions of several cryptographic primitives, including Trapdoor Functions/Permutations (TDF/TDP), Public Key Encryption (PKE), Deterministic PKE (DPKE), and Signature (SIG).

Definition A.1 (TDF/TDP). *Let $\mathcal{F} := \{F_{index}\}$ be a collection of functions, a family of TDF can be described as a tuple of PPT algorithms* $(\mathsf{G}, \mathsf{F}, \mathsf{F}^{-1})$ *as follows:*

- $\mathsf{G}(1^\lambda) \to (e, t)$: *The generation algorithm takes the security parameter 1^λ as input and outputs an index e of a function in $\mathcal{F}$ and a trapdoor t.*
- $\mathsf{F.Evl}(e, x) \to y$: *The evaluation algorithm takes an index e and an element x from the domain of F_e as input and outputs $y := F_e(x)$.*
- $\mathsf{F.Inv}(t, y) \to x/\bot$: *The inverting algorithm takes a trapdoor t and y as input and outputs x which satisfies $F_e(x) = y$ or failure symbol $\bot$.*

Specially, $(\mathsf{G}, \mathsf{F.Evl}, \mathsf{F.Inv})$ *is a family of TDP when $\mathcal{F} := \{F_{index}\}$ denotes a collection of permutations, it is a family of TDP.* $(\mathsf{G}, \mathsf{F.Evl}, \mathsf{F.Inv})$ *can be described as follows*

Definition A.2 ((D)PKE). *A PKE scheme consists of a tuple of PPT algorithms* $(\mathsf{Gen}, \mathsf{Enc}, \mathsf{Dec})$ *as follows:*

- $\mathsf{Gen}(1^\lambda) \to (pk, sk)$: *The generation algorithm takes the security parameter 1^λ as input and outputs a (public, secret) key pair (pk, sk).*
- $\mathsf{Enc}(pk, m) \to c$: *The encryption algorithm takes pk and a message m as input and outputs a ciphertext $c := \mathsf{Enc}(pk, m; r)$, r is the randomness.*
- $\mathsf{Dec}(sk, c) \to m/\bot$: *The decryption algorithm takes sk and a ciphertext c as input, and outputs a message m or the failure symbol $\bot$.*

Specially, $(\mathsf{Gen}, \mathsf{Enc}, \mathsf{Dec})$ *is DPKE scheme when the encryption algorithm* Enc *is deterministic.*

Definition A.3 (KEM). *A KEM scheme consists of a tuple of PPT algorithms* $(\mathsf{KGen}, \mathsf{KEnc}, \mathsf{KDec})$ *as follows:*

- $\mathsf{KGen}(1^\lambda) \to (pk, sk)$: *The generation algorithm takes the security parameter 1^λ as input and outputs a public/secret keys pair (pk, sk).*
- $\mathsf{KEnc}(pk) \to (c, k)$: *The encapsulation algorithm takes a public key pk as input and outputs a key k and an encapsulation of the key k.*
- $\mathsf{KDec}(sk, c) \to k/\bot$: *The decapsulation algorithm takes a secret key sk and an encapsulation c as input, and outputs a key k or $\bot$.*

Definition A.4 (SIG). *A SIG scheme consists of a tuple of PPT algorithms* $(\mathsf{Gen}, \mathsf{Sig}, \mathsf{Ver})$ *as follows:*

- $\mathsf{Gen}(1^\lambda) \to (pk, sk)$: *The key generation algorithm takes the security parameter 1^λ as input and outputs a (public, secret) key pair (pk, sk).*
- $\mathsf{Sig}(sk, m) \to \sigma$: *The signature algorithm takes a secret key sk and a message m as input and outputs a signature $\sigma \leftarrow \mathsf{Sig}(sk, m)$.*
- $\mathsf{Ver}(pk, m, \sigma) \to 0/1$: *The verification algorithm takes a public key sk, a message m and a signature σ as input and outputs a bit $b \in \{0, 1\}$. Here, $b = 1$ indicates that the σ is valid, while $b = 0$ indicates an invalid signature.*

A.3 RPRO

A RPRO $(O_{Evl}, O_{Prg}, O_{Rnd})$ can be described as in Fig. 3.

$O_{Evl}(x)$	$O_{Prg}(x, y)$	$O_{Rnd}(y)$
if $T[x] = \bot$	$T[x] := R[y]$	**if** $R[y] = \bot$
$\quad T[x] \xleftarrow{\$} Y$	**return** $T[x]$	$\quad R[y] \xleftarrow{\$} Y$
return $T[x]$		**return** $R[y]$

Fig. 3. RPRO $(O_{Evl}, O_{Rrg}, O_{Rnd})$

The evaluation oracle O_{Evl} behaves as a RO mapping $X \to Y$. The O_{Rnd} oracle implements a random mapping $\{0,1\}^* \to Y$. The programming interface O_{Prg} oracle takes $x \in X$ and $Y \in \{0,1\}^*$ as input, and sets $T[x]$to be the same as $R[y]$.

References

1. Ananth, P., Bhaskar, R.: Non observability in the random oracle model. In: ProvSec. LNCS, vol. 8209, pp. 86–103. Springer (2013)
2. Bellare, M., Boldyreva, A., O'Neill, A.: Deterministic and efficiently searchable encryption. In: CRYPTO. LNCS, vol. 4622, pp. 535–552. Springer (2007)
3. Bellare, M., Davis, H., Günther, F.: Separate your domains: NIST PQC kems, oracle cloning and read-only indifferentiability. In: EUROCRYPT (2). LNCS, vol. 12106, pp. 3–32. Springer (2020)
4. Bellare, M., Rogaway, P.: Random oracles are practical: a paradigm for designing efficient protocols. In: CCS, pp. 62–73. ACM (1993)
5. Bellare, M., Rogaway, P.: Optimal asymmetric encryption. In: EUROCRYPT. LNCS, vol. 950, pp. 92–111. Springer (1994)
6. Bellare, M., Rogaway, P.: The exact security of digital signatures - how to sign with RSA and rabin. In: EUROCRYPT. LNCS, vol. 1070, pp. 399–416. Springer (1996)
7. Bellare, M., Rogaway, P.: The security of triple encryption and a framework for code-based game-playing proofs. In: EUROCRYPT. LNCS, vol. 4004, pp. 409–426. Springer (2006)
8. Bernstein, D.J.: On the looseness of FO derandomization. IACR Cryptology ePrint Archive, p. 912 (2021). https://eprint.iacr.org/2021/912
9. Boneh, D., Dagdelen, Ö., Fischlin, M., Lehmann, A., Schaffner, C., Zhandry, M.: Random oracles in a quantum world. In: ASIACRYPT. LNCS, vol. 7073, pp. 41–69. Springer (2011)
10. Feistel, H.: Cryptography and computer privacy. Sci. Am. 15–23 (1973)
11. Fiat, A., Shamir, A.: How to prove yourself: practical solutions to identification and signature problems. In: CRYPTO. LNCS, vol. 263, pp. 186–194. Springer (1986)

12. Fischlin, M., Lehmann, A., Ristenpart, T., Shrimpton, T., Stam, M., Tessaro, S.: Random oracles with(out) programmability. In: ASIACRYPT. LNCS, vol. 6477, pp. 303–320. Springer (2010)
13. Fujisaki, E., Okamoto, T.: Secure integration of asymmetric and symmetric encryption schemes. In: CRYPTO. LNCS, vol. 1666, pp. 537–554. Springer (1999)
14. Fujisaki, E., Okamoto, T., Pointcheval, D., Stern, J.: RSA-OAEP is secure under the RSA assumption. In: CRYPTO. LNCS, vol. 2139, pp. 260–274. Springer (2001)
15. Hofheinz, D., Hövelmanns, K., Kiltz, E.: A modular analysis of the Fujisaki-Okamoto transformation. In: TCC (1). LNCS, vol. 10677, pp. 341–371. Springer (2017)
16. Reingold, O., Trevisan, L., Vadhan, S.P.: Notions of reducibility between cryptographic primitives. In: TCC. LNCS, vol. 2951, pp. 1–20. Springer (2004)
17. Zhandry, M.: Augmented random oracles. In: CRYPTO (3). LNCS, vol. 13509, pp. 35–65. Springer (2022)

Quantum-Safe Cryptography

BDEC: Enhancing Learning Credibility via Post-quantum Digital Credentials

Zoey Ziyi Li[1], Xinyu Zhang[1,2(✉)], Hui Cui[1], Jun Zhao[1], and Xuan Chen[1]

[1] Monash University, Melbourne, Australia
{Ziyi.Li,Xinyu.Zhang1,Hui.Cui,Jun.Zhao1,Xuan.Chen1}@monash.edu
[2] Data61, CSIRO, Sydney, Australia

Abstract. Digital credentials can streamline the verification process, reduce fraud, and enhance the portability and accessibility of academic records, and thus digital credentials become increasingly essential for verifying academic achievements and qualifications in a rapidly digitizing world. However, current research on digital credentials in the education scenario falls into two categories: 1) blockchain-verifiable credentials, which either rely on blockchain security or classical cryptographic problems and are not quantum-safe; and 2) post-quantum anonymous credentials, primarily lattice-based, facing challenges in achieving conditional linkability and efficient revocation.

In this paper, we propose a generic framework for constructing an anonymous credential system named Blockchain-based Digital Education Credential (BDEC). Our framework requires only a digital signature scheme and a zkSNARK. We formally prove the unforgeability, anonymity, and unlinkability of the proposed framework and show that it additionally supports conditional linkability and revocability. By instantiating the framework with the post-quantum signature Loquat [Crypto'24] and zkSNARK Aurora [Eurocrypt'19], we construct a post-quantum anonymous credential system whose security relies on collision-resistant hash functions and the Legendre PRF. Furthermore, our resulting system offers significant improvements in its concrete performance over the lattice-based system [Crypto'23].

Keywords: Digital Credential · Anonymous · Post-Quantum · Blockchain

1 Introduction

Traditionally, education certificates have served as the primary means to prove an individual's educational achievements, skills, and employability in the job market [23]. However, recent incidents have seriously challenged the credibility

Z. Z. Li and X. Zhang—First and second authors contributed equally to this work, and their sequence is according to alphabetical order.

J. K. Liu et al. (Eds.): ProvSec 2024, LNCS 14904, pp. 45–64, 2025.
https://doi.org/10.1007/978-981-96-0957-4_3

of educational certificates. For example, a private university in India sold 36,000 fake degrees for $1,362 each, causing graduates in Singapore, Malaysia, the US, and Canada to face pressure from employers worldwide to verify their qualifications [22]. Additionally, 150 Indian students in Canada faced deportation after being victims of an immigration scam that provided them with forged college admission letters [15]. On the other hand, honest students holding authentic certificates are at risk of credential misuse and theft, as demonstrated by LinkedIn's 2021 breach, which resulted in 700 million users' profiles being sold on the Dark Web [27]. In addition, the rise of micro-credentials, defined by the European Commission [9], as proofs of learning outcomes acquired through short learning experiences, often results in fragmented learning records. This fragmentation not only makes it difficult to track continuous progress but also leads to repetitive proofs of the same skills [10]. These issues underscore the urgent need for a more credible digital credential scheme with the following desired properties, which is the focus of our study:

- Unforgeability: Ensures that credentials cannot be counterfeited.
- Anonymity: Protects user privacy by preventing the linkage of credentials to their identity.
- Unlinkability: Guarantees user privacy one step further as different shown credentials cannot be linked to same identity.
- Conditional Linkability: Supports selective linkability to address fragmented learning records.
- Revocation: Enables the ability to revoke credentials if they are compromised or invalidated, ensuring that only legitimate credentials remain active.

1.1 Related Work

To address the above-mentioned issues, the most state-of-art approaches fall into two categories: blockchain-verifiable credentials and post-quantum anonymous credentials. These recent works build upon the foundational concept of pseudonymous credentials, first proposed by Chaum in 1984 [4], which enables users to sign documents without revealing their identity. The Camenisch and Lysyanskaya (CL) signature scheme [3] further advanced this field by providing a framework for creating secure and efficient anonymous credentials using group signatures and zero-knowledge proofs. Until 2014, Garman et al. introduced decentralized anonymous credentials (DAC), leveraging the benefits of distributed technology to enhance privacy and security [11].

Blockchain-Verifiable Credentials: In the recent blockchain domain, significant efforts have been made to combat credential forgery and theft. Notably, Damgard et al. introduced a credential identity layer that balances accountability and privacy in blockchain systems to mitigate "Anti Money Laundering" issues [7]. Other proposals have utilized Verifiable Credentials (VC) and blockchain Non-Fungible Tokens (NFTs) for various applications, such as electric vehicle authentication [20] and education credentials [16]. Traceability has also gained considerable research attention in blockchain proposals. Zhuang et al. proposed a privacy-preserving and traceability scheme for intellectual property [29], and similar efforts have been made for numerous supply chain management systems [17,18]. Regarding conditional linkability, Coconut introduced the first selective disclosure attribute-based credential scheme supporting threshold issuance, although it lacked support for traceability or revocation [26]. Shi et al. addressed this limitation by incorporating threshold tracing and revocation properties [24]. In terms of updatability, Garman et al. [11] discussed the creation of updatable (e.g., stateful) anonymous credentials, although their work did not fully implement this feature. Despite these advancements, current approaches largely rely on blockchain security or classical cryptographic problems (strong RSA or Diffie-Hellman assumption) and are not quantum-safe. None of them can satisfy all the desired security properties comprehensively.

Quantum-Resistant Credential: Jeudy et al. [12] proposed the first lattice-based anonymous credentials system, leveraging the hardness of the Short Integer Solution (SIS) and Learning With Errors (LWE) problems. Their approach marks a significant step towards quantum-resistant credentials, but it currently supports only a single message, making its use for anonymous verifiable credentials (VCs) cumbersome in terms of data size and performance. Other notable quantum-based proposals include the work of Blazy et al. [2], who provided a generic framework for constructing anonymous credential schemes, and Kazmi et al. [13], who introduced a pseudonymous credential scheme specifically designed for use in payment systems. The only education-focused study is by Shrivas et al. [25], who proposed a quantum-resistant university credentials verification system using lattice-based cryptography and hash-based signatures within a consortium blockchain. However, this study lacks comprehensive security proofs and code implementation. Overall, the current quantum-resistant credential proposals are primarily lattice-based, facing challenges in achieving conditional linkability and efficient revocation, thus highlighting the need for further research, possibly exploring symmetric-key primitives based schemes [8].

1.2 Our Contributions

Our contributions are twofold:

- **Contribution I**. We propose a generic framework for constructing anonymous credential systems that also achieve conditional linkability and revocability. Our framework assumes only *black-box* access to a digital signature scheme and a zero-knowledge succinct non-interactive argument of knowledge (zkSNARK) protocol, allowing for efficient instantiation with post-quantum building blocks. We provide a formal security analysis of the proposed framework, proving its unforgeability, anonymity, and unlinkability. Notably, if the underlying signature and zkSNARK schemes achieve perfect zero-knowledge, which is commonly the case, our system achieves perfect anonymity and unlinkability.

- **Contribution II.** We provide a post-quantum instantiation of our framework using LOQUAT [28], a post-quantum signature scheme based solely on collision-resistant hash functions and the Legendre PRF. We instantiate the underlying zkSNARK with Aurora [1] and Fractal [5], respectively. To demonstrate the practicality of our system, we analyze and compare the sizes of key pairs, credentials, and credential proofs with those of existing post-quantum anonymous credential systems. Assuming 128-bit security, our instantiation with LOQUAT and Aurora results in public key, private key, credential size, and credential proof size reductions of 2,447, 86,752, 5.56, and 4.82 times, respectively, compared to the lattice-based anonymous credential scheme proposed by Jeudy et al. [12] (Table 1).

Table 1. Properties Comparison with Existing Anonymous Credential Systems

Studies	Garman et al. [11]	Damgard et al. [7]	Coconut [26]	Jeudy et al. [12]	Shrivas et al. [25]	This study
Unforgeability	✓	✓	✓	✓	✓	✓
Anonymity	✓	✓	✓	✓	✓	✓
Unlinkability	–	–	✓	✓	✓	✓
Conditional Linkability	–	–	–	–	–	✓
Quantum-resistance	–	–	–	✓	✓	✓

1.3 Organizations

The rest of the paper is organized as follows. Section 2 provides a brief review of definitions used in this paper. Section 3 presents the framework of a blockchain-based digital education credential system (BDEC). In Sect. 4, we detail BDEC based on decentralized anonymous credential schemes, and analyze its security. We evaluate the performance of our proposed BDEC system in Sect. 5 and conclude the paper in Sect. 6.

2 Preliminaries

In this section, we briefly describe relevant definitions to be used in this paper.

2.1 ZkSNARKs

Let $\mathcal{R}$ be an efficiently decidable binary relation for an NP language $L_{\mathcal{R}}$.

Definition 1 (zkSNARK). *A zero-knowledge succinct non-interactive argument of knowledge (zkSNARK) consists of a tuple of probabilistic polynomial algorithms, denoted as* $(\mathcal{S}, \mathcal{P}, \mathcal{V})$ *such that*

- $\texttt{crs} \leftarrow \mathcal{S}(1^\lambda, \mathcal{R})$. *On input a security parameter* λ *in unary, the algorithm outputs a common reference string* $\texttt{crs}$.
- $\pi \leftarrow \mathcal{P}(\texttt{crs}, w, x)$. *On input a common reference string* $\texttt{crs}$ *and a witness-statement pair* (w, x), *the algorithm outputs a succinct argument* π.
- $0/1 \leftarrow \mathcal{V}(\texttt{crs}, x, \pi)$. *On input a common reference string* $\texttt{crs}$, *a claimed statement* x *and the argument* π, *the algorithm outputs* 1 *(accept) if* π *is convincing (i.e., the prover knows a witness* w *such that* $(w, x) \in R$ *for some NP relation* R*).*

2.2 Digital Signature

Definition 2 (Digital Signature). *A signature scheme consists of the following algorithms* ($\texttt{Sig.Setup}, \texttt{Sig.KeyGen}, \texttt{Sig.Sign}, \texttt{Sig.Verify}$)*:*

1. $\texttt{Sig.pp} \leftarrow \texttt{Sig.Setup}(1^\lambda)$. *On input a security parameter* λ *in unary, the algorithm generates a set of public parameters denoted as* $\texttt{Sig.pp}$.
2. $(sk, pk) \leftarrow \texttt{Sig.KeyGen}(\texttt{Sig.pp})$*: On input public parameters* $\texttt{Sig.pp}$ *generated in the setup phase, the algorithm outputs a key pair* (sk, pk).
3. $\sigma \leftarrow \texttt{Sig.Sign}(\texttt{Sig.pp}, sk, m)$*: On input public parameters* $\texttt{Sig.pp}$, *a secret key* sk, *and a message* m, *the (randomized) algorithm outputs a signature* σ.
4. $(0/1) \leftarrow \texttt{Sig.Verify}(\texttt{Sig.pp}, pk, m, \sigma)$*: On input public parameters* pp, *a public key* pk, *a message* m, *and a signature* σ, *the algorithm outputs 1 (accept) if the signature is valid. Otherwise, outputs 0 (reject).*

Due to page limits, we refer readers to the standard security notions of zkSNARKs and digital signatures as detailed in [19] and [28], respectively.

2.3 Blockchain

Since its adoption in the Bitcoin cryptocurrency [21], the blockchain platform, which is essentially a chain of blocks storing relevant digital data, has been proposed to a wide range of applications. As a distributed ledger, the blockchain enables the data to be stored on a number of nodes (or computers). Due to the fact that the data can be accessed by anybody, it is challenging for any single entity to fully control of the whole blockchain network. Such a distributed feature of the blockchain, integrating with smart contracts [6], allows users to deploy applications on the blockchain without the involvement of any trusted authority.

3 System Framework

In this section, we describe the framework of a blockchain-based digital education credential system, as well as its security requirements.

3.1 System Architecture

Let $N \in \mathbb{Z}^+$ be the maximum attributes $\{a_1, ..., a_N\}$ (here $\{a_i\}_{i\in[1,N]}$ could be Student Name: ABC, University: XYZ University, Major: Law, Year: 2023, etc.) that each student U in the blockchain-based digital education credential BDEC scheme can claim. At the beginning, each student U randomly selects a secret sk_U as the private user-key, and then derives a series of pseudonym public and private keys $(ppk_{U,TA}, psk_{U,TA})$ to communicate with different educational authority TA (e.g., colleges, universities, tertiary training organizations). The public key $ppk_{U,TA}$ plays the role of the pseudonym identity between the student U and the authority TA. When the student U needs to obtain an education credential on certain eligible attributes $\mathbf{A} = \{a_1, ..., a_m\}$ (where $m \in \mathbb{Z}^+ \leq N$), the student U creates a credential $c_{U,TA}$ on attributes $\mathbf{A}$ to the relevant educational institute TA from its keys $(ppk_{U,TA}, psk_{U,TA})$ established with the authority TA, as well as a corresponding proof $\pi_{c_{U,TA}}$ on the credential $c_{U,TA}$. Once the authority TA verifies the authenticity of the credential $c_{U,TA}$ over attributes $\mathbf{A}$ and the proof $\pi_{c_{U,TA}}$ provided by the student U, the information including $(ppk_{U,TA}, c_{U,TA}, \pi_{c_{U,TA}})$ will be published to the blockchain by the authority TA. In Fig. 1, we briefly describe the architecture of a blockchain-based digital education credential (BDEC) scheme.

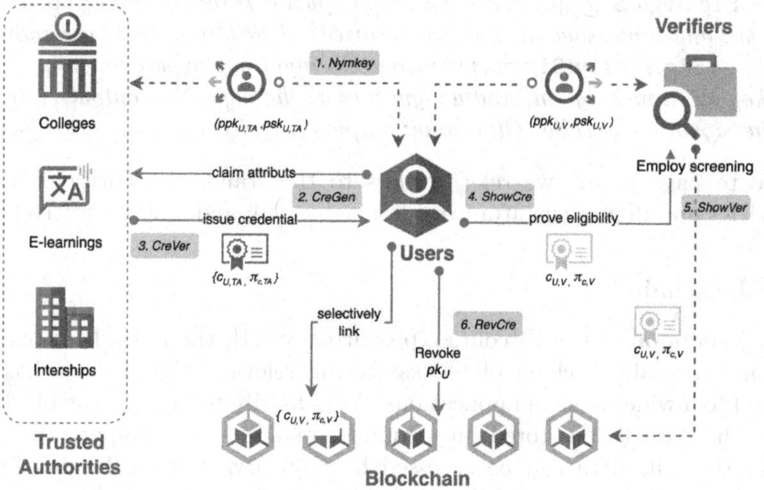

Fig. 1. The Architecture of A Blockchain-based Digital Education Credential Scheme.

Assume that an IT graduate (say Bob) owns two credentials: one on attributes (Name: ABC, University: XYZ University, Degree: Bachelor of Software Engineering, Year: 2023, GPA: 4.8/5) approved by the XYZ University and a credential, and the other one on attributes (Name: ABC, Company: Q Tech, Job: Junior Software Engineer, Level: Internship, Duration: 3 months, Year:

2022). Considering that a technology company V posts a software engineer job and Bob is willing to apply this job, in this scenario, Bob U needs to prove its capacity to the company V to become short listed. Bob U firstly generates a pseudonym public and private key pair $(ppk_{U,V}, psk_{U,V})$ to communicate with the company V, and then it extracts a shown credential $c_{U,V}$ on a statement that "($ppk_{U,V}$ has a bachelor degree and work experiences in Software Engineer from the XYZ University" and a proof $\pi_{c_{U,V}}$ for the ownership of the shown credential $c_{U,V}$. The company V checks the validity of the credential $c_{U,V}$, as well as the associated proof $\pi_{c_{U,V}}$, and accepts them to the blockchain if it would like to.

Once the shown credential $c_{U,V}$, the proof $\pi_{c_{U,V}}$, and other related information (in one transaction between the student U and the verifier V) is included in the blockchain, it is helpful for the student U to avoid repeatedly proving the ownership of the same attributes to various verifiers. Take the previous scenario as an example, Bob may need to apply several software engineer jobs posted by different companies. Bob may not want to repeatedly generating the ownership proof $\pi_{c_{U,V}}$ about the shown credentials $c_{U,V}$ proving the same statement about his eligibility. In this case, Bob U can simply generate a proof linking the previously approved shown credential on the blockchain rather than a "duplicate" proof on the shown credential.

3.2 Blockchain-Based Digital Education Credentials

A blockchain-based digital education credential BDEC scheme is composed of the following algorithms.

- $(par, L_R) \leftarrow Setup(1^\lambda)$. Taking the security parameter λ as the input, this algorithm, run by the system, outputs the public parameter par and an initially empty revocation list L_R.
- $(sk_U, pk_U) \leftarrow PriGen(par)$. Taking the public parameter par as the input, this algorithm, run by each user U, outputs a long term key pair (sk_U, pk_U). Note that both the secret and public keys will remain hidden unless the user decides to publish pk_U through the $RevCre$ algorithm.
- $(ppk_{U,TA}, psk_{U,TA}) \leftarrow NymKey(par, sk_U)$. Taking the public parameter par and the private user key sk_U as the input, this algorithm, run by the user (and authenticated by the trusted entity TA), outputs a pair of pseudonym public and private keys $(ppk_{U,TA}, psk_{U,TA})$.
- $(c_{U,TA}, \pi_{c_{U,TA}}) \leftarrow CreGen(par, sk_U, pk_U, ppk_{U,TA}, psk_{U,TA}, \mathbf{A}, aux)$. Taking the public parameter par, the user's long term key pair (sk_U, pk_U), the pseudonym public and private key pair $(ppk_{U,TA}, psk_{U,TA})$ and an attribute set $\mathbf{A}$ (and the description aux of attributes $\mathbf{A}$) as the input, this algorithm, run by the user U, outputs a credential $c_{U,TA}$ for attributes $\mathbf{A}$ and a proof $\pi_{c_{U,TA}}$ proving the credential ownership.
- $\{0,1\} \leftarrow CreVer(par, c_{U,TA}, \pi_{c_{U,TA}}, ppk_{U,TA}, \mathbf{A}, aux)$. Taking the public parameter par, the credential $c_{U,TA}$, the proof $\pi_{c_{U,TA}}$ for the credential $c_{U,TA}$, the pseudonym public key $ppk_{U,TA}$ and the attributes $\mathbf{A}$ (as well as the description aux of attributes) as the input, this algorithm, run by the issuing authority, outputs 1 for a valid proof $\pi_{c_{U,TA}}$ or 0 otherwise.

- $(c_{U,V},\ \pi_{c_{U,V}}) \leftarrow ShowCre(par,\ sk_U,\ pk_U,\ \{ppk_{U,TA},\ psk_{U,TA},\ c_{U,TA},\ csk_{U,TA}\},\ \mathbf{A},\ aux)$. Taking the public parameter par, the private user key sk_U, a set of the pseudonym public key $ppk_{U,TA}$ and private key $psk_{U,TA}$, the credential $c_{U,TA}$ over attributes $\mathbf{A}$ and the corresponding credential private key $csk_{U,TA}$, this algorithm, run by the user U, outputs a shown credential $c_{U,V}$ on attributes $\mathbf{A}$ and the corresponding proof $\pi_{c_{U,V}}$ for the shown credential $c_{U,V}$.
- $\{0,1\} \leftarrow ShowVer(par,\ c_{U,V},\ \pi_{c_{U,V}},\ ppk_{U,TA},\ \mathbf{A}',\ aux)$. Taking the public parameter par, the shown credential $c_{U,V}$ over attribute $\mathbf{A}'$ and its proof $\pi_{c_{U,V}}$ as the input, this algorithm, run by the verifier V, outputs 1 for a valid poof $\pi_{c_{U,TA}}$ and 0 otherwise.
- $pk_U \cup L_R \leftarrow RevCre(par,\ pk_U,\ c_{U,TA})$. Taking the public parameter par, the user's long term public key pk_U, the credential $c_{U,TA}$ to be revoked as the input, this algorithm, run by the user U, adds pk_U to the revocation list L_R.

A BDEC scheme is correct if for any security parameter λ, all participants run algorithms as above, it always hold $CreVer(par,\ c_{U,TA},\ \pi_{c_{U,TA}},\ ppk_{U,TA},\ \mathbf{A},\ aux) \rightarrow 1$ and $ShowVer(par,\ c_{U,V},\ \mathbf{A},\ \pi_{c_{U,V}}) \rightarrow 1$.

3.3 Security Definitions

A BDEC scheme must meet three basic security requirements, including unforgeability, anonymity and unlinkability.

- **Unforgeability**. This means that anybody, without knowing the private user key of the student U, should not be able to forge a credential $c_{U,TA}$ on behalf of the pseudonym public key established between the user U and the trusted entity TA.
  We define the security game of Unforgeability for the BDEC scheme between an adversary $\mathcal{A}$ and a challenger $\mathcal{B}$ as follows.
  - Setup. The algorithm $\mathcal{B}$ generates the public parameter par as in the Setup algorithm and sends par to $\mathcal{A}$. In addition, $\mathcal{B}$ initializes an empty list L_U storing each user U's long term key pair (sk_U, pk_U), pseudonym key pair $(ppk_{U,TA},\ psk_{U,TA})$, the credential $c_{U,TA}$ on attributes $\mathbf{A}$, and the credential proof $\pi_{c_{U,TA}}$ authenticated by each trusted entity TA.
  - Query. $\mathcal{A}$ issues the following queries to the algorithm $\mathcal{B}$.
    * $\mathcal{A}$ sends a user-key queries to the `PriGen` oracle on a user U. If there exists a long term user key pair (sk_U, pk_U) for U in the list L_U, $\mathcal{B}$ responds with the corresponding key pair. Otherwise, $\mathcal{B}$ generates (sk_U, pk_U) by running the $PriGen$ algorithm and adds the key pair (sk_U, pk_U) to the list L_U. $\mathcal{B}$ sends (sk_U, pk_U) to $\mathcal{A}$.
    * $\mathcal{A}$ sends a pseudonym key query to the `NymKey` oracle on a user U and a trusted entity TA. If there is already a pseudonym public and private key pair in the list L_U between the user U and the trusted entity TA, $\mathcal{B}$ responds with the pseudonym public key $ppk_{U,TA}$. Otherwise, $\mathcal{A}$ generates a pseudonym public and private key

pair $(ppk_{U,TA}, psk_{U,TA})$ via running the *NymKey* algorithm, adds them to the list L_U, and sends the pseudonym public and private key $(ppk_{U,TA}, psk_{U,TA})$ to $\mathcal{A}$.

∗ $\mathcal{A}$ sends a credential generation query to the CreGen oracle on a user U, attributes $(\mathbf{A}, aux)$ and a trusted entity TA. $\mathcal{B}$ returns a user credential $c_{U,TA}$ to $\mathcal{A}$ if the credential $c_{U,TA}$ is already in the list L_U. Otherwise, $\mathcal{B}$ runs the *CreGen* algorithm to create a credential $c_{U,TA}$ over attributes $\mathbf{A}$, along with the credential proof $\pi_{c_{U,TA}}$. $\mathcal{B}$ adds them to the list L_U, and sends the credential and the proof $(c_{U,TA}, \pi_{c_{U,TA}})$ to $\mathcal{A}$.

- Output. $\mathcal{A}$ outputs a pseudonym public key $ppk^*_{U,TA}$ for the user U^*, an attribute set $\mathbf{A}^*$, a user credential $c^*_{U,TA}$ and a proof $\pi^*_{c_{U,TA}}$ between the user U^* and the trusted entity TA^*. $\mathcal{A}$ wins this game if $CreVer(par, c^*_{U,TA}, \pi^*_{c_{U,TA}}, ppk^*_{U,TA}, \mathbf{A}^*, aux^*) = 1$, and the following conditions hold.
  ∗ The user U^* has never been queried to the PriGen oracle, and
  ∗ $ppk^*_{U,TA}$ is not the output of NymKey oracle, and
  ∗ $c^*_{U,TA}$ is not the output of CreGen oracle.

We say that the BDEC system is unforgeable if the advantage function referring to the above security game

$$\mathbf{Adv}^{\mathsf{UNF}}_{\mathsf{BDEC}} = \mathbf{Pr}[\mathsf{BDEC}^{\mathcal{A}} \Longrightarrow 1]$$

is negligible in the security parameter λ for any probabilistic polynomial-time (PPT) adversary algorithm $\mathcal{A}$.

– **Anonymity**. This means that given any pseudonym public key $ppk_{U,TA}$ and the associated credential $c_{U,TA}$, anybody, should not be able to distinguish the real identities of the user U.

We define the anonymity security game for the BDEC system between an adversary $\mathcal{A}$ and a challenger $\mathcal{B}$ as follows.

- Setup. The same as that in the Unforgeability game.
- Query 1. The same as that in the Unforgeability game except that $\mathcal{A}$ is not allowed to issue queries to the PriGen oracle on users in the Challenge Phase.
- KeyGen. $\mathcal{A}$ sends to $\mathcal{B}$ a list of attributes $\mathbf{A}^*$ (along with the *aux* that describes the attributes). On input the message from $\mathcal{A}$, $\mathcal{B}$ first generates two pseudonym key pairs $(psk^{(0)}_{U,TA}, ppk^{(0)}_{U,TA})$ and $(psk^{(1)}_{U,TA}, ppk^{(1)}_{U,TA})$. $\mathcal{B}$ forwards $(psk^{(0)}_{U,TA}, psk^{(1)}_{U,TA})$ to $\mathcal{A}$.
- Query 2. The same as that in Query 1.
- Challenge. $\mathcal{B}$ randomly selects $b \in \{0,1\}$ and generates credential $c^{(b)}_{U,TA}$ and credential proof $\pi^{(b)}_{U,TA}$ using $psk^{(b)}_{U,TA}$. $\mathcal{B}$ forwards $(ppk^{(b)}_{U,TA}, c^{(b)}_{U,TA}, \pi^{(b)}_{U,TA})$ to $\mathcal{A}$.
- Query 3. The same as that in Query 1.
- Output. The algorithm $\mathcal{A}$ outputs a guess b' and wins this game if $b' = b$.

We say that the BDEC system is anonymous if the advantage function referring to the above security game

$$\mathbf{Adv}^{\mathsf{ANON}}_{\mathsf{BDEC}} = |\mathbf{Pr}[b' = b] - 1/2|$$

is negligible in the security parameter λ for any probabilistic polynomial-time (PPT) adversary algorithm $\mathcal{A}$.

- **Unlinkability.** This considers the anonymity one step further, which means that given any two pseudonym public keys $ppk_{U,V}$ and their corresponding credentials $c_{U,V}$, anybody should not be able to tell whether they belong to the same user U or not.
  We define the unlinkability security game for BDEC between an adversary $\mathcal{A}$ and a challenger $\mathcal{B}$ as follows.
  - Setup. The same as that in the Unforgeability game.
  - Query 1. The same as that in the Unforgeability game except that $\mathcal{A}$ is not allowed to issue queries to the `PriGen` oracle on users in the Challenge Phase.
  - Challenge. The algorithm $\mathcal{B}$ creates two pseudonym key pairs $(psk_{U,V}^{(0)}, ppk_{U,V}^{(0)}$ and $(psk_{U,V}^{(1)}, ppk_{U,V}^{(1)})$ and an attribute set $\mathbf{A}^*$. Then, $\mathcal{B}$ randomly selects $b \in \{0,1\}$, and creates a credential $c_{U,V}^{(b)}$ with respect to $ppk_{U,V}^{(b)}$ on attributes $\mathbf{A}^*$. $\mathcal{B}$ forwards the credential $c_{U,V}^{(b)}$ to the algorithm $\mathcal{A}$.
  - Query 2. The same as that in Query 1.
  - Output. The algorithm $\mathcal{A}$ outputs a guess b' and wins this game if $b' = b$.

  We say that the BDEC scheme is unlinkable if the advantage function referring to the above security game

$$\mathbf{Adv}_{\mathsf{BDEC}}^{\mathsf{UNL}} = |\mathbf{Pr}[b' = b] - 1/2|$$

  is negligible in the security parameter λ for any probabilistic polynomial-time (PPT) adversary algorithm $\mathcal{A}$.

In addition to the aforementioned three properties, we require the BDEC system to satisfy the conditional linkability and revocability.

- Conditional linkability. This serves two primary purposes: solving the issue of discontinuous learning records (fragmented learning) and avoiding repetitive verification of the same attributes. First, Students often accumulate learning outcomes through various courses and platforms, leading to fragmented records. Conditional linkability allows students to link these fragmented records together, providing a continuous and coherent learning history. Second, students may need to present the same attributes to different verifiers multiple times, requiring repeated generation of shown credentials and proofs. To reduce this workload, the BDEC scheme should be armed with a mechanism enabling students to reuse previous shown credentials and proofs. Specifically, conditional linkability in the BDEC scheme allows students to link previous credentials and proofs to current ones, claiming ownership of the same attributes without regenerating them, as long as these credentials and proofs are included in the blockchain. If privacy is a concern, students can opt not to link, as their credentials and proofs under various pseudonyms on the blockchain do not reveal their real identities.

- Revocability. In the BDEC scheme, students need to store their private user-keys and pseudonym private keys in private. If any of those secrets is compromised, all associated (shown) credentials need to become inaccessible immediately. To prevent any compromised credential from being continuously utilised by malicious entities, it is of necessity for the BDEC scheme to achieve Revocability such that students can disqualify their approved credentials if they found that their private keys might be compromised.

4 Construction

In this section, we detail a blockchain-based digital education credential system based on decentralized anonymous credential schemes, and analyze its security.

4.1 A Generic Construction

Below, we describe a generic construction of our BDEC system based on digital signature schemes and zkSNARKs. For definitions and further details of the building blocks, we refer readers to Sect. 2.

- $par \leftarrow Setup(1^\lambda)$. On input a security parameter λ in unary, the algorithm runs $\texttt{Sig.pp} \leftarrow \texttt{Sig.Setup}(1^\lambda)$ and $\texttt{crs} \leftarrow \mathcal{S}(1^\lambda)$, where $\mathcal{S}$ denotes the setup algorithm of the underlying zkSNARK. The algorithm outputs $par = (\texttt{Sig.pp}, \texttt{crs})$. Note that we assume the security parameter λ is an implicit input to all later algorithms.
- $(sk_U, pk_U) \leftarrow PriGen(par)$. On input the public parameters $par = (\texttt{Sig.pp}, \texttt{crs})$, the algorithm runs $(sk_U, pk_U) \leftarrow \texttt{Sig.KeyGen}(\texttt{Sig.pp})$ and outputs (sk_U, pk_U). Note that both the secret and public keys will remain hidden unless the user decides to publish pk_U through the *RevCre* algorithm.
- $(ppk_{U,TA},\ psk_{U,TA}) \leftarrow NymKey(par,\ sk_U)$. On input the public parameters $par = (\texttt{Sig.pp}, \texttt{crs})$ and the user's long term secret key sk_U, the algorithm randomly selects the pseudonym public key $ppk_{U,TA} \xleftarrow{\$} \{0,1\}^\lambda$. The algorithm computes the corresponding pseudonym secret key as $psk_{U,TA} \leftarrow \texttt{Sig.Sign}(\texttt{Sig.pp}, sk_U, ppk)$ (i.e., the psk is the signature generated by treating ppk as a message and using sk_U as the signing key). Note that a user U can have as many pseudonym public and secret key pairs as it expects. For privacy concerns, the user U can use different pseudonym public and private key pairs to communicate with different TAs.
- $(c_{U,TA},\ \pi_{c_{U,TA}}) \leftarrow CreGen(par,\ sk_U,\ pk_U,\ ppk_{U,TA},\ psk_{U,TA},\ \mathbf{A},\ aux)$. On input the public parameter $par = (\texttt{Sig.pp}, \texttt{crs})$, user's long term key pair (sk_U, pk_U), a pseudonym public and secret key pair $(ppk_{U,TA}, psk_{U,TA})$, a list of attributes $\mathbf{A} = (a_1, \ldots, a_m)$ (together with attributes descriptions aux), the algorithm computes the credential $c_{U,TA} \leftarrow \texttt{Sig.Sign}(\texttt{Sig.pp}, sk_U, h_{U,TA})$. Note that $h_{U,TA} = \mathcal{H}(\mathbf{A})$ is the hash digest of all attributes, where the definition of the collision-resistant $\mathcal{H}$ is defined in $\texttt{Sig.pp}$. Finally, the algorithm generates a proof $\pi_{c_{U,TA}}$ with respect

to the zkSNARK statement $x = (c_{U,TA}, h_{U,TA}, ppk_{U,TA})$ and the witness $w = (pk_U, psk_{U,TA})$:

$$\pi_{c_{U,TA}} = \mathcal{P}(\texttt{crs}, x, w) : \\ \texttt{Sig.Verify}(\texttt{Sig.pp}, pk_U, h_{U,TA}, c_{U,TA}) = 1 \wedge \\ \texttt{Sig.Verify}(\texttt{Sig.pp}, pk_U, ppk_{U,TA}, psk_{U,TA}) = 1.$$

In other words, the circuit to be proven by zkSNARK is defined as the AND concatenation of two signature verification algorithms. The algorithm outputs $(c_{U,TA}, \pi_{c_{U,TA}})$. The user may submit $(c_{U,TA}, \pi_{c_{U,TA}}, \mathbf{A}, aux, ppk_{U,TA})$ to the blockchain.

- $\{0,1\} \leftarrow CreVer(par,\ c_{U,TA},\ \pi_{c_{U,TA}},\ ppk_{U,TA},\ \mathbf{A},\ aux)$. On input the public parameter $par = (\texttt{Sig.pp}, \texttt{crs})$, a credential $c_{U,TA}$ on attributes $\mathbf{A}$, a pseudonym public key $ppk_{U,TA}$, a proof $\pi_{c_{U,TA}}$, and the attributes description aux, the algorithm verifies if $\pi_{c_{U,TA}}$ is valid. In particular, the algorithm first computes $h_{U,TA} = \mathcal{H}(\mathbf{A})$. It then defines the NIZKPoK statement $x = (c_{U,TA}, h_{U,TA}, ppk_{U,TA})$ and invokes the zkSNARK verifier $\mathcal{V}(\texttt{crs}, x, \pi_{c_{U,TA}})$. The algorithm outputs 1 if and only if the zkSNARK verifier algorithm $\mathcal{V}$ outputs 1. Otherwise, outputs 0. The TA nodes should only accepts the credential if and only if $CreVer$ returns 1.
- $(c_{U,V},\ \pi_{c_{U,V}}) \leftarrow ShowCre(par,\ sk_U,\ pk_U,\ \{ppk_{U,TA},\ psk_{U,TA},\ c_{U,TA},\ csk_{U,TA}\},\ \mathbf{A},\ aux)$. Assume the user U owns a list of tuples $(ppk_{U,TA}, psk_{U,TA}, c_{U,TA}, \mathbf{A})$, and it intends to prove the eligibility of $\mathbf{A}' = (a_1, \ldots, a_n) \subseteq A$ to a verifier V, where n attributes are embedded in k $(k \leq n)$ credentials $\{c^{(j)}_{U,TA}\}^k_{j=1}$. On input the public parameters $par = (\texttt{Sig.pp}, \texttt{crs})$, user's long term key pair (sk_U, pk_U), a list of the selected pseudonym public key $ppk_{U,TA}$ and corresponding private key $psk_{U,TA}$, the credential $c_{U,TA}$ over attributes $\mathbf{A}$, the algorithm first generates pseudonym keys for communicating with the verifier: $(ppk_{U,V}, ppk_{U,V}) \leftarrow NymKey(par,\ sk_U)$. The user generates the credential $c_{U,V} \leftarrow \texttt{Sig.Sign}(\texttt{Sig.pp}, sk_U, h_{U,V})$ where $h_{U,V} \leftarrow \mathcal{H}(\mathbf{A}')$ and a proof $\pi_{c_{U,V}}$ with respect to statement $x = ((h^j_{U,TA}, ppk^{(j)}_{U,TA})^k_{j=1}, h_{U,V}, c_{U,V}, ppk_{U,V})$ and witness $w = ((psk^{(j)}_{U,TA})^k_{j=1}, pk_U, psk_{U,V})$:

$$\pi_{c_{U,V}} = \mathcal{P}(\texttt{crs}, x, w) : \\ \wedge^k_{j=1} \texttt{Sig.Verify}(pk_U, ppk^{(j)}_{U,TA}, psk^{(j)}_{U,TA}) = 1 \\ \wedge \texttt{Sig.Verify}(pk_U, ppk_{U,V}, psk_{U,V}) = 1 \\ \wedge \texttt{Sig.Verify}(pk_U, h_{U,V}, c_{U,V}) = 1$$

The circuit proven by NIZKPoK is $k + 2$ AND concatenation of signature verification algorithm.
Considering the list of attributes $\mathbf{A}'$ may need to be repeatedly prove to different verifiers. We would recommend first uploading the tuple $(c_{U,V}, \mathbf{A}', aux, \pi_{c,V}, ppk_{U,V})$ which was shown to verifier V to the blockchain. Then,

for any future proofs on attributes $\mathbf{A}'$ to a distinct verifier V', the user U can generate a proof $\pi'_{c_{U,V}}$ with respect to the statement $x = (ppk_{U,V}, ppk'_{U,V})$ and witness $w = (pk_U, psk_{U,V}, psk'_{U,V})$, where $(ppk'_{U,V}, ppk'_{U,V}) \leftarrow NymKey(par, sk_U)$:

$$\pi'_{c_{U,V}} = \mathcal{P}(\texttt{crs}, x, w): \\ \wedge\, \texttt{Sig.Verify}(pk_U, psk_{U,V}, ppk_{U,V}) = 1 \\ \wedge\, \texttt{Sig.Verify}(pk_U, psk'_{U,V}, ppk'_{U,V}) = 1$$

The circuit is an AND concatenation of two signature verification algorithms. The user can simply append $(\pi'_{c,V}, ppk'_{U,V})$ to the tuple which was already uploaded to blockchain.

- $\{0,1\} \leftarrow ShowVer(par,\ c_{U,V},\ \pi_{c_{U,V}},\ ppk_{U,TA},\ \mathbf{A}',\ aux)$. On input the public parameter $par = (\texttt{Sig.pp}, \texttt{crs})$, the shown credential $c_{U,V}$ over attributes $\mathbf{A}' = (a_1, \ldots, a_n)$ (together with aux, the attributes description), a proof of credential possession $\pi_{c_{U,V}}$, and the pseudonym public key attached with each credential $ppk_{U,TA}$, the algorithm verifies if $\pi_{c_{U,V}}$ is valid. In particular, the algorithm computes $h_{U,V} \leftarrow \mathcal{H}(\mathbf{A}')$ and $h^{(j)}_{U,TA} \leftarrow \mathcal{H}(\mathbf{A})$ for $j \in [k]$. It defines the zkSNARK statement $x = ((h^{(j)}_{U,TA}, ppk^{(j)}_{U,TA})^k_{j=1}, h_{U,V}, c_{U,V}, ppk_{U,V})$ and invokes the zkSNARK verifier algorithm $\mathcal{V}(\texttt{crs}, x, \pi_{c_{U,V}})$. The algorithm returns 1 if and only if the zkSNARK verifier returns 1. Otherwise, the algorithm returns 0.
- $pk_U \cup L_R \leftarrow RevCre(par,\ pk_U,\ c_{U,TA})$. On input the public parameter par, the user's long term public key pk_U, the credential $c_{U,TA}$ to be revoked, this algorithm publishes pk_U and adds pk_U to the revocation list L_R. For any future submission $(c_{U,V},\ \pi_{c_{U,V}},\ \mathbf{A}, aux)$ to the blockchain, the verifier node V selects a public key pk_U from the list L_U and then run an initial check on the proof about the pseudonym public key: $\texttt{Sig.Verify}(pk_U, \pi_{c_{U,V}}, h_{U,V})$, where $h_{U,V} \leftarrow \mathcal{H}(\mathbf{A}')$. If there exists pk_U that makes the verification pass (Sig.Verify returns 1), the submission will be rejected.

4.2 Security Analysis

Theorem 1 (Unforgeability). *The* BDEC *system is unforgeable under the assumption that the underlying signature scheme is existentially unforgeable under chosen-message attacks (EUF-CMA) and that the underlying zkSNARK proof system is knowledge sound.*

Proof Sketch: Assume the adversary is able to forge the credential and credential proof (without user's long term secret and public key), then it means the adversary must either forge a valid signature or forge a valid zkSNARK proof.

Theorem 2 (Anonymity). *The* BDEC *system is anonymous under the assumption that both the underlying signature scheme and the zkSNARK are zero-knowledge.*

Proof Sketch: Since pseudonym public keys are just random bit strings chosen by the user, no one should be able to identify the read signer based on these pseudonym public keys. Furthermore, since the signature and zkSNARK are both zero-knowledge, the credential and the credential proof should not leak any information about user's real identity.

Theorem 3 (Unlinkability). *The* BDEC *system is unlinkable under the assumption that both the underlying signature scheme and the zkSNARK are zero-knowledge.*

Proof Sketch: The pseudonym public keys should not be linked to the same user as they are random bit strings. Since the signature scheme is randomized and the zkSNARK is zero-knowledge, the credential and the credential proof should not be linked to the same user.

We show the formal security proofs of unforgeability, anonymity, and unlinkability in Appendix A.

Conditional Linkability. In the *ShowCre* algorithms, the user U is able to link any pseudonym public keys in the proof by showing that two pseudonym keys are generated with the same long term secret key. Thus, for any previously proven attributes (which have been accepted by the blockchain), the user U has the capability to include them in the current credential shown process without proving the ownership of those attributes for a second time.

Revocability. The *RevCre* algorithm supports the credential revocation. Once the user U finds out that its private user key sk_U is lost or leaked, the user U can publish the corresponding public user key pk_U to the revocation list L_R. For any submitted credential $c_{U,V}$ and the proof $\pi_{U,V}$, the verifier nodes will run the signature verification algorithm to check whether the submitted credential $c_{U,V}$ is a valid signature with respect to any public key pk_U in the list L_R.

We further discuss the approach to achieve hidden attributes from verifier in Appendix B.

4.3 Symmetric-Key Primitives Based Post-quantum Instantiation

We describe the post-quantum instantiation of our BDEC system using the state-of-the-art SNARK-friendly signature scheme LOQUAT [28]. The security of LOQUAT relies solely on collision-resistant hash functions and the Legendre PRF, making it post-quantum secure. The primary advantage of LOQUAT is its balanced performance between signature size/speed and SNARK-friendliness. Since our framework requires the user to prove signature validity during *CreGen* and *ShowCre*, it is crucial that the underlying signature scheme has a relatively small verification circuit. Although one-time signatures such as Lamport+ [14] have better verification complexity, they are unsuitable for system instantiation because the user needs a long-term key pair for signature generation. It is impractical for the user to maintain a state that ensures one-time secret keys are never reused.

We instantiate the zkSNARK with Aurora [1] and Fractal [5], which rely solely on collision-resistant hash functions and features a transparent setup. Both zkSNARKs has proof size polylogarithmic in the circuit size it proves, ensuring small overhead for the credential proof generated in *ShowCre*, especially when the number of TAs is large. Thus, the system is highly scalable. Furthermore, by leveraging recursive proof generation of Fractal, the credential proof produced by *ShowCre* can maintain a size independent of the number of involved TAs.

5 Performance Evaluation

To provide a general idea of the performance of our proposed **BDEC** system, we analyse two main metrics, namely credential size and running time for *CreGen*, *CreVer*, *ShowCre*, and *ShowVer* algorithms.

For *CreGen*, the running time is mainly depending on the signing time for the signature and the time for generating the zkSNARK proof for the verification of two signatures. In this analysis, we take Loquat [28] and Aurora [1] as concrete signature and zkSNARK schemes for our generic construction. The signing time for Loquat signature is $O(\lambda)$, where λ is the system security parameter. The proof generation time for Aurora is $O(N \log N)$, where N is the number of gates in the circuit. Since N is a polynomial of λ, this can be written as $O(poly(\lambda) \log \lambda)$. Correspondingly, the running time for *CreVer* is mainly depending on the verification time for the zkSNARK proof, and for Aurora it is $O(N)$, or $O(poly(\lambda))$.

Similarly, for *showCre* the running time is mainly depending on the signing time for the signature and the time for generating the zkSNARK proof for the verification of $k + 2$ signatures. In this case, the signing time is $O(\lambda)$ and the proof generation time is $O(k \cdot poly(\lambda) \log \lambda)$, where λ is the system security parameter and k is the number of TAs involved and in the worst case $k = |\mathbf{A}'|$. Correspondingly, the running time for *ShowVer* is mainly depending on the verification time for the zkSNARK proof, hence $O(k \cdot poly(\lambda))$.

For credential size, it is depending on the sizes of the signature and the zkSNARK proof. Table 2 shows empirical data for the running times and credential sizes with 100 bit security, for different k values. We note that the performances get less practical when the parameter k increases to a relatively large value. However, this is due to the performances of the state-of-the-art zkSNARK schemes. Given that our proposed construction is generic and modular, this can be improved by switching the zkSNARK component to a future scheme with better prover time, verifier time and proof size.

Table 3 compares the concrete performance of our scheme, instantiated with LOQUAT and Aurora, to the previously proposed post-quantum anonymous credential system in [12]. To ensure a fair comparison, we use LOQUAT with 128-bit security. For the credential proof size comparison, we assume both the number of attributes and TAs to be 10, aligning with the assumptions in [12]. It is important to note that in practice, the number of TAs is often greately smaller than the number of attributes, and the credential proof size in our scheme depends only on the number of TAs, not the number of attributes.

Table 2. Performance of Credential Proof in *ShowCre* using Aurora, Fractal, and Recursive Fractal (Fractal-R) (adapted from [28, Table 5]). t_I = indexer time, t_P = proving time, t_V = verification time, k = the number of TAs involved.

	Aurora					Fractal			Fractal-R (est.)			
	$k = 2$	6	14	30	62	2	6	14	2	6	14	30
t_I (s)	–	–	–	–	–	33	88	218	5K	13K	32K	32K
t_P (s)	14	33	67	160	553	119	251	556	3K	6K	14K	14K
t_V (s)	2.4	4.3	10	20	62	0.2	0.47	0.78	2.4	5.64	9.6	9.6
$\|\sigma\|$ (KB)	126	137	182	197	207	131	140	145	131	140	145	145

Table 3. Concrete Performance Comparison of Post-Quantum Anonymous Credential Systems. $|pk_U|$ & $|sk_U|$: User's long term public-secret key pairs; $|ppk_U|$ & $|psk_U|$: User's pseudonym public-secret key pairs; $|c|$: credential size; $|\pi|$: credential proof size. All sizes are in KB. SK denotes Symmetric-Key Based Assumptions (Legendre PRF and Collision-Resistant Hash).

Scheme	$\|pk_U\|$	$\|sk_U\|$	$\|ppk_U\|$	$\|psk_U\|$	$\|c\|$	$\|\pi\|$	Assump.
[12]	9,789	10,844	–	–	317	724	Lattice
Ours	4	0.125	0.125	57	57	150	SK

6 Conclusions

In this work, we propose a generic framework for an anonymous credential system. The framework requires only two building blocks: a digital signature scheme and a zkSNARK. We demonstrate that our framework satisfies unforgeability, anonymity, and unlinkability with formal security proofs. Additionally, our framework achieves conditional linkability and revocability, two features absent in existing works.

By instantiating the framework with the post-quantum signature scheme LOQUAT [28] and the post-quantum zkSNARK named Aurora [1], we obtain a post-quantum anonymous credential system whose security relies solely on collision-resistant hash functions and the Legendre PRF. The concrete performance of the resulting system is significantly more practical than existing anonymous credential systems based on lattices [12].

Appendix

A Security Proofs

A.1 Proof of Theorem 1: Unforgeability

Proof. Assume there exists an adversary $\mathcal{A}$ that wins the unforgeability game with non-negligible probability ϵ, we show that there exists an algorithm $\mathcal{B}$ that can break the EUF-CMA of the underlying signature scheme with probability at least $\epsilon - \epsilon_\pi$, where ϵ_π is the knowledge error of the zkSNARK.

Let $\mathcal{A}$ output a tuple $(ppk^*_{U,TA}, \mathbf{A}^*, c^*U, TA, \pi^*_{cU,TA})$ such that $CreVer(par, c^*_{U,TA}, \pi^*_{cU,TA}, ppk^*_{U,TA}, \mathbf{A}^*, aux^*) = 1$. Recall that the $CreVer(\cdot)$ algorithm invokes the zkSNARK verification algorithm $\mathcal{V}(\texttt{crs}, x^*, \pi^*_{cU,TA})$, where $x^* = (c^*_{U,TA}, h^*_{U,TA}, ppk^*_{U,TA})$ for $h^*_{U,TA} = \mathcal{H}(\mathbf{A}^*)$. Since the proof $\pi^*_{cU,TA}$ is valid and the zkSNARK is knowledge sound, there exists a polynomial time extractor of the zkSNARK that can extract a valid witness $w^* = (pk^*_U, psk^*_{U,TA})$ with probability at least $\epsilon - \epsilon_\pi$, where ϵ_π denotes the knowledge error of the zkSNARK. In other words, the extractor outputs a valid signature $psk^*_{U,TA}$ with respect to the message $ppk^*_{U,TA}$ and the signing key sk_U, breaking the existential unforgeability of the underlying signature scheme. □

A.2 Proof of Theorem 2: Anonymity

Proof. We construct a simulator $\mathcal{S}$ that outputs an indistinguishable transcript (including the pseudonym key, the credential, and the credential proof) from the real transcript generated by *CreGen*. Assume that our simulator $\mathcal{S}$ has black box access to the signature's simulator algorithm, denoted as $\mathcal{S}_\sigma$.

On input the adversary messages $\mathbf{A}^*$ and aux, the simulator $\mathcal{S}$ selects a random long term public key pk^*_U and a random pseudonym public key $ppk^*_{U,TA}$. $\mathcal{S}$ invokes the signature simulator $\mathcal{S}_\sigma$ with input $(ppk^*_{U,TA}, pk^*_U)$ to generate a simulated signatures $psk^*_{U,TA}$. Note that pseudonym key pair $(psk^*_{U,TA}, ppk^*_{U,TA})$ is indistinguishable from the real pseudonym key pairs as the signature scheme is zero-knowledge. Similarly, to simulate the credential, $\mathcal{S}$ invokes $\mathcal{S}_\sigma$ with inputs $(h^*_{U,TA}, pk^*_U)$, where $h^*_{U,TA} = \mathcal{H}(\mathbf{A}^*)$. Under the same reason, the simulated credential is indistinguishable from the real credential owing to zero-knowledgeness of the signature scheme.

Finally, $\mathcal{S}$ runs the zkSNARK prover algorithm $\pi^*_{cU,TA} \leftarrow \mathcal{P}(\texttt{crs}, x, w)$ with respect to the statement $x = (c^*_{U,TA}, h^*_{U,TA}, ppk^*_{U,TA})$ and witness $w = (pk^*_U, psk^*_{U,TA})$. As the proof is honestly generated, both $psk^*_{U,TA}$ and $c^*_{U,TA}$ are valid signatures, the credential proof $\pi^*_{cU,TA}$ is valid. Furthermore, due to the zkSNARK achieves zero-knowledge, the proof hides pk^*_U.

Note that if the underlying signature scheme and zkSNARK achieve perfect zero-knowledge, then our system achieves perfect anonymous (i.e., the simulated transcript is perfectly indistinguishable from the real transcript). □

A.3 Proof of Theorem 3: Unlinkability

Proof. We construct a simulator $\mathcal{S}$ that outputs an indistinguishable transcript (the pseudonym key, the credential, and the credential proof) from the real transcript generated from *ShowCre*. Assume that our simulator $\mathcal{S}$ has black box access to the signature's simulator algorithm and zkSNARK's simulator algorithm, denoted as $\mathcal{S}_\sigma$ and $\mathcal{S}_\pi$, respectively.

The simulator $\mathcal{S}$ selects a random long term public key pk^*_U and a random pseudonym public key $ppk^*_{U,V}$. $\mathcal{S}$ invokes the signature simulator $\mathcal{S}_\sigma$ with input

$(ppk^*_{U,V}, pk^*_U)$ to generate a simulated signatures $psk^*_{U,V}$. Note that pseudonym key pair $(psk^*_{U,V}, ppk^*_{U,V})$ is indistinguishable from the real pseudonym key pairs as the signature scheme is zero-knowledge. Similarly, to simulate the credential, $\mathcal{S}$ invokes $\mathcal{S}_\sigma$ with inputs $(h^*_{U,V}, pk^*_U)$, where $h^*_{U,V} = \mathcal{H}(\mathbf{A}^*)$. Under the same reason, the simulated credential is indistinguishable from the real credential owing to zero-knowledgeness of the signature scheme.

Finally, $\mathcal{S}$ invokes the zkSNARK simulator $\mathcal{S}_\pi$ on input $(\texttt{crs}, x)$, where $x = ((h^{(j)*}_{U,TA}, ppk^{(j)*}_{U,TA}), h^*_{U,V}, c^*_{U,V}, ppk^*_{U,V})$ to obtain a simulated proof $\pi^*_{c_{U,V}}$. The proof is indistinguishable from the real proof due to the zero-knowledgeness of the underlying zkSNARK.

Note that if the underlying signature scheme and zkSNARK achieve perfect zero-knowledge, then our system achieves perfect unlinkability (i.e., the simulated transcript is perfectly indistinguishable from the real transcript). □

B Hidden Attributes from Verifier

In our **BDEC** system, we assume users publishes the credential, credential proof, along with all attributes to the public ledger (e.g., blockchain). Given that many attributes cover general information without sensitive data, this is sufficient for many applications. Nevertheless, there might exist scenarios where a user would like to hide attributes shown to verifiers in *ShowVer* phase. We recommend the system to incorporate the Merkle tree accumulator to enforce such requirement. To be specific, in the *CreGen* algorithm, instead of signing the hash digest of all attributes, the user signs the Merkle root of the accumulated attributes (i.e., treating each attribute as a leaf of the tree). Then, the user only needs to publish the Merkle root, credential, and credential proof on chain. The proof can still be verified by TA if we assume TAs have full list of attributes of each user. If the user wants to show a subsets of attributes to a verifier, it can produces an authentication path (a.k.a. the membership proof) for each attribute. Hence, the verifier can effectively verify whether provided attributes were approved by TA, without knowing any additional attributes outside of the subset.

References

1. Ben-Sasson, E., Chiesa, A., Riabzev, M., Spooner, N., Virza, M., Ward, N.P.: Aurora: transparent succinct arguments for R1CS. In: Eurocrypt, pp. 103–128. Springer (2019)
2. Blazy, O., Chevalier, C., Renaut, G., Ricosset, T., Sageloli, E., Senet, H.: Efficient implementation of a post-quantum anonymous credential protocol. In: Proceedings of the 18th International Conference on Availability, Reliability and Security. Association for Computing Machinery, New York (2023). https://doi.org/10.1145/3600160.3600188
3. Camenisch, J., Lysyanskaya, A.: A signature scheme with efficient protocols. In: Security in Communication Networks: Third International Conference, SCN 2002, Amalfi, Italy, 11–13 September 2002, Revised Papers 3, pp. 268–289. Springer (2003)

4. Chaum, D.: Security without identification: transaction systems to make big brother obsolete. Commun. ACM **28**(10), 1030–1044 (1985)
5. Chiesa, A., Ojha, D., Spooner, N.: Fractal: post-quantum and transparent recursive proofs from holography. In: Eurocrypt, pp. 769–793. Springer (2020)
6. Cuccuru, P.: Beyond bitcoin: an early overview on smart contracts. Int. J. Law Inf. Technol. **25**(3), 179–195 (2017). https://doi.org/10.1093/ijlit/eax003
7. Damgård, I., Ganesh, C., Khoshakhlagh, H., Orlandi, C., Siniscalchi, L.: Balancing privacy and accountability in blockchain identity management. In: Paterson, K.G. (ed.) CT-RSA 2021. LNCS, vol. 12704, pp. 552–576. Springer, Cham (2021). https://doi.org/10.1007/978-3-030-75539-3_23
8. Dutto, S., Margaria, D., Sanna, C., Vesco, A.: Toward a post-quantum zero-knowledge verifiable credential system for self-sovereign identity. Cryptology ePrint Archive (2022)
9. European Commission: A European approach to micro-credentials: final report (2020). https://education.ec.europa.eu/education-levels/higher-education/micro-credentials
10. Fitzgerald, R., Huijser, H.: The opportunities and challenges in the portability and authentication of micro-credentials and short courses in a post-COVID landscape. In: Technology-Enhanced Learning and the Virtual University, pp. 465–477 (2023)
11. Garman, C., Green, M., Miers, I.: Decentralized anonymous credentials. IACR Cryptology ePrint Archive 2013/622 (2014). https://api.semanticscholar.org/CorpusID:6055016
12. Jeudy, C., Roux-Langlois, A., Sanders, O.: Lattice signature with efficient protocols, application to anonymous credentials. Cryptology ePrint Archive, Paper 2022/509 (2022). https://eprint.iacr.org/2022/509
13. Kazmi, R.A., Le, D.P., Minwalla, C.: Privacy-preserving post-quantum credentials for digital payments. In: International Conference on Financial Cryptography and Data Security, pp. 118–137. Springer (2022)
14. Khaburzaniya, I., Chalkias, K., Lewi, K., Malvai, H.: Aggregating and thresholdizing hash-based signatures using STARKs. In: Asia CCS. ACM (2022)
15. Khare, V.: Indian students face exit from Canada over fake papers (2023). https://www.bbc.com/news/world-us-canada-65898527. bBC Hindi
16. Li, Z.Z., Wang, H., Gasevic, D., Yu, J., Liu, J.K.: Enhancing blockchain adoption through tailored software engineering: an industrial-grounded study in education credentialing. Distrib. Ledger Technol. Res. Pract. **2**(4), 1–24 (2023)
17. Manoj, T., Makkithaya, K., Narendra, V.: A blockchain-based credentials for food traceability in agricultural supply chain. In: 2023 IEEE International Conference on Distributed Computing, VLSI, Electrical Circuits and Robotics (DISCOVER), pp. 19–24. IEEE (2023)
18. Musamih, A., Yaqoob, I., Salah, K., Jayaraman, R., Omar, M., Ellahham, S.: Using NFTS for product management, digital certification, trading, and delivery in the healthcare supply chain. IEEE Trans. Eng. Manag. (2022)
19. Nitulescu, A.: zk-SNARKs: a gentle introduction. Ecole Normale Superieure (2020)
20. Parameswarath, R.P., Gope, P., Sikdar, B.: User-empowered privacy-preserving authentication protocol for electric vehicle charging based on decentralized identity and verifiable credential. ACM Trans. Manag. Inf. Syst. (TMIS) **13**(4), 1–21 (2022)
21. Ruffing, T.: Cryptography for bitcoin and friends. Ph.D. thesis, Saarland University, Germany (2020). https://d-nb.info/1209947285
22. Sarkar, S.: India's fake degrees: hundreds in Singapore, Malaysia, US, Canada left questioning qualifications after Manav Bharti University scandal (2021). https://

www.scmp.com/week-asia/people/article/3123929/indias-fake-degrees-hundreds-singapore-malaysia-us-canada-left. South China Morning Post
23. Selvaratnam, R.M., Sankey, M.D.: An integrative literature review of the implementation of micro-credentials in higher education: implications for practice in Australasia. J. Teach. Learn. Graduate Employability **12**(1), 1–17 (2021)
24. Shi, R., et al.: Threshold attribute-based credentials with redactable signature. IEEE Trans. Serv. Comput. (2023)
25. Shrivas, M.K., Kachhwaha, S., Bhansali, A., Singh, S.V.: Quantum-resistant university credentials verification system on blockchain. In: 2022 IEEE Nigeria 4th International Conference on Disruptive Technologies for Sustainable Development (NIGERCON), pp. 1–6. IEEE (2022)
26. Sonnino, A., Al-Bassam, M., Bano, S., Meiklejohn, S., Danezis, G.: Coconut: threshold issuance selective disclosure credentials with applications to distributed ledgers. arXiv preprint arXiv:1802.07344 (2018)
27. UpGuard: The 72 biggest data breaches of all time (2023). https://www.upguard.com/blog/biggest-data-breaches. Accessed 17 Oct 2023
28. Zhang, X., Steinfeld, R., Esgin, M.F., Liu, J.K., Liu, D., Ruj, S.: Loquat: a SNARK-friendly post-quantum signature based on the legendre PRF with applications in ring and aggregate signatures. Cryptology ePrint Archive, Paper 2024/868 (2024). https://eprint.iacr.org/2024/868
29. Zhuang, C., Dai, Q., Zhang, Y.: BCPPT: a blockchain-based privacy-preserving and traceability identity management scheme for intellectual property. Peer-to-Peer Netw. Appl. **15**(1), 724–738 (2022)

Semi-compressed CRYSTALS-Kyber

Shuiyin Liu[1(✉)] and Amin Sakzad[2]

[1] Holmes Institute, Melbourne, VIC 3000, Australia
SLiu@holmes.edu.au

[2] Monash University, Melbourne, VIC 3800, Australia
Amin.Sakzad@monash.edu

Abstract. In this paper, we investigate the communication overhead of the Kyber, which has recently been standardized by the National Institute of Standards and Technology (NIST). Given the same decryption failure rate (DFR) and security argument, we show it is feasible to reduce the communication overhead of the Kyber by 54%. The improvement is based on two technologies: ciphertext quantization and plaintext encoding. First, we prove that the Lloyd-Max quantization is optimal to minimize the decryption decoding noise. The original Kyber compression function is not optimal. Second, we propose an encoding scheme, which combines Pulse-Amplitude Modulation (PAM), Gray mapping, and a binary error correcting code. An explicit expression for the DFR is derived. The minimum possible communication overhead is also derived. Finally, we demonstrate that with the Lloyd-Max quantization, 8-PAM, Gray mapping, and a shortened binary BCH(768, 638, 13) code, the proposed scheme encapsulates 638 bits (e.g., 2.5 AES keys) in a single ciphertext.

Keywords: Module leaning with errors · Lattice-based cryptography · Quantization · Encoding · Ciphertext expansion rate

1 Introduction

CRYSTALS-Kyber, the first post-quantum encryption algorithm selected by the National Institute of Standards and Technology (NIST), has attracted great attention from researchers and engineers [17]. The security of Kyber derives from cautious parameterizations of the Module Learning with Errors (M-LWE) problem, which is widely believed to be post-quantum secure. M-LWE based encryption approaches have a small failure probability during decryption, which is referred to as decryption failure rate (DFR). Observed decryption errors might leak the secret information to an adversary [8]. Since the DFR is proportional to the value of the M-LWE module q, M-LWE based encryption approaches commonly choose a large q to reduce the DFR. However, this choice leads to a large ciphertext size: for example, KYBER1024 converts a 32-byte plaintext into a 1568-byte ciphertext [17]. Large ciphertexts are hard to communicate over

J. K. Liu et al. (Eds.): ProvSec 2024, LNCS 14904, pp. 65–82, 2025.
https://doi.org/10.1007/978-981-96-0957-4_4

the network and this is an obstacle to the adoption of Kyber in applications like Internet-of-Things (IoT).

The communication overhead is measured by the ciphertext expansion rate (CER). To reduce the CER, Kyber uses an almost uniform (lossy) compression function, denoted as, $\mathsf{Compress}_q(x, d)$, to compress its ciphertexts [4], where $x \in \mathbb{Z}_q$ and $d < \lceil \log_2(q) \rceil$. Since the function $\mathsf{Compress}_q(x, d)$ maps the fraction x/q to the nearest fraction with denominator 2^d, it can be viewed as an almost uniform quantization [3]. From the decryption decoding perspective, the function $\mathsf{Compress}_q(x, d)$ introduces a $(\lceil \log_2(q) \rceil - d)$-bit quantization noise, resulting in a larger DFR. To reduce the DFR, Kyber uses two values $\{0, \lceil q/2 \rfloor\}$ to represent one information bit, which is equivalent to an *uncoded* binary Pulse Amplitude Modulation (2-PAM) [19]. The large Euclidean distance between $\{0, \lceil q/2 \rfloor\}$ ensures that the DFR is sufficiently small. In summary, to reduce the CER and DFR, Kyber uses an almost uniform quantization and a 2-PAM encoder.

From the plaintext encoding perspective, given the same DFR, it is possible to use error correcting codes to encode more information bits in a single ciphertext. The CER is thereby reduced. In [13], by replacing the 2-PAM by the Leech lattice constellation, a 380-bit plaintext (about 1.5 AES keys) can be encrypted into a single ciphertext. The CER of Kyber is reduced by 32.6%. In [16], a 471-bit plaintext (about 1.8 AES keys) is embedded in a single ciphertext, by using 5-PAM and a Q-ary BCH code. The CER of Kyber is reduced by about 45.6%. In the broader literature of LWE, a variety of coding approaches have been proposed for different encryption schemes, including a concatenation of BCH and LDPC codes for NewHope-Simple [11] and lattice codes for FrodoKEM [15]. Both approaches offer a CER reduction less than 15%. In practice, however, exchanging a slightly larger plaintext may have limited application, as only one AES key can be extracted from one ciphertext. An interesting question is if it is possible to encapsulate multiple 256-bit secretes (e.g., AES keys, random seeds, initialization vectors) in a single ciphertext.

From the ciphertext compression perspective, Kyber uses an almost uniform quantization to compress the ciphertext [4]. It is known that for a continuous uniform input, the uniform quantization is optimal to minimize the mean squared error (MSE) [3]. However, the ciphertext of Kyber is discrete and the quantization codebook size does not divide the module q (i.e., a prime number). Kyber compression function is not necessarily optimal to decrease the MSE. Therefore, it is possible to reduce both the DFR and CER of Kyber by simply using a better quantization. In the literature, a few attempts have been made to develop better quantisation, including D_4 lattice quantizer for NewHope [1] and E_8 lattice quantizer for M-LWE [20]. However, the CERs of [1,20] are larger than that of Kyber, leaving an important question open: whether an optimal ciphertext quantization can help reducing both the DFR and CER of Kyber.

From the security perspective, compressing the ciphertext is equivalent to adding an extra noise term to the ciphertext. It does not affect the security level of M-LWE based approaches. Although the error correcting code has no influence on the distribution of the ciphertext [16], the implementation of error correcting decoding might be vulnerable to side-channel attacks. In [10], the authors point out that error correcting decoding usually recovers valid codewords faster than the codewords that contain errors. This time information can be used to distinguish between valid ciphertexts and failing ciphertexts. However, this attack can be thwarted using a constant-time decoder. For example, a constant-time BCH decoder was proposed in [24]. A constant-time Leech lattice decoder was given in [18]. With an optimal quantization and a constant-time encoding scheme, we expect that the CER can be reduced significantly with no security implications.

In this paper, we aim at reducing the CER of Kyber by more than 50%. First, we prove that the optimal quantization for M-LWE based approaches is the Lloyd-Max quantization [14], which minimizes the MSE. Second, we present a variant of Kyber, where only the first part of ciphertext is quantized. This scheme is referred to as Semi-Compressed CRYSTALS-Kyber (SC-Kyber). This design is based on the fact that compressing the second part of ciphertext has little impact on reducing the CER, but at the cost of adding a 7 or 8-bit quantization noise to the decoding. Third, we show that the decryption decoding in the SC-Kyber is equivalent to the detection in the Additive white Gaussian noise (AWGN) channel. This result allows us to derive the maximum possible plaintext size, or equivalently, the minimum possible CER. Finally, we propose an encoding scheme for SC-Kyber. An explicit expression for the DFR is derived for such an encoding. We finally demonstrate that with the Lloyd-Max quantization, an 8-PAM constellation, Gray mapping, and a shortened binary BCH(768, 638, 13) code, the proposed scheme encrypts 638 bits (e.g., 2.5 AES keys) into a single ciphertext, given the same DFR and security level as in KYBER1024. We summarize our results in Table 1.

Table 1. Comparison of Variants of KYBER1024

	Plaintext Size	CER	DFR	Source
KYBER1024-Uncoded	256 (1 AES Key)	49	2^{-174}	[2,17]
KYBER1024-Leech	380 (1.5 AES Keys)	33	2^{-226}	[13]
KYBER1024-Q-BCH	471 (1.8 AES Keys)	26.6	2^{-174}	[16]
SC-KYBER1024-B-BCH	638 (2.5 AES Keys)	22.5	2^{-174}	This work

2 Preliminaries

2.1 Notation

Rings: Let R_q denote the polynomial ring $\mathbb{Z}_q[X]/(X^n + 1)$, where $n = 256$ and $q = 3329$ in this work. Elements in R_q will be denoted with regular font letters, while a vector of the coefficients in R_q is represented by bold lower-case letters.

Matrices and vectors will be denoted with bold upper-case and lower-case letters, respectively. The transpose of a vector $\mathbf{v}$ or a matrix $\mathbf{A}$ is denoted by $\mathbf{v}^T$ or $\mathbf{A}^T$, respectively. The default vectors are column vectors.

Sampling and Distribution: For a set $\mathcal{S}$, we write $s \leftarrow \mathcal{S}$ to mean that s is chosen uniformly at random from $\mathcal{S}$. If $\mathcal{S}$ is a probability distribution, then this denotes that s is chosen according to the distribution $\mathcal{S}$. For a polynomial $f(x) \in R_q$ or a vector of such polynomials, this notation is extended coefficient-wise. We use $\text{Var}(\mathcal{S})$ to represent the variance of the distribution $\mathcal{S}$. Let x be a bit string and S be a distribution taking x as the input, then $y \sim S := \mathsf{Sam}(x)$ represents that the output y generated by distribution S and input x can be extended to any desired length. We denote $\beta_\eta = B(2\eta, 0.5) - \eta$ as the central binomial distribution over $\mathbb{Z}$. The uniform distribution is represented as $\mathcal{U}$. The Cartesian product of two sets A and B is denoted by $A \times B$. We write $A \times A = A^2$.

Kyber Compress and Decompress Functions: Let $x \in \mathbb{R}$ be a real number, then $\lceil x \rfloor$ means rounding to the closet integer with ties rounded up. The operations $\lfloor x \rfloor$ and $\lceil x \rceil$ mean rounding x down and up, respectively. Let $x \in \mathbb{Z}_q$ and $d \in \mathbb{Z}$ be such that $2^d < q$. Kyber compression and decompression functions are [17]:

$$\begin{aligned} \mathsf{Compress}_q(x, d) &= \lceil (2^d/q) \cdot x \rfloor \mod 2^d, \\ \mathsf{Decompress}_q(x, d) &= \lceil (q/2^d) \cdot x \rfloor. \end{aligned} \tag{1}$$

Decryption Failure Rate (DFR) and Ciphertext Expansion Rate (CER): We let $\text{DFR} = \delta := \Pr(\hat{m} \neq m)$, where m is a shared secret. It is desirable to have a small δ, in order to be safe against decryption failure attacks [9]. In this work, the communication cost refers to the ciphertext expansion rate (CER), i.e., the ratio of the ciphertext size to the plaintext size.

2.2 Kyber Key Encapsulation Mechanism (KEM)

Each message $m \in \{0,1\}^n$ can be viewed as a polynomial in R with coefficients in $\{0,1\}$. We recall Kyber.CPA = (KeyGen; Enc; Dec) [2] as described in Algorithms 1 to 3. The values of δ, CER, and $(q, k, \eta_1, \eta_2, d_u, d_v)$ are given in Table 2. Note that the parameters (q, k, η_1, η_2) determine the security level of Kyber, while the parameters (d_u, d_v) describe the ciphertext compression rate.

Algorithm 1. Kyber.CPA.KeyGen(): key generation

1: $\rho, \sigma \leftarrow \{0,1\}^{256}$
2: $\mathbf{A} \sim R_q^{k \times k} := \mathsf{Sam}(\rho)$
3: $(\mathbf{s}, \mathbf{e}) \sim \beta_{\eta_1}^k \times \beta_{\eta_1}^k := \mathsf{Sam}(\sigma)$
4: $\mathbf{t} := \mathbf{As} + \mathbf{e}$
5: **return** $(pk := (\mathbf{t}, \rho), sk := \mathbf{s})$

Algorithm 2. Kyber.CPA.Enc ($pk = (\mathbf{t}, \rho), m \in \{0,1\}^n$)

1: $r \leftarrow \{0,1\}^{256}$
2: $\mathbf{A} \sim R_q^{k\times k} := \mathsf{Sam}(\rho)$
3: $(\mathbf{r}, \mathbf{e}_1, e_2) \sim \beta_{\eta 1}^k \times \beta_{\eta 2}^k \times \beta_{\eta 2} := \mathsf{Sam}(r)$
4: $\mathbf{u} := \mathsf{Compress}_q(\mathbf{A}^T\mathbf{r} + \mathbf{e}_1, d_u)$
5: $v := \mathsf{Compress}_q(\mathbf{t}^T\mathbf{r} + e_2 + \lceil q/2 \rfloor \cdot m, d_v)$
6: **return** $c := (\mathbf{u}, v)$

Algorithm 3. Kyber.CPA.Dec($sk = \mathbf{s}, c = (\mathbf{u}, v)$)

1: $\mathbf{u} := \mathsf{Decompress}_q(\mathbf{u}, d_u)$
2: $v := \mathsf{Decompress}_q(v, d_v)$
3: **return** $\mathsf{Compress}_q(v - \mathbf{s}^T\mathbf{u}, 1)$

Table 2. Parameters of Kyber [2,17]

	k	q	η_1	η_2	d_u	d_v	δ	CER	Information Bits
KYBER512	2	3329	3	2	10	4	2^{-139}	24	256 (1 AES key)
KYBER768	3	3329	2	2	10	4	2^{-164}	34	256 (1 AES key)
KYBER1024	4	3329	2	2	11	5	2^{-174}	49	256 (1 AES key)

2.3 Kyber Decryption Decoding

Let n_e be the decryption decoding noise in Kyber. According to [2], we have

$$\begin{aligned} n_e &= v - \mathbf{s}^T\mathbf{u} - \lceil q/2 \rfloor \cdot m \\ &= \mathbf{e}^T\mathbf{r} + e_2 + c_v - \mathbf{s}^T(\mathbf{e}_1 + \mathbf{c}_u), \end{aligned} \tag{2}$$

where c_v and $\mathbf{c}_u$ are rounding noises generated due to the compression operation. We let ψ_{d_v} and $\psi_{d_u}^k$ be their respective distribution. The elements in c_v or $\mathbf{c}_u$ are assumed to be i.i.d. and independent of other terms in (2). The distribution ψ_d is almost uniform over the integers in $[-\lceil q/2^{d+1} \rfloor, \lceil q/2^{d+1} \rfloor]$ [4].

Kyber decoding problem can thus be formulated as

$$y = v - \mathbf{s}^T\mathbf{u} = \lceil q/2 \rfloor \cdot m + n_e, \tag{3}$$

i.e., given the observation $y \in R_q$, recover the value of m.

The encoding scheme in (3) can be viewed as a *uncoded* 2-PAM [19], which can be easily generalized to the coded case [13,16]:

$$y = \lceil q/p \rfloor \cdot \mathsf{ENC}(m) + n_e, \tag{4}$$

where $p \in [2, \sqrt{2q})$ is an integer and the function $\mathsf{ENC}(\cdot)$ represents an encoder. For example, [13] uses a lattice encoder, while [16] uses a Q-ary BCH encoder.

The distribution of n_e can be evaluated numerically [2]. To gain more insight, [13] shows that n_e is well-approximated by the sum of multivariate normal and a discrete uniform random vector, i.e.,

$$n_e \leftarrow \mathcal{N}(0, \sigma_G^2 I_n) + \mathcal{U}(-\lceil q/2^{d_v+1} \rfloor, \lceil q/2^{d_v+1} \rfloor), \tag{5}$$

where $\sigma_G^2 = kn\eta_1^2/4 + kn\eta_1/2 \cdot (\eta_2/2 + \mathrm{Var}(\psi_{d_u})) + \eta_2/2$.

Equation (5) explains how the compression parameters (d_u, d_v) affect the decoding noise. An open question is if the Kyber compression function in (1) is optimal to minimize the DFR. We will answer this question in the next section.

3 Optimal Quantization for Kyber

We consider the compression, or more generally, the quantization in Kyber. Without loss of generality, we define a general quantization function

$$\hat{\mathbf{x}} = Q_L(\mathbf{x}, \mathcal{C}_L, T_L), \tag{6}$$

where a random vector $\mathbf{x} \in \mathbb{Z}_q^n$ is quantized to a quantizer $\hat{\mathbf{x}} \in \mathcal{C}_L$, according to the quantization codebook $\mathcal{C}_L \in \mathbb{R}^n$ and the corresponding decision regions $T_L \subset \mathbb{R}^n$. The number L represents the number of quantizers in $\mathcal{C}_L$.

We define the unique index of $\hat{\mathbf{x}}$ in $\mathcal{C}_L$ as $\mathsf{Index}_L(\hat{\mathbf{x}})$, i.e.,

$$\mathcal{C}_L(\mathsf{Index}_L(\hat{\mathbf{x}})) = \hat{\mathbf{x}}. \tag{7}$$

When storing/transmitting $\hat{\mathbf{x}}$, we only need to save/send $\mathsf{Index}_L(\hat{\mathbf{x}})$. Let $\mathbf{e}_L = \mathbf{x} - \hat{\mathbf{x}}$ be the quantization error vector. The mean squared error (MSE), denoted as

$$\mathsf{MSE}(\mathbf{e}_L) = \mathsf{E}(\|\mathbf{x} - \hat{\mathbf{x}}\|^2), \tag{8}$$

is almost invariably used in this text to measure distortion. The optimal quantization should achieve minimum MSE (MMSE):

$$(\mathcal{C}_L, T_L) = \arg \min_{\mathcal{C}'_L \in \mathbb{R}^n, T'_L \subset \mathbb{R}^n} \mathsf{E}(\|\mathbf{x} - Q_L(\mathbf{x}, \mathcal{C}'_L, T'_L)\|^2). \tag{9}$$

For simplicity of notation, we define the MMSE quantization as

$$\hat{\mathbf{x}} = Q_{\mathsf{MMSE},L}(\mathbf{x}). \tag{10}$$

In this section, we will show Kyber compression function in (1) is not optimal to decrease the MSE. We will prove that the Lloyd-Max quantization [14] produces the optimal quantization codebook and decision regions for the Kyber.

3.1 The Lloyd-Max Quantization (LMQ)

The Lloyd-Max quantization [14] is a scalar quantization, which minimizes MSE distortion with a fixed number of regions. We consider the situation with L quantizers $\mathcal{C}_L = \{\hat{x}_1, \dots, \hat{x}_L\}$. Let the corresponding quantization intervals be

$$T_L = \{(\beta_{i-1}, \beta_i), i = 1, \dots, L\}, \tag{11}$$

where $\beta_0 = -\infty$ and $\beta_L = \infty$. Given a bounded random variable x, let $x_{\min} = \min(x)$, $x_{\max} = \max(x)$, and $\Pr(x)$ be the probability mass function (PMF) of x. The Lloyd-Max algorithm takes inputs $(x, \Pr(x))$ and produces $(\mathcal{C}_L, T_L)$.

1. Choose an arbitrary initial set of L representation points $\{\hat{x}_i\}_{i=1}^{L}$ in ascending order. A common choice is $\hat{x}_i = x_{\min} + i \cdot (x_{\max} - x_{\min})/L, i = 1, \dots, L$.
2. For each i; $1 \le i \le L - 1$, set $\beta_i = (\hat{x}_i + \hat{x}_{i+1})/2$.
3. For each i; $1 \le i \le L$, set $\hat{x}_i$ equal to the conditional mean of x given $x \in (\beta_{i-1}, \beta_i]$. See line 8 of Algorithm 4.
4. Repeat Steps 2 and 3 until further improvement in MSE is negligible.

The MSE decreases (or remains the same) for each iteration. As shown in Step 2, each decision threshold β_i is in the middle of two consecutive quantizers. Therefore, the input x will be quantized to the nearest quantizer, i.e.,

$$\hat{x} = Q_{\mathsf{MMSE},L}(x) = \arg\min_{\hat{x}' \in \mathcal{C}_L} \|x - \hat{x}'\|. \tag{12}$$

The pseudocode is given in Algorithm 4 (the discrete version of LMQ in [21]).

Algorithm 4. $[\mathcal{C}_L, T_L] = \mathsf{LloydMax}(x, \Pr(x))$

1: $\hat{x}_i := x_{\min} + i \cdot (x_{\max} - x_{\min})/L, i = 1, \dots, L$ ▷ initial set of $\mathcal{C}_L$
2: $\hat{\beta}_0 := -\infty$ and $\hat{\beta}_L := \infty$
3: **repeat**
4:     **for** $i \leftarrow 1$ to $L - 1$ **do**
5:         $\beta_i := (\hat{x}_i + \hat{x}_{i+1})/2$
6:     **end for** ▷ update T_L
7:     **for** $i \leftarrow 1$ to L **do**
8:         $\hat{x}_i := \dfrac{\sum_{x \in (\beta_{i-1}, \beta_i]} \Pr(x) x}{\sum_{x \in (\beta_{i-1}, \beta_i]} \Pr(x)}$ ▷ the conditional mean
9:     **end for**
10: **until** T does not change
11: **return** $\mathcal{C}_L, T_L$

Since the M-LWE samples are assumed to be uniformly distributed, the following lemma gives the optimal quantization for the Kyber.

Lemma 1 (Global Minimum). *Let* $\mathbf{x} = [x_1, \dots, x_n]^T \leftarrow \mathbb{Z}_q^n$ *and* $L_i \in \mathbb{Z}_q \backslash \{0\}$ *for* $i = 1, \dots, n$. *If* $[\mathcal{C}_{L_i}, T_{L_i}] = \mathsf{LloydMax}(x_i, \Pr(x_i))$ *for* $i = 1, \dots, n$, *then* $C_L =$

$C_{L_1} \times \cdots \times C_{L_n}$ and $T_L = T_{L_1} \times \cdots \times T_{L_n}$ is the global solution to the following MMSE quantization problem

$$(\mathcal{C}_L, T_L) = \arg \min_{\mathcal{C}'_L \in \mathbb{R}^n, T'_L \subset \mathbb{R}^n} \mathsf{E}(\|\mathbf{x} - Q_L(\mathbf{x}, \mathcal{C}'_L, T'_L)\|^2). \tag{13}$$

Proof. For x_i, $i = 1, \ldots, n$, we define L_i quantizers $C_{L_i} = \{\hat{x}_{i,1}, \ldots, \hat{x}_{i,L_i}\}$ and the corresponding quantization intervals

$$T_{L_i} = \{(\beta_{i,j-1}, \beta_{i,j}), j = 1, \ldots, L_i\}, \tag{14}$$

where $\beta_{i,0} = -\infty$ and $\beta_{i,L_i} = \infty$.

Since $\mathbf{x} \leftarrow \mathbb{Z}_q^n$, the MSE can be written as follows:

$$\sum_{\mathbf{x} \in \mathbb{Z}_q^n} \Pr(\mathbf{x}) \|\mathbf{x} - Q_L(\mathbf{x}, \mathcal{C}_L, T_L)\|^2 = \Pr(\mathbf{x}) \sum_{i=1}^{n} \left(D_i \prod_{\ell \neq i} L_\ell \right), \tag{15}$$

where

$$D_i = \sum_{j=1}^{L_i} \sum_{x_i \in (\beta_{i,j-1}, \beta_{i,j}]} \|x_i - \hat{x}_{i,j}\|^2. \tag{16}$$

To minimize the MSE, we take derivatives of Eq. (15) with respect to $(\hat{x}_{i,j}, \beta_{i,j})$ and set them equal to zero, leading to the following conditions for the optimum quantizers $\hat{x}_{i,j}$ and quantization interval boundaries $\beta_{i,j}$ [21,22]:

$$\begin{aligned} \beta_{i,j} &= \frac{\hat{x}_{i,j} + \hat{x}_{i,j+1}}{2} \\ \hat{x}_{i,j} &= \frac{\sum_{x_i \in (\beta_{i,j-1}, \beta_{i,j}]} x_i}{|(\beta_{i,j-1}, \beta_{i,j}] \cap \mathbb{Z}|}. \end{aligned} \tag{17}$$

We observe that the optimal $(\hat{x}_{i,j}, \beta_{i,j})$ only depends on x_i. Therefore, any local minimum is also a global minimum.

A way to solve Eq. (17) is to first generate an initial set $\{\hat{x}_{i,1}, \ldots, \hat{x}_{i,L_i}\}$, then apply Eq. (17) alternately until convergence is obtained. This iteration is well known as the Lloyd-Max quantization [14].

In Table 3, we compare the values of MSE for Lloyd-Max quantization and Kyber compression. We quantize $x \leftarrow \mathbb{Z}_q$ with $L = 2^d$ quantization levels. In the Kyber, $d = 10$ or 11 is used to compress the first part of ciphertext, i.e., $\mathbf{u}$. For $d = 11$, we observe that Lloyd-Max quantization has a much smaller MSE.

Remark 1. With a continuous uniform input, the Lloyd-Max algorithm returns a set of evenly-spaced intervals that span the range of the input [3]. With a discrete uniform input $x \leftarrow \mathbb{Z}_q$, however, the optimal intervals are not necessarily evenly-spaced. Considering the fact that q is prime, the intervals returned by Lloyd-Max algorithm will have different sizes. The quantization codebook is not obvious.

Example 1. With $x \leftarrow \mathbb{Z}_q$ and $L = 2^d$, we present the distribution of $e_L = x - \hat{x}$ in Tables 4 and 5. We observe that for the Lloyd-Max quantization, the e_L is not uniformly distributed. It confirms that with the discrete uniform input, a uniform quantization is not necessarily optimal to reduce the MSE.

Table 3. $\mathsf{MSE}(e_L)$: Kyber Compression vs. Lloyd-Max Quantization

d	11	10
Kyber Compression	0.38 [13]	0.92 [2]
Lloyd-Max	0.1924	0.8468

Table 4. PMF of e_L with $L = 2^{11}$

Kyber Compression			
e_L	−1	0	1
$\Pr(e_L)$	0.1916	0.6138	0.1946
Lloyd-Max			
e_L	−0.5	0	0.5
$\Pr(e_L)$	0.3848	0.2304	0.3848

3.2 Kyber with the Lloyd-Max Quantization

We replace the Kyber compression function in Algorithm 2 by the Lloyd-Max quantization in Algorithm 4. The quantized ciphertext $(\mathbf{u}, v)$ is given by

$$(\mathbf{u} = Q_{\mathsf{MMSE},L_u}(\mathbf{A}^T\mathbf{r} + \mathbf{e}_1), v = Q_{\mathsf{MMSE},L_v}(\mathbf{t}^T\mathbf{r} + e_2 + \lceil q/2 \rfloor \cdot m)). \quad (18)$$

where $L_u = 2^{knd_u}$ and $L_v = 2^{nd_v}$. The corresponding quantization codebooks and decision regions are given by $(\mathcal{C}_{L_u} = \mathcal{C}_{2^{d_u}}^{kn}, T_{L_u} = T_{2^{d_u}}^{kn})$ and $(\mathcal{C}_{L_v} = \mathcal{C}_{2^{d_v}}^{n}, T_{L_v} = T_{2^{d_v}}^{n})$, respectively. They are obtained from Lemma 1 and Algorithm 4.

When storing/transmitting a ciphertext, we only need to save/send the indices of the quantized ciphertext coefficients:

$$(\mathsf{Index}_{L_u}(\mathbf{u}), \mathsf{Index}_{L_v}(v)). \quad (19)$$

The size of the ciphertext remains the same as the original Kyber. With the Lloyd-Max quantization, the updated Kyber encryption and decryption algorithms are described below. The key generation function is the same as Algorithm 1. Thus we omit details here.

Table 5. PMF of e_L with $L = 2^{10}$

Kyber Compression							
e_L	−2	−1	0	1	2		
$\Pr(e_L)$	0.0390	0.3061	0.3068	0.3088	0.0393		
Lloyd-Max							
e_L	−1.5	−1	−0.5	0	0.5	1	1.5
$\Pr(e_L)$	0.0772	0.2304	0.0772	0.2304	0.0772	0.2304	0.0772

Algorithm 5. Kyber.LloydMax.CPA.Enc ($pk = (\mathbf{t}, \rho), m \in \{0,1\}^n$)

1: $r \leftarrow \{0,1\}^{256}$
2: $\mathbf{A} \sim R_q^{k \times k} := \mathsf{Sam}(\rho)$
3: $(\mathbf{r}, \mathbf{e}_1, e_2) \sim \beta_{\eta_1}^k \times \beta_{\eta_2}^k \times \beta_{\eta_2} := \mathsf{Sam}(r)$
4: $\mathbf{u} := Q_{\mathsf{MMSE}, L_u}(\mathbf{A}^T \mathbf{r} + \mathbf{e}_1)$
5: $v := Q_{\mathsf{MMSE}, L_v}(\mathbf{t}^T \mathbf{r} + e_2 + \lceil q/2 \rfloor \cdot m)$
6: **return** $c := (\mathsf{Index}_{L_u}(\mathbf{u}), \mathsf{Index}_{L_v}(v))$

Algorithm 6. Kyber.LloydMax.CPA.Dec($sk = \mathbf{s}, c = (\mathsf{Index}_{L_u}(\mathbf{u}), \mathsf{Index}_{L_v}(v))$)

1: $\mathbf{u} := \mathcal{C}_{L_u}(\mathsf{Index}_{L_u}(\mathbf{u}))$
2: $v := \mathcal{C}_{L_v}(\mathsf{Index}_{L_v}(v))$
3: **return** $\mathsf{Compress}_q(v - \mathbf{s}^T \mathbf{u}, 1)$

We then study the DFR of the optimized Kyber in Algorithms 5 and 6. Let $(\mathbf{e}_{L_u}, e_{L_v})$ be the quantization noise for $(\mathbf{u}, v)$, respectively. The Kyber decoding noise n_e in (2) can be rewritten as

$$n_e = \mathbf{e}^T \mathbf{r} + e_2 + e_{L_v} - \mathbf{s}^T (\mathbf{e}_1 + \mathbf{e}_{L_u}). \tag{20}$$

Following the same line of Kyber [2], the elements in $\mathbf{e}_{L_u}$ or e_{L_v} are assumed to be i.i.d. and independent of other terms in (20).

Without loss of generality, we use $e_L^{(1)} \in \mathcal{S}$ to present an element in $\mathbf{e}_L$ or e_L. Since $\mathrm{E}\left(e_L^{(1)}\right) = 0$, we use a variant of [13, Theorem 1]:

Theorem 1. *According to the Central Limit Theorem (CLT), the distribution of n_e asymptotically approaches the sum of multivariate normal and quantization error e_{L_v}:*

$$n_e \leftarrow \mathcal{N}(0, \sigma_G^2 I_n) + e_{L_v}, \tag{21}$$

where $L_u = 2^{knd_u}$, $L_v = 2^{nd_v}$, and $\sigma_G^2 = kn\eta_1^2/4 + kn\eta_1/2 \cdot \left(\eta_2/2 + \mathsf{MSE}\left(e_{L_u}^{(1)}\right)\right) + \eta_2/2$. The values of $\mathsf{MSE}(e_{L_u}^{(1)})$ are given in Table 3.

Remark 2. Theorem 1 shows how the choice of quantization affects the Kyber decoding noise. For a fixed $(q, k, \eta_1, \eta_2, d_u, d_v)$ in Table 2, a MMSE quantization can minimize the decoding noise variance $\mathrm{Var}(n_e)$. The CLT assumption has been made in the Ring/Module-LWE literature. In [6], the noise coefficients of TFHE scheme after bootstrapping are assumed to be independent Gaussians. The assumption is experimentally verified in [6, Figure 10]. In [7], the noise coefficients of CKKS scheme [5] are assumed to be independent Gaussians. In [16], the noise coefficients of Kyber are assumed to be independent. Based on the CLT assumption, an upper bound on DFR is derived in [13], which is very close to the numerical bound in [2]. We will verify the CLT assumption below.

Consider the noise term $Y = \mathbf{e}^T\mathbf{r} + e_2 - \mathbf{s}^T(\mathbf{e}_1 + \mathbf{e}_{L_u})$. Let $Y = [Y_1, \ldots, Y_n]^T$ be the coefficients in Y. In Fig. 1, we compare the cumulative distribution functions (CDF) of Y_1/σ_G (in blue) and the standard normal distribution (in red). We observe that the curves are almost indistinguishable. Experimental result confirms the distribution of Y_1 is Gaussian. This experimentally validates our independent assumption in Theorem 1, since Y_i, for $i = 1, \ldots, n$, are uncorrelated and identically distributed random variables.

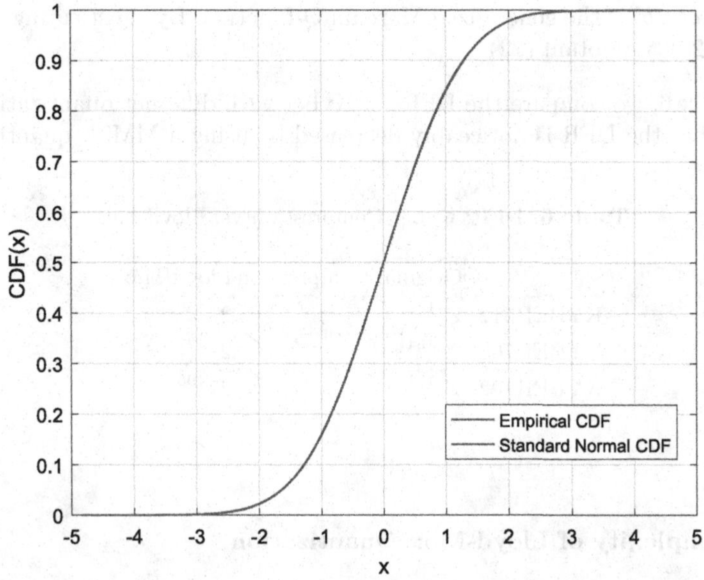

Fig. 1. KYBER1024: Comparing the CDF of Y_1/σ_G to the standard normal distribution with 1,000,000 samples, experimental validation of CLT assumption (Color figure online)

Using Theorem 1, we derive the DFR as follows.

Theorem 2. *With the Lloyd-Max quantization, the DFR of Kyber is given by*

$$\delta = 1 - \left(1 - \sum\nolimits_{e_{L_v}^{(1)} \in \mathcal{S}} \Pr\left(e_{L_v}^{(1)}\right) Q_{1/2}\left(\|e_{L_v}^{(1)}\|/\sigma_G, \lceil q/4 \rfloor/\sigma_G\right)\right)^n, \tag{22}$$

where σ_G is given in Theorem 1, and $Q_M(a, b)$ is the generalized Marcum Q-function. Both $e_{L_v}^{(1)}$ and $\Pr\left(e_{L_v}^{(1)}\right)$ can be found by Algorithm 4.

Proof. Given Theorem 1, we can write $n_e = x + e_{L_v}$, where $x \leftarrow \mathcal{N}(0, \sigma_G^2 I)$. Since the elements in n_e are i.i.d., for simplicity, we consider one element in n_e, denoted as $n_e^{(1)} = x^{(1)} + e_{L_v}^{(1)}$. The DFR can be written as

$$\delta = 1 - \Pr(\|n_e^{(1)}\| \leq \lceil q/4 \rfloor)^n. \tag{23}$$

We have

$$\Pr\left(\|n_e^{(1)}\| \le z\right) = \sum\nolimits_{e_{L_v}^{(1)} \in \mathcal{S}} \Pr\left(\|x^{(1)} + e_{L_v}^{(1)}\| \le z \,\middle|\, e_{L_v}^{(1)}\right) \Pr\left(e_{L_v}^{(1)}\right). \quad (24)$$

Given $e_{L_v}^{(1)}$, $\|x^{(1)} + e_{L_v}^{(1)}\|$ follows non-central chi distribution, i.e.,

$$\Pr\left(\|x^{(1)} + e_{L_v}^{(1)}\| \le z \,\middle|\, e_{L_v}^{(1)}\right) = 1 - Q_{1/2}\left(\|e_{L_v}^{(1)}\|/\sigma_G, z/\sigma_G\right), \quad (25)$$

where $Q_M(a, b)$ is the generalized Marcum Q-function. By substituting (25) and (24) for (23), we obtain (22).

In Table 6, we compare the DFRs of Kyber with different quantizations. We observe that the DFR is noticeably decreased by using a MMSE quantization.

Table 6. DFR: Kyber Compression vs. Lloyd-Max

	Original Compression	Lloyd-Max
KYBER512	2^{-139}	2^{-150}
KYBER768	2^{-164}	2^{-177}
KYBER1024	2^{-174}	2^{-196}

3.3 Complexity of Lloyd-Max Quantization

Kyber compression function in (1) involves one multiplication and one division operations, which imply time complexity $O(\log_2(q)^2)$. Here we assume that the rounding and modulo operations have very low computational cost and are treated as constant-time operations. The complexity of the decompression function is the same as the compression function.

For the Lloyd-Max quantization, an input x will be mapped to the nearest quantizer. Given a pre-stored codebook $\mathcal{C}_L$, we can use a binary search method to find the nearest quantizer, with time complexity $O(\log_2(L))$. Considering that the Lloyd-Max quantization does not require a reconstruction function, we conclude that the Lloyd-Max quantization takes less time than Kyber compression.

Note that the security levels of Kyber are computed independent of the compression method and the compression noise level [2]. Therefore, using Lloyd-Max quantization does not affect the security argument of Kyber.

4 Semi-compressed Kyber

4.1 The Design

We first revisit the ciphertext compression strategy in Kyber (Algorithm 2):

- Step 4: compress the first part of ciphertext, $\mathbf{u}$, to knd_u bits.
- Step 5: compress the second part of ciphertext, $\mathbf{v}$, to nd_v bits.

The CER of Kyber can be computed as

$$\mathrm{CER} = \frac{knd_u + nd_v}{K}, \tag{26}$$

where K represents the number of information bits. In the original Kyber, K is set to be 256 bits. Considering the values of (n, k, d_u, d_v) in Table 2, we notice that compressing $\mathbf{v}$ has little impact on reducing CER, but at the cost of adding a 7 or 8-bit quantization noise to the decoding.

Definition 1 (SC-Kyber). *We consider a variant of Kyber as follows.*

$$(Q_{\mathsf{MMSE},L_u}(\mathbf{A}^T\mathbf{r} + \mathbf{e}_1), \mathbf{t}^T\mathbf{r} + e_2 + \lceil q/p \rfloor \cdot \mathsf{ENC}(m)), \tag{27}$$

where $p \geq 2$, $m \leftarrow \{0,1\}^K$, and $\mathsf{ENC}(m) : \{0,1\}^K \mapsto \mathbb{Z}_p^n$. Since only the first part of ciphertext is quantized, this scheme is referred to as Semi-Compressed Kyber *(SC-Kyber). The CER reduces to*

$$CER = \frac{knd_u + 12n}{K}. \tag{28}$$

We expect that the reduced decryption decoding noise enables encoding a larger plaintext than [13,16], i.e., a larger K. Let $\mathsf{DEC}((v - \mathbf{s}^T\mathbf{u})/\lceil q/p \rfloor) : \mathbb{Z}_p^n \mapsto \{0,1\}^K$ be the decoding function. The choices of $\mathsf{ENC}(\cdot)$ and $\mathsf{DEC}(\cdot)$ are discussed in the Subsect. 4.3. The key generation function of SC-Kyber is the same as Algorithm 1. Thus we omit details here. The encryption and decryption algorithms of SC-Kyber are described in Algorithms 7 and 8.

Algorithm 7. $\mathsf{SC-Kyber.CPA.Enc}$ $(pk = (\mathbf{t}, \rho), m \in \{0,1\}^K)$

1: $r \leftarrow \{0,1\}^{256}$
2: $\mathbf{A} \sim R_q^{k \times k} := \mathsf{Sam}(\rho)$
3: $(\mathbf{r}, \mathbf{e}_1, e_2) \sim \beta_{\eta_1}^k \times \beta_{\eta_2}^k \times \beta_{\eta_2} := \mathsf{Sam}(r)$
4: $\mathbf{u} := Q_{\mathsf{MMSE},L_u}(\mathbf{A}^T\mathbf{r} + \mathbf{e}_1)$
5: $v := \mathbf{t}^T\mathbf{r} + e_2 + \lceil q/p \rfloor \cdot \mathsf{ENC}(m)$
6: **return** $c := (\mathsf{Index}_{L_u}(\mathbf{u}), v)$

Algorithm 8. $\mathsf{SC-Kyber.CPA.Dec}(sk = \mathbf{s}, c = (\mathsf{Index}_{L_u}(\mathbf{u}), v))$

1: $\mathbf{u} := \mathcal{C}_{L_u}(\mathsf{Index}_{L_u}(\mathbf{u}))$
2: **return** $\mathsf{DEC}((v - \mathbf{s}^T\mathbf{u})/\lceil q/p \rfloor)$

4.2 Information Theoretic Analysis of SC-Kyber

We study the maximum possible plaintext size K, or equivalently, the minimum possible CER for SC-Kyber. Since v remains uncompressed, according to Theorem 1, the decoding problem in SC-Kyber can be formulated by

$$y = \lceil q/p \rfloor \cdot \mathsf{ENC}(m) + n_e, \tag{29}$$

where $n_e \leftarrow \mathcal{N}(0, \sigma_G^2 I_n)$ and the value of σ_G is given in Theorem 1.

It is evident that the SC-Kyber decoding problem is equivalent to the detection problem in an AWGN channel with a p-PAM modulation and n independent channel uses. An upper bound on the plaintext size, i.e., K, is given below.

Lemma 2 (Maximum Plaintext Size). *For any* $\mathsf{ENC}(m) : \{0,1\}^K \mapsto \mathbb{Z}_p^n$*, the maximum amount of error-free information that can theoretically be decrypted is*

$$K \leq n/2 \log_2 \left(\frac{1+\gamma}{1+\gamma/p^2} \right) \triangleq K_{\mathsf{UB}}, \tag{30}$$

where

$$\gamma = \frac{\lceil q/p \rfloor^2 \sum_{i=0}^{p-1} (i-(p-1)/2)^2}{p\sigma_G^2}, \tag{31}$$

and the value of σ_G *is given in Theorem 1.*

Proof. We subtract $\lceil q/p \rfloor (p-1)/2$ from both sides of (29), obtaining

$$\hat{y} = \lceil q/p \rfloor \hat{m} + n_e, \tag{32}$$

where $\hat{y} = y - \lceil q/p \rfloor (p-1)/2$ and $\hat{m} = \mathsf{ENC}(m) - (p-1)/2$. Note that shifting a random variable does not change its entropy. Since $n_e \leftarrow \mathcal{N}(0, \sigma_G^2 I_n)$, the model (32) is equivalent to an AWGN channel with a p-PAM modulation and n independent channel uses. The maximum achievable information rate (bit per channel use) can be well-approximated by [23]

$$\max_{\Pr(\hat{m})} \frac{I(\hat{y}, \hat{m})}{n} \approx 1/2 \log_2 \left(\frac{1+\gamma}{1+\gamma/p^2} \right) \geq \frac{K}{n}, \tag{33}$$

where γ is given in (31).

Remark 3. Using Lemma 2, a lower bound on CER is given by

$$\mathsf{CER} \geq \frac{knd_u + 12n}{K_{\mathsf{UB}}} \triangleq \mathsf{CER}_{\mathsf{LB}}. \tag{34}$$

In Table 7, we compute the values of K_{UB} and $\mathsf{CER}_{\mathsf{LB}}$ for different p. We observe that with $p = 8$, it is theoretically possible to encapsulate two 256-bit AES keys in a single ciphertext. In the next subsection, we will present a practical encoding scheme to achieve this goal.

Table 7. SC-KYBER1024: K_{UB} and $\mathsf{CER}_{\mathsf{LB}}$

p	2	4	8	16
K_{UB}	255	505	742	935
$\mathsf{CER}_{\mathsf{LB}}$	56.2	28.4	19.3	15.3

4.3 Encoding, Decoding, and DFR

We consider a binary error correcting code (N, K, t), where $N = n\log_2(p)$ is the codeword length and t is the number of correctable errors [12]. Let $c_{\mathsf{B}} \in \{0,1\}^N$ be a binary codeword. The binary encoder $\{0,1\}^K \mapsto \{0,1\}^N$ and the corresponding binay decoder $\{0,1\}^N \mapsto \{0,1\}^K$ are defined by

$$\begin{aligned} c_{\mathsf{B}} &= \mathsf{B\text{-}Enc}(m) \\ m &= \mathsf{B\text{-}Dec}(c_{\mathsf{B}}). \end{aligned} \tag{35}$$

Gray code [19] is used to map every $\log_2(p)$ bits in c_{B} to a (shifted) p-PAM symbol. The bit mapper $\{0,1\}^N \mapsto \mathbb{Z}_p^n$ and demapper $\mathbb{Z}_p^n \mapsto \{0,1\}^N$ are given by

$$\begin{aligned} x &= \mathsf{Gray}(c_{\mathsf{B}}) \\ c_{\mathsf{B}} &= \mathsf{Gray}^{-1}(x). \end{aligned} \tag{36}$$

Example 2. In Table 8, we show the bit-to-symbol mapping on (shifted) 8-PAM. With Gray Code, only one bit changes state from one position to another.

Table 8. Bit-to-symbol mapping on (shifted) 8-PAM

Symbol	0	1	2	3	4	5	6	7
Bits	000	001	011	010	110	111	101	100

Combining (35) and (36), the encoding and decoding functions in Algorithms 7 and 8 are given by

$$\begin{aligned} x &= \mathsf{ENC}(m) = \mathsf{Gray}(\mathsf{B\text{-}Enc}(m)) \\ m &= \mathsf{DEC}(x) = \mathsf{B\text{-}Dec}(\mathsf{Gray}^{-1}(\lceil x \rfloor \bmod p)). \end{aligned} \tag{37}$$

We then derive the DFR for the proposed encoding scheme.

Lemma 3. *With p-PAM, Gray mapping, and a binary code (N, K, t), for a large γ in (31), the DFR of SC-Kyber can be computed by*

$$\delta = \sum_{j=t+1}^{N} \binom{N}{j} \mathsf{RBER}^j (1 - \mathsf{RBER})^{N-j}, \tag{38}$$

where $\mathsf{RBER} < 2Q(\lceil q/(2p) \rfloor / \sigma_G)/\log_2(p)$*, $Q(\cdot)$ is the Q-function, and the value of σ_G is given in Theorem 1.*

Proof. Since SC-Kyber decoding is equivalent to decoding in a p-PAM input AWGN channel, the raw symbol error rate (RSER) is

$$\mathsf{RSER} = \begin{cases} 2Q(\lceil q/(2p) \rfloor / \sigma_G), & \text{interior points} \\ Q(\lceil q/(2p) \rfloor / \sigma_G), & \text{end points} \end{cases} \tag{39}$$

Since Gray code makes sure that the most likely symbol errors cause only one bit error, for a large γ, the raw bit error rate (RBER) is well-approximated by

$$\mathsf{RBER} \approx \mathsf{RSER} / \log_2(p). \tag{40}$$

For a binary code (N, K, t), the DFR can be computed by (38).

Example 3. We consider an encoding approach with 8-PAM, Gray mapping, and binary BCH(768, 638, 13) [12], which is shortened from BCH(1023, 893, 13). For the SC-KYBER1024, we have $\delta = 2^{-174}$ and $\mathsf{CER} = 22.5$. Since the original KYBER1024 has $\mathsf{CER} = 49$, the communication overhead is reduced by 54%. Compared with the bounds in Table 7, there is a gap of about 0.4 bit per channel use between the theoretical limit and the rate achieved by the BCH code.

In Table 9, we compare the performances of different variants of KYBER1024, given the same security parameters $(n, q, k, \eta_1, \eta_2)$. With the proposed semi-compressed variant, we can easily encrypt two 256-bit AES keys into a single ciphertext. By changing the code rate, either DFR or CER can be minimized.

Table 9. Parameters for different variants of KYBER1024: $(n = 256, q = 3329, k = 4, \eta_1 = 2, \eta_2 = 2)$

Codes	Compression	p	K	d_u	d_v	CER	DFR	Source
Uncoded	Original [17]	2	256	11	5	49	2^{-174}	[17]
Leech lattice	Original [17]	8	380	11	5	33	2^{-226}	[13]
Q-BCH	Original [17]	5	471	11	5	26.6	2^{-174}	[16]
B-BCH(768, 513, 26)	Lloyd-Max	8	513	10	12	26	2^{-268}	This work
B-BCH(768, 638, 13)	Lloyd-Max	8	638	11	12	22.5	2^{-174}	This work

4.4 Security

As shown in [16], the encoding has no influence on the distribution of the ciphertext. Moreover, the proposed encoding scheme uses a constant-time BCH decoder in [24], thus it is resistant to timing attacks. Analysis of potential security issues and mitigation strategies is left for future work.

5 Conclusion

In this paper, we prove that the communication overhead of Kyber can be reduced by more than 50%, i.e., encapsulating two 256-bit AES keys in a single ciphertext. Our solution involves a provably optimal quantization and a constant-time encoding scheme. Closed-form expressions of the DFR is derived. From the information theoretic perspective, we derive the maximum possible plaintext size for Kyber, which tells the minimum possible communication overhead. Our results also imply that it is possible to design a more compact M-LWE encryption scheme than Kyber, using advanced quantization and coding technologies.

References

1. Alkim, E., Ducas, L., Pöppelmann, T., Schwabe, P.: Post-quantum key exchange—a new hope. In: 25th USENIX Security Symposium (USENIX Security 16), pp. 327–343. USENIX Association, Austin (2016). https://www.usenix.org/conference/usenixsecurity16/technical-sessions/presentation/alkim
2. Avanzi, R., et al.: Algorithm specifications and supporting documentation (version 3.02). Technical report, Submission to the NIST post-quantum project (2021). https://pq-crystals.org/kyber/resources.shtml
3. Azimi, M.: Digital Image Processing Lectures 7 & 8. Colorado State University (2011). https://www.engr.colostate.edu/ECE513/SP09/lectures/lectures7_8.pdf
4. Bos, J., et al.: CRYSTALS - kyber: a CCA-secure module-lattice-based KEM. In: 2018 IEEE European Symposium on Security and Privacy (EuroS&P), pp. 353–367 (2018). https://doi.org/10.1109/EuroSP.2018.00032
5. Cheon, J.H., Kim, A., Kim, M., Song, Y.: Homomorphic encryption for arithmetic of approximate numbers. In: Advances in Cryptology–ASIACRYPT 2017: 23rd International Conference on the Theory and Applications of Cryptology and Information Security, Hong Kong, China, 3–7 December 2017, Proceedings, Part I 23, pp. 409–437. Springer (2017)
6. Chillotti, I., Gama, N., Georgieva, M., Izabachène, M.: TFHE: fast fully homomorphic encryption over the torus. J. Cryptol. **33**, 34–91 (2020). https://doi.org/10.1007/s00145-019-09319-x
7. Costache, A., Curtis, B.R., Hales, E., Murphy, S., Ogilvie, T., Player, R.: On the precision loss in approximate homomorphic encryption. In: Selected Areas in Cryptography – SAC 2023, pp. 325–345. Springer, Cham (2024). https://doi.org/10.1007/978-3-031-53368-6_16
8. D'Anvers, J.P., Batsleer, S.: Multitarget decryption failure attacks and their application to saber and kyber. In: Hanaoka, G., Shikata, J., Watanabe, Y. (eds.) Public-Key Cryptography – PKC 2022, pp. 3–33. Springer, Cham (2022). https://doi.org/10.1007/978-3-030-97121-2_1
9. D'Anvers, J.-P., Guo, Q., Johansson, T., Nilsson, A., Vercauteren, F., Verbauwhede, I.: Decryption failure attacks on IND-CCA secure lattice-based schemes. In: Lin, D., Sako, K. (eds.) PKC 2019. LNCS, vol. 11443, pp. 565–598. Springer, Cham (2019). https://doi.org/10.1007/978-3-030-17259-6_19
10. D'Anvers, J.P., Tiepelt, M., Vercauteren, F., Verbauwhede, I.: Timing attacks on error correcting codes in post-quantum schemes. In: Proceedings of ACM Workshop on Theory of Implementation Security Workshop, TIS'19, pp. 2–9. Association for Computing Machinery, New York (2019). https://doi.org/10.1145/3338467.3358948

11. Fritzmann, T., Pöppelmann, T., Sepulveda, J.: Analysis of error-correcting codes for lattice-based key exchange. In: Cid, C., Jacobson Jr, M.J. (eds.) Selected Areas in Cryptography – SAC 2018, pp. 369–390. Springer, Cham (2019). https://doi.org/10.1007/978-3-030-10970-7_17
12. Lin, S., Costello, D.J.: Error Control Coding, 2nd edn. Prentice-Hall Inc. (2004)
13. Liu, S., Sakzad, A.: Lattice codes for CRYSTALS-kyber (2023). https://arxiv.org/abs/2308.13981
14. Lloyd, S.: Least squares quantization in PCM. IEEE Trans. Inf. Theory **28**(2), 129–137 (1982). https://doi.org/10.1109/TIT.1982.1056489
15. Lyu, S., Liu, L., Ling, C., Lai, J., Chen, H.: Lattice codes for lattice-based PKE. Des. Codes Cryptogr. (2023). https://doi.org/10.1007/s10623-023-01321-6
16. Maringer, G., Puchinger, S., Wachter-Zeh, A.: Information- and coding-theoretic analysis of the RLWE/MLWE channel. IEEE Trans. Inf. Forensics Secur. **18**, 549–564 (2023). https://doi.org/10.1109/TIFS.2022.3226907
17. National Institute of Standards and Technology: Module-Lattice-Based Key Encapsulation Mechanism Standard. Federal Information Processing Standards Publication (FIPS) NIST FIPS 203 ipd. (2023). https://doi.org/10.6028/NIST.FIPS.203.ipd
18. van Poppelen, A.: Cryptographic decoding of the Leech lattice. Cryptology ePrint Archive, Paper 2016/1050 (2016). https://eprint.iacr.org/2016/1050
19. Proakis, J.G.: Digital Communications, 4th edn. McGraw-Hill, New York (2000)
20. Saliba, C., Luzzi, L., Ling, C.: A reconciliation approach to key generation based on module-LWE. In: 2021 IEEE International Symposium on Information Theory (ISIT), pp. 1636–1641 (2021). https://doi.org/10.1109/ISIT45174.2021.9517882
21. Scheunders, P.: A genetic Lloyd-Max image quantization algorithm. Pattern Recogn. Lett. **17**(5), 547–556 (1996). https://doi.org/10.1016/0167-8655(96)00011-6
22. Tang, Y., Clapp, R.G.: Selection of reference-anisotropy parameters for wavefield extrapolation by Lloyd's algorithm. In: SEG Technical Program Expanded Abstracts, pp. 189–193 (2006). https://doi.org/10.1190/1.2369897
23. Urlea, M., Loyka, S.: Simple closed-form approximations for achievable information rates of coded modulation systems. J. Lightwave Technol. **39**(5), 1306–1311 (2021). https://doi.org/10.1109/JLT.2020.3039178
24. Walters, M., Roy, S.S.: Constant-time BCH error-correcting code. In: 2020 IEEE International Symposium on Circuits and Systems (ISCAS), pp. 1–5 (2020). https://doi.org/10.1109/ISCAS45731.2020.9180846

Blocklistable Anonymous Credential for Circuits with Post-quantum Security

Zuoxia Yu[1(✉)], Rupeng Yang[1], Willy Susilo[1], and Man Ho Au[2]

[1] Institute of Cybersecurity and Cryptology, School of Computing and Information Technology, University of Wollongong, Wollongong, NSW, Australia
{zuoxia_yu,rupeng_yang,willy_susilo}@uow.edu.au

[2] Department of Computing, The Hong Kong Polytechnic University, Hong Kong, China
mhaau@polyu.edu.hk

Abstract. A blocklistable anonymous credential system (BLAC) allows a service provider to decide if it would like to accept an anonymous user according to his historical behaviors. Security of such systems requires that 1) a user can be authenticated if and only if his historical behaviors satisfy a given policy and that 2) no additional information (besides the result of the authentication) is revealed to the service provider. Existing constructions of BLAC only consider very restricted access policies, e.g., blocking a user if he has an authentication record that is marked as misbehaved. Besides, most of them are constructed from number theoretical assumptions, which are vulnerable to the quantum attacks.

In this work, we advance the state-of-the-art for BLAC. First, we present the notion of BLAC for circuits, where the service provider can use general policies that are represented by any boolean circuits and admit a user if and only if his historical records satisfy the circuit. Then, we construct BLAC systems for arbitrary circuits from lattice assumptions, which offer post-quantum security. To obtain our constructions, we propose efficient lattice-based zero-knowledge arguments for various relations, which may be of independent interest. Besides, we demonstrate the practicality of our constructions by providing an estimation of the communication cost of our system.

1 Introduction

In order to protect users' privacy, anonymity and unlinkability are usually desirable when designing online authentication mechanisms. However, people may abuse their anonymity via breaching the rules from the service providers (SP), e.g., posting rumor, defacing webpages, etc. Thus, the authentication protocol should allow the service provider to revoke users with misbehaviors while guaranteeing privacy of users.

In some cases, the service provider cannot decide whether a user has misbehaved unless it learns all historical behaviors of the user. For example, in a forum, the author of a post should be rewarded if the post receives many supports; however, the author should be penalized if all supports come from the

J. K. Liu et al. (Eds.): ProvSec 2024, LNCS 14904, pp. 83–105, 2025.
https://doi.org/10.1007/978-981-96-0957-4_5

author himself. The question is can the service provider still detect such misbehaviors without compromising unlinkability of the system.

Blocklistable Anonymous Credential. Towards providing both anonymity/unlinkability and accountability for users, blocklistable anonymous credential (BLAC) systems are introduced [10,34]. Generally speaking, a BLAC system is similar to an anonymous credential system [11], where registered users authenticate with service providers in an anonymous way, but in a BLAC system, each SP additionally maintains a blocklist to record users with misbehaviors. For a registered user who wants to access the services provided by a SP, he should first request a blocklist from the SP and proves to the SP that he is legitimately registered and he is not on the blocklist. Here, to guarantee the privacy of users, service providers cannot learn the real identity of users when maintaining the blocklist. To achieve this, in the system, each authentication event is attached with a ticket, which binds the user's secret key in an anonymous and unlinkable way.[1] The SP puts tickets of authentication events with misbehaviors into blocklist and the user needs to prove that all tickets in the blocklist is not generated by him.

Early works [10,34] in this area only consider basic policy, where a user is blocked once he is put on a blocklist. Then in [36], d-strikes-out policies are supported, where a user is revoked if he appears in the blocklist for d-times. Next, in [5,37,40], BLAC systems with reputation (BLACR) are constructed. In a BLACR system, the service provider can assign positive or negative score to each authentication event in the "blocklist", and a user will be admitted if and only if the sum of his scores is above some threshold.

There are also some subsequent works considering improving efficiency of BLAC systems, by using techniques that "compress" blocklist for either basic blocklist [27,35] or blocklist with reputation [4,38,42]. In a nutshell, in these systems, the user would get a token from the service provider (which shows that the user has not been put in the blocklist or his score equals to a particular secret value) at some point in time and then all historical records before this time point are useless in the future authentications. In this way, the communication cost in these systems is greatly reduced. Another way to reduce the communication cost is to apply a ZK-SNARK in the protocol [32].

However, in all previous BLAC systems, the SP must decide if an authentication event is misbehaved (or assign scores to the authentication event) according to the public information. As the protocol can guarantee that users are anonymous and unlinkable, the service providers have to make the decision for each record independently. This makes the systems not applicable in scenarios that misbehaviors depend on the user's behaviors in several different authentication events.

Post-quantum Security. Another problem of current BLAC systems is that most of them will become insecure in the near future, when practical quan-

[1] For example, the ticket can be (g, g^s), where g is a random group element and s is the user's secret.

tum computers are available. Recently, due to the rapid development in implementing practical quantum computers, it is a trend to migrate traditional number-theoretic assumptions based cryptographic schemes into lattice-based ones, which are believed to remain secure under quantum attacks. Many fundamental cryptographic primitives, such as public-key encryption schemes and signature schemes, have found practical constructions from lattice. Moreover, great efforts have been made on constructing lattice-based privacy-preserving primitives (namely, authentication protocol with user privacy protection). Well known examples include group signature [14], ring signature [17], electronic cash [41], anonymous credential [9,21], etc. However, little attention has been paid on constructing post-quantum secure BLAC systems. The only known BLAC system from lattice is constructed by Yang et al. in [39], but they mainly explore the existence of lattice-based BLAC system and it is unknown to what extend the constructed scheme can be applied in practice.

To solving the above problems, we aim at giving an affirmative answer to the following question:

Can we construct a BLAC system that allows the service provider to judge a user according to all his historical behaviors while keeping anonymity and unlinkability of users? Also, can we enhance it with post-quantum security?

Our Contributions. In this work, we give answers to the question by presenting a lattice-based BLAC system for general circuit. Our system allows the service provider to specify a circuit as its policy. Then a user can access services from the service provider if and only if his historical behaviors[2] satisfy the circuit. In this way, the service provider does not need to identify which authentication event should be marked as "misbehaved" and instead it can embed the misbehavior detection program into the circuit.

The core components of our constructions is a set of efficient lattice-based zero-knowledge arguments of knowledge (ZKAoK) for various relations, including ZKAoK for circuits satisfiability, ZKAoK for historical records correctness, etc. We construct these ZKAoKs under the general framework proposed in [41]. We also introduce several new techniques to deal with specific issues in our constructions, and they can enrich the arsenal of privacy-preserving techniques in the post-quantum setting.

It is worth noting that we construct our BLAC systems in three different settings, namely, the static registration setting, where all users enroll in the beginning, the dynamic registration setting, where users could join or leave the system in a dynamic manner, and the decentralized setting, where no trusted registration center is needed. The third construction additionally exploit a public ledger to manage registration of users, which can be implemented by the blockchain technique.

To show the practicability of our proposed systems, we evaluate the communication cost of our schemes under different security levels and compare it with some previous schemes in Table 1. The communication costs of schemes in

[2] Here, the historical behaviors are defined by a binary string $\boldsymbol{x}$ s.t. $\boldsymbol{x}[i] = 1$ iff the i-th valid authentication record belongs to the user.

[4,5,34,40] are from the original paper. The communication costs of schemes in [27,35,39] are estimated in this work according to the complexity analysis shown in the original paper. Note that practical BLAC systems such as PEREA, PERM, etc. use some techniques that compress the historical behaviors of users to achieve a smaller communication size (in Table 1, we category such systems as "not stateless"). However, the techniques are not applicable in our setting, where all historical behaviors are potentially useful.

One may notice that there is still a large gap (about 3 orders of magnitude) between the efficiency of our system and that of schemes constructed from traditional number theoretical assumptions. We stress that such gap is common when comparing state-of-the-art lattice-based privacy-preserving primitives and traditional number theoretical assumptions based one, e.g., group signature (203 KB in [28] **vs** 200 Bytes in [8]), ring signature (22 KB in [29] **vs** 220 Bytes in [30]), E-Cash (262 MB in [41] **vs** 596 Bytes in [6]), etc.

2 Preliminaries

Notations. We will use bold lower-case letters (e.g., $\boldsymbol{v}$) to denote vectors, and use bold upper-case letters (e.g., $\boldsymbol{A}$) to denote matrices. All elements in vectors and matrices are integers unless otherwise specified. For a vector $\boldsymbol{v}$ of length n, we use $\boldsymbol{v}[i]$ to denote the ith element of $\boldsymbol{v}$ for $i \in [1, n]$. For a finite set $\mathcal{S}$, we use $|\mathcal{S}|$ to denote the size of $\mathcal{S}$ and use $s \xleftarrow{\$} \mathcal{S}$ to denote sampling an element s uniformly from set $\mathcal{S}$. For a distribution $\mathcal{D}$, we use $d \leftarrow \mathcal{D}$ to denote sampling d

Table 1. Comparisons of different BLAC systems.

	Policy	Post-Quantum Security	Stateless*	Decentralized	Communication cost◇
BLAC [36]	blocklist†	✗	✓	✗	700 KB
PEREA [35]	blocklist	✗	✗	✗	10.3 KB
FAUST [27]	blocklist	✗	✗	✗	1.7 KB
L-BLAC [39]	blocklist	✓	✓	✗	2.21 TB
SNARKBlock [32]	blocklist	✗	✓	✗	100KB
BLACR [5]	reputation‡	✗	✓	✗	865 KB
PERM [4]	reputation	✗	✗	✗	28 KB
DBLACR [40]	reputation	✗	✓	✓	1.03MB
Ours Scheme 1	circuit*	✓	✓	✗	1.9 GB
Scheme 2	circuit	✓	✓	✗	1.9 GB
Scheme 3	circuit	✓	✓	✓	1.9 GB

*: Stateless means that no token that compresses user's historical behaviors is needed;
†: "blocklist" means the basic policy used in BLAC [36];
‡: "reputation" means the policy used in BLACR [5];
*: "circuit" means the kind of policy denoted by any polynomial-size boolean circuit.
◇: The communication costs are estimated when the blocklist size is1000 and the circuit size is 10000 (if applicable).

according to $\mathcal{D}$. For integers $a \leq b$, we write $[a, b]$ to denote all integers from a to b, and use $[a]$ to denote all integers from 1 to a.

Boolean Circuit Representation. Let C be a boolean circuit with ℓ input wires and N gates. Here, a boolean circuit means that the value on each wire is either 0 or 1. The functionality of each gate considered in this paper is AND, OR, XOR or NOT calculation. The input wires are indexed by $1, 2, \ldots, \ell$, the internal wires are labeled by $\ell+1$, $\ell+2$, ..., $\ell+N-1$, the output wire is labeled as $\ell+N$. We assume each AND, OR and XOR gate has two input wires and each NOT gate has one input wire. All gates mentioned above support multiple-fan-out wires, where all fan-out wires are indexed with the same label. Following [16], we use mapping function **topo** to denote the topology of a circuit. Specifically,

$$\mathbf{topo} : \{\ell+1, \ldots, \ell+N\} \to \{\mathsf{AND}, \mathsf{OR}, \mathsf{XOR}, \mathsf{NOT}\} \times \{1, \ldots, \ell+N-1\} \times \{1, \ldots, \ell+N-1\}.$$

This function is used to map each non-input wire to its input wires and the gate used to connecting them. For each mapping $\mathbf{topo}(i) \to (\blacktriangleright_i, i_1, i_2)$, we require $i_1, i_2 < i$ and $\blacktriangleright_i \in \{\mathsf{AND}, \mathsf{OR}, \mathsf{XOR}, \mathsf{NOT}\}$, where $i_2 = \perp$ when $\blacktriangleright_i$ is NOT gate. Throughout this paper, we use C_ℓ to denote all boolean circuits with ℓ input wires.

Hardness Assumptions and Its Concrete Hardness. The security of our schemes relies on the short integer solution (SIS) assumption [1], the learning with errors (LWE) assumption [31] and learning with rounding (LWR) assumption [7].

When designing practical lattice-based cryptographic schemes, parameters are usually set to be robust against best known cryptanalysis. This approach has been adopted in many previous works, such as [2,3,15,20]. We also adopt the same approach when analyzing concrete efficiency of schemes in this work. Concretely, we examine the root Hermite factor (RHF) [18] for each lattice problem.

Then we use the estimator from [33] to estimate the cost of BKZ [12] algorithm with quantum-core-sieving [2,3,22] to arrive those root Hermite factors. In general, to achieve a 80/100/128-bit security, the corresponding RHF are 1.0048/1.0042/1.0035, respectively.

Building Blocks. In addition, our constructions are built on several cryptographic schemes, including a non-interactive zero-knowledge arguments of knowledge (NIZKAoK), accumulator scheme and weak pseudorandom function. The details are given below.

Zero-Knowledge Argument of Knowledge System (ZKAoK). A ZKAoK [19] system allows a prover to prove to a verifier that he possesses the witness for a statement without revealing any additional information. We refer readers to [19] for the definition of ZKAoK system. Although there already exists ZKAoK systems for general language, they are inefficient. In this work, we propose an efficient (non-interactive) ZKAoK system for some lattice-based relations.

Lattice-based Accumulator Scheme. We will employ the lattice-based accumulator proposed by Libert et al. in [23], which relies on the Merkle hash tree structure to accumulate a set of values into the root of the tree. As shown in [26], the Merkle tree accumulator scheme in [23] can be equipped with an efficient updating algorithm, which supports editing the accumulated value set without the need of reconstructing the whole tree. Due to the space limitation, we refer readers to works [23,26] for the accumulator schemes and the updating algorithm.

Weak Pseudorandom Function. Our constructions also use a variant of the weak pseudorandom function (wPRF) constructed implicitly by Banerjee et al. in [7]. Below, we give the construction of the variant and show that it achieves both weak pseudorandomness and key-injectivity, which requires that it is hard to compute two distinct secret keys $\boldsymbol{s}_1, \boldsymbol{s}_2$ s.t. $\mathbf{Eval}(\boldsymbol{s}_1, \boldsymbol{A}) = \mathbf{Eval}(\boldsymbol{s}_2, \boldsymbol{A})$ given a random input $\boldsymbol{A}$.

Let λ be the security parameter. Let q_0 be a prime, e_1, e_2 be positive integers and $p = q_0^{e_1}, q = q_0^{e_2}$. Let n_1, n_2 be positive integers that are polynomial in λ. The weak PRF $\mathbf{PRF} = (\mathbf{KeyGen}, \mathbf{Eval})$ works as follows:

- **KeyGen.** The key generation algorithm samples $\boldsymbol{s} \leftarrow \mathcal{ZO}_{n_2}(2/3)$ and outputs the key $\boldsymbol{s}$. Following [13], we use $\mathcal{ZO}_{n_2}(2/3)$ to denote a uniform distribution over $\{0, \pm 1\}^{n_2}$.
- **Eval.** On input an input $\boldsymbol{A} \xleftarrow{\$} \mathbb{Z}_q^{n_1 \times n_2}$, the evaluation algorithm outputs $\boldsymbol{y} = \lfloor \boldsymbol{A} \cdot \boldsymbol{s} \rfloor_p \mod p$.

Weak pseudorandomness of $\mathbf{PRF}$ comes from the $\mathrm{LWR}_{n_2,q,p}$ assumption with secret over $\mathcal{ZO}_{n_2}(\cdot)$. As claimed in [2,13], this is as hard as a standard LWE assumption $\mathrm{LWE}_{n,q,\alpha}$, where $n = \frac{3n_2}{2\log q}$ and $\alpha = \sqrt{\frac{2\pi((q/p)^2-1)}{120 n_2' q^2}}$.

Key-injectivity comes from the SIS assumption. In particular, for a random matrix $\boldsymbol{A}$, if the adversary is able to find two secret keys $\boldsymbol{s}_1, \boldsymbol{s}_2 \in \{0, \pm 1\}^{n_2}$ s.t. $\lfloor \boldsymbol{A} \cdot \boldsymbol{s}_1 \rfloor_p = \lfloor \boldsymbol{A} \cdot \boldsymbol{s}_2 \rfloor_p \mod p$, then it can find a solution $\boldsymbol{s} \in [-2, 2]^{n_2}, \boldsymbol{e} \in [-q/p+1, q/p-1]^{n_1}$ for $\boldsymbol{A} \cdot \boldsymbol{s} + \boldsymbol{e} = 0$. That is to say, it solves the normal form $SIS_{n,q,\beta}$ problem, where $\beta = \sqrt{4n_2 + (q/p-1)^2 \cdot n_1}$.

3 BLAC: Syntax Definitions

In this section, we give the definition of blocklistable anonymous credential (BLAC) system for circuits, where the access policy is specified by polynomial-size boolean circuits.

There are three kinds of entities in a BLAC system, including a group manager (GM), a set of service providers (SPs) and a set of users. The GM issues a credential to a user and ensures that each user could only get one credential. For each access of the service, the SP will specify an access policy and require the user to prove that his historical behaviors satisfy the access policy.

The BLAC system for general policy contains the following protocols:

Setup: this algorithm is run by the GM to set up the system. In particular, on input security parameters, the algorithm generates a pair of group keys $(\mathsf{gpk}, \mathsf{gsk})$, where the group secret key gsk is kept private by GM, and group public key gpk is an implicit input to all other protocols.

SP Setup: this algorithm is run by a service provider to setup its public parameters. In particular, it initializes an empty list used to record the access history of all users.

Registration: this algorithm is executed between the GM and a legitimate user to register the user into the system. Upon successful completion of the protocol, the user obtains a credential usk, and becomes a member in the group of registered users. Here the credential should be kept private and is only known to the user, i.e., the GM issues it in a blind way.

Authentication: this algorithm is executed between a SP and a user, and SP outputs success or failure to indicate whether user has successfully authenticated himself or not. More specifically, SP sends a historical list $\mathcal{L}$ and the policy circuit $\mathsf{C}_{\mathsf{Pol}}$to the user. Next, user generates his own historical string $\boldsymbol{x}$[3] from list $\mathcal{L}$ and prove to the SP that $\mathsf{C}_{\mathsf{Pol}}(\boldsymbol{x}) = 1$ to complete the authentication.

Security Definition. We follow the security requirements used in traditional BLAC system. Here, we only highlight a few security properties implied by the formal security definition.

Authenticity. The authenticity requires that SPs should accept authentication only from users who satisfy the authentication policy.

Mis-authentication Resistance. Mis-authentication occurs when an unregistered user successfully authenticates himself to a SP. A BLAC system has mis-authentication resistance if SPs are assured to accept authentication only from registered users.

Anonymity. The anonymity requires that all that SPs can infer about the identity of an authenticating user is whether the user satisfies the policy at the time of the execution of the protocol, regardless of whatever SPs do afterwards.

Non-frameability. We say a user is framed if he satisfies the authentication policy but is unable to successfully authenticate himself to an honest SP. In a BLAC system, property non-frameability holds if users satisfying the authentication policy can always successfully authenticate themselves to honest SPs.

4 Constructions of BLAC For Circuits From Lattice

In this section, we give several constructions of blocklistable anonymous credential (BLAC) system for circuits in different settings, namely, static BLAC system,

[3] Here, $\boldsymbol{x}_i = 1$ if and only if the i-th access event on list $\mathcal{L}$ is done by the user, otherwise, $\boldsymbol{x}_i = 0$.

dynamic BLAC system and decentralized BLAC system. Due to space limitation, here we only give the construction of static BLAC system. We refer readers to Appendix A for the constructions of dynamic BLAC system and decentralized BLAC system.

Parameter Settings. In all constructions proposed in this paper, we will employ the parameters given below. Let λ be the security parameter. Let q_0 be a prime, e_1, e_2, ℓ be positive integers and $p = q_0^{e_1}, q = q_0^{e_2}$. Let n, n_1, n_2 be positive integers that are polynomial in λ. Let $k_p = \lceil \log p \rceil$, $k_q = \lceil \log q \rceil$ and $m = 2nk_q$.

In addition, we utilize the following gadget matrix $\mathbf{G}_j$ to to achieve the transformation between vector in Z_j^t and its binary representation, where $(j,t) \in \{(p, n_1), (q, n)\}$.

$$\mathbf{G}_j = \begin{bmatrix} 1\ 2\ 2^2 \ldots 2^{k_j-1} & & & \\ & 1\ 2\ 2^2 \ldots 2^{k_j-1} & & \\ & & \ddots & \\ & & & 1\ 2\ 2^2 \ldots 2^{k_j-1} \end{bmatrix} \in Z_j^{t \times tk_j}$$

Then, we have $G_p \in Z_p^{n_1 \times n_1 k_p}$ and $G_q \in Z_q^{n \times nk_q}$. For any vector $\boldsymbol{y}_1 \in Z_p^{n_1}$, $\boldsymbol{y}_2 \in Z_q^n$, we have $\boldsymbol{y}_1 = \mathbf{G}_p \cdot \mathsf{bin}(\boldsymbol{y}_1)$ and $\boldsymbol{y}_2 = \mathbf{G}_q \cdot \mathsf{bin}(\boldsymbol{y}_2)$, where $\mathsf{bin}(\boldsymbol{y})$ is the binary representation of the vector $\boldsymbol{y}$.

Building Blocks. Our constructions are built on several cryptographic schemes, including a weak pseudorandom function (wPRF) scheme described in Sect. 2, the lattice-based Merkle-tree accumulator scheme proposed in [23,26]. We also employ non-interactive zero-knowledge arguments of knowledge system, which can be instantiated using techniques proposed in Sect. 5 and in [41]. Throughout this section, we assume $\mathbf{PRF} = (\mathbf{PRF.KeyGen}, \mathbf{PRF.Eval})$ to be the wPRF mapping from $Z_q^{n_1 \times n_2} \times \{-1, 0, 1\}^{n_2}$ to $Z_p^{n_1}$. Let $\mathbf{ACC}=$ $(\mathbf{ACC.Setup}, \mathbf{ACC.Acu}, \mathbf{ACC.Witness}, \mathbf{ACC.Verify}, \mathbf{ACC.Update})$ be the accumulator scheme with public parameter in $Z_q^{n \times m}$. We also use $\mathcal{H}$: $\{0,1\}^n \rightarrow Z_q^{n_1 \times n_2}$ as a hash function that is modeled as a random oracle.

4.1 Construction of Static BLAC

In this section, we give a lattice-based construction of static blocklistable anonymous credential (BLAC) system for circuits, where all system users are enrolled in the beginning when registration protocol executes. The construction of static BLAC works as follows:

- **Setup.** The setup protocol is done by the group manger (GM), which proceeds as follows.
  - Sample a random input $\boldsymbol{A} \in Z_q^{n_1 \times n_2}$ for **PRF**;
  - Sample a random matrix $\boldsymbol{D} \in Z_q^{n \times m}$ which is the public parameter for **ACC**;

  - Pick $\boldsymbol{P} \in Z_q^{n \times n_1 k_p}$, which maps an output of **PRF** to a member of accumulator;
  - The expected number of users in system is bounded by $N = 2^\ell$;
  - Set the group public key as $(N, \boldsymbol{A}, \boldsymbol{D}, \boldsymbol{P})$.
- **Registration.** This protocol consists of two steps: 1) each user generates his own secret/public key and send his public key as well as a proof for the ownership of the secret key to the GM; 2) for those users whose proofs are valid, GM enrolls them into the system.

  1) For each user $j \in [N]$, he interacts with GM as follows:

  1. User j sends a registration request to the GM and obtains a challenge $\mathtt{m}_j \in \{0,1\}^\lambda$ back.
  2. He generates his own secret key $\boldsymbol{s}_j \leftarrow$ **PRF.KeyGen** (1^λ), then computers $\boldsymbol{y}_j \leftarrow$ **PRF.Eval** $(\boldsymbol{s}_j, \mathbf{A})$.
  3. Next, user j generates a signature proof of knowledge $\Pi_{RES,j}$, i.e.,

  $$\Pi_{RES,j} = SPK\{\boldsymbol{s}_j \in \{-1,0,1\}^{n_2} : \boldsymbol{y}_j \leftarrow \mathbf{PRF.Eval}(\boldsymbol{s}_j, \mathbf{A})\}[\mathtt{m}_j],$$

  then sends $(\boldsymbol{y}_j, \Pi_{RES,j})$ to the GM.
  4. Upon receiving $(\boldsymbol{y}_j, \Pi_{RES,j})$, GM first checks the validity of $\Pi_{RES,j}$. If not, returns $reject_j$ to the user.

  Let $\tilde{S}$ be the set consisting of the binary representations of public-keys of all users, namely, $\tilde{S} = \{\tilde{\boldsymbol{y}}_1, \tilde{\boldsymbol{y}}_2, \ldots, \tilde{\boldsymbol{y}}_N\}$, where $\tilde{\boldsymbol{y}}_j$ is the binary representation of $\boldsymbol{y}_j$, i.e., $\boldsymbol{y}_j = \boldsymbol{G}_p \cdot \tilde{\boldsymbol{y}}_j$ and $|\tilde{\boldsymbol{y}}_j| = n_1 k_p$.[4] Next, for each element $\tilde{\boldsymbol{y}}_j \in \tilde{S}$, GM computes $\boldsymbol{y}'_j = \boldsymbol{P} \cdot \tilde{\boldsymbol{y}}_j \mod q$ and $\boldsymbol{y}^*_j = \mathsf{bin}(\boldsymbol{y}'_j)$, i.e., $\boldsymbol{y}'_j = \boldsymbol{G}_q \cdot \boldsymbol{y}^*_j$. Then define $S^* = \{\boldsymbol{y}^*_1, \boldsymbol{y}^*_2, \cdots, \boldsymbol{y}^*_N\}$.

  2) Then GM enrolls all users in S^* into the system as follows:

  1. GM runs $\boldsymbol{u} \leftarrow$ **ACC.Acu**$(\boldsymbol{D}, S^*)$ and makes accumulator value $\boldsymbol{u}$ public.
  2. The for each user $j \in [N]$, GM
     - first runs $\omega_j \leftarrow$ **ACC.Witness**$(\boldsymbol{D}, S^*, \boldsymbol{y}^*_j)$;
     - then returns witness ω_j to the j-th user.

  Until now, for each user $j \in [N]$, he completes the registration process with private credential $\boldsymbol{s}_j$ and public key $(\boldsymbol{y}_j, \omega_j)$.
- **Authentication.** In this protocol, a user with credential $\boldsymbol{s}$ and public key $(\boldsymbol{y}, \omega)$ authenticates himself to a SP, which proceeds as below:
  1. The user sends an access request to the SP and obtains a challenge $\mathtt{m} \in \{0,1\}^\lambda$, the historical access list $\mathcal{L} = \{(\mu_i, \boldsymbol{t}_i)\}_{i \in [1,|\mathcal{L}|]}$ and the policy circuit C, where μ_i is a random string of length λ and $\boldsymbol{t}_i$ is an output of **PRF**.
  2. Then user generates $\boldsymbol{x} = (x_1, \ldots, x_{|\mathcal{L}|})$ as follows. For each record $(\mu_i, \boldsymbol{t}_i) \in \mathcal{L}$, the user first computes $\boldsymbol{B}_i = \mathcal{H}(\mu_i)$, then he sets $x_i = 1$ if $\boldsymbol{t}_i = \mathbf{PRF.Eval}(\boldsymbol{s}, \boldsymbol{B}_i)$ and sets $x_i = 0$ otherwise.

---

[4] Notably, here we only consider the public-keys of those users who successfully prove the ownership of the corresponding secret keys, i.e., proof $\Pi_{RES,j}$s are valid. For the failed users, the group user just sets their public keys as a string of **0**s with length $n_1 k_p$.

3. Next, user picks $\mu \xleftarrow{*} \{0,1\}^n$ and computes $\boldsymbol{B} = \mathcal{H}(\mu)$, $\boldsymbol{t} = \textbf{PRF. Eval}(\boldsymbol{s}, \boldsymbol{B})$.
4. Then user generates a NIZKAoK proof Π for the following conditions:
   (a) $\boldsymbol{y} = \mathbf{G}_p \cdot \tilde{\boldsymbol{y}} \mod p$, where $\tilde{\boldsymbol{y}}$ is the binary representation of $\boldsymbol{y}$;
   (b) $\boldsymbol{y}' = \mathbf{P} \cdot \tilde{\boldsymbol{y}} \mod q$;
   (c) $\boldsymbol{y}' = \mathbf{G}_q \cdot \boldsymbol{y}^* \mod q$, where $\boldsymbol{y}^*$ is the binary representation of $\boldsymbol{y}'$;
   (d) $\boldsymbol{y}^* \neq \mathbf{0}^{nk_q}$;
   (e) $\textbf{ACC.Verify}(\boldsymbol{D}, \boldsymbol{y}^*, \boldsymbol{u}, \omega) = 1$;
   (f) $\boldsymbol{y} = \textbf{PRF. Eval}(\boldsymbol{s}, \boldsymbol{A})$;
   (g) $\boldsymbol{t} = \textbf{PRF. Eval}(\boldsymbol{s}, \boldsymbol{B})$;
   (h) For all $i \in [1, |\mathcal{L}|]$, the value of x_i is correctly assigned;
   (i) $\mathsf{C}(\boldsymbol{x}) = 1$.

   Actually, this proof is a signature proof of knowledge, which could be written in the following form:

$$\Pi = SPK\{(\boldsymbol{s}, \boldsymbol{y}, \tilde{\boldsymbol{y}}, \boldsymbol{y}', \boldsymbol{y}^*, \omega, \boldsymbol{x}) \in \{-1,0,1\}^{n_2} \times Z_p^{n_1} \times \{0,1\}^{n_1 k_p} \times Z_q^n \times \{0,1\}^{nk_q} \times \{0,1\}^{\ell + nk_q \ell} \times \{0,1\}^{|\mathcal{L}|} : \textit{Conditions (a) - (i) hold}\}[\mathtt{m}].$$

5. Finally, user sends $(\mu, \boldsymbol{t}, \Pi)$ to the SP.

At the end of the authentication procedure, SP outputs *success* or *failure* to indicate whether user has successfully authenticated himself or not.

- The procedure **SP Setup** is determined by the definition. We omit them here.

On Instantiating the ZKAoK Proof Π. In our construction, the user needs to generate a proof that proves Conditions (a) - (i) hold. To complete this task, we use the general framework presented in [41], which provides an efficient lattice-based ZKAoK for a basic relation $\mathcal{R}^*$ (formal description of $\mathcal{R}^*$ is given in Sect. 5.1) and shows how to reduce common lattice relations to $\mathcal{R}^*$. Here, conditions (a)-(c) and condition (e) can be reduced to $\mathcal{R}^*$ by using the techniques provided in [41]. Also, we show how to reduce conditions (d), (f)-(i) to $\mathcal{R}^*$ in Sect. 5.2 to Sect. 5.5. The size of the proofs is analyzed in Sect. 6.

Security. Regarding the security of our proposal, we have the following theorem whose proof shall appear in the full version of the paper.

Theorem 4.1. *Assume the worst-case hardness of GapSVP$_\gamma$ (or SIVP$_\gamma$) for some polynomial γ, then the blocklistable anonymous credential system constructed above is a secure BLAC system in the random oracle model.*

5 Supporting Zero-Knowledge Arguments for Circuit Satisfiability

In this section, we provide the supporting zero-knowledge arguments of knowledge that is used in our constructions. The strategy we employed is to reduce the satisfiability of circuits into the relation $\mathcal{R}^*$ defined by Yang et al. in [41], and then construct the argument under Yang et al.'s framework. For completeness, we first give a brief recall of the relation $\mathcal{R}^*$ and the framework in Sect. 5.1. Then we show how to complete the reduction in the remaining sections.

5.1 Warm-Up: The General Framework in [41]

In [41], Yang et al. propose a basic relation, to which many natural lattice relation can be reduced, and present an efficient (non-interactive) zero-knowledge arguments of knowledge for it. The basic relation, which is denoted as $\mathcal{R}^*$ therein, includes linear equations and quadratic constraints over witnesses. Formally, let $\mathfrak{m}, \mathfrak{n}, \mathfrak{l}$ be positive integers and let q be a power-of-prime (i.e., $q = q_0^e$ for some prime q_0 and some postive integer $e \geq 1$), then $\mathcal{R}^*$ is defined as follows:

$$\mathcal{R}^* = \{(\boldsymbol{P}, \boldsymbol{v}, \mathcal{M}), (\boldsymbol{w}) \in (\mathbb{Z}_q^{\mathfrak{m}\times\mathfrak{n}} \times \mathbb{Z}_q^{\mathfrak{m}} \times ([1,\mathfrak{n}]^3)^{\mathfrak{l}}) \times (\mathbb{Z}_q^{\mathfrak{n}}) : \\ \boldsymbol{P}\cdot\boldsymbol{w} = \boldsymbol{v} \wedge \forall (h,i,j) \in \mathcal{M}, \boldsymbol{w}[h] = \boldsymbol{w}[i]\cdot\boldsymbol{w}[j]\}.$$

Here, $\boldsymbol{P}, \boldsymbol{v}, \mathcal{M}$ are public, where matrix $\boldsymbol{P}$ and vector $\boldsymbol{v}$ are used to specify the linear relation over witness, and $\mathcal{M}$ is a set of tuples used to indicate the quadratic relations on witness.

5.2 Zero-Knowledge Arguments for Boolean Circuits

In this section, we show how to construct zero-knowledge arguments of knowledge for the satisfiability of boolean circuits. Formally, let C be a boolean circuit with ℓ inputs and N gates, then the relation can be described as follows:

$$\mathcal{R}_{circuit} = \{(\mathsf{C}), (\boldsymbol{a}) \in \mathcal{C}_\ell \times \{0,1\}^\ell : \mathsf{C}(\boldsymbol{a}) = 1\}$$

Let **topo** be the topology of C. Also, for all $i \in [\ell+1, \dots, \ell+N]$, let $\mathbf{topo}(i) \rightarrow (\blacktriangleright_i, i_1, i_2)$ and let

$$\begin{cases} a_i = a_{i_1} \wedge a_{i_2} & if \ \blacktriangleright_i = \mathsf{AND} \\ a_i = a_{i_1} \vee a_{i_2} & if \ \blacktriangleright_i = \mathsf{OR} \\ a_i = a_{i_1} \oplus a_{i_2} & if \ \blacktriangleright_i = \mathsf{XOR} \\ a_i = \neg a_{i_1} & if \ \blacktriangleright_i = \mathsf{NOT} \end{cases} \quad (1)$$

Then it is sufficient to argue knowledge of $(a_1, \dots, a_{\ell+N-1}) \in \{0,1\}^{\ell+N-1}$ s.t. Equation (1) holds for $a_{\ell+N} = 1$.

Equation (1) requires that each gate is correctly evaluated and next, we will show how to argue the correct evaluation of common logic gate.

The "AND Gate" with 2-Fan-In. This is the basic AND gate and can be described by the following relation:

$$\mathcal{R}_{\mathsf{AND}} = \{(), (a_1, a_2, b) \in \{0,1\}^3 : b = a_1 \wedge a_2\}$$

We reduce $\mathcal{R}_{\mathsf{AND}}$ into $\mathcal{R}^*$ via setting the witness $\boldsymbol{w} = (a_1, a_2, b)^\mathsf{T}$ and setting the set $\mathcal{M} = \{(i,i,i) : i \in [1,3]\} \cup \{(3,1,2)\}$. Note that no linear equation is needed to argue $\mathcal{R}_{\mathsf{AND}}$. Also, the length of $\boldsymbol{w}$ and the size of $\mathcal{M}$ are 3 and 4, respectively.

The "OR Gate" with 2-Fan-In. This is the basic OR gate and can be described by the following relation:

$$\mathcal{R}_{\mathsf{OR}} = \{(), (a_1, a_2, b) \in \{0,1\}^3 : b = a_1 \vee a_2\}$$

By the De Morgan's laws, we have $b = \neg(\neg a_1 \wedge \neg a_2)$. Also, as $\neg x = 1 - x$ for binary x, we have $1 - b = (1 - a_1)(1 - a_2)$. Thus, we can reduce $\mathcal{R}_{\mathsf{OR}}$ into $\mathcal{R}^*$ via setting $\boldsymbol{w} = (a_1, a_2, b, c)^\top$, $\boldsymbol{P} = (1, 1, -1, -1)$, $\boldsymbol{v} = 0$ and $\mathcal{M} = \{(i,i,i) : i \in [1,3]\} \cup \{(4,1,2)\}$, where $c = a_1 a_2$. Here, both length of $\boldsymbol{w}$ and the size of $\mathcal{M}$ are 4.

The "NOT Gate". A NOT gate can be described by the following relation:

$$\mathcal{R}_{\mathsf{NOT}} = \{(), (a, b) \in \{0,1\}^2 : b = \neg a\}$$

We reduce $\mathcal{R}_{\mathsf{NOT}}$ into $\mathcal{R}^*$ via setting $\boldsymbol{w} = (a, b)^\top$, $\boldsymbol{P} = (1, 1)$, and $\boldsymbol{v} = 1$, and $\mathcal{M} = \{(i,i,i) : i \in [1,2]\}$. Here, length of $\boldsymbol{w}$ is 2 and the size of $\mathcal{M}$ is 2.

The "XOR Gate". An XOR gate can be described by the following relation:

$$\mathcal{R}_{\mathsf{XOR}} = \{(), (a_1, a_2, b) \in \{0,1\}^3 : b = a_1 \oplus a_2\}$$

As $a_1 + a_2 + b$ is either 2 or 0, we can reduce $\mathcal{R}_{\mathsf{XOR}}$ into $\mathcal{R}^*$ via setting $\boldsymbol{w} = (a_1, a_2, b, c)^\top$, $\boldsymbol{P} = (1, 1, 1, 2)$, $\boldsymbol{v} = 2$ and $\mathcal{M} = \{(i,i,i) : i \in [1,4]\}$, where $c = 1$ if $a_1 + a_2 + b = 0$ and $c = 0$ otherwise. Here, both length of $\boldsymbol{w}$ and the size of $\mathcal{M}$ are 4.

Putting them All Together. We can reduce $\mathcal{R}_{circuit}$ to $\mathcal{R}^*$. Let ℓ and N be the number of input wires and the number of gates for a circuit C. Then after reducing the satisfiability of C into $\mathcal{R}^*$, both the length of witness and the size of $\mathcal{M}$ does not exceed $\ell + 2N$.

5.3 Zero-Knowledge Arguments for Non-zero Binary Vector

In this section, we show how to argue that a binary vector $\boldsymbol{x} \in \{0,1\}^m$ is not zero.

Let $d = \sum_{i=1}^{m} \boldsymbol{x}[i]$, then, it is sufficient to show that $d \in [1, m]$. Alternatively, it equals to prove that $e = d - 1$ is in $[0, m-1]$.

To argue that $e \in [0, m-1]$, we decompose it into a binary vector $\boldsymbol{e}$ using the decomposition technique proposed in [25]. More precisely, let $l = \lfloor \log(m-1) \rfloor + 1$ and let $\boldsymbol{g} = (\lfloor m/2 \rfloor \| \lfloor (m+1)/4 \rfloor \| \ldots \| \lfloor (m - 1 + 2^{i-1})/2^i \rfloor \| \ldots \| \lfloor (m - 1 + 2^{l-1})/2^l \rfloor)$ be a row vector. As shown in [25]: 1) the integer $e \in [0, m-1]$ iff there exists a binary vecotr $\boldsymbol{e} \in \{0,1\}^l$ that $\boldsymbol{g} \cdot \boldsymbol{e} = e$; 2) one can decompose the integer $e \in [0, m-1]$ into the l-dimension binary vector $\boldsymbol{e}$ efficiently.

Finally, we define $\boldsymbol{i} = (1, \ldots, 1)$ to be a row vector of length m, and define $\boldsymbol{P} = (\boldsymbol{i} \| -\boldsymbol{g})$. Also, we define the new witness $\boldsymbol{w} = (\boldsymbol{x}^\top \| \boldsymbol{e}^\top)^\top$ and the vector $\boldsymbol{v} = 1$. Besides, we set $\mathcal{M} = \{(i,i,i) : i \in [1, m+l]\}$, which indicates that $\boldsymbol{x}, \boldsymbol{e}$ are binary vectors. Here, the length of $\boldsymbol{w}$ is $m + l$ and the size of $\mathcal{M}$ is $m + l$.

5.4 Zero-Knowledge Arguments for Weak PRF

In this section, we give an argument for the weak pseudorandom function recalled in Sect. 2. In particular, the argument claims knowledge of a key that evaluates a public input to a private output. Our ZKAoK is similar to the one proposed in [41]. But here we do not need to hide the input matrix and instead we need to hide the output. Also, we should additionally prove that each entry of the secret key is in $\{0, \pm 1\}$.

More precisely, let n_1, n_2 be positive integers, q_0 be a prime and $p = q_0^{e_1}$, $q = q_0^{e_2}$, where $1 \leq e_1 < e_2$, we propose a ZKAoK for the following relation:

$$\mathcal{R}_{PRF} = \{(\boldsymbol{A}), (\boldsymbol{s}, \boldsymbol{y}) \in (\mathbb{Z}_q^{n_1 \times n_2}) \times ([-1,1]^{n_2} \times \mathbb{Z}_p^{n_1}) : \boldsymbol{y} = \lfloor \boldsymbol{A} \cdot \boldsymbol{s} \rfloor_p \mod p\}$$

We construct the argument via reducing the relation $\mathcal{R}_{PRF}$ to an instance of the relation $\mathcal{R}^*$. First, we rewrite the equation $\boldsymbol{y} = \lfloor \boldsymbol{A} \cdot \boldsymbol{s} \rfloor_p \mod p$ as follows:

$$\begin{cases} \boldsymbol{A} \cdot \boldsymbol{s} = \boldsymbol{u} \mod q \\ \lfloor \frac{p}{q} \cdot \boldsymbol{u} \rfloor = \boldsymbol{y} \mod p \end{cases}$$

The first equation is a linear equation. The second equation, as shown in [24], holds iff each element of the vector $\boldsymbol{u} - \frac{q}{p}\boldsymbol{y}$ is in $[0, \frac{q}{p})$, and thus can be transformed into a linear equation with short solution. Besides, to prove that $\boldsymbol{s}[i] \in \{-1, 0, 1\}$, we argue that $\boldsymbol{s}[i]^3 = \boldsymbol{s}[i]$. Next, we describe the reduction in more details. We remark that in the remaining part of this section, all arithmetic operations are under the modulus q, so we omit the moduli in the remaining part of this section.

Let $\boldsymbol{e} = \boldsymbol{u} - \frac{q}{p}\boldsymbol{y}$, then we decompose the vector $\boldsymbol{e}$ into a binary vector $\bar{\boldsymbol{e}}$ using the decomposition technique proposed in [25]. Let $\gamma = \frac{q}{p} - 1$ and $k = \lfloor \log \gamma \rfloor + 1$, then the length of $\bar{\boldsymbol{e}}$ is $k \cdot n_1$.

Also, let $\boldsymbol{g} = (\lfloor (\gamma + 1)/2 \rfloor \| \ldots \| \lfloor (\gamma + 2^{i-1})/2^i \rfloor \| \ldots \| \lfloor (\gamma + 2^{k-1})/2^k \rfloor)$ be a row vector. Then, we define the gadget matrix $\boldsymbol{G} = \boldsymbol{I}_{n_1} \otimes \boldsymbol{g}$, and it satisfies that $\boldsymbol{G} \cdot \bar{\boldsymbol{e}} = \boldsymbol{e}$.

Next, we define $t_i = \boldsymbol{s}[i]^2$ and define $\boldsymbol{t} = (t_1, \ldots, t_{n_2})^\top$.

Finally, we set

$$\boldsymbol{P} = \begin{pmatrix} \boldsymbol{A} & -\boldsymbol{I}_{n_1} & 0 & 0 & 0 \\ 0 & \boldsymbol{I}_{n_1} & -\frac{q}{p} \cdot \boldsymbol{I}_{n_1} & -\boldsymbol{G} & 0 \end{pmatrix}$$

$$\boldsymbol{w} = (\boldsymbol{s}^\top \quad \boldsymbol{u}^\top \quad \boldsymbol{y}^\top \quad \bar{\boldsymbol{e}}^\top \quad \boldsymbol{t}^\top)^\top, \quad \boldsymbol{v} = (0 \quad 0)^\top$$

Besides, we define

$$\begin{cases} \mathcal{M}_1 = \{(i, i, i)\}_{i \in [2n_1 + n_2 + 1, 2n_1 + n_2 + kn_1]} \\ \mathcal{M}_2 = \{(2n_1 + n_2 + kn_1 + i, i, i)\}_{i \in [1, n_2]} \cup \{(i, 2n_1 + n_2 + kn_1 + i, i)\}_{i \in [1, n_2]} \end{cases}$$

where $\mathcal{M}_1$ indicates that $\bar{\boldsymbol{e}}$ is a binary vector and $\mathcal{M}_2$ indicates that $\boldsymbol{s}[i]^3 = \boldsymbol{s}[i]$. Then we set $\mathcal{M} = \mathcal{M}_1 \cup \mathcal{M}_2$. In the new relation, the length of the witness is $n_2 + 2n_1 + kn_1 + n_2$, and the size of $\mathcal{M}$ is $kn_1 + 2n_2$.

5.5 Proving the Correctness of Historical Behavior $\boldsymbol{x}$

In this section, we show how to argue the correctness of $\boldsymbol{x}$. More precisely, we need to prove knowledge of

$$\{\boldsymbol{s} \in \{0, \pm 1\}^{n_2}; \boldsymbol{x} \in \{0, 1\}^{|\mathcal{L}|}\}$$

that satisfies

$$\begin{cases} \text{For } i \in [1, |\mathcal{L}|]: \\ (\boldsymbol{t}_i = \lfloor \boldsymbol{B}_i \cdot \boldsymbol{s} \rceil_p \mod p \wedge x_i = 1) \vee (\boldsymbol{t}_i \neq \lfloor \boldsymbol{B}_i \cdot \boldsymbol{s} \rceil_p \mod p \wedge x_i = 0) \end{cases} \tag{2}$$

for public

$$\{(\boldsymbol{B}_i)_{i \in [1, |\mathcal{L}|]} \in (\mathbb{Z}_q^{n_1 \times n_2})^{|\mathcal{L}|}; (\boldsymbol{t}_i)_{i \in [1, |\mathcal{L}|]} \in (\mathbb{Z}_p^{n_1})^{|\mathcal{L}|}\}$$

For $i \in [1, |\mathcal{L}|]$, let $\boldsymbol{t}'_i = \textbf{PRF. Eval}(\boldsymbol{s}, \mathbf{B}_i)$, then we can rewrite Eq. (2) as follows:

$$\begin{cases} \text{For } i \in [1, |\mathcal{L}|]: \\ (1)\ \boldsymbol{t}'_i = \lfloor \boldsymbol{B} \cdot \boldsymbol{s} \rceil_p \mod p \\ (2)\ (\boldsymbol{t}_i = \boldsymbol{t}'_i \mod p \wedge x_i = 1) \vee (\boldsymbol{t}_i \neq \boldsymbol{t}'_i \mod p \wedge x_i = 0) \end{cases} \tag{3}$$

Next, for $i \in [1, |\mathcal{L}|], j \in [1, n_1]$ let $x_{i,j} = 1$ iff $\boldsymbol{t}'_i[j] = \boldsymbol{t}_i[j] \mod p$, then we have $x_i = \bigwedge_{j=1}^{n_1} x_{i,j}$ and can rewrite Eq. (3) as follows:

$$\begin{cases} \text{For } i \in [1, |\mathcal{L}|]: \\ (1)\ \boldsymbol{t}'_i = \lfloor \boldsymbol{B} \cdot \boldsymbol{s} \rceil_p \mod p \\ (2)\ \text{For } j \in [1, n_1]: \\ \quad (\boldsymbol{t}_i[j] = \boldsymbol{t}'_i[j] \mod p \wedge x_{i,j} = 1) \vee (\boldsymbol{t}_i[j] \neq \boldsymbol{t}'_i[j] \mod p \wedge x_{i,j} = 0) \\ (3)\ x_i = \bigwedge_{j=1}^{n_1} x_{i,j} \end{cases} \tag{4}$$

It is easy to see that Eq. (4) is identical to the following equation:

$$\begin{cases} \text{For } i \in [1, |\mathcal{L}|]: \\ (1)\ \boldsymbol{t}'_i = \lfloor \boldsymbol{B} \cdot \boldsymbol{s} \rceil_p \mod p \\ (2)\ \text{For } j \in [1, n_1]: \\ \quad \boldsymbol{t}'_i[j] + (1 - x_{i,j}) + (1 - x_{i,j}) \cdot d_{i,j} = \boldsymbol{t}_i[j] \mod p \\ \quad d_{i,j} \in [0, p-2] \\ (3)\ x_i = \bigwedge_{j=1}^{n_1} x_{i,j} \end{cases} \tag{5}$$

where $d_{i,j} = \boldsymbol{t}_i[j] - \boldsymbol{t}'_i[j] - 1$ if $\boldsymbol{t}_i[j] \neq \boldsymbol{t}'_i[j]$ and $d_{i,j} = 0$ otherwise.

Next, we show how to reduce a relation defined by Eq. (5) to the basic relation $\mathcal{R}^* = \{(\boldsymbol{P}, \boldsymbol{v}, \mathcal{M}), (\boldsymbol{w}) : \boldsymbol{P} \cdot \boldsymbol{w} = \boldsymbol{v} \wedge \forall (h, i, j) \in \mathcal{M}, \boldsymbol{w}[h] = \boldsymbol{w}[i] \cdot \boldsymbol{w}[j]\}$. Let

$$\mathcal{R}_{1,i} = \{(\boldsymbol{B}_i), (\boldsymbol{s}, \boldsymbol{t}'_i) \in \mathbb{Z}_q^{n_1 \times n_2} \times \{0, \pm 1\}^{n_2} \times \mathbb{Z}_p^{n_1} : \boldsymbol{t}'_i = \lfloor \boldsymbol{B} \cdot \boldsymbol{s} \rfloor_p \mod p\}$$

$$\mathcal{R}_{2,i,j} = \{(\boldsymbol{t}_i[j]), (\boldsymbol{t}'_i[j], x_{i,j}, d_{i,j}) \in \mathbb{Z}_p \times \mathbb{Z}_p \times \{0,1\} \times [0, p-2] : \\ \boldsymbol{t}'_i[j] + (1 - x_{i,j}) + (1 - x_{i,j}) \cdot d_{i,j} = \boldsymbol{t}_i[j] \mod p\}$$

$$\mathcal{R}_{3,i} = \{(), (x_i, x_{i,1} \ldots, x_{i,n_1}) \in \{0,1\}^{n_1+1} : x_i = \bigwedge_{j=1}^{n_1} x_{i,j}\}$$

It is sufficient to show how $\mathcal{R}_{1,i}, \mathcal{R}_{2,i,j}, \mathcal{R}_{3,i}$ can be reduced to $\mathcal{R}^*$.

Dealing with $\mathcal{R}_{1,i}$. As shown in Sect. 5.4, we can reduce $\mathcal{R}_{1,i}$ to $\mathcal{R}^*$, where the length of witness is $2n_1 + 2n_2 + \ell_1 n_1$ and the size of $\mathcal{M}$ is $2n_2 + \ell_1 n_1$ for $\ell_1 = \lfloor \log (q_0^{e_2 - e_1} - 1) \rfloor + 1$.

Dealing with $\mathcal{R}_{2,i,j}$. Let $d'_{i,j} = x_{i,j} \cdot d_{i,j}$. Also, let $\ell_3 = \lfloor \log (p-2) \rfloor + 1$, $\boldsymbol{d}_{i,j} \in \{0,1\}^{\ell_3}$ be the binary decomposition of $d_{i,j}$ (using the decomposition technique proposed in [25]) and let $\boldsymbol{g} = (\lfloor (p-1)/2 \rfloor \| \lfloor p/4 \rfloor \| \ldots \| \lfloor (p-2+2^{i-1})/2^i \rfloor \| \ldots \| \lfloor (p-2+2^{\ell_3 - 1})/2^{\ell_3} \rfloor)$ be a row vector. Finally, we define $\boldsymbol{w} = (\boldsymbol{t}'_i[j], x_{i,j}, d_{i,j}, d'_{i,j}, \boldsymbol{d}_{i,j}^\mathsf{T})^\mathsf{T}$, $\boldsymbol{v} = (q(\boldsymbol{t}_i[j] - 1)/p, 0)^\mathsf{T}$ and

$$\boldsymbol{P} = \begin{bmatrix} q/p & -q/p & q/p & -q/p & \boldsymbol{0} \\ 0 & 0 & 1 & 0 & -\boldsymbol{g} \end{bmatrix}$$

and set $\mathcal{M} = \{(4+i, 4+i, 4+i)\}_{i \in [\ell_3]} \cup \{(2,2,2)\} \cup \{(4,2,3)\}$. Here, the length of witness is $4 + \ell_3$ and the size of $\mathcal{M}$ is $2 + \ell_3$.

Dealing with $\mathcal{R}_{3,i}$. Finally, we reduce $\mathcal{R}_{3,i}$ to $\mathcal{R}^*$. A straightforward way to deal with $\mathcal{R}_{3,i}$ is to divide it into n_1 standard AND gates and reduce each of them into $\mathcal{R}^*$. However, this will bring an extra communication cost linear in n_1. Next, we give a new approach to reduce $\mathcal{R}_{3,i}$ to $\mathcal{R}^*$, which only introduce an additional logarithm overhead.

Observe that $x_i = 1$ if and only if $x_{i,j} = 1$ for all $j \in [n_1]$. Thus, it is sufficient to argue that

$$(\sum_{j=1}^{n_1} x_{i,j} = n_1 \wedge x_i = 1) \vee (\sum_{j=1}^{n_1} x_{i,j} < n_1 \wedge x_i = 0) \tag{6}$$

for bits $x_{i,1}, \ldots, x_{i,n_1}, x_i$. It is easy to see Eq. (6) holds iff the following equation holds:

$$\sum_{j=1}^{n_1} x_{i,j} + (1 - x_i) \cdot d = n_1 \tag{7}$$

where $d \in [1, n_1]$ (we can set $d = n_1 - (x_{i,1} + \ldots + x_{i,n_1})$ if $x_{i,1} + \ldots x_{i,n_1} < n_1$ and set $d = 1$ otherwise).

Next, we set $e = d - 1$ and transform Eq. (7) as follows:

$$\sum_{j=1}^{n_1} x_{i,j} + (1 - x_i) + (1 - x_i) \cdot e = n_1 \tag{8}$$

where $e \in [0, n_1 - 1]$.

To argue that $e \in [0, n_1 - 1]$, we decompose it into a binary vector $\boldsymbol{e}$ using the decomposition technique proposed in [25]. Also, let $\ell_2 = \lfloor \log(n_1 - 1) \rfloor + 1$ and let $\boldsymbol{g} = (\lfloor n_1/2 \rfloor \| \lfloor (n_1+1)/4 \rfloor \| \ldots \| \lfloor (n_1 - 1 + 2^{i-1})/2^i \rfloor \| \ldots \| \lfloor (n_1 - 1 + 2^{\ell_2 - 1})/2^{\ell_2} \rfloor)$ be a row vector.

Finally, we define $\boldsymbol{a} = (x_{i,1}, \ldots, x_{i,n_1})^\top$, $e' = x_i \cdot e$ and define the new witness $\boldsymbol{w} = (\boldsymbol{a}^\top \| x_i \| e \| e' \| \boldsymbol{e}^\top)^\top$. Also, we define $\boldsymbol{v} = (n_1 - 1 \| 0)^\top$ and define

$$\boldsymbol{P} = \begin{bmatrix} \boldsymbol{i} & -1 & 1 & -1 & \boldsymbol{0} \\ \boldsymbol{0} & 0 & 1 & 0 & -\boldsymbol{g} \end{bmatrix}$$

where $\boldsymbol{i} = (1, \ldots, 1)$ is a row vector of length n_1. Besides, we set $\mathcal{M}_1 = \{(i, i, i) : i \in [1, n_1 + 1] \cup [n_1 + 4, n_1 + 3 + \ell_2]\}$, $\mathcal{M}_2 = \{(n_1 + 3, n_1 + 1, n_1 + 2)\}$, and define $\mathcal{M} = \mathcal{M}_1 \cup \mathcal{M}_2$, where $\mathcal{M}_1$ indicates that $\boldsymbol{a}, \boldsymbol{e}$ are binary vectors and x_i is binary, and $\mathcal{M}_2$ indicates that $e' = x_i \cdot e$. Here, the length of $\boldsymbol{w}$ is $n_1 + \ell_2 + 3$ and the size of $\mathcal{M}$ is $n_1 + \ell_2 + 2$ for $\ell_2 = \lfloor \log(n_1 - 1) \rfloor + 1$.

Putting it All Together. By combining above techniques, we can reduce a statement arguing the correctness of $\boldsymbol{x}$ into a statement for a relation $\mathcal{R}^*$, where the length of the witness is $2n_2 + |\mathcal{L}| \cdot (2n_1 + \ell_1 n_1 + n_1 + \ell_2 + 3 + (2 + \ell_3) n_1)$ and the size of $\mathcal{M}$ is $2n_2 + |\mathcal{L}| \cdot (\ell_1 n_1 + n_1 + \ell_2 + 2 + (1 + \ell_3) n_1)$ (the overlapped parts should be counted only once).

6 Performance Evaluation

In this section, we demonstrate the practicability of our constructions via estimating their efficiency. In particular, we focus on the communication cost of the authentication protocol. As the authentication protocol in all three constructions are similar. Here, as an example, we only test the efficiency of the static BLAC system.

In the authentication protocol, the service provider first sends a challenge, a list of tags (i.e., access list) and a circuit to the user. Then the user sends a tag and a proof to the service provider.

The challenge is of length λ. Each tag consists of a base and a PRF output, where the base is of length λ and the PRF output is of $n_1 k_p$. Thus, the downlink communication cost from the service provider to the sender is $\lambda + |\mathcal{L}| \cdot (\lambda + n_1 k_p) + |\mathsf{C}| \cdot (3 \cdot \lceil \log(|\mathcal{L}| + |\mathsf{C}|) \rceil + 1)$.

Next, we analyze the size of the proof. The proof consists of six parts:

- The first part, which is defined by Condition (a) to (c), claims relation between $\boldsymbol{y}, \tilde{\boldsymbol{y}}, \boldsymbol{y}', \boldsymbol{y}^*$. This part can be reduced to an instance of the relation $\mathcal{R}^*$, where the length of its witness is $n_1 + n_1 k_p + n + n k_q$ and the size of $\mathcal{M}$ is $n_1 k_p + n k_q$.
- The second part, which is defined by Condition (d), claims that $\boldsymbol{y}^*$ is not zero. As analyzed in Sect. 5.3, this part can be reduced to an instance of the relation $\mathcal{R}^*$, where the length of its witness is $nk_q + \lfloor \log (nk_q - 1) \rfloor + 1$ and the size of $\mathcal{M}$ is $nk_q + \lfloor \log (nk_q - 1) \rfloor + 1$.
- The third part, which is defined by Condition (e), claims that $\boldsymbol{y}^*$ is properly accumulated. As analyzed in [41] (Sect. 4.4), this part can be reduced to an instance of the relation $\mathcal{R}^*$, where the length of its witness is $2\lceil \log N \rceil + 4n\lceil \log N \rceil + 4nk_q \cdot \lceil \log N \rceil$ and the size of $\mathcal{M}$ is $2\lceil \log N \rceil + 2n\lceil \log N \rceil + 4nk_q \cdot \lceil \log N \rceil$.
- The fourth part, which is defined by Condition (f) and (g), claims that $\boldsymbol{y}, \boldsymbol{t}$ are the correct outputs of PRF. As analyzed in Sect. 5.4, this part can be reduced to an instance of the relation $\mathcal{R}^*$, where the length of its witness is $2n_2 + 3n_1 + 2n_1(\lfloor \log(q/p - 1) \rfloor + 1)$ and the size of $\mathcal{M}$ is $2n_2 + 2n_1(\lfloor \log(q/p - 1) \rfloor + 1)$. Note that the overlapped part should be counted only once.
- The fifth part, which is defined by Condition (h), claims that input of the circuit is correct. As analyzed in Sect. 5.5, this part can be reduced to an instance of the relation $\mathcal{R}^*$, where the length of its witness is $2n_2 + |\mathcal{L}| \cdot (2n_1 + (\lfloor \log (q/p - 1) \rfloor + 1)n_1 + n_1 + \lfloor \log (n_1 - 1) \rfloor + 1 + 3 + (2 + \lfloor \log (p - 2) \rfloor + 1)n_1)$ and the size of $\mathcal{M}$ is $2n_2 + |\mathcal{L}| \cdot ((\lfloor \log (q/p - 1) \rfloor + 1)n_1 + n_1 + \lfloor \log (n_1 - 1) \rfloor + 1 + 2 + (1 + \lfloor \log (p - 2) \rfloor + 1)n_1)$.
- The sixth part, which is defined by Condition (i), claims that the circuit is correctly evaluated. As analyzed in Sect. 5, this part can be reduced to an instance of the relation $\mathcal{R}^*$, where the length of its witness is $|\mathcal{L}| + 2|\mathsf{C}|$ and the size of $\mathcal{M}$ is $|\mathcal{L}| + 2|\mathsf{C}|$.

So, after combing these statements, the length of the witness will not exceed

$$\begin{aligned}\mathfrak{n} = n_1 + n_1 k_p + n + \lfloor \log (nk_q - 1) \rfloor + 1 + (2 + 4n + 4nk_q) \cdot \lceil \log N \rceil + 2n_2 + 2n_1 \\ + 2n_1(\lfloor \log(q/p - 1) \rfloor + 1) + |\mathcal{L}| \cdot (3n_1 + (4 + k_q)n_1 + \lfloor \log (n_1 - 1) \rfloor + 4) + 2|\mathsf{C}|\end{aligned}$$

and the size of $\mathcal{M}$ will be

$$\begin{aligned}\mathfrak{l} = n_1 k_p + \lfloor \log (nk_q - 1) \rfloor + 1 + (2 + 2n + 4nk_q) \cdot \lceil \log N \rceil + 2n_2 \\ + 2n_1(\lfloor \log(q/p - 1) \rfloor + 1) + |\mathcal{L}| \cdot ((3 + k_q)n_1 + n_1 + \lfloor \log (n_1 - 1) \rfloor + 3) + 2|\mathsf{C}|\end{aligned}$$

(the overlapped part should be counted only once).

Now, let $\hat{l}_1, \hat{l}_2, \hat{\sigma}_1, \hat{\sigma}_2, \hat{p}, \hat{\kappa}, \hat{N}$ be parameters used in the main protocol. Then, as shown in [41], the proof contains

$$\|\pi\| = (\log (2\hat{p} + 1) + \hat{\kappa} + (3\hat{l}_1 + 2\hat{l}_2 + 2\mathfrak{n} + 2\mathfrak{l}) \cdot k_q) \cdot \hat{N} + (\hat{l}_1 + \mathfrak{n}) \cdot k_q$$

bits.

In summary, the uplink communication cost from the user to the services provider is $\|\pi\| + \lambda + n_1 k_p$.

Choosing the Parameters. Next, we estimate the concrete communication cost via setting concrete values of parameters involved. Note that security of the scheme relies on the following 7 assumptions:

$SIS_{\hat{l}_1,q,\beta_1}$	$SIS_{\hat{l}_1,q,\beta_2}$	$LWE_{\hat{l}_2,q,\alpha_1}$	SIS_{n,q,β_3}	SIS_{n,q,β_4}	LWE_{n_2',q,α_2}	SIS_{n_1,q,β_5}

where $\beta_1 = 16\hat{p} \cdot \sqrt{\hat{l}_1 + \hat{l}_2 + \mathfrak{n}} \cdot (\hat{\sigma}_2 + \hat{p} \cdot \hat{\sigma}_1)$, $\beta_2 = 16\hat{p} \cdot \sqrt{\hat{l}_1 + \hat{l}_2 + \mathfrak{l}} \cdot (\hat{\sigma}_2 + \hat{p} \cdot \hat{\sigma}_1)$, $\alpha_1 = \frac{\sqrt{2\pi} \cdot \hat{\sigma}_1}{q}$; $\beta_3 = \sqrt{n_1 k_p}$, $\beta_4 = \sqrt{2nk_q}$; $n_2' = \frac{3n_2}{2\log q}$, $\alpha_2 = \sqrt{\frac{2\pi((q/p)^2-1)}{120 n_2' q^2}}$, $\beta_5 = \sqrt{4n_2 + (q/p-1)^2 \cdot n_1}$. Thus, we should guarantee that the above assumptions are valid while picking parameters. As discussed in Sect. 2, this can be achieved by setting the parameters in a way that a small root-Hermite factor is required to break the assumptions.

More concretely, we set these parameters as per Table 2. Our parameters are set to achieve 80-bit security, 100-bit security and 128-bit security respectively in a setting that we fix $L = 1000, C = 10000, N = 1000$ and $\hat{\kappa} = 128$.

Table 2. Concrete Parameters for Our Scheme.

Soundness Error	2^{-80}	2^{-100}	2^{-128}
δ_0	1.0048	1.0042	1.0035
$\hat{p}$	2^5	2^6	2^6
$\hat{l}_1$	1500	2100	2200
$\hat{l}_2$	1900	2300	2700
$\hat{N}$	16	17	22
$\lceil \log q \rceil$	60	63	63
n	20	25	30
n_1	55	70	85
n_2	100000	120000	145000
$\lceil \log p \rceil$	54	56	56
Downlink	3.37 MB	4.34 MB	5.21 MB
Uplink	1.90 GB	2.79 GB	4.37 GB

Communication Cost of BLAC System in [39]**.** Here, we give a rough estimation of the concrete communication cost for the authentication protocol of the BLAC system constructed in [39]. We omit several less significant parts in the estimation and thus the real communication cost will be larger than we have estimated here.

Let n_1, n_2, p, q be positive integers. Let $k_p = \lceil \log p \rceil$, $k_q = \lceil \log q \rceil$, $\sigma = 1.6 k_s \cdot \sqrt{n_1}$ and $k_\sigma = \lceil \log(12\sigma) \rceil$. Also, fixing the historical records set size as $|\mathcal{L}| = 1000$. Then the communication cost of their spend protocol is at least

$$\mathfrak{C}_S \approx (960 \cdot n_1 \cdot k_q^2 \cdot k_\sigma + 6000 n_2 k_q^2 + 3000 n_2 k_q^2 \cdot (k_q - k_p)/k_p) \cdot 137$$

bits and security of their system relies on $\mathrm{SIS}_{n_1,q,\beta}$ and $\mathrm{LWR}_{n_2,q,p}$, where $\beta = \sigma^2 \cdot (2 \cdot k_s \cdot n_1)^{1.5} \cdot 80$.

To achieve a 80-bits security level, we can set $n_1 = 1900$, $n_2 = 70$, $p = 2^8$, $q = 2^{65}$, and the communication cost $\mathfrak{C}_S \approx 2.21$ TB.

A Construction of Dynamic BLAC and Decentralized BLAC

In this section, we give the constructions of lattice-based dynamic BLAC system and decentralized BLAC system.

A.1 Construction of Dynamic BLAC

In this section, we give the construction of dynamic BLAC system, where system users could dynamically join and leave (or being revoked from) the system. Despite it may seem useless to design a BLAC system with user revocation functionality, as it can be simply achieved by embedding the list of revocation users into the access policy. However, this will introduce additional increase to the size of policy circuit, especially in the case that the number of revocation users is huge. Consequently, the proof size generated in authentication protocol will get increased. While, the revocation method used in our construction avoids these disadvantages.

The construction of our dynamic BLAC works as follows:

- **Setup.** This protocol is nearly the same as the **Setup** algorithm in static BLAC system, except with the follows:
  - Sample a random matrix $\mathbf{M} \in Z_q^{n \times nk_q}$, and a random string $\mathbf{msk} \in \{0,1\}^{nk_q}$, then compute $\mathbf{mpk} = \mathbf{M} \cdot \mathbf{msk} \mod q$.
  - GM maintains a table named as $S^* = (\boldsymbol{y}_1^*, \boldsymbol{y}_2^*, \ldots, \boldsymbol{y}_N^*)$, where for $i \in [N]$, $\boldsymbol{y}_i^* = \mathbf{0}^{nk_q}$. Here, $\boldsymbol{y}_i^*$ is used to store the information about the public-key of the legitimately registered users. Then build an updatable accumulator based on S^*, namely, the Merkle-tree is an all-zero tree at the current stage.
  - Counter of registered users $c = 0$.

  Finally, it sets the group public key as $(N, \boldsymbol{A}, \boldsymbol{D}, \boldsymbol{P}, \mathbf{M}, \mathbf{mpk})$, while the master secret key hold by group manager is $\mathbf{msk}$.
- **Registration.** This protocol works nearly the same way as the **Registration** protocol in Sect. 4.1, except the way that GM enrolls user into the system. More precisely, for a user with public key $\boldsymbol{y}$, GM first issues a unique identifier to the user as $\mathsf{bin}(c) \in \{0,1\}^\ell$, then calculate $\boldsymbol{y}^*$ from $\boldsymbol{y}$. Next, GM runs $\mathbf{ACC.Update}(\mathsf{bin}(c), \boldsymbol{y}^*)$ to update the c-th leaf in the Merkle-tree to be $\boldsymbol{y}^*$ and get the new root value. Finally, GM increases the counter $c = c + 1$. The user completes the registration process with private credential $\boldsymbol{s}$ and public key $(\mathsf{bin}(c), \boldsymbol{y})$.
- **Update.** This protocol is run by GM to update the group information, namely, the witness for a user that he is enrolled in the system and advance the system time clock τ.

1. Let set $R = \{\boldsymbol{y}^*_{j_1}, \boldsymbol{y}^*_{j_2}, \ldots, \boldsymbol{y}^*_{j_t}\}$ be the set of revoked users. If R is empty, then go to Step 2 directly. Otherwise, for each $j \in \{j_1, j_2, \ldots, j_t\}$, GM updates the corresponding j-th element of the accumulated set S^* to be $\boldsymbol{y}^*_j = \mathbf{0}^{nk_q}$, and updates accumulator by running $\mathbf{ACC.Update}(\mathsf{bin}(j), \boldsymbol{y}^*_j)$. Note that only user with non-zero public key could authenticate himself to SP in the new epoch τ.
2. Next, GM broadcasts the system information of current system time clock τ. In particular, the public system information is denoted as $\mathsf{Info}_\tau = (\tau, \mathbf{u}_\tau, \{\omega_j\}_{j\in[N]})$,i.e., the latest accumulator value and witness for each legitimated user. Note that, Info_τ is signed by GM to guarantee the integrity and the Merkle-tree based accumulator can only be modified by GM.

- **Authentication.** In this protocol, a user (with private credential $\boldsymbol{s}$ and public key $(\mathsf{bin}(c), \boldsymbol{y})$) first checks the validity of the signature for Info_τ and whether Info_τ contains a witness for node indexed as $\mathsf{bin}(c)$. If both yes, user proceeds in the same way as the **Authentication** protocol of static DBLC system. Otherwise, outputs $\bot$.

The security of our proposed dynamic BLAC system is guaranteed by the following theorem whose proof will be presented in the full version of the paper.

Theorem A.1. *Assume the worst-case hardness of GapSVP$_\gamma$ (or SIVP$_\gamma$) for some polynomial γ, then the blocklistable anonymous credential system constructed above is a secure BLAC system in the random oracle model.*

A.2 Construction of Decentralized BLAC

In this section, we give a construction of decentralized blocklistable anonymous credential system for circuits, where no trusted party is needed to register users. To achieve this, our construction employs a public append-only ledger $\mathcal{F}^*_{BB}$ (see [40] for its formal description), which can guarantee the integrity of data uploaded, provide a consistent view of the ledger and the latest data on the ledger for every party, and be instantiated by blockchain technology.

The construction of the system works as follows:

- **Setup.** This protocol proceeds in the same way as it in Sect. 4.1 and outputs public parameter as $(N, \boldsymbol{A}, \boldsymbol{D}, \boldsymbol{P})$.
- **Registration.** In this protocol, a user with auxiliary information aux and attributes att conducts some operations to register himself to the system. Here auxiliary information aux and attributes att are used to aid the service provider in deciding whether to accept the user as a valid candidate user for accessing their services. In particular, user generates his own public/privates keys and proof Π_{RES} as before except that Π_{RES} is on message aux and att. Then user stores $(\mathsf{Nym}, \boldsymbol{y}, \Pi_{RES}, \mathsf{aux}, \mathsf{att})$ to the public ledger and completes the registration.

- **Authentication.** Here, a user with private credential $\boldsymbol{s}$ and public key $(\boldsymbol{y}, \mathsf{aux}, \mathsf{att})$ attempts to authenticates himself to a SP *sid*. Firstly, the user downloads the access requirement $(U, \mathsf{C}, \mathcal{L})$ from the public ledger, where $U = \{\boldsymbol{y}_1, \boldsymbol{y}_2, \cdots, \boldsymbol{y}_N\}$ is the candidate user set specified by sid, C is the policy circuit and $\mathcal{L} = \{(\mu_i, \boldsymbol{t}_i)\}_{i \in [1,|\mathcal{L}|]}$ is the historical access list.

  Then the protocol proceeds nearly the same as the **Authentication** protocol in Sect. 4.1 except that user (resp. SP) needs to build the accumulator on set U by himself and performs all relevant computations on that accumulator value.
- **Interaction with The Ledger.** There are mainly two kinds of interactions among system participants and the public ledger, namely, uploading data to and obtaining data from the public ledger. To obtain data from the ledger, any participant of the system just needs to submit a "retrieve" request to $\mathcal{F}^*_{BB}$. Both users and service providers could upload data to the ledger through submitting a "store" request together with its pseudonym and its data to $\mathcal{F}^*_{BB}$. Recall that, a user needs to upload personal information in the registration process. A service provider could upload the access requirement $(U, \mathsf{C}, \mathcal{L})$ and access history $(\mu, \mathbf{t})$ of a successfully authenticated user to the historical access list $\mathcal{L}$.

Security of the decentralized BLAC system given above is guaranteed by the following theorem whose proof will appear in the full version of the paper.

Theorem A.2. *Assume the worst-case hardness of GapSVP$_\gamma$ (or SIVP$_\gamma$) for some polynomial γ, $\mathcal{F}^*_{BB}$ is a secure public append-only ledger, then the blocklistable anonymous credential system constructed above is a secure BLAC system in the random oracle model.*

References

1. Ajtai, M.: Generating hard instances of lattice problems. In: STOC, pp. 99–108. ACM, 1996
2. Albrecht, M.R., et al.: Estimate all the LWE, NTRU schemes! In: SCN, pp. 351–367. Springer, 2018
3. Alkim, E., Ducas, L., Pöppelmann, T., Schwabe, P.: Post-quantum key exchange-a new hope. In: USENIX Security Symposium, vol. 2016, 2016
4. Au, M.H., Kapadia, A.: PERM: practical reputation-based blacklisting without TTPS. In: CCS, pp. 929–940. ACM, 2012
5. Au, M.H., Kapadia, A., Susilo, W.: Blacr: ttp-free blacklistable anonymous credentials with reputation. In: NDSS (2012)
6. Au, M.H., Susilo, W., Mu, Y.: Practical compact e-cash. In: ACISP, pp. 431–445. Springer, 2007
7. Banerjee, A., Peikert, C., Rosen, A.: Pseudorandom functions and lattices. In: EUROCRYPT, pp. 719–737. Springer, 2012
8. Boneh, D., Boyen, X., Shacham, H.: Short group signatures. In: CRYPTO, pp. 41–55. Springer, 2004

9. Bootle, J., Lyubashevsky, V., Nguyen, N.K., Sorniotti, A.: A framework for practical anonymous credentials from lattices. In: Annual International Cryptology Conference, pp. 384–417. Springer, 2023
10. Brickell, E., Li, J.: Enhanced privacy id: a direct anonymous attestation scheme with enhanced revocation capabilities. In: Proceedings of the 2007 ACM Workshop on Privacy in Electronic Society, pp. 21–30. ACM (2007)
11. Chaum, D.: Security without identification: transaction systems to make big brother obsolete. Commun. ACM **28**(10), 1030–1044 (1985)
12. Chen, Y., Nguyen, P.Q.: BKZ 2.0: better lattice security estimates. In: ASIACRYPT, pp. 1–20. Springer, 2011
13. Cheon, J.H., Kim, D., Lee, J., Song, Y.: Lizard: cut off the tail! A practical post-quantum public-key encryption from lwe and lwr. In: SCN, pp. 160–177. Springer, 2018
14. Del Pino, R., Lyubashevsky, V., Seiler, G.: Lattice-based group signatures and zero-knowledge proofs of automorphism stability. In: CCS, pp. 574–591. ACM, 2018
15. Ducas, L., Lepoint, T., Lyubashevsky, V., Schwabe, P., Seiler, G., Stehlé, D.: CRYSTALS – dilithium: digital signatures from module lattices. Cryptology ePrint Archive, Report 2017/633, 2017. https://eprint.iacr.org/2017/633
16. El Kaafarani, A., Katsumata, S.: Attribute-based signatures for unbounded circuits in the rom and efficient instantiations from lattices. In: PKC. Springer (2018)
17. Esgin, M.F., Steinfeld, R., Liu, J.K., Liu, D.: Lattice-based zero-knowledge proofs: new techniques for shorter and faster constructions and applications. In: CRYPTO, pp. 115–146. Springer, 2019
18. Gama, N., Nguyen, P.Q.: Predicting lattice reduction. In: EUROCRYPT, pp. 31–51. Springer, 2008
19. Goldwasser, S., Micali, S., Rackoff, C.: The knowledge complexity of interactive proof-systems. In: STOC, pp. 291–304. ACM (1985)
20. Hoffstein, J., Pipher, J., Schanck, J.M., Silverman, J.H., Whyte, W., Zhang, Z.: Choosing parameters for ntruencrypt. In: CT-RSA, pp. 3–18. Springer, 2017
21. Jeudy, C., Roux-Langlois, A., Sanders, O.: Lattice signature with efficient protocols, application to anonymous credentials. In: Annual International Cryptology Conference, pp. 351–383. Springer, 2023
22. Laarhoven, T.: Sieving for shortest vectors in lattices using angular locality-sensitive hashing. In: CRYPTO, pp. 3–22. Springer, 2015
23. Libert, B., Ling, S., Nguyen, K., Wang, H.: Zero-knowledge arguments for lattice-based accumulators: logarithmic-size ring signatures and group signatures without trapdoors. In: EUCRYPT, pp. 1–31. Springer, 2016
24. Libert, B., Ling, S., Nguyen, K., Wang, H.: Zero-knowledge arguments for lattice-based PRFs and applications to E-cash. In: ASIACRYPT, pp. 304–335. Springer, 2017
25. Ling, S., Nguyen, K., Stehlé, D., Wang, H.: Improved zero-knowledge proofs of knowledge for the ISIS problem, and applications. In: PKC, pp. 107–124. Springer, 2013
26. Ling, S., Nguyen, K., Wang, H., Xu, Y.: Lattice-based group signatures: achieving full dynamicity with ease. In: ACNS, pp. 293–312. Springer, 2017
27. Lofgren, P., Hopper, N.: Faust: efficient, TTP-free abuse prevention by anonymous whitelisting. In: Proceedings of the 10th Annual ACM Workshop on Privacy in the Electronic Society, pp. 125–130 (2011)

28. Lyubashevsky, V., Nguyen, N.K., Plancon, M., Seiler, G.: Shorter lattice-based group signatures via "almost free" encryption and other optimizations. In: International Conference on the Theory and Application of Cryptology and Information Security, pp. 218–248. Springer, 2021
29. Lyubashevsky, V., Nguyen, N.K., Seiler, G.: SMILE: set membership from ideal lattices with applications to ring signatures and confidential transactions. In: Annual International Cryptology Conference, pp. 611–640. Springer, 2021
30. Nguyen, L.: Accumulators from bilinear pairings and applications. In: CT-RSA, pp. 275–292. Springer, 2005
31. Regev, O.: On lattices, learning with errors, random linear codes, and cryptography. In: STOC, pp. 84–93. ACM (2005)
32. Rosenberg, M., Maller, M., Miers, I.: Snarkblock: federated anonymous blocklisting from hidden common input aggregate proofs. In: 2022 IEEE Symposium on Security and Privacy (SP), pp. 948–965. IEEE (2022)
33. Schanck, J .: Estimator. https://github.com/jschanck/estimator
34. Tsang, P.P., Au, M.H., Kapadia, A., Smith, S.W.: Blacklistable anonymous credentials: blocking misbehaving users without TTPS. In: CCS, pp. 72–81. ACM (2007)
35. Tsang, P.P., Au, M.H., Kapadia, A., Smith, S.W.: PEREA: towards practical ttp-free revocation in anonymous authentication. In: CCS, pp. 333–344. ACM (2008)
36. Tsang, P.P., Au, M.H., Kapadia, A., Smith, S.W.: BLAC: revoking repeatedly misbehaving anonymous users without relying on TTPS. ACM Trans. Inf. Syst. Secur. (TISSEC) **13**(4), 1–33 (2010)
37. Wang, W., Feng, D., Qin, Y., Shao, J., Xi, L., Chu, X.: Exblacr: extending blacr system. In: Australasian Conference on Information Security and Privacy, pp. 397–412. Springer, 2014
38. Xi, L., Feng, D.: FARB: fast anonymous reputation-based blacklisting without ttps. In: Proceedings of the 13th Workshop on Privacy in the Electronic Society, pp. 139–148 (2014)
39. Yang, R., Au, M.H., Lai, J., Xu, Q.: Lattice-based techniques for accountable anonymity: Composition of abstract stern's protocols and weak PRF with efficient protocols from LWR. Cryptology ePrint Archive, Report 2017/781, 2017. http://eprint.iacr.org/2017/781
40. Yang, R., Au, M.H., Xu, Q., Yu, Z.: Decentralized blacklistable anonymous credentials with reputation. Comput. Secur. **85**, 353–371 (2019)
41. Yang, R., Au, M.H., Zhang, Z., Xu, Q., Yu, Z., Whyte, W.: Efficient lattice-based zero-knowledge arguments with standard soundness: construction and applications. In: CRYPTO, pp. 147–175. Springer, 2019
42. Yu, K.Y., Yuen, T.H., Chow, S.S., Yiu, S.M., Hui, L.C.: PE (AR) 2: privacy-enhanced anonymous authentication with reputation and revocation. In: European Symposium on Research in Computer Security, pp. 679–696. Springer, 2012

Distributed System and Blockchain Security

Asynchronous Byzantine Fault Tolerance Reliable Broadcast Based on Directed Acyclic Graph

Haibo Tian(✉) and Jiajun Chen

Guangdong Province Key Laboratory of Information Security Technology, School of Computer Science and Engineering, Sun Yat-Sen University, Guangzhou, China
tianhb@sysu.edu.cn, chenjj368@mail2.sysu.edu.cn

Abstract. Asynchronous Byzantine Fault Tolerance (BFT) reliable broadcast serves as a core component in constructing asynchronous BFT consensus algorithms, which are crucial to blockchain technology. Despite its significant role in the blockchain domain, BFT reliable broadcast still exhibits relatively high communication complexity. We propose a novel reliable broadcast protocol tailored for asynchronous network environments, leveraging Directed Acyclic Graph (DAG) technology to reduce communication complexity. Processes in the new protocol are responsible for sending response messages when they receive a broadcast message. These response messages contain both the broadcast message and references to previously received response messages, thereby forming a DAG of response messages. By analyzing the referencing patterns of response messages in the graph, the process can determine whether a message can be delivered. Under the condition of continuously receiving new broadcast messages, we show that the protocol satisfies agreement, integrity, and validity, achieving reliable broadcast. Comparative results reveal that it exhibits the lowest amortised communication complexity and amortised number of communication rounds for each broadcast message.

Keywords: BFT Reliable Broadcast · Asynchronous Network · Directed Acyclic Graph · Communication Complexity

1 Introduction

The consensus mechanism of blockchain, as a core element of blockchain technology, plays a crucial role in ensuring the consistency of distributed ledgers. Currently, various consensus mechanisms coexist and play significant roles in different scenarios. Bitcoin proposes the Proof of Work (POW) consensus mechanism to ensure ledger consistency by solving computational puzzles. Ethereum, on the other hand, has chosen Proof of Stake (POS) as its core consensus mechanism, allowing token holders to participate in the bookkeeping process through staking, thereby improving efficiency and reducing energy consumption.

J. K. Liu et al. (Eds.): ProvSec 2024, LNCS 14904, pp. 109–123, 2025.
https://doi.org/10.1007/978-981-96-0957-4_6

In the field of consortium blockchains, the Byzantine Fault Tolerance (BFT) consensus mechanism has gained widespread application. Derived from the Byzantine Generals Problem, BFT consensus aims to solve the issue of process consensus in untrusted environments. Within this framework, numerous notable consensus mechanisms have emerged, such as PBFT [6], Dashing and Star [1], HoneyBadger [13], Dumbo [10], and DAG-Rider [12]. Through innovative algorithm and protocol designs, these mechanisms ensure that honest processes can still form bookkeeping consensus even in the presence of malicious processes, safeguarding the consistency of blockchain systems.

Within BFT consensus protocols, the BFT reliable broadcast serves as a fundamental component. For instance, in HoneyBadger, Dumbo, and DAG-Rider [10,12,13], all operating in asynchronous network environments, asynchronous BFT reliable broadcast plays a pivotal role. Notably, both HoneyBadger and Dumbo have developed specific asynchronous BFT reliable broadcast protocols tailored to their respective consensus mechanisms. For protocols operating in semi-synchronous environments, such as PBFT and Dashing and Star [1,6], the security properties achieved inherently encompass the attributes of BFT reliable broadcast in such semi-synchronous settings.

Currently, several proposals for BFT reliable broadcast protocols in asynchronous network environments have been put forward. For n processes, when broadcasting a message M, the communication complexity has been reduced from $O(n^2|M|)$ [3] to $O(n|M| + nh + n^2 \log n)$ [2], where h represents a length parameter determined by cryptographic algorithms, and $|M|$ denotes the size of the message. Typically, $|M|$ is significantly larger than h.

We observe that current reliable broadcast protocols process messages individually without considering the sequential order of message transmission. Therefore, a new message format called the response message is designed, and a Directed Acyclic Graph (DAG) constructed from the messages is utilized to complete reliable broadcast. As a result, the amortised communication complexity required for a broadcast message can be further reduced to $O(n|M| + nh)$.

1.1 Related Works

In 1987, Bracha [3] proposed a classical BFT reliable broadcast protocol that included three rounds of messages: "initial-echo-ready". His protocol could be proven to satisfy the security properties of reliable broadcast even under conditions where the adversary had unlimited computing resources, with a communication complexity of $O(n^2|M|)$. Subsequently, researchers divided the technical approaches into two lines based on whether the adversary's computing resources were limited or not. We assume that the adversary is probabilistic polynomial time (PPT) bounded, and thus we focus on the efforts made by researchers to reduce communication complexity under this assumption.

The first approach aims to reduce the overall communication cost by allowing all honest processes to broadcast only a portion of the message. In 2005, Cachin and Tessaro [5] employed techniques such as hash functions and erasure codes to enable all honest processes to broadcast only fragments of the message along with hash values derived from a Merkle tree. The communication complexity of this protocol is $O(n|M| + hn^2 \log n)$. It was utilized in the HoneyBadger protocol [13]. In 2007, Hendricks et al. [11] proposed appending fingerprint functions to message fragments during the message broadcast process, indicating the message associated with each fragment. The communication complexity of the corresponding protocol is $O(n|M| + hn^3)$. More recently, in 2020, Nayak et al. [14] introduced a reliable broadcast protocol based on accumulators and error-correcting codes, achieving a communication complexity of $O(n|M| + hn^2)$.

The second approach focuses on optimizing the steps of the Bracha protocol [3] to reduce the overall communication cost. In 2021, Das et al. [9] presented a protocol for asynchronous data dissemination along with a corresponding BFT reliable broadcast protocol, with a communication complexity of $O(n|M| + hn^2)$. In 2022, Alhaddad et al. [2] comprehensively utilized the research findings of Bracha, Cachin and Tessaro, and Das et al. [3,5,9], proposing two BFT reliable broadcast protocols. The first one further reduced computational overhead while maintaining the same communication complexity of $O(n|M| + hn^2)$, while the second one further lowered the communication complexity to $O(n|M| + hn + n^2 \log n)$. Additionally, Zhao et al. [16] introduced a BFT reliable broadcast protocol leveraging a trusted execution environment. Their protocol modifies the basic structure of the traditional "initial-echo-ready" process to a simplified "initial-echo" two-step approach, significantly reducing communication overhead. Nevertheless, it is important to note that trusted execution environments are not immune to attacks, and various methods, including side-channel attacks [4,15], pose significant threats to their security.

Moreover, in recent years, several asynchronous BFT consensus mechanisms have emerged, accompanied by customized asynchronous BFT reliable broadcast protocols tailored specifically for these consensus mechanisms. The design objectives of these protocols are to reduce the overall communication complexity of the consensus mechanisms and enhance efficiency. Guo et al. [10] shortened the size of broadcast messages in the Bracha protocol to improve the overall efficiency of the Dumbo2 consensus mechanism. Dai et al. [8] embedded hierarchical information into the Bracha protocol to reduce the time delay in submitting data within their GradedDAG consensus mechanism. Chen et al. [7] added timing assumptions to the Bracha protocol, resulting in a consensus protocol that falls between the asynchronous and semi-synchronous categories.

Therefore, under the assumption of PPT adversaries and without relying on a trusted execution environment, the lowest communication complexity of asynchronous BFT reliable broadcast is $O(n|M| + nh + n^2 \log n)$. Distinct from all previously existing reliable broadcast protocols, we incorporate the sequential order of broadcast messages into the references of a DAG. The decision of whether to deliver a broadcast message is determined by the referential relationships within the DAG. Through this innovative design, the amortised communication complexity of each broadcast message is reduced to $O(n|M| + nh)$.

1.2 Our Contributions

The main contribution of this paper is the asynchronous reliable broadcast protocol based on DAG, which reduces communication complexity. In more detail:

- We introduce response messages for reliable broadcast to construct the DAG.
- We present detailed algorithms to show how to use the DAG.
- We prove that the protocol satisfies the requirements of a reliable broadcast protocol.
- We provide the performance analysis of our protocol and compare our protocol with classic and recent proposals.

Section 2 introduces preliminaries for our protocol, while Sect. 3 details the protocol itself. Section 4 examines its security and performance, and the conclusion summarizes the paper.

2 Preliminaries

2.1 Hash Function

A collision-resistant hash function $H : \{0,1\}^* \to \{0,1\}^h$ is a cryptographic primitive that maps arbitrary bit string inputs of variable length to a fixed-size output, known as a hash value. The key property of such a function is its resistance to collisions, meaning it is computationally infeasible to find two distinct inputs that produce the same hash value. More formally, for any PPT adversary, the probability of successfully finding two distinct bit strings $M \neq M' \in \{0,1\}^*$, such that $H(M) = H(M')$, is negligible.

2.2 DAG

A DAG is a graph structure consisting of nodes and directed edges. Each edge in a DAG has a direction, and no cycles or loops exist. Let's represent the graph as $G = (V, E)$, where V represents the nodes and E represents the directed edges. In this context, each node in V denotes a response message created by a process, and the directed edges E represent the referential relationships among these response messages. In our design, each response message sent out must include the hash values of at least two previously received response messages. Therefore, the referential relationships indicate the order of reception of response messages at a process. Since a DAG is acyclic, a process can deduce whether a particular response message has been received by another process based on the referential relationships among all the received response messages, thus enabling reliable broadcasting.

The referential relationships in a DAG can be categorized into direct and indirect references. A direct reference occurs when one node points directly to another node, and each directed edge represents a direct referential relationship. An indirect reference, on the other hand, occurs when a node indirectly points to another node through a series of direct references. By tracing the path of the directed edges, one can establish the indirect referential relationships among nodes in the DAG. For any given response message, the messages it directly or indirectly references were received earlier at an honest sending process.

2.3 Asynchronous BFT Reliable Broadcast

We define the reliable broadcast in the same way as DAG-Rider [12]. There are n processes $(p_1, \ldots, p_n)$. At most $t_n \leq \frac{n-1}{3}$ processes have Byzantine behavior. Byzantine processes may delay messages, drop messages, or unicast a message that should be broadcasted, and so on. These processes are in an asynchronous network environment, where the only requirement is that messages between honest processes can be eventually received, without any stipulation on the delay of final delivery. There are authenticated channels between each pair of processes, which could be implemented by usual transport layer secure protocols.

As a reliable broadcast protocol, a sender process p_k can send messages by calling $bcast_k(m, w)$ where m is a message and $w \in \mathbb{N}$ is a round number. Every honest process $p_i \neq p_k$ should have an output $deliver_i(m, w, p_k)$ where p_k is the honest process that called the $bcast_k(m, w)$. There are three properties about the protocol:

1. Agreement: If an honest process p_i outputs $deliver_i(m, w, p_k)$, then every other honest process p_j eventually outputs $deliver_j(m, w, p_k)$ with probability 1.
2. Integrity: For each round $w \in \mathbb{N}$ and process p_k, an honest process p_i outputs $deliver_i(m, w, p_k)$ at most once regardless of m.
3. Validity: If an honest process p_k calls $bcast_k(m, w)$, then every honest process p_i eventually outputs $deliver_i(m, w, p_k)$ with probability 1.

3 The Protocol

The protocol consists of five algorithms: initialization, sender broadcasting messages, process sending response messages, process receiving response messages, and process buffer handling. As shown in Algorithm 1, a sender process p_k runs Algorithm 3 to broadcast a message m to all processes in the form of $v_k = (SEND, m, w, p_k)$ where $SEND$ is a message flag, m is the message, w is the round number, and p_k is the sender identity. Each process except the sender runs Algorithm 2 to initialize some buffers and data structures. On receiving v_k, a process p_i runs Algorithm 4 to possibly create a response message

$$r_{ik} = (RESPONSE, v_k, ref_{p_i}, p_i) \tag{1}$$

where $RESPONSE$ is a message flag, ref_{p_i} is the reference field including (ref_1, ref_2) and an optional ref_3, and p_i is the process identity. On receiving a response message r_{jk} from p_j, a process p_i runs Algorithm 5 to put r_{jk} in a DAG and update the reference counters with a possibility to produce some outputs such as $deliver_i(m', w', p_k)$. That is, a received response message r_{jk} may cause the delivery of another broadcast message m'. If there are too many messages in buffers, a process runs Algorithm 6 to reduce their sizes. In the next subsections, we detail the five algorithms.

Algorithm 1: The DAG Based Reliable Broadcast Protocol

if $p_i \neq p_k$ **then**
  p_i invokes Algorithm 2 to set initial data structures.
upon *p_k calls $bcast_k(m, w)$* **do**
  p_k invokes Algorithm 3 to broadcast v_k.
upon *$p_i \neq p_k$ receives a message v_k from p_k* **do**
  p_i invokes Algorithm 4 to create r_{ik}.
upon *$p_i \neq p_k$ receives a message r_{jk} from p_j* **do**
  p_i invokes Algorithm 5 to update the DAG for delivery.
upon *the buffers in p_i (where $p_i \neq p_k$) for v_k or r_{jk} overflow* **do**
  p_i invokes Algorithm 6 to update buffers.

Algorithm 2: Process p_i Initialization

Input: A hash function H, a public initial message m_0, and two threshold values x_1, x_2.
Output: A DAG graph G_i and six empty data structures: $votes_i$, vk_i, $echo_i$, $ready_i$, $inbuffer_i$, and $buffer_i$.
Initialize $G_i = (V_i, E_i)$ with $V_i = \{H(m_0)\}$ and $E_i = \varnothing$ to store the hash values of response messages and their reference relationships.
Initialize $votes_i$ as an empty dictionary to store entries $(key, \{refs, ids_e, ids_r\})$, where key is a hash value of a response message, $refs$ is a set containing hash values of response messages referencing the message with hash key, ids_e is a set containing different process identities that reference a message with hash in $\{key\} \cup refs$ using references in $\{ref_1, ref_2\}$, and ids_r is a set containing different process identities that reference a message using ref_3.
Initialize vk_i as an empty dictionary to store entries $(key, index)$, where key is a hash value of a sender message and $index$ is a set containing different values of the keys in $votes_i$.
Initialize $echo_i$ and $ready_i$ as empty dictionaries to store entries $((w, p_k), m)$.
Initialize $inbuffer_i = \varnothing, buffer_i = \varnothing$, with the maximal capacity of $inbuffer_i$ set to x_1 and the maximal capacity of $buffer_i$ set to x_2, respectively.
return $G_i, votes_i, vk_i, echo_i, ready_i, inbuffer_i, buffer_i$.

3.1 Initialization

As shown in Algorithm 2, an honest process is tasked with initializing a DAG, four dictionaries, and two buffer sets. The initialization process receives, as inputs, a public initial message m_0 along with two small integers x_1 and x_2, and a hash function H. The message m_0 can be arbitrary, including common announcements or a version number. Initially, the DAG contains only a single node representing the hash value of m_0, denoted as $H(m_0)$. Both the dictionaries and the buffer sets are initially empty.

The dictionary $votes_i$ maintains a portion of the referential relationships within a DAG. Each entry in the dictionary has a key that corresponds to the hash value of a response message. The value field associated with each key holds the hash values of response messages that refer to the keyed message, directly or indirectly, including the key itself for convenience. The dictionary vk_i is used to record the response messages that contain v_k. The dictionaries $echo_i$ and $ready_i$ are used to simulate the functions of "echo" and "ready" in Bracha's protocol [3]. The two buffer sets serve distinct purposes: one is designated for sender messages, while the other is reserved for process response messages.

3.2 Sender Broadcasting Messages

Algorithm 3 outlines the process by which sender p_k broadcasts messages. Given inputs of a message m and a round number w, the sender process makes a broadcast message $v_k = (SEND, m, w, p_k)$, and sends the message to all other processes.

Algorithm 3: Sender Process p_k Broadcasting ($bcast_k(m, w)$)

Input: A message m and a round number w
Output: v_k
1 Send $v_k = (SEND, m, w, p_k)$ to all other processes.

3.3 Process Sending Response Messages

Algorithm 4 outlines the process by which process p_i broadcasts a response message. We use some convenient symbols for dictionaries. Take $echo_i$ as an example. $echo_i.keys$ means a set that contains all the keys in the dictionary. $echo_i[(w, p_k)]$ means to get the value in the dictionary with the key (w, p_k).

After receiving a message v_k, the process p_i first parses the message and performs potential message compliance checks (Line 1). Subsequently, with a probability of $1 - \frac{1}{2t_n+1}$, the message v_k is placed into the set $inbuffer_i$ and the process exits. With a probability of $\frac{1}{2t_n+1}$, a response message

$$r_{ik} = (RESPONSE, v_k, ref_{p_i}, i)$$

is generated and sent (Line 2).

Lines 5-23 in Algorithm 4 specify the selection rules for the reference field ref_{p_i}:

1. First, two processes $p_{j_1}, p_{j_2} \neq p_i$ are selected (Line 5).
2. Then, choose response messages sent by the two processes as ref_1, ref_2. Lines 7–12 guarantee that an honest process only references the same broadcast message for a specific round.

Algorithm 4: Process p_i Handles v_k

Input: A message v_k
Output: A response message r_{ik} or $\perp$
1 Parse $v_k = (SEND, m, w, p_k)$ and make any necessary checks.
2 With probability $1 - \frac{1}{2t_n+1}$, add v_k to the $inbuffer_i$ set and return $\perp$. Otherwise, continue.
3 Construct a response message $r_{ik} = (RESPONSE, v_k, ref_{p_i}, p_i)$ where the reference set ref_{p_i} is constructed as follows:
4 **begin**
5   Select two processes $p_{j_1}, p_{j_2} \neq p_i$ in a round-robin manner.
6   **for** *each process* $p_{j_b} \in \{p_{j_1}, p_{j_2}\}$ **do**
7   Choose a response message r^* from $votes_i$ or V_i sent by process p_{j_b} as ref_b
8   Extract $v_k^* = (SEND, m^*, w^*, p_k)$ from r^*.
9   **if** $(w^*, p_k) \in echo_i.keys$ *and* $m^* \neq echo_i[(w^*, p_k)]$ **then**
10   Goto line 7.
11   **else if** $(w^*, p_k) \notin echo_i.keys$ **then**
12   Add $((w^*, p_k), m^*)$ to $echo_i$.
13   **for** $(key, index) \in vk_i$ **do**
14   Initialize temp sets $s_e = \emptyset$ and $s_r = \emptyset$.
15   **for** $H(r') \in index$ **do**
16   Add the ids_e with $key = H(r')$ in $votes_i$ to the set s_e.
17   Add the ids_r with $key = H(r')$ in $votes_i$ to the set s_r.
18   **if** $|s_e| \geq 2t_n + 1$ *or* $|s_r| \geq t_n + 1$ **then**
19   Parse $v'_k = (SEND, m', w', p_k)$ where $H(v'_k) = key$.
20   **if** $(w', p_k) \notin ready_i.keys$ **then**
21   Select a hash value $H(r') \in index$ and set $ref_3 = H(r')$.
22   Add $((w', p_k), m')$ to the $ready_i$ dictionary and break.
23   Set $ref_{p_i} = \{ref_1, ref_2, [ref_3]\}$ where ref_3 is optional.
24 Broadcast r_{ik} to all.
25 **return** r_{ik}.

3. Finally, if a broadcast message v'_k indexed by the vk_i dictionary is included in some response messages that have been referenced by at least $t_n + 1$ different honest processes, or if there is an honest process that is preparing to deliver v'_k (Lines 14–18), and the process p_i has not prepared to deliver v'_k (Line 20), the hash value of a response message containing v'_k is added to ref_{p_i} as ref_3.

Generally, in the selection process, priority should be given to unreferenced response messages. If no available response messages are found, the value $H(m_0)$ of the initial message can be used as a replacement. If there are multiple unreferenced response messages, they may be referenced in the order of receipt.

3.4 Process Receiving Response Messages

Algorithm 5 shows the process by which process p_i receives a response message from a process p_j.

Algorithm 5: Process p_i Receiving Response Messages

Input: A response message r_{jk} from process p_j
Output: *True* or *False*

1 Parse $r_{jk} = (RESPONSE, v_k, ref_{p_j}, j)$ and make any necessary checks.
2 If $v_k \in inbuffer_i$, delete v_k from $inbuffer_i$.
3 If $H(r_{jk}) \in V_i$, return *False*. Otherwise, continue.
4 If $ref_{p_j} \not\subset V_i$, put r_{jk} in $buffer_i$. Otherwise, continue.
5 Set $V_i = V_i \cup \{H(r_{jk})\}$, $E_i = E_i \cup \{(H(r_{jk}), ref^*) | ref^* \in ref_{p_j}\}$.
6 **for** $(key, \{refs, ids_e, ids_r\}) \in votes_i$ **do**
7   **for** $ref \in ref_{p_j}$ **do**
8   If $ref \in refs$ and $ref \in \{ref_1, ref_2\}$ of ref_{p_j}, set $ids_e = ids_e \cup \{p_j\}$.
9   If $ref \in refs$ and $ref \in \{ref_3\}$ of ref_{p_j}, set $ids_r = ids_r \cup \{p_j\}$.
10   If $ref \in refs$, set $refs = refs \cup \{H(r_{jk})\}$.
11 Put $((H(r_{jk}), \{\{H(r_{jk})\}, \{p_j\}, \{p_j\}\}))$ in $votes_i$.
12 **for** $(key, index) \in vk_i$ **do**
13   If $key = H(v_k)$, set $index = index \cup \{H(r_{jk})\}$.
14   Set a temp set $s_t = \emptyset$.;
15   **for** $H(r^*) \in index$ **do**
16   Add ids_r from $votes_i$, where the key is $H(r^*)$, to the set s_t.
17   If $|s_t| \geq 2t_n + 1$, then parse $v^* = (SEND, m^*, w^*, p_k)$ where $H(v^*) = key$, output $deliver_i(m^*, w^*, p_k)$, remove the entries in $votes_i$ with their keys in $index$, and remove the entry in vk_i.
18 If $H(v_k) \notin vk_i.keys$, put $(H(v_k), \{H(r_{jk})\})$ in vk_i.
19 **for** $r^* \in buffer_i$ **do**
20   If r^* makes the response messages referenced by r^* all in V_i, run the algorithm from step 1 for r^*.
21 **return** *True*.

After receiving a response message r_{jk} from process p_j, process p_i first needs to parse r_{jk} and perform message compliance checks (Line 1). If the sender message v_k in the $inbuffer_i$ matches the received response, process p_i removes it from $inbuffer_i$ set (Line 2). Then, p_i checks if all the referenced response messages in r_{jk} are present in G_i. If not all the referenced messages are in G_i, the received message will be added to the buffer $buffer_i$. Otherwise, the response message will be added to G_i if r_{jk} is not already in G_i (Lines 3–5).

Lines 6–11 deal with the dictionary $votes_i$. For each entry in the dictionary $votes_i$, it checks whether r_{jk} directly or indirectly references the response message with the hash value key. If r_{jk} references the response message corresponding to key through the ref_1 or ref_2 fields, the process identity p_j is added to the ids_e set (Line 8). If it is through the ref_3 field, the p_j is added to the ids_r set (Line 9). In both cases, the hash value of r_{jk} needs to be added to the $refs$ set corresponding to key (Line 10).

Lines 12–18 deal with the dictionary vk_i. If the hash value of v_k in r_{jk} is not a key in vk_i, it means that the response message r_{jk} contains a new broadcast message v_k, which is then put into vk_i as in Line 18. Otherwise, it means that the response message r_{jk} also contains v_k, which is then put into the $index$ field as in Line 13. To check whether a broadcast message could be delivered, we count the number of processes that signal "ready" via the ref_3 field (Lines 13-16). If the number is greater than $2t_n + 1$, deliver the message indexed by the key and remove related states (Line 17).

Lines 19–20 in Algorithm 5 update the $buffer_i$ set. For a response message r^* in $buffer_i$, p_i checks whether r_{jk} is the missing last reference. If it is, p_i removes r^* from the $buffer_i$ set and executes Algorithm 5 for r^*.

3.5 Process Buffer Handling

Algorithm 6 describes the process through which process p_i handles its buffers.

Algorithm 6: Process p_i Buffer Handling

Input: $buffer_i$, $inbuffer_i$
Output: True

if $|buffer_i| \geq x_2$ **then**
    for $j \in \{1, \ldots, n\}$ **do**
        Send a synchronization request $(SYNC, buffer_i, p_i)$ to p_j.
    Clear $buffer_i$.
upon receiving a synchronization request $(SYNC, buffer_j, p_j)$ from process p_j **for** $r^* \in buffer_j$ **do**
    if V_i *contains all responses messages referenced by* r^* **then**
        Send the referenced messages and r^* back to p_j.
if $|inbuffer_i| \geq x_1$ **then**
    for $v_k^* \in inbuffer_i$ **do**
        Run Algorithm 4 from Line 3.
        Remove v_k^* from $inbuffer_i$.
return *True*

Process p_i will monitor the sizes of the local buffers $buffer_i$ and $inbuffer_i$. If the size of $buffer_i$ exceeds a predefined threshold x_2, a synchronization request will be broadcast for these response messages, and all the response messages in the buffer will be removed. On receiving the synchronization request, an honest process holding response messages referenced by the request in its local DAG will unicast the referenced response messages back to process p_i. If the size of $inbuffer_i$ exceeds another threshold x_1, Algorithm 4 will be executed starting from line 3 so that the messages in $inbuffer_i$ can be sent.

4 Security and Performance

4.1 Security Analysis

We next prove that the protocol has the three properties of reliable broadcast.

Lemma 1. *Assume that a sender process always broadcasts new messages. Then, an honest process p_i can send new response messages with probability 1.*

Proof. When p_i receives a broadcast message, it sends a response message with a probability $\frac{1}{2t_n+1}$. Suppose the sender sends z messages. The probability of no response being generated by p_i is $(1-\frac{1}{2t_n+1})^z$. Then, the probability of sending a response message is $\alpha = 1-(1-\frac{1}{2t_n+1})^z$. Since $t_n > 1$, $\alpha \approx 1$ when z increases. So, p_i can send new responses with probability 1.

Lemma 2. *If an honest process p_i sends a response message r^* to all other processes, every other honest process p_j eventually puts r^* in their DAG graph G_j.*

Proof. When r^* reaches an honest process p_j, according to Algorithm 5, there are several different situations. Firstly, $H(r^*) \in V_j$, which means that the response message is already in the graph G_j. Secondly, r^* is put into $buffer_j$ due to the lack of some referenced response messages. Then, the response message r^* may enter the graph G_j when some new response message reaches p_j according to lines 19-20 in Algorithm 5. Or, the response message r^* is sent in a synchronization request in Algorithm 6. In the second case, since r^* is sent by an honest process, the references of r^* will eventually reach p_j, and r^* enters the graph G_j. Thirdly, the response message r^* enters the graph G_j directly. So, we conclude that in all situations, the response message r^* enters the graph G_j.

Lemma 3. *If an honest process p_i puts $((w, p_k), m)$ in $ready_i$ and another honest process p_j puts $((w, p_k), m')$ in $ready_j$, then $m = m'$.*

Proof. According to Algorithm 4, process p_i puts $((w, p_k), m)$ in $ready_i$ when there are at least $2t_n + 1$ different processes referencing the response messages related to (w, p_k). This implies that at least $t_n + 1$ different honest processes have put $((w, p_k), m)$ in their respective *echo* dictionaries. Similarly, process p_j puts $((w, p_k), m')$ in $ready_j$ under the same conditions, meaning at least $t_n + 1$ honest processes have included $((w, p_k), m')$ in their *echo* dictionaries. Due to the properties of Byzantine quorums, there must be an honest process p^* that has put both $((w, p_k), m)$ and $((w, p_k), m')$ into its $echo_{p^*}$ dictionary. However, Algorithm 4 (lines 9-12) specifies that an honest process cannot simultaneously include both $((w, p_k), m)$ and $((w, p_k), m')$ in its *echo* dictionary. This contradiction leads us to conclude that $m = m'$.

Theorem 1. Agreement: *Assume that a sender process always broadcasts new messages. If an honest process p_i outputs $deliver_i(m, w, p_k)$, every other honest process p_j eventually outputs $deliver_j(m, w, p_k)$ with probability 1.*

Proof. Since the honest process p_i outputs $deliver_i(m, w, p_k)$, according to Algorithm 5 (Line 17), $|s_t| \geq 2t_n+1$. Suppose v_k includes (m, w, p_k) and the response messages containing v_k are in a set res_{vk}. Then s_t contains the identities of processes that sent response messages referencing some response messages in res_{vk}

via their ref_3 field. Since there are at most t_n Byzantine processes, there are at least $t_n + 1$ honest processes in s_t. The response messages of these honest processes can be received by the honest processes not in the set s_t according to Lemma 2.

The honest processes not in the set s_t will set their ref_3 field in their new response messages according to Algorithm 4 (Lines 18-22) when they send new response messages with probability 1 according to Lemma 1. The honest processes are ready for the same (w, p_k) due to Lemma 3. Therefore, every honest process will eventually receive at least $2t_n + 1$ response messages with ref_3 fields referencing some response messages in res_{vk}. This leads to the same output about (m, w, p_k) for all honest processes.

Theorem 2. Integrity: *For each round $w \in \mathbb{N}$ and process p_k, an honest process p_i outputs $deliver_i(m, w, p_k)$ at most once regardless of m.*

Proof. If an honest process p_i outputs $\text{deliver}_i(m, w, p_k)$, according to Algorithm 5 (Line 17), $|s_t| \geq 2t_n + 1$. Note that $|s_r|$ in Algorithm 4 (Line 18) is equivalent to $|s_t|$. Therefore, process p_i has put $((w, p_k), m)$ in the $ready_i$ dictionary. If process p_i outputs another $\text{deliver}_i(m', w, p_k)$, it must have put $((w, p_k), m')$ in the $ready_i$ dictionary too. However, Algorithm 4 (Lines 20–22) ensures that this does not happen. The contradiction shows that process p_i outputs $\text{deliver}_i(m, w, p_k)$ at most once regardless of m.

Theorem 3. Validity: *Assume that a sender process always broadcasts new messages. If an honest process p_k calls $bcast(m, w)$, then every honest process p_i will eventually output $deliver_i(m, w, p_k)$ with probability* 1.

Proof. If an honest p_k calls $bcast(m, w)$, a message $v_k = (\text{SEND}, m, w, p_k)$ is broadcasted. According to Algorithm 4, an honest process p_i will create a response message containing v_k with a probability of $1/(2t_n + 1)$. There are three scenarios. In the first scenario, multiple honest processes, including p_i, send multiple response messages containing the same v_k. According to Algorithm 5, this case will only accelerate the delivery of v_k since we set a dictionary vk_i for each v_k in p_i. In the second scenario, no process sends a response message containing v_k. In this case, for p_i, v_k is put into the $inbuffer_i$ set. Then there are two subcases. The first subcase is that v_k is removed by p_i later due to receiving a response message r^* containing the same v_k. The second subcase is that when $|inbuffer_i| \geq x_1$, according to Algorithm 6, v_k will be sent in a response message from p_i. In the third scenario, only p_i sends a response message containing v_k.

Now suppose only one response message r_{ik} containing v_k is sent by an honest process. By Lemma 2, r_{ik} will eventually be included in the local DAG of other honest processes. According to Algorithm 4 (Lines 5–12), the response message r_{ik} has a chance to be referenced in each honest process. Since p_k is honest, the condition in line 9 will not be triggered. So r_{ik} will eventually be referenced by honest processes when the processes broadcast new response messages with probability 1. When $2t_n + 1$ new response messages referencing r_{ik} reach p_i,

p_i will send a new response message referencing r_{ik} with the ref_3 field. When $2t_n+1$ response messages referencing r_{ik} with the ref_3 field reach p_i, the message v_k in r_{ik} will be delivered by p_i. Then, by Theorem 1, all honest processes will eventually deliver v_k.

4.2 Performance Analysis

We undertake an analysis of the communication performance between our protocol and existing alternatives in Table 1. Firstly, while most protocols require four rounds, our protocol reduces this to three rounds, as the response message serves dual purposes: it disseminates sender messages and references other response messages. Secondly, our protocol relies solely on cryptographic hash functions, similar to many other protocols. Finally, the communication complexity of our approach is the lowest.

Table 1. Communication Complexity Comparison with Cryptographic Tools and Rounds

Protocols	Sender Process	Other Process	Tools	Rounds
Bracha [3]	$O(n\|M\|)$	$O(n^2\|M\|)$	–	4
Cachin-Tessaro [5]	$O(\|M\| + hn \log n)$	$O(n\|M\| + hn^2 \log n)$	Hash	4
Das [9]	$O(n\|M\| + hn)$	$O(n\|M\| + hn^2)$	Hash	4
Nayak [14]	$O(n\|M\| + hn)$	$O(n\|M\| + hn^2)$	Accumulator	7
Alhaddad1 [2]	$O(\|M\| + hn^2)$	$O(n\|M\| + hn^2)$	Hash	4
Alhaddad2 [2]	$O(n\|M\| + hn + n \log n)$	$O(n\|M\| + hn + n^2 \log n)$	Threshold Signature	7
Ours	$O(n\|M\|)$	$O(n\|M\| + hn)$	Hash	3

Our communication complexity is calculated as follows. When a sender process broadcasts a message, it triggers a response message in a single process with a probability of $\frac{1}{2t_n+1}$. For a message to be delivered, there must be $2t_n + 1$ references from different processes in the ref_3 field. However, to generate a response message containing ref_3, there should be $2t_n + 1$ references in the ref_1 or ref_2 positions. Given that each response message carries at least two references, approximately $\lceil(2t_n + 1)/2\rceil + (2t_n + 1)$ response messages are required. Consequently, the communication overhead of a process to deliver a message is approximately $(3t_n + 2) \cdot \frac{n}{2t_n+1} \cdot (n|M| + 3nh)$. However, since each response message encapsulates a broadcast message, the amortised communication overhead per message becomes $\frac{(3t_n+2)n(n|M|+3nh)}{(3t_n+2)(2t_n+1)}$, resulting in a complexity of $O(n|M| + nh)$ for $n = 3t_n + 1$. However, in the worst case, where every sender message is broadcasted by each process due to Algorithm 6, the communication complexity goes back to $O(n^2|M| + n^2h)$.

In assessing the computational performance of our protocol, it is noteworthy that, apart from the scheme proposed in [3], all other protocols rely on cryptographic tools, introducing additional computational overhead. For instance, the computational cost in [2] scales as $\tilde{O}(n|M|)$, where $\tilde{O}$ hides poly-logarithmic terms to simplify the complexity expression, and $\tilde{O}(|M|)$ denotes the computations required by various tools, such as hashing, coding, and threshold signature operations. We use this symbol $\tilde{O}(|M|)$ to denote the computation cost of operations in lines 7–10 of the Algorithm 5.

The primary computational bottleneck of our protocol resides in Algorithm 5. Specifically, line 6 of this algorithm requires the inspection of each entry in the $votes_i$ dictionary. Note that a sender message to be delivered typically requires approximately $3t_n+2$ response messages. Assuming the sender transmits c messages per second, the number of entries in $votes_i$ can be approximated as $c \cdot \frac{n}{2t_n+1} \cdot (3t_n + 2)$. Using the $\tilde{O}(|M|)$ symbol, the overall computational complexity of our protocol can then be expressed as $\tilde{O}(cn|M|)$. We believe that this computational complexity highlights the cost of designing protocols based on DAGs, suggesting that in order to achieve higher system performance, it is necessary to enhance the computational capabilities of processes.

5 Conclusion

We have presented an asynchronous reliable broadcast protocol based on DAGs. In this protocol, the sender process continuously broadcasts messages, while other processes relay these messages through the sending of response messages that encode reference relationships of response messages. This approach not only relays sender messages but also emulates the fundamental procedures of the Bracha protocol using the reference relationships, resulting in a provably secure reliable broadcast protocol while reducing the amortised communication overhead. Looking ahead, our future endeavors will aim to strengthen experimental verification and integrate the reliable broadcast protocol with existing DAG consensus, thereby achieving a more efficient DAG consensus protocol.

Acknowledgement. This work is supported by the National Key R&D Program of China under Grant No. 2022YFB2701500 and Guangdong Provincial Key Laboratory of Information Security Technology (No. 2023B1212060026).

References

1. Dashing and star: byzantine fault tolerance using weak certificates. In: Proceedings of the 2024 ACM SIGOPS European Conference on Computer Systems, pp. 1–22. EuroSys'24, ACM (2024). https://eprint.iacr.org/2022/625
2. Alhaddad, N., et al.: Balanced byzantine reliable broadcast with near-optimal communication and improved computation. In: Proceedings of the 2022 ACM Symposium on Principles of Distributed Computing, pp. 399–417. PODC'22, Association for Computing Machinery, New York, NY, USA (2022). https://doi.org/10.1145/3519270.3538475
3. Bracha, G.: Asynchronous byzantine agreement protocols. Inf. Comput. **75**(2), 130–143 (1987). https://doi.org/10.1016/0890-5401(87)90054-X

4. Brasser, F., Müller, U., Dmitrienko, A., Kostiainen, K., Capkun, S., Sadeghi, A.R.: Software grand exposure: sgx cache attacks are practical. In: Proceedings of the 11th USENIX Conference on Offensive Technologies, p. 11. WOOT'17, USENIX Association, USA (2017)
5. Cachin, C., Tessaro, S.: Asynchronous verifiable information dispersal. In: 24th IEEE Symposium on Reliable Distributed Systems (SRDS'05), pp. 191–201. IEEE (2005). https://doi.org/10.1109/RELDIS.2005.9
6. Castro, M., Liskov, B.: Practical byzantine fault tolerance. In: Proceedings of the Third Symposium on Operating Systems Design and Implementation, pp. 173–186. OSDI'99, USENIX Association, USA (1999)
7. Chen, Z., Fan, L., Liu, S., Vukolić, M., Wang, X., Zhang, J.: Bridging the gap of timing assumptions in byzantine consensus. In: Proceedings of the 24th International Middleware Conference, pp. 178–191. Middleware'23, Association for Computing Machinery, New York, NY, USA (2023). https://doi.org/10.1145/3590140.3629114
8. Dai, X., Zhang, Z., Xiao, J., Yue, J., Xie, X., Jin, H.: Gradeddag: an asynchronous dag-based bft consensus with lower latency. In: 2023 42nd International Symposium on Reliable Distributed Systems (SRDS), pp. 107–117 (2023). https://doi.org/10.1109/SRDS60354.2023.00020
9. Das, S., Xiang, Z., Ren, L.: Asynchronous data dissemination and its applications, pp. 2705–2721. CCS'21, Association for Computing Machinery, New York, NY, USA (2021). https://doi.org/10.1145/3460120.3484808
10. Guo, B., Lu, Z., Tang, Q., Xu, J., Zhang, Z.: Dumbo: faster asynchronous bft protocols. In: Proceedings of the 2020 ACM SIGSAC Conference on Computer and Communications Security, pp. 803–818. CCS'20, Association for Computing Machinery, New York, NY, USA (2020). https://doi.org/10.1145/3372297.3417262
11. Hendricks, J., Ganger, G.R., Reiter, M.K.: Verifying distributed erasure-coded data. In: Proceedings of the Twenty-Sixth Annual ACM Symposium on Principles of Distributed Computing, pp. 139–146. PODC'07, Association for Computing Machinery, New York, NY, USA (2007). https://doi.org/10.1145/1281100.1281122
12. Keidar, I., Kokoris-Kogias, E., Naor, O., Spiegelman, A.: All you need is dag. In: Proceedings of the 2021 ACM Symposium on Principles of Distributed Computing, pp. 165–175. PODC'21, Association for Computing Machinery, New York, NY, USA (2021). https://doi.org/10.1145/3465084.3467905
13. Miller, A., Xia, Y., Croman, K., Shi, E., Song, D.: The honey badger of bft protocols. In: Proceedings of the 2016 ACM SIGSAC Conference on Computer and Communications Security, pp. 31–42. CCS'16, Association for Computing Machinery, New York, NY, USA (2016). https://doi.org/10.1145/2976749.2978399
14. Nayak, K., Ren, L., Shi, E., Vaidya, N.H., Xiang, Z.: Improved extension protocols for byzantine broadcast and agreement. In: Attiya, H. (ed.) 34th International Symposium on Distributed Computing (DISC 2020). Leibniz International Proceedings in Informatics (LIPIcs), vol. 179, pp. 28:1–28:17. Schloss Dagstuhl – Leibniz-Zentrum für Informatik, Dagstuhl, Germany (2020). https://drops-dev.dagstuhl.de/entities/document/10.4230/LIPIcs.DISC.2020.28
15. Zhang, X., et al.: Interface-based side channel in tee-assisted networked services. IEEE/ACM Trans. Netw. **32**(1), 613–626 (2024). https://doi.org/10.1109/TNET.2023.3294019
16. Zhao, L., Decouchant, J., Liu, J., Lu, Q., Yu, J.: Trusted hardware-assisted leaderless byzantine fault tolerance consensus. IEEE Trans. Dependable Secure Comput. **Early Access**, 1–12 (2024). https://doi.org/10.1109/TDSC.2024.3357521

PDTS: Practical Data Trading Scheme in Distributed Environments

Kun Wang[1], Qianhong Wu[1(✉)], Tianxu Han[1], Sipeng Xie[1], Qin Wang[2], Yingmiao Zhang[1], Bo Qin[3], and Xiaopeng Dai[1]

[1] School of Cyber Science and Technology, Beihang University, Beijing, China
{kun_wang,qianhong.wu,hantianxu,sipengxie, zy2339126,xiaopeng.dai}@buaa.edu.cn

[2] School of Computer Science and Engineering, UNSW, Sydney, Australia

[3] School of Information, Renmin University of China, Beijing, China
bo.qin@ruc.edu.cn

Abstract. Blockchain solves the problem of loss of data control and the single point of failure faced by centralized content platforms. Despite the huge potential, existing blockchain-based data trading solutions still suffer from major issues, such as data privacy breaches, difficulty in ensuring fairness among participants, significant resource consumption due to interaction with the chain, and computational consumption during the file preprocessing phase.

To fill the gap, this paper introduces PDTS (short for *practical data trading scheme*), an innovative enhancement of the fairswap protocol that utilizes state channels and Proof of Delivery. Our scheme is specifically designed to facilitate efficient data trading between entities dealing with large data volumes. We provide a formal security analysis and developed a prototype to rigorously evaluate the effectiveness of PDTS. Experimental results demonstrate that our scheme not only significantly reduces resource consumption but also maintains high system availability, thereby offering a robust solution that addresses the key drawbacks of current blockchain-based data trading frameworks and significantly enhances trading efficiency and security.

Keywords: Blockchain · Data trading · Fair exchange · State channel

1 Introduction

Many emerging technologies have become inextricably linked to our lives in the age of digitalisation [5] and Web3 [21], such as the mobile Internet, social networks, intelligent systems based on the Internet of Things, and various content distribution platforms. At the same time, more and more data is being generated and collected [22]. According to World Economic Forum statistics [6], from 2018 to 2025, data grew from 35 to 175 Zettabytes, with a growth rate of 500%. These data are held by various entities, thus forming data silos, which seriously impede the flow of data [23]. With data becoming an increasingly valued asset,

J. K. Liu et al. (Eds.): ProvSec 2024, LNCS 14904, pp. 124–142, 2025.
https://doi.org/10.1007/978-981-96-0957-4_7

people gradually realize the importance of data trading. The emergence of the data trading market makes it possible.

Traditionally, data trading is facilitated through centralized data exchanges where the *data seller* (DS) uploads data and sets prices, while the *data buyer* (DB) pays the exchange to access it. Upon receiving payment, the exchange delivers the data to DB and remits payment to DS. These exchanges handle various data formats such as images (e.g., ShutterStock, iStockphoto), videos (e.g., Netflix, HBO, Apple TV, Youtube), and texts (e.g., Apple Books, Kindle).

Data exchanges typically rely on centralized yet *credible* platforms, categorized into two main types. The first type involves well-funded entities like government agencies or large corporations that own extensive data resources and operate platforms such as AWS Data Exchange. The second type includes platforms created by third parties who facilitate data exchanges between Data Sellers (DS) and Data Buyers (DB). Both types suffer from issues such as single points of failure, high resource consumption, data privacy breaches, and challenges in ensuring fairness. These inherent problems in data trading are difficult to address without involving a third party [2].

Blockchain [20] offers a promising solution to the challenges of data trading and sharing due to its decentralized, transparent, immutable, and traceable nature [15]. As a system maintained collectively by the entire network and not owned by any single entity, blockchain minimizes risks like single points of failure, enhancing system availability. Trading on the blockchain are facilitated through smart contracts, which automatically execute trading conditions and enforce obligations. The immutable nature of smart contracts [15] ensures that penalties agreed upon are enforced, making it difficult for parties such as DB to refuse payment or DS to withhold data, thereby lending credibility to the data trading process.

While blockchain offers solutions to issues in centralized data trading platforms, achieving a fully blockchain-based data trading system presents several challenges. Existing methods fall into three categories: *zero-knowledge proof*-based data trading [10], *fair exchange*-based data trading [7], and *other* types of data trading [9,12,13]. Zero-knowledge proof-based trading faces inefficiency due to trusted setups and the nature of the proofs, high costs, and potential unfairness if dishonest participants cause honest ones to incur unnecessary expenses. Fair exchange-based methods struggle with high resource consumption due to on-chain dispute arbitration. Other trading methods, like those using sampling and authentication techniques, often suffer from poor availability due to algorithmic overheads.

Contribution. We aim to mitigate the above problems by proposing a new data trading scheme called PDTS. Our scheme is practical due to its high efficiency for several reasons: (i) constructions run with the help of a state channel network, reducing resource consumption without affecting the operation of the native chain, thus improving the availability; (ii) we utilize the improved fair exchange to solve the problem of excessive computational overhead in zero-knowledge proof-based approaches; (iii) our scheme encrypts the data using lightweight cryptography methods to protect data privacy.

Based on such designs, PDTS is expected to be used in future data trading scenarios, such as content acquisition and data transfer between IoT devices. In short, the main contributions of this paper are as follows:

- We introduce PDTS, a fair data trading scheme tailored for distributed environments. PDTS addresses challenges including privacy concerns, high resource consumption, and fairness assurance difficulties. An improved file encoding algorithm allows PDTS to support proof of delivery.
- We provide a concrete construction leveraging state channel. Our construction performs reduced resource consumption and increased availability in contrast to existing solutions. Additionally, it demonstrates high scalability and can be adaptable to any blockchain that supports smart contracts (i.e., EVM-compatible).
- We further implement a prototype and conduct experiments assessing computational costs and token consumption during PDTS interactions on the blockchain. We measure the time required to encode a file. The results affirm the scheme's feasibility and its ability to provide adequate security.

Paper Organization. Section 2 provides the related work. Sec.3 presents preliminaries. Section 4 describes the system model and design object. Section 5 describes our PDTS solution. Section 6 & Sect. 7 analyze security and performance, respectively. Section 8 presents conclusions.

2 Related Work

The unfairness issue in data trading has been studied for decades. With blockchain technologies, fair data trading can be conducted without relying on trusted third parties (TTPs). Blockchain provides a public ledger with persistent evidence for each participant. Any malicious activity can later be traced for claims. Researchers have devoted many efforts [14,16,19,24] to achieve better decentralization. We present two mainstream technical routes.

FairSwap Approach. Fairswap [7] employs a Proof-of-Misbehavior (PoM) to establish a fair swap protocol on the blockchain emphasizing fairness. The protocol assumes that the data DS provided is correct until DB proves otherwise through proof submitted to the blockchain. Fairswap is designed for trading data represented as a binary string, such as purchasing digital files like films or music online. A crucial prerequisite for the traded data is that its hash value serves as a unique identifier. In the illustrated example, the Merkle hash of the file functions as this identifier, known to both parties at the protocol's outset. OptiSwap [8] extends FairSwap by mitigating trading costs and preventing honest parties from incurring high fees due to malicious intervention. Although the data preprocessing overheads for claim or refund agreements are generally minimal, additional measures are necessary to address potential disputes introduced by attackers during the process.

Blockchain as TTP. Another category is blockchain as a TTP solution. Huang et al. [12] implemented fair signing of electronic contracts involving three parties based on blockchain. They used a blockchain system and verifiable cryptographic signatures to ensure the fairness of the process, with dishonest participants being monetarily penalized. Guo et al. [11] implemented a multiparty fair exchange protocol based on Bitcoin. S Janin et al. [13] implemented a two and multiparty scenario under which documents are purchased in a fair exchange protocol. In their protocol, the dishonest party is financially penalized. The current multi-party fair data exchange does not guarantee atomic fairness and does not reduce both on-chain and off-chain overheads.

Table 1. The comparison of PDTS with state-of-the-art schemes.

Scheme	Without TTP	Optimistic Proof	Public Verifiable	Succinct	Proof of Delivery	Scalable
[13]	✓	✗	✗	✗	✗	✗
[4]	✗	✗	✓	✗	✗	✗
[17]	✓	✗	✓	✗	✓	✗
[7]	✓	✓	✓	✓	✗	✗
[14]	✓	✗	✓	✗	✓	✓
[25]	✓	✓	✓	✗	✓	✓
PDTS	✓	✓	✓	✓	✓	State Channel

Zero-Knowledge Proof (ZKP) Approach. The zero-knowledge proof protocol enhances blockchain-based fair data exchanges by ensuring atomic fairness between DB and DS without requiring their interaction, making it suitable for validating proofs based on NP problems to multiple parties without added costs. Introduced by G. Maxwell [10], the Zero-Knowledge Contingent Payment (ZKCP) scheme on the Bitcoin network employs zk-SNARKs for data availability validation. M. Campanelli [4] et al. later developed the Zero-Knowledge Continuous Service Payment protocol (ZKCSP) for fair trading in outsourced data storage, based on ZKCP. However, zk-SNARKs require a trusted setup, posing a security vulnerability. To overcome this, transparent zero-knowledge proof (ZKP) protocols [1,26] like those proposed in recent studies offer security without a trusted setup and are not yet applied in multiparty data exchanges. ZKCPlus [17] introduces a Commit-and-Prove Non-interactive zero-knowledge (CP-NIZK) argument that is significantly more efficient than zkSNARKs, with proofs and verifications under one second, enhancing practical applicability.

Table 1 shows the comparison of our proposed PDTS with some state-of-the-art schemes. Our analysis shows that existing schemes are unable to achieve programmatic utility while guaranteeing data delivery. The most notable gaps are that current schemes either incur high costs due to interaction with chains or consume limited computational resources in processing files. To address these two issues, this paper improves the data preprocessing phase and the dispute arbitration phase. To guarantee both parties, we add interactions in the beginning phase of the scheme to ensure that the user is indeed subjected to the target data. To make the proposed scheme more practical, we deploy the protocol in a Layer 2 network.

3 Preliminaries

FairSwap. We summarize FairSwap [7], which aims to ensure the fair exchange of digital goods. Initially, the seller starts by sending an encrypted message containing the good x to the buyer. This message includes the encryption z of the witness evaluation $\phi(x)$ under key k. Upon receiving and confirming this message, the buyer sends payment of p coins to the trading contract, which then secures both the payment and a concise commitment to z and ϕ.

Subsequently, the seller reveals the key through the contract, enabling the buyer to decrypt the witness. The funds are eventually transferred to the seller if the witness proves accurate. However, if the buyer receives a witness that fails to satisfy the agreed-upon predicate (i.e., $\phi(x) \neq 1$), triggering a divergence or pessimistic case, the buyer can submit a *proof of misbehavior* (PoM) to the contract. Despite its compact size relative to the witnesses and the predicate, this proof convincingly demonstrates that the received witness $x = Dec(k, z)$ does not align with the predicate.

Upon successful proof submission to the judge contract, the buyer regains possession of the coins. Notably, the protocol safeguards against theft or locking of funds prevents fraudulent trading (i.e., the seller getting paid for an incorrect proof), and empowers the buyer to contest a valid proof. The inclusion of a minimal PoM, coupled with all data storage within the contract, contributes to cost reduction in the overall protocol.

State Channel. State channels [18] enable the transfer of states between participants, which can involve various applications like voting or auctions. These channels, often built on multi-signatures and time-lock instructions, allow participants to sign contracts and lock funds for transfers, utilizing smart contracts. The state is exchanged off-chain, enhancing speed by avoiding on-chain delays. After trading, the final state is submitted to the main chain via a contract. State channels are especially beneficial for frequent state exchanges, significantly accelerating blockchain transaction speeds.

Lifecycle: The typical lifecycle of a state channel includes three phases: establishment, execution, and termination. Initially, participants lock funds or assets in a smart contract on the main chain, setting the channel's capacity. They then wait for this transaction to be confirmed. These locked funds are restricted for use exclusively within the channel. During execution, participants exchange states and reallocate funds based on the most recently agreed state. Each new state, once validated by participants, is shared and recorded in sequence. Finally, participants submit the channel's final state to the smart contract, which verifies the signatures to close the channel.

State Replacement: Trading in a state channel involves replacing old states with new ones, ideally occurring just once for trading finality. However, to address disputes from disagreements over new states, four primary techniques have been identified [9]: *replace-by-incentive* (RbI), *replace-by-timielock* (RbT), *replace-by-revocation* (RbR), and *replace-by-version* (RbV).

4 System Model and Design Object

4.1 System Model

Our PDTS scheme consists of four types of entities (cf. Fig. 1) as below.

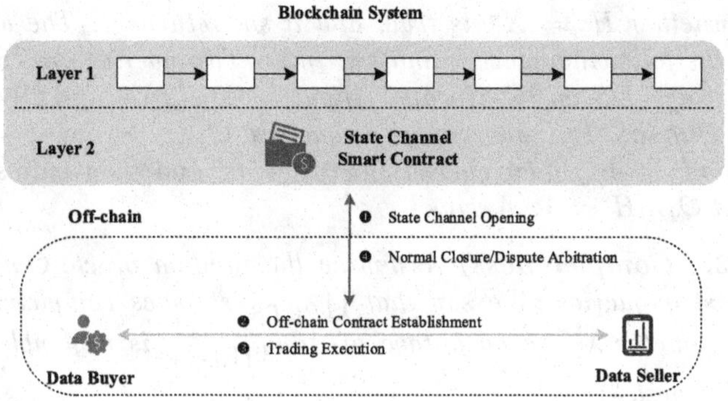

Fig. 1. System model

- *Data seller* (DS): DS owns valuable data and seeks to profit from trading this data.
- *Data buyer* (DB): DB is an individual desiring access to data and is prepared to pay tokens for it.
- *Smart contract*: A Turing-complete smart contract is in place to support the operation of the state channel.
- *Blockchain*: Diverging from conventional centralized data trading solutions, PDTS facilitates data trading through a blockchain that supports Turing-complete smart contracts.

This trading scenario is typically employed when a single entity possesses the target data and the data volume is substantial. The scheme leverages a layer-two network and an improved Fairswap to implement the data trading function. This approach reduces trading costs while ensuring fairness for both parties.

4.2 Design Object

To enable data trading in a distributed environment, PDTS needs to satisfy the following security model and other properties.

Security Model

Definition 1. *(**Completeness Game.**) For a polynomial-time adversary $\mathcal{A}$, we define the completeness game $\boldsymbol{Exp}^{Complete}_{\mathcal{A},\prod_{PDTS}}(\lambda)$ with respect to the $\prod_{PDTS}$ scheme and Completeness property. The completeness game $\boldsymbol{Exp}^{Complete}_{\mathcal{A},\prod_{PDTS}}(\lambda)$ consists of two phases: the setup phase and the challenge phase.*
Setup Phase. *$\mathcal{O}_{DB}$ is a random oracle and has an internal variable X^*. When receiving a query with X as input, $X^* \leftarrow X$ is executed. Then DB asks $\mathcal{O}_{SC} = (id = DB, op = \text{“query”}, input = \text{“}X^*\text{”})$. DB receives the output of $\mathcal{O}_{SC}$ as X, then uses X as input to query $\mathcal{O}_H$, receives the output of $\mathcal{O}_H$, recorded as H_x, DB verifies whether $H_x \stackrel{?}{=} X^*$ is true, and if so, returns 1. The adversary $\mathcal{A}$ can perform the following query at most q times. Two queries are executed each time, $\mathcal{O}_{SC} = (id = DS, op = \text{“Storage”}, input = \text{“}\mathcal{O}_H(y_i)\text{”})$ and $\mathcal{O}_{DB}(y_i)$.*
Challenge Phase. *The adversary $\mathcal{A}$ queries $\mathcal{O}_{SC} = (id = DS, op = \text{“Storage”}, input = h^*$, then queries $\mathcal{O}_H(\overline{y}) = \overline{h}$, and then quires $\mathcal{O}_{DB}(h^*)$. If $h^* \neq \overline{h}$, but $\mathcal{O}_{DB}H^* = 1$, $\mathcal{A}$ wins.*

Definition 2. *(**Completeness**) Assuming the random oracle $\mathcal{O}_{SC}, \mathcal{O}_{DB}, \mathcal{O}_H$ accept at most q queries. We say that $\prod_{PDTS}$ satisfies completeness, if for a security parameter λ, the advantage of $Adv^{Complete}_{\mathcal{A},\prod_{PDTS}}$ is negligible, satisfying $Adv^{Complete}_{\mathcal{A},\prod_{PDTS}} < negl(\lambda)$.*

Definition 3. *(**Fairness**) At the end of the protocol, either DB receives valid data, DS obtains payment equal to the worth of its trading data, or neither DB nor DS gets anything.*

Other Properties

- *Data confidentiality*: During the trading process, data should be transmitted in ciphertext or over a secure channel that any entity cannot access without a private key or session key.
- *Publicly verifiable*: Unlike traditional centralized data trading solutions, PDTS should achieve public verifiability, making the solution process transparent.
- *Incentive compatibility*: PDTS should ensure that entities that correctly execute data trading protocols are rewarded with data or tokens, and entities that incorrectly implement protocols are penalized. The system should safeguard the rights and interests of participants through reasonable reward and punishment mechanisms and verifiable data trading protocols.

5 PDTS Detailed Scheme

General Assumption. Our scheme is based on an existing distributed storage network in which nodes operate without incentives, and data trading originates from spontaneous forwarding between nodes. Moreover, we assume that the addressing and data characteristics are determined before the data trading.

Before executing a data trading, DB needs to determine the relevant information of the DS. Taking IPFS [3] as an example, the user addresses the data through the data feature Cid to find the relevant information about the target data. DS first applies symmetric encryption to the data to solve data privacy leakage in data trading. To preprocess the data, this paper improves the Encoding method in FairSwap [7].

5.1 File Pre-processing

In the file preprocessing phase, our idea of processing files is derived from FairSwap [7], but we have made some improvements. DS needs to additionally compute the hash value of the overall hash value of the ciphertext and the hash value of the hash value of the ciphertext after a simple modification. In this paper, the operation for the modified ciphertext value is to add a bit to the end of the original ciphertext data, and the bit is 1, represented by +1 in this paper. Take ciphertext C, for example. The modified ciphertext C' is $C + 1$. DS needs to calculate $H(C)$ and $H(H(C')) = H(H(C + 1))$ in the preprocessing phase. In addition, calculating the hash value of the tree's leaf nodes is also +1 after the ciphertext. Combined with the data encoding in FairSwap, we call this overall new encoding algorithm improved encoding, as shown in Algorithm 1. The algorithm gives the construction process from C to C' and the ciphertext tree, but not the hash operation for C and the hash operation for C'.

Algorithm 1. Improved encoding algorithm

Require: Plain file chunks $P[\cdot]$, symmetric key k
Ensure: Encrypted file chunks $C[\cdot]$, modified encrypted file chunks $C'[\cdot]$, merkel commitment c_m, c'_m

$PlainTree[\cdot] \leftarrow Merkel(P).Flatten()$
for $i = 0$; $i < P.Length$; $i = i + 1$ **do**
  $C[i] \leftarrow Encrypt(P[i], key, i)$
  $C'[i] \leftarrow C[i] + 1$ \\ Calculate the value of the modified ciphertext.
  $CipherLeaf[i] \leftarrow Hash(C[i])$
  $CipherLeaf'[i] \leftarrow Hash(C'[i])$
end for\\ Generate ciphertext Merkle tree.
for $i = 0; i < PlainTree.Length; i = i + 1$ **do**
  $CipherLeaf[i + P.Length]$
  $\leftarrow Encrypt(PlainTree[i], key, i + P.Length)$
  $CipherLeaf'[i + P.Length] =$
  $CipherLeaf[i + P.Length] + 1$
end for\\ Generate the modified ciphertext Merkle tree.
$c_m \leftarrow Merkel(CipherLeaf).Root$
$c'_m \leftarrow Merkel(CipherLeaf').Root$ \\ Calculate the root hash of the modified Merkle tree.
return $C[\cdot], C'[\cdot], c_m, c'_m$

5.2 State Channel Opening

The purpose of this phase is to open the state channel. DS and DB will initiate the state channel smart contract. They each initiate a transaction into the contract to transfer enough tokens as a $Value_{Deposit}$ to prepare the protocol for execution. The amount invested by both parties must be greater than or equal to twice the total value required to execute the one-to-one trading protocol for subsequent use in arbitration against malicious actors.

5.3 Contract Establishment

This phase aims to negotiate and establish the protocol for the off-chain interaction, parameters and corresponding definitions are given in Table 3.

The operation of this phase is to carry out off-chain protocol negotiation and can be divided into two steps: *price negotiation* and *trading protocol negotiation.* The detailed process of the two protocols is given below.

- *Negotiation of data purchase price and time.* The operation of this stage can be divided into the negotiation on the price of data and the negotiation on the time of data delivery. The specific flow is as follows: DB first asks DS for the data price, and DS sends the price and the signature for the request. After that, DB asks DS for the data delivery time, and DS sends the data delivery time and the signature for the request, as shown in Fig. 2.
- *Trading protocol negotiation.* After determining the price and delivery time, DB requests DS for the data trading contract. DS sends the message that it has received the request and prepares to draft the data trading contract. DS sends the prepared data trading contract to DB, and DB sends the signed and signature information to DS, as detailed in Fig. 3.

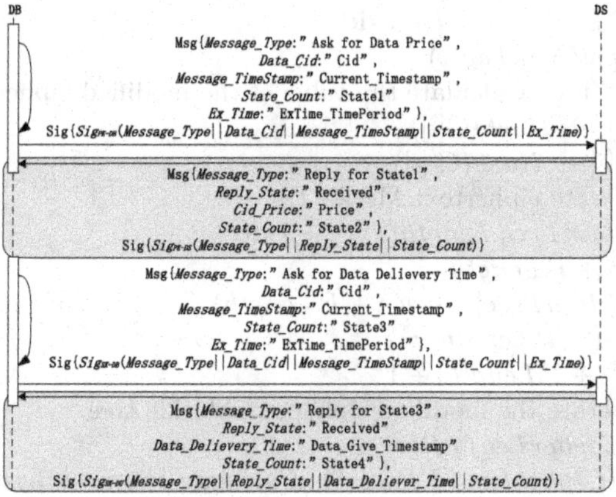

Fig. 2. Data trading price and delivery time negotiations

5.4 Trading Execution

An overview diagram of off-chain protocol execution is given herein, as shown in Fig. 4. For ease of understanding, Fig. 5 is used herein to explain Fig. 4. Figure 5 illustrates the key steps of the off-chain data trading protocol, divided into four steps. In *Step-(1)*, DS sends the Hash value of the ciphertext C and the modified ciphertext $C+1$ message processed by two Hash functions to DB. The purpose of this step is to be able to determine whether the DB has received the ciphertext message. *Step-(2)*, DS sends the ciphertext message to DB. The ciphertext is the value of plaintext M encrypted with symmetric key K. In *Step-(3)*, DB gets the

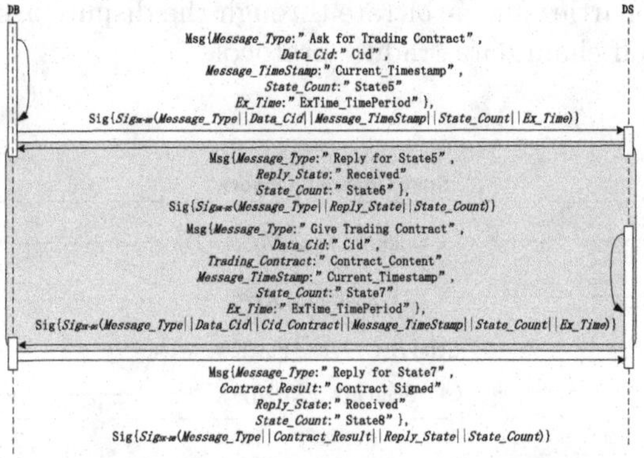

Fig. 3. Data trading protocol negotiation

Fig. 4. Details of the off-chain data trading protocol

data and sends the modified ciphertext message processed by the Hash function and the file purchase token. This step can be used to prove that DB received the data. *Step-(4)*, DS encrypts the data encryption key K through DB's secret key and sends the ciphertext of the key K to DB.

5.5 Completion

There are two ways of completing this stage: *normal closure* and *dispute arbitration*. Normal closure means that the off-chain data trading is under the protocol, and the entities have agreed on the final state. The second situation is that one entity has not executed the off-chain data trading under the existing protocol. In this case, both parties may arbitrate through the dispute arbitration method stipulated in the off-chain data trading protocol.

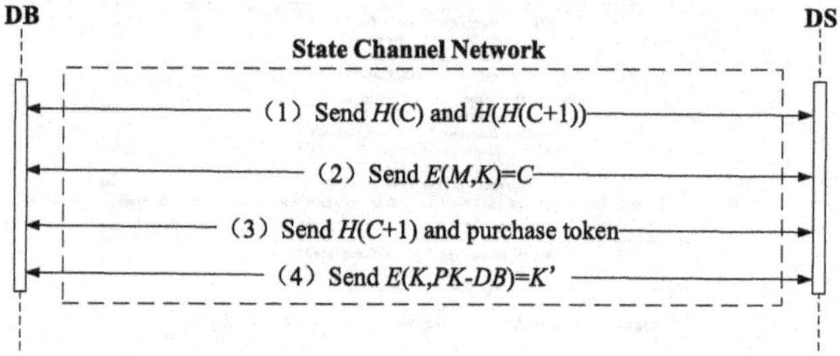

Fig. 5. Overview of the off-chain data trading protocol

- *Normal closure.* If no dispute arises, both parties proceed to the final state after DB acquires data from DS, submitting it to the on-chain state channel smart contract for settlement. This final state, the 14th state shown in Fig 4, follows the pre-negotiated protocol. The smart contract then executes fund settlements based on off-chain data. In the absence of disputes, the contract performs a normal settlement where DS and DB settle accounts with DB's final amount calculated as $Value_{Deposit}$ - $Value_D$ and DS's as $Value_{Deposit}$ + $Value_D$. If a dispute occurs, it is addressed by dispute arbitration module.
- *Dispute arbitration.* Dispute arbitration is divided into two aspects: dispute arbitration for data and process, corresponding to the two situations:
  - *DS does not send the data encryption key after DB sends feedback on receipt of data.* In our scheme, protocol signing information is submitted to the blockchain, and data feedback is used for dispute arbitration. If DB raises a dispute, the on-chain state channel smart contract reviews the data trading contract and feedback. If DS fails to provide the required information within the specified time, the contract conducts dispute arbitration, penalizing DS by transferring a penalty of $Value_D$ to DB for breaking the protocol.

- *DS sends incorrect data encryption key or data.* In our scheme, if key or data mismatches occur, DB submits a fraud-proof using the improved encoding algorithm to the state channel smart contract. If DS is found to have violated the agreement, DS is penalized by deducting tokens equal to $Value_D$ and transferring them to DB. This form of arbitration deters malicious behavior by imposing significant costs on the malicious party, ensuring that tokens equivalent to $Value_D$ are deducted from the violator and awarded to the aggrieved party. This method effectively prevents malicious actions and guarantees correct execution of the scheme through robust arbitration.

Incentive Mechanism. The incentives specify that the number of tokens deposited to the state channel contract is twice the number required to execute the one-to-one data trading protocol. Parties that correctly execute off-chain agreements transfer tokens according to pre-agreed rules. In dispute arbitration, the state channel smart contract will arbitrate against the party at fault by deducting tokens from the $Value_{\mathbf{Deposit}}$ in the same amount as $Value_D$. Under normal circumstances, the tokens required to purchase data will be deducted from DB's deposit and transferred to DS.

6 Security Analysis

6.1 Formal Security

Completeness. Completeness means data trading can be executed successfully if both parties are honest and trustworthy. Each has a strong incentive to complete the data trading, and DB can verify that the information provided by DS is consistent with its description. At the end of the protocol, DS is rewarded with a pre-agreed amount of tokens and the DB obtains the target data.

Theorem 1 (Completeness). *The construction of scheme PDTS has the security property of completeness.*

Proof (Completeness). **Query Phase.** We use simulator $\mathcal{B}$ to simulate the interaction between the adversary $\mathcal{A}$ and $\mathcal{O}_H, \mathcal{O}_{SC}$ and $\mathcal{O}_{DB}$. The output distribution obtained by $\mathcal{A}$ between $\mathcal{O}_H, \mathcal{O}_{SC}$ and $\mathcal{O}_{DB}$ is statistically indistinguishable from the output obtained by $\mathcal{B}$. The above query can be executed at most q times.

Challenge Phase. The adversary $\mathcal{A}$ generates C, asks $\mathcal{O}_H$, and the simulator $\mathcal{B}$ returns x_1. The adversary quires $\mathcal{O}_{SC} = (id = DS, op = \text{“}storage\text{”}, input = \text{“}x_1\text{”})$. The adversary generates $C^* \neq C$ and asks $\mathcal{O}_{DB}(C^*)$. If the simulator $\mathcal{B}$ returns 1. The simulator $\mathcal{B}$ can construct $H(C^*) = H(C)$. This means that the adversary $\mathcal{A}$ wins the **Completeness Game** with a probability greater than or equal to negl(λ). The simulator $\mathcal{B}$ can construct a collision of C with probability a probability greater than or equal to negl(λ). This completes the proof. □

Fairness. DB fairness means that an honest DB will ensure the payment of the corresponding token reward (the value corresponding to the acquired data) only if the DS provides the correct data. DS fairness is that the honest DB will ensure the correct data acquisition if the DB pays the token reward. This two-way fairness ensures that the rights of both parties are reasonably safeguarded throughout the exchange process.

Theorem 2 (Fairness). *The construction of scheme PDTS in Chaps. 5.1 and 5.4 has the security property of fairness.*

Proof (Fairness). We systematically assess the fairness property for our constructions and each entity involved.

- DS fairness: DS fairness in our scheme ensures that DB accesses the plaintext of data D only after DS receives the agreed reward. Initially, DB only has the ciphertext of D and its hash value, which prevents DB from knowing the actual content until DS releases the encryption key. If DB maliciously disputes the authenticity of D', they would need to forge a Merkle proof linked to the data, a task requiring the detection of hash function collisions, not feasible in polynomial time. Therefore, the likelihood of DB successfully forging this proof is less than or equal to negl(λ), ensuring DS's fairness.
- DB fairness: If DS sends a commit $H(H(C+1))$, DB will continue to execute the protocol by freezing tokens as agreed. DB fairness is safeguarded as a malicious DS cannot send a false promise $H(H(C+1))'$ without making it possible for DB to generate valid proof of misbehavior that the contract would reject. For such a deception to succeed, DS would need to find an encoding C_fake that hashes to $H(H(C+1))$. However, the probability of finding such a C_fake is negligible (negl(λ)) since it would require breaking the hash function's collision resistance. Therefore, DB's fairness is assured, as any disputes can be efficiently arbitrated using proof of misbehavior. □

Theorem 3 (Fairness-FairSwap). *The construction of the scheme FairSwap [7] has the security property of fairness.*

Proof (Fairness-PDTS). Refer to FairSwap [7]. □

Theorem 4 (Fairness-PDTS). *Assuming Chaps. 5.1 and 5.4 are fairness, FairSwap [7] is fairness, then our proposed scheme PDTS is fairness.*

Proof (Fairness-PDTS). Our proposed scheme differs from FairSwap [7] in that we include a process to guarantee that the data is indeed delivered, which can be referred to as Proof of Delivery. Other parts of our scheme are almost the same as FairSwap. In addition, the stateful channel network we utilize not only does not change the trust assumptions of the blockchain but also increases the utility of the scheme by reducing the overhead. In summary, the fairness of the proposed scheme PDTS is proved. □

6.2 Other Properties

Data Confidentiality. Confidentiality ensures that only authorized entities with the correct keys can access data. Unauthorized individuals lacking these keys cannot view or manipulate the data. To protect privacy, data is encrypted using symmetric encryption before trading. Without the decryption key, the data content remains inaccessible. Additionally, to enhance security, the input for hashing includes the hash of the ciphertext plus a 1-bit, making it impossible to determine the ciphertext unless the hash function's collision resistance is compromised. This approach effectively safeguards data privacy.

Publicly Verifiable. Our solution significantly advances traditional methods by eliminating dependence on trusted third parties (TTP). It securely automates critical steps such as data delivery and dispute resolution through blockchain-stored information. We incorporate state channels to reduce trading costs and ensure public verifiability. In disputes, either party can efficiently resolve issues by submitting them to a designated smart contract on the blockchain, which triggers a rule-based judgment process, streamlining dispute resolution. Our designed arbitration mechanisms are lightweight, minimizing blockchain resource use, and enhancing system efficiency and availability.

Incentive Compatibility. Our proposed construction is designed to promote accurate protocol execution by incentivizing rational behavior among participants. In data trading, DS receives a reward for selling data, and DB pays tokens to obtain the data, encouraging adherence to the protocol. Additionally, our solution includes mechanisms to manage deviations from protocol execution. For instance, if a participant fails to submit the required data to the blockchain within the allotted time, they face a penalty equal to twice $Value_D$. This penalty acts as a strong deterrent, ensuring participants follow the protocol guidelines and supporting the proper execution of the data trading process.

7 Performance Analysis

We conducted a series of experiments, operating on a MacBook Pro with 32 GB 6400 Mpbs LPDDR5 RAM and an M1 Pro CPU. The Ethereum testnet adopted Truffle v5.7.3, Ganache, Solidity v0.8.17, and Goreli testnet.We build state channel smart contracts and file processor programs and use XOR encryption for file preprocessing. The file encoding uses our improved encoding algorithm for data slicing with different file block sizes. We also deployed the contract on an Ethereum testnet and performed token consumption during dispute arbitration.

Before the experimental analysis, we conducted a theoretical analysis (cf. Table 2). It can be seen that although our scheme has a slight increase in consumption during file preprocessing and decryption, it exchanges for the Proof of Delivery function. Compared with FairSwap [7], our scheme has better performance in dispute arbitration by leveraging the layer two network.

Table 2. Theoretical analysis.

	File preprocessing and Decryption	Dispute arbitration	Proof of Delivery
[7]	$\frac{\lvert\mathbf{X}\rvert}{n}(\mathcal{H}_{\mathcal{MHT}} + Enc_{XOR})$	$\frac{\lvert\mathbf{X}\rvert}{n}\mathcal{H}_{\mathcal{MHT}} + Layer_{one}$	✗
PDTS	$\frac{\lvert\mathbf{X}\rvert+n(bit)}{n}(\mathcal{H}_{\mathcal{MHT}} + Enc_{XOR})$	$\frac{\lvert\mathbf{X}\rvert+n(bit)}{n}\mathcal{H}_{\mathcal{MHT}} + Layer_{two}$	✓

File Preprocessing and Decryption. The purpose of file preprocessing is to construct the ciphertext of the data, which is convenient for smart contracts to handle dispute arbitration. The file size used for testing is 1 GB, and the preprocessing time of the data is tested based on different file block sizes. Figure 6a shows that different block sizes (256, 512, 1024, 2048, 4096, 8192, 16384, 32768, and 65536 Byte) correspond to different file preprocessing times in milliseconds. Similarly, we have tested for file decryption, and the data is the same as the file preprocessing, shown in Fig. 6b.

Dispute Arbitration. Dispute arbitration is tested in three dimensions: root node dispute arbitration, non-leaf node dispute arbitration, and leaf node dispute arbitration. Due to the large gap in gas consumption between arbitration for leaf nodes and the first two, this result is presented in two figures: Fig. 6c shows the case for root and non-leaf nodes, and Fig. 6d shows the case for leaf nodes. This paper uses different block sizes of node divisions (256, 512, 1024, 2048, 4096, 8192, 16384, 32768, and 65536 bytes) for testing. Horizontal coordinates are in Byte, and vertical coordinates are in Gas.

Comparison with FairSwap. In this paper, the proposed scheme is compared with FairSwap, and the proposed scheme is much less expensive than FairSwap due to the scaling of the blockchain using the layer two technique. The file size of the test is 1 GB, and the chunk size is 32 bytes. The ETH price at the time of the test was 1961.61 USD, and the gas price was 48 GWei. The results of the experiments are shown in the following figures, with the gas cost illustrated in Fig. 6e and the cost of fee illustrated in Fig. 6f. Experimental results show that the proposed scheme has similar gas consumption for contract deployment and dispute arbitration but a much smaller fee cost than FairSwap.

7.1 Application and Scalability of the Scheme

Application. The PDTS solution is principally employed for the conveyance of data in distributed systems. The solution's primary advantage lies in its utilization of state channels and Proof of Delivery, which serve to markedly diminish resource consumption and enhance system availability. The following section will present several real-world scenarios in which PDTS is employed.

1. Content acquisition: The process of acquiring content is facilitated by the utilization of the PDTS solution. The PDTS solution may be employed for the acquisition of voluminous data files, including video, audio, and images. By

employing stateful channel technology, PDTS is capable of reducing transaction costs while maintaining data privacy and transaction fairness.

2. Internet of Things (IoT): In the context of the IoT, data transfers between devices are characterized by high volumes and frequent occurrence. The use of stateful channel networking enables PDTS to address these data transfer requirements efficiently and securely.

Scalability. The scalability of PDTS is a further advantage, allowing it to be applied in a variety of contexts. The scalability of PDTS is indicative of its flexibility and adaptability in a range of application scenarios.

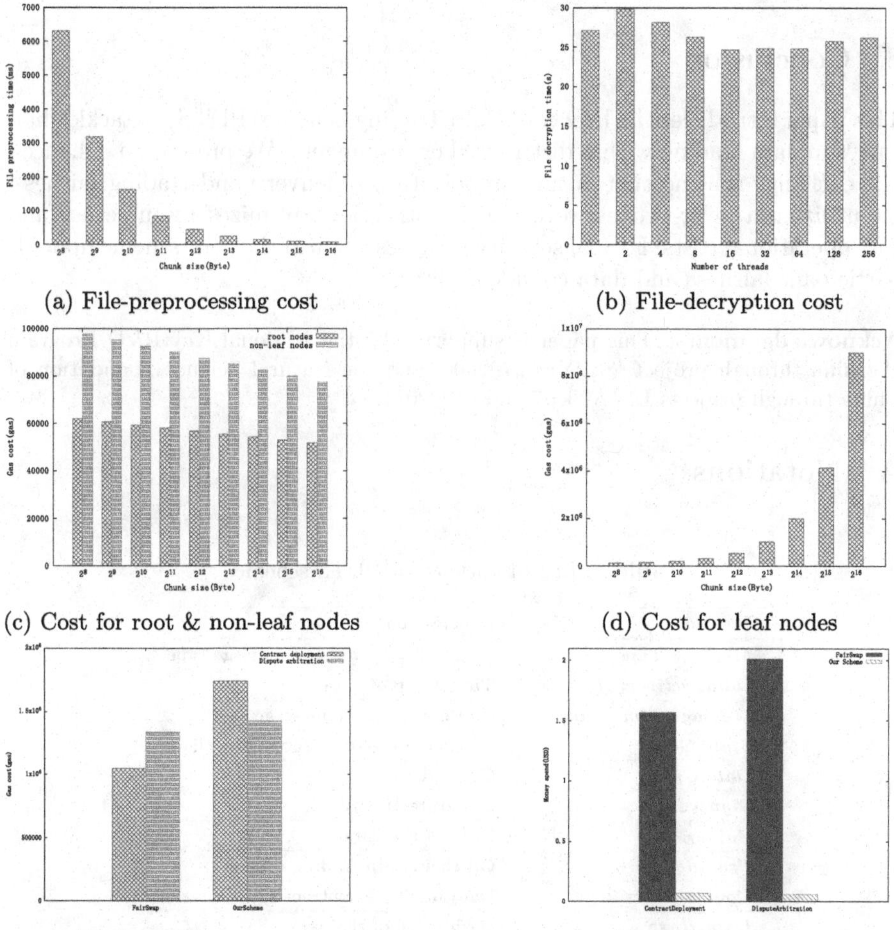

(a) File-preprocessing cost (b) File-decryption cost

(c) Cost for root & non-leaf nodes (d) Cost for leaf nodes

(e) Gas cost compare (f) Fee cost compare

Fig. 6. Performance analysis

1. The system is designed in a modular fashion. The PDTS employs a modular design that permits the individual upgrading and expansion of its constituent components. Regarding data encryption methods and state channel protocols, they can be modified and enhanced as required to align with the specific demands of different applications and advancements in technology.
2. The utilization of layer 2 networks is a key aspect of the system. PDTS operates on state channels, reducing dependence on the main chain while lowering transaction costs. This approach not only improves the scalability of the system but also enhances its performance under high load.
3. Flexible Dispute Arbitration Mechanism: PDTS is designed with a flexible dispute arbitration mechanism that can be adapted to different transaction scenarios and dispute types. This flexibility ensures that the system can maintain efficiency and fairness in a variety of complex situations.

8 Conclusion

This paper introduces the Practical Data Trading Scheme (PDTS) to tackle challenges in data trading within distributed environments. We present an enhanced fair exchange scheme that ensures proof of data delivery and trading fairness. By utilizing a layer-two network, our construction optimizes resource use and cuts operational costs. Formal security analyses confirm that our scheme upholds participant fairness and data confidentiality.

Acknowledgements. This paper is supported by the National Key R&D Program of China through project 2022YFB2702900, and the Natural Science Foundation of China through projects U21A20467 and 61932011.

A Notations

Table 3. List of notions for PDTS scheme.

Notation	Explanation
$Message\_Type$	Off-chain transmission message type
$Data\_Delivery\_Time$	Timestamp of data sent
$Message\_TimeStamp$	Timestamp of the message sent
$State\_Count$	Count of messages sent off the chain
$Data\_Cid$	Cid of data
$Sign_{sk-x}()$	Signature of entity X
$Value_D$	Price of the data
$Trading\_Contract$	Off-chain data trading contract
$Contract\_Result$	Data purchase contract signing result
$Data\_Hash$	Hash value of the data
$Reply\_State$	Feedback on the off-chain message
$Data\_Modification\_Hash$	Hash value of data after modification
$Data$	Data information
Ex_Time	Data transmission tolerance latency

B Future Work

Our solution currently overlooks scenarios where users face limited storage resources, often leading them to outsource storage for large files. This outsourcing necessitates interaction with third-party storage providers, raising significant access control challenges to manage data efficiently given the restricted storage capacity. Additionally, our scheme utilizes a layer-two network for data trading operations, yet the execution still relies on the network's storage capabilities. Theoretically, tasks like setting up contracts for off-chain data trading could be shifted to the off-chain, but this raises concerns about data availability. Addressing these challenges is crucial for practical implementation. Moreover, our system requires predefined roles for buyers and sellers, which restricts dynamic role interchangeability in trading. Future enhancements should aim to allow flexible two-way trading within the state channel to overcome the limitation.

References

1. Ames, S., Hazay, C., Ishai, Y., Venkitasubramaniam, M.: Ligero: lightweight sublinear arguments without a trusted setup. In: Proceedings of the ACM SIGSAC Conference on Computer and Communications Security (CCS), pp. 2087–2104 (2017)
2. Asokan, N., Schunter, M., Waidner, M.: Optimistic protocols for fair exchange. In: Proceedings of the ACM Conference on Computer and Communications Security (CCS), pp. 7–17 (1997)
3. Benet, J.: Ipfs-content addressed, versioned, p2p file system. arXiv preprint arXiv:1407.3561 (2014)
4. Campanelli, M., Gennaro, R., Goldfeder, S., Nizzardo, L.: Zero-knowledge contingent payments revisited: attacks and payments for services. In: Proceedings of the ACM SIGSAC Conference on Computer and Communications Security (CCS), pp. 229–243 (2017)
5. Deng, H., et al.: Achieving fine-grained data sharing for hierarchical organizations in clouds. IEEE Trans. Depend. Secure Comput. (TDSC) **20**(2), 1364–1377 (2022)
6. Dimitri, Z., Tomonori, Y., Tomoaki, N.: The world is drowning in data. why don't we trade it like on a stock exchange? (2022). https://www.weforum.org/agenda/2022/01/data-trading-stock-exchange/
7. Dziembowski, S., Eckey, L., Faust, S.: Fairswap: how to fairly exchange digital goods. In: Proceedings of the ACM SIGSAC Conference on Computer and Communications Security (CCS), CCS 2018, pp. 967-984. Association for Computing Machinery, New York (2018)
8. Eckey, L., Faust, S., Schlosser, B.: Optiswap: fast optimistic fair exchange. In: Proceedings of the ACM Asia Conference on Computer and Communications Security (CCS), pp. 543–557 (2020)
9. Gangwal, A., Gangavalli, H.R., Thirupathi, A.: A survey of layer-two blockchain protocols. J. Netw. Comput. Appl. **209**, 103539 (2023)
10. Gregory, M.: Zero knowledge contingent payment (2011). https://en.bitcoin.it/wiki/Zero_Knowledge_Contingent_Payment
11. Guo, L., Li, X., Gao, J.: Multi-party fair exchange protocol with smart contract on Bitcoin. Int. J. Netw. Secur. **21**(1), 71–82 (2019)

12. Huang, H., Li, K.-C., Chen, X.: A fair three-party contract singing protocol based on blockchain. In: Wen, S., Wu, W., Castiglione, A. (eds.) CSS 2017. LNCS, vol. 10581, pp. 72–85. Springer, Cham (2017). https://doi.org/10.1007/978-3-319-69471-9_6
13. Janin, S., Qin, K., Mamageishvili, A., Gervais, A.: Filebounty: fair data exchange. In: IEEE European Symposium on Security and Privacy Workshops (EuroSP-W), pp. 357–366. IEEE (2020)
14. Jiang, E., et al.: Bdts: blockchain-based data trading system. In: International Conference on Information and Communications Security (ICICS), pp. 645–664. Springer, Heidelberg (2023). https://doi.org/10.1007/978-981-99-7356-9_38
15. Li, R., Wang, Q., Wang, Q., Galindo, D.: How do smart contracts benefit security protocols? arXiv preprint arXiv:2202.08699 (2022)
16. Li, Y.N., Feng, X., Xie, J., Feng, H., Guan, Z., Wu, Q.: A decentralized and secure blockchain platform for open fair data trading. Concurr. Comput. Pract. Exp. **32**(7), e5578 (2020)
17. Li, Y., et al.: Zkcplus: optimized fair-exchange protocol supporting practical and flexible data exchange. In: Proceedings of the ACM SIGSAC Conference on Computer and Communications Security (CCS), pp. 3002–3021 (2021)
18. Miller, A., Bentov, I., Bakshi, S., Kumaresan, R., McCorry, P.: Sprites and state channels: payment networks that go faster than lightning. In: Goldberg, I., Moore, T. (eds.) FC 2019. LNCS, vol. 11598, pp. 508–526. Springer, Cham (2019). https://doi.org/10.1007/978-3-030-32101-7_30
19. Nguyen, L.D., Hoang, J., et al.: Bdsp: a fair blockchain-enabled framework for privacy-enhanced enterprise data sharing. In: IEEE International Conference on Blockchain and Cryptocurrency (ICBC), pp. 1–9. IEEE (2023)
20. Nguyen, L.T., Nguyen, L.D., Hoang, T., Bandara, D., et al.: Blockchain-empowered trustworthy data sharing: fundamentals, applications, and challenges. arXiv preprint arXiv:2303.06546 (2023)
21. Wang, Q., Li, R., Wang, Q., Chen, S., Ryan, M., Hardjono, T.: Exploring web3 from the view of blockchain. arXiv preprint arXiv:2206.08821 (2022)
22. Wang, Y., Ding, Y., Wu, Q., Wei, Y., Qin, B., Wang, H.: Privacy-preserving cloud-based road condition monitoring with source authentication in vanets. IEEE Trans. Inf. Forensics Secur. (TIFS) **14**(7), 1779–1790 (2018)
23. Wang, Y., et al.: Secure server-aided data sharing clique with attestation. Inf. Sci. **522**, 80–98 (2020)
24. Wu, Q., Zhou, X., Qin, B., Hu, J., Liu, J., Ding, Y.: Secure joint bitcoin trading with partially blind fuzzy signatures. Soft. Comput. **21**, 3123–3134 (2017)
25. Xue, L., Ni, J., Liu, D., Lin, X., Shen, X.: Blockchain-based fair and fine-grained data trading with privacy preservation. IEEE Trans. Comput. **72**(9), 2440–2453 (2023)
26. Zhang, J., Xie, T., Zhang, Y., Song, D.: Transparent polynomial delegation and its applications to zero-knowledge proof. In: IEEE Symposium on Security and Privacy (SP), pp. 859–876. IEEE (2020)

Communication-Efficient Secure Neural Network via Key-Reduced Distributed Comparison Function

Peng Yang[1], Zoe Lin Jiang[1(✉)], Shiqi Gao[1], Hongxiao Wang[2], Jun Zhou[3], Yangyiye Jin[3], Siu-Ming Yiu[2], and Junbin Fang[4]

[1] Harbin Institute of Technology, ShenZhen, China
{stuyangpeng,200111514}@stu.hit.edu.cn, zoeljiang@hit.edu.cn
[2] The University of Hong Kong, Hong Kong, China
{hxwang,smyiu}@cs.hku.hk
[3] Shanghai Pudong Development Bank, Shanghai, China
{zhoujun,jinyyy}@spdb.com.cn
[4] Jinan University, Guangzhou, China
tjunbinfang@jnu.edu.cn

Abstract. In privacy-preserving neural network, the high communication costs of securely computing non-linear functions is the primary performance bottleneck. For commonly used non-linear functions, such as ReLU, existing methods adopt an offline-online computation paradigm and utilizes distributed comparison function (DCF) to reduce communication costs. Specifically, these methods prepare DCF keys in the offline phase and perform secure non-linear function computation using these keys in the online phase. However, the practicality of these methods is limited due to the substantial size of DCF keys and the heavy reliance on a trusted third party during the offline phase.

In this work, we introduce FssNN, a communication-efficient secure two-party neural network framework, which features a key-reduced DCF scheme without a trusted third party to enable practical secure training and inference. Firstly, by analyzing the correlations between DCF keys to eliminate redundant parameters, we propose a key-reduced DCF scheme with a compact additive construction, decreasing the size of DCF keys by about 17.9% and offline communication costs by approximately 28.0%. Secondly, leveraging an MPC-friendly pseudorandom number generator, we propose a secure two-party distributed key generation protocol for our key-reduced DCF, eliminating the need for a trusted third party. Finally, we utilize the key-reduced DCF and additive secret sharing to compute non-linear and linear functions, and design secure computation protocols with constant online communication rounds for neural network operations, reducing online communication costs by 28.9%–43.4%.

We provide formal security proofs and evaluate the performance of FssNN on various models and datasets. Experimental results show that compared to the state-of-the-art framework AriaNN, our framework reduces the total communication costs of secure training and inference by approximately 25.4% and 26.4% respectively.

J. K. Liu et al. (Eds.): ProvSec 2024, LNCS 14904, pp. 143–163, 2025.
https://doi.org/10.1007/978-981-96-0957-4_8

Keywords: Privacy-preserving neural network · Secure multi-party computation · Distributed comparison function · Additive secret sharing

1 Introduction

Machine learning using neural networks is widely applied in many practical scenarios such as healthcare prediction, financial services and policy making. To improve the models' accuracy and generalization capability, many organizations wish to collect data from multiple parties to jointly train neural network models, but privacy concerns and regulations prevent them from openly sharing their data [20]. Privacy-preserving neural network based on secure multi-party computation (MPC), such as homomorphic encryption [12], garbled circuit [28] and secret sharing [14], provides a promising solution by allowing different parties to train various models on their joint data without revealing any sensitive information. Compared with privacy-preserving neural network based on homomorphic encryption and garbled circuit, privacy-preserving neural network based on secret sharing has significant advantages in computation efficiency and communication efficiency respectively, making it widely used for neural network training and inference in the real-life scenarios [11].

However, compared to plaintext neural network training, privacy-preserving neural network based on secret sharing still incurs substantial communication costs. The main source of inefficiency in prior work [20,21,24] is that the bulk of secure computation of non-linear functions in neural network, such as ReLU and MaxPool. Within secure computation protocols, these non-linear functions need to be represented as Boolean and arithmetic circuits, which have a high circuit depth, and the communication complexity of securely computing these nonlinear functions is proportional to the circuit depth [8]. Therefore, the high communication costs of secure non-linear functions computation protocols is the primary performance bottleneck in privacy-preserving neural network. To decrease the communication costs of secure non-linear function computation protocols, existing work [2,15,16,22] adopts an offline-online computation paradigm [7] and utilizes distributed comparison function (DCF) [3,4] to design efficient protocols. Specifically, these works precompute DCF keys in the offline phase and perform secure non-linear function computation using these DCF keys in the online phase. However, these work requires generating a large number of DCF keys in the offline phase and relies on a trusted third party to generation DCF keys, incurring massive communication costs in the training and inference process.

To address these issues, we introduce a communication-efficient secure two-party neural network framework, called FssNN, to enable practical secure training and inference. First, by analyzing the correlations between DCF keys to eliminate redundant parameters, we propose a key-reduced DCF scheme with a compact additive construction, which decreases the size of DCF keys by about 17.9% and the offline communication costs by approximately 28.0%. Secondly, by leveraging an MPC-friendly pseudorandom number generator (PRG) [9], we propose a secure two-party distributed DCF key generation protocol for our key-reduced DCF, thereby eliminating the reliance on the trusted third party and supporting a larger input domain ($\mathbb{Z}_{2^{32}}$ and above) than the state-of-the-art DCF key generation shceme [2]. Finally, we utilize our key-reduced DCF and additive secret sharing to compute non-linear and linear functions, respectively, and design secure computation protocols with constant online communication rounds for neural network operators, reducing the online communication costs by 28.9%–43.4%.

Theoretical analysis indicates that, compared with existing work ABY2.0 [21] and AriaNN [22], our FssNN achieves fewer online communication rounds and lower communication costs. Experimental results show that, compared to the state-of-the-art framework AriaNN [22], the communication costs for secure training and inference in FssNN is reduced by approximately 25.4% and 26.4%, respectively, with the accuracy difference between secure and plaintext training and inference being only about 0.05%.

1.1 Related Work

Privacy-preserving neural network built on MPC has emerged as a flourishing research area in the past few years. Existing works use secure computation protocols based on secret sharing to compute linear functions and protocols based on secret sharing (SS), garbled circuit (GC), or function secret sharing (FSS) to compute non-linear functions. These works also adopt the offline-online computation mode [7] to obtain an efficient online phase by moving a majority of computation and communication costs to the offline phase.

In SS-based and GC-based solutions, SecureML [20] is the first privacy-preserving neural network framework and implementation with secure two-party computation (2PC) based on SS and GC. It enables the secure training by combining Boolean secret sharing, arithmetic secret sharing and Yao's secret sharing [8], but the conversion between three types of secret shares incurs huge communication costs. ABY2.0 [21] reduces online communication rounds and communication costs by designing an efficient secret shares conversion protocol, and improves the efficiency of secure two-party neural network. However, these 2PC frameworks have a number of communication rounds linear to the circuit depth, resulting in extremely high communication costs and latency. ABY3 [19] and Falcon [25] are proposed to tackle secure training by leveraging three-party computation (3PC), and Trident [6] and Tetrad [17] are the secure four-party computation (4PC) framework for privacy-preserving neural network training. Compared with 2PC frameworks, these 3PC and 4PC frameworks have fewer communication rounds (still linear with circuit depth) [11], but impose a stronger security assumption (honest-majority rather than the dishonest-majority), the practicality is greatly limited.

In FSS-based solutions, non-linear functions are evaluated by using FSS-based 2PC protocols, which are optimal in terms of online communication and rounds [2]. AriaNN [22] is a low-interaction privacy-preserving neural network framework based on FSS by reducing the key sizes of distributed comparison function (DCF, a FSS scheme for comparisons) However, it still requires considerable online communication costs, and the secure protocols within AriaNN designed for ReLU incorporate a 1-bit error. BCG+21 [2], LLAMA [15] and Grotto [23] provide secure computation protocols based on DCF for computing various math functions (e.g., comparison, reciprocal square root and piecewise polynomial), yet they currently can not provide support for training neural networks. Orca [16] enables secure inference and training by accelerating the computation of FSS-based 2PC protocols with GPUs, but the online phase in Orca requires additional communication rounds compared with other FSS-based solutions, incurring the high communication latency. However, AriaNN [22], LLAMA [15], Grotto [23] and Orca [16] rely heavily on a unrealistic trusted party to generate DCF key in the offline phase. Although BCG+21 [2] designs a distributed DCF key generation scheme by extending the Doerner-Shelat protocol [10] to replace the trusted party, it is only suitable to a small input domain ($\mathbb{Z}_{2^{16}}$ or smaller), which greatly limits its practicality. The FSS-based secure neural network frameworks are summarized in Table 1.

Table 1. The FSS-based secure neural network frameworks.

Framework	Training	Inference	Online Gate Evaluation Rounds	Without Trusted Party	GPUs
BCG+21 [2]	×	×	1	✓	×
AriaNN [22]	✓	✓	1	×	✓
LLAMA [15]	✓	×	1	×	×
Grotto [23]	×	×	1	×	×
Orca [16]	✓	✓	$O(1)$	×	✓
FssNN (Ours)	✓	✓	1	✓	×

1.2 Our Contributions

We propose a communication-efficient secure two-party neural network framework called FssNN, which to enable practical secure training and inference. In details, our contributions can be summarized in the following three aspects:

- **Key-reduced DCF with a compact additive construction**. By analyzing the correlations between DCF keys to eliminate redundant parameters, we propose a key-reduced DCF scheme with a compact additive construction with fewer key sizes than the state-of-the-art DCF construction [2] from $n(\lambda + 3) + \lambda + 1$ bits to $(\lceil n - \log \lambda \rceil)(\lambda + 3) + 2\lambda$ bits where n is the input size and λ is the security parameter, thus reduce offline communication costs by 26.8%–28.3%.
- **Distributed DCF key generation based on MPC-friendly pseudorandom generators**. by leveraging an MPC-friendly pseudorandom number generator, we propose a secure two-party DCF distributed key generation protocol for our key-reduced DCF, thereby eliminating the reliance on a trusted third party and supporting a larger input domain ($\mathbb{Z}_{2^{32}}$ and above) than the state-of-the-art DCF key generation shceme [2].

- **Online efficient secure neural network operators.** By utilizing the proposed key-reduced DCF and additive secret sharing, we construct online-efficient secure computation protocols for neural network operators, such as matrix multiplication, Hadamard product, ReLU and Maxpool, and reduce the online communication costs by 43.4% and 28.9%, respectively.

2 Preliminaries

Notations. $\mathbb{Z}_{2^n}$ is a ring with arithmetic operations with each element identified by its n-bit binary representation. We parse $x \in \{0,1\}^n$ as $x_{n-1}||\cdots||x_0$ where $x_{[i]} \in \mathbb{Z}_2$ denotes x_i and $x_{[i,j)} \in \mathbb{Z}_{2^{j-i}}$ denotes the ring element corresponding to the bit-string $x_{j-1}||\cdots||x_i$ for $0 \leq i < j \leq n$. Denote scalar, vector and matrix by lowercase letter x, lowercase bold letter $\mathbf{x}$ and uppercase bold letter $\mathbf{X}$ respectively. Denote security parameter by λ, and $\mathbf{1}\{b\}$ by the indicator function that outputs 1 when b is true and 0 otherwise.

2.1 Neural Network

Let $D = \{(\mathbf{x}_i, y_i)|i \in \{0,1,\cdots,m\}\}$ denotes training datasets where each data sample $\mathbf{x}_i$ contains d features with the corresponding output label y_i. Neural network is a computational process to learn a function g such that $g(\mathbf{x}_i) \approx y_i$ where g can be represented as a function of weight matrix $\mathbf{W}$ and input data $\mathbf{x}_i$. The neural network training procedure consists of two phases, namely forward propagation and backward propagation. The phase to calculate the predicted output $\hat{y}_i = g(\mathbf{W}, \mathbf{x}_i)$ is called *forward propagation*, which comprises of linear operations and a non-linear activation function. One of the most popular activation functions is the rectified linear unit (ReLU).

To learn the weight $\mathbf{W}$, a cost function $C(\mathbf{W})$ that quantifies the error between predicted value $\hat{y}_i$ and actual value y_i is defined, and $\mathbf{W}$ is calculated and updated by solving the optimization problem of $\mathsf{argmin}_{\mathbf{W}} C(\mathbf{W})$. The solution for this optimization problem can be computed by using stochastic gradient descent (SGD), which is an effective approximation algorithm for approaching a local minimum of a function step by step. SGD algorithm works as follows: $\mathbf{W}$ is initialized as a vector of random values or all 0s. In each iteration, a sample $(\mathbf{x}_i, y_i)$ is selected randomly and the coefficient matrix $\mathbf{W}$ is updated by $\mathbf{W} := \mathbf{W} - \alpha\nabla C(\mathbf{W})$, where α is the learning rate and $\nabla C(\mathbf{W})$ is the partial derivatives of the cost with respect to the changes in weight. The phase to calculate the change $\alpha\nabla C(\mathbf{W})$ is called *backward propagation*, where error rates are fed back through a neural network to update weight $\mathbf{W}$.

In practice, instead of selecting one sample of data per iteration, a small batch of samples are selected randomly and $\mathbf{W}$ is updated by averaging the partial derivatives of all samples on the current $\mathbf{W}$. This is called a mini-batch SGD, and its advantage is to allow for the use of vectorization techniques.

2.2 Additive Secret Sharing

An additive secret sharing (SS) scheme splits a secret value into multiple shares that add up to the original secret, ensuring no individual share reveals the secret. In a two-party SS scheme, party P_0 with secret share $\langle x\rangle_0$ and party P_1 with secret share $\langle x\rangle_1$ share the secret value $x \in \mathbb{Z}_{2^n}$, such that $x = (\langle x\rangle_0 + \langle x\rangle_1) \bmod 2^n$. We say that P_0 and P_1 together hold the secret share pair $\langle x\rangle$, meaning that P_0 holds $\langle x\rangle_0$ and P_1 holds $\langle x\rangle_1$.

Sharing and Reconstruction. To realize the functionality $\mathcal{F}_{\mathsf{Share}}$ which additively shares a secret value $x \in \mathbb{Z}_{2^n}$, secret owner samples random $r \in \mathbb{Z}_{2^n}$, and sends $\langle x\rangle_b = (x - r) \bmod 2^n$ to P_b and sends $\langle x\rangle_{1-b} = r$ to P_{1-b}. To implement the functionality $\mathcal{F}_{\mathsf{Recon}}$ which opens an additively shared value $\langle x\rangle$, P_b sends $\langle x\rangle_b$ to P_{1-b} who computes $(\langle x\rangle_0 + \langle x\rangle_1) \bmod 2^n$ for $b = \{0, 1\}$. In the following text, we omit the modular operation for simplicity.

Addition and Multiplication. Functionalities $\mathcal{F}_{\mathsf{Add}}$ and $\mathcal{F}_{\mathsf{Mul}}$ add and multiply two shared values $\langle x\rangle$ and $\langle y\rangle$ respectively. It is easy to non-interactively add the shared values by having P_b compute $\langle z\rangle_b = \langle x\rangle_b + \langle y\rangle_b$. We overload the addition operation to denote the secure addition by $\langle x\rangle + \langle y\rangle$. To realize $\mathcal{F}_{\mathsf{Mul}}$, taking the advantage of Beaver's precomputed multiplication triples technique [1], the specific protocol Π_{Mul} works as follows: assume that P_0 and P_1 hold multiplication triples $\langle u\rangle, \langle v\rangle, \langle uv\rangle$ where $u, v \in_R \mathbb{Z}_{2^n}$, P_b locally computes $\langle e\rangle_b = \langle x\rangle_b - \langle u\rangle_b$ and $\langle f\rangle_b = \langle y\rangle_b - \langle v\rangle_b$ and then the two parties reconstruct $\langle e\rangle, \langle f\rangle$ to get e, f. Finally, P_b lets $\langle z\rangle_b = b \cdot e \cdot f + f \cdot \langle u\rangle_b + e \cdot \langle v\rangle_b + \langle uv\rangle_b$.

Specifically, functionality $\mathcal{F}_{\mathsf{GenMT}}$ generates multiplication triples $(\langle u\rangle, \langle v\rangle, \langle uv\rangle)$ consumed in Π_{Mul}. Typically, multiplication triples can be generated based on oblivious transfer (OT). In this paper, the protocol Π_{GenMT} for $\mathcal{F}_{\mathsf{GenMT}}$ is achieved by directly using OT-based generation scheme [20, 26].

In the case of $n > 1$ (e.g., $n = 32$) which supports arithmetic operations (e.g., addition and multiplication), arithmetic share pair is denoted by $\langle\cdot\rangle^A$. In the case of $n = 1$ which supports Boolean operations (e.g., XOR and AND), Boolean share pair is denoted by $\langle\cdot\rangle^B$. In this paper, we mostly use the arithmetic share pair and denote it by $\langle\cdot\rangle$ for short.

2.3 Function Secret Sharing

Intuitively, a two-party function secret sharing (FSS) scheme [2] splits a function $f \in \mathcal{F}$ into two shares f_0, f_1, such that: (1) each f_b hides f; (2) for each input x, $f_0(x) + f_1(x) = f(x)$. This section follows the definition of FSS from [2].

Definition 1. *A two-party FSS scheme is a pair of algorithms* (Gen, Eval)*:*

(1) $\mathsf{Gen}(1^\lambda, \hat{f})$ *is a probabilistic polynomial-time (PPT) key generation algorithm that given* 1^λ *and* $\hat{f} \in \{0,1\}^*$ *(description of a function* $f : \mathbb{G}^{\mathsf{in}} \to \mathbb{G}^{\mathsf{out}}$*) outputs a pair of keys* (k_0, k_1)*. We assume that* $\hat{f}$ *explicitly contains descriptions of input and output groups* $\mathbb{G}^{\mathsf{in}}, \mathbb{G}^{\mathsf{out}}$*.*

(2) $\mathsf{Eval}(b, k_b, x)$ *is a polynomial-time evaluation algorithm that given* $b \in \{0,1\}$ *(party index),* k_b *(key defining* $f_b : \mathbb{G}^{\mathsf{in}} \to \mathbb{G}^{\mathsf{out}}$*) and* $x \in \mathbb{G}^{\mathsf{in}}$ *(input for* f_b*) outputs a group element* $y_b \in \mathbb{G}^{\mathsf{out}}$ *(the value of* $f_b(x)$*).*

Distributed Comparison Function and Its Variant. A special piecewise function, $f^{<}_{\alpha,\beta}(x)$, also referred to as a comparison function, outputs β if $x < \alpha$ and 0 otherwise. We refer to a FSS scheme for comparison functions as distributed comparison function (DCF). And the variant of DCF, called dual distributed comparison function (DDCF), is considered and denoted by $f^{<}_{\alpha,\beta_0,\beta_1}(x)$ that outputs β_0 for $0 \le x < \alpha$ and β_1 for $x \ge \alpha$. Obviously, $f^{<}_{\alpha,\beta_0,\beta_1}(x) = \beta_1 + f^{<}_{\alpha,\beta_0-\beta_1}(x)$ and thus DDCF can be constructed by DCF.

Secure Two-Party Computation via FSS. Recent work of Boyle et al. [2, 5] shows that FSS paradigm can be used to efficiently evaluate some function families in the two-party computation in the offline-online model, where Gen and Eval correspond to the offline phase and the online phase respectively. Refer [2] for more details.

2.4 Threat Model

We consider two-party computation secure against a *semi-honest* adversary, i.e., the corrupted party running the protocol honestly while trying to learn as much information as possible about others' input or function share. In this paper, we directly follow the definition of semi-honest security from [18].

In addition, modular sequential composition theorems [13,18] are considered, and we prove protocols secure under the definition of semi-honest security from [18] and immediately derive their security under sequential composition. Our protocols invoke several sub-protocols and for ease of exposition we describe them using the hybrid model, which is the same as a real interaction except that the sub-protocol executions are replaced with calls to the corresponding trusted functionalities - protocol invoking $\mathcal{F}$ is said to be in the $\mathcal{F}$-hybrid model.

3 The Proposed FssNN

In this section, we present a high-level overview of FssNN framework in Subsect. 3.1, and provide detailed construction of secure linear layer functions and secure non-linear layer functions in Subsect. 3.2 and Subsect. 3.3 respectively. Due to space limitations, the security proof of the proposed protocols is in the full version of this paper [27].

3.1 The FssNN Overview

In FssNN, we consider parties P_0 and P_1 who want to train various models on their joint data. We denote the training datasets D_0 and D_1 holding by parties P_0 and P_1 respectively. To distribute the secret shares of training datasets between

P_0 and P_1, P_0 generate $(\langle D_0\rangle_0, \langle D_0\rangle_1) \leftarrow \mathcal{F}_{\mathsf{Share}}(D_0)$ and send $\langle D_0\rangle_1$ to P_1, and P_1 generate $(\langle D_1\rangle_0, \langle D_1\rangle_1) \leftarrow \mathcal{F}_{\mathsf{Share}}(D_1)$ and send $\langle D_1\rangle_0$ to P_0. P_0 compute $\langle D\rangle_0 = \langle D_0\rangle_0 + \langle D_1\rangle_0$ and P_1 compute $\langle D\rangle_1 = \langle D_0\rangle_1 + \langle D_1\rangle_1$ locally.

Specifically, as shown in Fig. 1 (a), FssNN works as follows: parties P_0 and P_1 hold the secret shares of training datasets $\langle D\rangle_0$ and $\langle D\rangle_1$ respectively, and initialize $\langle \mathbf{W}\rangle_0$ and $\langle \mathbf{W}\rangle_1$ to be the all **0**s locally. Then, for $b = 0, 1$, P_b randomly selects a training sample $(\langle \mathbf{x}_i\rangle_b, \langle y_i\rangle_b)$ for $\langle D\rangle_b$, and engages in a secure two-party SGD protocol (2PC-SGD) with P_{1-b} to update $\langle \mathbf{W}\rangle$ interactively, which involves two steps: ① forward propagation and ② backward propagation. During the forward propagation and the backward propagation, we need to securely compute linear layers (denoted by green solid line boxes) and non-linear layers (denoted by blue dashed line boxes). Finally, P_0 and P_1 select a new sample randomly and repeat the above process until the samples are used up, and finally P_b gets $\langle \mathbf{W}\rangle_b$ and sends $\langle \mathbf{W}\rangle_b$ to P_{1-b} to reconstruct $\mathbf{W}$.

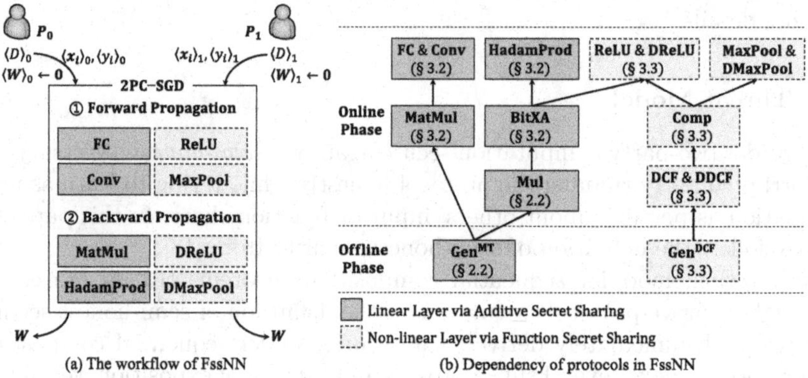

Fig. 1. The high level overview of FssNN

To reduce the communication rounds and communication costs required to compute linear layers and non-linear layers, we propose a hybrid method combing additive secret sharing (SS) and function secret sharing (FSS) and adopt the offline-online paradigm to compute linear layers in one round of online communication and compute non-linear layers in a constant round of online communication. Figure 1 (b) shows our secure linear layer protocols (denoted by blue dashed line boxes) and secure non-linear layer protocols (denoted by blue dashed line boxes) in the offline-online paradigm.

For linear layers, by leveraging a SS-based secure two-party computation protocol, we generate multiplication triples ($\mathsf{Gen}^{\mathsf{MT}}$) in the offline phase and utilize these multiplication triples to compute linear layer functions such as MatMul, Conv, FC and $\mathsf{HadamProd}$ in one round of communication in the online phase. Among them, we propose a protocol, BitXA, that supports direct multiplication of a bit and an integer to reduce online communication costs, and extend it to

HadamProd through vectorization techniques. **For non-linear layers**, we propose a key-reduced DCF scheme with compact additive construction and design a distributed DCF key generation scheme based on an MPC-friendly pseudo-random generator (PRG). In the offline phase, we design a distributed DCF key generation scheme ($\mathsf{Gen}^{\mathsf{DCF}}$) for the proposed key-reduced DCF to generate the DCF key rather than relying on a trusted party, and utilize the DCF key to compute non-linear layer functions such as ReLU, DReLU, MaxPool and DMaxPool with a constant-round online communication.

3.2 Construction of Secure Linear Layers

In this section, we present the detailed construction of linear layer functions, i.e., matrix multiplication MatMul and Hadamard product HadamProd.

Secure Matrix Multiplication. A fully-connected layer is exactly a matrix multiplication, thus secure fully-connected layer (FC) can be implemented directly using Π_{MatMul}. Likewise, convolutional layer can also be expressed as a matrix multiplication using an unrolling technique (see Fig. 3 in [22]), so secure convolution layer (Conv) can also be implemented using Π_{MatMul}.

By leveraging the vectorization technique in [20], secure scalar multiplication (Mul) introduced in Sect. 2.2 can be easily extended to secure matrix multiplication (MatMul) where the multiplication triples are replaced by matrix multiplication triples. Given secret shares of matrices $\langle \mathbf{X} \rangle, \langle \mathbf{Y} \rangle$ held by P_0 and P_1 where $\mathbf{X} \in \mathbb{Z}_{2^n}^{m_1 \times m_2}, \mathbf{Y} \in \mathbb{Z}_{2^n}^{m_2 \times m_3}$, functionality $\mathcal{F}_{\mathsf{MatMul}}$ computes $\langle \mathbf{Z} \rangle$ such that $\mathbf{Z} = \mathbf{X} \times \mathbf{Y}$. Π_{MatMul} realizes the functionality $\mathcal{F}_{\mathsf{MatMul}}$ as follows: 1) In offline phase, P_b samples $\langle \mathbf{U} \rangle_b, \langle \mathbf{V} \rangle_b$ randomly, and then parties invoke $\mathsf{Gen}^{\mathsf{MT}}(\langle \mathbf{U} \rangle, \langle \mathbf{V} \rangle)$ to generate matrix multiplication triples $(\langle \mathbf{U} \rangle, \langle \mathbf{V} \rangle, \langle \mathbf{UV} \rangle)$. 2) In the online phase, parties open $\mathbf{X} - \mathbf{U}$ and $\mathbf{Y} - \mathbf{V}$, and then P_b computes $\langle \mathbf{Z} \rangle_b = b \cdot (\mathbf{X} - \mathbf{U}) \times (\mathbf{Y} - \mathbf{V}) + (\mathbf{X} - \mathbf{U}) \times \langle \mathbf{V} \rangle_b + \langle \mathbf{U} \rangle_b \times (\mathbf{Y} - \mathbf{V}) + \langle \mathbf{UV} \rangle_b$ locally. This requires an online communication of $(m_1 m_2 + m_2 m_3) \cdot n$ bits in 1 round.

Secure Hadamard Product. Neural network training makes extensive use of Hadamard product in backpropagation. Observe that Hadamard product operations (denoted by $\odot$) have a specific structure that can be leveraged to reduce communication costs: when computing $\mathbf{X} \odot \mathbf{Y}$ where $\mathbf{X} \in \mathbb{Z}_{2^n}^{m_1 \times m_2}, \mathbf{Y} \in \mathbb{Z}_{2}^{m_2 \times m_3}$, the each element x in $\mathbf{X}$ is a n-bit integer and the each element y in $\mathbf{Y}$ is a bit. However, the arithmetic share $\langle x \rangle^A$ can not be directly multiplied by the Boolean share $\langle y \rangle^B$ since they are calculated with different moduli. Existing works first convert $\langle y \rangle^B$ to the arithmetic share $\langle y \rangle^A$ and then perform the multiplication of $\langle x \rangle^A$ and $\langle y \rangle^A$, incurring an online communication of $2 m_1 m_2 n$ bits in 2 rounds.

In order to reduce online communication costs, we propose an online-efficient Hadamard product protocol to support the direct computation of $\mathbf{X} \odot \mathbf{Y}$ by moving the share conversion into the offline phase, which requires an online communication of $m_1 m_2 (n+1)$ bits in 1 round. We present a scalar protocol, Π_{BitXA}, to support the product of $\langle x \rangle^A$ and $\langle y \rangle^B$, which can be easily extended to the vector protocol $\Pi_{\mathsf{HadamProd}}$ through the vectorization technique.

Given the arithmetic share $\langle x\rangle^A$ and Boolean share $\langle y\rangle^B$, functionality $\mathcal{F}_{\mathsf{BitXA}}$ generates $\langle z\rangle^A$ with $z = x \cdot y$ and the protocol is shown in Algorithm 1. Π_{BitXA} needs an online communication of $n+1$ bits per party in 1 round.

Algorithm 1. BitXA: $\Pi_{\mathsf{BitXA}}(\langle y\rangle^B, \langle x\rangle^A)$

Input: P_0 and P_1 hold $\langle x\rangle^A$ and $\langle y\rangle^B$.
Output: P_b gets $\langle z\rangle_b^A$ such that $\langle z\rangle_0^A + \langle z\rangle_1^A = (\langle x\rangle_0^A + \langle x\rangle_1^A)\cdot((\langle y\rangle_0^B)\oplus\langle y\rangle_1^B)$.

- **Offline Phase**

1: P_b samples $\langle\hat{\delta}_y\rangle_b^B \in_R \mathbb{Z}_2$, and then P_0 and P_1 convert it to arithmetic share:
(1) P_0 lets $\langle e\rangle_0^A = \langle\hat{\delta}_y\rangle_0^B, \langle f\rangle_0^A = 0$, and P_1 lets $\langle e\rangle_1^A = 0, \langle f\rangle_1^A = \langle\hat{\delta}_y\rangle_1^B$.
(2) P_0 and P_1 compute $(\langle ef\rangle_0^A, \langle ef\rangle_1^A) \leftarrow \Pi_{\mathsf{Mul}}(\langle e\rangle^A, \langle f\rangle^A)$.
(3) P_b computes $\langle\delta_y\rangle_b^A = \langle e\rangle_b^A + \langle f\rangle_b^A - 2\cdot\langle ef\rangle_b^A$ locally.
2: P_b samples $\langle\delta_x\rangle_b^A \in_R \mathbb{Z}_{2^n}$, and then parties compute $(\langle\delta_z\rangle_0^A, \langle\delta_z\rangle_1^A) \leftarrow \Pi_{\mathsf{Mul}}(\langle\delta_x\rangle^A, \langle\delta_y\rangle^A)$ such that $\delta_z = \delta_x\cdot\delta_y$.
3: P_0 and P_1 hold $\langle\delta_x\rangle^A, \langle\delta_y\rangle^A, \langle\delta_z\rangle^A$ and $\langle\hat{\delta}_y\rangle^B$.

- **Online Phase**

1: P_b locally computes $\langle x\rangle_b^A + \langle\delta_x\rangle_b^A, \langle y\rangle_b^B \oplus \langle\hat{\delta}_y\rangle_b^B$, and sends to P_{1-b}.
2: P_b reconstructs $\Delta_x = x + \delta_x, \Delta_y = y \oplus \hat{\delta}_y$, and sets $\Delta_y' = \Delta_y$ where $\Delta_y' \in \mathbb{Z}_{2^n}$.
3: P_b computes locally $\langle z\rangle_b^A = b\cdot\Delta_y'\cdot\Delta_x + \langle\delta_y\rangle_b^A\cdot\Delta_x - 2\cdot\Delta_y'\cdot\Delta_x\cdot\langle\delta_y\rangle_b^A - \Delta_y'\cdot\langle\delta_x\rangle_b^A - \langle\delta_z\rangle_b^A + 2\cdot\Delta_y'\cdot\langle\delta_z\rangle_b^A$.

Security Analysis. Theorem 1 captures the security of Π_{BitXA}, and the proof is in the full version of this paper [27]. The security of HadamProd follows in the $\mathcal{F}_{\mathsf{BitXA}}$-hybrid model.

Theorem 1. *In the $\mathcal{F}_{\mathsf{Mul}}$-hybrid model, Π_{BitXA} securely computes the functionality $\mathcal{F}_{\mathsf{BitXA}}$ in the presence of semi-honest adversaries.*

3.3 Construction of Secure Non-linear Layers

In this section, we present the construction of non-linear layer functions (i.e., DReLU and ReLU) by using a key-reduced distributed comparison function (DCF) scheme with compact additive construction. To replace the trusted party in the offline phase, we propose a DCF key generation scheme based on MPC-friendly pseudorandom generators, which supports a larger input domain. In this paper, we directly use the secure maxpool algorithm proposed in [22] (see algorithm 7 in [22]) and its derivative, but utilize our proposed DCF construction.

Secure DReLU and ReLU. In neural network, ReLU is one of the most popular activation functions in neural network training. For a signed value x, ReLU is define as $\mathsf{max}(0, x)$ and its derivative is defined as $\mathbf{1}\{x \geq 0\}$. Given an arithmetic share $\langle x\rangle$, the functionality $\mathcal{F}_{\mathsf{ReLU}}$ outputs the arithmetic share of $\mathsf{max}(0, x)$, and the functionality $\mathcal{F}_{\mathsf{DReLU}}$ outputs the Boolean share of $\mathbf{1}\{x \geq 0\}$. It can be seen that $\mathsf{ReLU}(x) = x\cdot\mathsf{DReLU}(x)$. In this section, by leveraging the

DDCF scheme constructed by using the proposed DCF, we first design a signed integer comparison gate scheme to implement DReLU, and then compute ReLU using $\Pi_{\mathsf{ReLU}}(\langle x\rangle^A) = \Pi_{\mathsf{BitXA}}(\langle x\rangle^A, \langle \Pi_{\mathsf{DReLU}}(\langle x\rangle^A)\rangle^B)$.

Secure. DReLU To implement $\mathcal{F}_{\mathsf{DReLU}}$, we first propose signed integer comparison gate Comp in Algorithm 2 which is derived from [2]. In the Algorithm 2, $(\mathsf{Gen}_{n-1}^{\mathsf{DDCF}}, \mathsf{Eval}_{n-1}^{\mathsf{DDCF}})$ is used to evaluate $f^{<}_{\alpha^{(n-1)},\beta_0,\beta_1}(x)$ that outputs β_0 for $0 \le x < \alpha^{(n-1)}$ and β_1 for $x \ge \alpha^{(n-1)}$, and its detailed construction is shown in the Appendix A. Comp requires 1 call of DDCF and the key sizes are $(\lceil n-1-\log\lambda\rceil)(\lambda+3)+2\lambda$ bits per party where λ is the security parameter.

Base on Comp, Π_{DReLU} is proposed to compute $\mathbf{1}\{x \ge 0\}$, and this protocol is in Algorithm 3 where a trusted party is used to precompute FSS keys of Comp. The trusted party can be instantiated via using our proposed distributed DCF key generation scheme (Algorithm 5). Π_{DReLU} requires 1 call of Comp in the offline phase, and requires requires 1 round with n bits in the online phase.

Secure. ReLU $\mathcal{F}_{\mathsf{ReLU}}$ is implemented by computing $\Pi_{\mathsf{ReLU}}(\langle x\rangle^A) = \Pi_{\mathsf{BitXA}}(\langle x\rangle^A, \langle \Pi_{\mathsf{DReLU}}(\langle x\rangle^A)\rangle^B)$, which needs the same key sizes as Π_{DReLU} and requires 1 round with $2n+1$ bits in the online phase.

Algorithm 2. Signed Integer Comparison Gate Comp : $(\mathsf{Gen}_n^{\mathsf{Comp}}, \mathsf{Eval}_n^{\mathsf{Comp}})$

- $\mathsf{Gen}_n^{\mathsf{Comp}}(1^\lambda, \mathsf{r}_1^{\mathsf{in}}, \mathsf{r}_2^{\mathsf{in}}, \mathsf{r}^{\mathsf{out}})$
  - Let $r = (2^n - (\mathsf{r}_1^{\mathsf{in}} - \mathsf{r}_2^{\mathsf{in}})) \in \mathbb{Z}_{2^n}$, and $\alpha^{(n-1)} = r_{[0,n-1)}$.
  - $(k_0^{(n-1)}, k_1^{(n-1)}) \leftarrow \mathsf{Gen}_{n-1}^{\mathsf{DDCF}}(1^\lambda, \alpha^{(n-1)}, \beta_0, \beta_1)$, where $\beta_0 = 1 \oplus r_{[n-1]}, \beta_1 = r_{[n-1]}$.
  - Sample randoms $\mathsf{r}_0, \mathsf{r}_1 \in_R \mathbb{Z}_2$, such that $\mathsf{r}_0 \oplus \mathsf{r}_1 = \mathsf{r}^{\mathsf{out}}$.
  - Let $k_b = k_b^{(n-1)} || \mathsf{r}_b$
  - **return** (k_0, k_1).
- $\mathsf{Eval}_n^{\mathsf{Comp}}(b, k_b, \hat{x}, \hat{y})$
  - P_b parses $k_b = k_b^{(n-1)} || \mathsf{r}_b$, and lets $z = (\hat{x} - \hat{y}) \in \mathbb{Z}_{2^n}$.
  - P_b computes $m_b \leftarrow \mathsf{Eval}_{n-1}^{\mathsf{DDCF}}(b, k_b^{(n-1)}, z^{(n-1)})$, where $z^{(n-1)} = 2^{n-1} - z_{[0,n-1)} - 1$.
  - P_b lets $v_b = (b \cdot z_{[n-1]}) \oplus m_b \oplus \mathsf{r}_b$.
  - **return** v_b.

Security Analysis. Theorem 2 captures the security of Π_{DReLU}, and the proof is given in the full version of this paper [27]. The security of Π_{ReLU} follows in $(\mathcal{F}_{\mathsf{BitXA}}, \mathcal{F}_{\mathsf{DReLU}})$-hybrid model.

Theorem 2. *In the $\mathcal{F}_{\mathsf{Gen}_n^{\mathsf{Comp}}}$-hybrid model, Π_{DReLU} securely computes the functionality $\mathcal{F}_{\mathsf{DReLU}}$ in the presence of semi-honest adversaries.*

Key-Reduced DCF with a Compact Additive Construction. A central building block in FssNN is a distributed comparison function (DCF), which is intensively used in neural network to build activation functions like ReLU (and

Algorithm 3. $\mathsf{DReLU} : \Pi_{\mathsf{DReLU}}(\langle x\rangle^A)$

Input: P_0 and P_1 hold arithmetic share $\langle x\rangle^A$.
Output: P_0 and P_1 obtain Boolean share $\langle y\rangle^B$, such that $\langle y\rangle_0^B \oplus \langle y\rangle_1^B = \mathbf{1}\{x \geq 0\}$.

• **Offline Phase**
1: Compute $(k_0, k_1) \leftarrow \mathsf{Gen}_n^{\mathsf{Comp}}(1^\lambda, \mathsf{r}_1^{\mathsf{in}}, \mathsf{r}_2^{\mathsf{in}}, \mathsf{r}^{\mathsf{out}})$.
2: Send k_b, $\langle \mathsf{r}_1^{\mathsf{in}}\rangle_b^A$,$\langle \mathsf{r}^{\mathsf{out}}\rangle_b^B$ and $\mathsf{r}_2^{\mathsf{in}}$ to P_b.

• **Online Phase**
1: P_b computes $\langle x + \mathsf{r}_1^{\mathsf{in}}\rangle_b^A = \langle x\rangle_b^A + \langle \mathsf{r}_1^{\mathsf{in}}\rangle_b^A$ and sends $\langle x + \mathsf{r}_1^{\mathsf{in}}\rangle_b^A$ to P_{1-b}.
2: P_b computes $x + \mathsf{r}_1^{\mathsf{in}} = \langle x + \mathsf{r}_1^{\mathsf{in}}\rangle_0^A + \langle x + \mathsf{r}_1^{\mathsf{in}}\rangle_1^A$.
3: P_b computes $\langle y\rangle_b^B \leftarrow b \oplus \mathsf{Eval}_n^{\mathsf{Comp}}(b, k_b, x + \mathsf{r}_1^{\mathsf{in}}, \mathsf{r}_2^{\mathsf{in}}) \oplus \langle \mathsf{r}^{\mathsf{out}}\rangle_b^B$ locally.
4: **return** $\langle y\rangle_b^B$.

its derivative). We examine the case of $x, \alpha \in \mathbb{Z}_{2^n}$ and $\beta \in \mathbb{Z}_2$ and propose a key-reduced DCF scheme with compact additive construction for comparison function $f^<_{\alpha,\beta}(x)$. Our construction draws inspiration from the distributed point function of [4], and our construction involves the algorithm $(\mathsf{Gen}_n^<, \mathsf{Eval}_n^<)$. The proposed DCF construction has the following two differences compared the state-of-the-art work, called BCG+21 [2]:

(1) We maintain input group $\mathbb{G}^{\mathsf{in}} = \mathbb{Z}_{2^n}$ but let the output group $\mathbb{G}^{\mathsf{out}} = \mathbb{Z}_2$ rather than $\mathbb{G}^{\mathsf{out}} = \mathbb{Z}_{2^m}$ where m, n are integers, and propose a key-reduced DCF construction by integrating correction words and designing a more compact key generation algorithm.
(2) We apply the idea of early termination in [4] to reduce the number of actually required correction words, thereby further reducing the DCF key sizes. Therefore, our proposed DCF construction only supports the output group $\mathbb{G}^{\mathsf{out}} = \mathbb{Z}_2$, but it has smaller key sizes than BCG+21 [2] from $n(\lambda+3)+\lambda+1$ bits to $(\lceil n - \log\lambda\rceil)(\lambda+3) + 2\lambda$ bits where λ is the security parameter.

Distributed Comparison Function. $(\mathsf{Gen}_n^<, \mathsf{Eval}_n^<)$ are presented by Algorithm 4, where $G : \{0,1\}^\lambda \rightarrow \{0,1\}^{2(\lambda+2)}$ be a PRG, and $||$ is a concatenation operator. In Algorithm 4, the number of PRG invocations in $\mathsf{Gen}_n^<$ is $2n$ and the number of PRG invocations in $\mathsf{Eval}_n^<$ is n. The gray parts are the differences between our DCF scheme and the DCF scheme in BCG+21 [2].

Early Termination Optimization. According to the description of the early termination technique in Boyle's distributed point function scheme [4], if the length of elements in the output group of a point function is short than the length of random string generated for each node, then several outputs can be packed into a single correction word. We can further improve the complexity of $(\mathsf{Gen}_n^<, \mathsf{Eval}_n^<)$ by using the "early termination" optimization, which works as follows: for any node V of depth v in the tree, there are 2^{n-v} leaf nodes in its sub-tree, or 2^{n-v} input elements with a shared prefix that ends at V. If the size of $CW^{(v+1)}$ is at least 2^{n-v} times the output length then the subsequent correction words, especially v^L_{CW}, can be computed and packed into a single $CW^{(v+1)}$

Algorithm 4. Distributed Comparison Function (DCF): $(\mathsf{Gen}_n^<, \mathsf{Eval}_n^<)$

- Key Generation Algorithm $\mathsf{Gen}_n^<(1^\lambda, \alpha, \beta)$

1: Let $\alpha_1||\cdots||\alpha_n \in \{0,1\}^n$ be the bit decomposition of α.
2: Sample randoms $s_0^{(0)} \in_R \{0,1\}^\lambda$ and $s_1^{(0)} \in_R \{0,1\}^\lambda$, and $t_0^{(0)} = 0, t_1^{(0)} = 1$.
3: Let $v_0^{(0)} = 0, v_1^{(0)} = 0$.
4: **for** $i = 1$ to n **do**
5: $s_0^L||v_0^L||t_0^L||s_0^R||v_0^R||t_0^R \leftarrow G(s_0^{(i-1)})$, and $s_1^L||v_1^L||t_1^L||s_1^R||v_1^R||t_1^R \leftarrow G(s_1^{(i-1)})$.
6: **if** $\alpha_i = 0$ **then** $\mathsf{Keep} \leftarrow L, \mathsf{Lose} \leftarrow R$.
7: **else** $\mathsf{Keep} \leftarrow R, \mathsf{Lose} \leftarrow L$.
8: $s_{CW} \leftarrow s_0^{\mathsf{Lose}} \oplus s_1^{\mathsf{Lose}}$, and $v_{CW}^L \leftarrow v_0^L \oplus v_1^L \oplus (\alpha_i \cdot \beta)$.
9: $t_{CW}^L \leftarrow t_0^L \oplus t_1^L \oplus \alpha_i \oplus 1$, and $t_{CW}^R \leftarrow t_0^R \oplus t_1^R \oplus \alpha_i$.
10: $CW^{(i)} = s_{CW}||v_{CW}^L||t_{CW}^L||t_{CW}^R$.
11: $s_0^{(i)} = s_0^{\mathsf{Keep}} \oplus t_0^{(i-1)} \cdot s_{CW}, s_1^{(i)} = s_1^{\mathsf{Keep}} \oplus t_1^{(i-1)} \cdot s_{CW}$.
12: $t_0^{(i)} = t_0^{\mathsf{Keep}} \oplus t_0^{(i-1)} \cdot t_{CW}^{\mathsf{Keep}}, t_1^{(i)} = t_1^{\mathsf{Keep}} \oplus t_1^{(i-1)} \cdot t_{CW}^{\mathsf{Keep}}$.
13: **end for**
14: Let $k_b = s_b^{(0)}||CW^{(1)}||\cdots||CW^{(n)}$.
15: **return** (k_0, k_1).

- Evaluation Algorithm $\mathsf{Eval}_n^<(b, k_b, x)$

1: Parse $k_b = s^{(0)}||CW^{(1)}||\cdots||CW^{(n)}$, and let $x = x_1||\cdots||x_n$, $v = 0$, and $t^{(0)} = b$.
2: **for** $i = 1$ to n **do**
3: Parse $CW^{(i)} = s_{CW}||v_{CW}^L||t_{CW}^L||t_{CW}^R$, and compute $G(s^{(i-1)}) = \hat{s}^L||\hat{v}^L||\hat{t}^L||\hat{s}^R||\hat{v}^R||\hat{t}^R$.
4: $\tau^{(i)} \leftarrow [\hat{s}^L||\hat{v}^L||\hat{t}^L||\hat{s}^R||\hat{v}^R||\hat{t}^R] \oplus (t^{(i-1)} \cdot [s_{CW}||v_{CW}^L||t_{CW}^L||s_{CW}||v_{CW}^L||t_{CW}^R])$.
5: Parse $\tau^{(i)} = s^L||v^L||t^L||s^R||v^R||t^R$.
6: **if** $x_i = 0$ **then** $v \leftarrow v \oplus v^L$, $s^{(i)} \leftarrow s^L, t^{(i)} \leftarrow t^L$.
7: **else** $s^{(i)} \leftarrow s^R, t^{(i)} \leftarrow t^R$.
8: **end for**
9: **return** v

instead of involving all subsequent correction words. In this case, $CW^{(v+1)}$ will be a sequence of $v_{CW}^{L,\hat{\alpha}} = v_{CW}^{L,v+1} \oplus \cdots \oplus v_{CW}^{L,n}$ where $\hat{\alpha} \in \mathbb{Z}_{2^{n-v}}$ and $v_{CW}^{L,i}$ is the last $n-v$ values in all v_{CW}^Ls (i.e., $v_{CW}^{L,i}$ for $i = v+1, \cdots, n$) where v_{CW}^L is defined in the line 11 in Algorithm 4. The sequence will output β in the location specified by $\alpha_{[v+1,n]} = \alpha_{v+1}||\cdots||\alpha_n$, and 0 in every other location.

In this paper, we let $v = \lceil n - \log \lambda \rceil$ to satisfy the above conditions. Therefore, there are only v correction words of size $\lambda + 3$, plus a $CW^{(v+1)}$ of size $2^{n-v} = \lambda$, thus the total DCF key sizes are $(\lceil n - \log \lambda \rceil)(\lambda + 3) + 2\lambda$ bits.

Security Analysis. Theorem 3 captures the correctness and security of the DCF construction, and its full proof can be found in the full paper [27].

Theorem 3. *(Correctness and Security) The scheme* $(\mathsf{Gen}_n^<, \mathsf{Eval}_n^<)$ *from Algorithm 4 is a DCF for the family of comparison functions* $f_{\alpha,\beta}^<(x) : \mathbb{Z}_{2^n} \rightarrow \mathbb{Z}_2$ *with key sizes* $(\lceil n - \log \lambda \rceil)(\lambda + 3) + 2\lambda$ *bits, where* λ *is the security parameter.*

Distributed DCF Key Generation via MPC-friendly PRG. A trusted party is required to execute the procedure $\mathsf{Gen}_n^{\mathsf{Comp}}$ for Comp in Algorithm 3, and since Comp is constructed based on the proposed DCF, the DCF key needs to be computed indeed. To realize the functionality $\mathcal{F}_{\mathsf{Gen}^{\mathsf{DCF}}}$, we present $\Pi_{\mathsf{Gen}^{\mathsf{DCF}}}$ based on a secure two-party PRG to generate DCF key, and this protocol is in Algorithm 5, where $\mathcal{F}_{\mathsf{SecPRG}}$ can be realized by the MPC-friendly PRG [9] and $\mathcal{F}_{\mathsf{2PC}}$ can be instantiate via using a secure two-party protocol based on secret sharing [7,8,21]. Note that Algorithm 5 is naturally extended to the case of using the early termination optimization.

The scheme in BCG+21 [2] (Fig. 9 in BCG+21 [2]) needs $O(2^n)$ invocations of PRG and is restricted to moderate domain sizes. By comparison, $\Pi_{\mathsf{Gen}^{\mathsf{DCF}}}$ only requires $O(n)$ invocations of PRG and can be used with larger domain sizes. Although the Appendix A.2 in [2] also mentions a distributed DCF key generation scheme via a generic 2PC with $O(n)$ evaluations of PRG, it does not give a specific construction. More importantly, the scheme mentioned in BCG+21 [2] is only applicable to the DCF construction proposed in BCG+21 [2] and cannot be used to generate the key of our proposed DCF construction, because our proposed DCF construction is essentially different from the DCF construction of BCG+21 [2].

Algorithm 5. $\Pi_{\mathsf{Gen}^{\mathsf{DCF}}}(1^\lambda, b, \{\langle\alpha_i\rangle_b^B\}_{i=1,\cdots,n}, \langle\beta\rangle_b^B)$

Input: Party index b, and P_b holds $\{\langle\alpha_i\rangle_b^B\}_{i=1,\cdots,n}$ and $\langle\beta\rangle_b^B$.
Output: P_b gets DCF key k_b.

P_b samples randoms $s_b^{(0)} \in_R \{0,1\}^\lambda, t_b^{(0)} = b$.
P_b invokes $\Pi_{\mathsf{Share}}(s_b^{(0)}), \Pi_{\mathsf{Share}}(t_b^{(0)})$ to generate secret shares of $s_b^{(0)}$ and $t_b^{(0)}$, then P_b obtains $\langle s_0^{(0)}\rangle_b^B, \langle t_0^{(0)}\rangle_b^B, \langle s_1^{(0)}\rangle_b^B, \langle t_1^{(0)}\rangle_b^B$.
for $i = 1$ to n **do**
  P_0 and P_1 engage in a secure two-party PRG to compute (for $j \in \{0,1\}$):

$$(\langle G(s_j^{(i-1)})\rangle_0^B, \langle G(s_j^{(i-1)})\rangle_1^B) \leftarrow \mathcal{F}_{\mathsf{SecPRG}}(\langle s_j^{(i-1)}\rangle_0^B, \langle s_j^{(i-1)}\rangle_1^B)$$

  where $\langle G(s_j^{(i-1)})\rangle_0^B \oplus \langle G(s_j^{(i-1)})\rangle_1^B = s_j^{L,i-1}||v_j^{L,i-1}||t_j^{L,i-1}||s_j^{L,i-1}||v_j^{L,i-1}||t_j^{L,i-1}$.
  P_0 and P_1 make access to $\mathcal{F}_{\mathsf{2PC}}$ to compute:

$$(s_{CW}, v_{CW}^L) \leftarrow \begin{cases} (s_0^{R,i-1} \oplus s_1^{R,i-1}, v_0^{L,i-1} \oplus v_1^{L,i-1}) & \alpha_i = 0 \\ (s_0^{L,i-1} \oplus s_1^{L,i-1}, v_0^{L,i-1} \oplus v_1^{L,i-1} \oplus \beta) & \alpha_i = 1 \end{cases}$$

$$(t_{CW}^L, t_{CW}^R) \leftarrow \begin{cases} (t_0^{L,i-1} \oplus t_1^{L,i-1} \oplus 1, t_0^{R,i-1} \oplus t_1^{R,i-1}) & \alpha_i = 0 \\ (t_0^{L,i-1} \oplus t_1^{L,i-1}, t_0^{R,i-1} \oplus t_1^{R,i-1} \oplus 1) & \alpha_i = 1 \end{cases}$$

  P_0 and P_1 obtain $s_{CW}; v_{CW}^L; t_{CW}^L, t_{CW}^R$.
  P_b computes $CW^{(i)} = s_{CW}||v_{CW}^L||t_{CW}^L||t_{CW}^R$ locally.
  P_0 and P_1 make access to $\mathcal{F}_{\mathsf{2PC}}$ to compute:

$$s_b^{(i)} \leftarrow \begin{cases} s_b^{L,i-1} \oplus t_b^{(i-1)} \cdot s_{CW} & \alpha_i = 0 \\ s_b^{R,i-1} \oplus t_b^{(i-1)} \cdot s_{CW} & \alpha_i = 1 \end{cases}, \quad t_b^{(i)} \leftarrow \begin{cases} t_b^{L,i-1} \oplus t_b^{(i-1)} \cdot t_{CW}^L & \alpha_i = 0 \\ t_b^{R,i-1} \oplus t_b^{(i-1)} \cdot t_{CW}^R & \alpha_i = 1 \end{cases}$$

  P_0 and P_1 obtain $(\langle s_b^{(i)}\rangle_0^B, \langle t_b^{(i)}\rangle_0^B), (\langle s_b^{(i)}\rangle_1^B, \langle t_b^{(i)}\rangle_1^B)$ respectively, where $b = 0, 1$.
end for
P_b lets $k_b \leftarrow s_b^{(0)}||CW^{(1)}||...||CW^{(n)}$.

---

4 Theoretical Analysis and Experiment

In the section, we present the theoretical analysis of the communication and computation complexity in Sect. 4.1, and show the experiment results in Sect. 4.2.

4.1 Theoretical Analysis

Online Round and Communication Complexity. The online rounds and communication costs of each neural network operation in ABY2.0 [21], AriaNN [22] and FssNN (Ours) are presented in Table 2. The function $\mathsf{MatMul}_{m_1,m_2,m_3}$ denotes a matrix multiplication of dimension $m_1 \times m_2$ with $m_2 \times m_3$, and $\mathsf{HadamProd}_{m_1,m_2}$ denotes a Hadamard product of dimension $m_1 \times m_2$. ReLU_{m_1,m_2} and DReLU_{m_1,m_2} denotes ReLU and its derivative over a $m_1 \times m_2$ matrix, and $\mathsf{MaxPool}_{m,k,s}$ denotes maxpool with input the $m \times m$ where k stands for the kernel size and s stands for the stride. All communication is measured for n-bit inputs and missing entries mean that data was not available.

For round complexity, all neural network operators are computed with constant online communication rounds in AriaNN and FssNN, while linear functions (i.e., MatMul and $\mathsf{HadamProd}$) computation requires 1 round and non-linear (i.e., DReLU, ReLU and $\mathsf{MaxPool}$) computation requires $O(\log n)$ rounds in ABY2.0. For online communication costs, FssNN achieves lower online communication costs in $\mathsf{HadamProd}$ and ReLU than AriaNN due to our communication efficient protocol Π_{BitXA}.

Table 2. Online rounds and communication of ABY2.0 [21], AriaNN [22] and FssNN (Ours)

Operators	Rounds			Communication		
	ABY2.0	AriaNN	**FssNN**	ABY2.0	AriaNN	**FssNN**
$\mathsf{MatMul}_{m_1,m_2,m_3}$	1	1	1	m_1m_3n	$(m_1m_2 + m_2m_3)n$	$(m_1m_2 + m_2m_3)n$
$\mathsf{HadamProd}_{m_1,m_2}$	1	1	1	$2m_1m_2n$	$2m_1m_2n$	$m_1m_2(n+1)$
DReLU_{m_1,m_2}	$1 + \log n$	1	1	$\sim 3m_1m_2n$	m_1m_2n	m_1m_2n
ReLU_{m_1,m_2}	$2 + \log n$	2	2	$\sim 5m_1m_2n$	$3m_1m_2n$	$m_1m_2(2n+1)$
$\mathsf{MaxPool}_{m,k,s}$	-	3	3	-	$(\frac{m-k}{s} + 1)^2(k^4 + 2)n$	$(\frac{m-k}{s} + 1)^2(k^4 + 2)n$

Offline Communication and Computation Complexity. In the online phase, ABY2.0 [21], AriaNN [22] and FssNN (Ours) all have an order of magnitude of online computation complexity since they all adopt the offline-online paradigm. In the offline phase, FssNN uses the same multiplication triples generation scheme as ABY2.0 and AriaNN. However, FssNN needs to generate correlated randomness (i.e., DCF key) to compute DReLU, ReLU and $\mathsf{MaxPool}$, while ABY2.0 requires smaller correlated randomness and it can be generated more efficiently using 2PC-based offline phase (but leads to $4-5\times$ more rounds and $3-6\times$ more communication of online communication [2]) and AriaNN relies on a trusted party to correlated randomness (but leads to stronger assumptions). Therefore, FssNN requires more communication and computation in the offline phase, but has less online communication compared with ABY2.0 and does not rely on the trusted leader compared with AriaNN.

DCF Key Sizes. The communication criteria of DCF construction is the sizes of key k_b (i.e., the output of $\mathsf{Gen}_n^{<}$), so the DCF key sizes in BCG+21 [2], AriaNN [22] and FssNN are shown in Table 3. It is clear that the DCF key sizes of FssNN is the smallest, which decreases the size of DCF keys by about 17.9%.

Table 3. The DCF key sizes in BCG+21 [2], AriaNN [22] and FssNN (Ours)

Para. (bits)	BCG+21 [2]	AriaNN [22]	FssNN (Ours)
(n, λ)	$n(\lambda+3)+\lambda+1$	$n(\lambda+2n+4)+\lambda+2n$	$(\lceil n-\log\lambda\rceil)(\lambda+3)+2\lambda$
(32, 127)	4424	6431	3634

4.2 Experiment

In this section, we present the implement of FssNN and the detailed experiment results and analysis. We implement FssNN in Python and run the experiments on Aliyun ESC using ecs.hfr7.xlarge machines with 32 cores and 256 GB of CPU RAM in a LAN setting. In order to simplify comparison with existing works, we follow a setup very close to AriaNN [22] and use same neural network models and datasets. AriaNN [22] is the state-of-the-art seucre neural network training and inference framework based on function secret sharing, and outperform other works such as FALCON [25] and ABY2.0 [21].

Evaluations for Secure Layer Functions. First, we present the offline and online communication costs of linear layer functions (i.e., MatMul and HadamProd) and non-linear layer functions (i.e., DReLU, ReLU and MaxPool) in Table 4.

Table 4. Offline and online communication of neural network operators in AriaNN [22] and FssNN where (784, 128, 10), (128, 128) and (24, 2, 2) are typical parameters.

Operators	Input Sizes	Offline Comm. (MB)		Online Comm. (MB)	
		AriaNN	FssNN (Ours)	AriaNN	FssNN (Ours)
$\mathsf{MatMul}_{m_1,m_2,m_3}$	(784, 128, 10)	0.842	0.842	0.775	0.775
$\mathsf{HadamProd}_{m_1,m_2}$	(128, 128)	0.381	0.272 (↓ 28.6%)	0.251	0.142 (↓ 43.4%)
DReLU_{m_1,m_2}	(128, 128)	14.377	10.314 (↓ 28.3%)	0.126	0.126
ReLU_{m_1,m_2}	(128, 128)	14.758	10.586 (↓ 28.3%)	0.377	0.268(↓ 28.9%)
$\mathsf{MaxPool}_{m,k,s}$	(24, 2, 2)	0.399	0.292 (↓ 26.8%)	0.020	0.020

For linear layer functions, compared with AriaNN, the offline and online communication costs of HadamProd decreases by 28.6% and 43.4% respectively. For non-linear layer functions, we improve the offline communication costs by 26.8%–28.3% over AriaNN due to the proposed key-reduced DCF in FssNN. The online communication improvement of ReLU is attributed to our communication efficient Π_{BitXA}.

Evaluations for Secure Neural Network. We benchmark secure training and inference on MNIST (60,000 training samples and 10,000 test samples) and evaluate following 3 neural networks: (1) a 3-layer fully-connected network (FCNN), (2) a 4-layer convolutional neural network (CNN) and (3) a 4-layer LeNet network (LeNet). It should be noted that FssNN, like AriaNN [22], can support to more machine learning tasks and datasets, such as models AlexNet and VGG16 in datasets CIFAR10 and Tiny Imagenet.

Time, communication and accuracy of secure training and inference in the LAN setting are presented in Table 5, where accuracy of plaintext training and inference are also reported for comparison. The time and communication for secure training are given in hours and GB per epoch, and secure inference is evaluated over pre-trained neural network models and the total time and communication are reported.

It is observed that accuracy of secure training and inference are a little lower than their plaintext counterparts, but the gap between them isn't significant.

Table 5. Time, communication and accuracy of secure training and inference in FssNN

FssNN	Model	Epochs	Time (h)	Comm. (GB)	Private Acc.	Plaintext Acc.
Training	FCNN	15	0.23	27.35	98.00%	98.04%
	CNN	10	2.24	439.78	98.60%	98.73%
	LeNet	10	3.46	648.83	98.93%	99.03%
Inference	FCNN	–	0.01	2.14	98.15%	98.17%
	CNN	–	0.30	72.84	98.95%	99.02%
	LeNet	–	0.56	107.63	99.22%	99.27%

Compare with AriaNN [22]. The total communication and time for secure training and inference are presented in Table 6. Compared with AriaNN [22], the communication for training declined by 24.3% – 25.4% and the communication for inference decreased by 22.9% – 26.4%. This is attributed to our online-efficient protocol Π_{BitXA}, and key-reduced DCF scheme which improves the communication efficiency of protocols Π_{DReLU}, Π_{ReLU} and Π_{MaxPool}.

Table 6. The communication and time for secure training and inference

	Model	Training		Inference	
		Comm. (GB)	Time (h)	Comm. (GB)	Time (h)
AriaNN [22]	FCNN	36.11	0.28	2.84	0.02
	CNN	589.91	2.24	94.49	0.37
	LeNet	869.75	3.50	146.24	0.56
FssNN(Ours)	FCNN	27.35 (↓ 24.3%)	0.23	2.14 (↓ 24.8%)	0.02
	CNN	439.78 (↓ 25.4%)	2.24	72.84 (↓ 22.9%)	0.30
	LeNet	648.83 (↓ 25.4%)	3.46	107.63 (↓ 26.4%)	0.56

5 Conclusion

Privacy-preserving neural network based on secure multiparty computation has emerged as a flourishing research area in the past few years, but its practicality is greatly limited due to the low efficiency caused by massive communication costs and a deep dependence on a trusted party. In this work, we proposed a communication-efficient secure neural network framework, FssNN, to enable practical training and inference. Theoretical analysis and experiment show the practical performance of FssNN, and the substantial performance advantage over existing works. Compared with the state-of-the-art solution AriaNN, the communication costs of secure training and inference are decreased by 25.4% and 26.4% respectively. More attempts might be made to construct actively secure protocols to defend against a malicious adversary.

Acknowledgements. We sincerely thank the anonymous reviewers of ProvSec 2024 for their valuable comments. The work is supported by Shenzhen Science and Technology Major Project (KJZD20230923114908017), National Natural Science Foundation of China (62272131), and Guangdong Provincial Key Laboratory of Novel Security Intelligence Technologies (2022B1212010005).

A Dual Distributed Comparison Function

Dual DCF (DDCF) is a variant of DCF, is defined as:

$$f^{<}_{\alpha,\beta_0,\beta_1}(x) = \begin{cases} \beta_0 & x < \alpha \\ \beta_1 & \text{else} \end{cases} \tag{1}$$

where $x, \alpha \in \mathbb{Z}_{2^n}, \beta_0, \beta_1 \in \mathbb{Z}_2$, and $\beta_0 \neq \beta_1$.

We present a DDCF scheme based on the DCF scheme, its detailed construction is shown in Algorithm 6. Compared with [2], our DDCF construction is slightly modified: the output group is constrained to be $\mathbb{Z}_2$, and more importantly, our DDCF construction relies on the proposed key-reduced DCF (i.e., $(\mathsf{Gen}^{<}_{n}, \mathsf{Eval}^{<}_{n})$, § 3.3). Our DDCF construction requires 1 call of DCF, and the key sizes are $(\lceil n - \log \lambda \rceil)(\lambda + 3) + 2\lambda$ bits where λ is the security parameter.

Algorithm 6. DDCF: $(\mathsf{Gen}_n^{\mathsf{DDCF}}, \mathsf{Eval}_n^{\mathsf{DDCF}})$

• $\mathsf{Gen}_n^{\mathsf{DDCF}}(1^\lambda, \alpha, \beta_0, \beta_1)$

1: Compute $(k_0^{(n)}, k_1^{(n)}) \leftarrow \mathsf{Gen}_n^{<}(1^\lambda, \alpha, \beta_0 \oplus \beta_1)$.
2: Sample $r_0, r_1 \in_R \{0,1\}$, such that $r_0 \oplus r_1 = \beta_1$.
3: Let $k_b = k_b^{(n)} || r_b$ for $b \in \{0,1\}$.
4: **return** (k_0, k_1).

• $\mathsf{Eval}_n^{\mathsf{DDCF}}(b, k_b, x)$

1: Parse $k_b = k_b^{(n)} || r_b$, and compute $y_b^{(n-1)} \leftarrow \mathsf{Eval}_n^{<}(b, k_b^{(n)}, x)$.
2: Let $v_b = y_b^{(n-1)} \oplus r_b$.
3: **return** v_b.

References

1. Beaver, D.: Efficient multiparty protocols using circuit randomization. In: Feigenbaum, J. (ed.) CRYPTO 1991. LNCS, vol. 576, pp. 420–432. Springer, Heidelberg (1992). https://doi.org/10.1007/3-540-46766-1_34
2. Boyle, E., et al.: Function secret sharing for mixed-mode and fixed-point secure computation. In: Canteaut, A., Standaert, F.-X. (eds.) EUROCRYPT 2021. LNCS, vol. 12697, pp. 871–900. Springer, Cham (2021). https://doi.org/10.1007/978-3-030-77886-6_30
3. Boyle, E., Gilboa, N., Ishai, Y.: Function secret sharing. In: Oswald, E., Fischlin, M. (eds.) EUROCRYPT 2015. LNCS, vol. 9057, pp. 337–367. Springer, Heidelberg (2015). https://doi.org/10.1007/978-3-662-46803-6_12
4. Boyle, E., Gilboa, N., Ishai, Y.: Function secret sharing: improvements and extensions. In: 2016 ACM SIGSAC Conference on Computer and Communications Security, pp. 1292–1303. ACM, Vienna (2016). https://doi.org/10.1145/2976749.2978429
5. Boyle, E., Gilboa, N., Ishai, Y.: Secure computation with preprocessing via function secret sharing. In: Hofheinz, D., Rosen, A. (eds.) TCC 2019. LNCS, vol. 11891, pp. 341–371. Springer, Cham (2019). https://doi.org/10.1007/978-3-030-36030-6_14
6. Chaudhari, H., Rachuri, R., Suresh, A.: Trident: efficient 4PC framework for privacy preserving machine learning. In: Network and Distributed System Security Symposium (2020). https://doi.org/10.14722/ndss.2020.23005
7. Damgård, I., Pastro, V., Smart, N., Zakarias, S.: Multiparty computation from somewhat homomorphic encryption. In: Safavi-Naini, R., Canetti, R. (eds.) CRYPTO 2012. LNCS, vol. 7417, pp. 643–662. Springer, Heidelberg (2012). https://doi.org/10.1007/978-3-642-32009-5_38
8. Demmler, D., Schneider, T., Zohner, M.: ABY - a framework for efficient mixed-protocol secure two-party computation. In: Network and Distributed System Security Symposium (2015). https://doi.org/10.14722/ndss.2015.23113
9. Dinur, I., et al.: MPC-friendly symmetric cryptography from alternating moduli: candidates, protocols, and applications. In: Malkin, T., Peikert, C. (eds.) CRYPTO 2021. LNCS, vol. 12828, pp. 517–547. Springer, Cham (2021). https://doi.org/10.1007/978-3-030-84259-8_18
10. Doerner, J., Shelat, A.: Scaling ORAM for secure computation. In: Proceedings of the 2017 ACM SIGSAC Conference on Computer and Communications Security, pp. 523–535. ACM, Dallas (2017). https://doi.org/10.1145/3133956.3133967

11. Feng, D., Yang, K.: Concretely efficient secure multi-party computation protocols: survey and more. In: Security and Safety, p. 2021001 (2022). https://doi.org/10.1051/sands/2021001
12. Gentry, C.: Fully homomorphic encryption using ideal lattices. In: 41st Annual ACM Symposium on Theory of Computing, pp. 169–178. ACM, Bethesda (2009). https://doi.org/10.1145/1536414.1536440
13. Goldreich, O.: Foundations of Cryptography: volume 2, Basic Applications. Cambridge university press, Cambridge (2004). https://doi.org/10.1017/CBO9780511721656
14. Goldreich, O., Micali, S., Wigderson, A.: How to play any mental game. In: Proceedings of the 19th ACM Symposium on Theory of Computing, pp. 218–229. ACM, New York (1987). https://doi.org/10.1145/28395.28420
15. Gupta, K., Kumaraswamy, D., Chandran, N., Gupta, D.: LLAMA: a low latency math library for secure inference. In: Proceedings on Privacy Enhancing Technologies, pp. 274–294 (2022). https://doi.org/10.56553/popets-2022-0109
16. Jawalkar, N., Gupta, K., Basu, A., Chandran, N., Gupta, D., Sharma, R.: Orca: FSS-based secure training and inference with GPUs. In: 2024 IEEE Symposium on Security and Privacy, pp. 66–66. IEEE, San Francisco (2024). https://doi.org/10.1109/SP54263.2024.00063
17. Koti, N., Patra, A., Rachuri, R., Suresh, A.: Tetrad: actively secure 4PC for secure training and inference. In: Network and Distributed System Security Symposium (2022). https://doi.org/10.14722/ndss.2022.24058
18. Lindell, Y.: How to simulate it–a tutorial on the simulation proof technique. In: Tutorials on the Foundations of Cryptography: Dedicated to Oded Goldreich, pp. 277–346 (2017). https://doi.org/10.1007/978-3-319-57048-8_6
19. Mohassel, P., Rindal, P.: ABY3: a mixed protocol framework for machine learning. In: Proceedings of the 2018 ACM SIGSAC Conference on Computer and Communications Security, pp. 35–52. ACM, Toronto (2018). https://doi.org/10.1145/3243734.3243760
20. Mohassel, P., Zhang, Y.: SecureML: a system for scalable privacy-preserving machine learning. In: 2017 IEEE Symposium on Security and Privacy, pp. 19–38. IEEE, San Jose (2017). https://doi.org/10.1109/SP.2017.12
21. Patra, A., Schneider, T., Suresh, A., Yalame, H.: ABY2.0: improved mixed-protocol secure two-party computation. In: 30th USENIX Security Symposium, pp. 2165–2182. USENIX Association (2021). https://www.usenix.org/conference/usenixsecurity21/presentation/patra
22. Ryffel, T., Tholoniat, P., Pointcheval, D., Bach, F.: AriaNN: low-interaction privacy-preserving deep learning via function secret sharing. In: Proceedings on Privacy Enhancing Technologies, pp. 291–316 (2022). https://doi.org/10.2478/popets-2022-0015
23. Storrier, K., Vadapalli, A., Lyons, A., Henry, R.: Grotto: screaming fast $(2+1)$-PC for $\mathbb{Z}_{2^n}$ via (2, 2)-DPFs. In: 2023 ACM SIGSAC Conference on Computer and Communications Security, pp. 2143–2157. ACM, Copenhagen (2023). https://doi.org/10.1145/3576915.3623147
24. Wagh, S., Gupta, D., Chandran, N.: SecureNN: 3-party secure computation for neural network training. In: Proceedings on Privacy Enhancing Technologies, pp. 26–49 (2019). https://doi.org/10.2478/popets-2019-0035
25. Wagh, S., Tople, S., Benhamouda, F., Kushilevitz, E., Mittal, P., Rabin, T.: Falcon: honest-majority maliciously secure framework for private deep learning. In: Proceedings on Privacy Enhancing Technologies, pp. 188–208 (2021). https://doi.org/10.2478/popets-2021-0011

26. Yang, K., Weng, C., Lan, X., Zhang, J., Wang, X.: Ferret: fast extension for correlated OT with small communication. In: 2020 ACM SIGSAC Conference on Computer and Communications Security, pp. 1607–1626. ACM, Virtual Event (2020). https://doi.org/10.1145/3372297.3417276
27. Yang, P., et al.: FssNN: communication-efficient secure neural network training via function secret sharing. Cryptology ePrint Archive, Paper 2023/073 (2023). https://eprint.iacr.org/2023/073
28. Yao, A.C.C.: How to generate and exchange secrets. In: 27th Annual Symposium on Foundations of Computer Science, pp. 162–167. IEEE (1986). https://doi.org/10.1109/SFCS.1986.25

Enabling Efficient Cross-Shard Smart Contract Calling via Overlapping

Zixu Zhang[1], Hongbo Yin[2], Ying Wang[3](✉), Guangsheng Yu[4], Xu Wang[1], Wei Ni[4], and Ren Ping Liu[1]

[1] University of Technology Sydney, Ultimo, Australia
zixu.zhang@student.uts.edu.au, {xu.wang,renping.liu}@uts.edu.au
[2] Chongqing University of Posts and Telecommunications, Chongqing, China
s210101168@stu.cqupt.edu.cn
[3] Hangzhou Dianzi University, Hangzhou Dianzi University Hangzhou, China
90023@hdu.edu.cn
[4] Data61, CSIRO, Sydney, Australia
{saber.yu,wei.ni}@data61.csiro.au

Abstract. As blockchain networks grow, sharding offers a promising solution to scalability challenges by dividing the network into smaller segments. However, managing cross-shard transactions, especially those involving smart contract calling, introduces significant complexities due to the extensive coordination required between shards. This paper introduces a novel framework for blockchain architectures with overlapping shards to address these challenges in cross-shard smart contract calling. The framework introduces overlapping shards and an optimized PBFT consensus mechanism, xPBFT. This framework simplifies cross-shard transaction management by treating them as intra-shard activities, reducing latency and improving security by enabling nodes to operate across multiple shards. Through experimental results, it is demonstrate that this framework decreases latency by up to 40% compared to traditional PBFT methods while effectively maintaining transaction security.

Keywords: blockchain · sharding · cross-shard transaction · smart contract · consensus

1 Introduction

Blockchain technology has significantly transformed the landscape of decentralized systems, offering unparalleled security and transparency across numerous applications. As blockchain networks grow, the scalability trilemma [1–4]-balancing scalability, security, and decentralization-becomes increasingly challenging. Sharding emerges as a compelling solution to this trilemma by partitioning the network into smaller, manageable segments, or shards, that process transactions concurrently, thereby boosting throughput significantly [5–7].

J. K. Liu et al. (Eds.): ProvSec 2024, LNCS 14904, pp. 164–178, 2025.
https://doi.org/10.1007/978-981-96-0957-4_9

While sharding improves scalability and maintains robust security, it introduces complexities in managing cross-shard transactions, especially those involving smart contracts function calling [8]. These transactions frequently suffer from high latency due to the need for coordination between multiple shards and are vulnerable to security risks posed by malicious nodes within the network [9–11]. Specifically, the integrity of cross-shard transactions hinges on the reliable exchange of information, such as transaction proofs or commitment evidence, between shard leaders, who may act maliciously or become compromised [12–15].

This paper presents a novel framework designed for managing cross-shard smart contract transactions within blockchain architectures that utilize overlapping shards. The framework introduces a refined version of the Practical Byzantine Fault Tolerance (PBFT) consensus mechanism, termed xPBFT, optimized for overlapping shards. By converting cross-shard transactions into intra-shard transactions, xPBFT simplifies transaction management. Leaders are randomly selected from each shard to form an overlapping shard, where they access comprehensive transaction data across all shards. This setup enables efficient consensus directly within the central shard, with outcomes subsequently synchronized across all individual shards.

Key contributions of this paper include:

- This paper introduces a framework that leverages overlapping shards to convert cross-shard transactions into intra-shard transactions, thereby reducing latency.
- A cross-shard-optimized PBFT consensus mechanism, referred to as xPBFT, is proposed for overlapping shard architectures, which achieves a latency reduction of up to 40% while enhancing security against adversarial threats.

The remainder of the paper is organized as follows: Sect. 2 reviews related work of blockchain sharding. Section 3 describes the proposed PBFT consensus mechanism based on overlapping shards. Section 4 presents a comprehensive evaluation of the system. Finally, the conclusions are given in Sect. 5.

2 Related Work

Sharding has emerged as a critical solution to enhance throughput and address the scalability challenges in blockchain technology by dividing the blockchain into smaller, independently operating segments known as shards. This configuration introduces complexities, particularly in managing cross-shard transactions involving smart contracts, which require extensive coordination between shards. To address these complexities, Hong *et al.* [2] introduce the PYRAMID model, a novel approach to blockchain scalability that leverages layered sharding. In this model, shards can overlap, allowing some nodes to participate in multiple shards. This design enables nodes that store blockchain data from these overlapping shards to validate and execute cross-shard transactions directly, without needing to decompose them into multiple sub-transactions. While sharding improves system throughput, it raises significant security concerns, particularly regarding the integrity and security of cross-shard transactions. Liu *et al.* [13] propose a secure cross-shard view-change protocol to mitigate risks associated with potentially malicious shard leaders, ensuring transaction integrity across shards and preventing data censorship by compromised leaders. Concurrently, Sonnino *et al.* [8] delve into consensus mechanisms tailored for sharded blockchains, focusing on BFT-based algorithms to achieve strong consistency and fault tolerance within and across shards, ensuring secure and reliable transaction validation and commitment.

Further studies, such as those by Zamani *et al.* [10] have explored sharding protocols aimed at optimizing network resources and maintaining scalability amid an increasing number of nodes and transactions. Furthermore, Yang *et al.* [16] introduce overlapping shards that enable nodes to belong to multiple shards, simplifying transaction processes by converting cross-shard to intra-shard transactions, thereby enhancing security and reducing latency while employing machine learning for dynamic shard configuration optimization based on real-time network conditions.

Despite these advancements, existing solutions [2,5,8,10,16] often struggle with high latency during cross-shard smart contract transactions and may not effectively handle the intricate dynamics of such operations. Therefore, this paper introduces a novel framework designed for cross-shard smart contract transaction function calling. It incorporates overlapping shards and xPBFT consensus mechanism, which simplifies the management of cross-shard transactions by treating them as intra-shard transactions. This approach significantly reduces latency and enhances security, providing a robust solution to scalability challenges in blockchain architectures.

3 Cross-Shard Smart Contract Framework: Overlapping Shards and xPBFT Consensus

In this section, we detail the architecture of overlapping shards designed to address the high latency and security challenges inherent in cross-shard transactions involving smart contracts. Several leaders are randomly selected from each shard to form an overlapping shard, ensuring that these leaders have access to comprehensive transaction data from all shards. Within this novel framework, the xPBFT consensus mechanism operates through an overlapping shard structure.

3.1 Sharding with Overlapping Shard

Each shard maintains its ledger in the proposed architecture, but the leader within the overlapping shard can access the full transaction data across the network. This setup is crucial for managing both intra-shard and cross-shard transactions effectively. The role of overlapping shard leaders is not only to facilitate cross-shard transactions but also to ensure that intra-shard transactions adhere to the global state of the blockchain, thereby preserving consistency and integrity throughout the system. Table 1 presents the notations used throughout the paper.

Table 1. Notations

Notation	Description
n	Total number of nodes
n_k	Total number of nodes in the k-th shard
K	Total number of shards
m	Total number of leader nodes in overlapping shard
m_k	Total number of leader nodes in the k-th shard
$\mathbb{M}$	Set of nodes in overlapping shard
T^{ε}	Total latency in the ε consensus round
T^{ε}_{pkg}	Block packing latency in the ε consensus round
T^{ε}_{cp}	Consensus latency in the ε consensus round
	including phases: $T^{\varepsilon}_{cp,pre-prepare}$, $T^{\varepsilon}_{cp,prepare}$,
	$T^{\varepsilon}_{cp,submit}$, $T^{\varepsilon}_{cp,result}$, $T^{\varepsilon}_{cp,verify}$
$B^{\varepsilon}_{pre-prepare}$	Block data size in the pre-prepare stage at the ε
$B^{\varepsilon}_{prepare}$	Block data size in the prepare stage at the ε
B^{ε}_{submit}	Block data size in the commitment stage at the ε
B^{ε}_{result}	Block data size in the reply stage at the ε
S	Transmission rate
c_k	Total CPU cycle requirement in the k-th shard
f_i	Computational Capability (CPU cycles per second) for i-th node
F	Total number of signatures
V	Total number of Message Authentication Codes
D	Total storage requirement
$\mathcal{B}_k$	Block storage requirement in the k-th shard

Figure 1 illustrates the process of proposing and broadcasting a transaction to the overlapping shard. It highlights the central role of leaders from each shard in the initial transaction handling. Each shard operates independently and includes multiple nodes, designated as n_k. From these, a subset, m_k, are chosen as leaders. These leaders collectively form the overlapping shard, consisting of m total nodes, thus representing the combined leadership from all participating shards.

3.2 The Proposed xPBFT Consensus

As depicted in Fig. 2, the workflow of the proposed xPBFT consensus within the overlapping sharding framework is designed to optimize both the speed and security of transaction processing. Utilizing an overlapping shard that exists for all shard leaders, the system can rapidly reach consensus on intra-shard and cross-shard transactions, significantly reducing the communication overhead typically associated with such operations.

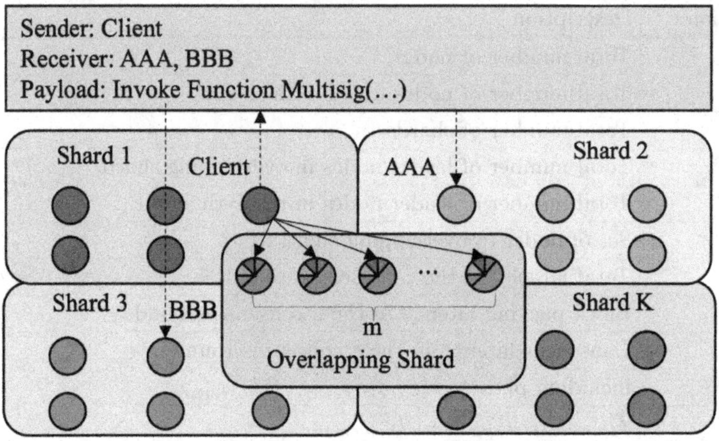

Fig. 1. A client proposes a transaction and broadcasts it to the overlapping shard containing several leaders from each shard.

Algorithm 1: PBFT Consensus for Overlapping Shards

Input: $REQ(C, op, t, Sig)$: The transaction request from client C with operation op, timestamp t, and signature Sig;
Output: Confirmation of transaction commitment;

$v \leftarrow$ **GetCurrentViewNumber(*REQ*)** ;
$\phi \leftarrow$ **GetUniqueSequenceNumber(*REQ*)** ;
$d \leftarrow$ **ComputeDigest**(REQ) ;
BroadcastToAllLeaders$(PP(v, \phi, d, REQ))$;
// Broadcast pre-prepare message to all leaders in the overlapping shard.
foreach leader $\in \mathbb{M}$ **do**
  $P \leftarrow$ **ReceivePrepareMessage**$(PP(v, \phi, d, REQ))$;
  // Each leader receives prepare messages from others.
  if **ValidatePrePrepare**$(\mathcal{P}(v, \phi, d, i).)$ **then**
    AddToPreparedList$(\mathcal{P}(v, \phi, d, i).)$;
    // Validate and add to prepared list if valid.
if **ConsensusReached**$(\mathcal{P}(v, \phi, d, i).)$ **then**
  $\mathcal{C} \leftarrow$ **CommitTransaction**$(\mathcal{P}(v, \phi, d, i))$;
  BroadcastToAllNodesInShards$(\mathcal{C}(v, \phi, d, i, s))$;
  //Commit the transaction and notify all nodes. ;
  return "Transaction Committed Successfully" ;
else
  return "Transaction Failed to Reach Consensus" ;

The xPBFT consensus process, as outlined in Algorithm 1, starts when a client submits a transaction request to the overlapping shard's leaders during the **Pre-prepare Phase**. This request, denoted as $REQ(C, op, t, \mathrm{Sig})$, consists of the client submitting an operation op, client identifier C, timestamped with t, and secured by a digital signature Sig. During this phase, each transaction is encapsulated with a view number v, sequence number ϕ, and a digest d of the request, represented as $\mathcal{PP}(v, \phi, d, REQ)$. This initial phase guarantees uniform receipt and verification of transaction data by all leaders in the overlapping shard, mitigating the risk of double spending attacks and promoting a consistent approach to transaction validation.

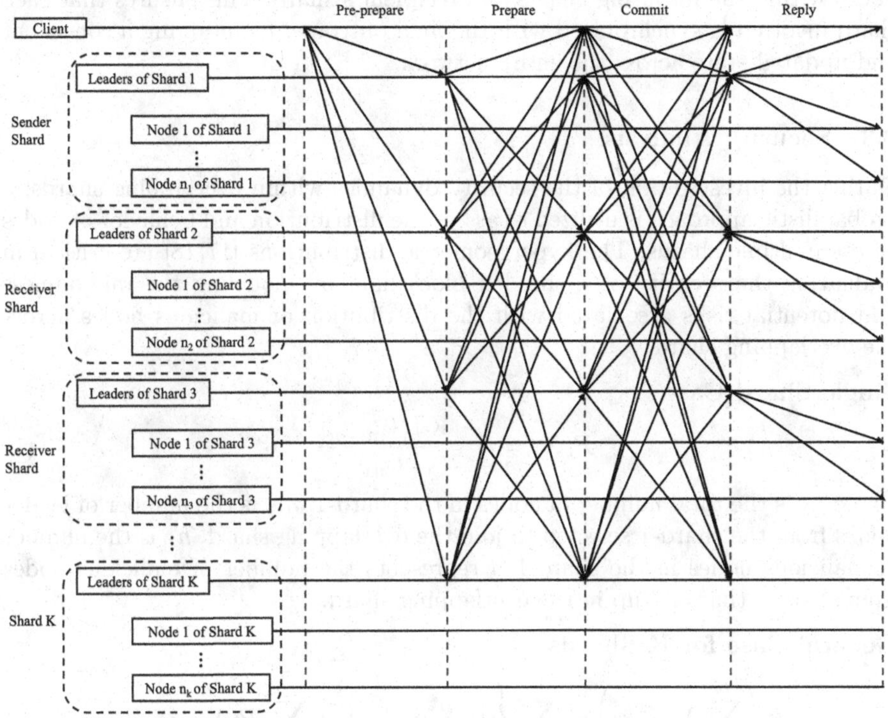

Fig. 2. The proposed PBFT workflow based on the overlapping sharding framework. The security is ensured by keeping malicious nodes in the overlapping shard below the threshold α, defined as one-third of all leader nodes ($\alpha = \frac{1}{3}(m_1 + m_2 + \cdots + m_k)$). Only the sender and receiver shards involved in the transaction require replies. The client can be any node initiating a transaction from any shard. Leaders from Shard 1 to Shard K form the overlapping shard, coordinating to reach a consensus on cross-shard smart contract transactions.

After the Pre-prepare Phase, the transaction enters the **Prepare Phase**, where the detailed transaction data is further verified and prepared for final consensus. The Prepare message includes the view number v, sequence number

ϕ, a digest d of the request and identification of the node that sent this prepare message i, represented as $\mathcal{P}(v, \phi, d, i)$. During the Prepare Phase, each leader within the overlapping shard independently validates the transaction, facilitating a consensus-driven verification process.

Upon achieving consensus, the transaction advances to the **Commitment Phase**, where it is formally committed to the blockchain. This phase marks the definitive agreement among the leaders, ensuring the transaction's integrity and finality. The commitment is denoted as $\mathcal{C}(v, \phi, d, i, s)$, representing a complete and verified transaction.

Following the commitment, the **Reply Phase** initiates. During this phase, leaders from the overlapping shard communicate the transaction results to all nodes within the initiating clients and recipient's shard. This ensures that each shard involved is synchronized with the final outcome, maintaining a consistent and updated state across the entire network.

3.3 Security Analysis

During the investigation of the security dynamics within overlapping shards, a probabilistic approach is utilized to assess the distribution and behavior of nodes across multiple shards. The hypergeometric distributions [17,18] are critical in evaluating the security of a sharded blockchain by modeling the randomness and potential risks associated with the distribution of malicious nodes across the overlapping shard.

Single Shard Case

$$P(X_1 = i) = \frac{C_{h_1}^{i} C_{n_1-h_1}^{m_1-i}}{C_{n_1}^{m_1}}, \tag{1}$$

where n_1 is the total number of nodes in the shard-1. m_1 is the number of leader nodes from the shard-1 selected to join the overlapping shard. h_1 is the number of malicious nodes in the shard-1. i represents the number of malicious nodes from shard-1 that end up in the overlapping shard.

General Case for K Shards

$$\begin{aligned} P\left(\sum_{k=1}^{K} X_k \le \alpha\right) = \sum_{i_1=0}^{\alpha} \Bigg\{ P(X_1 = i_1) \times \Bigg[\sum_{i_2=0}^{\alpha-i_1} P(X_2 = i_2) \times \\ \cdots \times \sum_{i_{K-1}=0}^{\alpha-(\sum_{j=1}^{K-2} i_j)} \Bigg[P(X_{K-1} = i_{K-1}) \times \\ P(X_K \le \alpha - \left(\sum_{j=1}^{K-1} i_j\right)) \Bigg]\Bigg]\Bigg\} \end{aligned} \tag{2}$$

where $P(X_1 = i_1)$ represents the probability that i_1 node joins the overlapping shard from shard-1. X_k is defined as the random variable representing the number of malicious nodes assigned to the k-th shard. The formula shown aims to compute the security probability P that the aggregate number of malicious nodes $\sum_{k=1}^{K}$ across all shards K remains below a specific threshold α. This threshold α is defined as one-third of the total number of nodes joining the overlapping shard from all shards involved, expressed as $\alpha = \frac{1}{3}\lfloor(m_1 + m_2 + \cdots + m_k)\rfloor$. The significance of α is to establish a bound at which the presence of malicious leaders within the overlapping shard would not pose a security risk. The term $P(X_K \leq \alpha - \left(\sum_{j=1}^{K-1} i_j\right)$ represents the cumulative probability that the number of malicious nodes in the K-th shard does not exceed $\alpha - \left(\sum_{j=1}^{K-1} i_j\right)$. This term ensures that the sum of malicious nodes across all K shards stays within the threshold α.

The cumulative probability function for X_K is defined as:

$$P\left(X_K \leq y\right) = \sum_{i=0}^{y} P\left(X_K = i\right), \tag{3}$$

where $y = \alpha - \left(\sum_{j=1}^{K-1} i_j\right)$ indicates the maximum allowable number of malicious nodes in shard-K that, when combined with the malicious nodes from other shards, does not exceed α. Each probability $P\left(X_K = i\right)$ within the sum is computed based on the hypergeometric distribution, which accounts for the likelihood of having exactly i malicious nodes in shard-K given the total nodes in that shard and the overall number of malicious nodes.

3.4 Complexity Analysis

Communication Complexity. Reducing communication complexity is pivotal in scaling distributed blockchain networks in public blockchain environments that utilize PBFT mechanisms. Traditionally, PBFT implementations suffer from a communication complexity of $O(n^2)$, where n is the total number of nodes in the network [19]. This inefficiency arises because each node must broadcast messages to every other node to achieve consensus, leading to significant operational challenges as the network expands.

The introduction of sharding, especially with an overlapping shard design where only select leaders from each shard participate in the consensus process, significantly reduces the communication complexity to $O(m^2)$, where m represents the number of nodes in the overlapping shard. This reduction from $O(n^2)$ to $O(m^2)$ enhances scalability and allows the network to support more nodes and handle a higher volume of transactions without a proportional increase in resource demand or latency.

Consensus Latency Costs. The latency T^{ε} for a consensus round ε is a critical metric in evaluating the efficiency of the proposed PBFT consensus mechanism for overlapping shards. The equation for total latency is expressed as:

$$T^{\varepsilon} = \min(T^{\varepsilon}_{\text{pkg}} + T^{\varepsilon}_{\text{cp}}), \tag{4}$$

where $T^{\varepsilon}_{\text{pkg}}$ denotes the block packing latency, and $T^{\varepsilon}_{\text{cp}}$ represents the overall consensus latency, encompassing all critical phases of the consensus protocol. Each phase's latency depends on the maximum transmission time of data blocks and the node transmission rate, which is affected by the number of participating leaders, potentially leading to congestion.

In each shard, reaching consensus involves two key operations [20]: 1) the message transmission between nodes, including signature verification, and 2) the validation of the message authentication code (MAC) by the nodes. The total latency involved in a cross-shard transaction process, considering multiple phases of a consensus protocol, is detailed as follows:

$$\begin{aligned} T^{\varepsilon}_{\text{cp}} &= T^{\varepsilon}_{\text{cp,pre-prepare}} + T^{\varepsilon}_{\text{cp,prepare}} + T^{\varepsilon}_{\text{cp,submit}} \\ &+ T^{\varepsilon}_{\text{cp,result}} + T^{\varepsilon}_{\text{cp,verify}} \\ &= \max\left\{\left(\frac{B^{\varepsilon}_{\text{pre-prepare}}}{S(m)}\right)\middle| i,j \in \mathbb{M}, i \neq j\right\} \\ &+ \max\left\{\left(\frac{B^{\varepsilon}_{\text{prepare}}}{S(m)}\right)\middle| i,j \in \mathbb{M}, i \neq j\right\} \\ &+ \max\left\{\left(\frac{B^{\varepsilon}_{\text{submit}}}{S(m)}\right)\middle| i,j \in \mathbb{M}, i \neq j\right\} + \frac{\sum_{k=1}^{K} c_k}{f_i} \\ &+ \max\left\{\left(\frac{B^{\varepsilon}_{\text{result}}}{S(m)}\right)\middle| i \in \mathbb{M}, j \in \mathbb{P}\right\} \\ &+ \max\left\{\left(T^{\varepsilon}_{\text{cp,verify},i}, T^{\varepsilon}_{\text{cp,verify},j}\right)\middle| i,j \in \mathbb{N}, i \neq j\right\}, \end{aligned} \tag{5}$$

where $T^{\varepsilon}_{\text{cp}}$ represents the total latency in a cross-shard transaction, comprising stages like *pre-prepare, prepare, commitment, reply, and verification.* Each stage's latency depends on the maximum transmission time of data blocks ($B^{\varepsilon}_{\text{pre-prepare}}$, $B^{\varepsilon}_{\text{prepare}}$, etc.) and the transmission rate $S(m)$, which decreases as more leaders (m) participate, indicating potential congestion. $\mathbb{M}$ denotes a set of leaders in overlapping shards, critical in coordination across shards. $\mathbb{P}$ denotes all node sets in the sender shards and receiver shards involved in processing the transaction. c_k represents the CPU cycles the k-th shard requires to process a part of a cross-shard smart contract transaction. f_i defines the computational capability of the unit CPU cycles per second for the i-th node. $T^{\varepsilon}_{\text{cp,verify},i}$, $T^{\varepsilon}_{\text{cp,verify},j}$ represents the maximum verification delay encountered by any pair of nodes in the network, encompassing the time taken for computational tasks such as signature and MAC verification.

The verification latency for each node involved in the consensus process within a shard is quantified using the following formulas:

$$T^{\varepsilon}_{\text{cp,verify},i} = \frac{\alpha F + \beta[F(1+V) + 4(n_k - 1)]}{f_i}, \tag{6}$$

$$T^{\varepsilon}_{\text{cp,verify},j} = \frac{\alpha F + \beta[FV + 4(n_k - 1)]}{f_j}, \tag{7}$$

where F represents the total number of signatures that need to be verified. V represents the number of MACs that need to be verified for each request. The term $1 + V$ in node i's equation includes verifying each transaction's signature along with an additional signature for the block itself. n_k indicates the number of nodes within the k-th shard. Coefficients α and β measure the CPU cycles needed to verify one signature and one MAC, respectively, quantifying the computational effort required for cryptographic tasks. f_i and f_j denote the computational capability of nodes i and j, measured in CPU cycles per second, which is pivotal in determining the speed at which these nodes can handle cryptographic verification.

Storage Costs. The storage costs in a blockchain system, which includes both overlapping and non-overlapping shards, can be modeled using the following equation:

$$D = \sum_{k=1}^{K} m_k \mathcal{B}_k + \sum_{k=1}^{K} (n_k - m_k) \mathcal{B}_k, \tag{8}$$

where D represents the total storage overhead for the entire system, accounting for both overlapping and non-overlapping shards. K is the total number of shards in the system. Each shard has its specific storage requirements and node configurations. n_k denotes the number of non-leader nodes in the k-th shard. m_k indicates the number of leader nodes in the k-th shard. These leaders typically handle additional storage responsibilities due to managing data across multiple shards. $\mathcal{B}_k$ is the block storage requirement in the k-th shard, representing the data capacity needed to store in the chain. The first term of the equation, $\sum_{k=1}^{K} m_k \mathcal{B}_k$, calculates the total storage requirements for leader nodes in all shards. Leader nodes are crucial as they might store information from their shard and others, particularly in systems with overlapping shards. The second term, $\sum_{k=1}^{K} (n_k - m_k) \mathcal{B}_k$, represents the storage required for all non-leader nodes across each shard, which typically store only data relevant to their specific shard.

4 Experiments

To validate the performance of our proposed framework with overlapping shards and xPBFT consensus mechanism, experimental tests are conducted on a MacBook Pro equipped with a 2.5 GHz Quad-Core Intel Core i7 processor and 16GB of RAM.

Figure 3 shows a linear rise in storage requirements as the number of nodes within overlapping shards and the total number of shards increases. Systems with more shards, such as 48 shards, experience a sharper rise in storage needs compared to systems with fewer shards, such as 4 or 8. This indicates that higher shard counts naturally require more storage due to increased data replication to ensure transaction integrity and system robustness across a diverse network.

Figure 4 illustrates the relationship between the delay and the ratio of leaders to total nodes (m/n) across different shard configurations. The graph shows

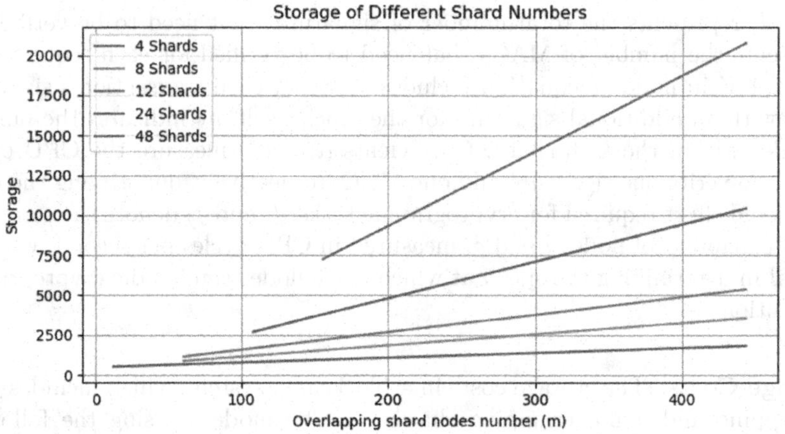

Fig. 3. Storage escalation with shard number and leader number, $n_k = 100$, $m_k \geq 3$.

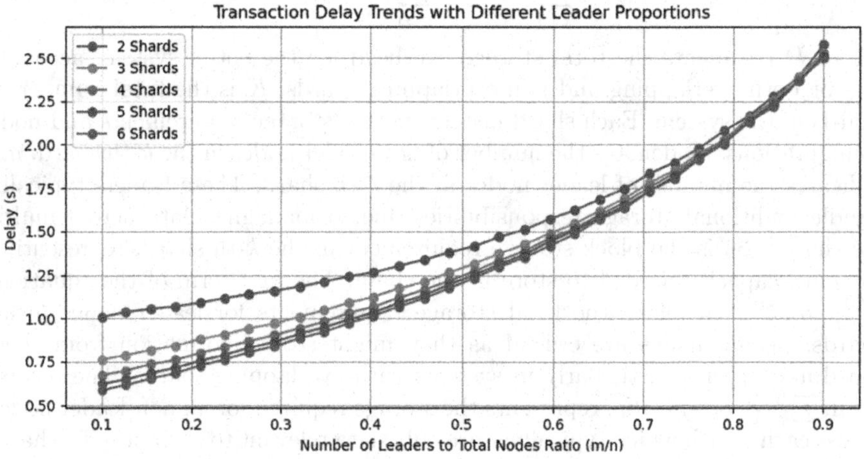

Fig. 4. Transaction delay variations with different leader proportions, $n = 200$, $k = \{2, 3, 4, 5, 6\}$.

that with an increase in the number of shards, from 2 to 6, the delay decreases, indicating that fewer leaders relative to the total number of nodes can efficiently handle consensus processes and minimize communication overhead. However, as the m/n ratio nears 1, the delay significantly increases across all shard configurations. This suggests that a higher proportion of leaders leads to improved communication and coordination overhead, slowing down the system. This pattern indicates an optimal m/n ratio where the delay is minimized, and this optimal point shifts slightly with changes in the number of shards.

Figure 5 illustrates the latency differences between the proposed xPBFT consensus and the traditional PBFT used in Omniledger [5], emphasizing the

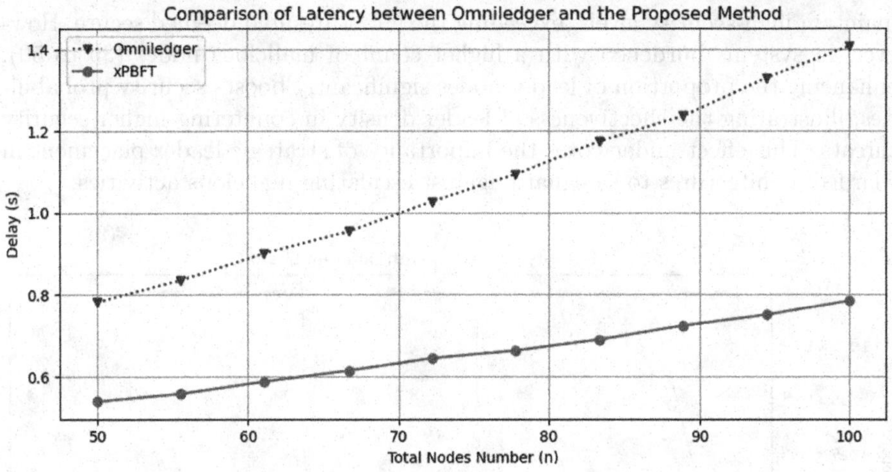

Fig. 5. Comparison of transaction delays between traditional PBFT consensus (Omniledger) and the proposed xPBFT consensus, $n = [50, 100]$.

improvements across varying node counts. The xPBFT demonstrates a consistent 40% reduction in latency compared to Omniledger, underscoring its enhanced efficiency in transaction handling. This efficiency is achieved through xPBFT's optimized design, which reduces communication overhead and accelerates transaction processing.

Figure 6 focuses on the variation in security probability with different counts of malicious nodes. As the number of leader nodes increases relative to the total nodes, systems with a low count of malicious nodes (10 and 20) consistently

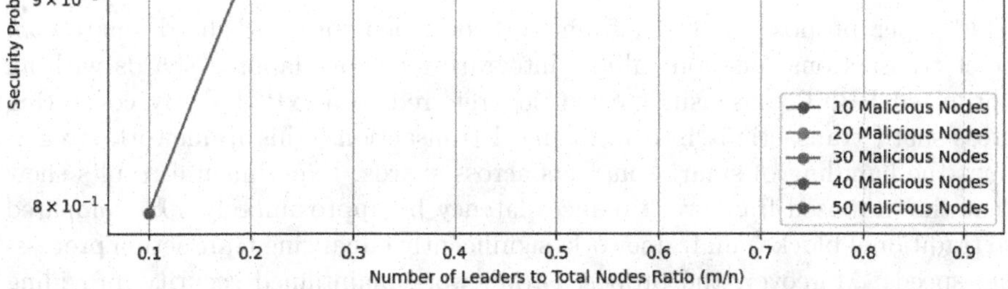

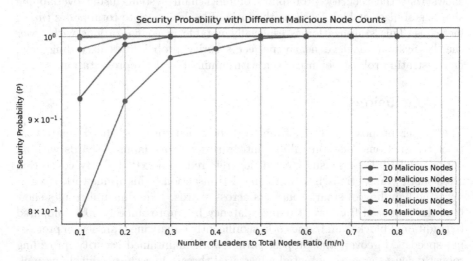

Fig. 6. Security enhancements with varying leader counts and malicious scenarios, $n = 200$, $k = 2$, $h = \{10, 20, 30, 40, 50\}$.

maintain high-security levels, exceeding the 99% threshold deemed secure. However, in systems burdened with a higher count of malicious nodes (30 to 50), enhancing the proportion of leader nodes significantly boosts security probabilities, illustrating the effectiveness of leader density in countering higher security threats. This effect underscores the importance of strategic leader placement in sharded architectures to safeguard against escalating malicious activities.

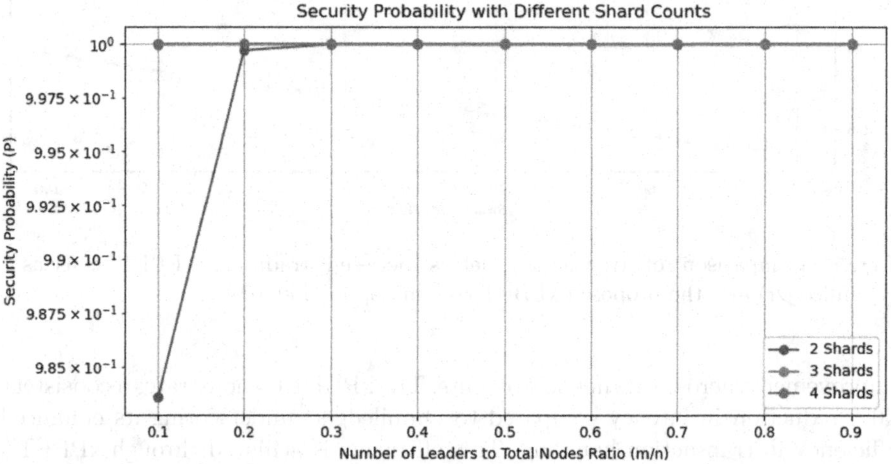

Fig. 7. Security enhancements with varying leader counts and malicious scenarios, $n_k = 100$, $k = \{2, 3, 4\}$, $h = 30$.

Figure 7 evaluates the security probability across different shard counts and shows that the security probability of blockchain systems using overlapping shards stabilizes at high levels as the ratio of leader nodes to total nodes (m/n) increases. This stabilization is especially notable in configurations with fewer shards. Systems achieve nearly perfect security probabilities exceeding 99%, demonstrating robust defenses even with minimal leader representation.

5 Conclusions

This paper proposed a novel framework designed for cross-shard smart contract transactions function calling, integrating the overlapping shards with an optimized PBFT consensus mechanism, referred to as xPBFT. By converting cross-shard transactions into intra-shard transactions, this framework streamlines the handling of smart contracts across shards. Experimental results show that the proposed framework reduces latency by approximately 40% compared to traditional blockchain framework, significantly enhancing transaction processing speeds. Moreover, the proposed framework maintained security, providing robust defenses against potential adversarial threats in scenarios involving multiple recipients.

References

1. Monte, G.D., Pennino, D., Pizzonia, M.: Scaling blockchains without giving up decentralization and security: a solution to the blockchain scalability trilemma. In: Proceedings of the 3rd Workshop on Cryptocurrencies and Blockchains for Distributed Systems, pp. 71–76 (2020)
2. Hong, Z., Guo, S., Li, P.: Scaling blockchain via layered sharding. IEEE J. Sel. Areas Commun. **40**(12), 3575–3588 (2022)
3. Yu, G., et al.: Survey: sharding in blockchains. IEEE Access **8**, 14155–14181 (2020)
4. Wang, X., et al.: Blockchain-enabled fish provenance and quality tracking system. IEEE Internet Things J. **9**(11), 8130–8142 (2021)
5. Kokoris-Kogias, E., Jovanovic, P., Gasser, L., Gailly, N., Syta, E., Ford, B.: Omniledger: a secure, scale-out, decentralized ledger via sharding. In: IEEE Symposium on Security and Privacy (SP), pp. 583–598. IEEE (2018)
6. Wang, G., Shi, Z.J., Nixon, M., Han, S.: Sok: sharding on blockchain. In: Proceedings of the 1st ACM Conference on Advances in Financial Technologies, pp. 41–61 (2019)
7. Zhang, Z., et al.: A community detection-based blockchain sharding scheme. In: International Conference on Blockchain, pp. 78–91. Springer, Heidelberg (2022)
8. Sonnino, A., Bano, S., Al-Bassam, M., Danezis, G.: Replay attacks and defenses against cross-shard consensus in sharded distributed ledgers. In: IEEE European Symposium on Security and Privacy (EuroS&P), pp. 294–308. IEEE (2020)
9. Al-Bassam, M., Sonnino, A., Bano, S., Hrycyszyn, D., Danezis, G.: Chainspace: a sharded smart contracts platform. arXiv preprint arXiv:1708.03778 (2017)
10. Zamani, M., Movahedi, M., Raykova, M.: Rapidchain: scaling blockchain via full sharding. In: Proceedings of the 2018 ACM SIGSAC Conference on Computer and Communications Security, pp. 931–948 (2018)
11. Liu, Y., et al.: Building blocks of sharding blockchain systems: concepts, approaches, and open problems. Comput. Sci. Rev. **46**, 100513 (2022)
12. Luu, L., Narayanan, V., Zheng, C., Baweja, K., Gilbert, S., Saxena, P.: A secure sharding protocol for open blockchains. In: Proceedings of the 2016 ACM SIGSAC Conference on Computer and Communications Security, pp. 17–30 (2016)
13. Liu, Y., Liu, J., Hei, Y., Xia, Yu., Wu, Q.: A secure cross-shard view-change protocol for sharding blockchains. In: Baek, J., Ruj, S. (eds.) ACISP 2021. LNCS, vol. 13083, pp. 372–390. Springer, Cham (2021). https://doi.org/10.1007/978-3-030-90567-5_19
14. Zhang, Z., et al.: Tbdd: a new trust-based, drl-driven framework for blockchain sharding in iot. Comput. Netw. **244**, 110343 (2024)
15. Yu, G., et al.: Adaptive resource scheduling in permissionless sharded-blockchains: a decentralized multiagent deep reinforcement learning approach. IEEE Trans. Syst. Man Cybern. Syst. (2023)
16. Yang, X., Xu, T., Zan, F., Ye, T., Mao, Z., Qiu, T.: An overlapping self-organizing sharding scheme based on DRL for large-scale IIoT blockchain. IEEE Internet Things J. (2023)
17. Aiyar, K., Halgamuge, M.N., Mohammad, A.: Probability distribution model to analyze the trade-off between scalability and security of sharding-based blockchain networks. In: IEEE 18th Annual Consumer Communications & Networking Conference (CCNC), pp. 1–6. IEEE (2021)
18. Hafid, A., Hafid, A.S., Samih, M.: A novel methodology-based joint hypergeometric distribution to analyze the security of sharded blockchains. IEEE Access **8**, 179389–179399 (2020)

19. Li, W., Feng, C., Zhang, L., Xu, H., Cao, B., Imran, M.A.: A scalable multi-layer pbft consensus for blockchain. IEEE Trans. Parallel Distrib. Syst. **32**(5), 1146–1160 (2020)
20. Cui, Z., Xue, Z., Ma, Y., Cai, X., Chen, J.: A many-objective optimized sharding scheme for blockchain performance improvement in end-edge enabled internet of things. IEEE Internet Things J. (2023)

Key Exchange and Privacy

Subversion-Resilient Authenticated Key Exchange with Reverse Firewalls

Jiahao Liu[1], Rongmao Chen[1(✉)], Yi Wang[1], Xincheng Tang[1], and Jinshu Su[2(✉)]

[1] College of Computer Science and Technology, National University of Defense Technology, Changsha 410073, Hunan, China
{liujiahao14,chromao,wangyi14,tangxincheng19}@nudt.edu.cn
[2] Academy of Military Science, Beijing, China
sjs@nudt.edu.cn

Abstract. Authenticated key exchange (AKE) protocol is an essential tool for secure communication in practice. To defend against subversion attacks that compromise the security of cryptosystem by subverting the implementation of algorithms, Dodis et al. (CRYPTO'16) introduced the first subversion-resilient AKE protocol utilizing the reverse firewalls (RFs) by Mironov and Stephens-Davidowitz (EUROCRYPT'15), and proved its security within a non-standard model.

In this paper, we propose a generic subversion-resilient AKE construction under the classic game-based AKE model. Compared to Dodis et al.'s model, our model is more strict and captures the standard multi-challenge and "single-bit-guess" security, which requires all the test keys to be real-or-random. Our AKE construction follows the standard "$1 \times \mathsf{KEM} + 2 \times \mathsf{SIG}$" paradigm for designing AKE protocols, with the key encapsulation mechanism (KEM) providing some specific properties like malleability and universal decryptability. The security of our AKE construction is tightly based on the security of the underlying KEM and the underlying signature scheme. We instantiate our construction using the plain Diffie-Hellman key encapsulation, resulting in a protocol that is tightly secure based on the strong Diffie-Hellman assumption. Finally, using the strong twin Diffie-Hellman technique of Cash et al. (EUROCRYPT'08), we obtain an AKE protocol with reverse firewalls that achieves tight security based on the standard computational Diffie-Hellman assumption.

Keywords: Subversion resilience · Authenticated key exchange · Security model · Reverse firewalls

1 Introduction

Authenticated key exchange (AKE) protocol, which allows two parties to authenticate each other and to negotiate a session key, has found wide application in

J. K. Liu et al. (Eds.): ProvSec 2024, LNCS 14904, pp. 181–200, 2025.
https://doi.org/10.1007/978-981-96-0957-4_10

practice. Most security models for AKE protocol assume that the implementation of underlying algorithms strictly follows the specification, which may not be the case in reality. In particular, the Snowden revelations warned us that the implementation of cryptosystem can be subverted to leak secret information subliminally, and it is difficult for ordinary users to distinguish the output of subverted cryptosystem from that of honest one [6].

To defend against such subversion attacks, Dodis et al. [19] proposed the first AKE protocol with subversion resilience by utilizing reverse firewalls (RFs) introduced by Mironov and Stephens-Davidowitz [26]. In general, an RF is placed between a party and the external network to protect the party against subversion attacks. During protocol execution, the RF usually sanitizes the outgoing messages by performing rerandomization (i.e., changing the underlying randomnesses of messages). The action of RF preserves the functionality of protocol and prevents the exfiltration of secret information. Bossuat et al. [7] extended the concept of RFs from AKE protocol to record-layer protocol and presented a generic formalization of RFs. Specifically, they defined a new model for both AKE and record-layer protocols where each RF is assigned with a public key and the party would send encrypted message under this public key to RF. Also, they proposed an AKE protocol of unilateral authentication with such RFs.

Although the RFs by Bossuat et al. [7] could provide subversion resilience at the record layer, it is preferable to construct RFs that do not have to maintain long-term state (e.g., public key), as in [19]. In Dodis et al.'s protocol [19], unique signature over bilinear pairings is cleverly used to facilitate the sanitation by RF. However, the computation of bilinear pairings is less efficient than the plain Diffie-Hellman key exchange. Also, the security of this protocol is proved under a non-standard AKE model, instead of standard models, such as the Bellare-Rogaway-like models [4] and the Canetti-Krawczyk-like models [9,24]. Thus, our aim is to construct a pairing-free AKE protocol with RFs under standard model.

Contributions. We propose a generic framework of AKE protocol with RFs under the classic security model. This generic construction is built on key encapsulation mechanism (KEM) of multi-user one-wayness under plaintext-checking attacks (MU-OW-PCA) and signature scheme of multi-user existential unforgeability under chosen-message attacks (MU-EUF-CMA).

Then, we instantiate proposed framework with the plain Diffie-Hellman key encapsulation. The security of this instantiation is tightly based on the strong Diffie-Hellman (SDH) assumption. Using the strong twin DH technique [10], we get a tightly secure AKE with subversion-resilience based on the computational Diffie-Hellman (CDH) assumption.

1.1 Results Overview

Our primary contribution is a generic AKE protocol that is secure against subversion attacks when augmented with RFs. This is accomplished through a two-step process. First, we propose a generic plain AKE protocol that is secure within the conventional AKE security model. Next, we enhance the AKE protocol by designing RFs for both parties. By demonstrating the properties of RFs, we prove the security of our AKE protocol in a subversion setting.

Our Generic AKE Construction. We propose a general construction of AKE based on a KEM, a signature scheme and a commitment scheme. The basic idea of our protocol is the classic "$1 \times \mathsf{KEM} + 2 \times \mathsf{SIG}$" approach used in many AKE protocols [21,27]. Despite signatures for entity authentication, this approach is essentially a process of key encapsulation: the initiator of the protocol contributes an ephemeral public key and the responder contributes a ciphertext by encapsulating the public key. The session key results from the encapsulation of the ephemeral public key. However, to prevent either party from controlling the session key, referred to as the *key control* problem, we incorporate a commitment scheme into the protocol, following the method of Dodis et al. [19]. This ensures that each party contributes to the final session key. Specifically, the initiator first commits to its "key share". Upon receiving a key share from the responder, the initiator opens the commitment. The "key shares" of two parties are an ephemeral public key and a ciphertext, respectively. The responder should generate the ciphertext without knowing the public key, which requires the KEM to be *universally decryptable* defined in [15]. Before the commitment is opened, neither party can determine even a single bit of the final session key. We show that the security of the proposed construction can be tightly based on the MU-OW-PCA security of the KEM and the MU-EUF-CMA security of the signature scheme.

RFs for Our AKE. In the AKE protocol, an RF is required to sanitize the messages and the corresponding key shares generated by the protected party. In the aforementioned AKE construction, signatures are generated over the key shares of both parties. Any modification by the RFs to the key shares would be detected by the parties, as the signature would become invalid. Therefore, constructing RFs that remain undetected by both parties in such a protocol appears to be challenging. Inspired by the work of Chakraborty et al. [14], we consider more powerful RFs which are allowed to send *feedback messages* to parties, i.e., a party may receive some feedback messages from its RFs to modify the messages it sent previously. To avoid extra interactions between a party and its RFs, the feedback messages are piggybacked onto the protocol messages. This approach requires the underlying KEM scheme to exhibit specific properties of rerandomizability and malleability to modify the public keys and ciphertexts. Additionally, the commitment scheme is also required to be rerandomizable and malleable to prevent subversions. Furthermore, our construction utilizes a unique signature to overcome possibly subverted implementation problem of the signature scheme.

Instantiations. We instantiate the MU-OW-PCA secure KEM using a Diffie-Hellman based KEM. The security of this KEM is based on the SDH assumption. To instantiate our construction under a more standard assumption, we modify the scheme to employ a twin Diffie-Hellman key exchange, whose security is based on the strong twin Diffie-Hellman (S2DH) assumption [10]. By the tight reduction from the S2DH assumption to the CDH assumption, we obtain the tight security of an instantiation based on the CDH assumption. Moreover, we can instantiate our construction in a group of signed quadratic residues $\mathbb{QR}_N^+$ [23], which results in a tightly secure AKE under the factoring assumption.

1.2 Related Work

Resistance Against Subversion Attacks. Reverse firewalls are used extensively to resist subversion attacks against many cryptographic primitives [2,16] and protocols [11,12,19]. Chakraborty et al. [14] considered universal composability (UC) security in the subversion setting and proposed a UC subversion-resilient framework. They "sanitized" the GMW compiler that transforms a multiparty computation (MPC) protocol secure against semi-honest adversaries into an MPC protocol secure against malicious adversaries. Recently, Chakraborty et al. [13] proposed the first subversion-resilient password-authenticated key exchange (PAKE) protocol using reverse firewalls and proved its security in the model of [14]. Note that since AKE is a special two-party computation, RFs in [13,14] seem to be suitable for it. However, solutions presented in [13,14] lack practicality for AKE. Particularly, their general constructions of RF increases the communication cost and number of rounds compared to the initial protocols, rendering AKE protocols impractical. There are also some other defense mechanisms against subversion attacks, including the *watchdogs* [5,17,28–30] and the *self-guarding* mechanism [20], which rely on different architectural assumptions compared to those of RFs.

AKE Security with Optimal Tightness. Several AKE protocols with tight security have been proposed over the last few years. Gjøsteen et al. [21] proposed a modified "signed Diffie-Hellman" protocol that achieved tight security, but in a "multi-bit-guess" model. Cohn-Gordon et al. [18] gave a nearly tight reduction for implicitly authenticated Diffie-Hellman protocols in the "single-bit-guess" model. Han et al. [22] proposed the first AKE protocols that have been proven to be tightly secure without random oracle. Their general constructions are based on the hash proof system (HPS) and a signature scheme secure in the multi-user setting. Their security model extends that of [21] to the "single-bit-guess" model and security against replay attacks. Inspired by the proof technique of Cohn-Gordon et al. [21], Pan et al. [27] provided a tight reduction proof of the signed Diffie-Hellman key exchange protocol in a "single-bit-guess" model.

2 Preliminaries

Notations. Let $\emptyset$ denote the empty string. Let g be a generator of a cycle group $\mathbb{G}$ of a prime order p. Let $1_{\mathbb{G}}$ denote the identity element. Let $\mathcal{S} := \mathcal{S} \cup \{s\}$ denote appending an element s to a list $\mathcal{S}$. Let $[y]$ denote the set $\{1, \cdots, y\}$ for a positive integer $y > 1$. Let $x \leftarrow_\$ \mathcal{X}$ denote picking a uniformly random value from a set $\mathcal{X}$. Let $y \leftarrow_\$ f(x)$ denote a random output from a probabilistic function f which takes x as input. Let λ denote the security parameter throughout this paper. $\mathsf{negl}(\varphi)$ represents a negligible function h of φ s.t. for all sufficiently large φ and all polynomials $p(\varphi)$, it holds that $h(\varphi) < \frac{1}{p(\varphi)}$.

2.1 Cryptographic Assumptions

We define two variants of the CDH assumption: SDH assumption [1] and S2DH assumption [10]. First, we define the *restricted DDH oracle* $\mathcal{O}_{g^x}(\cdot,\cdot)$ as follows: given a number $x \in \mathbb{Z}_p$, on input $(Y, Z) \in \mathbb{G}^2$, return 1 if $Y^x = Z$, otherwise return 0.

Definition 1 (Strong Diffie-Hellman Assumption). *Let $\mathbb{G}$ be a cyclic group of a generator g and a prime order p such that $2^{\lambda+1} \geq p \geq 2^\lambda$. We define the advantage of an adversary $\mathcal{A}$ in breaking the strong Diffie-Hellman assumption for $\mathbb{G}$ as* $\mathrm{SDHAdv}[\mathcal{A}, \mathbb{G}, \lambda] := \Pr[(x, y) \leftarrow_{\$} \mathbb{Z}_p^2 : \mathcal{A}^{\mathcal{O}_{g^x}(\cdot,\cdot)}(g, g^x, g^y) = g^{xy}]$. *The SDH assumption holds if for all PPT adversaries $\mathcal{A}$, it holds that* $\mathrm{SDHAdv}[\mathcal{A}, \mathbb{G}, \lambda] \leq \mathsf{negl}(\lambda)$.

We define *twin DDH oracle* $\mathcal{O}_{g^{x_1}, g^{x_2}}(\cdot,\cdot,\cdot)$ as follows: given $(x_1, x_2) \in \mathbb{Z}_p^2$, on input $(Y, Z_1, Z_2) \in \mathbb{G}^3$, return 1 if $Y^{x_1} = Z_1$ and $Y^{x_2} = Z_2$, otherwise return 0.

Definition 2 (Strong Twin Diffie-Hellman Assumption). *Let $\mathbb{G}$ be a cyclic group of a generator g and a prime order p such that $2^{\lambda+1} \geq p \geq 2^\lambda$. We define the advantage of an adversary $\mathcal{A}$ in breaking the strong twin Diffie-Hellman assumption for $\mathbb{G}$ as*

$$\mathrm{S2DHAdv}[\mathcal{A}, \mathbb{G}, \lambda] := \Pr[(x_1, x_2, y) \leftarrow_{\$} \mathbb{Z}_p^3 : \\ \mathcal{A}^{\mathcal{O}_{g^{x_1}, g^{x_2}}(\cdot,\cdot,\cdot)}(g, g^{x_1}, g^{x_2}, g^y) = (g^{x_1 y}, g^{x_2 y})].$$

The S2DH assumption holds if for all PPT adversaries $\mathcal{A}$, it holds that

$$\mathrm{S2DHAdv}[\mathcal{A}, \mathbb{G}, \lambda] \leq \mathsf{negl}(\lambda).$$

We provide the basic definitions of the KEM and commitment below. More definitions about the commitment [12,19] and the signature scheme [21] (i.e., MU-EUF-CMA^{corr} security) are deferred to the full version of this paper.

2.2 Key Encapsulation Mechanism

A KEM scheme [31] KEM is defined by four algorithms (Setup, Gen, Encap, Decap):

- Setup(1^λ) takes 1^λ as input and generates the public parameters pp, which include the key space $\mathcal{K}$, the public key space $\mathcal{PK}$, the secret key space $\mathcal{SK}$, the ciphertext space $\mathcal{C}$ and the randomness space $\mathcal{R}_{\mathsf{KEM}}$.
- Gen(pp) takes the public parameters pp as input and outputs a key pair (pk, sk).
- Encap(pk) takes the public key pk as input, and outputs a ciphertext C and a key K.
- Decap(sk, C) takes a secret key sk and a ciphertext C as input, and outputs a key K.

Correctness. Let $\mathsf{KEM} = (\mathsf{Setup}, \mathsf{Gen}, \mathsf{Encap}, \mathsf{Decap})$ be a KEM scheme. We say that KEM is *correct* if for any λ, for any $\mathsf{pp} \leftarrow_{\$} \mathsf{Setup}(1^\lambda)$, for any $(pk, sk) \leftarrow_{\$} \mathsf{Gen}(\mathsf{pp})$, for any $(K, C) \leftarrow_{\$} \mathsf{Encap}(pk)$, it holds that $\mathsf{Decap}(sk, C) = K$.

OW-PCA Security. The *one-wayness under plaintext-checking attacks* (OW-PCA) security [32] is a slightly stronger security notion than the one-wayness under chosen-plaintext attacks (OW-CPA) security. Compared to the OW-CPA security game, there is additionally a *plaintext checking oracle* (PCO) in the OW-PCA security game. The PCO takes (C, K) as input and outputs 1 if $K = \mathsf{Decap}(sk, C)$, otherwise it outputs 0. In this paper, we consider OW-PCA security in the multi-user setting [8], referred to as *MU-OW-PCA* security. The MU-OW-PCA security game is shown in Fig. 1, which is a modified version of the OW-PCA definition in [8].

Exp $\mathsf{MU\text{-}OW\text{-}PCA}(\mathcal{A}, \lambda, \mathsf{KEM})$	$\textsc{Enc}(i)$
$\mathsf{pp} \leftarrow_{\$} \mathsf{Setup}(1^\lambda)$	$(C_i, K_i) \leftarrow_{\$} \mathsf{Encap}(pk_i)$
for $n \in [N]$	**return** C_i
$\quad (pk_n, sk_n) \leftarrow_{\$} \mathsf{Gen}(\mathsf{pp})$	$\textsc{Pco}(pk_i, C, K)$
$(i, (C, K)) \leftarrow \mathcal{A}^{\mathcal{O}}(pk_1, \cdots, pk_N)$	$K' \leftarrow \mathsf{Decap}(sk_i, C)$
if $C \neq C_i$: **return** $\perp$	**return** $K == K'$
return $K == K_i$	

Fig. 1. The MU-OW-PCA security game for KEM. $\mathcal{A}$ has access to oracles $\mathcal{O} := \{\textsc{Enc}, \textsc{Pco}\}$. However, $\mathcal{A}$ is only allowed to make an $\textsc{Enc}(i)$ query for each $i \in [N]$.

Definition 3 (MU-OW-PCA). *Let N be the number of users. Let $\mathcal{A}$ be an adversary that plays the* MU-OW-PCA *security game against the key encapsulation mechanism* KEM. *The advantage of $\mathcal{A}$ is defined as* $\mathrm{Adv}_{\mathsf{KEM}}^{N\text{-}\mathsf{MU\text{-}OW\text{-}PCA}}(\mathcal{A}, \lambda) := \Pr[\mathsf{MU\text{-}OW\text{-}PCA}(\mathcal{A}, \lambda, \mathsf{KEM}) = 1]$.

Fuzziness and Anonymity. Informally, if pk output by Gen is uniformly distributed over $\mathcal{PK}$, then we say that KEM is *fuzzy.* If C output by Encap is uniformly distributed over $\mathcal{C}$, then we say that KEM is *anonymous.* The formal definitions follow those in [3].

Universal Decryptability. We utilize the notion of *universal decryptability* defined in [15]. To achieve this property, Encap is composed of three sub-algorithms $(\mathsf{Rg}, \mathsf{Kg}, \mathsf{Cg})$:

- $\mathsf{Rg}(\mathsf{pp})$ takes public parameters pp as input, and outputs a randomness $r \in \mathcal{R}_{\mathrm{kem}}$.
- $\mathsf{Kg}(pk, r)$ takes the public key pk and a randomness r as input, and outputs a key K.

– $\mathsf{Cg}(r)$ takes the randomness r as input, and outputs a ciphertext C.

A formal definition of the universal decryptability property is shown below.

Definition 4 (Universal Decryptability [15]**).** *We say that a KEM scheme* $\mathsf{KEM} = (\mathsf{Setup}, \mathsf{Gen}, \mathsf{Encap}, \mathsf{Decap})$, *with* $\mathsf{Encap} = (\mathsf{Rg}, \mathsf{Kg}, \mathsf{Cg})$, *is* universally decryptable *if for any* $\lambda \in \mathbb{N}$ *and* $\mathsf{pp} \leftarrow_{\$} \mathsf{Setup}(1^\lambda)$, $r \leftarrow_{\$} \mathsf{Rg}(\mathsf{pp})$ *and* $C := \mathsf{Cg}(r)$, $(pk, sk) \leftarrow_{\$} \mathsf{Gen}(\mathsf{pp})$, *it holds that* $\mathsf{Decap}(sk, C) = \mathsf{Kg}(pk, r)$.

Malleability. An additional property required for KEM is *malleability* of the ciphertexts and the public keys. We say that a KEM scheme is *malleable* if it is both *ciphertext-malleable* and *key-malleable.*

Definition 5 (Ciphertext Malleability). *We say that a KEM scheme* KEM $= (\mathsf{Setup}, \mathsf{Gen}, \mathsf{Encap}, \mathsf{Decap})$ *is* ciphertext-malleable *if for all* $(pk, sk) \leftarrow_{\$} \mathsf{Gen}(\mathsf{pp})$ *where* $\mathsf{pp} \leftarrow_{\$} \mathsf{Setup}(1^\lambda)$, *there exist a pair of algorithms* $(\mathsf{CMaul}, \mathsf{KMaul})$ *that works as follows: let* $\mathcal{R}_{\mathrm{maul}}$ *denote the randomness space in* CMaul *and* KMaul. *For any ciphertext-key pair* $(C, K) \leftarrow_{\$} \mathsf{Encap}(pk)$ *and any randomness* $r \leftarrow_{\$} \mathcal{R}_{\mathrm{maul}}$, CMaul *takes* C *and* r *as inputs, and outputs a new ciphertext* C'. C' *are uniformly distributed over* $\mathcal{C}$. *Let* $K' := \mathsf{Decap}(sk, C')$. *It holds that* $K' = \mathsf{KMaul}(K, r)$.

Definition 6 (Key Malleability). *Let* $\mathsf{KEM} = (\mathsf{Setup}, \mathsf{Gen}, \mathsf{Encap}, \mathsf{Decap})$ *be a KEM scheme. Let* PKMaul *and* SKMaul *be two algorithms. Let* $\mathcal{R}_{\mathrm{maul}}$ *denote the randomness space in* PKMaul. KEM *is* key-malleable *if for all* $\mathsf{pp} \leftarrow_{\$} \mathsf{Setup}(1^\lambda), (pk, sk) \leftarrow_{\$} \mathsf{Gen}(\mathsf{pp})$, $r \leftarrow_{\$} \mathcal{R}_{\mathrm{maul}}$, $pk' \leftarrow \mathsf{PKMaul}(pk, r)$ *and* $(C, K) \leftarrow_{\$} \mathsf{Encap}(pk')$, *it holds that* $K = \mathsf{Decap}(sk', C)$ *where* $sk' = \mathsf{SKMaul}(sk, r)$, *and* pk' *is uniformly distributed over* $\mathcal{PK}$.

2.3 Commitment

A commitment scheme $\Pi_{\mathsf{com}} = (\mathsf{Gen}, \mathsf{Com}, \mathsf{Open}, \mathsf{Ver})$ is defined as follows:

– $\mathsf{Gen}(1^\lambda)$ takes 1^λ as input, and outputs the public parameters ρ, which include the message space $\mathcal{M}_{\mathsf{com}}$, the randomness space $\mathcal{R}_{\mathsf{com}}$ and the commitment space $\mathcal{C}_{\mathsf{com}}$.
– $\mathsf{Com}(m, \rho; r)$ takes a message $m \in \mathcal{M}_{\mathsf{com}}$, the security parameters ρ and a randomness $r \in \mathcal{R}_{\mathsf{com}}$ as input, and outputs a commitment $c \in \mathcal{C}_{\mathsf{com}}$.
– $\mathsf{Open}(c, \rho, r)$ takes the commitment c, the security parameter ρ and the randomness r as input, and outputs an opening x.
– $\mathsf{Ver}(c, x)$ takes a commitment c and an opening x as input, and outputs a message m or $\perp$.

Correctness. The above commitment scheme is correct if for any message $m \in \mathcal{M}_{\mathsf{com}}$, any commitment $c \leftarrow_{\$} \mathsf{Com}(m, \rho; r)$, any opening $x \leftarrow \mathsf{Open}(c, \rho, r)$ where $r \in \mathcal{R}_{\mathsf{com}}$, it holds that $\mathsf{Ver}(c, r) = m$.

Definition 7 (Malleable Commitment). *Let* $\Pi_{\mathsf{com}} = (\mathsf{Gen}, \mathsf{Com}, \mathsf{Open}, \mathsf{Ver})$ *be a commitment scheme.* Π_{com} *is* malleable *if there exist three efficient algorithms* $(\mathsf{MaulCom}, \mathsf{mMaul}, \mathsf{xMaul})$ *such that for any commitment* c*, its opening* x *and a mauling randomness* r*, if we compute* $c' \leftarrow \mathsf{MaulCom}(c, r)$*, then it holds that* $m' = \mathsf{mMaul}(m, r)$ *and* $\mathsf{Ver}(c', x') = m'$ *where* $\mathsf{Ver}(c, x) = m, x' \leftarrow \mathsf{xMaul}(x, r)$.

Definition 8 (Rerandomizable Commitment [19]). *A commitment is* rerandomizable *if there exist two efficient algorithms* $(\mathsf{Rerand}, \mathsf{OpenRerand})$*, such that for any commitment* c*, its opening* x *and a randomness* $r \in \mathcal{R}_{\mathsf{rand}}$ *where* $\mathcal{R}_{\mathsf{rand}}$ *is the randomness space for rerandomization,* $c' \leftarrow \mathsf{Rerand}(c, r)$ *is a uniformly random value in commitment space, and it holds that* $\mathsf{Ver}(c, x) = \mathsf{Ver}(c', x')$ *where* $x' \leftarrow \mathsf{OpenRerand}(x, r)$.

2.4 Reverse Firewalls

There are three requirements for an RF [19,26]: (1) *functionality maintaining.* The RF should not break the functionality of the original protocol if the user implementation of the protocol is honest. (2) *security preservation.* An RF preserves the security of the original protocol, which means that a malicious RF should not compromise the security of the protocol. Therefore, an RF does not hold any secret information of the protected party; otherwise, the security of the original protocol is not guaranteed. (3) *exfiltration resistance.* An RF for a party prevents exfiltration of secret information from that party, regardless of the behaviors of that (possibly subverted) party. Formal definitions of these properties can be found in [19].

3 Security Model for AKE

Definition of AKE. We follow Han et al. [22] to define an AKE protocol.

Definition 9 (AKE [22]). *An AKE scheme* AKE *includes three algorithms:*

- $\mathsf{AKE.Setup}$*: output the public parameters* pp.
- $\mathsf{AKE.Gen}$*: take the public parameters* pp *and a party identity* P_i *as input, and output a long-term key pair* (pk_i, sk_i).
- $\mathsf{AKE.Protocol}$*: an interactive protocol executed between* P_i *and* P_j*. Each party holds its own long-term key pair, the public parameters and the public keys of the other parties. Finally, each party outputs a flag* $\psi \in \{\emptyset, \mathtt{accept}, \mathtt{reject}\}$ *and a session key* $k \in \mathcal{K}_{\mathsf{ake}}$ *where* $\mathcal{K}_{\mathsf{ake}}$ *is the session key space.*

Correctness. For two honest parties P_i and P_j, they get the same flag (i.e., $\psi_i = \psi_j = \mathtt{accept}$) and session key (i.e., $k_i = k_j \neq \emptyset$) after the protocol execution.

Our game-based model for AKE follows the Bellare-Rogaway model and is formalized in the paradigm of [21] except that we use a single bit for all test queries and each oracle is indexed by a party identifier and a session identifier.

Execution Environment. Assume that there are N parties $P_1, \cdots, P_N$, where each party runs no more than s protocol instances. Each instance has a unique session identifier sid. Therefore, we represent a protocol instance of party P_i with session identifier sid as an oracle π_i^{sid}. Each oracle π_i^{sid} corresponds to a protocol execution of party P_i. Moreover, π_i^{sid} has access to the long-term key pair (pk_i, sk_i) of P_i and the public keys of all the other parties. There are four internal state variables for an oracle π_i^{sid}:

- ρ_i^{sid}: The randomness tape of π_i^{sid}.
- $\mathsf{Pid}_i^{\mathsf{sid}}$: The identity of the intended peer.
- k_i^{sid}: The session key computed by π_i^{sid}.
- $\psi_i^{\mathsf{sid}} \in \{\texttt{accept}, \texttt{reject}\}$: whether π_i^{sid} has completed the protocol execution and accepted the session key computed by π_i^{sid}.

We initialize the above variables by setting $(\rho_i^{\mathsf{sid}}, \mathsf{Pid}_i^{\mathsf{sid}}, k_i^{\mathsf{sid}}, \psi_i^{\mathsf{sid}}) = (\emptyset, \emptyset, \emptyset, \emptyset)$. The session key k_i^{sid} is not empty if and only if π_i^{sid} accepts the result session key, i.e., $k_i^{\mathsf{sid}} \neq \emptyset \Leftrightarrow \psi_i^{\mathsf{sid}} = \texttt{accept}$.

Upon receiving an input (m, j), an oracle π_i^{sid} checks the value of $\mathsf{Pid}_i^{\mathsf{sid}}$. If it holds that $\mathsf{Pid}_i^{\mathsf{sid}} = \emptyset$, then π_i^{sid} sets $\mathsf{Pid}_i^{\mathsf{sid}} := j$; else if $\mathsf{Pid}_i^{\mathsf{sid}} = j$, then π_i^{sid} generates the next message according to the protocol specification and updates the internal states. Otherwise, π_i^{sid} outputs $\perp$.

Attacker Model. An adversary $\mathcal{A}$ interacts with oracles by queries. As in other AKE models, $\mathcal{A}$ controls the communications between all parties. Moreover, five types of queries are provided to $\mathcal{A}$ for simulation of the real-world adversarial behaviors. Before $\mathcal{A}$ makes any query, a bit $b \in \{0, 1\}$ is randomly sampled for the TEST queries. The five types of queries are specified as follows.

- SEND(sid, i, j, m): $\mathcal{A}$ sends a message m to an oracle π_i^{sid} in the name of P_j. The oracle π_i^{sid} generates the response according to the protocol specification and the internal state of π_i^{sid}. If ψ_i^{sid} is set to be $\texttt{accept}$ after the φ-th query (which is a SEND query), then we say that π_i^{sid} is *φ-accepted* [22]. This query simulates the scheduling of protocol messages by the adversary.
- REGCORRUPT(i, pk): If P_i has been registered, then $\mathcal{A}$ receives $\perp$. Else (i, pk) is sent to other parties and P_i is registered. This query simulates that an adversary registers a party with a public key pk.
- REVEAL(i, sid): The variable $\mathsf{reveal}_i^{\mathsf{sid}}$ is set to be $\texttt{true}$ and k_i^{sid} is returned to $\mathcal{A}$. This query simulates that $\mathcal{A}$ gets a session key of an oracle that has accepted the key.
- CORRUPT(i): The label $\mathsf{corr}[i]$ is set to be $\texttt{true}$ and the long-term secret key sk_i of P_i is returned to $\mathcal{A}$. P_i is called *φ-corrupted* if CORRUPT(i) is the φ-th query of the adversary [22]. This query simulates the corruption of a party.
- TEST(i, sid): π_i^{sid} responds with $\perp$ if $\psi_i^{\mathsf{sid}} \neq \texttt{accept}$; otherwise sets $k_0 \leftarrow_\$ \mathcal{K}_{\mathsf{ake}}, k_1 \leftarrow k_i^{\mathsf{sid}}$, and responds with k_b.

Security Experiment. The security experiment $\mathrm{Exp}_{\mathsf{AKE},\mathcal{A}}(\lambda)$ for an AKE protocol is shown in Fig. 2. To evaluate security of an AKE scheme, the AKE experiment allows the adversary $\mathcal{A}$ to make TEST queries to multiple oracles, referred to as *test oracles*, but does not allow $\mathcal{A}$ to test the same oracle more than once.

To prevent $\mathcal{A}$ from making TEST queries of oracles whose session key can be trivially computed by $\mathcal{A}$, we use the notion of *partnering* [21] which is defined based on *original key* [25].

Definition 10 (Original key [25]). *Let π_i^{sid} and π_j^{sid} be two oracles that execute the protocol with each other and π_i^{sid} sends the first message. The* original key $K_{i,j}^{\mathsf{sid}}$ *is the session key computed by both oracles in the presence of a passive adversary which honestly forwards the messages between oracles.*

It is easy to see that the original key only relies on the long-term keys of both parties and the randomness ρ_i^{sid} and ρ_j^{sid} used by both parties.

Definition 11 (Partnering [21]). *We say that π_i^{sid} is partnered to π_j^{sid} (denoted as $\pi_i^{\mathsf{sid}} = \mathsf{Partner}(\pi_j^{\mathsf{sid}})$) if either of the following conditions holds:*

- *The first protocol message has been sent by π_i^{sid} and $k_i^{\mathsf{sid}} = K_{i,j}^{\mathsf{sid}}$,*
- *The first protocol message has been received by π_i^{sid} and $k_i^{\mathsf{sid}} = K_{j,i}^{\mathsf{sid}}$.*

$\mathsf{Exp}_{\mathsf{AKE},\mathcal{A}}(\lambda)$

$b \leftarrow_{\$} \{0,1\}, \mathcal{L}_{pk} \leftarrow \emptyset$
$\mathsf{pp} \leftarrow_{\$} \mathsf{AKE.Setup}(1^\lambda)$
for $n \in [N]$
  $(pk_n, sk_n) \leftarrow \mathsf{AKE.Gen}(\mathsf{pp})$
  $\mathcal{L}_{pk} := \mathcal{L}_{pk} \cup \{pk_n\}$
  $\mathsf{corr}[n] \leftarrow$ **false**
$\mathcal{T} \leftarrow \phi$
$b' \leftarrow \mathcal{A}^{\mathcal{O}}(pk_1, \cdots, pk_n)$
return $b == b'$

$\mathrm{CORRUPT}(i)$

$\mathsf{corr}[i] :=$ **true**
return sk_n

$\mathrm{SEND}(\mathsf{sid}, i, j, m)$

if $\psi_i^{\mathsf{sid}} = \mathsf{accept}$: **return** $\perp$
return $\pi_i^{\mathsf{sid}}(m, j)$

$\mathrm{REVEAL}(i, \mathsf{sid})$

$\mathsf{reveal}_i^{\mathsf{sid}} :=$ **true**
return k_i^{sid}

$\mathrm{REGCORRUPT}(i, pk)$

if $i \in [N]$
  return $\perp$
$\mathcal{L}_{pk} := \mathcal{L}_{pk} \cup \{pk\}$
return $\mathcal{L}_{pk}$

$\mathrm{TEST}(i, \mathsf{sid})$

if $(i, \mathsf{sid}) \in \mathcal{T} \vee k_i^{\mathsf{sid}} = \perp$, **return** $\perp$
if $\mathrm{FRESH}(i, \mathsf{sid}) =$ **false**, **return** $\perp$
$\mathcal{T} := \mathcal{T} \cup \{(i, \mathsf{sid})\}$
$K_0^* \leftarrow k_i^{\mathsf{sid}}, K_1^* \leftarrow_{\$} \mathcal{K}_{\mathsf{ake}}$
return K_b^*

Fig. 2. The AKE security experiment with perfect forward security. $\mathcal{A}$ has access to oracle $\mathcal{O} :=$ {CORRUPT, SEND, REVEAL, REGCORRUPT, TEST}. The FRESH procedure is shown in Fig. 3.

We follow the model of Cohn-Gordon et al. [18] to require that all test oracles should be *fresh*. Our definition of freshness differs from theirs in two aspects: first, we do not require two partnered oracles to have identical transcript. This is to avoid the no-match attacks [25]. Second, we allow the intended peer of a fresh oracle π_i^{sid} to be corrupted after π_i^{sid} accepts, regardless of whether π_i^{sid} has a partner oracle or not. This guarantees *perfect forward secrecy*. Specifically, An oracle π_i^{sid} is called *fresh* if all the following conditions hold:

- $\mathsf{reveal}_i^{\mathsf{sid}} = \mathbf{false}$ and $\mathsf{reveal}_j^{\mathsf{sid}} = \mathbf{false}$ where $\pi_j^{\mathsf{sid}} = \mathsf{Partner}(\pi_i^{\mathsf{sid}})$.
- The adversary did not make a Test-query on (j, sid), i.e., $(j, \mathsf{sid}) \notin \mathcal{T}$, where $\pi_j^{\mathsf{sid}} = \mathsf{Partner}(\pi_i^{\mathsf{sid}})$.
- $\mathsf{Pid}_i^{\mathsf{sid}}$ is not corrupted before π_i^{sid} accepts.

The last condition captures the perfect forward secrecy: to exclude trivial impersonation attacks, an adversary is only allowed to corrupt the intended peer of P_i *after* π_i^{sid} has accepted. KCI attacks are also implicitly captured by the definition of freshness: the adversary is allowed to corrupt the owner of a test oracle without limitation, which makes sure that the session key of an oracle is secure even though the secret key of its owner is revealed.

Definition 12 (AKE Security). *Let* $\mathrm{Adv}_{\mathsf{AKE}}(\mathcal{A}, \lambda)$ *denote the advantage of an adversary* $\mathcal{A}$ *in breaking the security of protocol* AKE, *where* λ *is a security parameter. We define* $\mathrm{Adv}_{\mathsf{AKE}}(\mathcal{A}, \lambda) := |\Pr[\mathrm{Exp}_{\mathsf{AKE},\mathcal{A}}(\lambda) \Rightarrow 1] - \frac{1}{2}|$. *If for all PPT adversaries* $\mathcal{A}$, $\mathrm{Adv}_{\mathsf{AKE}}(\mathcal{A}, \lambda)$ *is negligible, then we say that the protocol* AKE *is secure.*

Note that the above security definition captures attacks against the authentication of AKE protocols, i.e., the $\mathsf{break}_\mathsf{A}$ event defined in [21]. Recall that $\mathsf{break}_\mathsf{A}$ occurs if there exists an oracle π_i^{sid} such that $\psi_i^{\mathsf{sid}} = \mathtt{accept}$, $\mathsf{Pid}_i^{\mathsf{sid}} = j$ and P_j is never corrupted, and there exists no unique oracle π_j^{sid} that π_i^{sid} is partnered to. This includes two sub-cases: First, π_i^{sid} is partnered to two different oracles.

FRESH(i, sid)

if $\mathsf{reveal}_i^{\mathsf{sid}}$ or $(\exists\ \pi_j^{\mathsf{sid}} = \mathsf{Partner}(\pi_i^{\mathsf{sid}}) \wedge \mathsf{reveal}_j^{\mathsf{sid}})$
  return false
if $\exists\ \pi_j^{\mathsf{sid}} = \mathsf{Partner}(\pi_i^{\mathsf{sid}})$ s.t. $(j, \mathsf{sid}) \in \mathcal{T}$
  return false
if $\varphi' < \varphi$
  return false
return true

Fig. 3. The FRESH procedure used in the security experiment, where the oracle π_i^{sid} is φ-accepted and party $\mathsf{Pid}_i^{\mathsf{sid}}$ is φ'-corrupted.

However, we assume that each run of the protocol has a unique session identifier. Therefore, this case cannot occur. Second, π_i^{sid} is partnered to no oracle, which means that an active adversary interacts with π_i^{sid} such that $\psi_i^{\mathsf{sid}} = \mathtt{accept}$. It is evident that π_i^{sid} is a *fresh* oracle, and the adversary is permitted to make a Test query on π_i^{sid}, thereby compromising AKE security, which is already captured in the security experiment.

Corruption Cases. We consider the security of an AKE protocol in different corruption cases. The above security model implicitly assumes that the implementation of the protocol is honest, and the RF is honest whenever the party is honest. We assume that subversion can only occur at the beginning of the protocol execution, i.e., the adversary is not allowed to subvert the implementation during the execution of the protocol. A party equipped with an RF is desired to be subversion-resilient if the RF is honest. The caveat is that the RFs are not always honest. Therefore, we additionally consider three other corruption cases of a party and its RF: (1) An honest party and a malicious RF. In this case, the RF acts as part of the adversary. However, since RF does not possess any secret information of the party, the security of the protocol should still hold; (2) A subverted party and an honest RF. Due to the exfiltration resistance property of the RF, the security of the protocol is maintained; (3) A subverted party and a malicious RF. In this situation, the security of the party is not guaranteed due to subversion attacks.

4 Our Construction of AKE

Construction Overview. Our generic AKE construction Π_{AKE} is shown in Fig. 4, which is a four-round AKE protocol. It consists of a KEM scheme $\mathsf{KEM} = (\mathsf{Setup}, \mathsf{KEM.Gen}, \mathsf{Encap}, \mathsf{Decap})$ with $\mathsf{Encap} = (\mathsf{Rg}, \mathsf{Kg}, \mathsf{Cg})$, a commitment scheme $\Pi_{\mathsf{com}} = (\Pi_{\mathsf{com}}.\mathsf{Gen}, \mathsf{Com}, \mathsf{Open}, \Pi_{\mathsf{com}}.\mathsf{Ver})$ and a unique signature scheme $\Sigma = (\Sigma.\mathsf{KeyGen}, \Sigma.\mathsf{Sig}, \Sigma.\mathsf{Vrf})$ in which each message has a unique signature. To support an RF, KEM is required to be fuzzy, anonymous, universally decryptable and malleable. In addition to being binding and hiding, Π_{com} is required to be both malleable and rerandomizable. The light gray parts in Fig. 4 refer to the additional operations of parties due to the running of RFs. For simplicity, we implicitly require that the mMaul algorithm used in Π_{com} is identical to the CMaul algorithm used in KEM, both of which are used to maul the public keys.

Let A be an initiator and $\mathsf{F_A}$ be its RF. Let B be a responder and $\mathsf{F_B}$ be its RF. Let $(\mathsf{sk_A}, \mathsf{vk_A})$ and $(\mathsf{sk_B}, \mathsf{vk_B})$ denote the signature key pairs for A and B, respectively, which are generated by running $\Sigma.\mathsf{Gen}(1^\lambda)$. Let $(\mathsf{sid}, (\mathsf{sk_A}, \mathsf{vk_A}))$ and $(\mathsf{sid}, (\mathsf{sk_B}, \mathsf{vk_B}))$ be the input to A and B, where sid represents the session identifier. Initially, A runs $\mathsf{Setup}(1^\lambda)$ to get public parameters pp for KEM, and executes $\Pi_{\mathsf{com}}.\mathsf{Gen}(1^\lambda)$ to get the public parameters ρ for the commitment scheme.

Sanitization of the messages is performed by each RF. $\mathsf{F_A}$ mauls and rerandomizes the commitment $\widetilde{com}$ using $\mathsf{MaulCom}$ and Rerand, respectively. The "feedback message" $\tilde{r}_1$ is returned to A along with the second protocol message v'. A updates the public key $\widetilde{pk}' \leftarrow \mathsf{mMaul}(\widetilde{pk}, \tilde{r}_1)$ and the opening mes-

$\mathsf{A}(\mathsf{sid}, (\mathsf{sk_A}, \mathsf{vk_A}))$		$\mathsf{F_A}$		$\mathsf{F_B}$		$\mathsf{B}(\mathsf{sid}, (\mathsf{sk_B}, \mathsf{vk_B}))$
$\mathsf{pp} \leftarrow\!\!\$\ \mathsf{Setup}(1^\lambda)$						
$\rho \leftarrow\!\!\$\ \Pi_{\mathsf{com}}.\mathsf{Gen}(1^\lambda), r \leftarrow\!\!\$\ \mathcal{R}_{\mathsf{com}}$						
$(\widetilde{pk}, \widetilde{sk}) \leftarrow \mathsf{KEM.Gen}(\mathsf{pp})$						
$\widetilde{com} \leftarrow \mathsf{Com}(\widetilde{pk}, \rho; r)$	$\xrightarrow{u := \widetilde{com}}$					
		$\tilde{r}_1 \leftarrow\!\!\$\ \mathcal{R}_{\mathsf{com}}, \tilde{r}_2 \leftarrow\!\!\$\ \mathcal{R}_{\mathsf{rand}}$				
		$u' \leftarrow \mathsf{MaulCom}(u, \tilde{r}_1)$				
		$u'' \leftarrow \mathsf{Rerand}(u', \tilde{r}_2)$				
			$\xrightarrow{u''}$		$\xrightarrow{u''}$	
						$\tilde{r} \leftarrow\!\!\$\ \mathsf{Rg}(\mathsf{pp}), \tilde{c} := \mathsf{Cg}(\tilde{r})$
					$\xleftarrow{v := \tilde{c}}$	
				$\tilde{r}_3 \leftarrow \mathcal{R}_{\mathsf{maul}}$		
				$v' \leftarrow \mathsf{CMaul}(v, \tilde{r}_3)$		
	$\xleftarrow{(v', \tilde{r}_1)}$		$\xleftarrow{v'}$			
$\widetilde{pk}' \leftarrow \mathsf{mMaul}(\widetilde{pk}, \tilde{r}_1)$						
$x \leftarrow \mathsf{Open}(\widetilde{com}, \rho, r)$						
$x' \leftarrow \mathsf{xMaul}(x, \tilde{r}_1)$						
$\sigma_1 \leftarrow \mathsf{Sig}(\mathsf{sk_A}, tr)$	$\xrightarrow{(x', \sigma_1)}$					
$\widetilde{sk}' \leftarrow \mathsf{SKMaul}(\widetilde{sk}, \tilde{r}_1)$		$x'' \leftarrow \mathsf{OpenRerand}(x', \tilde{r}_2)$				
$K \leftarrow \mathsf{Decap}(\widetilde{sk}', v')$		$\widetilde{pk}' \leftarrow \Pi_{\mathsf{com}}.\mathsf{Ver}(u', x')$				
		$\Sigma.\mathsf{Ver}(\mathsf{vk_A}, (tr, \sigma_1)) \stackrel{?}{=} 1$				
			$\xrightarrow{(x'', \sigma_1)}$		$\xrightarrow{(x'', \sigma_1, \tilde{r}_3)}$	$v' \leftarrow \mathsf{CMaul}(v, \tilde{r}_3)$
						$\widetilde{pk}' \leftarrow \Pi_{\mathsf{com}}.\mathsf{Ver}(u'', x'')$
						$\Sigma.\mathsf{Ver}(\mathsf{vk_A}, (tr, \sigma_1)) \stackrel{?}{=} 1$
						$\sigma_2 \leftarrow \mathsf{Sig}(\mathsf{sk_B}, tr)$
					$\xleftarrow{\sigma_2}$	
				$\widetilde{pk}' \leftarrow \Pi_{\mathsf{com}}.\mathsf{Ver}(u'', x'')$		
				$\Sigma.\mathsf{Ver}(\mathsf{vk_B}, (tr, \sigma_2)) \stackrel{?}{=} 1$		
	$\xleftarrow{\sigma_2}$		$\xleftarrow{\sigma_2}$			$K \leftarrow \mathsf{Kg}(\widetilde{pk}', \tilde{r})$
$\Sigma.\mathsf{Ver}(\mathsf{vk_B}, (tr, \sigma_2)) \stackrel{?}{=} 1$						$K' \leftarrow \mathsf{KMaul}(K, \tilde{r}_3)$
$K \leftarrow H(\mathsf{sid}, \widetilde{pk}', \tilde{v}', \widetilde{K})$						$K \leftarrow H(\mathsf{sid}, \widetilde{pk}', \tilde{v}', \widetilde{K})$

Fig. 4. Our general AKE protocol Π_{AKE}, where $tr := (\widetilde{pk}', v', \mathsf{sid})$.

sage $x' \leftarrow \mathsf{xMaul}(x, \tilde{r}_1)$, and generates a signature over $(\widetilde{pk}', v', \mathsf{sid})$. On the responder side, B first outputs a ciphertext $v := \tilde{c}$. Upon receiving v, $\mathsf{F_B}$ picks $\tilde{r}_3 \leftarrow_{\$} \mathcal{R}_{\text{maul}}$ and updates $v' \leftarrow \mathsf{CMaul}(v, \tilde{r}_3)$. After receiving the third protocol message (x'', σ_1), $\mathsf{F_B}$ returns the feedback message $\tilde{r}_3$ to B along with (x'', σ_1). Then B computes $\widetilde{pk}' \leftarrow \Pi_{\mathsf{com}}.\mathsf{Ver}(u'', x'')$ and checks the correctness of σ_1. If σ_1 is invalid, then B aborts the protocol execution. Else, B computes $\sigma_2 \leftarrow \mathsf{Sig}(sk_{\mathsf{B}}, (\widetilde{pk}', v', \mathsf{sid}))$ and sends σ_2 to A. Finally, both parties compute the session key $K \leftarrow H(\mathsf{sid}, \widetilde{pk}', \tilde{v}', \widetilde{K})$.

Subversion Resilience. By the malleability of Π_{com} and KEM, and the rerandomizability of Π_{com}, we have that u'', x' and $\widetilde{pk}'$ are all uniformly random, despite of A's behaviors. By the universal decryptability and ciphertext-malleability of KEM, the message v' output by $\mathsf{F_B}$ is uniformly random regardless of the behaviors of B. Moreover, the signatures output by both parties are free of subversion attacks. Therefore, the output messages of both parties are sanitized successfully and both RFs are exfiltration-resistant.

Security Analysis. First, we consider the security of Π_{AKE} in the classic AKE security model defined in Sect. 3. This implies treating a party and its RF as a single entity, with interactions between them considered internal. Subsequently, we consider subversion attacks and demonstrate that an honest RF can prevent a subverted party from exfiltrating secret information.

Theorem 1. *Π_{AKE} is secure if H is modeled as a random oracle,* KEM *is* MU-OW-PCA *secure, and Σ is* MU-EUF-CMA^{corr} *secure.*

Proof. The proof involves several games played between an adversary $\mathcal{A}$ and a challenger $\mathcal{C}$ that executes Π_{AKE}. The first game is identical to the experiment $\mathrm{Exp}_{\Pi_{\mathsf{AKE}},\mathcal{A}}(\lambda)$. In the last game, the test session keys are randomly chosen from $\mathcal{K}_{\mathsf{ake}}$. Let G_n denote the event that the experiment in Game n outputs 1.

Game 0. This game is the same as the AKE security experiment $\mathrm{Exp}_{\Pi_{\mathsf{AKE}},\mathcal{A}}(\lambda)$. $\mathcal{C}$ simulates the protocol execution and answers all queries made by $\mathcal{A}$. It holds that $\Pr[\mathsf{G}_0] = \Pr[\mathrm{Exp}_{\Pi_{\mathsf{AKE}},\mathcal{A}}(\lambda) \Rightarrow 1]$.

Game 1. If two oracles of different initiators output the same transcript, then we abort the game. Due to the assumption that each run of a protocol has a unique sid, the abortion probability is 0. Thus we have $\Pr[\mathsf{G}_1] = \Pr[\mathsf{G}_0]$.

Game 2. If $\mathcal{A}$ makes a query $\textsc{Send}(\mathsf{sid}, \mathsf{B}, \mathsf{A}, (r, \sigma_1))$ s.t. $\Sigma.\mathsf{Ver}(\mathsf{vk_A}, (tr, \sigma_1)) = 1$ where $tr = (\widetilde{pk}'', \tilde{v}', \mathsf{sid})$ and $\widetilde{pk}''$ is not originated from the initiator in session sid, then we abort the game. Let W_1 be the event that $\mathcal{A}$ did not make a $\textsc{Corrupt}$ query on A while successfully making the oracle $\pi_{\mathsf{B}}^{\mathsf{sid}}$ accept with a different public key $\widetilde{pk}''$. $\mathcal{A}$ cannot distinguish Game 1 and Game 2 except that W_1 happens.

We bound the probability that event W_1 happens by building a forger $\mathcal{B}$ that breaks the MU-EUF-CMA security of Σ. First $\mathcal{B}$ receives $(\mathsf{vk}_1, \mathsf{vk}_2, \cdots, \mathsf{vk}_N)$ from its challenger. In the AKE protocol execution, $\mathcal{B}$ follows the protocol specifications: generates $\widetilde{pk}'$ and $v' := \tilde{c}'$ using KEM.Gen. When $\mathcal{A}$ corrupts a party

P_i, $\mathcal{B}$ queries $\text{CORR}(i)$ and forwards sk_i to $\mathcal{A}$. Since $\mathcal{B}$ has no knowledge of signing keys of honest parties, when $\mathcal{B}$ simulates a signature for an honest initiator, it makes a SIG query to its challenger and obtains the signature. If W_1 happens, then $\mathcal{B}$ returns $(\mathsf{vk_B}, ((\widetilde{pk}'', \tilde{v}', \mathsf{sid}), \sigma_1))$ to its challenger and breaks the MU-EUF-CMA security of Σ. It holds that $|\Pr[\mathsf{G}_2] - \Pr[\mathsf{G}_1]| = \Pr[W_1] \leq \mathrm{Adv}_{\Sigma}^{(N,\mu)\text{-MU-EUF-CMA}^{\mathsf{corr}}}(\mathcal{B}, \lambda)$.

Game 3. If $\mathcal{A}$ makes a query $\text{SEND}(\mathsf{sid}, \mathsf{A}, \mathsf{B}, \sigma_2)$ s.t. $\Sigma.\mathsf{Ver}(\mathsf{vk_B}, (\widetilde{pk}', \tilde{v}'', \mathsf{sid})) = 1$ and $\tilde{v}''$ is not originated from $\pi_{\mathsf{B}}^{\mathsf{sid}}$, then we abort the game. Let W_2 denote the event that $\mathcal{A}$ did not corrupt B while successfully making $\pi_{\mathsf{A}}^{\mathsf{sid}}$ accept with a different $\tilde{v}''$ than original $\tilde{v}'$. $\mathcal{A}$ cannot distinguish Game 3 from Game 2 except that the event W_2 happens. If W_2 happens, we can construct a forgery $\mathcal{B}'$ to break the MU-EUF-CMA security of Σ. The construction of $\mathcal{B}'$ is analogous to $\mathcal{B}$ in Game 2 and is omitted here due to space constraints. We have $|\Pr[\mathsf{G}_3] - \Pr[\mathsf{G}_2]| = \Pr[W_2] \leq \mathrm{Adv}_{\Sigma}^{(N,\mu)\text{-MU-EUF-CMA}^{\mathsf{corr}}}(\mathcal{B}', \lambda)$.

Game 4. This game is identical to Game 3, except that the session keys of all pairs of partnered oracles are set to be random without maintaining the consistency of the random oracle. Note that since Game 3, the adversary $\mathcal{A}$ is not allowed to perform active attacks against the protocol. Therefore, each oracle $\pi_{\mathsf{A}}^{\mathsf{sid}}$ has a partnered oracle $\pi_{\mathsf{B}}^{\mathsf{sid}}$. Let M denote the event that $\mathcal{A}$ makes a random oracle query on $(\mathsf{sid}, \widetilde{pk}', \tilde{v}', \widetilde{K})$, where $\widetilde{K} \leftarrow \mathsf{Decap}(\widetilde{sk}', \tilde{v}')$. Here $\tilde{v}'$ is output by the oracle $\pi_{\mathsf{B}}^{\mathsf{sid}}$ and $\widetilde{sk}'$ is the ephemeral secret key generated by $\pi_{\mathsf{A}}^{\mathsf{sid}}$. $\mathcal{A}$ cannot distinguish Game 4 from Game 3 unless the event M happens. Given that event M happens, we can construct an adversary $\mathcal{D}$ that breaks the MU-OW-PCA security of KEM using $\mathcal{A}$ as a subroutine. $\mathcal{D}$ is constructed as follows.

Initially, $\mathcal{D}$ receives a set of public keys $(pk_1, \cdots, pk_S)$ in the MU-OW-PCA security game, where S denotes the number of session identifiers. $\mathcal{D}$ takes challenge ciphertexts $\{C_1, \cdots, C_S\}$ from its challenger $\mathcal{C}$, and is required to return a key K s.t. $K = \mathsf{Decap}(sk_i, C^*)$, where $C^* \in \{C_1, \cdots, C_S\}$, given the PCO.

$\mathcal{D}$ interacts with $\mathcal{A}$ as in Game 4, with the following modifications: $\mathcal{D}$ takes $pk_1, \cdots, pk_S$ as the ephemeral public keys of the initiators, and $C_1, \cdots, C_S$ as the KEM ciphertexts of the responders, respectively. More specifically, let $\widetilde{pk}'$ denote the public key and $\tilde{v}'$ denote the ciphertext corresponding to a session identifier in the AKE security game. $\mathcal{D}$ picks $(\widetilde{pk}', \tilde{v}')$ from the set $\{(pk_1, C_1), \cdots, (pk_S, C_S)\}$.

Since $\mathcal{D}$ has no knowledge of the secret keys $sk_1, \cdots, sk_N$ in the MU-OW-PCA security game, we need to identify some random oracle queries related to $sk_1, \cdots, sk_N$ carefully. In particular, we should identify whether it holds that $\widetilde{K} = \mathsf{Decap}(sk_i, \tilde{v}')$ for some secret key $sk_i \in \{sk_1, \cdots, sk_N\}$ and $\widetilde{K}$ in a random oracle query $(\mathsf{sid}, pk_i, \tilde{v}', \widetilde{K})$ where $pk_i \in \{pk_1, \cdots, pk_N\}$. This is achieved by querying $\text{PCO}(pk_i, \widetilde{K}, \tilde{v}')$. If the output is 1, which means that $(\tilde{v}', \widetilde{K})$ is a valid ciphertext-key pair for pk_i, then $\mathcal{D}$ outputs $(i, (\tilde{v}', \widetilde{K}))$ and wins the MU-OW-PCA security game against KEM. We have $\mathrm{Adv}_{\mathsf{KEM}}^{N\text{-MU-OW-PCA}}(\mathcal{D}, \lambda) \geq \Pr[M]$. Therefore, it holds that $|\Pr[\mathsf{G}_4] - \Pr[\mathsf{G}_3]| = \Pr[M] \leq \mathrm{Adv}_{\mathsf{KEM}}^{N\text{-MU-OW-PCA}}(\mathcal{D}, \lambda)$.

Essentially, in Game 4, the adversary has no advantage in distinguishing the challenge keys from random. Therefore, we have $\Pr[\mathsf{G}_4] = \frac{1}{2}$. We conclude that

$$\begin{aligned}\mathrm{Adv}_{\Pi_{\mathsf{AKE}}}(\mathcal{A},\lambda) &:= |\Pr[\mathrm{Exp}_{\mathsf{AKE},\mathcal{A}}(\lambda) \Rightarrow 1] - \frac{1}{2}| \\ &= |\mathsf{G}_4 - \mathsf{G}_0| \\ &\leq \mathrm{Adv}_{\Sigma}^{(N,\mu)\text{-}\mathsf{MU\text{-}EUF\text{-}CMA}^{\mathsf{corr}}}(\mathcal{B},\lambda) \\ &+ \mathrm{Adv}_{\Sigma}^{(N,\mu)\text{-}\mathsf{MU\text{-}EUF\text{-}CMA}^{\mathsf{corr}}}(\mathcal{B}',\lambda) + \mathrm{Adv}_{\mathsf{KEM}}^{N\text{-}\mathsf{MU\text{-}OW\text{-}PCA}}(\mathcal{D},\lambda).\end{aligned}$$

Properties of the RFs. Now we analyze the security of our AKE construction in the presence of subversion attacks.

- An honest party and a malicious RF. We assume that A is honest and F_{A} is malicious. The adversary is allowed to maul the public key sent by A and obtain the signature corresponding to a specific sid. Observe that the security of the protocol is still guaranteed since no secret information is leaked. The analysis for the case of honest B and malicious F_{B} is essentially the same.
- A subverted party and an honest RF. By the exfiltration resistance property of the RFs, our AKE protocol is secure in this corruption case.
- A subverted party and a malicious RF. The adversary may obtain secret information of the subverted party and break the AKE security. Therefore, the AKE security in this case is not guaranteed any more.

Note that our AKE protocol works well without installing the RFs: since the feedback messages are piggybacked onto the messages sent by parties, they can be optional. If a party receives a protocol message without a corresponding feedback message, it simply follows the protocol specification as if there were no RFs involved.

5 Instantiations

5.1 Using the Plain Diffie-Hellman Key Encapsulation

The instantiation based on the plain Diffie-Hellman key encapsulation is shown in Fig. 5. The KEM is derived from the ElGamal encryption and is referred to as ElGamal KEM in [3]. The instantiation of the commitment follows the construction by Dodis et al. [19]. A detailed description of the instantiation is shown in the full version of this paper due to space constraints. To avoid covert channel through signature, the signature scheme Σ is instantiated with a unique signature [2]. Notice that this instantiation is similar to the AKE protocol proposed by Dodis et al. [19] except that our instantiation generates signatures over the DH key shares instead of bilinear pairings. Consequently, our framework can be viewed as an extension and generalization of their AKE protocol. The MU-OW-PCA security of the ElGamal KEM is tightly based on the SDH assumption, which is proved in the full version of this paper. We omit the detailed proof of the protocol in Fig. 5 as it is an instantiation of our generic construction.

A(sid, (sk$_A$, vk$_A$))		F$_A$		F$_B$		B(sid, (sk$_B$, vk$_B$))
$a \leftarrow\$ \mathbb{Z}_p^*;\ A \leftarrow g^a$						
$(r, s) \leftarrow\$ \mathcal{R}_{\mathsf{com}}^2$						
$(c_1, c_2) \leftarrow (g^r h^s, h^s A)$						
$u := (c_1, c_2)$	$\xrightarrow{u}$					
		$\alpha \leftarrow\$ \mathbb{Z}_p$				
		$(r_1, s_1) \leftarrow\$ \mathcal{R}_{\mathsf{com}}^2$				
		$c_1' \leftarrow g^{r_1} h^{s_1} c_1^{\alpha}$				
		$c_2' \leftarrow h^{s_1} c_2^{\alpha}$				
		$u' := (c_1', c_2')$	$\xrightarrow{u'}$		$\xrightarrow{u'}$	$b \leftarrow\$ \mathbb{Z}_p^*, v \leftarrow g^b$
					$\xleftarrow{v}$	
				$\beta \leftarrow\$ \mathbb{Z}_p^*, v' \leftarrow v^{\beta}$		
	$\xleftarrow{(v', \alpha)}$		$\xleftarrow{v'}$			
if $v' = 1_{\mathbb{G}}$, **output** $\perp$						
$A' \leftarrow A^{\alpha}, x := (r, s)$						
$\sigma_1 \leftarrow \mathsf{Sig}(\mathsf{sk}_A, tr)$	$\xrightarrow{(x, \sigma_1)}$					
		$r' \leftarrow r\alpha + r_1$				
		$s' \leftarrow s\alpha + s_1$				
		$A' \leftarrow \Pi_{\mathsf{com}}.\mathsf{Ver}(u', (r', s'))$				
		if $A' \notin \mathbb{G}\backslash\{1_{\mathbb{G}}\}$, **output** $\perp$				
		$\Sigma.\mathsf{Ver}(\mathsf{vk}_A, (tr, \sigma_1)) \stackrel{?}{=} 1$				
		$x' := (r', s')$	$\xrightarrow{(x', \sigma_1)}$		$\xrightarrow{(x', \sigma_1, \beta)}$	$v' \leftarrow v^{\beta}$
						$A' \leftarrow \Pi_{\mathsf{com}}.\mathsf{Ver}(u', x')$
						if $A' \notin \mathbb{G}\backslash\{1_{\mathbb{G}}\}$, **output** $\perp$
						$\Sigma.\mathsf{Ver}(\mathsf{vk}_A, (tr, \sigma_1)) \stackrel{?}{=} 1$
						$\sigma_2 \leftarrow \mathsf{Sig}(\mathsf{sk}_B, tr)$
					$\xleftarrow{\sigma_2}$	
				$\Sigma.\mathsf{Ver}(\mathsf{vk}_B, (tr, \sigma_2)) \stackrel{?}{=} 1$		
	$\xleftarrow{\sigma_2}$		$\xleftarrow{\sigma_2}$			
$\Sigma.\mathsf{Ver}(\mathsf{vk}_B, (tr, \sigma_2)) \stackrel{?}{=} 1$						
Output $H(\mathsf{sid}, A', v', v'^{a\alpha})$						Output $H(\mathsf{sid}, A', v', A'^{b\beta})$

Fig. 5. The AKE scheme based on the plain Diffie-Hellman key encapsulation, where $tr := (A', v', \mathsf{sid})$.

5.2 A Tightly-Secure Construction Based on CDH Assumption

By using the twin DH technique [10], we obtain a variant of our instantiation, which has a tight reduction to the CDH assumption. The detailed description of this variant is shown in the full version. Compared with the previous scheme, this variant uses double group elements in the ciphertext, which makes security of this scheme tightly based on the S2DH assumption. The proof is analogous to the proof of Theorem 1, except that PCO is replaced by the twin DDH oracle. Moreover, as shown in Theorem 3 of [10], the S2DH assumption is implied by the CDH assumption. We conclude that this variant is tightly secure under the CDH assumption in the random oracle model.

Acknowledgements. This work is supported in part by the National Natural Science Foundation of China (No.62122092, No.62202485, No.62032005), Young Elite Scientists Sponsorship Program by China Association for Science and Technology (No.YESS20230028) and Science and Technology Research Plan Program by NUDT (No.ZK22-03).

Funding. The National Natural Science Foundation of China (No.62372462).

References

1. Abdalla, M., Bellare, M., Rogaway, P.: The Oracle Diffie-Hellman assumptions and an analysis of DHIES. In: Naccache, D. (ed.) CT-RSA 2001. LNCS, vol. 2020, pp. 143–158. Springer, Heidelberg (2001). https://doi.org/10.1007/3-540-45353-9_12
2. Ateniese, G., Magri, B., Venturi, D.: Subversion-resilient signature schemes. In: Ray, I., Li, N., Kruegel, C. (eds.) ACM CCS 2015: 22nd Conference on Computer and Communications Security, pp. 364–375. ACM Press, Denver (2015). https://doi.org/10.1145/2810103.2813635
3. Beguinet, H., Chevalier, C., Pointcheval, D., Ricosset, T., Rossi, M.: GeT a CAKE: generic transformations from key encaspulation mechanisms to password authenticated key exchanges. In: ACNS 23: 21st International Conference on Applied Cryptography and Network Security, Part II. Lecture Notes in Computer Science, pp. 516–538. Springer, Heidelberg (2023). https://doi.org/10.1007/978-3-031-33491-7_19
4. Bellare, M., Rogaway, P.: Entity authentication and key distribution. In: Stinson, D.R. (ed.) CRYPTO 1993. LNCS, vol. 773, pp. 232–249. Springer, Heidelberg (1994). https://doi.org/10.1007/3-540-48329-2_21
5. Bemmann, P., Berndt, S., Diemert, D., Eisenbarth, T., Jager, T.: Subversion-resilient authenticated encryption without random oracles. In: ACNS 23: 21st International Conference on Applied Cryptography and Network Security, Part II. Lecture Notes in Computer Science, pp. 460–483. Springer, Heidelberg (2023). https://doi.org/10.1007/978-3-031-33491-7_17
6. Berndt, S., Wichelmann, J., Pott, C., Traving, T.H., Eisenbarth, T.: ASAP: algorithm substitution attacks on cryptographic protocols. In: Suga, Y., Sakurai, K., Ding, X., Sako, K. (eds.) ASIACCS 22: 17th ACM Symposium on Information, Computer and Communications Security, pp. 712–726. ACM Press, Nagasaki (2022). https://doi.org/10.1145/3488932.3517387

7. Bossuat, A., Bultel, X., Fouque, P.-A., Onete, C., van der Merwe, T.: Designing reverse firewalls for the real world. In: Chen, L., Li, N., Liang, K., Schneider, S. (eds.) ESORICS 2020. LNCS, vol. 12308, pp. 193–213. Springer, Cham (2020). https://doi.org/10.1007/978-3-030-58951-6_10
8. Brunetta, C., Heum, H., Stam, M.: Multi-instance secure public-key encryption. In: Boldyreva, A., Kolesnikov, V. (eds.) PKC 2023: 26th International Conference on Theory and Practice of Public Key Cryptography, Part II. Lecture Notes in Computer Science, vol. 13941, pp. 336–367. Springer, Heidelberg (2023). https://doi.org/10.1007/978-3-031-31371-4_12
9. Canetti, R., Krawczyk, H.: Analysis of key-exchange protocols and their use for building secure channels. In: Pfitzmann, B. (ed.) EUROCRYPT 2001. LNCS, vol. 2045, pp. 453–474. Springer, Heidelberg (2001). https://doi.org/10.1007/3-540-44987-6_28
10. Cash, D., Kiltz, E., Shoup, V.: The Twin Diffie-Hellman problem and applications. In: Smart, N. (ed.) EUROCRYPT 2008. LNCS, vol. 4965, pp. 127–145. Springer, Heidelberg (2008). https://doi.org/10.1007/978-3-540-78967-3_8
11. Chakraborty, S., Dziembowski, S., Nielsen, J.B.: Reverse firewalls for actively secure MPCs. In: Micciancio, D., Ristenpart, T. (eds.) CRYPTO 2020. LNCS, vol. 12171, pp. 732–762. Springer, Cham (2020). https://doi.org/10.1007/978-3-030-56880-1_26
12. Chakraborty, S., Ganesh, C., Pancholi, M., Sarkar, P.: Reverse firewalls for adaptively secure MPC without setup. In: Tibouchi, M., Wang, H. (eds.) ASIACRYPT 2021. LNCS, vol. 13091, pp. 335–364. Springer, Cham (2021). https://doi.org/10.1007/978-3-030-92075-3_12
13. Chakraborty, S., Magliocco, L., Magri, B., Venturi, D.: Key exchange in the post-snowden era: UC secure subversion-resilient PAKE. Cryptology ePrint Archive, Paper 2023/1827 (2023). https://eprint.iacr.org/2023/1827
14. Chakraborty, S., Magri, B., Nielsen, J.B., Venturi, D.: Universally composable subversion-resilient cryptography. In: Dunkelman, O., Dziembowski, S. (eds.) Advances in Cryptology – EUROCRYPT 2022, Part I. Lecture Notes in Computer Science, vol. 13275, pp. 272–302. Springer, Heidelberg (2022). https://doi.org/10.1007/978-3-031-06944-4_10
15. Chen, R., Huang, X., Yung, M.: Subvert KEM to break DEM: practical algorithm-substitution attacks on public-key encryption. In: Moriai, S., Wang, H. (eds.) ASIACRYPT 2020. LNCS, vol. 12492, pp. 98–128. Springer, Cham (2020). https://doi.org/10.1007/978-3-030-64834-3_4
16. Chen, R., Mu, Y., Yang, G., Susilo, W., Guo, F., Zhang, M.: Cryptographic reverse firewall via malleable smooth projective hash functions. In: Cheon, J.H., Takagi, T. (eds.) ASIACRYPT 2016. LNCS, vol. 10031, pp. 844–876. Springer, Heidelberg (2016). https://doi.org/10.1007/978-3-662-53887-6_31
17. Chow, S.S.M., Russell, A., Tang, Q., Yung, M., Zhao, Y., Zhou, H.-S.: Let a non-barking watchdog bite: cliptographic signatures with an offline watchdog. In: Lin, D., Sako, K. (eds.) PKC 2019. LNCS, vol. 11442, pp. 221–251. Springer, Cham (2019). https://doi.org/10.1007/978-3-030-17253-4_8
18. Cohn-Gordon, K., Cremers, C., Gjøsteen, K., Jacobsen, H., Jager, T.: Highly efficient key exchange protocols with optimal tightness. In: Boldyreva, A., Micciancio, D. (eds.) CRYPTO 2019. LNCS, vol. 11694, pp. 767–797. Springer, Cham (2019). https://doi.org/10.1007/978-3-030-26954-8_25
19. Dodis, Y., Mironov, I., Stephens-Davidowitz, N.: Message transmission with reverse firewalls—secure communication on corrupted machines. In: Robshaw, M., Katz, J.

(eds.) CRYPTO 2016. LNCS, vol. 9814, pp. 341–372. Springer, Heidelberg (2016). https://doi.org/10.1007/978-3-662-53018-4_13
20. Fischlin, M., Mazaheri, S.: Self-guarding cryptographic protocols against algorithm substitution attacks. In: Chong, S., Delaune, S. (eds.) CSF 2018: IEEE 31st Computer Security Foundations Symposium, pp. 76–90. IEEE Computer Society Press, Oxford (2018). https://doi.org/10.1109/CSF.2018.00013
21. Gjøsteen, K., Jager, T.: Practical and tightly-secure digital signatures and authenticated key exchange. In: Shacham, H., Boldyreva, A. (eds.) CRYPTO 2018. LNCS, vol. 10992, pp. 95–125. Springer, Cham (2018). https://doi.org/10.1007/978-3-319-96881-0_4
22. Han, S.: Authenticated key exchange and signatures with tight security in the standard model. In: Malkin, T., Peikert, C. (eds.) CRYPTO 2021. LNCS, vol. 12828, pp. 670–700. Springer, Cham (2021). https://doi.org/10.1007/978-3-030-84259-8_23
23. Hofheinz, D., Kiltz, E.: The group of signed quadratic residues and applications. In: Halevi, S. (ed.) CRYPTO 2009. LNCS, vol. 5677, pp. 637–653. Springer, Heidelberg (2009). https://doi.org/10.1007/978-3-642-03356-8_37
24. LaMacchia, B., Lauter, K., Mityagin, A.: Stronger security of authenticated key exchange. In: Susilo, W., Liu, J.K., Mu, Y. (eds.) ProvSec 2007. LNCS, vol. 4784, pp. 1–16. Springer, Heidelberg (2007). https://doi.org/10.1007/978-3-540-75670-5_1
25. Li, Y., Schäge, S.: No-match attacks and robust partnering definitions: defining trivial attacks for security protocols is not trivial. In: Thuraisingham, B.M., Evans, D., Malkin, T., Xu, D. (eds.) ACM CCS 2017: 24th Conference on Computer and Communications Security, pp. 1343–1360. ACM Press, Dallas (2017https://doi.org/10.1145/3133956.3134006
26. Mironov, I., Stephens-Davidowitz, N.: Cryptographic reverse firewalls. In: Oswald, E., Fischlin, M. (eds.) EUROCRYPT 2015. LNCS, vol. 9057, pp. 657–686. Springer, Heidelberg (2015). https://doi.org/10.1007/978-3-662-46803-6_22
27. Pan, J., Qian, C., Ringerud, M.: Signed (group) Diffie-Hellman key exchange with tight security. J. Cryptol. **35**(4), 26 (2022). https://doi.org/10.1007/s00145-022-09438-y
28. Russell, A., Tang, Q., Yung, M., Zhou, H.-S.: Cliptography: clipping the power of kleptographic attacks. In: Cheon, J.H., Takagi, T. (eds.) ASIACRYPT 2016. LNCS, vol. 10032, pp. 34–64. Springer, Heidelberg (2016). https://doi.org/10.1007/978-3-662-53890-6_2
29. Russell, A., Tang, Q., Yung, M., Zhou, H.S.: Generic semantic security against a kleptographic adversary. In: Thuraisingham, B.M., Evans, D., Malkin, T., Xu, D. (eds.) ACM CCS 2017: 24th Conference on Computer and Communications Security, pp. 907–922. ACM Press, Dallas (2017). https://doi.org/10.1145/3133956.3133993
30. Russell, A., Tang, Q., Yung, M., Zhou, H.-S.: Correcting subverted random oracles. In: Shacham, H., Boldyreva, A. (eds.) CRYPTO 2018. LNCS, vol. 10992, pp. 241–271. Springer, Cham (2018). https://doi.org/10.1007/978-3-319-96881-0_9
31. Shoup, V.: A proposal for an ISO standard for public key encryption. Cryptology ePrint Archive, Report 2001/112 (2001). https://eprint.iacr.org/2001/112
32. Steinfeld, R., Baek, J., Zheng, Y.: On the necessity of strong assumptions for the security of a class of asymmetric encryption schemes. In: Batten, L., Seberry, J. (eds.) ACISP 2002. LNCS, vol. 2384, pp. 241–256. Springer, Heidelberg (2002). https://doi.org/10.1007/3-540-45450-0_20

On Sealed-Bid Combinatorial Auction with Privacy-Preserving Dynamic Programming

Hong Yen Tran(✉), Jiankun Hu, and Shabnam Kasra Kermanshahi

School of Systems and Computing at UNSW, Canberra, Australia
{hongyen.tran,jiankun.hu,s.kasra_kermanshahi}@unsw.edu.au

Abstract. Privacy-preserving combinatorial auctions, also known as sealed-bid combinatorial auctions, allow bidders to place bids on combinations of homogeneous or heterogeneous items without revealing the bidding prices (except for the winning ones) to any individual party. There is a significant lack of literature addressing this crucial and practical issue. We are bridging this gap by introducing two novel protocols for centralized and distributed auction systems. In the centralised approach, we integrate homomorphic encryption and DGK/Veugen secure comparison in a 2-server protocol for sealed-bid auctions. In the distributed approach we introduce a novel protocol based on homomorphic encryption and perturbation to allow an auction issuer and bidders to collaborate without any third party.

Keywords: sealed-bid combinatorial auction · privacy-preserving dynamic programming · secure comparison · homomorphic encryption · perturbation

1 Introduction

An *auction* is a mechanism to trade commodities among buyers and sellers [1]. Auction models can be classified into different types according to different factors [19], e.g., the number of bidding items (single-item auctions, multi-item auctions or combinatorial auctions), the roles of sellers/buyers (forward auctions, reverse auctions), the rules to determine the winners (first-price sealed-bid auctions, and (M+1)-price sealed-bid auctions), etc. In combinatorial auctions, bidders can place their bids on a set of items which can be of the same type or different types [1]. An auctioneer determines the optimal allocation to maximize the seller's revenue (in forward auctions) or minimize the buyer's cost (in reverse auctions). The optimal solution can be obtained by dynamic programming [10,18].

In *sealed-bid auctions*, also known as *privacy-preserving auctions*, bidders submit their protected (sealed) bids to ensure that their bids remain confidential throughout the auction process. After the auction finishes, the losing bids are still kept private to protect the losing bidders' privacy. If the losing bids are revealed to the auctioneer or the sellers, their competitive advantage in future auctions

J. K. Liu et al. (Eds.): ProvSec 2024, LNCS 14904, pp. 201–220, 2025.
https://doi.org/10.1007/978-981-96-0957-4_11

might be negatively affected. For example, the starting price or the minimum value of the bid in future auctions might be increased, and the bidders might not be offered a lower price than their past bidding prices. This auction type helps to promote a fair trading market. However, computing the outcome of such an auction is a significant challenge, as solving the winner determination problem of general combinatorial auctions, even without privacy, is already NP-hard.

In the literature on sealed-bid auctions, very few works tackle the combinatorial auction problem, which requires solving a combinatorial optimization problem rather than just determining the maximum or the minimum of bidding prices. A general method for solving any sealed-bid auction protocol is to use the garbled circuit [14]. However, this method requires expensive computation and a different combinatorial circuit for different inputs [20]. The most challenging problem in solving the optimization problems of combinatorial auctions is balancing the privacy/level of trust assumption and the efficiency. In existing sealed-bid auction protocols, there are different assumptions and models of trust that with efficiency at the cost of privacy: fully trusted auctioneers, trusted third parties, distributed-auctioneer trust, distributed-bidder trust, and two-server trust. Most of the proposed protocols are on the model of distributed auctioneer trust where a large number of distributed auctioneers are required (i.e. the number of optimization subproblems in dynamic programming [15,20,22]). Additionally, several works add multiple third parties to their model of trust (e.g., notaries in [9]) to support secure comparison operations which increases the risk of data leakage.

In this work, we propose two protocols, one for centralised auctions and the other for distributed auctions, aiming to balance the level of trust and efficiency. The first protocol assumes the two-server trust model and the second one works with the distributed-bidder trust model. These protocols minimize the participation of third parties in the system compared to related works, which also helps minimise the leakage risk. More specifically, there is only a semi-honest auctioneer in the centralised protocol and no auctioneer or any third parties in the distributed approach. Both protocols guarantee that only the auction issuer knows the bidding prices of the winners, and the losing bidding prices are always kept private even after releasing the auction outcome. Not only bidding prices but also the values of intermediate computations of dynamic programming are also protected (by encryption in the centralised protocol and by encryption and perturbation in the distributed protocol). This helps eliminate the private information leakage from the intermediate computation which has not been addressed in previous works [15,20,22]. More details of our contributions are summarized below:

- We design two novel auction protocols, one for centralized auctions and another for distributed auctions, both of which provide secure computation of dynamic programming and achieve a balance between trust and efficiency in combinatorial auctions. Our protocols address potential issues of private information leakage from the intermediate computation of dynamic programming in previous works.

- In the centralised protocol, we integrate homomorphic encryption and DGK-Veugen secure comparison in a two-server trust model to execute secure dynamic programming. The optimal solution is only known by the auction issuer (i.e., the buyer in procurement auctions). The auctioneer does not know any bidding prices or the minimum cost of any intermediate sub-problems.
- In the distributed protocol, we design a novel collaboration mechanism among the auction issuer and bidders to implement a secure dynamic programming algorithm without any auctioneer. Thanks to perturbation techniques and the homomorphic property of ElGamal encryption, bidding prices are kept on the bidder side for local computation without being sent to any party, and bidders only obtain the distorted values of the intermediate dynamic programming computation from their immediate predecessor.

2 Preliminaries

2.1 Related Works

Many of the existing works focus on non-combinatorial sealed-bid auctions [2,4,6,11–13,23]. These works deal with more simplified auction types, which only determine the bid with the maximum or minimum price instead of finding the set of bids whose combination results in the optimal price, as our work does. In the line of research on combinatorial sealed-bid auctions, there are only a few works [8,9,14,15,17,22]. Naor *et al.* [14] proposed a general method for any sealed-bid auction protocol using the garbled circuit technique. In dealing with combinatorial auctions, this method requires constructing a specific combinatorial circuit that implements a dynamic programming algorithm corresponding to each fixed input. Yokoo and Suzuki [22] presented secure multi-agent dynamic programming based on homomorphic encryption which can be applied to solve sealed-bid combinatorial auctions. They proposed a representation of secret weights (bidding prices) which supports determining the maximum of weights and adding a constant to a weight given only the encryption of the weight. Their protocol requires many semi-honest non-colluding evaluators (auctioneers), and each auctioneer corresponds to a subproblem, which is impractical considering the large number of subproblems in dynamic programming (e.g., $k \cdot N$ subproblems in a reverse multi-unit combinatorial auction, where k is the number of bidders and N is the order quantity). Additionally, because a secret weight is encrypted using an auctioneer's public key, if that auctioneer can obtain the weight encryption over the communication, then the weight is revealed. In our approach, bidding prices are kept locally for computation, not sent out over the network even in encryption form, which helps eliminate this leakage risk. Another problem with Yokoo and Suzuki's protocol is that if there is only one link connecting two subproblems, it always leaks the weight of this link. This problem also does not occur in our protocols. The same authors also proposed another protocol for secure dynamic programming using polynomial secret sharing in another work [20]. This protocol also requires multiple semi-honest auctioneers, which makes their protocols fail to scale. The same leakage of weights (bidding prices) as in [22] also occurs in this work.

Nojoumian and Stinson [15] added verifiability to [20] and prevented the leakage of exact bidding prices via noise addition. The key idea is to mask bidding prices ($p_i + r$ or $a \cdot p_i + r$), which helps preserve the order for comparison without revealing the exact bidding prices p_i. A verifiable secret-sharing scheme is applied in sharing the masked prices among auctioneers to resist corruption among $\leq t$ auctioneers. Their protocol inherits the vulnerabilities of the protocol in [20]. Moreover, their masking scheme reveals either the difference between bidding prices or the ratios among them. Parkes *et al.* [17] solved a privacy-preserving combinatorial clock-proxy auction. The protocol only protects bidding prices in the clock phase. In the winner determination phase, bidding prices are revealed to the auctioneer to compute the solution. Damle *et al.*[9] proposed a blockchain-based multi-agent secure comparison and applied it to design a sealed-bid combinatorial auction protocol for single-minded bidders. Their secure comparison requires many semi-trusted third parties (notaries and a central server).

2.2 Reverse Multi-unit Combinatorial Auction

We investigate a specific type of combinatorial auction, which involves finding the optimal allocation that minimizes the buyer's cost, also known as the reverse multi-unit combinatorial auction (RMUCA) or procurement auction. Our protocols can still apply to other types of sealed-bid combinatorial auctions or privacy-preserving optimization problems that can be solved with the dynamic programming approach. First, we present the definition of RMUCA.

Let N be the total number of units requested by a buyer; $\mathcal{B}_1, \mathcal{B}_2, \ldots, \mathcal{B}_k$ are k bidders with the corresponding bids $b_1, b_2, \ldots, b_k$. Each bid b_i is in the format $b_i = (l_i, u_i, p_i)$, where p_i is the offer price per unit of bid b_i, and l_i and u_i ($l_i < u_i \leq N$) are the lower bound and the upper bound, respectively, of the number of units to which p_i is applicable. An allocation π is a subset of bids, comprising chosen bids b_i with corresponding allocated quantities $x_i \in [l_i, u_i]$ such that $\sum_{b_i \in \pi} x_i = N (1 \leq i \leq k)$. Denote the set of all possible allocations by Π. The RMUCA problem is to find the minimum cost $\mathsf{mincost} = \mathsf{min}_{\pi \in \Pi} \sum_{b_i \in \pi} p_i x_i$ and the corresponding optimal allocation $\pi_{\min} = \mathsf{argmin}_{\pi \in \Pi} \sum_{b_i \in \pi} p_i x_i$ that assigns quantities to bidders within their applicable quantity intervals.

Dynamic programming [3] has been used to solve various combinatorial optimization problems. The main idea of dynamic programming is to break down the original problem into sub-problems and solve each sub-problem only once, storing the solutions to sub-problems in a *table* to avoid redundant computations and improve efficiency. The recursive relation in dynamic programming includes both arithmetic operations and comparison operations. The RMUCA problem can be solved in pseudo-polynomial time with an exact dynamic programming algorithm, as described in Algorithm 1. We define a cost table C of the height $k + 1$ and the width $N + 1$ (i.e. a dynamic programming table) consisting of $(k+1) \cdot (N+1)$ entries $C(i, n)$ $(0 \leq i \leq k, 0 \leq n \leq N)$, where $C(i, n)$ represents the minimum cost of n units provided by a subset of the first i suppliers. We

Algorithm 1. Reverse Multi-unit Combinatorial Auctions (RMUCA)

```
Input: {l_i, u_i, p_i}_{i=1}^k      // Bids of k bidders
Output: C(k, N) and π_min           // The mincost and optimal allocation
for i ∈ [0, k] do
    C(i, 0) = 0
for j ∈ [1, N] do
    C(0, j) = MAX
for i from 1 to k do
    for n from 1 to N do
        min = C(i − 1, n)
        for x ∈ Q_{i,n}\{0} do
            if if min > C(i − 1, n − x) + x · p_i then
                min = C(i − 1, n − x) + x · p_i
        C(i, n) = min
mincost = C(k, N)
R = N
π_min = ∅
for i from k to 0 do
    for x ∈ Q_{i,n} do
        if C(i, R) == C(i − 1, R − x) + x · p_i then
            R = R − x
            π_min = π_min ∪ (i, x)
```

denote by $\mathsf{MAX} = N \cdot p_{\max}$ the maximum value of N items, where $p_{\max}$ is the maximum unit price that the buyer can accept. Initial assignments are set as follows: $\{C(i,0) = 0\}_{i=0}^{k}, \{C(0,j) = \mathsf{MAX}\}_{j=1}^{N}$. We iterate through each row and column to fill C by using the following recurrence relation for $C(i,n)$:

$$C(i,n) = \min_{x \in Q_{i,n}} \big(C(i-1, n-x) + x \cdot p_i\big) \tag{1}$$

where $Q_{i,n} \triangleq \{0\} \cup ([1,n] \cap [l_i, u_i])$ is the set of all trial quantities x corresponding to bidder $\mathcal{B}_i$ in the sub-problem $C(i,n)$.

Let $t(i,n,x) = C(i-1, n-x) + x \cdot p_i$ denote the cost of the trial having x units from $\mathcal{B}_i$ in the sub-problem $C(i,n)$, we have $C(i,n) = \min_{x \in Q_{i,n}} \big(t(i,n,x)\big)$. Once C is filled, $C(k,N)$ is the minimum cost and we can trace back to get the selected suppliers of this optimal solution. See Table 1 for a toy example.

Table 1. Table C of an RMUCA toy example with $N = 6, k = 3, b_1 = (3,5,2), b_2 = (3,5,3), b_3 = (1,8,4)$. The optimal allocation is $x_1 = 5, x_2 = 0, x_3 = 1$ with the minimum cost $5 \times 2 + 0 \times 3 + 1 \times 4 = 14$.

0	MAX	MAX	MAX	MAX	MAX	MAX
0	MAX	MAX	6	8	10	MAX
0	MAX	MAX	6	8	10	15
0	4	8	6	8	10	14

2.3 Notations and Cryptographic Primitives

In this section, we present the frequently used notations (shown in Table 2) and the cryptographic primitives that we used in our design.

Table 2. List of notations

Notation	Description
N	The requested number of good units announced by $\mathcal{AI}$
p_{max}	The maximum acceptable unit price
MAX	$= N \cdot p_{max}$ The maximum acceptable cost of N units
k	The number of bidders
$b_i = (l_i, u_i, p_i)$	The bid of bidder $\mathcal{B}_i$, including the bidding price p_i
	the lower bound l_i, and the upper bound u_i that p_i is applicable)
$\langle C \rangle, \tilde{C}$	The encrypted and perturbed dynamic programming cost table
$C(i, j)$	The entry at row i column j of table C
$\langle C(i, j) \rangle, \tilde{C}(i, j)$	The encrypted and perturbed value of $C(i, j)$
$t(i, n, x)$	$= C(i-1, n-x) + x \cdot p_i$: The cost of the trial having x units
	from $\mathcal{B}_i$ in the sub-problem $C(i, n)$
$\tilde{t}(i, n, x)$	The perturbed value of $t(i, n, x)$

Building Blocks for Scheme 1, The main idea of the centralised sealed-bid RMUCA protocol is to utilise homomorphic encryption and a secure comparison protocol in a two-non-colluded-server setting. Paillier encryption scheme [16] and DGK secure comparison protocol [7] are the two main adopted blocks to encrypt the bidding price and compute the encrypted dynamic programming table $\langle C \rangle$.

- *Paillier encryption* [16] of plaintext $m \in \mathbb{Z}_N$ is denoted by $\langle m \rangle$ and computed as $\langle m \rangle = g^m r^N \bmod N^2$, where N is a product of two large primes, r is a random integer satisfying $0 < r < N$ and $\gcd(r, N) = 1$. We choose $g = N + 1$ to reduce g^m to $1 + N \cdot m$ modulo N^2. Paillier crypto system has homomorphic properties: homomorphic addition ($\langle m_1 \rangle \cdot \langle m_2 \rangle = \langle m_1 + m_2 \rangle \bmod N^2$), and homomorphic multiplication ($\langle m \rangle^k = \langle k * m \rangle \bmod N^2$), where $0 \le m, m_1, m_2 < N$ are plaintexts. The multiplicative inverse of x modulo n is denoted by x^{-1} and equals the integer $y, 0 \le y < n$, such that $x \cdot y = 1 \bmod n$. The multiplicative inverse is used to negate an encrypted integer: $\langle x \rangle^{-1} = \langle -x \rangle \bmod n$.
- *DGK encryption* [7] of plaintext $m \in \mathbb{Z}_u$ is computed as $[m] = g^m h^r \bmod n$, where r is a fresh random integer, u is a small prime divisor (16 or 32-bit) of both $(p-1, q-1)$, (p, q) are two large primes. The public key is (n, g, h, u) and the private key is (p, q, v_p, v_q). The ciphertext modulus n is the product of p and q. The numbers g and h are elements of $\mathbb{Z}_*^n$ of order uv_pv_q and v_pv_q respectively.

- *DGK/Veugen secure comparison protocol* [7,21] utilises both Paillier encryption and DGK encryption to compare two ciphertexts with small computational and communication costs. There are two non-colluded servers in this protocol. Server A has two Paillier encrypted inputs while server B has the Paillier decryption key and DGK decryption key. After two communication rounds, server A obtains the encrypted comparison result of its two encrypted inputs. DGK/Veugen protocol provides computational security towards server A and statistical security towards server B.

Building Blocks for Scheme 2. ElGamal encryption scheme, representation of private non-negative integers, and additive noise perturbation are the main techniques adopted in this protocol.

- *ElGamal encryption*: Let $q, p = 2q + 1$ be two large primes and $\mathbb{G} = \langle g \rangle$ be a cyclic group of order q generated by g. A common choice for G is a subgroup of the multiplicative group of integers modulo a prime p, denoted as $\mathbb{Z}_p^*$. The secret key is $x \in \mathbb{Z}_q$, where $\mathbb{Z}_q = \{0, 1, \ldots q-1\}$. The public key is $(g, y = g^x)$. Encryption of a message $M \in \mathbb{G}$ is $E(M) = (A = g^r, B = y^r M)$, where $r \in \mathbb{Z}_q$ is a random number. Decryption using the private key $M = B/A^x$. ElGamal encryption is homomorphic: $E(M_1) \cdot E(M_2) = E(M_1 \cdot M_2)$
- *Representation of private non-negative integers*: We utilise the representation of private non-negative integers [22] with modification as follows to represent a private non-negative integer m $(0 \leq m \leq L)$ as a vector $\mathbf{e}(m)$ of L ElGamal ciphertexts:

$$\begin{aligned}\mathbf{e}(m) &= (e_1, \ldots, e_L) \\ &= (\underbrace{E(1), \ldots, E(1)}_{m}, \underbrace{E(z), \ldots, E(z)}_{L-m})\end{aligned} \tag{2}$$

where $E(1)$ and $E(z)$ are the ElGamal encryptions of 1 and z, respectively ($z \neq 1$ and is public known).

By representing a private non-negative integer this way, we can obtain the private sum of that non-negative integer and a known integer (*Adding a constant*) and the private minimum of a list of private non-negative integers given their representations (*Finding the minimum*).

Adding a constant: Having $\mathbf{e}(m)$ and a constant a, we can create the representation of $m + a$ without knowing m by inserting (removing) $(\underbrace{E(1), \ldots, E(1)}_{a})$ on the left and removing (inserting) $(\underbrace{E(z), \ldots, E(z)}_{a})$ on the right if a is positive (negative):

$$\mathbf{e}(m) = (\underbrace{E(1), \ldots, E(1)}_{m}, \underbrace{E(z), \ldots, E(z)}_{L-m})$$

$$\mathbf{e}(m+a) = (\underbrace{E(1), \ldots, E(1)}_{a}, \underbrace{E(1), \ldots, E(1)}_{m}, \underbrace{E(z), \ldots, E(z)}_{L-m-a}) \tag{3}$$

$e(m+a)$ needs to be randomized by element-wise product with $\underbrace{(E(1),\ldots,E(1))}_{L}$ so that one has seen $e(m)$ and $e(m+a)$ cannot deduce the value of a. The randomization utilises the homomorphic property of ElGamal encryption: $E(1)\cdot E(1) = E(1\cdot 1) = E(1), E(z)\cdot E(1) = E(z\cdot 1) = E(z)$

$$e(m+a) \xrightarrow{randomize} e'(m+a) \tag{4}$$

where $e'(m+a)$ is another valid representation of $(m+a)$
Finding the minimum: Having representations $e(m_1), e(m_2), \ldots, e(m_k)$, we can create a representation of the minimum $\mu = \min(m_1, m_2, \ldots, m_k)$ by doing the element-wise product of these representations.

$$\begin{aligned}\prod_{i=1}^{k} e(m_i) &= (\prod_{i=1}^{k} e_{1,i}, \ldots, \prod_{i=1}^{k} e_{L,i}) \\ &= (\underbrace{E(1),\ldots,E(1)}_{\mu}, \underbrace{E(z^{s_1}),\ldots,E(z^{s_{L-\mu}})}_{L-\mu})\end{aligned} \tag{5}$$

Denote $\bar{e}(\mu) = (\underbrace{E(1),\ldots,E(1)}_{\mu}, \underbrace{E(z^{s_1}),\ldots,E(z^{s_{L-\mu}})}_{L-\mu})$. By decrypting each ElGamal encryption component from left to right until reaching the first value $\neq 1$, we obtain the minimum value μ. In our protocol, we use the subscript i in $e_i(m), \bar{e}_i(m)$ to indicate the public key pk_i used in Elgamal encryption.
- Additive noise perturbation: Random noises are generated from a discrete Gaussian distribution [5] $\mathcal{N}(0, \frac{\mathsf{MAX}}{\varepsilon})$ to perturb table C with ε-differential privacy guarantee.

3 Scheme 1: Centralised Sealed-Bid RMUCA (cRMUCA)

3.1 Overview

System Model. The system consists of k bidders $\mathcal{B}_i$, $(i = 1\cdots k)$, an auctioneer server $\mathcal{AS}$, and an auction issuer $\mathcal{AI}$ (i.e. a buyer in RMUCA). The public key pk of $\mathcal{AI}$ is publicly known by all parties of the system. We assume public communication channels exist between $\mathcal{AS}$ and $\mathcal{AI}$ and between $\mathcal{AS}$ and each bidder $\mathcal{B}_i$.

The auctioneer issuer $\mathcal{AI}$ starts an auction by sending an order to $\mathcal{AS}$, which contains (N, MAX). $\mathcal{AS}$ broadcasts the order to all members of the system. The members, who are interested in the order, submit their encrypted bids to the auctioneer server $\mathcal{AS}$. $\mathcal{AS}$ performs the computation to find the optimal allocation for $\mathcal{AI}$'s order over the encrypted bids with the cooperation of $\mathcal{AI}$ to reduce the complexity of secure computation. Finally, $\mathcal{AS}$ assists $\mathcal{AI}$ to determine the optimal solution (Fig. 1).

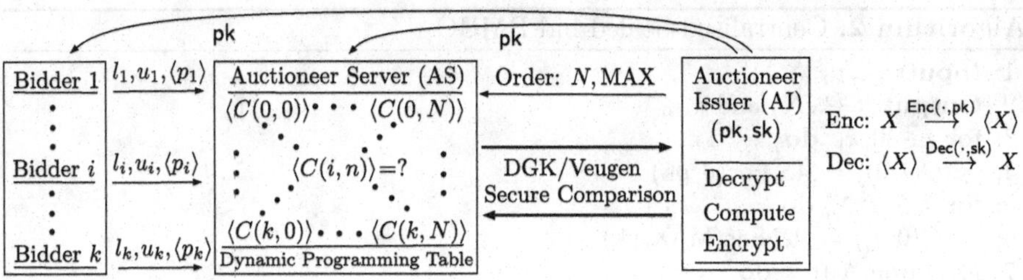

Fig. 1. A centralised 2-server protocol for sealed-bid combinatorial auction using DKG/Veugen secure comparison.

Theat Model. We consider a semi-honest (also known as honest-but-curious) adversary $\mathcal{A}$, who follows the protocol correctly but attempts to collect the bidding prices of (losing) bidders. $\mathcal{A}$ can corrupt a group of bidders (but not all of k bidders). $\mathcal{A}$ can also corrupt $\mathcal{AS}$ or $\mathcal{AI}$, but not both of the servers (i.e. $\mathcal{AS}$ and $\mathcal{AI}$ are assumed not to collude).

3.2 Description

The centralised sealed-bid RMUCA protocol includes the following steps:

Setup: $\mathcal{AI}$ generates a key pair $(\mathsf{pk}, \mathsf{sk})$ of Paillier encryption scheme, where pk is public known and sk is kept private.

Bidding: Bidders using pk to encrypt their bidding prices. $\langle p_i \rangle = \mathcal{B}_i.\mathsf{Enc}(p_i, \mathsf{pk})$

Finding the optimal allocation: $\mathcal{AS}$ solves RMUCA by implementing privacy-preserving dynamic programming in collaboration with $\mathcal{AI}$ (see Algorithm. 2).

1. First, $\mathcal{AS}$ initializes the encrypted table $\langle C \rangle$ by filling the encrypted values to row 0 and column 0.
2. Given the encrypted bidding price $\langle p_i \rangle$, the encryptions $\langle C(i-1, n-x) \rangle$, and a trial quantity $x \in Q_{i,n}$, $\mathcal{AS}$ computes $\langle C(i-1, n-x) + x \cdot p_i \rangle = \langle C(i-1, n-x) \rangle \cdot \langle p_i \rangle^x$ (without knowing p_i) thanks to the homomorphic properties of the Paillier encryption.
3. $\mathcal{AS}$ needs to obtain $\langle C(i,n) \rangle = \langle \min\{C(i-1, n-x) + x \cdot p_i\}_{x \in Q_{i,n}} \rangle$ given the ciphertexts $\{\langle C(i-1, n-x) + x \cdot p_i \rangle\}_{x \in Q_{i,n}}$. The DGK secure comparison protocol proposed by Damgard [7] and improved by Veugen in [21] is utilised, in which $\mathcal{AS}$ plays the role of server A having two ciphertexts and $\mathcal{AI}$ plays the role of server B who has the decryption keys.
4. After computing all the encrypted values of $\langle C \rangle$, $\mathcal{AS}$ sends $\mathcal{AI}$ $\langle C(k, N) \rangle$, which is the encryption of the $\mathsf{mincost}$. $\mathcal{AS}$ also assists $\mathcal{AI}$ to determine the optimal allocation x_i for each bidder B_i. In order to achieve this, for each row i with R being the updated remaining quantity, $\mathcal{AS}$ creates a list $\langle \mathcal{L} \rangle$ of encrypted values $\{\langle C(i-1, R-x) \rangle \cdot \langle p_i \rangle^x \cdot \langle C(i,R) \rangle^{-1}\}_{x \in Q_{i,n}}$, which is equivalent to $\{\langle C(i-1, R-x) + x \cdot p_i - C(i,R) \rangle\}_{x \in Q_{i,n}}$. Then $\mathcal{AS}$ sends $\langle \mathcal{L} \rangle$ to $\mathcal{AI}$ with the corresponding $Q_{i,n}$. $\mathcal{AI}$ decrypts to get $\mathcal{L}$, and determines the position j that $\mathcal{L}_j = 0$. The corresponding value at this position in $Q_{i,n}$ is the correct allocation x_i for bidder $\mathcal{B}_i$.

Algorithm 2. Centralised Sealed-bid RMUCA

Input: $\{l_i, u_i, \langle p_i \rangle\}_{i=1}^{k}$ //Bids of k bidders
Output: $C(k, N)$ and $\pi_{\min}$ // The mincost and optimal allocation
for $i \in [0, k]$ **do**
  $\langle C(i, 0)\rangle = \mathcal{AS}.\mathsf{Enc}(0, \mathsf{pk})$
for $j \in [1, N]$ **do**
  $\langle C(0, j)\rangle = \mathcal{AS}.\mathsf{Enc}(\mathsf{MAX}, \mathsf{pk})$
for i from 1 to k **do**
  for n from 1 to N **do**
    $\langle \min \rangle = \langle C(i-1, n)\rangle$
    for $x \in Q_{i,n} \backslash \{0\}$ **do**
      $\langle e\rangle = \mathsf{SecComp}_{\mathcal{AS},\mathcal{AI}}(\langle \min\rangle, \langle C(i-1, n-x)\rangle \cdot \langle p_i\rangle^x)$ //$e = \min \le C(i-1, n-x) + x \cdot p_i$
      if $\mathcal{AI}.\mathsf{Dec}(\langle e\rangle, \mathsf{sk}) == 0$ **then**
        $\langle \min\rangle = \langle C(i-1, n-x)\rangle \cdot \langle p_i\rangle^x$
    $\langle C(i, n)\rangle = \langle \min\rangle$
$\mathsf{mincost} = \mathcal{AI}.\mathsf{Dec}(\langle C(k, N)\rangle, \mathsf{sk})$
$R = N$
$\pi_{\min} = \emptyset$
for i from k to 1 **do**
  $\langle \mathcal{L}\rangle = \emptyset$
  for $x \in Q_{i,R}$ **do**
    $\langle \mathcal{L}\rangle.\text{append}(\langle C(i-1, R-x)\rangle \cdot \langle p_i\rangle^x \cdot \langle C(i, R)\rangle^{-1})$
  $\mathcal{L} = \mathcal{AI}.\mathsf{Dec}(\langle \mathcal{L}\rangle, \mathsf{pk})$
  Determine the position j s.t. $\mathcal{L}_j == 0$. The allocation x_i for $\mathcal{B}_i$ is the j-th element in $Q_{i,R}$
  $R = R - x_i$
  $\pi_{\min} = \pi_{\min} \cup (i, x_i)$
return $\mathsf{mincost}$, $\pi_{\min}$

5. Finally, $\mathcal{AI}$ requests the winning bidders (i.e. with non-zero quantity allocation) to reveal the bidding prices.

3.3 Discussion

Correctness Analysis

Theorem 1. *Assuming the correctness of DGK/Veugen secure comparison, Paillier encryption, and the dynamic programming algorithm, in an honest-but-curious setting, where all parties follow the protocol correctly but may attempt to learn private information from others, the correctness of* cRMUCA *is guaranteed.*

Proof. The DGK/Veugen secure comparison protocol allows two parties to compare encrypted integers without revealing the plaintext values. If $E(m_1)$ and $E(m_2)$ are Paillier encrypted messages of m_1 and m_2, respectively, the protocol correctly determines whether $m_1 \le m_2$ or $m_1 > m_2$.

Paillier encryption is an additively homomorphic encryption scheme. Given two ciphertexts $E(m_1)$ and $E(m_2)$, there exists an operation on the ciphertexts such that $E(m_1) \cdot E(m_2) = E(m_1 + m_2)$. The correctness of Paillier encryption ensures that encrypted computations yield correct results when decrypted.

The dynamic programming algorithm employed in our centralised RMUCA protocol solves a specific optimization problem (e.g., minimum cost allocation). The correctness of the dynamic programming algorithm ensures that given correct inputs, it produces correct outputs (e.g., optimal solutions).

Since the correctness of each individual component (DGK/Veugen secure comparison, Paillier encryption, and dynamic programming) is established, the correctness of the centralized sealed-bid RMUCA protocol follows directly.

Performance Analysis. See Algorithm 2 for an easier understanding of the following analysis. The initialization of the encrypted dynamic programming table $\langle C \rangle$ requires $O(N + k)$ Paillier encryptions (lines 3–6), $O(kN^2)$ ciphertext multiplications, exponentiation, and decriptions, $O(kN^2)$ secure comparison operations (DGK/Veugen) (lines 7–14). Note that in line 10, x is at most n. The traceback requires $O(kN)$ ciphertext multiplications, exponentiations, and inverses, and $O(kN)$ decryptions (lines 18–22).

Security Analysis

Theorem 2 (Security of cRMUCA). *Assuming no collusion between AI and AS, and that all parties follow the protocol as specified, the security of the DGK/Veugen secure comparison and Paillier encryption guarantees the security of* cRMUCA *protocol. As long as AS (who can access the encrypted dynamic programming table $\langle C \rangle$ and encrypted bidding prices) and AI (who has the decryption key sk) do not collude, all intermediate dynamic programming values and bidding prices are protected by the Paillier encryption.*

Proof. Paillier encryption is semantically secure. Given a ciphertext $E(m)$ and the corresponding public key, it is computationally infeasible for an adversary to derive any information about the plaintext m without access to the private decryption key sk. This property ensures that any encrypted value, whether it be an intermediate dynamic programming value or a bidding price, remains confidential as long as the private key sk is not compromised.

The DGK/Veugen secure comparison protocol allows for secure comparisons between encrypted values without revealing the plaintext values involved in the comparison. This protocol ensures that the outcome of the comparison does not leak information about the underlying plaintexts. The protocol's security relies on cryptographic assumptions such as the hardness of the Decisional Diffie-Hellman (DDH) problem.

It is assumed that AS and AI do not collude. AS can access the encrypted dynamic programming table $\langle C \rangle$ and encrypted bidding prices, but cannot decrypt them without AI's private key sk. Conversely, AI has the private key sk but does not have access to the encrypted values held by AS.

Since AS and AI do not collude, AS cannot decrypt any values without AI, and AI cannot access the encrypted values held by AS. Therefore, all intermediate dynamic programming values and bidding prices remain encrypted and secure. The semantic security of Paillier encryption ensures that even if AS and AI were to share their public data, they still could not learn any meaningful information about the encrypted values without colluding.

4 Scheme 2: Distributed Sealed-Bid RMUCA (dRMUCA)

4.1 Overview

System Model. The system consists of k bidders $\mathcal{B}_1, \cdots, \mathcal{B}_k$ and an auction issuer $\mathcal{AI}$. We assume public communication channels exist among bidders and between the auction issuer $\mathcal{AI}$ and each bidder $\mathcal{B}_i$.

The auction issuer $\mathcal{AI}$ starts an auction by announcing an auction order (N, MAX). Assume there are k bidders in the auction, $\{\mathcal{B}_1, \mathcal{B}_2, \ldots, \mathcal{B}_k\}$, sorted by $\mathcal{AI}$. In the "bidder chain" $\mathcal{B}_0, \mathcal{B}_1, \ldots, \mathcal{B}_{k+1}$, $\mathcal{AI}$ is considered as "bidder" $\mathcal{B}_0$ and also "bidder" $\mathcal{B}_{k+1}$. All bidders sequentially transmit their protected rows in table C (row i corresponding to bidder B_i) to the next bidder in the chain. More specifically, bidder $\mathcal{B}_i$ will send bidder $\mathcal{B}_{i+1}$ the noisy row $\tilde{C}_i$, which is in a secure representation form of Elgamal encryptions that only $\mathcal{B}_{i+1}$ can decrypt. $\mathcal{AI}$ controls the start and the end of the whole bidding process and finally can remove the accumulated noise at $\tilde{C}_k$ to obtain the minimum cost.

Threat Model. We consider a semi-honest (also known as honest-but-curious) adversary $\mathcal{A}$, who follows the protocol correctly but attempts to collect the bidding prices of bidders. $\mathcal{A}$ can corrupt a "bidder" (note that $\mathcal{AI}$ is also considered as "bidder" 0 and "bidder" $k+1$). $\mathcal{A}$ can also obtain all the transmitted messages.

4.2 Description

The distributed sealed-bid RMUCA (see Fig. 2) includes the following steps:

Setup:

- $\mathcal{AI}$ chooses two large primes $q, p = 2q + 1$, group $\mathbb{G}$. and generates a key pair $(\mathsf{sk}_0, \mathsf{pk}_0 = g^{\mathsf{sk}_0})$ where sk_0 is randomly chosen from $\mathbb{Z}_q$ (note that $\mathcal{AI}$ is considered as "bidder" $\mathcal{B}_0$ and $\mathcal{B}_{k+1}$ in the scheme). Next, $\mathcal{AI}$ chooses k secret values $M_0, M_1, \ldots, M_{k-1}$ where $\forall M_i > \mathsf{MAX}$ and sets $L = \mathsf{MAX} + M_0 + \ldots + M_{k-1}$. $\mathcal{AI}$ broadcasts public parameters $\mathsf{pp} = \{\mathbb{G}, g, z, \{\mathsf{pk}_i\}_{i=0}^{N+1}, \mathsf{MAX}, L, \varepsilon\}$ and sends $e_i(M_i)$ to bidder $\mathcal{B}_i$ $(i = 1, \ldots, k-1)$.
- Each bidder $\mathcal{B}_i$ $(i = 1, \ldots, k)$ generates a key pair $(\mathsf{sk}_i, \mathsf{pk}_i = g^{\mathsf{sk}_i})$ where sk_i is randomly chosen from $\mathbb{Z}_q$.

Finding the optimal allocation: $\mathcal{AI}$ and k bidders cooperate to solve RMUCA

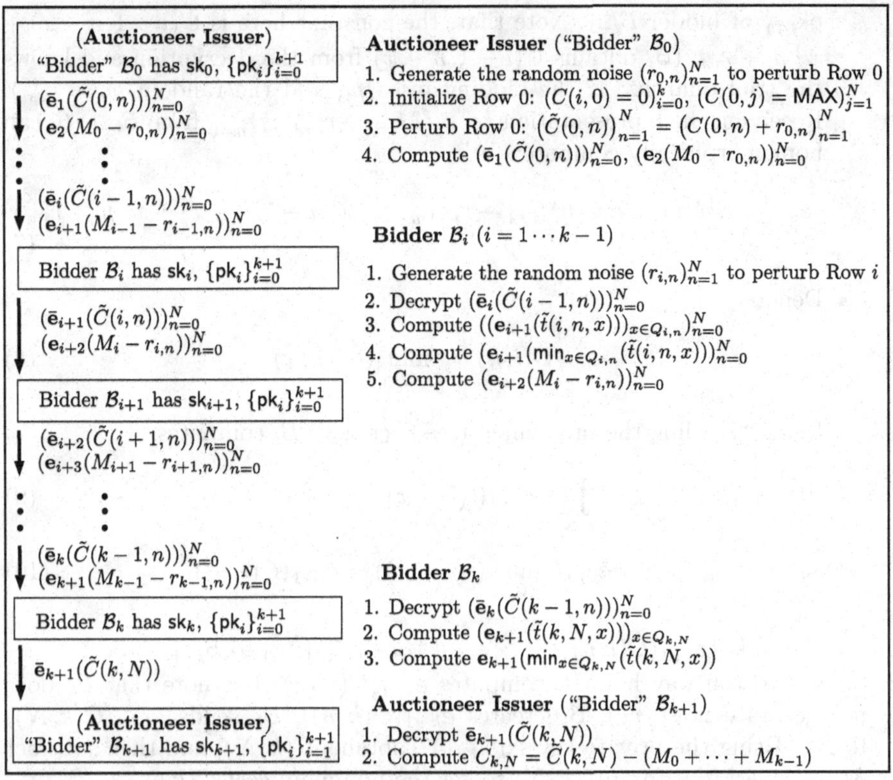

Fig. 2. Distributed sealed-bid RMUCA protocol, in which bidders and $\mathcal{AI}$ collaborate to compute the optimal solution.

1. $\mathcal{AI}$ ("bidder" $\mathcal{B}_0$) initializes row 0 of table C: $\{C(i,0)=0\}_{i=0}^k$, $\{C(0,j) = \mathsf{MAX}\}_{j=1}^N$. $\mathcal{AI}$ generates a random vector of length N within $(-\mathsf{MAX}, \mathsf{MAX})$ from a discrete Gaussian distribution $r_0 \leftarrow \mathcal{N}(0, \frac{\mathsf{MAX}}{\varepsilon})$ to perturb row 0 ($\{\tilde{C}(0,n) = C(0,n) + r_{0,n}\}_{n=1}^N$). Next, $\mathcal{AI}$ creates $\{\bar{e}_1(\tilde{C}(0,n))\}_{n=0}^N$ using the public key pk_1, $\{e_2(M_0 - r_{0,n})\}_{n=0}^N$ using the public key pk_2 and sends them to $\mathcal{B}_1$.
2. For each bidder $\mathcal{B}_i$, $i = 1, \ldots, k-1$, the following steps are implemented:
   - $\mathcal{B}_i$ decrypts $\{\bar{e}_i(\tilde{C}(i-1,n))\}_{n=0}^N$ using the secret key sk_i to get $\tilde{C}_{i-1}$
   - $\mathcal{B}_i$ generates a random vector of length N within $(-\mathsf{MAX}, \mathsf{MAX})$ from a discrete Gaussian distribution $r_i \leftarrow \mathcal{N}(0, \frac{\mathsf{MAX}}{\varepsilon})$ to perturb row i
   - $\mathcal{B}_i$ decrypts $e_i(M_i)$ to get M_i and then creates $\{e_{i+2}(M_i - r_{i,n})\}_{n=0}^N$ using the public key pk_{i+2}
   - Denote:

$$\tilde{t}(i,n,x) = M_{i-1} - r_{i-1,n-x} + \tilde{C}(i-1, n-x) + x \cdot p_i + r_{i,n} \qquad (6)$$

   $\mathcal{B}_i$ homomorphically computes the representation $e_{i+1}(\tilde{t}(i,n,x))$ thanks to the property "Adding a constant" (see Sect. 2.3) with the public key

pk_{i+1} of bidder $\mathcal{B}_{i+1}$. Note that, the constant here is $\tilde{C}(i-1, n-x) + x \cdot p_i + r_{i,n}$ ($\mathcal{B}_i$ obtains $\tilde{C}(i-1, n-x)$ from the decryption and knows the trial quantity x, the bidding price p_i, and the random noise $r_{i,n}$). Receiving the representation $\{\mathbf{e}_{i+1}(M_{i-1} - r_{i-1,n})\}_{n=0}^{N}$ from $\mathcal{B}_{i-1}$, $\mathcal{B}_i$ can homomorphically compute:

$$\mathbf{e}_{i+1}(\tilde{t}(i,n,x)) = \mathbf{e}_{i+1}(M_{i-1} - r_{i-1,n-x} + \tilde{C}(i-1, n-x) + x \cdot p_i + r_{i,n}) \tag{7}$$

- Denote:

$$\tilde{C}(i,n) = \min_{x \in Q_{i,n}} (\tilde{t}(i,n,x) \tag{8}$$

Using "Finding the minimum" (see Sect. 2.3), $\mathcal{B}_i$ computes:

$$\prod_{x \in Q_{i,n}} \mathbf{e}_{i+1}(\tilde{t}(i,n,x)) \tag{9}$$

$$= \bar{\mathbf{e}}_{i+1}(\min_{x \in Q_{i,n}} (\tilde{t}(i,n,x)) = \bar{\mathbf{e}}_{i+1}(\tilde{C}(i,n)) \tag{10}$$

- $\mathcal{B}_i$ sends $\{\bar{\mathbf{e}}_{i+1}(\tilde{C}(i,n)\}_{n=0}^{N}$, $\{\mathbf{e}_{i+2}(M_i - r_{i,n})\}_{n=0}^{N}$ to $\mathcal{B}_{i+1}$.

3. Similar to the way how B_i computes $\bar{\mathbf{e}}_{i+1}(\tilde{C}(i,n))$ (but note that $\mathcal{B}_k$ does not generate noise $\boldsymbol{r}_k$), $\mathcal{B}_k$ creates $\bar{\mathbf{e}}_{k+1}(\tilde{C}(k,n))$. $\mathcal{B}_k$ sends $\bar{\mathbf{e}}_{k+1}(\tilde{C}(k,N))$ to $\mathcal{AI}$. Using the private key sk_{k+1}, $\mathcal{AI}$ obtains $\tilde{C}(k,N)$, and then subtract $M_0 + \ldots + M_{k-1}$ from $\tilde{C}(k,N)$ to get the minimum cost $C(k,N)$.
5. The optimal allocation $\pi_{\min}$ of $C(k,N)$ is traced back as follows:
   - First, $\mathcal{AI}$ requests $\mathcal{B}_k$ to send $\mathcal{AI}$ the $(\tilde{C}(k,N)+1)$-th components of $\{\mathbf{e}_{k+1}(\tilde{t}(k,N,x_k))\}_{x_k \in Q_{k,N}}$ and $Q_{k,N}$. Then, $\mathcal{AI}$ decrypts these encryptions using the public key $\mathsf{pk}_{k+1} (= \mathsf{pk}_0)$. If any decryption results in the value $\neq 1$ then the corresponding value in $Q_{k,N}$ is the allocation x_k for $\mathcal{B}_k$ in the optimal solution.
   - Next, $\mathcal{AI}$ asks $\mathcal{B}_{k-1}$ to send $\mathcal{B}_k$ the $(\tilde{C}(k-1, N-x_k)+1)$-th components of $\{\mathbf{e}_k(\tilde{t}(k-1, N-x_k, x_{k-1}))\}_{x_{k-1} \in Q_{k-1,N-x_k}}$ and send $Q_{k-1,N-x_k}$ to $\mathcal{AI}$. $\mathcal{B}_k$ decrypts these encryptions using the public key pk_k and sends the results to $\mathcal{AI}$. If any decryption results in the value $\neq 1$ then $\mathcal{AI}$ determines the respective value in $Q_{k-1,N-x_k}$ be the allocation x_{k-1} for $\mathcal{B}_{k-1}$.
   - $\mathcal{AI}$ repeats the same process with the remaining bidders $\mathcal{B}_{k-2}, \ldots, \mathcal{B}_1$ to determine the allocations for all bidders (a losing bidder $\mathcal{B}_i$ is allocated zero quantity).
   - Finally, $\mathcal{AI}$ requests the winning bidders (i.e. with non-zero quantity allocation) to reveal the bidding prices.

4.3 Discussion

Correctness Analysis

Theorem 3. *Assuming the correctness of Elgamal encryption and the dynamic programming algorithm, in an honest-but-curious setting, where all parties follow the protocol correctly but may attempt to learn private information from others, the correctness of* dRMUCA *is guaranteed.*

Proof. First, we prove by induction that each bidder $\mathcal{B}_{i+1}$ $(i = 1, \ldots, k-1)$ obtains the perturbed i-th row:

$$\{\tilde{C}(i,n) = C(i,n) + r_{i,n} + M_0 + \ldots + M_{i-1}\}_{n=0}^{N} \tag{11}$$

In fact, replace $i = 1$ in (7), bidder $\mathcal{B}_1$ computes:

$$\begin{aligned}
&\boldsymbol{e}_2(M_0 - r_{0,n-x_1} + \tilde{C}(0, n - x_1) + x_1 \cdot p_1 + r_{1,n}) \\
&= \boldsymbol{e}_2(M_0 - r_{0,n-x_1} + C(0, n - x_1) + r_{0,n-x_1} + x_1 \cdot p_1 + r_{1,n}) \\
&= \boldsymbol{e}_2(C(0, n - x_1) + x_1 \cdot p_1 + r_{1,n} + M_0)
\end{aligned}$$

We have:

$$\begin{aligned}
C(0, n - x_1) + x_1 \cdot p_1 + r_{1,n} + M_0 &= t(1, n, x_1) + r_{1,n} + M_0 \\
&= \tilde{t}(1, n, x_1)
\end{aligned} \tag{12}$$

Using the "Finding the minimum" property, $\mathcal{B}_1$ obtains:

$$\begin{aligned}
\bar{\boldsymbol{e}}_2(\tilde{C}(1,n)) &= \bar{\boldsymbol{e}}_2(\min_{x_1 \in Q_{1,n}} (\tilde{t}(1, n, x_1))) \\
&= \bar{\boldsymbol{e}}_2(\min_{x_1 \in Q_{1,n}} (t(1, n, x_1) + r_{1,n} + M_0)) \\
&= \bar{\boldsymbol{e}}_2(C(1, n) + r_{1,n} + M_0)
\end{aligned}$$

Thus, we have:

$$\tilde{C}(1, n) = C(1, n) + r_{1,n} + M_0 \tag{13}$$

Therefore, (11) is correct for $i = 1$. Assume that (11) applies for $i = m - 1$ $(m \geq 2)$, we prove that (11) also applies for $i = m$.

$$\begin{aligned}
&\boldsymbol{e}_{m+1}(M_{m-1} - r_{m-1,n-x_m} + \tilde{C}(m-1, n - x_m) + x_m \cdot p_m + r_{m,n}) \\
&= \boldsymbol{e}_{m+1}(M_{m-1} - r_{m-1,n-x_m} + C(m-1, n - x_m) + r_{m-1,n-x_m} \\
&\quad + M_0 + \ldots + M_{m-2} + x_m \cdot p_m + r_{m,n}) \\
&= \boldsymbol{e}_{m+1}(C(m-1, n - x_m) + x_m \cdot p_m + r_{m,n} + M_0 + \ldots + M_{m-1})
\end{aligned} \tag{14}$$

Thus, we have:

$$\begin{aligned}
&C(m-1, n - x_m) + x_m \cdot p_m + r_{m,n} + M_0 + \ldots + M_{m-1} \\
&= t(m, n, x_m) + r_{m,n} + M_0 + \ldots + M_{m-1} \\
&= \tilde{t}(m, n, x_m)
\end{aligned} \tag{15}$$

$\mathcal{B}_m$ obtains:

$$\begin{aligned}\bar{e}_{m+1}(\tilde{C}(m,n)) &= \bar{e}_{m+1}(\min_{x_m \in Q_{m,n}}(\tilde{t}(m,n,x_m))) \\ &= \bar{e}_{m+1}(\min_{x_m \in Q_{m,n}}(t(m,n,x_m) + r_{m,n} + M_0 + \ldots + M_{m-1})) \\ &= \bar{e}_{m+1}(C(m,n) + r_{m,n} + M_0 + \ldots + M_{m-1})\end{aligned}$$

$\mathcal{B}_m$ sends $\{\bar{e}_{m+1}(\tilde{C}(m,n))\}_{n=0}^{N}$ to $\mathcal{B}_{m+1}$. Then by using the secret key sk_{m+1} $\mathcal{B}_{m+1}$ obtains $\{\tilde{C}(m,n)\}_{n=0}^{N}$ and:

$$\tilde{C}(m,n) = C(m,n) + r_{m,n} + M_0 + \ldots + M_{m-1}$$

Next, we prove that the optimal allocation $\pi_{\min}$ is correctly computed. In fact, $\mathcal{B}_{i+1}$ receives the $\tilde{C}(i,R)+1$-th components of representations of perturbed trial costs $\mathbf{e}_{i+1}(\tilde{t}(i,R,x))_{x \in Q_{i,R}}$ from $\mathcal{B}_i$ (R is the remaining quantity, R is initialized to N). Having sk_{i+1}, $\mathcal{B}_{i+1}$ successfully finds the trial with the minimum value and then determines the corresponding $x \in Q_{i,R}$ as the correct allocated quantity for bidder $\mathcal{B}_i$ in the optimal solution. $\mathcal{AI}$ repeats the tracing with the updated remaining quantity $R = R - x$ until $R = 0$. □

Performance Analysis. We estimate the complexity of the protocol (Table 3) based on the number of ElGamal encryptions, decryptions, and ciphertext multiplications for each party. Note that, $L = \mathsf{MAX} + M_0 + \cdots + M_{k-1} \geq (k+1)\mathsf{MAX} = (k+1)Np_{\max}$. Consider $p_{\max}$ as a constant input. Each bidder B_i decrypts the previous perturbed row $\{\bar{e}_i(\tilde{C}(i-1,n))\}_{n=0}^{N}$ of $N+1$ elements, where each element is an array of L Elgamal encryptions, resulting $O(LN) = O(kN^2)$ decriptions. Regarding the encryption of noises $\{\mathbf{e}_{i+2}(M_i - r_{i,n})\}_{n=0}^{N}$, each bidder (except bidder B_k) carries on $O(LN) = O(kN^2)$ encryptions. For the homomorphic computation of $\{\{\langle \tilde{t}(i,n,x)\rangle\}_{x \in Q_{i,n}}\}_{n=0}^{N}$, note that $|Q_{i,n}| \leq n < N$ and the complexity of an "adding a constant" operation is $O(L)$ encryptions and $O(L)$ ciphertext multiplication (for re-randomization), thus the total complexity to have $\{\{\langle \tilde{t}(i,n,x)\rangle\}_{x \in Q_{i,n}}\}_{n=0}^{N}$ is $O(kN^3)$ encryptions and $O(kN^3)$ ciphertext multiplications. For computing $\{\langle \tilde{C}(i,n)\rangle\}_{n=0}^{N}$, each B_i computes N times "finding min" operations where the complexity of each "finding min" operation is $O(LN)$, resulting in $O(kN^3)$ ciphertext multiplications, except $O(kN^2)$ for bidder B_k who only computes $\tilde{C}_{k,N}$ instead of the entire row $\tilde{C}_k$. For $\mathcal{AI}$ (bidder B_0 and B_{k+1}), the complexity is $O(LN) = O(kN^2)$ for initial encryption $\{\bar{e}_1(\tilde{C}(0,n))\}_{n=0}^{N}$, $\{\mathbf{e}_2(M_0 - r_{0,n})\}_{n=0}^{N}$ and $O(kN)$ decriptions to obtain the $\mathsf{mincost}$ and the optimal allocation $\pi_{\min}$.

Security Analysis

Theorem 4 (Security of dRMUCA). *Assuming no collusion among participants and all participants are semi-honest and perform the protocol properly, if a semi-honest adversary $\mathcal{A}$ corrupts a bidder $\mathcal{B}_j$ ($j = 1, \cdots, k+1$, $\mathcal{AI}$ is*

Table 3. Computation complexity

Party	Decrypt	Encrypt	Add a constant		Find min
	$D(\cdot)$	$E(\cdot)$	$E(\cdot)$	$E(\cdot) \times E(\cdot)$	$E(\cdot) \times E(\cdot)$
$\mathcal{AI}(\mathcal{B}_0)$	n/a	$O(kN^2)$	n/a	n/a	n/a
$\mathcal{B}_1$	$O(kN^2)$	$O(kN^2)$	$O(kN^3)$	$O(kN^3)$	$O(kN^3)$
$\mathcal{B}_{k-1}$	$O(kN^2)$	$O(kN^2)$	$O(kN^3)$	$O(kN^3)$	$O(kN^3)$
$\mathcal{B}_k$	$O(kN^2)$	n/a	$O(kN^3)$	$O(kN^3)$	$O(kN^2)$
$\mathcal{AI}(B_{k+1})$	$O(kN)$	n/a	n/a	n/a	n/a

$\mathcal{B}_{j+1}$) and obtains all messages transmitted over the communication channel then dRMUCA *provides ε-differential privacy for bidder $\mathcal{B}_{j-1}$ and computational privacy for other bidders provided that the ElGamal encryption is CPA secure.*

Proof. Privacy for bidder $\mathcal{B}_i$ is the assurance of the privacy of the bidding price p_i and the corresponding dynamic programming values C_i.

First, we prove that dRMUCA provides ε-differential privacy for bidder $\mathcal{B}_{j-1}$. In fact, as $\mathcal{A}$ corrupts $\mathcal{B}_j$, then $\mathcal{A}$ obtains $\{\tilde{C}(j-1,n)\}_{n=0}^{N}$ by decrypting $\{\bar{e}_j(\tilde{C}(j-1,n))\}_{n=0}^{N}$ using sk_j. $\{C(j-1,n)\}_{n=0}^{N}$ is perturbed by random noises sampling from a discrete Gaussian distribution $\mathcal{N}(0, \frac{\mathsf{MAX}}{\varepsilon})$. The discrete Gaussian random noises help guarantee ε-differential privacy [5] for $\{C(j-1,n)\}_{n=0}^{N}$ and also for p_{j-1} as $\{C(j-1,n)\}_{n=0}^{N}$ is computed with the corresponding p_{j-1}.

Next, we prove that dRMUCA provides computational privacy for other bidders $\mathcal{B}_i$ $(i \neq j-1)$. We demonstrate that if there exists an adversary $\mathcal{A}$ that can break the computational privacy of those bidders with a non-negligible advantage $\mathsf{Adv}(\mathcal{A})$, then there exists an adversary that can break the ElGamal encryption scheme with the same non-negligible advantage.

We define an attack game to the privacy of bidders $\mathcal{B}_i$ $(i \neq j-1)$ as follows:

Definition 1 (Attack Game to dRMUCA). *For a given ElGamal encryption scheme $\mathcal{E}_{\mathsf{EG}} = (\mathbb{G}, E, D)$ and for an efficient semi-honest adversary $\mathcal{A}$, we define an experiment:*

- *The adversary $\mathcal{A}$ chooses a random l from $\{1, \cdots, k\}$ and submits a query $(l, \bar{p}_0, \bar{p}_1)$ to the challenger $\mathcal{C}$*
- *The challenger $\mathcal{C}$ generates key pairs $(\mathsf{sk}_i, \mathsf{pk}_i = g^{\mathsf{sk}_i})$ $(i = 1, \cdots, k)$ where sk_i is picked randomly from $\mathbb{Z}_q$, and all k bids $\{l_i, u_i, p_i\}_{i=1}^{k}$*
- *The challenger $\mathcal{C}$ chooses a random bit $b \xleftarrow{R} \{0,1\}$, a random value j from $\{0, 1, \cdots, k\}$ s.t. $j \neq l$*
- *If $l = j-1$ the challenger aborts, else the challenger $\mathcal{C}$ picks random $\{M_i\}_{i=0}^{k-1}$ s.t. $M_i > \mathsf{MAX}$, generates values of $k-1$ bids $\{(l_i, u_i, p_i)\}_{i \in \{1,\cdots,k\}, i \neq l}$ ($l_i \leftarrow U(1,N)$, $u_i \leftarrow U(l_i, N)$, $p_i \leftarrow U(1, p_{\max})$), and initializes $\{C(i,0) = 0\}_{i=0}^{k}, \{C(0,n) = \mathsf{MAX}\}_{n=1}^{N}$*

– *For* $(i = 0, \cdots k)$, $\mathcal{C}$ *computes:*
  - $\{r_{i,n} \xleftarrow{R} U(0, \mathsf{MAX})\}_{n=0}^{N}$ *if* $i \neq k$
  - $\{\{t(l, n, x) = C(l-1, n-x) + x \cdot \bar{p}_b\}_{x \in Q_{i,n}}\}_{n=0}^{N}$
  - $\{\{t(i, n, x) = C(i-1, n-x) + x \cdot p_i\}_{x \in Q_{i,n}}\}_{n=0}^{N}$ *if* $i \neq 0$ *and* $i \neq l$
  - $\{\{\tilde{t}(i, n, x) = t(i, n, x) + r_{i,n} + M_0 + \cdots + M_{i-1}\}_{x \in Q_{i,n}}\}_{n=0}^{N}$ *if* $i \neq 0$
  - $\{C(i, n) = \min(\{t(i, n, x)\}_{x \in Q_{i,n}})\}_{n=0}^{N}$ *if* $i \neq 0$
  - $\{\tilde{C}(0, n) = C_{0,n} + r_{0,n}\}_{n=0}^{N}$, *and* $\{\tilde{C}(i, n) = \min(\{\tilde{t}(i, n, x)\}_{x \in Q_{i,n}})\}_{n=0}^{N}$ *if* $i \neq 0$
  - $\{\bar{\mathsf{e}}_{i+1}(\tilde{C}(i, n))\}_{n=0}^{N}$
  - $\{\mathsf{e}_{i+2}(M_i - r_{i,n})\}_{n=0}^{N}$ *if* $i \neq k$

– *The challenger* $\mathcal{C}$ *sends to* $\mathcal{A}$ *message* $\mathcal{M}$ *which includes:*
  – $\{\mathsf{pk}_i\}$ *for all* $i = 1, \cdots, k$, $\{\bar{\mathsf{e}}_{i+1}(\tilde{C}(i, n))\}_{n=0}^{N}$ *and* $\{\mathsf{e}_{i+2}(M_i - r_{i,n})\}_{n=0}^{N}$ *for all* $i = 1, \cdots, k$ *(i.e.* $\mathcal{A}$ *eavesdrops the communication channel).*
  – $\mathsf{sk}_0, \{r_{0,n}\}_{n=0}^{N}, \{M_i\}_{i=1}^{k}, \{C(0, n)\}_{n=0}^{N}, C(k, N), (x_1, \cdots, x_k)$ *if* $j = 0$ *(i.e.* $\mathcal{A}$ *corrupts* $\mathcal{AI}$*).*
  – $\mathsf{sk}_j, \{r_{j,n}\}_{n=0}^{N}$ *if* $j \neq 0$ *(i.e.* $\mathcal{A}$ *corrupts bidder* $\mathcal{B}_j$*)*

– *The adversary* $\mathcal{A}$ *outputs a bit* $\hat{b} \in \{0, 1\}$.

The advantage of $\mathcal{A}$ *is defined as:*

$$\mathsf{Adv}(\mathcal{A}) = \left|\mathsf{Pr}(b = \hat{b}) - \frac{1}{2}\right| \tag{16}$$

Now we demonstrate that $\mathcal{C}$ can use $\mathcal{A}$ to attack the ElGamal encryption scheme as in Fig. 3. $\mathcal{C}$ will use two values $\bar{p}_0, \bar{p}_1$ received from $\mathcal{A}$ to generate two messages m_0, m_1 respectively. More specifically, $m_0 = \{\tilde{C}(l, n)\}_{n=0}^{N}$ where $p_l = \bar{p}_0$ and $m_1 = \{\tilde{C}(l, n)\}_{n=0}^{N}$ where $p_l = \bar{p}_1$. $\mathcal{C}$ sends m_0, m_1 to the ElGamal challenger who sends back to $\mathcal{C}$ the challenge (i.e. the Elgamal's encryptions $\mathsf{e}(m_b)$) with the corresponding encryption key pk. $\mathcal{C}$ sends to $\mathcal{A}$ message $\mathcal{M}'$ which is the same as message $\mathcal{M}$ (in Definition 1) but replacing all ElGamal ciphertexts encrypted by pk_{l+1} by the Elgamal ciphertexts received from the Elgamal challenger, pk_{l+1} is also replaced with the encryption key that $\mathcal{C}$ received from the Elgamal challenger. $\mathcal{C}$ responds to the ElGamal challenger with the bit $\hat{b}$ that $\mathcal{A}$ responds to $\mathcal{C}$. Therefore, the privacy of bidder $\mathcal{B}_l$ $(l \neq j-1)$ is reduced to the CPA security of the ElGamal encryption scheme. □

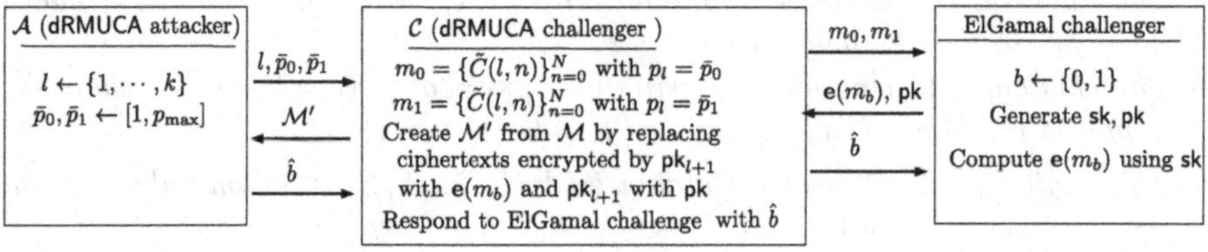

Fig. 3. $\mathcal{C}$ uses $\mathcal{A}$ to attack the ElGamal scheme.

5 Conclusion

We present two novel auction protocols for centralized and distributed scenarios, ensuring secure dynamic programming in combinatorial auctions while balancing trust and efficiency. Addressing privacy concerns, our centralized protocol utilizes homomorphic encryption and secure comparison, hiding bidding prices from all the parties including the auctioneer server and issuer. The distributed protocol introduces a novel collaboration between an auction issuer and bidders, employing perturbation and homomorphic encryption to keep bidding prices locally secured. The security and performance of our proposed protocols are presented in detail. We are committed to thoroughly exploring auction outcome verification in our upcoming work.

Acknowledgement. This research is partially supported by ARC Grants: DP190103660, DP200103207, and LP180100663.

References

1. Alvarez, R., Nojoumian, M.: Comprehensive survey on privacy-preserving protocols for sealed-bid auctions. Comput. Secur. **88**, 101502 (2020)
2. Bag, S., Hao, F., Shahandashti, S.F., Ray, I.G.: Seal: sealed-bid auction without auctioneers. IEEE Trans. Inf. Forensics Secur. **15**, 2042–2052 (2019)
3. Bellman, R.: Dynamic programming. Science **153**(3731), 34–37 (1966)
4. Blass, E.-O., Kerschbaum, F.: Strain: a secure auction for blockchains. In: Lopez, J., Zhou, J., Soriano, M. (eds.) ESORICS 2018. LNCS, vol. 11098, pp. 87–110. Springer, Cham (2018). https://doi.org/10.1007/978-3-319-99073-6_5
5. Canonne, C.L., Kamath, G., Steinke, T.: The discrete gaussian for differential privacy. Adv. Neural. Inf. Process. Syst. **33**, 15676–15688 (2020)
6. Chen, B., Li, X., Xiang, T., Wang, P.: Sbrac: blockchain-based sealed-bid auction with bidding price privacy and public verifiability. J. Inf. Secur. Appl. **65**, 103082 (2022)
7. Damgard, I., Geisler, M., Kroigard, M.: Homomorphic encryption and secure comparison. Int. J. Appl. Cryptogr. **1**(1), 22–31 (2008)
8. Damle, S., Faltings, B., Gujar, S.: A practical solution to yao's millionaires' problem and its application in designing secure combinatorial auction. arXiv preprint arXiv:1906.06567 (2019)
9. Damle, S., Faltings, B., Gujar, S.: Blockchain-based practical multi-agent secure comparison and its application in auctions. In: IEEE/WIC/ACM International Conference on Web Intelligence and Intelligent Agent Technology, pp. 430–437 (2021)
10. De Vries, S., Vohra, R.V.: Combinatorial auctions: a survey. INFORMS J. Comput. **15**(3), 284–309 (2003)
11. Galal, H.S., Youssef, A.M.: Verifiable sealed-bid auction on the ethereum blockchain. In: Zohar, A., et al. (eds.) FC 2018. LNCS, vol. 10958, pp. 265–278. Springer, Heidelberg (2019). https://doi.org/10.1007/978-3-662-58820-8_18
12. Ghasaei, E., Baniasadi, A.: Blockchain-based, privacy-preserving, first price sealed bid auction (fpsba) verifiable by participants. In: 2023 5th Conference on Blockchain Research & Applications for Innovative Networks and Services (BRAINS), pp. 1–8. IEEE (2023)

13. Guo, Z., Fu, Yu., Cao, C.: Secure first-price sealed-bid auction scheme. EURASIP J. Inf. Secur. **2017**(1), 1–6 (2017). https://doi.org/10.1186/s13635-017-0068-1
14. Naor, M., Pinkas, B., Sumner, R.: Privacy preserving auctions and mechanism design. In: Proceedings of the 1st ACM Conference on Electronic Commerce, pp. 129–139 (1999)
15. Nojoumian, M., Stinson, D.R.: Efficient sealed-bid auction protocols using verifiable secret sharing. In: Huang, X., Zhou, J. (eds.) ISPEC 2014. LNCS, vol. 8434, pp. 302–317. Springer, Cham (2014). https://doi.org/10.1007/978-3-319-06320-1_23
16. Paillier, P.: Public-key cryptosystems based on composite degree residuosity classes. In: International Conference on the Theory and Applications of Cryptographic Techniques, pp. 223–238. Springer, Heidelberg (1999). https://doi.org/10.1007/3-540-48910-x_16
17. Parkes, D.C., Rabin, M.O., Thorpe, C.: Cryptographic combinatorial clock-proxy auctions. In: Dingledine, R., Golle, P. (eds.) FC 2009. LNCS, vol. 5628, pp. 305–324. Springer, Heidelberg (2009). https://doi.org/10.1007/978-3-642-03549-4_19
18. Rothkopf, M.H., Pekeč, A., Harstad, R.M.: Computationally manageable combinational auctions. Manag. Sci. **44**(8), 1131–1147 (1998)
19. Shi, Z., de Laat, C., Grosso, P., Zhao, Z.: Integration of blockchain and auction models: a survey, some applications, and challenges. IEEE Commun. Surv. Tutor. (2022)
20. Suzuki, K., Yokoo, M.: Secure combinatorial auctions by dynamic programming with polynomial secret sharing. In: Blaze, M. (ed.) FC 2002. LNCS, vol. 2357, pp. 44–56. Springer, Heidelberg (2003). https://doi.org/10.1007/3-540-36504-4_4
21. Veugen, T.: Improving the dgk comparison protocol. In: 2012 IEEE International Workshop on Information Forensics and Security (WIFS), pp. 49–54. IEEE (2012)
22. Yokoo, M., Suzuki, K.: Secure multi-agent dynamic programming based on homomorphic encryption and its application to combinatorial auctions. In: Proceedings of the First International Joint Conference on Autonomous Agents and Multiagent Systems: Part 1, pp. 112–119 (2002)
23. Zhang, Z., et al.: A blockchain-based privacy-preserving scheme for sealed-bid auction. IEEE Trans. Dependable Secure Comput. (2024)

Short Papers

SePEnTra: A Secure and Privacy-Preserving Energy Trading Mechanism in the Transactive Energy Market

Rumpa Dasgupta(✉), Amin Sakzad, Carsten Rudolph, and Rafael Dowsley

Faculty of Information Technology, Monash University, Clayton, Australia
rumpa.dasgupta@monash.edu

Abstract. In this paper, we design and present a novel model called SePEnTra to ensure the security and privacy of energy data while sharing with other entities during energy trading to determine optimal price signals in Transactive Energy Market (TEM). A market operator can store and use this data to detect malicious activities (deviation of actual energy generation/consumption from forecast data beyond a threshold) of users in later stages of energy trading without violating privacy. We use two cryptographic primitives; additive secret sharing and Pedersen commitment, in SePEnTra. We analyze the security of our proposed model in this work. The performance of our proposed model is evaluated theoretically and numerically, considering practical TEM scenarios. The result shows that even though using two advanced cryptographic primitives in a large market framework, our proposed model has very low computational complexity and communication overhead. For example, in a TEM with 100 users, SePEnTra achieves an execution time of 0.92 s.

Keywords: Transactive energy market · Peer-to-Peer energy trading · False data injection attacks · User's privacy · Additive secret sharing

1 Introduction

An effective energy management system through TEM heavily relies on accurate energy demand/supply forecasts provided by market participants in the day-ahead TEM [1]. When participants can supply precise forecast data for a specific period, market operators can prepare generators for upcoming operations and make necessary arrangements for trading energy from external markets or the grid based on local community energy deficits or surpluses. Additionally, the determination of energy prices for a specific period depends on the total energy demand and supply of users. During the day-ahead TEM, market operators estimate energy prices in advance for the future period based on these predictions. These estimated prices are then utilized for real-time energy trading within the market. Any malicious and false information can mislead market operators

J. K. Liu et al. (Eds.): ProvSec 2024, LNCS 14904, pp. 223–235, 2025.
https://doi.org/10.1007/978-981-96-0957-4_12

in estimating market prices and balancing the energy supply and demand for the upcoming period. Unfortunately, malicious market participants and external attackers can exploit this opportunity and launch various attacks such as false data injection attacks (FDIAs) [2–4] to manipulate original forecast data either by targeting various system components or by injecting false forecasts directly using their controlled devices. The aim of these attacks is to escalate the financial advantages of malicious market participants while causing inconvenience for other participants. Furthermore, such attacks have the potential to disrupt regular market operations and may result in power outages [5,6].

In TEM, energy forecasting is not only crucial for effective energy management and optimal price determination but is also sensitive for market participants, as user privacy is linked to such information. Energy forecast data provides insights into users' day-to-day activities in advance, particularly during the daytime and weekends. This data can reveal critical information to unauthorized individuals, such as a user's presence at home, usage patterns of electrical equipment, and personal preferences, violating user privacy [7,8]. This information could empower attackers to target specific users and strategically plan FDIAs based on their roles. Additionally, it opens the door to planning theft or burglary, particularly when users are away, posing a serious security threat. Therefore, a novel TEM framework is required to address both aspects: first, preserving the privacy of market participants while sharing energy forecast with other entities, and second, identifying malicious market participants or devices responsible for injecting false forecasts while ensuring the security of forecast data.

Table 1. Comparison of existing schemes with SePEnTra

Ref.	Model			FDIA through		Attack	Technique	Privacy against		Comput.
	Market	Pricing	3rd-party[§]	Links	Malicious	Detection		Users	TO/DSO	Cost
[9,10]	Full-P2P	Auction	✓	X	X	X	Blockchain	✓	X	11.79 s
[11]	Full-P2P	Auction	X	X	X	X	Blockchain	✓	X	2.39 s
[12]	Hybrid	Distributed	X	✓	✓	X	Blockchain	✓	X	1.8 s
[13]	Full-P2P	Distributed	X	X	X	X	F-ADMM	✓	X	1 s
[14]	Community	Auction	✓	X	X	X	Paillier enc.	✓	✓	22.31 s
[15]	Community	Auction	✓	✓	X	✓	Paillier enc. & sig.	✓	✓	0.23 s
SePEnTra	Community	Distributed	X	✓	✓	✓	Secret sharing & Com.	✓	✓	0.62 s

Notations: TO: Transactive Market Operator, DSO: Distribution System Operator, F-ADMM: Fast Alternating Direction Method of Multipliers. [§]: Introducing an honest third party alongside the three regular market entities (market participants/transactive agents, TO, and DSO) to assist in the trading operations of TEM.

Table 1 depicts an overview of some existing literature related to security and privacy during energy trading in TEM. It summarizes the market type, pricing mechanism, introduction of another third party alongside the three regular market entities of TEM, FDIA through communication links and malicious users, attack detection, adopted techniques, and privacy considerations taken into account by these schemes. To be specific, Laszka et al. [9] introduced a distributed-ledger-based solution called Privacy-preserving Energy Transactions (PETra) during energy trading in transactive IoT microgrids to preserve prosumer privacy. Kvaternik et al. [10] extended the work of [9] and implemented PETra using a microgrid's original load profile data set. Samy et al. [11] presented a permissioned energy blockchain to perform secure energy transactions between energy sellers and buyers during P2P energy trading in a microgrid. Saha et al. [12] introduced the blockchain architecture for transactive energy with a distributed protocol for keeping constraints and bids private and a distributed algorithm to mitigate data attacks. Blockchain technology falls short of being an ideal solution for TEM due to certain limitations such as scalability issues and compromised user accountability. Hence, blockchain technology may not be useful in this scenario. In addition to blockchain technology, certain research endeavours explored alternative techniques for safeguarding user privacy in energy trading. For example, a privacy-preserved distributed energy pricing scheme for the full-Peer-to-Peer (P2P) TEM was developed in [13]. A homomorphic encryption-based approach was developed to preserve privacy during the market operation of TES in [14] and [15]. However, their schemes are unsuitable for real-time market operation due to the high computational cost [14] and introduction of an honest third party besides regular market entities to perform encrypted aggregations [15]. Prior research in this field often neglected the utilization of cryptographic primitives that combine computational efficiency with real-world applicability to ensure the security of energy data and the preservation of user privacy in TEM. In our work, we take a different approach by forgoing blockchain technology or homomorphic encryption.

1.1 Our Contributions

The main contributions of this paper are as follows:

SePEnTra Model and Construction.
We propose a new model, which we call SePEnTra, a secure multiparty computation (MPC) based framework for trading energy in TEM. The foundation of this framework is built upon two highly effective cryptographic primitives, namely the additive secret sharing scheme [16] and the Pedersen commitment scheme [17].

SePEnTra Functionality.
The functionalities of SePEnTra are mentioned here. *Preserving market participant's privacy*: SePEnTra allows market participants to share energy data with market operators while keeping their information private. Only the participant knows their energy demand/supply forecasts and actual consumption and/or generation; other participants or operators do not have access to this information. *Providing security of energy data*: SePEnTra ensures that energy data remains secure during transmission and cannot be viewed by external attackers or unauthorized users. *Detection of FDIAs*: SePEnTra can identify market participants whose actual energy consumption or production deviates significantly from their forecasted demand or supply, surpassing a predefined threshold. This detection

allows for the identification of individuals or devices responsible for injecting false forecasts. *Prevention of FDIAs*: SePEnTra prevents the manipulation of energy prediction data by external attackers, malicious market participants, or the participants themselves.

SePEnTra Efficiency Evaluation.
The proposed model's security is thoroughly examined, and security proofs are provided. We evaluate the computational costs, communication costs, and storage size of our SePEnTra scheme, considering practical TEM scenarios. The results demonstrate that SePEnTra maintains low computational and communication costs, despite the involvement of two cryptographic primitives that include numerous computationally demanding operations. For example, in a TEM with 100 users, SePEnTra achieves an execution time of 0.92 s.

2 System Design

Our proposed system has three main entities. A distribution system operator (DSO) monitors the trading activities of a community and maintains connectivity between the grid and the community. The community consists of N transactive agents (TAs). Each TA is equipped with a tamper-proofed smart meter, a HEMS, a set of appliances, and a set of DERs such as solar panels and photovoltaic batteries. All DERs and appliances are connected with HEMS. HEMS receives energy generation information from connected DERs and determines the optimal starting time of each connected device. HEMS estimates surplus/deficit energy for a particular period using device schedules and DER energy generation forecasts. TA receives information regarding surplus or deficit energy from HEMS. Based on the energy generation or consumption, TA can act as a prosumer/seller or consumer/buyer in TEM. TAs can talk and share information with each other. A transactive market operator (TO) coordinates and monitors trading activities inside the community. TO is equipped with high computational power hardware to perform necessary computation and has enough storage space. During energy trading among TAs, they need to communicate with others through TO. TO participates in the external market or maintains communication with DSO on behalf of TAs to trade energy from external markets or the main grid. Note that TAs can trade any deficit/surplus energy from outside through TO. However, energy prices at the grid and external market are fixed and can not be negotiated, whereas TAs can negotiate with TO for the price in the P2P market. The buying and selling energy price in the P2P is lower and higher, respectively than in the grid and external market. Hence, all TAs try to trade the maximum energy in the P2P market to maximize their profit.

Market Phases: This work divides the whole market process into 2 phases. One is the forecast phase, second is the online phase. We divide a whole day (24 h) into equal time slots such as $t = 1, 2, \ldots, T$, where T denotes the total number of time slots. The forecast phase occurs before the time addressed by t, and the online phase occurs after time t. More specifically, if we divide the whole day into 24 one-hour time slots, then 12 AM to 1 AM is addressed by $t = 1$. In our scheme, TO runs the forecast phase before 12 AM, where TAs join and make commitments with TO for energy generation or consumption at 12 to 1 AM based on HEMs' forecast. After 1 AM, the online phase checks the actual energy generation/consumption based on energy data received from the smart meter of each TA. We present our trading activities and proposed algorithms only for the one-time slot. We ignore time notation for the sake of simplicity.

Overview of Trading Process: Let $E_{n,tot}$ denotes the energy demand or supply forecast of TA_n, for $n \in [1, N]$. We have that $E_{n,tot} > 0$, if TA_n has surplus energy, and $E_{n,tot} < 0$, if TA_n has deficit energy at a particular period. E_n is defined as TA_n's traded energy in the P2P market. Since P2P market prices are beneficial for TAs, each TA aims to trade maximum energy in the P2P market. To clear P2P market, we consider the trading mechanism introduced in paper [18]. Authors defined a distributed iterative approach using Lagrangian multipliers, and the updating rules for multipliers can be expressed as follows [19]:

$$\underline{v}_n^{k+1} = [\underline{v}_n^k - \zeta(E_n^k)]^+ \tag{1}$$

$$\overline{v}_n^{k+1} = [\overline{v}_n^k + \zeta(E_n^k - E_{n,tot})]^+ \tag{2}$$

$$E_n^{k+1} = [E_n^k + \zeta(\frac{\psi_n - \gamma_k + \underline{v}_n^{k+1} - \overline{v}_n^{k+1}}{\chi_n} - E_n^k)]^+ \tag{3}$$

$$\gamma_{k+1} = [\gamma_k + \zeta(\sum_{n=1}^{N} E_n^{k+1})]^+ \tag{4}$$

$$|\gamma_{k+1} - \gamma_k| < \epsilon \quad \text{and} \quad k > \varsigma \tag{5}$$

where $\underline{v}_n$ and $\overline{v}_n$ are dual variables of minimum and maximum boundaries of TA_n in the P2P market, ζ is a small and positive tuning parameter, ψ_n and χ_n are two preference parameters of TA_n, and $[.]^+$ represents max(0, .). Initially, TO starts the P2P market by sending an initial price signal γ_k based on the market forecast to all TAs. Here, k is the iteration number, and $k \geq 1$. Each TA updates $\underline{v}_n^{k+1}$ and $\overline{v}_n^{k+1}$ using (1) and (2) and use them to update E_n^{k+1} following (3). The updated E_n^{k+1} is sent to TO. After receiving E_n^{k+1} from N TAs, TO updates its price signal γ_{k+1} using (4) and sent the new price signal γ_{k+1} to all TAs. This iterative process is stopped when 2 convergence criteria $\gamma_{k+1} - \gamma_k < \epsilon$ and $k > \varsigma$ are met. Here, ϵ = small positive number to indicate the algorithm termination and ς = maximum number of iterations. The price at convergence represents the clearing price or P2P market price for all TAs.

3 Threat Model and Security Goals

3.1 Threat Model

Our proposed model assumes that the DSO is a trusted entity, whereas the TO is semi-honest. That means TO is an honest but curious adversary. TO correctly follows the trading rules and has no intention of maliciously behaving to produce the wrong result. However, TO may try to gain more information regarding the supply or demand forecast of TAs. TAs can be malicious. They can inject false energy demand or supply prediction in the forecast phase. Besides malicious TAs, third-party attackers (external attackers) can sniff the communications and alter forecasting data during transmission from one entity to another entity.

3.2 Security and Privacy Goals

In this work, we set five security goals considering security assumptions and the threat model discussed in Sect. 3.1. *Goal 1 (Privacy against TAs)*: Not to let TAs learn anything about other TAs' energy demand/supply prediction or actual consumption/generation information. *Goal 2 (Privacy against TO)*: To hide each TA's demand or supply forecast from TO during the forecast phase. Note that TO will eventually gain access to the actual energy consumption or supply data of each TA for billing purposes at the end of the period. As a result, our emphasis is on keeping energy forecast information hidden from the TO until the forecast phase. *Goal 3 (Confidentiality)*: To keep data secure (not disclosed or view original information) from third-party attackers or unauthorized users/TAs during transmission from one entity (TA) to another entity (TO). *Goal 4 (Integrity)*: To prevent manipulation of TAs' promised energy demand or supply value by third-party attackers, malicious TAs, and TA him/herself. *Goal 5 (Detectability)*: To detect malicious TAs whose actual energy generation/consumption deviates significantly from forecast or committed value beyond a threshold.

4 SePEnTra: Secure and Privacy-Preserving Energy Trading Mechanism

In this section, we discuss a detailed framework of our proposed construction, called SePEnTra, with the designed algorithms. The pseudocodes of algorithms appear in [20]. SePEnTra consists of five phases: Π_S = (SePEnTra.Negotiation, SePEnTra.OneOffKeyGen, SePEnTra.Commitment, SePEnTra.CommitmentCheck, SePEnTra.Online). It is important to note that the first four phases of our algorithm are designed for the forecast phase of trading energy, and the fifth phase is developed for the online phase. In this work, SePEnTra.Negotitation, SePEnTra.Commitment, SePEnTra.CommitmentCheck, SePEnTra.Online run for each time slot of a day, whereas SePEnTra.OneOffKeyGen runs once a day. That is why we call the phase "One-Off" key generation. The details of all phases are discussed below.

SePEnTra.Negotiation: This algorithm takes the total number of TAs (N), energy demand or supply forecast of individual TA ($E_{n,tot}$), and minimum and maximum boundaries of particular TA to trade energy from the P2P market ($\underline{v}_n, \overline{v}_n$), two preference parameters of each TA to trade energy from the P2P market (ψ_n, χ_n), small tuning parameter (ζ), initial energy price (γ), maximum number of iteration (ς), and small positive number to terminate iteration (ϵ) as inputs. This algorithm generates the traded energy forecast of individual TA from the P2P market (E_n) after a round of negotiations. More specifically, TO starts the first round of the negotiation ($k = 1$) of the P2P market by sending $\gamma_k = \gamma$ to TAs. Each TA_n, $n \in N$, updates $\underline{v}_n^{k+1}, \overline{v}_n^{k+1}$ based on input value and using (1) and (2). Then, TA_n updates E_n^{k+1} using $\underline{v}_n^{k+1}, \overline{v}_n^{k+1}$ and (3). TA_n splits E_n^{k+1} to N parts following additive secret sharing scheme. TA_n keeps the first share of E_n^{k+1} to themself and distributes the rest of the share to $(N-1)$ TAs. Each TA holds one share of E_n^{k+1}. The whole process is applicable to all TAs. It is important to note that we assume every TA correctly adheres to the additive secret sharing rule, resulting in each TA holding one share from each of the N TAs after the split and distribution process. This ensures that each TA has N shares from N TAs. TA sums up N shares received from N TAs and sends the value to TO. TO adds all value received from N TAs, which is equivalent to $\sum_{n=1}^{N} E_n^{k+1}$ of (4). TO updates the price signal using (4) and broadcasts it to all TAs. Then, TO runs the next round of negotiation following the same process. This negotiation is stopped when (5) are satisfied. After the convergence, TAs receive a notification from TO. The traded energy at convergence is considered as the final energy demand/supply forecast that TA must fulfil with tolerable deviation during the actual period. TA_n stores E_n at the end of this algorithm.

SePEnTra.OneOffKeyGen: TO generates commitment key $ck = (\mathbb{G}, q, p, g, h)$ in this algorithm by taking security parameter λ as input. TO picks two prime numbers q, p in such a way that $p|q-1$, which is equivalent to $q = b \cdot p + 1$ for random b. Then it computes elements of $\mathbb{G}$ using $\{i^b \bmod q | i \in \mathbb{Z}_q \backslash \{0\}\}$ and $\mathbb{G}$ order must be equal to p. Since the order of $\mathbb{G}$ is prime, any element of $\mathbb{G}$ except 1 is a generator. TO chooses two numbers from $\mathbb{G}$ as generators g, h. TO outputs and broadcasts commitment key $ck = (\mathbb{G}, q, p, g, h)$ to all TAs. TO also stores ck for future reference.

SePEnTra.Commitment: This algorithm managed by TAs, inputs commitment key $ck = (\mathbb{G}, q, p, g, h)$ and outputs C_{TA_n}, E'_n, r'_n. TA_n picks a random number r_n from $\mathbb{Z}_p$ and stores r_n. Then it generates the commitment of $E_n \in \mathbb{Z}_p$, using $C_{TA_n} = g^{E_n} h^{r_n} \mod q$. It is worth mentioning that, generally, E_n is a real number, not an integer number. Hence, we convert E_n from real to an integer by multiplying a large integer number (in our case $10,000$) and rounding up the number using the ceiling and flooring function. After that, TA_n splits E_n and r_n following an additive secret sharing scheme, distributes one share of them to N TAs, and receives shares from other TAs, as we discussed in the SePEntra.Negotiation. Each TA calculates $\sum_{m=1}^{N} E_{mn}$ and $\sum_{m=1}^{N} r_{mn}$ to generate E'_n, r'_n. At the end, TA_n transmits C_{TA_n}, E'_n, r'_n to TO.

SePEnTra.CommitmentCheck: TO runs this phase by receiving C_{TA_n}, E'_n, r'_n inputs from N TAs, and notifies TAs about acceptance or rejection of inputs. To begin with, TO computes $C_{TA} = \prod_{m=1}^{N} C_{TA_m}$. TO also calculates $E = \sum_{m=1}^{N} E'_m$ and $r = \sum_{m=1}^{N} r'_m$. TO computes commitment of E using $C = g^E h^r \mod q$. Then it compares C and C_{TA}. The equality should hold according to additive homomorphic property of the Pedersen commitment scheme as TO performs computation over received commitment. Specifically, the multiplication of N TAs individual forecast commitments provides the same result as the commitment of N TAs total forecast according to the additive homomorphic property of the Pedersen commitment scheme. Therefore, if $C = C_{TA}$, TO stores E and the commitment of N users (C_{TA_1} to C_{TA_N}) and broadcasts a notification to all TAs. Otherwise, TO rejects commitments and notifies TAs also.

SePEnTra.Online: This algorithm receives the actual energy generation /consumption value (e_n) from each TA's smart meter, a threshold to deviation for N TAs (β), and a threshold to deviation for each TA (σ) as inputs. The algorithm outputs two lists; $T_{m.list}$ and $T_{f.list}$. Here, $T_{m.list}$ contains TAs whose actual energy consumption/generation deviates beyond the threshold from their forecast. On the other hand, $T_{f.list}$ contains TAs whose revealing forecasts under SePEnTra.Online is different than the committed forecast under SePEnTra.CommitmentCheck. In SePEnTra.Online, while the actual period is over, TA_n receives e_n from the smart meter. Then, e_n is split and shared with N TAs following an additive secret sharing scheme. TA_n sums up the N shares acquired from N TAs, generates e'_n, and sends to TO. TO aggregates e'_1 to e'_N received from N TAs to determine e. TO compares E and e to investigate whether the difference lies within the threshold (β). If the deviation between the total forecast (E) and the actual value (e) lies within β, SePEnTra outputs two null lists; $T_{m.list}$ and $T_{f.list}$. Then, the algorithm is terminated immediately. Otherwise, TO requests to all TAs to reveal respective E_n, r_n, and e_n. Using E_n, r_n, and ck, TO calculates C'_{TA_n} and compares it with C_{TA_n}, which the TA_n previously sent and TO stored under SePEnTra.CommitmentCheck. If $C'_{TA_n} = C_{TA_n}$, TO checks whether e_n deviates from E_n beyond σ or not. If deviation goes beyond σ, TO puts TA_n to $T_{m.list}$ and repeats the process for the next TA. If C'_{TA_n} does not match with C_{TA_n}, TO adds TA_n to $T_{f.list}$ and starts the whole process for next TA. While TO completes checking for all TAs and terminates the algorithm, TO outputs $T_{m.list}$ and $T_{f.list}$.

5 Security Analysis

This section conducts an analysis of the security of SePEnTra. All security definitions, developed theorems, and proof of theorems are provided in the [20].

As per Theorem 1 of [20], our protocol Π_S is $(N-1)$-private. Except TA_n, other TAs or TO not learn anything about TA_n's energy demand/supply forecast (E_n) or actual consumption/generation (e_n) information. Hence, our privacy goals (Goal 1 and Goal 2) are achieved. In Theorem 2 of [20], we prove that our protocol Π_S is hiding. Hence, TA's energy forecast is not disclosed to third-party attackers or unauthorized users/TAs, and the confidentiality (Goal

3) of our scheme is preserved. Our protocol Π_S is binding as per Theorem 3 of [20]. Adversaries cannot open TA's commitment with different randomness. Hence, attackers, including third-party and unauthorized users, can not manipulate the energy forecast, and Goal 4 (Integrity) of our scheme is achieved. The fifth objective of SePEnTra is to identify malicious TAs whose actual energy generation/consumption deviates beyond a specified threshold from the energy forecast. To achieve this goal, SePEnTra consists of a two-phase verification process during SePEnTra.Online phases. This two-phase verification process allows TO to detect activities such as an attacker manipulating C_{TA_n} or malicious TAs modifying their forecast value E_n after the negotiation phase. As a result, malicious TAs cannot intentionally introduce excessive demand or supply during the forecast phase to manipulate energy prices. Hence, we can say that our proposed scheme achieved Goal 5 listed in Sect. 3.2.

6 Performance Evaluation

We evaluate the effectiveness of SepEnTra examining the following 3 aspects; (i) computational cost: Time needed to execute each phase of SePEnTra (ii) communication overhead: The data transmitted from one TA to other TAs and TO in each phase (for TA). The data transmitted from TO to TA(s) in each phase (for TO). (iii) storage analysis: Storage space needed for each TA and TO during each individual phase of SePEnTra.

6.1 Analytical Performance Evaluation

The computational, communication, and storage size of each TA and TO for SePEnTras' phases are summarized in Table 2. As an example, we describe how the computational cost of SePEnTra.Negotiation is calculated for each TA and TO in a single round. In each round of SePEnTra.Negotiation, TA_n estimates $\underline{v}_n, \overline{v}_n$, E_n, splits E_n into N shares, and calculates E'_n (summation of $E_{1n}, \ldots, E_{Nn}$). Time taken to compute boundaries, energy prediction, split a secret into N shares, and summation of N numbers are τ_v, τ_E τ_S, and τ_A, respectively. Therefore, the computational cost of SePEnTra.Negotiation for TA is $\tau_v + \tau_E + \tau_S + \tau_A$. On the other hand, TO adds N numbers to get E, calculates the price signal λ and checks termination criteria in each round of SePEnTra.Negotiation. Thus, the computational complexity for TO is $\tau_A + \tau_\gamma + \tau_t$. We follow the same approach for rest of the parameters in Table 2.

Table 2. Computational and communication Costs of SePEnTra

Algorithm Name	TA/TO	Computational Cost	Communication Cost	Storage Size
Negotiation (1 iteration)	TA	$\tau_v + \tau_E + \tau_S + \tau_A$	$(N-1) \cdot \ell'_E + \ell_{E'}$	ℓ_E
	TO	$\tau_A + \tau_\gamma + \tau_t$	ℓ_γ	-
OneOffKeyGen	TO	$p \cdot \tau_{\mathbb{G}}$	$\ell_q + \ell_p + \ell_g + \ell_h$	$\ell_q + \ell_p + \ell_g + \ell_h$
Commitment	TA	$\tau_C + 2\tau_S + 2\tau_A$	$(N-1) \cdot \ell'_E + (N-1) \cdot \ell'_r + \ell_C + \ell_{E'} + \ell_{r'}$	ℓ_r
CommitmentCheck	TO	$\tau_M + 2\tau_A + \tau_C + \tau_D$	-	$N\ell_C + \ell_E$
Online	TA	$\tau_S + \tau_A$	$(N-1) \cdot \ell'_e + \ell_{e'} + \ell_E + \ell_r + \ell_e$	-
	TO	$\tau_A + N\tau_C + (N+1) \cdot \tau_D$	-	-

Notations: τ_v: Time needed to compute energy trading boundaries in P2P market; τ_E: Time needed to compute an energy supply/demand forecast; τ_S: Time needed to split a secret into N shares; τ_A: Time needed to sum N shares of energy supply/demand forecasts; τ_λ: Time needed to compute a price signal; τ_t: Time needed to check termination criteria; $\tau_{\mathbb{G}}$: Time needed to generate an element of $\mathbb{G}$; τ_C: Time needed to compute a commitment; τ_M: Time needed to multiply N commitments; τ_D: Time needed to compare two values; ℓ_x: Size (bit-length) of x; ℓ'_x: Size (bit-length) of one share of x; $\ell_{x'}$: Size of the sum of N shares of x

6.2 Simulation Setup

We develop our source code in Java, and our machine for running it is an Intel(R) Core(TM) i5-8265U CPU @ 1.60 GHz processor with 16 GB RAM running Windows 10. We implement energy trading of SepEnTra for the one-time slot, which is assumed to be one hour (1 h). A community with an equal number of sellers and buyers is considered. We follow [18] and [21] to set all major parameters of each TA and TO. We have chosen $E_{n,tot} \in$ [0, 20] kW for each TA. The boundaries of traded energy are chosen to $\underline{v}_n \in$ [0, 5] kWh and $\overline{v}_n \in$ [3, 20] kWh, respectively. The preference parameters are set to $\chi_n \in$ [0.09, 0.1]¢/kWh^2 and $\psi_n \in$ [24, 38] ¢/kWh. The price signal γ is 10 ¢/kWh. The maximum iteration (ς) and small positive number to terminate iteration (ϵ) are considered as 100 and 0.001, respectively. We use Miller-Rabin primality test [22] with 5,000 rounds to generate all prime numbers during SePEnTra implementation.

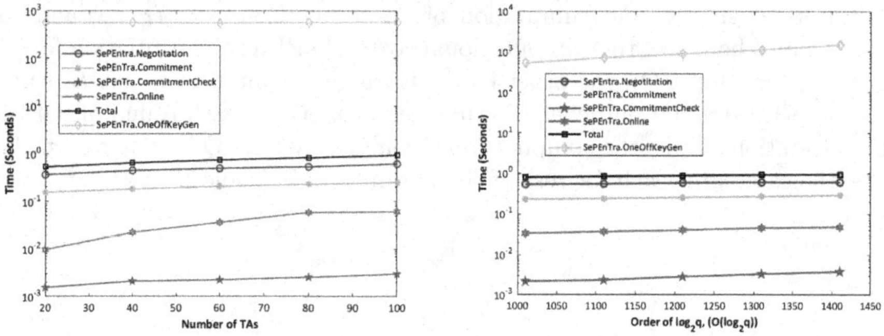

Fig. 1. Comparing computational time with various: (a) #TAs and (b) $\log_2 q$.

6.3 Computational Cost

This section demonstrates the computational costs of SepEnTra with various numbers of TAs and different orders of q to analyze the efficacy of SePEnTra.

Effects of the Number of TAs: In this section, we change the number of TAs (N) from 20 to 100. The execution time of five phases of SePEnTra separately and the total execution time of SePEnTra excludes the SePEnTra.OneOffKeyGen phase is illustrated in Fig. 1.(a). While the number of TAs in the community grows, the computation time of all phases of SePEnTra barely increases. The total execution time of SePEnTra lies under 1 s, even with 100 TAs. The generation of the commitments is computationally very challenging because multiple operations with higher bits of p, q are associated with this. In our proposed construction, SePEnTra.Commitment takes around 250 ms to generate 100 TAs commitment which is time-efficient. Hence, we can say that our proposed model is suitable for large scenarios/communities with a higher number of community members. In our implementation and comparison purposes, we consider the total number of TAs as 100 as default. Furthermore, it is evident from Fig. 1.(a) that among the 5 phases of SePEnTra, SePEnTra.OneOffKeyGen has the highest execution time, which is around 560 s (9.33 min). We had $O(\log_2 q) = 1,020$ and $O(\log_2 p) = 20$ to ensure security. As KeyGen executes only once in the whole day and it is performed by TO, which is equipped with proper hardware and has more computation power, the time is in tolerable range due to providing proper security and privacy of TAs.

Effects of $\log_2 q$: We consider the order of $\log_2 b$ from 990 to 1,390 to get a large order of $\log_2 q$ as $q = b \cdot p + 1$, and we set $O(\log_2 p) = 20$. The computation time of all phases of SePEnTra with varying order of $\log_2 q$ is depicted in Fig. 1.(b). There, the execution time of SePEnTra rises slightly with the orders of $\log_2 q$ except for SePEnTra.OneOffKeyGen. In SePEnTra.OneOffKeyGen, the time needed to generate the commitment key by TO is proportional to the order of $\log_2 q$. TO takes around 529.94 s (8.81 min) to 1,491.711 s (24.86 min) to generate the commitment key while the order of $\log_2 q$ is 1,010 to 1,410. The time is still suitable for real-time implementation as it is a one-off mechanism and managed by high computational power equipped TO.

7 Conclusion

In this paper, we have proposed a novel model named SePEnTra for TEM that integrates security and privacy during energy trading. SePEnTra has five phases and uses two well-known cryptographic techniques; additive secret sharing and Pedersen commitment. By employing these cryptographic techniques, the market user can share energy forecasts and actual data with the market operator and other users without violating individual's privacy while the market operator utilizes this information to determine honest price signals in the forecast phase and detect malicious users's activity in the online phase. We evaluate the performance of our model, taking into account large and practical scenarios. The results show that the proposed framework's computation complexity is low while providing security and privacy by using two advanced cryptographic techniques.

References

1. Dasgupta, R.: Cyber Attacks and Countermeasures in Transactive Energy Market-based Microgrid Systems (2024)
2. Dasgupta, R., Sakzad, A., Rudolph, C.: Cyber attacks in transactive energy market-based microgrid systems. Energies **14** (2021)
3. Dayaratne, T.T., Jaigirdar, F.T., Dasgupta, R., Sakzad, A., Rudolph, C.: Improving cybersecurity situational awareness in smart grid environments, pp. 115–134. Springer, Cham (2023). https://doi.org/10.1007/978-3-031-20360-2_5
4. He, Z., Khazaei, J., Moazeni, F., Freihaut, J.D.: Detection of false data injection attacks leading to line congestions using neural networks. Sustain. Urban Areas **82**, 103861 (2022)
5. Dasgupta, R., Sakzad, A., Rudolph, C.: Impact analysis of false data injection attacks in transactive energy market-based micro-grid systems. In: IEEE PES Asia (ISGT Asia), vol. 2021, pp. 1–5 (2021). https://doi.org/10.1109/ISGTAsia49270.2021.9715633
6. Dasgupta, R., Sakzad, A., Rudolph, C., Dowsley, R.: Fdias on hybrid trading transactive energy markets: attacks, impacts, and prevention. In: IEEE PES Innovative Smart Grid Technologies Europe (ISGT EUROPE), pp. 1–6 (2023). https://doi.org/10.1109/ISGTEUROPE56780.2023.10407432
7. Gong, Y., Cai, Y., Guo, Y., Fang, Y.: A privacy-preserving scheme for incentive-based demand response in the smart grid. IEEE Trans. Smart Grid **7**, 1304–1313 (2016)
8. Habibzadeh, H., Nussbaum, B.H., Anjomshoa, F., Kantarci, B., Soyata, T.: A survey on cybersecurity, data privacy, and policy issues in cyber-physical system deployments in smart cities. Sustain. Urban Areas **50**, 101660 (2019)
9. Laszka, A., Dubey, A., Walker, M., Schmidt, D.: Providing privacy, safety, and security in IoT-based transactive energy systems using distributed ledgers (2017). https://doi.org/10.1145/3131542.3131562
10. Kvaternik, K., et al.: Privacy-preserving platform for transactive energy systems (2017)
11. Samy, A., Yu, H., Zhang, H., Zhang, G.: Spets: secure and privacy-preserving energy trading system in microgrid. Sensors **21** (2021)
12. Saha, S., Ravi, N., Hreinsson, K., Baek, J., Scaglione, A., Johnson, N.G.: A secure distributed ledger for transactive energy: the electron volt exchange (eve) blockchain. Appl. Energy **282**, 116208 (2021)
13. Ullah, M.H., Park, J.-D.: Peer-to-peer energy trading in transactive markets considering physical network constraints. IEEE Trans. Smart Grid **12**, 3390–3403 (2021)
14. Lu, Y., Lian, J., Zhu, M., Ma, K.: Transactive energy system deployment over insecure communication links (2020)
15. Lu, Y., Lian, J., Zhu, M.: Privacy-preserving transactive energy system. In: 2020 American Control Conference, pp. 3005–3010 (2020). https://doi.org/10.23919/ACC45564.2020.9147486
16. Escudero, D.: An introduction to secret-sharing-based secure multiparty computation (2022). https://eprint.iacr.org/2022/062

17. Pedersen, T.P.: Non-interactive and information-theoretic secure verifiable secret sharing. In: Feigenbaum, J. (ed.) CRYPTO 1991, pp. 129–140. Springer, Heidelberg (1992)
18. Khorasany, M., Najafi-Ghalelou, A., Razzaghi, R.: A framework for joint scheduling and power trading of prosumers in transactive markets. IEEE Trans. Sustain. Energy **12**, 955–965 (2021)
19. Khorasany, M., Mishra, Y., Ledwich, G.: A decentralized bilateral energy trading system for peer-to-peer electricity markets. IEEE Trans. Ind. Electron. **67**, 4646–4657 (2020)
20. Dasgupta, R., Sakzad, A., Rudolph, C., Dowsley, R.: SePEnTra: a secure and privacy-preserving energy trading mechanisms in transactive energy market (2023). https://arxiv.org/abs/2304.06179
21. Khorasany, M., Mishra, Y., Ledwich, G.: Hybrid trading scheme for peer-to-peer energy trading in transactive energy markets. IET Gener. Transm. Distrib. (2020)
22. Rabin, M.O.: Probabilistic algorithm for testing primality. J. Number Theory **12**, 128–138 (1980)

On Multi-User Security of Lattice-Based Signature Under Adaptive Corruptions and Key Leakages

Masayuki Fukumitsu[1(✉)] and Shingo Hasegawa[2]

[1] University of Nagasaki, Nagayo 851-2195, Japan
fukumitsu@sun.ac.jp
[2] Fukushima University, Fukushima 960-1296, Japan
hasegawa@sss.fukushima-u.ac.jp

Abstract. We consider the multi-user security under the adaptive corruptions and key leakages ($\mathrm{MU}^{\mathrm{c\&l}}$ security) for lattice-based signatures. Although there exists an $\mathrm{MU}^{\mathrm{c\&l}}$ secure signature based on a number-theoretic assumption, or a leakage-resilient lattice-based signature in the single-user setting, $\mathrm{MU}^{\mathrm{c\&l}}$ secure lattice-based signature is not known.

We examine the existing lattice-based signature schemes from the viewpoint of $\mathrm{MU}^{\mathrm{c\&l}}$ security, and find that the security of the Lyubashevsky's signature, which is proven to have the ordinary single-user security only, can be extended to the multi-user security even if we take the adaptive corruptions and the key leakages into account.

Our security proof in the multi-user setting makes use of the feature of the SIS problem so that a SIS instance is set to the public parameter and a reduction algorithm can set a public key with a secret key in order to answer a corruption query. We also show that the entropy of the secret key is kept under the bounded leakage with a high probability and then the leakage resilience of signature holds.

Keywords: Lattice signature · Multi-user setting · Adaptive corruptions · Leakage resilience

1 Introduction

The signature scheme is a fundamental cryptographic primitive for proving the authenticity of a message. Its security is widely studied. The most basic notion is the existential unforgeability against the chosen message attack (EUF-CMA) [10] in which an adversary cannot generate a forgery even if it can obtain polynomially many pairs of a message and a signature. The original definition of EUF-CMA [10] considers the *single-user setting*, the adversary is required to attack the signature with respect to a given challenge public key. However, the adversary can see many public keys in the real world, and it is sufficient that the adversary produces a forgery with respect to one of the public keys the adversary obtains. This situation is captured as the security in the *multi-user setting*.

J. K. Liu et al. (Eds.): ProvSec 2024, LNCS 14904, pp. 236–245, 2025.
https://doi.org/10.1007/978-981-96-0957-4_13

The formal security of signatures in the multi-user setting is also studied. [8] showed a generic reduction from EUF-CMA, the security in the single-user setting, to the multi-user existential unforgeability against the chosen message attack (MU-EUF-CMA). However, the reduction is *loose* because it suffers the security loss depending on the number of users. Kiltz, Masny and Pan [16] clarified the relationship among security notions of the signature with respect to both the single-user setting and the multi-user setting. They showed the *tight* security reduction from EUF-CMA to MU-EUF-CMA in the random oracle model (ROM) [4], namely the security loss is independent of the number of users. Their reduction employs the random-self-reducibility (RSR).

For the security in the multi-user setting, we should take into account the *corruption* of users unlike the single-user setting. Namely the adversary can obtain secret keys of users that are designated adaptively, and can use it on generating a forgery with respect to a public key of an uncorrupted user. Such an attack and security is captured as the multi-user security under the adaptive corruptions. For signature schemes, this security notion is defined as the MU-EUF-CMA security under the adaptive corruptions (MU^{c}-EUF-CMA). The signature schemes having MU^{c}-EUF-CMA security are studied in the literature [1,6,9,11–13,20].

The multi-user security under the adaptive corruptions divides users into two types: corrupted users whose secret is fully revealed to the adversary and uncorrupted users whose secret is completely hidden. As the *intermediate* users, we can consider users whose secret is *partially leaked*. This situation is captured by MU-EUF-CMA security under the adaptive corruptions and *key leakages* ($\mathrm{MU}^{c\&l}$-EUF-CMA) formalized by [12]. In [12], an almost tightly $\mathrm{MU}^{c\&l}$-EUF-CMA secure signature scheme is proposed. The scheme is constructed based on the MDDH assumption [7] and its $\mathrm{MU}^{c\&l}$-EUF-CMA security is proven in the standard model. On the other hand, there are signature schemes [6,13,20] based on cryptographic assumptions other than the MDDH assumption if we consider the MU^{c}-EUF-CMA security (namely without key leakage) only. Especially, the post-quantum constructions [13,20] exist based on lattice assumptions. However, only the signature scheme in [12] is the example of $\mathrm{MU}^{c\&l}$-EUF-CMA secure signature and a post-quantum construction is not known.

1.1 Our Contribution

In this paper, we aim to construct a lattice-based $\mathrm{MU}^{c\&l}$-EUF-CMA secure signature, which remains open as described above. The $\mathrm{MU}^{c\&l}$-EUF-CMA secure signature of [12] is based on the publicly-verifiable quasi-adaptive hash proof system (PV-QA-HPS), which is a new primitive introduced in [12], and the quasi-adaptive non-interactive zero-knowledge proof (QA-NIZK) [14]. It is natural to consider a lattice-based PV-QA-HPS and then to apply the framework of [12] to it. However, it seems difficult to construct a PV-QA-HPS from a lattice assumption because a lattice-based construction does not satisfy the exact correctness [13] due to the noise arising in a lattice problem. One solution to address the problem is relaxing the requirement concerning the exact correctness. In fact, the probabilistic QA-HPS is proposed in [13] which is a variant of QA-HPS relaxing the correctness, and a lattice-based MU^{c}-EUF-CMA secure signature based on a probabilistic QA-HPS. The signature scheme satisfies the almost tight security in the standard model, however, it does not have the leakage resilience. Thus we take another approach to construct a lattice-based MU$^{\text{c\&l}}$-EUF-CMA secure signature. We directly consider whether or not the existing lattice-based signature schemes have the multi-user security under the adaptive corruptions and key leakages. Fortunately, we find that the security of the signature scheme by [19], denoted as Lyu, can be extended to the multi-user security even if we take the adaptive corruptions and the key leakages into account. We briefly describe the reason why our security proof works.

In [19], the ordinary EUF-CMA security (in the single-user setting) is proven in the ROM under the short integer solution (SIS) assumption. On a given SIS instance matrix $\boldsymbol{A} \in \mathbb{Z}_p^{n \times m}$ of row size n and column size m, the security reduction $\mathcal{R}$ constructed in [19] samples a secret key $\boldsymbol{S} \in \mathbb{Z}_p^{m \times \tilde{m}}$ of Lyu with small norm, and generates the corresponding public key $\boldsymbol{T} \leftarrow \boldsymbol{AS}$. Then, $\mathcal{R}$ invokes an adversary $\mathcal{A}$ against the EUF-CMA of Lyu twice to obtain pairs (μ, σ) and (μ', σ') of a message and a signature. By utilizing these pairs and the forking lemma [3], $\mathcal{R}$ finds a non-zero short vector $\boldsymbol{v}$ such that $\boldsymbol{Av} = \boldsymbol{0}$. The proof that $\boldsymbol{v}$ is non-zero proceeds by two facts (i) and (ii). The fact (i) states that there exist at least two secret keys $\boldsymbol{S}, \tilde{\boldsymbol{S}}$ of the challenge public key $\boldsymbol{T} = \boldsymbol{AS} = \boldsymbol{A}\tilde{\boldsymbol{S}}$ with overwhelming probability. This fact is used to guarantee that for the valid signatures σ and σ' under the public key $\boldsymbol{T}$, at least one of $\boldsymbol{S}$ and $\tilde{\boldsymbol{S}}$ induces that $\boldsymbol{v}$ is a non-zero vector. The fact (ii) states the upper bound for $\mathcal{A}$'s advantage to recognize which of $\boldsymbol{S}$ and $\boldsymbol{S}'$ is selected only from the challenge public key $\boldsymbol{T}$ during the EUF-CMA game. Namely, $\mathcal{A}$ can determine which of $\boldsymbol{S}$ and $\boldsymbol{S}'$ is used with at most $1/2 + \mathsf{negl}$. In particular, the latter result is proven by simulating the singing oracle without the secret key $\boldsymbol{S}$ and utilizing the honest-verifier zero-knowledge property and the random oracle.

On extending the security reduction $\mathcal{R}$ to the MU$^{\text{c\&l}}$-EUF-CMA case, the key observation is that $\mathcal{R}$ can select the challenge secret and public key pair by itself. Since a given SIS instance $\boldsymbol{A}$ is set to the public parameter, not the public key, $\mathcal{R}$ can generate secret keys of all users with corresponding public keys including the challenge secret and public key during the game, and $\mathcal{R}$ can naturally respond to any corrupting oracle query and any leakage oracle query by $\mathcal{A}$. Moreover, this feature helps us to prove the fact (ii) above under our situation where the corrupting oracle and the leakage oracle are provided to $\mathcal{A}$. In the security proof, $\mathcal{R}$ samples secret keys $\{\boldsymbol{S}_k\}_k$ for all K users independently and uniformly at random. The independent sampling implies that the information about secret keys of the other users is useless even when $\mathcal{A}$ can obtain these other secret keys from the corrupting oracle. In other words, we do not need to consider the impact of the corruption of other users. Then we can proceed to the proof in the same way as the single-user security and it means that the security loss can be independent of the number K of users. We eventually show the fact (ii) under the condition that some bits of the secret key $\boldsymbol{S}_{k^*}$ are given to $\mathcal{A}$, where k^*

indicates the target user. We evaluate the probability that the entropy of the challenge secret key $\boldsymbol{S}_{k^*}$ becomes 0 due to the leakage information. We can show that such a probability can be negligible by selecting parameters appropriately. Concretely, the probability that the conditional entropy is to be 0 can be $2^{-\rho}$ by setting ρ so that $\frac{\rho+n\tilde{m}\log_2 p}{2L} = o(1)$ for the length L of the secret key. This implies that Lyu is MU$^{c\&l}$-EUF-CMA secure under the leakage of $(1/2 - o(1))L$ bits of $\boldsymbol{S}_{k^*}$. Note that [17] discussed the (single-user) EUF-CMA of Lyu with key leakage, however they did not give a detailed parameter setting.

We finally note the signing oracle simulation in the security proof. Concerning the simulation of the signing oracle, [2,5] pointed out the incompleteness of the security proofs for most of the lattice-based Fiat-Shamir signatures, including [19]. More precisely, such security proofs did not consider simulating the singing oracle when it fails to respond to a query. To fix the incompleteness, they proposed the method to simulate this failure case by employing the leftover hash lemma. We also evaluate the parameters that make their method applicable to our case. Overall, the parameter settings are given in Table 1.

2 Preliminaries

$\mathbb{N}$, $\mathbb{P}$, $\mathbb{Z}$ and $\mathbb{R}$ denote the sets of the natural numbers, the primes, the integers and the reals, respectively. For any integers $a \le b$, we denote by $[a, b] \subseteq \mathbb{Z}$ the subset of integers x such that $a \le x \le b$. In particular, $[1, b]$ is simply represented by $[b]$. We set $\mathbb{Z}_{|d|} = [-d, d]$ for $d \in \mathbb{N}$.

For any probability distribution D over a set X, $x \leftarrow_{\$} D$ means that $x \in X$ is chosen according to D. When D is the uniform distribution over a finite set X, $x \leftarrow_{\$} D$ is simply represented by $x \leftarrow_{\$} X$. $|a|$ stands for the absolute value of a real $a \in \mathbb{R}$, $|X|$ stands for the cardinality of a set X, and $|s|$ stands for the length of a string $s \in \{0,1\}^*$. We say that a function ϵ on $\lambda \in \mathbb{N}$ is negligible if for any polynomial ν, there exists a natural number $\lambda_0 \in \mathbb{N}$ such that for any $\lambda \ge \lambda_0$, it holds that $\epsilon(\lambda) \le 1/\nu(\lambda)$. The notation **w/ prob.** is abbreviated from "with probability". PPT is abbreviated from probabilistic polynomial-time.

Entropy. The min-entropy of a random variable X is defined by $H_\infty(X) = \min_{x\in\{0,1\}^n}\{-\log_2 \Pr[X = x]\}$. The min-entropy of X under a condition that an event E happens is given by $H_\infty(X \mid E) = \min_{x\in\{0,1\}^n}\{-\log_2 \Pr[X = x \mid E]\}$.

Lemma 1 ([15, **Lemma 1**]). *Let X be a random variable of min-entropy H, let $\Delta \in [0, H]$, and let $f : \{0,1\}^* \to \{0,1\}^\gamma$ be a function. We set that $Y = \{y \in \{0,1\}^\gamma \mid H_\infty(X \mid y = f(X)) \le H - \Delta\}$. We have $\Pr[f(X) \in Y] \le 2^{\gamma-\Delta}$.*

2.1 Lattices

For any $p \in \mathbb{P}$, let $\mathbb{Z}_p$ be the residue ring modulo p. We represent all the elements in $\mathbb{Z}_p$ by using $\mathbb{Z}_{|(p-1)/2|}$. For any $\boldsymbol{x} = [x_1 \cdots x_n]^T \in \mathbb{Z}_p^n$, the ℓ_1-norm $\|\boldsymbol{x}\|_1$ and the ℓ_2-norm $\|\boldsymbol{x}\|$ are expressed as $\|\boldsymbol{x}\|_1 = \sum_{i=1}^n |x_i|$ and $\|\boldsymbol{x}\| = \sqrt{\sum_{i=1}^n |x_i|^2}$.

$\mathsf{Game}_{\mathcal{A},K,\iota}^{\mathsf{MU^{c\&l}\text{-}EUF\text{-}CMA}}(1^\lambda)$

$\mathsf{pp} \leftarrow\!\!\$\ \mathsf{Pgen}(1^\lambda);\ \mathfrak{L}_s \leftarrow \emptyset;\ \mathfrak{L}_c \leftarrow \emptyset;\ l \leftarrow 0$
for $k \in [K]$:
  $(\mathsf{sk}_k, \mathsf{pk}_k) \leftarrow\!\!\$\ \mathsf{KGen}(\mathsf{pp})$
$(k^*, \mu^*, \sigma^*) \leftarrow\!\!\$\ \mathcal{A}^{\mathsf{O}_c,\mathsf{O}_l,\mathsf{O}_s}(\mathsf{pp}, \{\mathsf{pk}_k\}_{k\in[K]})$
return 0 **if** $\mathsf{pk}_{k^*} \in \mathfrak{L}_c \vee (k^*, \mu^*) \in \mathfrak{L}_s$
  $\vee\ \mathsf{Vf}(\mathsf{pp}, \mathsf{pk}_{k^*}, \mu^*, \sigma^*) = 0$
return 1

$\mathsf{O}_s(k, \mu)$

$\sigma \leftarrow\!\!\$\ \mathsf{Sign}(\mathsf{pp}, \mathsf{sk}_k, \mu)$
$\mathfrak{L}_s \leftarrow \mathfrak{L}_s \cup \{(k, \mu)\}$
return σ

$\mathsf{O}_l(k, f)$

return $\perp$ **if** $l + |f(\mathsf{sk}_k)| > \iota$
$l \leftarrow l + |f(\mathsf{sk}_k)|$
return $f(\mathsf{sk}_k)$

$\mathsf{O}_c(k)$

$\mathfrak{L}_c \leftarrow \mathfrak{L}_c \cup \{k\}$
return sk_k

Fig. 1. $\mathsf{MU^{c\&l}}$-EUF-CMA game

Discrete Gaussian Distribution. The Gaussian distribution centered by $\boldsymbol{v} \in \mathbb{R}^m$ with the standard deviation s is defined by $\mathfrak{N}_{\boldsymbol{v},s}^m(\boldsymbol{x}) = (\frac{1}{\sqrt{2\pi s^2}})^m e^{-\frac{\|\boldsymbol{x}-\boldsymbol{v}\|^2}{2s^2}}$ for any $\boldsymbol{x} \in \mathbb{R}^m$. In particular, when $\boldsymbol{v} = \boldsymbol{0}$, $\mathfrak{N}_{\boldsymbol{v},s}^m$ is denoted by $\mathfrak{N}_s^m$. The discrete Gaussian distribution centered by $\boldsymbol{v} \in \mathbb{Z}^m$ with the standard deviation s is given by $\mathfrak{D}_{\boldsymbol{v},s}^m(\boldsymbol{x}) = \mathfrak{N}_{\boldsymbol{v},s}^m(\boldsymbol{x})/\mathfrak{N}_s^m(\mathbb{Z}^m)$ for any $\boldsymbol{x} \in \mathbb{Z}^m$, where $\mathfrak{N}_s^m(\mathbb{Z}^m) = \sum_{\boldsymbol{x}\in\mathbb{Z}^m} \mathfrak{N}_s^m(\boldsymbol{x})$.

ℓ_2 -Short Integer Solution (ℓ_2-SIS) Assumption [19] Let $p \in \mathbb{P}$, and let $n, m, \zeta \in \mathbb{N}$. ℓ_2-$\mathsf{SIS}_{p,n,m,\zeta}$ *problem* asks for finding a non-zero vector $\boldsymbol{v} \in \mathbb{Z}_p^m$ such that $\|\boldsymbol{v}\| \leq \zeta$ and $\boldsymbol{A}\boldsymbol{v} = \boldsymbol{0}$ for a given random matrix $\boldsymbol{A} \leftarrow\!\!\$\ \mathbb{Z}_p^{n\times m}$. $(T_{\mathsf{SIS}}, \epsilon_{\mathsf{SIS}})$-$\ell_2$-$\mathsf{SIS}_{p,n,m,\zeta}$ *assumption* states that for any probabilistic algorithm $\mathcal{A}$, which runs in time T_{SIS}, $\mathcal{A}$ solves the ℓ_2-$\mathsf{SIS}_{p,n,m,\zeta}$ problem with probability at most ϵ_{SIS}. For solving the ℓ_2-$\mathsf{SIS}_{p,n,m,\zeta}$ problem, we assume as in [19] that $\boldsymbol{A}$ is represented as the Hermite Normal Form. Namely, $\boldsymbol{A}$ is of the form $\boldsymbol{A} = [\overline{\boldsymbol{A}}\ \boldsymbol{I}]$.

2.2 Digital Signature

Syntax. A *digital signature* DS consists of the following four algorithms:

$\mathsf{Pgen}(1^\lambda)$ returns a public parameter pp for a security parameter λ.
$\mathsf{KGen}(\mathsf{pp})$ returns a key pair $(\mathsf{sk}, \mathsf{pk})$.
$\mathsf{Sig}(\mathsf{sk}, \mu)$ returns a signature σ for a message μ.
$\mathsf{Vf}(\mathsf{pk}, \mu, \sigma)$ returns 1 if σ is valid with respect to (pk, μ) or 0 otherwise.

Correctness. The correctness of DS is defined as follows: for any security parameter λ and any message μ, when $\mathsf{pp} \leftarrow\!\!\$\ \mathsf{Pgen}(1^\lambda)$, $(\mathsf{sk}, \mathsf{pk}) \leftarrow\!\!\$\ \mathsf{KGen}(1^\lambda)$ and then $\sigma \leftarrow\!\!\$\ \mathsf{Sig}(\mathsf{sk}, \mu)$, $\mathsf{Vf}(\mathsf{pk}, \mu, \sigma)$ always returns 1 if $\sigma \neq \perp$.

Security. The multi-user existential unforgeability against the chosen message attack under the adaptive corruptions and key leakages ($\mathsf{MU^{c\&l}}$-EUF-CMA) is defined by the game given in Fig. 1. Then, DS *is* $(T_{\mathsf{c\&l}}, \epsilon_{\mathsf{c\&l}}, K, Q_{\mathsf{H}}, Q_s, Q_c, Q_l, \iota)$-$\mathsf{MU^{c\&l}}$-EUF-CMA *in the random oracle model* if for any PPT adversary $\mathcal{A}$, which runs in time $T_{\mathsf{c\&l}}$ and can make Q_{H} queries to the random oracle O_{H}, Q_s queries to the signing oracle O_s, Q_c queries to the corrupting oracle O_c and Q_l queries to the leakage oracle O_l in order to obtain at most ι-bits information about secret keys $\{\mathsf{sk}_k\}_{k\in[K]}$, $\mathsf{Game}_{\mathcal{A},K,\iota}^{\mathsf{MU^{c\&l}\text{-}EUF\text{-}CMA}}(1^\lambda)$ returns 1 with probability at most $\epsilon_{\mathsf{c\&l}}$.

$\mathsf{Pgen}(1^\lambda)$

return $\mathsf{pp} \leftarrow \boldsymbol{A} = \mathbb{Z}_p^{n\times m}$

$\mathsf{KGen}(\mathsf{pp})$

$\boldsymbol{S} \leftarrow\!\!\$\ \mathbb{Z}_{|d|}^{m\times \tilde{m}}$; $\boldsymbol{T} \leftarrow \boldsymbol{AS}$

$(\mathsf{sk}, \mathsf{pk}) \leftarrow (\boldsymbol{S}, \boldsymbol{T})$

return $(\mathsf{sk}, \mathsf{pk})$

$\mathsf{Sign}(\mathsf{pp}, \mathsf{sk}, \mathsf{pk}, \mu)$

$\boldsymbol{y} \leftarrow\!\!\$\ \mathfrak{D}_s^m$; $\boldsymbol{w} \leftarrow \boldsymbol{Ay}$

$\boldsymbol{c} \leftarrow H(\mathsf{pk}, \boldsymbol{w}, \mu)$

$\boldsymbol{z} \leftarrow \boldsymbol{y} + \boldsymbol{Sc}$

w/ prob. $p(\boldsymbol{S}, (\boldsymbol{c}, \boldsymbol{z}))$:

  return $\sigma \leftarrow (\boldsymbol{c}, \boldsymbol{z})$

else : **return** $\bot$

$\mathsf{Vf}(\mathsf{pp}, \mathsf{pk}, \mu, \sigma)$

$\boldsymbol{w} \leftarrow \boldsymbol{Az} - \boldsymbol{Tc}$

return 1 **if** $\|\boldsymbol{z}\| \le \eta s\sqrt{m} \wedge \boldsymbol{c} = H(\mathsf{pk}, \boldsymbol{w}, \mu)$

return 0

Fig. 2. Plain Lyubashevesky Signature Scheme Lyu

Table 1. Parameters for Lyu

n	the row size of $\boldsymbol{A}$	a polynomial in λ
m	the column size of $\boldsymbol{A}$	$m \ge 2n$
p	modulo	prime and a polynomial in λ
ν	the expanding parameter for m	$m \approx \nu(n) + n\frac{\log_2 p}{\log_2(2d+1)}$ ($\nu = 64$ in [19])
$\tilde{m}$	the column size of $\boldsymbol{S}$	
d	the ℓ_1-norm of $\boldsymbol{S}$	$d \ge 1$
κ	the ℓ_1-norm of $\boldsymbol{c} \in \mathcal{CH}$	$\binom{\tilde{m}}{\kappa} \ge 2^{\nu(n)}$
η	the parameter for $\boldsymbol{z}$	
α'	the parameter for $p(\boldsymbol{S}, (\boldsymbol{c}, \boldsymbol{z}))$	$\frac{\mathfrak{D}_s^m(\boldsymbol{z})}{\mathfrak{D}_{\boldsymbol{v},s}^m} \le \exp(d\kappa\sqrt{2\alpha' m}/s + (d\kappa\sqrt{m}/(2s))^2)$ w/ prob. $1 - 2e^{-\alpha'}$ ($\alpha' = 72$ in [18, Lemma 4.5])
M	the constant in Rejection Sampling [19, Theorem 3.4]	$m \ge n\log_2 p + \log_2\left(1 - \frac{1-2e^{-\alpha'}}{M}\right) + 2\alpha' \log_2 e - 2$
s	the standard deviation for $\mathfrak{D}$	$M \approx \mathfrak{D}_s^m(\boldsymbol{z})/\mathfrak{D}_{\boldsymbol{v},s}^m$
L	the size of $\mathsf{sk} = \boldsymbol{S}$	$L = \lvert\mathsf{sk}\rvert = m\tilde{m}\log_2(2d+1)$
δ	the ratio of the leakage bit over L	$\iota = \delta L$
ρ	the adjusting parameter for δ	$\delta \le \frac{1}{2} - \frac{\rho(n) + n\tilde{m}\log_2 p}{2L} = \frac{1}{2} - o(1)$

3 MU[c&l]-EUF-CMA Security of Lyubashevesky Signature

The Lyubashevesky signature scheme Lyu [19] is described in Fig. 2 and the parameters for Lyu are listed in Table 1, where $\mathcal{CH} = \left\{\boldsymbol{c} \in \mathbb{Z}_{|1|}^{\tilde{m}} \mid \|\boldsymbol{c}\|_1 \le \kappa\right\}$ and $H : \{0,1\}^* \to \mathcal{CH}$. For any $\boldsymbol{S} \in \mathbb{Z}^{m\times\tilde{m}}$, any $\boldsymbol{c} \in \mathbb{Z}^{\tilde{m}}$ and any $\boldsymbol{z} \in \mathbb{Z}^m$, let $p(\boldsymbol{S}, (\boldsymbol{c}, \boldsymbol{z}))$ denote $\min\left\{\frac{\mathfrak{D}_s^m(\boldsymbol{z})}{MD_{\boldsymbol{Sc},s}^m(\boldsymbol{z})}, 1\right\}$. Then, the MU[c&l]-EUF-CMA of Lyu with $\iota = \left(\frac{1}{2} - o(1)\right) L$ bits leakages can be shown in the following way.

$\mathsf{Game}_1, \mathsf{Game}_2$

$\mathsf{pp} = \boldsymbol{A} \leftarrow\!\!\$\ \mathbb{Z}_p^{n\times m};\ l \leftarrow 0;\ q \leftarrow 0$
$\mathfrak{L}_{\mathsf{H}} \leftarrow \emptyset;\ \mathfrak{L}_s \leftarrow \emptyset;\ \mathfrak{L}_c \leftarrow \emptyset$
for $k \in [K]$:
  $\boldsymbol{S}_k \leftarrow\!\!\$\ \mathbb{Z}_{|d|}^{m\times \tilde{m}};\ \boldsymbol{T}_k \leftarrow \boldsymbol{A}\boldsymbol{S}_k$
  $(\mathsf{sk}_k, \mathsf{pk}_k) \leftarrow (\boldsymbol{S}_k, \boldsymbol{T}_k)$
$(k^*, \mu^*, \sigma^*) \leftarrow\!\!\$\ \mathcal{A}^{\mathsf{O}_{\mathsf{H}}, \mathsf{O}_c, \mathsf{O}_l, \mathsf{O}_s}(\mathsf{pp}, \{\mathsf{pk}_k\}_{k\in[K]})$
$(\mathbf{c}^*, \boldsymbol{z}^*) \leftarrow \sigma^*;\ \boldsymbol{w}^* \leftarrow \boldsymbol{A}\boldsymbol{z} - \boldsymbol{T}_{k^*}\mathbf{c}^*$
return 0 **if** $\mathsf{pk}_{k^*} \in \mathfrak{L}_c \vee (k^*, \mu^*) \in \mathfrak{L}_s \vee$
  $\|\boldsymbol{z}^*\| > \eta s\sqrt{m} \vee \mathbf{c}^* \neq \mathsf{O}_{\mathsf{H}}(\mathsf{pk}_{k^*}, \boldsymbol{w}^*, \mu^*)$
return 1

$\mathsf{O}_s(k, \mu)$

$\boldsymbol{y} \leftarrow\!\!\$\ \mathfrak{D}_s^m;\ \boldsymbol{w} \leftarrow \boldsymbol{A}\boldsymbol{y}$
$\mathbf{c} \leftarrow \mathsf{O}_{\mathsf{H}}(\mathsf{pk}_k, \boldsymbol{w}, \mu)$
$\boldsymbol{z} \leftarrow \boldsymbol{y} + \boldsymbol{S}_k\mathbf{c}$
w/ prob. $p(\boldsymbol{S}_k, (\mathbf{c}, \boldsymbol{z}))$:
  return $\sigma \leftarrow (\mathbf{c}, \boldsymbol{z})$
else : **return** $\perp$
$\mathfrak{L}_s \leftarrow \mathfrak{L}_s \cup \{(k, \mu)\}$

$\mathsf{O}_{\mathsf{H}}(\mathsf{pk}, \boldsymbol{w}, \mu)$

if $\mathfrak{L}_{\mathsf{H}}[\mathsf{pk}, \boldsymbol{w}, \mu] \neq \perp$:
  $q \leftarrow q + 1;\ \mathbf{c} \leftarrow\!\!\$\ \mathcal{CH}$
  $\mathfrak{L}_{\mathsf{H}}[\mathsf{pk}, \boldsymbol{w}, \mu] \leftarrow (\mathbf{c}, q)$
return $\mathfrak{L}_{\mathsf{H}}[\mathsf{pk}, \boldsymbol{w}, \mu]$

$\mathsf{O}'_s(k, \mu)$

$\boldsymbol{z} \leftarrow\!\!\$\ \mathfrak{D}_s^m$
$q \leftarrow q + 1;\ \mathbf{c} \leftarrow\!\!\$\ \mathcal{CH}$
w/ prob. $1/M$:
  $\boldsymbol{w} \leftarrow \boldsymbol{A}\boldsymbol{z} - \boldsymbol{T}_k\mathbf{c}$
  $\sigma \leftarrow (\mathbf{c}, \boldsymbol{z})$
else :
  $\boldsymbol{w} \leftarrow\!\!\$\ \mathbb{Z}_p^n;\ \sigma \leftarrow \perp$
abort if
  $\mathfrak{L}_{\mathsf{H}}[\mathsf{pk}_k, \boldsymbol{w}, \mu] \neq \perp$
$\mathfrak{L}_{\mathsf{H}}[\mathsf{pk}_k, \boldsymbol{w}, \mu] \leftarrow (\mathbf{c}, q)$
return σ
$\mathfrak{L}_s \leftarrow \mathfrak{L}_s \cup \{(k, \mu)\}$

Fig. 3. Sequential games for Theorem 1 where O_c and O_l are the same as Fig. 1

Theorem 1. *let $n, m, p, \nu, \tilde{m}, d, \kappa, \eta, M, s, L, \delta, \rho$ be parameters as in Table 1, and let $\zeta = 2(\eta s + d\kappa)\sqrt{m}$. Then, under the $(T_{\mathsf{SIS}}, \epsilon_{\mathsf{SIS}})$-$\ell_2$-$\mathsf{SIS}_{p,n,m,\zeta}$ assumption,* Lyu *is $(T_{\mathsf{c\&l}}, \epsilon_{\mathsf{c\&l}}, K, Q_{\mathsf{H}}, Q_s, Q_c, Q_l, \iota)$-$\mathsf{MU}^{\mathsf{c\&l}}$-EUF-CMA in the random oracle model, where for $\tilde{Q} = Q_{\mathsf{H}} + Q_s + 1$ and a negligible function ϵ_{tw},*

$$T_{\mathsf{c\&l}} = 2T_{\mathsf{SIS}} - O(Km(n + \tilde{m}) + Q_{\mathsf{H}} + Q_s) \text{ and}$$

$$\epsilon_{\mathsf{c\&l}} \leq \sqrt{2\tilde{Q}\epsilon_{\mathsf{SIS}} + \frac{\tilde{Q}}{|\mathcal{CH}|} + \frac{\tilde{Q}}{3^{\nu(n)}} + \frac{\tilde{Q}}{2^{\rho(n)}}} + \frac{Q_s\tilde{Q}}{2^{n+1}} + Q_s\left(\frac{2(1+M)}{Me^{\alpha'}} + \epsilon_{\mathsf{tw}}\right).$$

Proof (Sketch). We show this theorem by the hybrid argument. Let $\mathcal{A}$ be an adversary against $\mathsf{MU}^{\mathsf{c\&l}}$-EUF-CMA of Lyu.

Game_1. Game_1 is the original $\mathsf{MU}^{\mathsf{c\&l}}$-EUF-CMA game of Lyu. Then, we have

$$\Pr[\mathsf{Game}_1 = 1] = \epsilon_{\mathsf{c\&l}}. \tag{1}$$

Game_2. In the same way as the game change from Hybrid 1 to Hybrid 2 in [18, Fig. 3], O_s is replaced with O'_s given in Fig. 3. As pointed out in [5], the rejection case was not considered in Hybrid 2 in [18, Fig. 3] completely. Our $\mathsf{O}s'$ reflects the modification method for such an issue by [5]. It follows from the rejection sampling [19] and the leftover hash lemma [5] that the difference between the success probabilities of Game_1 and Game_2 is evaluated as follows for some negligible function ϵ_{tw}, although its proof will be given in our full version.

$$|\Pr[\mathsf{Game}_2 = 1] - \Pr[\mathsf{Game}_1 = 1]| \leq Q_s\left(\frac{2(1+M)}{Me^{\alpha'}} + \epsilon_{\mathsf{tw}}\right) + \frac{Q_s\tilde{Q}}{2^{n+1}}. \tag{2}$$

*Reduction of ℓ_2-*SIS *from* Game_2. We discuss converting Game_2 into an adversary against the ℓ_2-SIS probability. In the same way as the proof of [18, Lemma 5.3], we can show the following by applying the forking lemma [3] to Game_2.

Lemma 2. *For some index $k^* \in [K]$, two transcripts $(\boldsymbol{w}, \boldsymbol{c}, \boldsymbol{z})$ and $(\boldsymbol{w}', \boldsymbol{c}^*, \boldsymbol{z}^*)$, which satisfy that $\boldsymbol{w} = \boldsymbol{w}', \boldsymbol{c} \neq \boldsymbol{c}'$, $\boldsymbol{z}, \boldsymbol{z}' \leq \eta s\sqrt{m}$, $\boldsymbol{w} = \boldsymbol{Az} - \boldsymbol{AS}_{k^*}\boldsymbol{c}$ and $\boldsymbol{w}' = \boldsymbol{Az}' - \boldsymbol{AS}_{k^*}\boldsymbol{c}'$, are obtained in time $2T_{\mathsf{c\&l}} + O(Km(n+\tilde{m}) + Q_{\mathsf{H}} + Q_s)$ with probability $\mathsf{frk} \geq \frac{\Pr[\mathsf{Game}_2=1]^2}{\tilde{Q}} - \frac{1}{|\mathcal{CH}|}$.*

By letting $\boldsymbol{v} = \boldsymbol{z} - \boldsymbol{z}' - \boldsymbol{S}_{k^*}(\boldsymbol{c} - \boldsymbol{c}')$, it holds that $\boldsymbol{Av} = \boldsymbol{0}$. It follows from $\boldsymbol{S}_{k^*} \in \mathbb{Z}_{|d|}^{m \times \tilde{m}}$ and $\boldsymbol{c}, \boldsymbol{c}' \in \mathcal{CH}$ that $\|\boldsymbol{S}_{k^*}\boldsymbol{c}\|, \|\boldsymbol{S}_{k^*}\boldsymbol{c}'\| \leq \kappa d\sqrt{m}$, and hance $\|\boldsymbol{v}\| = \|\boldsymbol{z}\| + \|\boldsymbol{z}'\| + \|\boldsymbol{S}_{k^*}\boldsymbol{c}\| + \|\boldsymbol{S}_{k^*}\boldsymbol{c}'\| \leq 2(\eta s + d\kappa)\sqrt{m} = \zeta$. Therefore, $\boldsymbol{v}$ can be a solution of the ℓ_2-SIS problem under the condition that $\boldsymbol{v} \neq \boldsymbol{0}$.

The rest of the proof is devoted to showing that $\boldsymbol{v} = \boldsymbol{z} - \boldsymbol{z}' - \boldsymbol{S}_{k^*}(\boldsymbol{c} - \boldsymbol{c}') \neq \boldsymbol{0}$ with high probability. The following lemma guarantees that there exists at least two short vectors $\boldsymbol{S}_{k^*}, \tilde{\boldsymbol{S}}_{k^*}$ such that $\boldsymbol{AS}_{k^*} = \boldsymbol{A}\tilde{\boldsymbol{S}}_{k^*}$.

Lemma 3 (Generalized from [18, **Lemma 5.2**]**).** *Let $p \in \mathbb{P}$, let $n \in \mathbb{N}$, let $d \geq 1$, and let $m > \nu(n) + n \cdot \log p / \log(2d+1)$. We set $\boldsymbol{A} \in \mathbb{Z}_p^{n \times m}$. For any random vector $\boldsymbol{s} \leftarrow_{\$} \mathbb{Z}_{|d|}^n$, the probability that there exists another vector $\tilde{\boldsymbol{s}} \leftarrow_{\$} \mathbb{Z}_{|d|}^n$ such that $\boldsymbol{As} = \boldsymbol{A}\tilde{\boldsymbol{s}}$ is at least $1 - 3^{-\nu(n)}$.*

Since $\boldsymbol{c} \neq \boldsymbol{c}'$, this lemma implies that even if $\boldsymbol{z} - \boldsymbol{z}' + \boldsymbol{S}_{k^*}(\boldsymbol{c}' - \boldsymbol{c}) = \boldsymbol{0}$, then it is guaranteed that $\boldsymbol{z} - \boldsymbol{z}' + \tilde{\boldsymbol{S}}_{k^*}(\boldsymbol{c}' - \boldsymbol{c}) \neq \boldsymbol{0}$ and $\boldsymbol{A}(\boldsymbol{z} - \boldsymbol{z}' + \tilde{\boldsymbol{S}}_{k^*}(\boldsymbol{c}' - \boldsymbol{c})) = \boldsymbol{0}$.

For the information about $\boldsymbol{S}_{k^*}$, $\mathcal{A}$ obtains $\boldsymbol{T}_{k^*} = \boldsymbol{AS}_{k^*}$, signatures from O_s' and the ι bits from O_l. As in the procedure on Game_2, O_s no longer uses $\boldsymbol{S}_{k^*}$. The only chance to obtain such information is the use of the leakage oracle O_l. We now see that O_l does not affect to detect which of $\boldsymbol{S}_{k^*}$ or $\tilde{\boldsymbol{S}}_{k^*}$ is used. To show this fact, we consider the queries made by $\mathcal{A}$ to O_l during the first execution and the second execution of Game_2. We suppose that $\mathcal{A}$ has made a function f_i to O_l at i-th query during the first execution of Game_2 for each $i \in [Q_l]$, whereas it also has made a function f_i' to O_l at i-th query during the second execution of Game_2 for each $i \in [Q_l]$. The most significant information about $\boldsymbol{S}_{k^*}$ from O_l can be obtained when $\mathcal{A}$ makes queries (k^*, f_i) and (k^*, f_i') to O_l. The total bits of the obtained information in this case is 2ι bits, since $\mathcal{A}$ can obtain at most ι-bits information from O_l during each of the first execution and the second execution of Game_2. We set the function $f : \mathbb{Z}_{|d|}^{m \times \tilde{m}} \rightarrow \{0,1\}^{2\iota + n\tilde{m}\log_2 p}$ mapping a matrix $\boldsymbol{S} \in \mathbb{Z}_{|d|}^{m \times \tilde{m}}$ to the concatenated string $f_1(\boldsymbol{S})|\cdots|f_Q(\boldsymbol{S})|f_1'(\boldsymbol{S})|\cdots|f_Q'(\boldsymbol{S})|\boldsymbol{T}_{n^*} \in \{0,1\}^{2\iota} \times \mathbb{Z}_p^{n \times \tilde{m}}$. We note that $f(\boldsymbol{S}_{k^*})$ denotes all information on $\boldsymbol{S}_{k^*}$ that can be obtained by $\mathcal{A}$. Then, the entropy of $\boldsymbol{S}_{k^*}$ under the condition that $\mathcal{A}$ can obtain such leaked information about $\boldsymbol{S}_{k^*}$ is evaluated by the following lemma.

Lemma 4. *For $L = |\boldsymbol{S}_{k^*}| = m\tilde{m}\log_2(2d+1)$ and $\iota = \delta L$ such that there exists a polynomial ρ on n such that $\delta \leq \frac{1}{2} - \frac{\rho(n) + n\tilde{m}\log_2 p}{2L} = \frac{1}{2} - o(1)$, it holds that $H_\infty(\boldsymbol{S}_{k^*} \mid f(\boldsymbol{S}_{k^*})) = 0$ with probability at most $2^{-\rho(n)}$.*

Proof. We show this lemma by employing Lemma 1. Since $\boldsymbol{S}_{k^*}$ is chosen uniformly at random from $\mathbb{Z}_{|d|}^{m \times \tilde{m}}$, $H = H_\infty(\boldsymbol{S}_{k^*})$ is L. The length $|f(\boldsymbol{S}_{k^*})|$ can be evaluated as $2\iota + n\tilde{m}\log_2 p$. It follows from Lemma 1 and $\Delta = H$ that $H_\infty(\boldsymbol{S}_{k^*} \mid f(\boldsymbol{S}_{k^*})) = 0$ with probability at most $2^{|f(\boldsymbol{S}_{k^*})| - H}$. By $\iota = \delta L$, we have $2^{|f(\boldsymbol{S}_{k^*})| - H} = 2^{2\delta L + n\tilde{m}\log_2 p - L} \leq 2^{2(\frac{1}{2} - \frac{\rho(n) + n\tilde{m}\log_2 p}{2L})L + n\tilde{m}\log_2 p - L} = 2^{-\rho(n)}$. □

Under the conditions that there exists at least two secret keys $\boldsymbol{S}_{k^*}$ and $\tilde{\boldsymbol{S}}_{k^*}$ of $\boldsymbol{T}_{k^*}$ and $H_\infty(\boldsymbol{S}_{k^*} \mid f(\boldsymbol{S}_{k^*})) > 0$, $\mathcal{A}$ can distinguish which of $\boldsymbol{S}_{k^*}$ and $\tilde{\boldsymbol{S}}_{k^*}$ is used in Game_2 with probability at most 1/2. Lemmas 2, 3 and 4 imply that

$$\epsilon_{\mathsf{SIS}} \geq \frac{1}{2}\left(1 - \frac{1}{3^{\nu(n)}}\right)\left(1 - \frac{1}{2^{\rho(n)}}\right) \cdot \mathsf{frk} \geq \frac{1}{2}\mathsf{frk} - \frac{1}{2 \cdot 3^{\nu(n)}} - \frac{1}{2 \cdot 2^{\rho(n)}}. \tag{3}$$

By combining Eqs. (1)–(3), the success probability ϵ_{SIS} of solving ℓ_2-SIS satisfies

$$2\epsilon_{\mathsf{SIS}} \geq \frac{1}{\tilde{Q}}\left(\epsilon_{\mathsf{c\&I}} - \frac{Q_s\tilde{Q}}{2^{n+1}} - Q_s\left(\frac{2(1+M)}{Me^{\alpha'}} + \epsilon_{\mathsf{tw}}\right)\right)^2 - \frac{1}{|\mathcal{CH}|} - \frac{1}{3^{\nu(n)}} - \frac{1}{2^{\rho(n)}}.$$

This implies that

$$\epsilon_{\mathsf{c\&I}} \leq \sqrt{2\tilde{Q}\epsilon_{\mathsf{SIS}} + \frac{\tilde{Q}}{|\mathcal{CH}|} + \frac{\tilde{Q}}{3^{\nu(n)}} + \frac{\tilde{Q}}{2^{\rho(n)}}} + \frac{Q_s\tilde{Q}}{2^{n+1}} + Q_s\left(\frac{2(1+M)}{Me^{\alpha'}} + \epsilon_{\mathsf{tw}}\right).$$

□

Acknowledgments. We would like to thank anonymous reviewers for their valuable comments and suggestions. This work was supported by JSPS KAKENHI Grant Numbers JP22K12023 and JP23K11105.

References

1. Bader, C., Hofheinz, D., Jager, T., Kiltz, E., Li, Y.: Tightly-secure authenticated key exchange. In: Dodis, Y., Nielsen, J.B. (eds.) Theory of Cryptography, pp. 629–658. Springer, Heidelberg (2015)
2. Barbosa, M., et al.: Fixing and mechanizing the security proof of Fiat-Shamir with aborts and Dilithium. In: Handschuh, H., Lysyanskaya, A. (eds.) Advances in Cryptology - CRYPTO 2023, pp. 358–389. Springer, Cham (2023)
3. Bellare, M., Neven, G.: Multi-signatures in the plain public-key model and a general forking lemma. In: Proceedings of the 13th ACM Conference on Computer and Communications Security, CCS 2006, pp. 390–399. Association for Computing Machinery, New York (2006). https://doi.org/10.1145/1180405.1180453
4. Bellare, M., Rogaway, P.: Random oracles are practical: a paradigm for designing efficient protocols. In: Proceedings of the 1st ACM Conference on Computer and Communications Security, CCS 1993, pp. 62–73. Association for Computing Machinery, New York, NY, USA (1993). https://doi.org/10.1145/168588.168596
5. Devevey, J., Fallahpour, P., Passelègue, A., Stehlé, D., Xagawa, K.: A detailed analysis of Fiat-Shamir with aborts. Cryptology ePrint Archive, Paper 2023/245 (2023). https://eprint.iacr.org/2023/245
6. Diemert, D., Gellert, K., Jager, T., Lyu, L.: More efficient digital signatures with tight multi-user security. In: Garay, J.A. (ed.) Public-Key Cryptography - PKC 2021, pp. 1–31. Springer, Cham (2021)
7. Escala, A., Herold, G., Kiltz, E., Ràfols, C., Villar, J.: An algebraic framework for Diffie-Hellman assumptions. In: Canetti, R., Garay, J.A. (eds.) CRYPTO 2013. LNCS, vol. 8043, pp. 129–147. Springer, Heidelberg (2013). https://doi.org/10.1007/978-3-642-40084-1_8

8. Galbraith, S., Malone-Lee, J., Smart, N.: Public key signatures in the multi-user setting. Inf. Process. Lett. **83**(5), 263–266 (2002). https://doi.org/10.1016/S0020-0190(01)00338-6. https://www.sciencedirect.com/science/article/pii/S0020019001003386
9. Gjøsteen, K., Jager, T.: Practical and tightly-secure digital signatures and authenticated key exchange. In: Shacham, H., Boldyreva, A. (eds.) CRYPTO 2018. LNCS, vol. 10992, pp. 95–125. Springer, Cham (2018). https://doi.org/10.1007/978-3-319-96881-0_4
10. Goldwasser, S., Micali, S., Rivest, R.L.: A digital signature scheme secure against adaptive chosen-message attacks. SIAM J. Comput. **17**(2), 281–308 (1988). https://doi.org/10.1137/0217017
11. Han, S., et al.: Authenticated key exchange and signatures with tight security in the standard model. In: Malkin, T., Peikert, C. (eds.) CRYPTO 2021. LNCS, vol. 12828, pp. 670–700. Springer, Cham (2021). https://doi.org/10.1007/978-3-030-84259-8_23
12. Han, S., Liu, S., Gu, D.: Almost tight multi-user security under adaptive corruptions & leakages in the standard model. In: Hazay, C., Stam, M. (eds.) Advances in Cryptology - EUROCRYPT 2023, pp. 132–162. Springer, Cham (2023)
13. Han, S., Liu, S., Wang, Z., Gu, D.: Almost tight multi-user security under adaptive corruptions from LWE in the standard model. In: Handschuh, H., Lysyanskaya, A. (eds.) Advances in Cryptology - CRYPTO 2023, pp. 682–715. Springer, Cham (2023)
14. Jutla, C.S., Roy, A.: Shorter quasi-adaptive NIZK proofs for linear subspaces. In: Sako, K., Sarkar, P. (eds.) ASIACRYPT 2013. LNCS, vol. 8269, pp. 1–20. Springer, Heidelberg (2013). https://doi.org/10.1007/978-3-642-42033-7_1
15. Katz, J., Vaikuntanathan, V.: Signature schemes with bounded leakage resilience. In: Matsui, M. (ed.) ASIACRYPT 2009. LNCS, vol. 5912, pp. 703–720. Springer, Heidelberg (2009). https://doi.org/10.1007/978-3-642-10366-7_41
16. Kiltz, E., Masny, D., Pan, J.: Optimal security proofs for signatures from identification schemes. In: Robshaw, M., Katz, J. (eds.) CRYPTO 2016. LNCS, vol. 9815, pp. 33–61. Springer, Heidelberg (2016). https://doi.org/10.1007/978-3-662-53008-5_2
17. Liu, Y., Zhou, Y., Zhang, R., Tao, Y.: (Full) leakage resilience of Fiat-Shamir signatures over lattices. Front. Comput. Sci. **16**(5), 165819 (2022). https://doi.org/10.1007/s11704-021-0586-3
18. Lyubashevsky, V.: Lattice signatures without trapdoors. Cryptology ePrint Archive, Paper 2011/537 (2011). https://eprint.iacr.org/2011/537
19. Lyubashevsky, V.: Lattice signatures without trapdoors. In: Pointcheval, D., Johansson, T. (eds.) EUROCRYPT 2012. LNCS, vol. 7237, pp. 738–755. Springer, Heidelberg (2012). https://doi.org/10.1007/978-3-642-29011-4_43
20. Pan, J., Wagner, B.: Lattice-based signatures with tight adaptive corruptions and more. In: Hanaoka, G., Shikata, J., Watanabe, Y. (eds.) Public-Key Cryptography - PKC 2022, pp. 347–378. Springer, Cham (2022)

Reusable Fuzzy Extractor from Isogeny

Yu Zhou[1,2], Shengli Liu[1,2](✉), and Shuai Han[2,3]

[1] Department of Computer Science and Engineering, Shanghai Jiao Tong University, Shanghai 200240, China
{zhouyusjtu2019,slliu,dalen17}@sjtu.edu.cn
[2] State Key Laboratory of Cryptology, P.O. Box 5159, Beijing 100878, China
[3] School of Cyber Science and Engineering, Shanghai Jiao Tong University, Shanghai 200240, China

Abstract. We propose the *first* reusable fuzzy extractor (rFE) scheme from isogeny. Our rFE scheme supports linear fraction of errors. The reusability is based on the weak pseudorandomness of CSI-FiSh (Beullens et al., Asiacrypt 2019) in the standard model, and allows multiple extractions from the fuzzy source, which admits many applications of rFE with the same source.

Keywords: Reusable fuzzy extractor · Isogeny-based cryptography · Weak pseudorandomness

1 Introduction

In physical world, there are fuzzy sources which have high entropy and samplings from a fuzzy source result in close samples. Common fuzzy sources include biometric features like faces, fingerprints, palmprint, voice etc. [17,21,23]), physical unclonable functions (PUFs) [18,28], and quantum bits [4,9]. Extracting uniformly random strings from fuzzy sources is known as *fuzzy extractor (FE)*, a primitive first proposed by Dodis et al. [15].

A traditional FE is captured by two algorithms: the generation algorithm Gen and the reproduction algorithm Rep. One can sample a reading $\mathbf{x} \leftarrow X$ from the fuzzy source X, and then use $\mathsf{Gen}(\mathbf{x})$ to extract a string R and output public helper string P. Later, one can sample another reading $\mathbf{x}' \leftarrow X$, then use the reproduction algorithm $\mathsf{Rep}(\mathbf{x}', \mathsf{P})$ to output an extracted string R'. As long as $\mathbf{x}$ and $\mathbf{x}'$ are close enough, then the reproduce algorithm will successfully recover $\mathsf{R}' = \mathsf{R}$. The security of FE requires that R is uniformly distributed even when P is disclosed.

Reusable Fuzzy Extractor. FE is inherently limited to a single extraction, and this prevents FE from wide applications. In [8], Boyen introduced the concept of *reusable fuzzy extractor (rFE)*. rFE relaxes the uniformity of the extracted string to a pseudo-random one but allows multiple extractions from the same fuzzy source, which is captured by reusability of rFE. Boyen [8] also proposed a reusable FE scheme in the random oracle (RO) model. Later, Canetti et al.

J. K. Liu et al. (Eds.): ProvSec 2024, LNCS 14904, pp. 246–256, 2025.
https://doi.org/10.1007/978-981-96-0957-4_14

[10] and Alamélou et al. [2] proposed reusable FE schemes for the low-entropy source, which also relied on the RO model. In [32], Wen et al. proposed the first reusable FE scheme in the standard model from the DDH assumption.

To pursue post-quamtum security, Apon et al. [3] introduced the first reusable FE scheme from the learning with errors (LWE) assumption. However, their scheme only tolerates logarithmic fraction of errors. In 2018, Wen et al. [31] overcame this limitation by presenting the first reusable FE scheme which is capable of tolerating linear fraction of errors under the LWE assumption. Both works of [3] and [31] assume that the manipulation between two readings of the same source is adaptively controlled by a PPT adversary.

Isogeny-Based Cryptography. Another promising candidate for post-quantum security is isogeny-based cryptography, which can be traced back to 1997 by Couveignes. In 2006, Couveignes proposed authentication and key exchange schemes from isogeny [14]. In the mean time, Rostovtsev and Stolbunov [26] independently discovered these results. The Couveignes-Rostovtsev-Stolbunov scheme relies on the action of ideal class groups on ordinary elliptic curves as its foundation. However, its efficiency is far from practical, and it is vulnerable to a subexponential-time attack [13]. To seek efficiency, Jao and De Feo [19] turned to supersingular elliptic curves and proposed a Diffie-Hellman like key agreement protocol, known as the Supersingular Isogeny Diffie Hellman (SIDH). However, recent works [11,24] has shown that SIDH is no longer secure.

The well-accepted secure key-exchange protocol is the Commutative Supersingular Isogeny Diffie-Hellman (CSIDH) protocol, due to Castryck et al. [12]. By leveraging isogeny over supersingular elliptic curves instead of ordinary elliptic curves, CSIDH becomes a practical protocol. Up to now, CSIDH is believed to have post-quantum security since it avoids the leakage of some sensitive points. Later, Beullens et al. [7] constructed CSI-FiSh by computing the structure of the ideal class group for CSIDH-512.

In 2020, Alamati et al. [1] introduced the concept called *cryptographic group action*, which enabled the generalization of the work of CSIDH and CSI-FiSh, resulting in ranges of isogeny-based schemes [6,16,22]. However, up to now, there does not exist isogeny-based rFE scheme. It naturally arises a question:

How to construct an efficient reusable fuzzy extractor from isogeny-based assumptions?

1.1 Our Contributions

In this paper, we answer this question in the affirmative.

- We construct the *first* isogeny-based reusable fuzzy extractor in the standard model. Our rFE supports linear fraction of errors.
- The reusability of our construction is tightly reduced to the weak pseudorandomness of CSI-FiSh [7].
- Our construction is simple and efficient. Only one group action operation is involved in both generation and reproduction algorithm.

In Sect. 4, we present our isogeny-based rFE scheme $\mathsf{rFE}_{\mathsf{Isogeny}}$. We provide a comparison between our $\mathsf{rFE}_{\mathsf{Isogeny}}$ and some known rFE schemes in Table 1.

Table 1. Comparison with some known reusable fuzzy extractor schemes. Each source reading is denoted by W_i for $i \in [Q]$. Let $\Delta W_{i,j}$ denote $W_j - W_i$. Let $W_i[j]$ denotes the j-th element of W_i. "Linear Error Rate" denotes whether the scheme tolerates linear fraction of errors. "Source Requirement" denotes the requirements for the fuzzy source. "–" means the scheme is an information theoretical one. "weak" means that it is difficult for any PPT adversary to distinguish R_i from a uniform one solely based on observing public helper strings $\{\mathsf{P}_j\}_{j\in[Q]}$. "strong" means that it is difficult for any PPT adversary to distinguish R_i from a uniform one when given both $\{\mathsf{P}_j\}_{j\in[Q]}$ and $\{\mathsf{R}_j\}_{j\neq i, j\in[Q]}$.

rFE Schemes	Linear Error Rate	Assumptions	Reusability	Source Requirement
Boy04 [8]	✓	–	weak	$\widetilde{\mathbf{H}}_\infty(W_i\|\Delta W_{i,j}) = \mathbf{H}_\infty(W_i)$
ABCG16 [2]	✓	DDH	strong	$\widetilde{\mathbf{H}}_\infty(W_i[j]\|(W_i/W_i[j]))$ is high enough
CFPRS16 [10]	✗	strong DDH	strong	$\widetilde{\mathbf{H}}_\infty(W_i[j_1],\ldots,W_i[j_k]\|j_1,\ldots,j_k)$ is high enough
ACEK17 [3]	✗	LWE	strong	W follows the error distribution of LWE
WLH18 [32]	✓	DDH	strong	(m,ρ)-correlated
WL18 [31]	✓	LWE	strong	$\Delta W_{i,j}$ is chosen by PPT adversary $\mathcal{A}$
Our $\mathsf{rFE}_{\mathsf{Isogeny}}$	✓	Isogeny	strong	$\Delta W_{i,j}$ is chosen by PPT adversary $\mathcal{A}$

2 Preliminaries

Notation. Let λ denote the security parameter throughout this paper, and all algorithms, distributions, functions and adversaries take 1^λ as an implicit input. We use normal and bold letters like x, $\mathbf{x}$ to denote elements and column vectors respectively. For a set $\mathcal{X}$, $x \leftarrow_{\$} \mathcal{X}$ denotes the process of sampling x uniformly from $\mathcal{X}$. For a distribution X, $x \leftarrow X$ denotes the process of sampling x according to X. PPT abbreviates probabilistic polynomial time. Denote by negl some negligible function. For $n \in \mathbb{N}$, define $[n] := \{1, 2, ..., n\}$.

For two distributions X and Y, the min-entropy of X is defined by $\mathbf{H}_\infty(X) := -\log(\max_x \Pr[X = x])$, and the average min-entropy of X given Y is defined by $\widetilde{\mathbf{H}}_\infty(X|Y) := -\log(\mathbb{E}_{y\leftarrow Y}[\max_x \Pr[X = x|Y = y]])$. The statistical distance between X and Y is defined by $\mathsf{SD}(X, Y) := \frac{1}{2}\sum_u |\Pr[X = u] - \Pr[Y = u]|$. We denote $X \overset{s}{\approx}_\varepsilon Y$ if $\mathsf{SD}(X, Y) \le \varepsilon$. We denote $X \overset{c}{\approx}_\varepsilon Y$ if $|\Pr[\mathcal{D}(X) = 1] - \Pr[\mathcal{D}(Y) = 1]| \le \varepsilon$ for all PPT distinguishers $\mathcal{D}$. When $\varepsilon = \mathsf{negl}(\lambda)$, we simply denote $X \overset{s}{\approx} Y$ or $X \overset{c}{\approx} Y$.

For a primitive XX and a security notion YY, by $\mathsf{Exp}^{\mathrm{YY}}_{\mathrm{XX},\mathcal{A}}(\lambda) \Rightarrow 1$, we mean that the security experiment outputs 1 after interacting with an adversary $\mathcal{A}$, and by $\mathbf{Adv}^{\mathrm{YY}}_{\mathrm{XX},\mathcal{A}}(\lambda)$, we denote the advantage of $\mathcal{A}$ in the security experiment. Finally, we define $\mathbf{Adv}^{\mathrm{YY}}_{\mathrm{XX}}(\lambda) := \max_{\mathrm{PPT}\mathcal{A}} \mathbf{Adv}^{\mathrm{YY}}_{\mathrm{XX},\mathcal{A}}(\lambda)$.

2.1 Fuzzy Source and Secure Sketch

A *metric space* is a set $\mathcal{M}$ equipped with a distance function $\mathsf{dis} : \mathcal{M} \times \mathcal{M} \to [0, \infty)$. Especially, let $\mathsf{dis}(\mathbf{w}) := \mathsf{dis}(\mathbf{w}, \mathbf{0})$. Now we present the definitions of fuzzy source and secure sketch.

Definition 1 (($\mathcal{M}, m$)-Fuzzy Source). *Let W be a random variable over $\mathcal{M}$. If $\mathbf{H}_\infty(W) \geq m$, then W is called an $(\mathcal{M}, m)$-fuzzy source.*

Definition 2 (Secure Sketch [15]). *An $(\mathcal{M}, \mathcal{S}, m, \widetilde{m}, t)$-secure sketch for a metric space $\mathcal{M}$ consists a pair of PPT algorithms $\mathsf{SS} = (\mathsf{SS.Gen}, \mathsf{SS.Rec})$:*

- $\mathbf{s} \leftarrow \mathsf{SS.Gen}(\mathbf{w})$: *Taking $\mathbf{w} \in \mathcal{M}$ as input, it outputs a sketch $\mathbf{s} \in \mathcal{S}$.*
- $\hat{\mathbf{w}} \leftarrow \mathsf{SS.Rec}(\mathbf{w}', \mathbf{s})$: *Taking as input $\mathbf{w}' \in \mathcal{M}$ and $\mathbf{s} \in \mathcal{S}$, it outputs $\hat{\mathbf{w}}$.*

Moreover, it satisfies the following two properties.

- **Correctness.** *For any $\mathbf{w}, \mathbf{w}' \in \mathcal{M}$, if $\mathsf{dis}(\mathbf{w}, \mathbf{w}') \leq t$, then we have $\mathbf{w} = \mathsf{SS.Rec}(\mathbf{w}', \mathsf{SS.Gen}(\mathbf{w}))$.*
- **Privacy.** *For any distribution W over $\mathcal{M}$, if $\mathbf{H}_\infty(W) \geq m$, then we have $\widetilde{\mathbf{H}}_\infty(W | \mathsf{SS.Gen}(W)) \geq \widetilde{m}$.*

Moreover, a secure sketch is homomorphic if for any $\mathbf{w}, \mathbf{w}' \in \mathcal{M}$, it holds that $\mathsf{SS.Gen}(\mathbf{w} + \mathbf{w}') = \mathsf{SS.Gen}(\mathbf{w}) + \mathsf{SS.Gen}(\mathbf{w}')$.

2.2 Extractor

In this subsection, we recall the definition of average-case strong extractor, along with its homomorphic property.

Definition 3 (Average-Case Strong Extractor [15]). *An efficiently computable function $\mathsf{Ext} : \mathcal{K} \times \mathcal{X} \to \mathcal{Y}$ is an average-case $(\widetilde{m}, \varepsilon)$-strong extractor, if for any variable X over $\mathcal{X}$ and any variable Z such that $\widetilde{\mathbf{H}}_\infty(X|Z) \geq \widetilde{m}$, it holds that $\mathsf{SD}((\mathsf{Ext}(K, X), K, Z), (U, K, Z)) \leq \varepsilon$, where K and U are uniformly distributed over $\mathcal{K}$ and $\mathcal{Y}$, respectively.*

Definition 4 (Homomorphic Average-Case Strong Extractor). *An average-case $(\widetilde{m}, \varepsilon)$-strong extractor $\mathsf{Ext} : \mathcal{K} \times \mathcal{X} \to \mathcal{Y}$ is homomorphic, if for any $\mathbf{x}_1, \mathbf{x}_2 \in \mathcal{X}$ and all $\mathbf{k} \in \mathcal{K}$, we have $\mathsf{Ext}(\mathbf{k}, \mathbf{x}_1 + \mathbf{x}_2) = \mathsf{Ext}(\mathbf{k}, \mathbf{x}_1) \oplus \mathsf{Ext}(\mathbf{k}, \mathbf{x}_2)$, where $(\mathcal{X}, +)$ and $(\mathcal{Y}, \oplus)$ are both groups.*

2.3 Isogenies, Ideal Class Group Actions and CSI-FiSh

In this subsection, we provide a brief overview of the concepts and syntax of ideal class group action. Meanwhile, we present some essential results from CSI-FiSh [7]. Instead of recalling the background on elliptic curves over finite fields and isogenies, we refer the readers to [27,29] for more details.

Set of Isomorphism Classes of Elliptic Curves $\mathcal{E}(\mathcal{O})$. Let $\mathbb{F}_p$ be a prime field and E an elliptic curve defined over $\mathbb{F}_p$. Let $\mathcal{O} = \text{End}_{\mathbb{F}_p}(E)$ denote the set of the endomorphisms defined over $\mathbb{F}_p$, which is only an order in the imaginary quadratic field $\mathbb{K} = \mathbb{Q}(\sqrt{-p})$. Define $\mathcal{E}(\mathcal{O})$ as the set of $\mathbb{F}_p$-isomorphism classes of elliptic curves with $\mathbb{F}_p$-rational endomorphism ring $\mathcal{O}$.

Ideal Class Group $Cl(\mathcal{O})$ and Group Action $\star$. The ideal class group of $\mathcal{O}$, denoted by $Cl(\mathcal{O})$, is the quotient of the group of fractional invertable ideals in $\mathcal{O}$ by the principal fractional invertable ideals.

For any $[\mathfrak{a}] \in Cl(\mathcal{O})$ and $E \in \mathcal{E}(\mathcal{O})$, a group action $\star$ can be defined by $[\mathfrak{a}] \star E = E/\mathfrak{a}$ such that there exists an isogeny $\phi : E \to E'$ with $ker(\phi) = \cap_{\alpha \in [\mathfrak{a}]}\{P \in E(\bar{\mathbb{F}}_p) | \alpha(P) = 0\}$. The image curve of $[\mathfrak{a}] \star E$ is well-defined up to $\mathbb{F}_p$-isomorphism. Moreover, the ideal class group $Cl(\mathcal{O})$ acts freely and transitively on $\mathcal{E}(\mathcal{O})$, which gives us a regular abelian group operation according to [30].

CSI-FiSh. Given $p = 4 \times \ell_1 \times \cdots \times \ell_n - 1$ where ℓ_i are small odd primes. In this case, $p = 3 \mod 8$, then for any supersingular elliptic curve E defined over $\mathbb{F}_p$, the ring $\mathcal{O} = \mathbb{Z}[\sqrt{-p}]$ if and only if E is $\mathbb{F}_p$-isomorphic to $E_A : y^2 = x^3 + Ax^2 + x$ for some unique $A \in \mathbb{F}_p$. Then we can use the coefficient A to identify the isomorphism class of a curve $E_A : y^2 = x^3 + Ax^2 + x$. Now we simply denote

$$\mathcal{E}(\mathcal{O}) = \mathcal{E}(\mathbb{Z}[\sqrt{-p}]) = \{E_A \mid A \in \mathbb{F}_p \text{ and } E_A : y^2 = x^3 + Ax^2 + x \text{ is supersingular}\}. \tag{1}$$

In 2019, Beullens et al. [7] introduced CSI-FiSh, in which they proposed a method for precomputing the structure of the group $Cl(\mathcal{O}) = Cl(\mathbb{Z}[\sqrt{-p}])$ for CSIDH-512 [12]. This is achieved by representing it as a relation lattice of low norm generators. In this way, CSI-FiSh admits unique representation of group element and enables efficient uniform sampling from the group. Furthermore, they computed the group order $N = O(\sqrt{p})$ and obtained the generator $[\mathfrak{g}]$ of $Cl(\mathbb{Z}[\sqrt{-p}])$. In this way, any ideal $[\mathfrak{a}] \in Cl(\mathbb{Z}[\sqrt{-p}])$ can be represented by $[\mathfrak{g}]^a$ with $a \in \mathbb{Z}_N$, and the group action is given by

$$\begin{aligned} \star : Cl(\mathbb{Z}[\sqrt{-p}]) \times \mathcal{E}(\mathbb{Z}[\sqrt{-p}]) &\to \mathcal{E}(\mathbb{Z}[\sqrt{-p}]) \\ ([\mathfrak{g}]^a, E) &\mapsto [\mathfrak{g}]^a \star E. \end{aligned} \tag{2}$$

Based on CSIDH, Beullens et al. exploited a practical algorithm to compute the group action $[\mathfrak{g}]^a \star E$ from $[\mathfrak{g}], a, E$.

According to [1] and [25], the group action $\star$ from CSI-FiSh is believed to have weak pseudorandomness. That is, for $Q = \mathsf{poly}(\lambda)$,

$$\{E_i, [\mathfrak{g}]^a \star E_i\}_{i \in [Q]} \overset{c}{\approx} \{E_i, F_i\}_{i \in [Q]}, \tag{3}$$

where $a \leftarrow_{\$} \mathbb{Z}_N$, $E_i, F_i \leftarrow_{\$} \mathcal{E}(\mathbb{Z}[\sqrt{-p}])$, and $[\mathfrak{g}]$ is the generator of $Cl(\mathbb{Z}[\sqrt{-p}])$.

3 Reusable Fuzzy Extractor

In this section, we recall the definition of *reusable fuzzy extractor (rFE)*.

Definition 5 (Reusable Fuzzy Extractor (rFE)). *An* $(\mathcal{M}, m, \mathcal{R}, t)$*-reusable Fuzzy Extractor (rFE) for a metric space* $\mathcal{M}$ *consists of three PPT algorithms* $\mathsf{rFE} = (\mathsf{rFE.Setup}, \mathsf{rFE.Gen}, \mathsf{rFE.Rep})$*:*

- $\mathsf{crs} \leftarrow \mathsf{rFE.Setup}$: *The setup algorithm outputs a common reference string* crs.
- $(\mathsf{P}, \mathsf{R}) \leftarrow \mathsf{rFE.Gen}(\mathsf{crs}, \mathbf{w})$: *Taking as input* crs *and an element* $\mathbf{w} \in \mathcal{M}$*, it outputs a public helper string* P *and an extracted string* $\mathsf{R} \in \mathcal{R}$.
- $\mathsf{R}/\perp \leftarrow \mathsf{rFE.Rep}(\mathsf{crs}, \mathbf{w}', \mathsf{P})$: *Taking as input* crs*, an element* $\mathbf{w}' \in \mathcal{M}$ *and the public helper string* P*, it outputs an extracted string* R *or a rejection symbol* $\perp$.

Moreover, it satisfies the following properties.

- **Correctness.** *For any* $\mathbf{w}, \mathbf{w}' \in \mathcal{M}$*, if* $\mathsf{dis}(\mathbf{w}, \mathbf{w}') \leq t$*, then for all* $\mathsf{crs} \leftarrow \mathsf{rFE.Setup}$*,* $(\mathsf{P}, \mathsf{R}) \leftarrow \mathsf{rFE.Gen}(\mathsf{crs}, \mathbf{w})$ *and* $\mathsf{R}' \leftarrow \mathsf{rFE.Rep}(\mathsf{crs}, \mathbf{w}', \mathsf{P})$*, we have* $\mathsf{R}' = \mathsf{R}$.
- **Reusability.** *For any distribution* W *over* $\mathcal{M}$ *such that* $\mathbf{H}_\infty(W) \geq m$ *and any PPT adversary* $\mathcal{A}$*, it holds that*

$$\mathbf{Adv}^{\mathsf{reu}}_{\mathsf{rFE},W,\mathcal{A}}(\lambda) := |\Pr[\mathsf{Exp}^{\mathsf{reu}}_{\mathsf{rFE},W,\mathcal{A}}(\lambda) \Rightarrow 1] - 1/2| \leq \mathsf{negl}(\lambda),$$

where $\mathsf{Exp}^{\mathsf{reu}}_{\mathsf{rFE},W,\mathcal{A}}(\lambda)$ *describes the reusability experiment played between* $\mathcal{A}$ *and a challenger* $\mathcal{C}$ *is shown in Fig. 1.*

$\mathsf{Exp}^{\mathsf{reu}}_{\mathsf{rFE},W,\mathcal{A}}(\lambda)$:	$\mathcal{O}^b_{\mathsf{Gen}}(\delta_i \in \mathcal{M})$:
$b \leftarrow_\$ \{0,1\}$, $\mathsf{crs} \leftarrow \mathsf{rFE.Setup}$.	If $\mathsf{dis}(\delta_i) > t$, return $\perp$.
$\mathbf{w} \leftarrow W$.	$(\mathsf{P}_i, \mathsf{R}_i^{(1)}) \leftarrow \mathsf{rFE.Gen}(\mathsf{crs}, \mathbf{w} + \delta_i)$.
$b' \leftarrow \mathcal{A}^{\mathcal{O}^b_{\mathsf{Gen}}(\delta_i)}(\mathsf{crs})$.	$\mathsf{R}_i^{(0)} \leftarrow_\$ \mathcal{R}$.
Return 1 iff $b' = b$.	Return $(\mathsf{P}_i, \mathsf{R}_i^{(b)})$.

Fig. 1. The reusability experiment $\mathsf{Exp}^{\mathsf{reu}}_{\mathsf{rFE},W,\mathcal{A}}(\lambda)$.

In the above formalization of reusability, we assume that the adversary controls the differences δ between any two different readings of the source W, following Wen et al. [31].

4 Construction of Reusable Fuzzy Extractor from CSI-FiSh

In this section, we present our construction of isogeny-based reusable fuzzy extractor $\mathsf{rFE}_{\mathsf{Isogeny}}$, which uses the following building blocks.

- Let $\mathsf{SS} = (\mathsf{SS.Gen}, \mathsf{SS.Rec})$ be a homomorphic $(\mathcal{M}, \mathcal{S}, m, \widetilde{m}, t)$-secure sketch.
- Let $\mathsf{Ext} : \{0,1\}^\ell \times \mathcal{M} \rightarrow \mathbb{Z}_N$ be a homomorphic average-case $(\widetilde{m}, \varepsilon = \mathsf{negl}(\lambda))$-strong extractor.

- The group action $\star$ defined in CSI-FiSh (cf. Eq. (2) in Subsect. 2.3), that is

$$\star : Cl(\mathbb{Z}[\sqrt{-p}]) \times \mathcal{E}(\mathbb{Z}[\sqrt{-p}]) \to \mathcal{E}(\mathbb{Z}[\sqrt{-p}])$$
$$([\mathfrak{g}]^a, E) \mapsto [\mathfrak{g}]^a \star E,$$

where the group $Cl(\mathbb{Z}[\sqrt{-p}])$ is cyclic of order N with generator $[\mathfrak{g}]$, and the set $\mathcal{E}(\mathbb{Z}[\sqrt{-p}])$ is defined in Eq. (1).

The resulting isogeny-based rFE scheme $\mathsf{rFE}_{\mathsf{Isogeny}}$ is shown in Fig. 2.

$\underline{\mathsf{rFE.Setup}}$:	$\underline{\mathsf{rFE.Gen}(\mathsf{crs}, \mathbf{w})}$:	$\underline{\mathsf{rFE.Rep}(\mathsf{crs}, \mathbf{w}', \mathsf{P})}$:
$\mathsf{k}_{\mathsf{ext}} \leftarrow_{\$} \{0,1\}^{\ell}$. Return $\mathsf{crs} := (p, [\mathfrak{g}], N, \mathsf{k}_{\mathsf{ext}})$.	Parse $\mathsf{crs} = (p, [\mathfrak{g}], N, \mathsf{k}_{\mathsf{ext}})$. $\mathbf{s} \leftarrow \mathsf{SS.Gen}(\mathbf{w})$. $k \leftarrow \mathsf{Ext}(\mathsf{k}_{\mathsf{ext}}, \mathbf{w})$. $E \leftarrow_{\$} \mathcal{E}(\mathbb{Z}[\sqrt{-p}])$. $\mathsf{R} := [\mathfrak{g}]^k \star E$. Return $(\mathsf{P} := (\mathbf{s}, E), \mathsf{R})$.	Parse $\mathsf{crs} = (p, [\mathfrak{g}], N, \mathsf{k}_{\mathsf{ext}})$. Parse $\mathsf{P} = (\mathbf{s}, E)$. $\hat{\mathbf{w}}' \leftarrow \mathsf{SS.Rec}(\mathbf{w}', \mathbf{s})$. If $\mathsf{dis}(\hat{\mathbf{w}}', \mathbf{w}') > t$: return $\perp$. $k \leftarrow \mathsf{Ext}(\mathsf{k}_{\mathsf{ext}}, \hat{\mathbf{w}}')$. $\mathsf{R} \leftarrow [\mathfrak{g}]^k \star E$. Return R.

Fig. 2. The isogeny-based reusable fuzzy extractor $\mathsf{rFE}_{\mathsf{Isogeny}}$.

Theorem 1. *Let W be an $(\mathcal{M}, m)$-fuzzy source. Then the scheme $\mathsf{rFE}_{\mathsf{Isogeny}}$ proposed in Fig. 2 is an $(\mathcal{M}, m, \mathcal{R}, t)$-reusable fuzzy extractor, where $\mathcal{R} := \mathcal{E}(\mathbb{Z}[\sqrt{-p}])$.*

Proof. We prove the reusability of $\mathsf{rFE}_{\mathsf{Isogeny}}$ by a sequence of games. Denoted by $\Pr[\mathsf{G}_j \Rightarrow 1]$ the probability that $\mathcal{A}$ wins (i.e., $b = b'$) in G_j.

Game G_0: This is exactly the reusability experiment $\mathsf{Exp}^{\mathsf{reu}}_{\mathsf{rFE},W,\mathcal{A}}(\lambda)$ (cf. Definition 5). Then we have $\mathbf{Adv}^{\mathsf{reu}}_{\mathsf{rFE},W,\mathcal{A}}(\lambda) = |\Pr[\mathsf{G}_0 \Rightarrow 1] - 1/2|$.

Game G_1: G_1 is the same as G_0, except that when answering $\mathcal{A}$'s oracle query $\mathcal{O}^b_{\mathsf{Gen}}(\delta_i)$, $\mathcal{O}^b_{\mathsf{Gen}}(\delta_i)$ will generate $\mathbf{s}_i := \mathsf{SS.Gen}(\mathbf{w}) + \mathsf{SS.Gen}(\delta_i)$ and $k_i := \mathsf{Ext}(\mathsf{k}_{\mathsf{ext}}, \mathbf{w}) + \mathsf{Ext}(\mathsf{k}_{\mathsf{ext}}, \delta_i)$ instead of generating $\mathbf{s}_i \leftarrow \mathsf{SS.Gen}(\mathbf{w} + \delta_i)$ and $k_i \leftarrow \mathsf{Ext}(\mathsf{k}_{\mathsf{ext}}, \mathbf{w} + \delta_i)$ directly.

According to the homomorphic properties of SS and Ext, these changes are only conceptional. Thus, $\Pr[\mathsf{G}_0 \Rightarrow 1] = \Pr[\mathsf{G}_1 \Rightarrow 1]$.

Game G_2: G_2 is the same as G_1, except that $k \leftarrow \mathsf{Ext}(\mathsf{k}_{\mathsf{ext}}, \mathbf{w})$ in G_1 is changed to $k \leftarrow_{\$} \mathbb{Z}_N$ during step 2.

Note that when computing $\mathbf{s}_i := \mathbf{s} + \mathsf{SS.Gen}(\delta_i)$ and $k_i := k + \Delta k_i$, only $\mathbf{s} \leftarrow \mathsf{SS.Gen}(\mathbf{w})$ and $k \leftarrow \mathsf{Ext}(\mathsf{k}_{\mathsf{ext}}, \mathbf{w})$ may leak information of $\mathbf{w}$. Due to the fact that $\mathbf{H}_{\infty}(W) \geq m$ and the privacy of SS, we have $\widetilde{\mathbf{H}}_{\infty}(W \mid \mathbf{s}) \geq \widetilde{m}$. Moreover, Ext is an average-case $(\widetilde{m}, \varepsilon = \mathsf{negl}(\lambda))$-strong extractor, it holds that $\mathsf{SD}((k, \mathsf{k}_{\mathsf{ext}}, \mathbf{s}), (u, \mathsf{k}_{\mathsf{ext}}, \mathbf{s})) \leq \varepsilon$, where $k \leftarrow \mathsf{Ext}(\mathsf{k}_{\mathsf{ext}}, \mathbf{w})$ and $u \leftarrow_{\$} \mathbb{Z}_N$. Thus, $|\Pr[\mathsf{G}_1 \Rightarrow 1] - \Pr[\mathsf{G}_2 \Rightarrow 1]| \leq \varepsilon = \mathsf{negl}(\lambda)$.

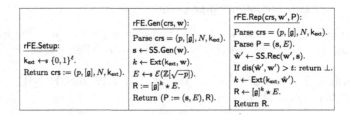

Game G_3: G_3 is the same as G_2, except that when answering $\mathcal{A}$'s oracle query, $\mathsf{R}_i^{(1)} \leftarrow [\mathfrak{g}]^{k_i} \star E_i$ is replaced with $\mathsf{R}_i^{(1)} \leftarrow [\mathfrak{g}]^{\Delta k_i} \star ([\mathfrak{g}]^k \star E_i)$.

Since $Cl(\mathbb{Z}[\sqrt{-p}])$ is a cyclic group, in G_2, $\mathsf{R}_i^{(1)}$ can be rewritten as $[\mathfrak{g}]^{k_i} \star E_i = [\mathfrak{g}]^{k+\Delta k_i} \star E_i = [\mathfrak{g}]^{\Delta k_i} \star ([\mathfrak{g}]^k \star E_i)$. These changes are just conceptional. Thus, $\Pr[\mathsf{G}_2 \Rightarrow 1] = \Pr[\mathsf{G}_3 \Rightarrow 1]$.

Game G_4: G_4 is the same as G_3, except that when generating $\mathsf{R}_i^{(1)}$, $\mathcal{C}$ samples $\mathsf{R}_i^{(1)} \leftarrow_\$ \mathcal{E}(\mathbb{Z}[\sqrt{-p}])$, instead of invoking $\mathsf{R}_i^{(1)} \leftarrow [\mathfrak{g}]^{\Delta k_i} \star ([\mathfrak{g}]^k \star E_i)$.

According to the weak pseudorandomness of CSI-FiSh (cf. Eq. (3)), given elements $\{E_i \leftarrow_\$ \mathcal{E}(\mathbb{Z}[\sqrt{-p}])\}_{i\in[Q]}$, the distribution of $\{\mathsf{R}_i^{(1)} \leftarrow_\$ \mathcal{E}(\mathbb{Z}[\sqrt{-p}])\}_{i\in[Q]}$ is computationally indistinguishable to the distribution of $\{\mathsf{R}_i^{(1)} \leftarrow [\mathfrak{g}]^{\Delta k_i} \star ([\mathfrak{g}]^k \star E_i)$, where $k \leftarrow_\$ \mathbb{Z}_N$. If $\mathcal{A}$ can distinguish G_3 and G_4 with a non-negligible probability, then we can construct a PPT adversary $\mathcal{B}$ to break the weak pseudorandomness of CSI-FiSh. As a result, $|\Pr[\mathsf{G}_3 \Rightarrow 1] - \Pr[\mathsf{G}_4 \Rightarrow 1]| \leq \mathsf{negl}(\lambda)$.

Finally, both $\mathsf{R}_i^{(0)}$ and $\mathsf{R}_i^{(1)}$ are sampled uniformly at random from $\mathcal{E}(\mathbb{Z}[\sqrt{-p}])$ in G_4. Thus, the challenge bit b is completely hidden to $\mathcal{A}$, and $\Pr[\mathsf{G}_4 \Rightarrow 1] = \frac{1}{2}$.

Taking all things together, we obtain the result that $\mathbf{Adv}^{\mathsf{reu}}_{\mathsf{rFE},W,\mathcal{A}}(\lambda) := |\Pr[\mathsf{G}_0 \Rightarrow 1] - 1/2| \leq \mathsf{negl}(\lambda)$. Consequently, Theorem 1 follows. □

5 Efficiency Analysis

Firstly, we show how to instantiate our isgogeny-based rFE scheme $\mathsf{rFE}_{\mathsf{Isogeny}}$.

- For the homomorphic secure sketch, we utilize a syndrome-based secure sketch [15].
- For the average-case strong extractor, we employ the Toeplitz matrix, which is a simple and straightforward tool for extracting uniform strings. Previous works [20, 32] also make use of Toplitz matrix as their extractors.
- We implement the CSI-FiSh group action with the code package on GitHub [5].

Next, we present the efficiency of our scheme with simulated experiments. We consider the fuzzy sources with two cases: one case is 256 bit readings from fuzzy sources, and the other is 1024 bit readings. In our experiments, we test the average running time of each building block and the total processing on platform of Apple M3 Pro. The results are shown in Table 2.

Notice that both our SS and Ext are implemented using information-theoretical cryptographic primitives, resulting in high efficiency. Therefore, the main factors affecting the performance of our scheme lie in the computations involving elliptic curves and group actions. Nevertheless, the total time for a single generation or reproduction process is still low, thanks to the work of [7], which saves us significant overhead in computing the relation lattice and the reduced basis. Additionally, the random sampling of elliptic curve E in the generation algorithm also consumes considerable time, reflected in more running time of rFE.Gen than rFE.Rep.

6 Conclusion

In this work, we propose the first isogeny-based reusable fuzzy extractor from CSI-FiSh in the standard model. The proposed rFE scheme is simple, since only one group action is involved in either the rFE's generation algorithm or the reproduction algorithm. Besides, it tolerates linear fraction of errors. Our simulation experiments show that our rFE from CSI-FiSh is practical with running time hundreds of milliseconds. Our work provides the first practical solution to rFE from isogeny.

Acknowledgments. Yu Zhou and Shengli Liu were partially sponsored by Guangdong Major Project of Basic and Applied Basic Research under Grant (No. 2019B030302008), National Natural Science Foundation of China under Grant (No. 61925207) and the National Key R & D Program of China under Grant (No. 2022YFB2701500). Shuai Han was partially supported by National Natural Science Foundation of China under Grant (No. 62372292), and Young Elite Scientists Sponsorship Program by China Association for Science and Technology under Grant (No. YESS20200185).

References

1. Alamati, N., Feo, L.D., Montgomery, H., Patranabis, S.: Cryptographic group actions and applications. In: ASIACRYPT 2020, vol. 12492, pp. 411–439 (2020)
2. Alamélou, Q., et al.: Pseudoentropic isometries: a new framework for fuzzy extractor reusability. In: AsiaCCS 2018, pp. 673–684 (2018)
3. Apon, D., Cho, C., Eldefrawy, K., Katz, J.: Efficient, reusable fuzzy extractors from LWE. In: CSCML 2017, pp. 1–18 (2017)
4. Bennett, C.H., Brassard, G., Robert, J.: Privacy amplification by public discussion. SIAM J. Comput. **17**(2), 210–229 (1988)
5. Beullens, W.: CSI-fish: Github repository (2019). https://github.com/KULeuven-COSIC/CSI-FiSh/tree/master/implementation

Table 2. Efficiency of our rFE scheme. "rFE.Gen-256 (resp., rFE.Rep-256)" denotes the rFE's generation (resp., reproduction) algorithm processing 256-bit readings of fuzzy source. "rFE.Gen-1024 (resp., rFE.Rep-1024)" denotes the generation (resp., reproduction) algorithm processing 1024-bit readings of fuzzy source. "Time of Algorithms" denotes the average running time of Algorithms, where Algorithms $\in$ {SS.Gen, SS.Rec, Ext, sampling E, group action $\star$}. "Total time" denotes the average running time of a whole rFE's generation or reproduction processing.

	Time of SS.Gen (ms)	Time of SS.Rec (ms)	Time of Ext (ms)	Time of Sampling E (ms)	Time of Group Action $\star$ (ms)	Total Time (ms)
rFE.Gen-256	0.001	–	0.003	147.054	92.587	239.679
rFE.Rep-256	–	0.002	0.003	–	90.243	90.256
rFE.Gen-1024	0.001	–	0.019	153.868	335.611	489.527
rFE.Rep-1024	–	0.003	0.024	–	351.111	351.160

6. Beullens, W., Dobson, S., Katsumata, S., Lai, Y., Pintore, F.: Group signatures and more from isogenies and lattices: generic, simple, and efficient. In: EUROCRYPT 2022, vol. 13276, pp. 95–126 (2022)
7. Beullens, W., Kleinjung, T., Vercauteren, F.: CSI-fish: efficient isogeny based signatures through class group computations. In: ASIACRYPT 2019, vol. 11921, pp. 227–247 (2019)
8. Boyen, X.: Reusable cryptographic fuzzy extractors. In: CCS 2004, pp. 82–91. ACM (2004)
9. Briët, J., Perdrix, S.: Quantum computation and information - introduction to the special theme. ERCIM News **2018**(112) (2018)
10. Canetti, R., Fuller, B., Paneth, O., Reyzin, L., Smith, A.D.: Reusable fuzzy extractors for low-entropy distributions. In: EUROCRYPT 2016, vol. 9665, pp. 117–146 (2016)
11. Castryck, W., Decru, T.: An efficient key recovery attack on SIDH. In: EUROCRYPT 2023, vol. 14008, pp. 423–447 (2023)
12. Castryck, W., Lange, T., Martindale, C., Panny, L., Renes, J.: CSIDH: an efficient post-quantum commutative group action. In: ASIACRYPT 2018, vol. 11274, pp. 395–427 (2018)
13. Childs, A.M., Jao, D., Soukharev, V.: Constructing elliptic curve isogenies in quantum subexponential time. J. Math. Cryptol. **8**(1), 1–29 (2014)
14. Couveignes, J.M.: Hard homogeneous spaces. IACR Cryptology ePrint Archive, p. 291 (2006)
15. Dodis, Y., Reyzin, L., Smith, A.D.: Fuzzy extractors: how to generate strong keys from biometrics and other noisy data. In: EUROCRYPT 2004, vol. 3027, pp. 523–540 (2004)
16. Feo, L.D., Galbraith, S.D.: Seasign: compact isogeny signatures from class group actions. In: EUROCRYPT 2019, vol. 11478, pp. 759–789 (2019)
17. Golic, J.D., Baltatu, M.: Entropy analysis and new constructions of biometric key generation systems. IEEE Trans. Inf. Theory **54**(5), 2026–2040 (2008)
18. Herder, C., Yu, M.M., Koushanfar, F., Devadas, S.: Physical unclonable functions and applications: a tutorial. Proc. IEEE **102**(8), 1126–1141 (2014)
19. Jao, D., Feo, L.D.: Towards quantum-resistant cryptosystems from supersingular elliptic curve isogenies. In: PQCrypto 2011, vol. 7071, pp. 19–34 (2011)
20. Jiang, M., Liu, S., Lyu, Y., Zhou, Y.: Face-based authentication using computational secure sketch. IEEE Trans. Mob. Comput. **22**(12), 7172–7187 (2023)
21. Kelkboom, E.J.C., Breebaart, J., Buhan, I., Veldhuis, R.N.J.: Maximum key size and classification performance of fuzzy commitment for gaussian modeled biometric sources. IEEE Trans. Inf. Forensics Secur. **7**(4), 1225–1241 (2012)
22. Lai, Y., Galbraith, S.D., de Saint Guilhem, C.D.: Compact, efficient and UC-secure isogeny-based oblivious transfer. In: EUROCRYPT 2021, vol. 12696, pp. 213–241 (2021)
23. Li, N., Guo, F., Mu, Y., Susilo, W., Nepal, S.: Fuzzy extractors for biometric identification. In: ICDCS 2017, pp. 667–677 (2017)
24. Maino, L., Martindale, C., Panny, L., Pope, G., Wesolowski, B.: A direct key recovery attack on SIDH. In: EUROCRYPT 2023, vol. 14008, pp. 448–471 (2023)
25. Montgomery, H., Zhandry, M.: Full quantum equivalence of group action DLOG and CDH, and more. In: ASIACRYPT 2022, vol. 13791, pp. 3–32 (2022)
26. Rostovtsev, A., Stolbunov, A.: Public-key cryptosystem based on isogenies. IACR Cryptology ePrint Archive, p. 145 (2006)
27. Silverman, J.H.: The Arithmetic of Elliptic Curves. Graduate Texts in Mathematics, vol. 106 (1986)

28. Suh, G.E., Devadas, S.: Physical unclonable functions for device authentication and secret key generation. In: DAC 2007, pp. 9–14 (2007)
29. Washington, L.C.: Elliptic curves: number theory and cryptography (2008)
30. Waterhouse, W.C.: Abelian varieties over finite fields. In: Annales scientifiques de l'École normale supérieure, vol. 2, pp. 521–560 (1969)
31. Wen, Y., Liu, S.: Reusable fuzzy extractor from LWE. In: ACISP 2018, vol. 10946, pp. 13–27 (2018)
32. Wen, Y., Liu, S., Han, S.: Reusable fuzzy extractor from the decisional Diffie-Hellman assumption. Des. Codes Cryptogr. **86**(11), 2495–2512 (2018)

Ensuring Fair Data Trading via Passive Proxy Re-encryption with Smart Contracts

Peng Zhang[1(✉)], Jiaquan Wei[1], Yuhong Liu[2], Jianzhou Ruan[1], and Hui Cui[3]

[1] College of Electronics and Information Engineering, Shenzhen University, Shenzhen, China
zhangp@szu.edu.cn

[2] Department of Computer Science and Engineering, Santa Clara University, Santa Clara, USA
yhliu@scu.edu

[3] Faculty of Information Technology, Monash University, Clayton, VIC, Australia
Hui.Cui@monash.edu

Abstract. With the massive amount of digital data generated everyday, data trading becomes a trend. As a result, the fairness of such transactions has drawn increasing attention in recent years. Ensuring fairness in these transactions, without relying on a Trusted Third-Party (TTP), has become a critical concern. Blockchain presents a promising solution as a fair transaction platform. When combined with Proxy Re-Encryption (PRE), smart contracts can take the role of a proxy, checking data consistency and transferring the decryption right after payment. In order to facilitate data trading, Passive Proxy Re-Encryption (PPRE) is defined and proposed. Unlike traditional PRE, where the seller (delegator) actively initiates delegation, PPRE allows delegation to occur upon the request of the buyer (delegatee). Further, by connecting the re-encryption key with the ciphertext, which means the delegation is just for the current data, the PPRE scheme is forward-secure and backward-secure. By adding the verification for the re-encryption key, PPRE supports arbitration when the interruption occurs. The proposed PPRE scheme is secure under Chosen-Ciphertext Attacks (CCA) based on the assumption of Divisible Computation Diffie-Hellman (DCDH). Theoretical analysis and experiment results validate the feasibility and effectiveness of the proposed PPRE scheme, demonstrating its potential to facilitate secure and fair data trading.

Keywords: Data Trading · Fairness · Proxy Re-encryption · Smart Contracts

1 Introduction

High-quality data has become one fundamental driving force of today's AI advancement. The high demand for data makes data trading a quickly growing

J. K. Liu et al. (Eds.): ProvSec 2024, LNCS 14904, pp. 257–266, 2025.
https://doi.org/10.1007/978-981-96-0957-4_15

market. For example, Reddit will make over $200 million in the coming years by selling its data to Google and other companies for AI training [19]. As data trading takes a large and rapidly growing share of our economy [5], how to ensure fair trading has attracted increasing attention. Similar to other types of trading, fair data trading requires the system to ensure that the two participating parties (i.e., the buyer and seller) can both get what they want, or neither. In addition, data trading has a unique challenge. That is, once the data is released to the buyer, the asset is transferred and cannot be returned. Therefore, the payment has to be made before the buyer can access the data. However, how can a buyer validate the legitimacy of the data without accessing the data?

To ensure fair transactions, most existing solutions introduce a Trusted Third-Party (TTP) to participate in data trading [1], who securely hosts the data on its own platform and facilitates the data validation and payment. However, the fairness of transactions then will depend on the behavior of TTP. A malicious TTP can easily damage the transaction. The emergence of Blockchain [13] and smart contracts [6] technologies provides another possibility for fair data trading. Blockchain's decentralization and transparency can effectively prevent it from taking sides in transactions, making it a potential fair transaction platform trusted by both the seller and the buyer. Nevertheless, information stored on Blockchain is by default open to the public, raising privacy concerns. Encrypting such data, however, brings new challenges to fairness, as after encryption, it is difficult to verify whether the original data is identical to the claimed data.

To address the issue of encrypted data verification, Proxy Re-Encryption (PRE), which enables a proxy to transform a ciphertext intended for one party (i.e., the delegator) into a ciphertext for another party (i.e., the delegatee) without revealing the underlying message, has been identified as a promising technology [12]. Using PRE, the proxy performs ciphertext transformation after payment to ensure that the buyer receives the data and the seller gets paid. Furthermore, as smart contracts deployed on blockchains are public programs that can be automatically executed without external interruptions, they can take on the role of a proxy, checking data consistency and transferring the decryption right after payment.

In this study, we attempt to design a novel proxy re-encryption scheme by addressing the above challenges. Our major contributions are summarized as follows.

- A passive PRE is designed in this work to facilitate data trading, where the delegation will only be enabled when a seller (as a delegator) receives a request from a buyer (as a delegatee).
- By connecting the re-encryption key with the ciphertext, the proposed passive PRE scheme is forward-secure and backward-secure. That means the delegation is just for the current data, and the sold and unsold ciphertexts even under the same private key are not open to the current buyer. This is a critical property to ensure fair data trading.

- By adding the verification for the re-encryption key, the proposed passive PRE scheme supports arbitration. When the interruption occurs, it can automatically judge who is dishonest, and such judgment is open for validation.

2 Related Work

The concept of proxy re-encryption was proposed a few decades ago by Blaze el al. [4], where a semi-trusted proxy can transform a ciphertext under Alice's public key into another ciphertext under Bob's public key, with the constraint that Bob can decrypt it with his own private key, but the proxy cannot learn anything about the plaintext. Since then, different versions of PRE schemes have been proposed. Ateniese et al. [2] proposed a PRE scheme using bilinear pairing, which, however, cannot resist Chosen-Ciphertext Attacks (CCA). Wang el al. [17] proposed a CCA secure PRE scheme using bilinear pairing. As the computational cost of bilinear pairing is much higher than that of modular exponentiation, which may lead to significantly higher economic costs on smart contracts.

Next, we are inclined to the PRE schemes without bilinear pairing. Deng et al. [8] and Weng et al. [18] constructed PRE schemes without bilinear pairing, which meet CCA security. Shao et al. [16] proposed a PRE scheme without bilinear pairing. However, it failed to satisfy CCA security when facing specific attacks [7]. Although a more efficient PRE scheme without bilinear pairing was proposed in [7], an important flaw in the security proof of PRE scheme was identified by [15], which then proposed an anti-collusion PRE scheme without bilinear pairing, which satisfied CCA security under the random oracle model.

Recently, PRE schemes have been applied for a broad range of applications. For example, Kan et al. [9] proposed a CCA-secure and collusion-resilient proxy re-encryption scheme for a decentralized storage network. Lin et al. [11] proposed a generalized autonomous path proxy re-encryption scheme for supporting branch functionality. In order to ensure the safe sharing of medical data among healthcare systems, Rastogi et al. [14] chose to integrate PRE into blockchains, reducing the risk of key leakage by not directly sharing private keys but using re-encrypted keys. Khashan et al. [10] improved the PRE efficiency by integrating symmetric and asymmetric cryptographic techniques, in order to customize for Wireless Sensor Networks (WSN). Lu et al. in [12] proposed a searchable PRE scheme to facilitate IoT data trading.

All the PRE schemes discussed above can be considered active PRE, where the delegator needs to decide to whom the decryption right should be delegated. However, in a data transaction, the seller, as a delegator, cannot predict who will make the purchase and therefore cannot identify the delegatee until receiving purchase request from a specific buyer. A passive PRE is required in this scenario.

3 Definition and Security Model

3.1 The Definition of Passive Proxy Re-encryption

In current literatures, (active) PRE assumes that the delegator is honest and active in transferring the decryption right to the specified delegatee and knows the delegatee's public key before generating a re-encryption key for him/her. However, in data trading, a delegator passively receives requests from delegatees and may often be motivated not to play fair. Formally, we define passive PRE by adding two new algorithms *Request* and $VerifyReKey$, based on the PRE definition $\{Setup, KeyGen, Encrypt, ReKeyGen, ReEncrypt, Decrypt\}$, as descried in [7]. *Request* is used by a delegatee to make a request and send his/her public key to the delegator. To prevent forgery from malicious delegators, $VerifyReKey$ is used to verify the re-encryption key. These two algorithms are defined as follows.

- $Request(pk_i, pk_j)$: With inputs as pk_i of the delegator i and pk_j of the delegatee j, this algorithm outputs a request R for requesting ciphertext conversion from the delegator i to the delegatee j.
- $VerifyReKey(rk_{ij}, CT_i, R)$: Use this algorithm to verify whether the delegator has honestly calculated the re-encryption key rk_{ij} which can transform CT_i into CT_j. This algorithm outputs 1 or 0, which means that rk_{ij} is valid or invalid, respectively.

3.2 The Security Model of Passive Proxy Re-Encryption

Definition 1 (CCA Security of a passive PRE). *The advantage of $\mathcal{A}$ in attacking the passive PRE scheme is define as* $Adv_{PRE,\mathcal{A}}^{IND-CCA} = |Pr[\theta' = \theta] - 1/2|$, *where the probability is taken over the random coins consumed by the challenger and the adversary. Run the KeyGen algorithm n_u times resulting a list of good public/private keys, and run the KeyGen algorithm for n_c times to get a list of corrupted public/private keys. A passive PRE scheme is defined to be $(t, n_u, n_c, q_{rq}, q_{rk}, q_{re}, q_d, \epsilon)$-IND-CCA secure, if for any t-time IND-CCA adversary $\mathcal{A}$, who makes at most q_{rq} request queries, q_{rk} re-encryption key generation queries, q_{re} re-encryption queries, and q_d decryption queries, we have* $Adv_{PRE,\mathcal{A}}^{IND-CCA} \leq \epsilon$.

For details about the adversary $\mathcal{A}$ and games with the challenger, please refer to [7]. Note that there is one more **OReq** oracle, which takes $\langle pk_i, pk_j \rangle$ and returns the request R. **OReK** oracle is different, taking $\langle pk_i, pk_j \rangle$, a request R, and a ciphertext CT_i, with the output of a re-encryption key rk_{ij}.

4 The Proposed Passive PRE

4.1 The Proposed Scheme

Inspired by PRE schemes of Chow et al. [7], we construct a passive PRE scheme (PPRE) without pairings, which consists of the following eight algorithms.

Setup(l_q): Given a security parameter l_q, two big primes p and q are chosen such that $q|p-1$, and the bit-length of q is l_q. Let $\mathbb{G}$ be a generator of group $\mathbb{G}$, which is a subgroup of $\mathbb{Z}_p^*$ with order q. Three collision-resistant hash functions can be chosen as follows: $H_1 : \{0,1\}^{l_0} \times \{0,1\}^{l_1} \to \mathbb{Z}_q^*$,

$H_2 : \mathbb{G} \rightarrow \{0,1\}^{l_0+l_1}$, and $H_3 : \{0,1\}^* \rightarrow \mathbb{Z}_q^*$. Here l_0 and l_1 are also security parameters, and the message space $\mathcal{M}$ is $\{0,1\}^{l_0}$. The global parameters are $param = (p, q, g, H_1, H_2, H_3, l_0, l_1)$. By default, the following algorithms all require the parameters $param$ as input.

$KeyGen(param)$: For a delegator i, this algorithm picks $x_{i1} \xleftarrow{\$} \mathbb{Z}_q^*$ and $x_{i2} \xleftarrow{\$} \mathbb{Z}_q^*$ randomly, and computes the private key $sk_i = \{sk_{i1}, sk_{i2}\} = \{x_{i1}, x_{i2}\}$ and public key $pk_i = \{pk_{i1}, pk_{i2}\} = \{g^{x_{i1}}(modp), g^{x_{i2}}(modp)\}$. In the same way, the private key $sk_j = \{sk_{j1}, sk_{j2}\} = \{x_{j1}, x_{j2}\}$ and the public key $pk_j = \{pk_{j1}, pk_{j2}\} = \{g^{x_{j1}}(modp), g^{x_{j2}}(modp)\}$ for a delegatee j can be generated.

$Encrypt(pk_i, m)$: On input pk_i and plaintext $m \in \mathcal{M}$, this algorithm outputs the original ciphertext CT_i under pk_i by following the procedure below.

- Pick $w \xleftarrow{\$} \{0,1\}^{l_1}$, and compute $r = H_1(m, w)$, $F = H_2(g^r) \oplus (m||w)$.
- Pick $u \xleftarrow{\$} \mathbb{Z}_q^*$, and compute $\Pi = {pk_{i1}}^{H_3(F)} pk_{i2}$, $D = \Pi^u$, $E = \Pi^r$.
- Compute $s = u + r \cdot H_3(D, E, F)(modq)$.
- Output ciphertext $CT_i = \{\Pi, D, E, F, s\}$.

$Request(pk_i, pk_j)$: Delegatee j makes a request to delegator i. On input pk_i of delegator i and pk_j of delegatee j, this algorithm outputs a request R for transferring the decryption right of m from delegator i to delegatee j by following the procedure below.

- Pick $h \xleftarrow{\$} \{0,1\}^{l_0}$ and $\pi \xleftarrow{\$} \{0,1\}^{l_1}$, and compute $v = H_1(h, \pi)$.
- Compute $V_i = pk_{i2}^v$, $V_j = pk_{j2}^v$, $W = H_2(g^v) \oplus (h||\pi)$, and $\Phi = g^h$.
- Output $R = \{pk_j, V_i, V_j, W, \Phi\}$.

$ReKeyGen(sk_i, R, CT_i)$: For a request R from delegatee j, the delegator i uses this algorithm to generate re-encryption key rk_{ij}, or output an error symbol $\perp$.

- Compute $(h||\pi) = W \oplus H_2({V_i}^{1/sk_{i2}})$.
- Check whether $V_i = pk_{i2}^{H_1(h,\pi)}$ holds. If not, output $\perp$.
- Compute $rk_{ij} = \frac{h}{x_{i1} H_3(F) + x_{i2}}$.
- Output the re-encryption key rk_{ij}.

$VerifyReKey(rk_{ij}, CT_i, R)$: This algorithm aims to verify if the delegator i has honestly calculated the re-encryption key rk_{ij} to transform the decryption right. On input rk_{ij}, $\Pi \in CT_i$, and $\Phi \in R$, this algorithm outputs 1 or 0, which indicates whether rk_{ij} is valid or not, respectively. Specifically, it follows the procedure below.

- Check whether $\Pi^{rk_{ij}} = \Phi$ holds.
- If not, output 0. Otherwise, output 1.

$ReEncrypt(CT_i, R, rk_{ij}, pk_i, pk_j)$: On input the original ciphertext CT_i under public key pk_i and the re-encryption key rk_{ij}, this algorithm transforms CT_i into CT_j, which is a ciphertext under the public key pk_j. It follows the procedure below.

- Check whether $({pk_{i1}}^{H_3(F)} pk_{i2})^s = D \cdot E^{H_3(D,E,F)}$ holds. If not, output $\perp$.
- Compute $E' = E^{rk_{ij}}$.
- Output a transformed ciphertext $CT_j = \{E', F, V_j, W\}$.

Decrypt$(sk_i/sk_j, CT_i/CT_j)$: On input a private key sk_i and an original ciphertext $CT_i = \{\Pi, D, E, F, s\}$, the delegator i can use this algorithm to decrypt CT_i, and output the plaintext m or error symbol $\perp$.

- If $({pk_{i1}}^{H_3(F)} pk_{i2})^s = D \cdot E^{H_3(D,E,F)}$ does not hold, output $\perp$.
- Else, compute $m||w = F \oplus H_2(E^{\frac{1}{x_{i1}H_3(F)+x_{i2}}})$.
- If $E = ({pk_{i1}}^{H_3(F)} pk_{i2})^{H_1(m,w)}$ holds, return m. Otherwise, output $\perp$.

On input the private key sk_j and a transformed ciphertext $CT_j = \{E', F, V_j, W\}$, the delegatee j can use this algorithm to decrypt CT_j, and it outputs the plaintext m or an error symbol $\perp$.

- Compute $(h||\pi) = W \oplus H_2(V_j^{1/sk_{j2}})$.
- Check whether $V_j = pk_{j2}^{H_1(h,\pi)}$ holds. If not, output $\perp$.
- Compute $m||w = F \oplus H_2(E'^{1/h})$.
- If $E' = g^{H_1(m,w) \cdot h}$ holds, return m. Otherwise, output $\perp$.

Compared to the (active) PRE, we add *Request* and *VerifyReKey* algorithms for PPRE. The *Request* algorithm is used to make a request by delegatee, and the *VerifyReKey* algorithm is used to verify the re-encryption key and avoid the delegator forging. In addition, as the *ReKeyGen* algorithm is related to a cipertext, the decryption right is just transferred for the specified message.

4.2 PPRE Deployed on Smart Contracts

In the data trading scenario, the process of securely and fairly transferring data between a seller and a buyer involves several steps, utilizing the proposed PPRE scheme and smart contracts.

The individual user generates a pair of public and private keys by *KeyGen*. The seller encrypts the data using a symmetric encryption algorithm. The symmetric key used for encryption is then encrypted using the proposed PPRE scheme with the *Encrypt* function. The encrypted data is uploaded to InterPlanetary File System (IPFS) [3], which returns a unique hash value. The seller uploads this hash value along with the encrypted symmetric key to smart contracts.

When a buyer wants to purchase the data, he/she interacts with smart contracts by submitting a purchase request and payment. Upon receiving the payment, smart contracts notify the seller to submit the re-encryption key. The re-encryption key is generated by the *ReKeyGen* function, which converts the seller's symmetric key into a key that the buyer can decrypt. The seller submits this re-encryption key to smart contracts.

Next, smart contracts verify the re-encryption key by *VerifyReKey*, and perform the re-encryption algorithm *ReEncrypt*. After re-encryption, the transformed ciphertext is sent to the buyer, and the payment is transferred to the seller. The buyer then decrypts the transformed ciphertext to obtain the symmetric key, downloads the encrypted data from IPFS using the hash value, and decrypts it using the symmetric key to obtain the purchased data.

5 Analysis

5.1 Security Analysis

Definition 2 (Divisible Computation Diffie-Hellman (DCDH) Assumption). *For an algorithm $\mathcal{B}$, its advantage in solving the DCDH problem is defined as $Adv_{\mathcal{B}}^{DCDH} \triangleq Pr\left[\mathcal{B}(g, g^a, g^b) = g^{b/a}\right]$, where the probability is taken over the random choices of a, b and those made by $\mathcal{B}$. We say that the (t, ϵ)-DCDH assumption holds in $\mathbb{G}$ if no t-time algorithm $\mathcal{B}$ has advantage at least ϵ in solving the DCDH problem in $\mathbb{G}$.*

Theorem 1. *The proposed scheme is CCA-secure for the original ciphertext under the DCDH assumption. If a $(t, n_u, n_c, q_{rq}, q_{rk}, q_{re}, q_d, \epsilon)$-IND-CCA adversary $\mathcal{A}_{orig}$ with an advantage ε breaks the IND-CCA security of the given scheme in time t, the algorithm $\mathcal{B}_{orig}$ can break the DCDH assumption in $\mathbb{G}$ with advantage ε' within time t'.*

For detailed proof, please refer to [7], with slight differences in the oracle models. The similar analysis is also for the transformed ciphertext.

5.2 Theoretical Analysis

We conduct theoretical comparisons between the proposed scheme and the most well-known (active) PRE schemes, including Shao et al. [16], Chow et al. [7], Wang et al. [17] and Selvi et al. [15].

Table 1 shows the performance comparisons of several PRE schemes. For the first time, a passive PRE is defined and proposed in this paper, where the delegator does not transfer the proxy right until after the delegatee makes a request. Second, there is no pairing computation used in [7,15,16], and the proposed scheme, which is more practical for resource-constrained environment, like smart contracts. In addition, the PRE schemes proposed in [7,16], and [15] can resist collusion attacks, which can avoid the exposure of the delegator's private key if the proxy colludes with the delegatee. However, all ciphtertext under this private key can be decrypted. The proposed scheme is forward and backward secure under the attacks launched by the colluded proxy and delegatee, which means the private key of delegator cannot be leaked, and the other ciphertext under this private key cannot be decrypted. Last but not least, except for [16], the other schemes are CCA-secure based on the related difficulty assumptions,

Table 1. The performance comparisons with existing PRE schemes

Schemes	[16]	[7]	[17]	[15]	PPRE
Active/Passive	Active	Active	Active	Active	Passive
Pairings	No	No	Yes	No	No
Collusion resistance	Yes	Yes	Uncertain	Yes	Yes
Security level	Not CCA	CCA	CCA	CCA	CCA
Standard model	No	No	Yes	No	No
Assumptions	DDH	CDH	DBDH	CDH, DCDH	DCDH

among which only [17] is secure in the standard model. In summary, the proposed scheme is the only passive PRE scheme, which is collusion-secure and CCA-secure in the random model based on the DCDH assumption.

Further, we analyze theoretical computational costs of different algorithms in these PRE schemes. In particular, t_{exp} and t_p denote the computational costs of an exponentiation and a bilinear pairings, respectively. *Orig.CT* and $Trans.CT$ denote the original ciphertext and the transformed ciphertext, respectively. $|\mathbb{G}|$, $|\mathbb{Z}_q|$, $|\mathbb{G}_1|$ and $|\mathbb{G}_T|$ denote the bit-length of an element in groups $\mathbb{G}$, $\mathbb{Z}_q$, $\mathbb{G}_1$ and $\mathbb{G}_T$, respectively. N_X and N_Y are the safe-prime modulus in scheme of Shao et al. [16]. In our calculation, the computational cost of $g^{r_1} \cdot g^{r_2}$ or $(g^{r1} \cdot g)^{r_2}$ will be considered as $2t_{exp}$. As shown in Table 2, the efficiency of the proposed scheme is higher than that of scheme in [15], and slightly lower than that of scheme in [7]. Please note that we specifically add *Request* and $VerifyReKey$ algorithms to propose the passive PRE which is more suitable for data trading.

Table 2. The efficiency comparisons with existing PRE schemes

Schemes		[16]	[7]	[17]	[15]	PPRE
Cost	*Encrypt*	$5t_{exp}$	$4t_{exp}$	$1t_p+5t_{exp}$	$5t_{exp}$	$4t_{exp}$
	Request	\	\	\	\	$3t_{exp}$
	ReKeyGen	$2t_{exp}$	$2t_{exp}$	$1t_p+6t_{exp}$	$2t_{exp}$	$2t_{exp}$
	$VerifyReKey$	\	\	\	\	$1t_{exp}$
	ReEncrypt	$5t_{exp}$	$4t_{exp}$	$5t_p+6t_{exp}$	$7t_{exp}$	$4t_{exp}$
	Decrypt Orig.CT	$6t_{exp}$	$5t_{exp}$	$3t_p+3t_{exp}$	$9t_{exp}$	$5t_{exp}$
	$Trans.CT$	$4t_{exp}$	$4t_{exp}$	$4t_p+4t_{exp}$	$4t_{exp}$	$4t_{exp}$
Length	*Orig.CT*	$2k + 3\|N_X^2\| + \|m\|$	$3\|\mathbb{G}\| + \|\mathbb{Z}_q\|$	$2\|\mathbb{G}_1\| + \|\mathbb{G}_T\|$	$3\|\mathbb{G}\| + \|\mathbb{Z}_q\|$	$4\|\mathbb{G}\| + \|\mathbb{Z}_q\|$
	$Trans.CT$	$k + 3\|N_X^2\| + 2\|N_Y^2\| + \|m\|$	$2\|\mathbb{G}\| + 2\|\mathbb{Z}_q\|$	$5\|\mathbb{G}_1\| + \|\mathbb{G}_T\|$	$4\|\mathbb{G}\|$	$4\|\mathbb{G}\|$

5.3 Experimental Analysis

In order to ensure a fair comparison, we chose schemes [7] and [15] to compare with the proposed scheme because they are also without paring and meet CCA security in the random oracle model. We implement these schemes through java programming language on a computer that consists of an Intel (R) Core (TM) i7-8750 processor and a RAM with total memory of 16 GB. In order to facilitate the experiments, we always set $p = 2q + 1$ and $l_0 = l_1$.

We execute each algorithm 50 times and present the average running time. Let l_q = 256, 512, 1024 respectively, and $p = 2q + 1$, $l_0 = l_1 = \frac{1}{2}l_q$. The experiment results are shown in Fig. 1. The total time cost of PPRE is lower than that of scheme in [15], but slightly higher than that of scheme in [7], due to our introduced *Request* and *VerifyRekey* algorithms.

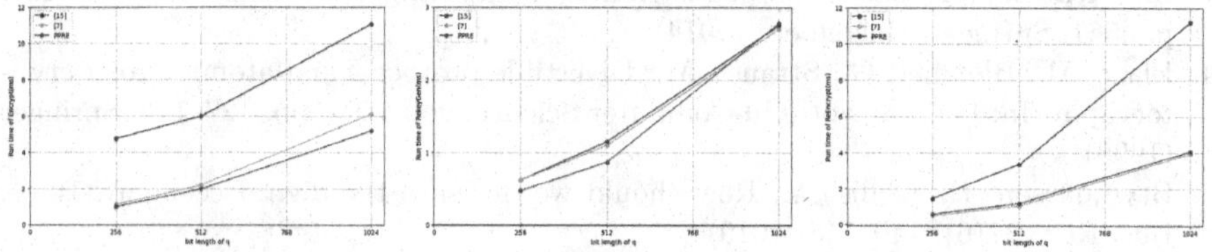

(a) *Encrypt* (b) *RekeyGen* (c) *ReEncrypt*

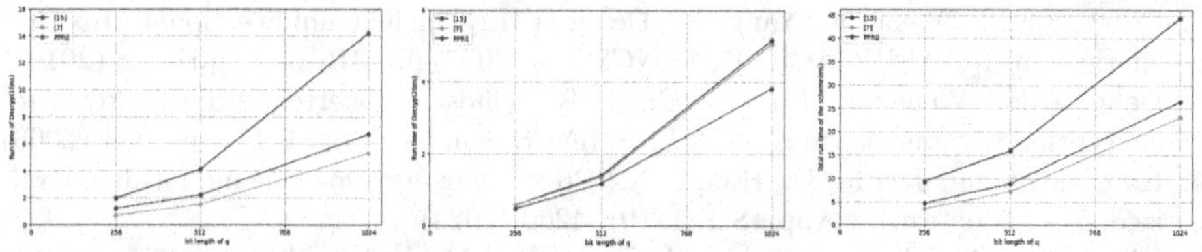

(d) *Decrypt* for Orig.CT (e) *Decrypt* for Trans.CT (f) Total

Fig. 1. The running time comparison of schemes

6 Conclusion

To achieve fair data trading on blockchain, this paper proposes a passive proxy re-encryption (PPRE) scheme, which leverages smart contracts to act as proxies, transferring the decryption right after payment. Unlike traditional Proxy Re-Encryption (PRE) schemes, where the seller (delegator) actively initiates delegation, PPRE allows the delegation process to be initiated by the buyer (delegatee). Since the re-encryption key is associated with the ciphertext, the scheme is forward-secure and backward-secure under collusion attacks, which means that a re-encryption key can only decrypt the corresponding ciphertext but cannot decrypt other ciphertexts. The re-encryption key is verified before its use. This verification process facilitates the identification of dishonest parties, and such judgment is open for validation. Nevertheless, the proposed PPRE scheme is secure and efficient in ensuring fair trading of data.

References

1. Abla, P., Li, T., He, D., Huang, H., Yu, S., Zhang, Y.: Fair and privacy-preserved data trading protocol by exploiting blockchain. IEEE Trans. Inf. Forensics Secur. (2024)
2. Ateniese, G., Fu, K., Green, M., Hohenberger, S.: Improved proxy re-encryption schemes with applications to secure distributed storage. In: Proceedings of the Network and Distributed System Security Symposium, NDSS 2005, San Diego, California, USA. The Internet Society (2005)
3. Benet, J.: IPFS - content addressed, versioned, P2P file system. In: Proceedings of the 14th Annual Conference on Distributed Computing Systems. LNCS, vol. 1407, p. 3561. Springer, Heidelberg (2014)
4. Blaze, M., Bleumer, G., Strauss, M.: Divertible protocols and atomic proxy cryptography. In: Lecture Notes in Computer Science, vol. 1403, pp. 127–144. Springer (1998)
5. Brynjolfsson, E., Collis, A.: How should we measure the digital economy. Harv. Bus. Rev. **97**(6), 140–148 (2019)
6. Buterin, V., et al.: A next-generation smart contract and decentralized application platform. White Paper **3**(37) (2014)
7. Chow, S.S.M., Weng, J., Yang, Y., Deng, R.H.: Efficient unidirectional proxy re-encryption. In: AFRICACRYPT. LNCS, vol. 6055, pp. 316–332. Springer (2010)
8. Deng, R.H., Weng, J., Liu, S., Chen, K.: Chosen-ciphertext secure proxy re-encryption without pairings. In: CANS. LNCS, vol. 5339, pp. 1–17. Springer (2008)
9. Kan, J., Zhang, J., Liu, D., Huang, X.: Proxy re-encryption scheme for decentralized storage networks. Appl. Sci. **12**(9), 4260 (2022)
10. Khashan, O.A., Khafajah, N.M., Alomoush, W., Alshinwan, M.: Innovative energy-efficient proxy re-encryption for secure data exchange in wireless sensor networks. IEEE Access (2024)
11. Lin, Z., Zhou, J., Cao, Z., Dong, X., Choo, K.K.R.: Generalized autonomous path proxy re-encryption scheme to support branch functionality. IEEE Trans. Inf. Forensics Secur. (2023)
12. Lu, X., et al.: Decentralized fair IoT data trading via searchable proxy re-encryption. IEEE Internet Things J. (2024)
13. Nakamoto, S.: Bitcoin: a peer-to-peer electronic cash system (2008) https://bitcoin.org/bitcoin.pdf. Accessed 24 Feb 2020
14. Rastogi, P., Singh, D., Bedi, S.: Fully decentralized block chain with proxy re-encryption algorithm for healthcare security. Int. J. Intell. Eng. Syst. **16**, 572–583 (2023)
15. Selvi, S.S.D., Paul, A., Rangan, C.P.: A provably-secure unidirectional proxy re-encryption scheme without pairing in the random oracle model. In: CANS. LNCS, vol. 11261, pp. 459–469. Springer (2017)
16. Shao, J., Cao, Z.: CCA-secure proxy re-encryption without pairings. In: Public Key Cryptography. LNCS, vol. 5443, pp. 357–376. Springer (2009)
17. Wang, H., Cao, Z.: More efficient CCA-secure unidirectional proxy re-encryption schemes without random oracles. Secur. Commun. Netw. **6**(2), 173–181 (2013)
18. Weng, J., Deng, R.H., Liu, S., Chen, K.: Chosen-ciphertext secure bidirectional proxy re-encryption schemes without pairings. Inf. Sci. **180**(24), 5077–5089 (2010)
19. Wired.com: Reddit's sale of user data for AI training draws FTC inquiry. https://www.wired.com/story/reddits-sale-user-data-ai-training-draws-ftc-investigation/

DPAC: A New Data-Centric Privacy-Preserving Access Control Model

Xu Wang(✉), Baihe Ma, Ren Ping Liu, and Ian Oppermann

Global Big Data Technologies Centre, Faculty of Engineering and Information Technology, University of Technology Sydney, Sydney, Australia
{Xu.Wang,Baihe.Ma,Renping.Liu,Ian.Oppermann}@uts.edu.au

Abstract. Access Control (AC) is a critical technology for protecting privacy in data sharing. Various AC models have been developed, but they generally focus on individual data instances without addressing the challenges posed by diverse data presentations and their associated privacy levels. This paper introduces a novel Data-centric, Privacy-preserving Access Control (DPAC) model to address this issue. The DPAC model enables the representation of a single piece of data in multiple views, each customized for specific applications, thus promoting a unified approach to data-centric privacy protection and controlled data processing and sharing. To support the DPAC model, we propose a new data product policy scheme that includes a data product creation function, sensitivity assessments, and a set of Attribute-Based Access Control (ABAC) policies. The data product policy scheme effectively manages privacy risks, access requirements, and control policies within a cohesive policy framework. To demonstrate the functionality of the DPAC model, we develop a Secure Multi-Organization Data Sharing (SMODS) platform and design data product policies for collaborative emergency response scenarios. This implementation showcases the effectiveness of DPAC in managing privacy risks during data sharing and the adaptability and practical utility in real-world applications.

Keywords: Access control · Privacy · Data sharing

1 Introduction

Data sharing among enterprises necessitates rigorous protections as firms serve as responsible custodians of this data-a duty enshrined in stringent regulations like Europe's General Data Protection Regulation and the California Consumer Privacy Act in certain jurisdictions [13]. In the commercial sector, enterprises utilize the enterprise data of their partners as well as the personal data of users to monitor compliance, forecast trends, and derive insights into market dynamics. Yet, this data, especially when personal or enterprise-sensitive, is often shared in cross-organization contexts, thereby elevating the risk of privacy breaches.

J. K. Liu et al. (Eds.): ProvSec 2024, LNCS 14904, pp. 267–276, 2025.
https://doi.org/10.1007/978-981-96-0957-4_16

To provide secure and private data sharing, Access Control (AC) models, including Identity-Based Access Control (IBAC) [2], Role-Based Access Control (RBAC) [4], Policy-aware Role-Based Access Control (P-RBAC) [7], and Attribute-Based Access Control (ABAC) [1,15,17], are introduced to manage permissions in various organizational environments. IBAC focuses on individual identification, granting access based on unique user identities, while RBAC assigns permissions based on predefined roles [4]. P-RBAC builds on RBAC by incorporating policies to enhance flexibility and scalability [7]. ABAC introduces a more dynamic approach by making access decisions based on a comprehensive set of user attributes, allowing for fine-grained and context-aware control. The attributes can include user roles, organizational affiliations, data sensitivity levels, and contextual factors such as time and location [3].

Existing AC models have primarily concentrated on managing secure access to individual data instances, which fails to adequately address the complexities arising from diverse data presentations and fluctuating privacy levels. In this paper, we introduce a Data-centric, Privacy-preserving Access Control (DPAC) model that formalizes and safeguards data processing and sharing, tailored to specific application needs and privacy requirements. Aligned with the Australian Computer Society (ACS) data sharing framework [10], our model features a novel data product policy scheme comprising creation functions, sensitivity analysis, and ABAC policies. This scheme transforms raw data into shareable, privacy-compliant data products, with comprehensive ABAC policies ensuring secure access and robust privacy protection across various user scenarios. This approach allows data owners to confidently manage and share their data, maintaining strict privacy controls. The key contributions of this paper are as follows:

- We propose the Data-centric and Privacy-preserving Access Control (DPAC) model featuring a new data product policy scheme. This scheme enables data to be processed, shared, and managed within a unified policy framework, accommodating various application and privacy requirements.
- We design a multi-view data sharing framework that illustrates the data processing and sharing workflow, incorporating the new DPAC model. This framework enables data providers to offer multiple views of the same data, adhering to predefined data product policies.
- We implement the model and framework on the Secure Multi-Organization Data Sharing (SMODS) platform, demonstrating video data sharing in an emergency response scenario accessible by various user attributes. The platform also leverages image processing functions to automatically detect and mask private information in video frames, enhancing privacy protection.

The rest of this paper is organized as follows. Related works are reviewed in Sect. 2. The proposed DPAC model platform is illustrated in Sect. 3, followed by a case study in Sect. 4. Section 5 concludes the paper.

2 Related Works

As a critical technology protecting privacy during data sharing, many access control models have been proposed, such as IBAC [2], RBAC [4] and ABAC [1]. These models govern the access to data objects based on users' identities, roles and attributes, respectively.

Privacy-Aware Access Control. Privacy-aware access control models incorporate privacy details like purpose and obligation to formulate complex privacy policies [9]. Ling et al. [16] enhanced privacy in mobile cloud computing with a system that integrates authentication and hierarchical access control, utilizing self-certified public key cryptography and the Chinese remainder theorem for mutual authentication and user anonymity. This system, however, faces challenges in updating access privileges due to complex bilinear pairing operations and does not support data processing based on privacy needs. Herrera et al. [7] introduced a context-sensitive, privacy-aware system for decentralized data sharing that allows users to set detailed access rules and manage data access, employing private function evaluation to protect data and user privacy, though it does not address the depth of information access. Sun et al. [14] developed a lightweight privacy-aware access control scheme for IoT-based smart health systems, optimizing data management and reducing computational overhead with an efficient encryption/decryption approach, though it encounters challenges related to attribute privacy and system efficiency.

Data-Centric Access Control: Data-centric AC models aim to provide comprehensive control over data processed across various modules, enhancing privacy and data sharing efficiency [11]. Li et al. [8] implemented ciphertext-policy attribute-based encryption to ensure data privacy, allowing only attribute access by authorized users and using a key chain mechanism to update data attributes efficiently. However, their system lacks the capability to provide fine-grained data products tailored to individual user needs. Focusing on data context, research in [6] enables providers to set AC rules based on data context, allowing users minimal personal attribute usage for access. Despite this, the lack of personalized data products limits privacy preservation. Henzen et al. [5] introduced a method allowing users to specify data handling requirements, adding an indirection layer to communicate these to the storage server for personalized views. Yet, this system fails to offer a unified policy framework and neglects the data lifecycle, highlighting a need for models that integrate comprehensive, user-specific AC mechanisms.

3 Data-Centric Privacy-Aware Access Control Model

The proposed DPAC model addresses the requirement for versatile data sharing, enabling a single data item to be presented in various views tailored to specific applications and privacy needs. The proposed model ensures both privacy preservation and data utility during data sharing. The section begins with an introduction to a new data product policy, which outlines the data processing for creating a data product, assesses the sensitivity of the generated data product, and establishes a set of ABAC policies for the derived data product. The data product policy scheme describes all data processing and access activities of the data product within a cohesive framework. Subsequently, a multi-view data-sharing process is delineated, illustrating cross-organizational data sharing under the new data product policy scheme.

3.1 The Proposed Data Product Policy Scheme

The proposed data product policy scheme consists of a creation function, sensitivity, and ABAC policies, and can be defined as

$$\mathcal{P}_p := \{\mathcal{F}, \mathcal{S}, \mathcal{P}_{AC}\}, \tag{1}$$

where $\mathcal{P}_p$ denotes a data product policy encompassing the creation function $\mathcal{F}$, sensitivity $\mathcal{S}$, and the ABAC policies $\mathcal{P}_{AC}$ linked to the data products.

The creation function $\mathcal{F}$ defines the input, typically raw data, the output data product, and the corresponding data processing method, as given by

$$\mathbf{D}_p, \mathbf{D}_{pm} = \mathcal{F}(\mathbf{D}), \tag{2}$$

where $\mathbf{D}$ represents the given data, $\mathbf{D}_p$ is the resulting data product, and $\mathbf{D}_{pm}$ denotes the metadata for the data product. Data products are manifestations resulting from the processing of raw data, encompassing aggregated versions, subsets of the original dataset, perturbed data, insights, charts, dashboards, and other outcomes derived from data utilization. The data products exhibit diverse sensitivity levels and incorporate varying degrees of personal information compared to the original data asset. The metadata describes the data product and is used to manage and index the derived data products.

The sensitivity $\mathcal{S}$ encompasses both the privacy level of the data product and the access requirements. The privacy level indicates the privacy risk associated with sharing the data product and can be defined using numerical ratings, textual descriptions, or other rating methods. Similarly, the access requirements specify the necessary control level for accessing the data product and can also be defined using methods analogous to those used for the privacy level.

A $\mathcal{P}_p$ also includes a set of ABAC policies $\mathcal{P}_{AC}$. Each ABAC policy $\mathcal{P}_{AC}$ consists of the required attributes to access the data product, an attribute-based description of the accessible objects, and the actions permitted. Popular ABAC languages, such as the eXtensible Access Control Markup Language (XACML) [1], can be employed here. The required attributes typically include the user's affiliation, role, and qualifications. The accessible objects could refer to the data products, described using metadata fields such as date range and location range, or to metadata only. The action field defines the mode of access, e.g., online access only or downloadable.

3.2 Multi-view Data Sharing Process

The proposed DPAC model facilitates the sharing of multi-view data products, centered on a single data copy, across various access environments. Each environment's control level is matched to the data accessing environment's requirements. The data sharing interaction between the Data User Organization (DUO) and Data Provider Organization (DPO) is illustrated in Fig. 1.

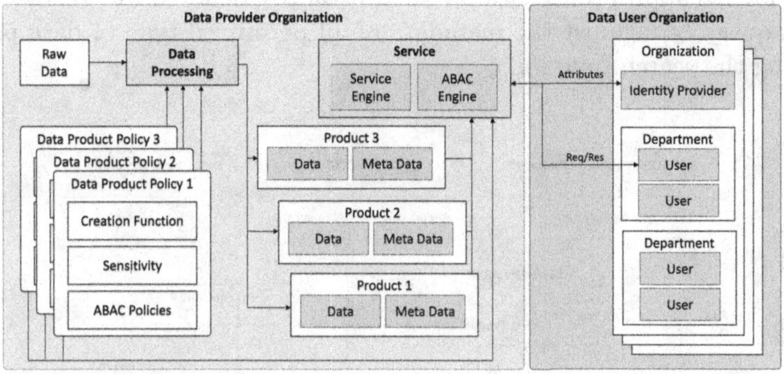

Fig. 1. Data sharing process. The raw data from the data owner organization is processed based on the data product policies as various products. This process allows users with different privileges to have multi-view products, ensuring privacy protection in data sharing.

DUO: Each DUO has an Identity Provider (IDP) that offers user authentication services and supplies trusted user attributes to DPOs. There are multiple data users in the DUO who apply the access from DPO, as given by

$$U_i = \{\mathcal{A}_i\}, \tag{3}$$

where U_i represents the i-th user in the DUO with the set of attributions $\mathcal{A}_i$ certified by the IDP. User U_i sends request R to the DPO, and the j-the request from U_i, denoted by $R_{i,j}$, is given by

$$R_{i,j} = \{\mathcal{A}_i, Q_j\}, \tag{4}$$

where Q_j is the data query sent to the DPO.

DPO: DPO contains a data processing module creating data products following data product policies, and a service module handling data access requests.

When new data arrives, the data processing module reviews all data product policies and executes the embedded product creation functions to generate data products. Simultaneously, the index of available data products is updated.

Once receiving a data query request $R_{i,j}$, the service module identifies the corresponding data products $\hat{\mathbf{D}}_p$ as the response to the request, following

$$\hat{\mathbf{D}}_p = \mathcal{S}\left(\mathcal{M}\left(\mathcal{A}_i, \bar{\mathcal{P}}_{AC}\right), Q_j, \bar{\mathbf{D}}_{pm}\right). \tag{5}$$

The service module firstly matches the user attributes $\mathcal{A}_i$ with all ABAC policies across all data product policies, denoted by $\bar{\mathcal{P}}_{AC}$, with function $\mathcal{M}$ to identify the type of data products that U_i can access. Then, the service module searches for the appropriate data product instances, denoted by $\hat{\mathbf{D}}_p$, by checking the data query Q_j against the metadata of all permitted type of data products $\bar{\mathbf{D}}_{pm}$ using the search function $\mathcal{S}$.

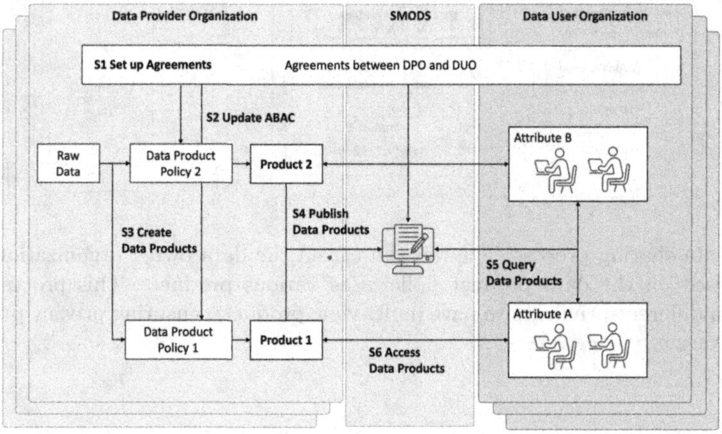

Fig. 2. The structure of the proposed SMODS. Step 1: DPO and DUO negotiate the data sharing agreements following the privacy level and requirement defined in data product policies. Step 2: DPO and SMODS update ABAC policies according to the agreements. Step 3: DPOs create data products following the data product policies. Step 4: DPOs publish the data products to SMODS. Step 5: DUs query accessible data products from SMODS. Step 6: DUs are redirected to DPOs and access data products.

4 Case Study

In this section, we present the Secure Multi-Organization Data Sharing (SMODS) platform, which exemplifies the implementation of the DPAC model for cross-organization privacy-preserving data sharing, as depicted in Fig. 2. The SMODS platform facilitates the discovery of available data products from various DPOs, effectively connecting data users with the appropriate data providers. Additionally, for secure and privacy-preserving cross-organization authentication, the platform employs the OpenID protocol [12].

4.1 SMODS

To facilitate cross-organization data sharing, a DUO and a DPO initially negotiate data sharing agreements that align users with accessible data products in accordance with the ABAC scheme. The DPO recommends appropriate data products and specifies the required attributes based on the sensitivity definitions outlined in the data product policies. Upon ratification of these agreements, the ABAC policies are integrated into the existing data product policies, enabling the DPO to regulate access to the data products. Additionally, these policies are synchronized to the SMODS platform, enhancing its capability to accurately identify and connect users with the appropriate data products. When the DPO generates new data products following the DPO's data product policies, the DPO also publishes the products to SMODS by transmitting the metadata associated with the data products to SMODS. The actual data products stay with the DPO to minimize the risk of data leakage.

The data product access process initiates when a user sends a query to SMODS to identify and access data products from appropriate DPOs. Users must log into SMODS using attributes transferred via the OpenID login process from the DUO's IDP, where SMODS functions as an OpenID client. The authentication follows the OpenID protocol, which does not require the user's real identity as per ABAC requirements, ensuring that private user information remains undisclosed. Once the relevant data product and DPO are identified, users are redirected to the DPO, who retrieves the user's attributes from the IDP using a similar OpenID client process. With trusted attributes in place, the ABAC engine at the DPO grants access to the data products if the user meets the necessary criteria.

4.2 Video Sharing for Emergency Response

An example of cross-organization video sharing for emergency responses is illustrated in Fig. 3, highlighting the integration of the DPAC model to manage privacy risks. Videos captured during emergencies may contain sensitive identifiable information, necessitating robust privacy controls. We categorize video data into four data product types based on their required privacy levels: high, moderate, low, and no control, each with tailored ABAC policies.

For the high control environment, the original video files are restricted to authorized emergency professionals within specific geographical areas, addressing the privacy concerns associated with bio-identifiable imagery like faces and body shapes. In the moderate control setting, videos are processed to mask identifiable features, allowing broader access to emergency support units within their jurisdictional boundaries. Low control data products consist of key still images for on-call responders, providing necessary visual information without full video access. Lastly, for the no control environment, a textual summary of events is made available to the public, ensuring no sensitive information is disclosed. These strategies demonstrate how video data can be effectively and securely shared across different organizational levels and control settings, ensuring compliance with privacy requirements.

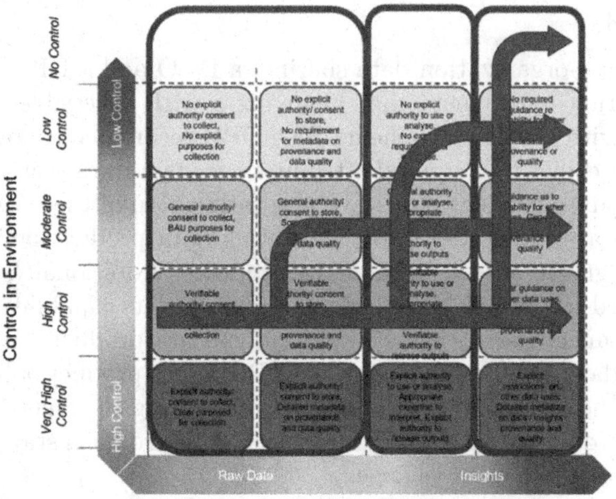

Fig. 3. The privacy and control levels for video sharing.

4.3 System Implementation

We implemented the SMODS platform and an emergency response scenario, which was then evaluated by stakeholders. The system runs on an Apple MacBook Pro, equipped with an M1 Max CPU and 64 GB of memory. For video processing, we utilized the Ultralytics YOLOv8 model[1], specifically employing a pre-trained YOLOv8n face detection model[2] for identifying faces. Frame processing was conducted using CV2[3]. To enhance performance, the device running the YOLO model was configured to use Metal Performance Shaders (MPS).

The developed SMODS platform with the video sharing case is shown in Fig. 4. The figure shows the four types of data products from high, moderate, low and no control environments. Specifically, Fig. 4a displays the high-control data product, featuring raw video footage of an incident with clearly visible faces. Figure 4b shows the moderate-control data product, where faces are masked for privacy. Figure 4c illustrates the low-control data product, represented by a single frame from the video, and Fig. 4d shows the no-control data product, which provides a textual description of the incident. The face identification and masking function can achieve above 25 FPS in our test across six videos, showing the function is capable to support real-time video streams.

[1] https://docs.ultralytics.com.

[2] https://github.com/derronqi/yolov8-face?tab=readme-ov-file.

[3] https://opencv.org.

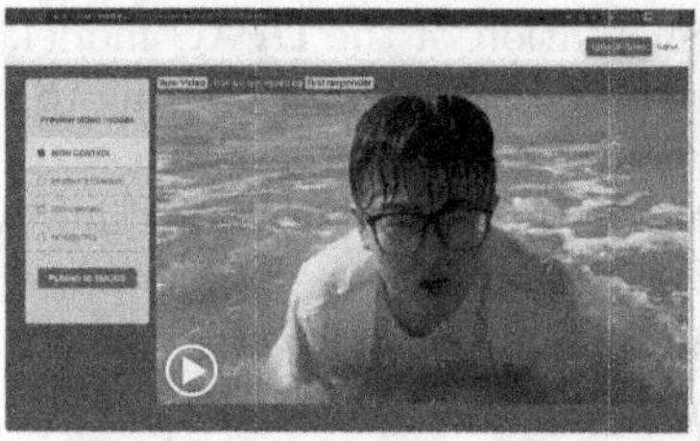

(a) "High Control" Data Product.

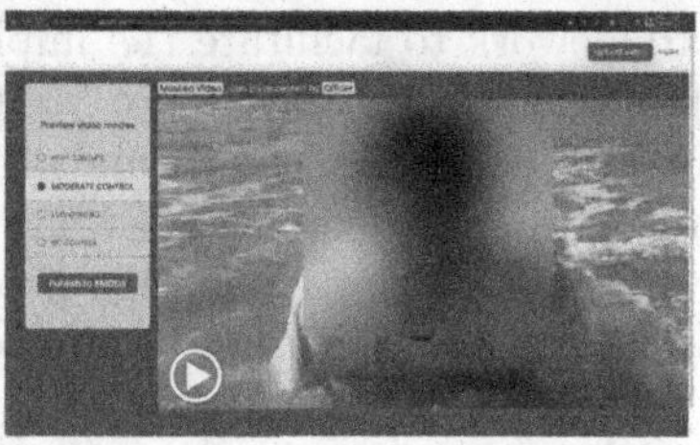

(b) "Moderate Control" Data Product

(c) "Low Control" Data Product

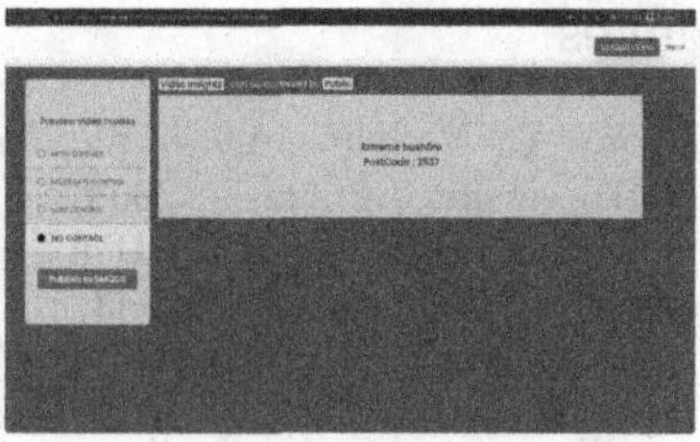

(d) "No Control" Data Product

Fig. 4. Four data products in SMODS.

5 Discussion and Conclusion

Data Privacy and Utility. The proposed DPAC model and its implementation via the SMODS platform significantly enhance privacy management and data-centric access control. The DPAC model enables data providers to assess privacy risks, align data product attributes with user needs, and effectively manage ABAC policies, facilitating tailored data customization for diverse users and scenarios. This enhances data utility and sharing across the data lifecycle, expanding beyond traditional models that focus on singular data items. Meanwhile, SMODS supports secure, privacy-preserving data sharing across organizations by transmitting only metadata for indexing, while actual data products are kept securely with DPOs, minimizing data leakage risks. Additionally, the platform's adoption of OpenID-based authentication bolsters the trustworthiness of user attributes without revealing sensitive personal information, thereby enhancing both security and usability across various operational contexts.

Conclusion. In this paper, we introduced the Data-centric, Privacy-preserving Access Control (DPAC) model designed to enhance data sharing across multiple organizational contexts. The DPAC model allows a single piece of data to be customized for various users, optimizing utility while preserving privacy effectively. Alongside the DPAC model, we developed a comprehensive data product policy scheme, aimed at providing robust management of privacy risks and access controls associated with data products. Furthermore, we designed a multi-view data sharing framework to facilitate the implementation of the DPAC model, which was then applied within the Secure Multi-Organization Data Sharing (SMODS) platform. This platform, using collaborative emergency response scenarios as a case study, effectively demonstrated how the DPAC model not only improves the security and privacy of data sharing processes but also ensures the preservation of data utility in complex, multi-organizational environments.

Acknowledgment. This paper is supported by Connectivity Innovation Network via the project Secure Multi-Organization Data Sharing project.

References

1. Anderson, A., Nadalin, A., et al.: Extensible access control markup language (XACML) version 1.0. Oasis (2003)
2. Belchior, R., Putz, B., et al.: SSIBAC: self-sovereign identity based access control. In: 19th TrustCom, pp. 1935–1943. IEEE (2020)
3. Chiquito, A., Bodin, U., Schelén, O.: Attribute-based approaches for secure data sharing in industrial contexts. IEEE Access **11**, 10180–10195 (2023)
4. Ding, F., Liu, Q., et al.: Firms' access to informal financing: The role of shared managers in trade credit access. J. Corp. Finan. **79**, 102388 (2023)
5. Henze, M., Matzutt, R., et al.: Complying with data handling requirements in cloud storage systems. IEEE Trans. Cloud Comput. **10**(3), 1661–1674 (2020)
6. Herrera, J.L., Chen, H.Y., et al.: Privacy-aware and context-sensitive access control for opportunistic data sharing. In: 21st CCGrid, pp. 762–769. IEEE (2021)
7. Herrera, J.L., Chen, H.Y., et al.: Context-aware privacy-preserving access control for mobile computing. Pervasive Mob. Comput. **87**, 101725 (2022)
8. Li, R., Asaeda, H., Li, J.: A distributed publisher-driven secure data sharing scheme for information-centric IoT. IEEE Internet Things J. **4**(3), 791–803 (2017)
9. Ni, Q., Bertino, E., et al.: Privacy-aware role-based access control. ACM Trans. Inf. Syst. Secur. **13**(3), 1–31 (2010)
10. Oppermann, I. (ed.): Frameworks and controls for data sharing. Australian Computer Society (2023). https://www.acs.org.au/insightsandpublications/reports-publications/Industry_Insights_Frameworks_and_Controls_for_Data_Sharing.html
11. Pasquier, T., et al.: Data-centric access control for cloud computing. In: Proceedings 21st ACM Symposium on Access Control Models Technology (2016)
12. Recordon, D., Reed, D.: OpenID 2.0: a platform for user-centric identity management. In: Proceedings of the 2nd ACM Workshop on Digital Identity Management, pp. 11–16 (2006)
13. Russo, M., Feng, T.: What B2B can learn from B2C about data privacy and sharing. Abrufdatum **20** (2022). https://www.bcg.com/de-de/publications/2020/imperative-of-data-privacy-plans-for-b2bcompanies-part-4
14. Sun, J., Xiong, H., et al.: Lightweight and privacy-aware fine-grained access control for IoT-oriented smart health. IEEE Internet Things J. **7**(7), 6566–6575 (2020)
15. Wang, X., Yu, G., et al.: Blockchain-enabled fish provenance and quality tracking system. IEEE Internet Things J. **9**(11), 8130–8142 (2022)
16. Xiong, L., Li, F., et al.: An efficient privacy-aware authentication scheme with hierarchical access control for mobile cloud computing services. IEEE Trans. Cloud Comput. **10**(4), 2309–2323 (2020)
17. Yu, G., Zha, X., et al.: Enabling attribute revocation for fine-grained access control in blockchain-IoT systems. IEEE Trans. Eng. Manage. **67**(4), 1213–1230 (2020)

Improving the Accuracy of Transaction-Based Ponzi Detection on Ethereum

Phuong Duy Huynh[1](✉), Son Hoang Dau[1], Xiaodong Li[1], Phuc Luong[2], and Emanuele Viterbo[2]

[1] RMIT University, Melbourne, VIC 3000, Australia
duy.huynh@student.rmit.edu.au
[2] Monash University, Clayton, VIC 3800, Australia

Abstract. The Ponzi scheme, an old-fashioned fraud, is now popular on the Ethereum blockchain, causing considerable financial losses to many crypto investors. A few Ponzi detection methods have been proposed in the literature, most of which detect a Ponzi scheme based on its smart contract source code. This *contract-code-based* approach, while achieving very high accuracy, is *not robust* because a Ponzi developer can fool a detection model by obfuscating the opcode or inventing a new profit distribution logic that cannot be detected. On the contrary, a *transaction-based* approach could improve the robustness of detection because transactions, unlike smart contracts, are harder to be manipulated. However, the current transaction-based detection models achieve fairly *low accuracy*. In this paper, we aim to improve the accuracy of the transaction-based models by employing *time-series features*, which turn out to be crucial in capturing the lifetime behaviour of a Ponzi application but were completely overlooked in previous works. We propose a new set of 85 features (22 known account-based and 63 new time-series features), which allows off-the-shelf machine learning algorithms to achieve up to 30% higher F1-scores compared to existing works.

1 Introduction

In recent years, crypto-crowdfunding via initial coin offerings (ICOs) has become a major fundraising method used by many businesses [1], providing an attractive alternative to traditional stock exchanges. By the end of December 2023, the global market capitalization of blockchains had reached a staggering amount of over $1.7 trillion with more than 2.2 million different cryptocurrencies [10]. However, this phenomenal success of blockchain technology in digital finance has also led to a rising number of cybercrimes. Smart-contract-supporting blockchains have now become a paradise for a plethora of devastating financial scams, such as Ponzi, Honeypots, Phishing, Rug Pull, and Trapdoor [4].

A Ponzi scheme is a scam that promises high returns to investors by using the funds from newcomers to pay earlier investors. This scam collapses when few or

J. K. Liu et al. (Eds.): ProvSec 2024, LNCS 14904, pp. 277–287, 2025.
https://doi.org/10.1007/978-981-96-0957-4_17

no new investors join, making most investors, except for the early ones and the scheme owner, lose their investment. According to Chainanalysis's 2021 Crypto Crime Report [5], from 2017 to 2020, most blockchain frauds were Ponzi schemes, which accounted for nearly $7 billion worth of cryptocurrency in 2019, more than double of all other scams in 2020. The development of Ponzi schemes on Ethereum have attracted some attention from the research community. The first work was done by Bartoletti *et al.* [2], who analysed Solidity *source codes* of smart contracts and proposed four criteria to identify a Ponzi scheme. They classified Ponzi schemes on the Ethereum chain into four different types according to their money distribution logic. They also constructed the very first Ponzi dataset on Ethereum, consisting of 184 Ponzi contracts by manually inspecting their source codes. To automatically detect Ponzi schemes, a number of detection models using machine learning methods [7,8,13,17,18,22] and symbolic execution techniques [9] have been developed in the literature. Most of the machine learning approaches employed both transaction-based features and contract-code-based features in their models to improve detection accuracy. However, a *contract-code-based approach*, while capable of achieving very high accuracy, is *not robust.* A *transaction-based approach* could improve the robustness of detection because transactions, unlike smart contracts, are harder to be manipulated (see Sect. 2). However, the current transaction-based detection models [7,8,18] achieve fairly poor performance.

In this work, we aim to develop more *robust* and *accurate* detection models that only rely on transaction data. To this end, we first analysed the transaction data collected from XBlock [23] of 1395 labelled applications provided in [9] to capture the way Ponzi applications work. We observed that Ponzi and non-Ponzi applications have distinctive behaviours and characteristics and the *time* factor, which has been overlooked in most studies, is crucial in identifying a Ponzi application. Based on such intuition, we designed a new feature list that consists of existing features and novel *time-series features* that capture the behaviours of an application throughout its lifetime. To evaluate the effectiveness of the proposed list of features, we ran different machine learning algorithms on this list and on the existing lists of features used by other studies [7,18], treated as the baselines. Analysing the list of important features from the best performing model (LGBM), we found that *time-series features* indeed contributed to the improvement of the F1-score of the model. The improvement is up to 5.7% as compared to models that only used *account features.* Furthermore, we trimmed our original feature set to obtain a much smaller one consisting of the 85 most important features. It is remarkable that the trimmed feature set outperforms the original one for *all* performance metrics. Last but not least, we demonstrated that our approach can also detect, with high accuracy, *new* types of Ponzi schemes that were not present in the training dataset.

2 Related Works

Existing Ponzi detection models can be divided into two groups, depending on whether they rely on smart contract codes or on transactions.

Contract-Code-Based Approaches: Bartoletti *et al.* [2] first proposed four criteria to detect a Ponzi application by inspecting their contract source codes. However, it turns out that the Solidity source codes of 77.3% contracts on Ethereum are not available [24]. To tackle this drawback and to detect Ponzi automatically, many researchers built Ponzi detection tools based on the frequency distribution of opcodes, which are always available on Ethereum. Chen *et al.* [7,8] proposed a detection tool on opcode features using machine learning models. Their experimental results showed that models using opcode features achieved greater performance than those using account features, which were aggregated from transactions. Wang *et al.* [22] adopted a deep learning technique to build a more accurate detection tool and also used oversampling techniques to deal with an imbalanced dataset. Jung *et al.* [18] and Sun *et al.* [20] focused more on crafting better representative features than improving data quality. A common drawback of previous studies is the *lack of robustness.* As pointed out by Chen *et al.* [9], scammers can use code obfuscation techniques [3] to counter opcode based models (see [9, Section 7.2.1]). Chen *et al.* [9] also proposed in their work a new detection tool called SADPonzi, which was built upon a semantic-aware approach and achieved 100% `Precision` and `Recall`. SADPonzi was proven to be more robust when facing code obfuscation techniques. However, SADPonzi requires a domain expert to analyse a Ponzi working logic to build the corresponding semantic pattern. On top of that, SADPonzi can only effectively detect known Ponzi types with predefined semantics and may fail to detect a new Ponzi variant (see [9, Section 8]).

Transaction-Based Approaches: Transactions are records that save historical activities between an application and its participants. Transaction data was used in some existing works [2,7,8] to capture the differences between Ponzi and non-Ponzi applications. Detection tools based on transaction data are more resilient to scammers' countermeasures because transaction information cannot be modified from the chain. Although scammers can add transaction records, they cannot manipulate transaction data as freely as they can for two reasons. *First*, any participant, not just the creator, can create transactions which is not under the control of the contract creator. *Second*, the cost to create a transaction on the chain is expensive ($14.26 on average per transaction [12]). These factors prevent the Ponzi scammer from manipulating their transaction data arbitrarily to elude detection, e.g. by flooding the system with fake transactions. Despite several advantages, existing transaction-based models [7–9] suffered from *low classification accuracy*. The key reason could be due to the fact that existing works have completely missed the *time dimension* when building their models. *In this work*, we explored the temporal behaviour of Ponzi applications and introduced *time-series features* alongside existing account features, aiming for *both* robustness and accuracy in detection.

3 Transaction-Based Features Extraction

Data Collection. We refined the dataset of labelled Ponzi and non-Ponzi addresses provided in the SADPonzi paper [9] by first downloading and extracting transaction histories of these contracts from the XBlock [23]. We then filtered out unsuccessful transactions that failed for various reasons, such as insufficient gas or errors in the contract codes. We also discarded applications with no transactions or having a lifetime shorter than one day. These are outliers whose behaviours do not resemble the whole group. Even if such an application was a Ponzi, it was also a failed scam. Therefore, removing those applications is important to build a clean dataset, especially for a transaction-based approach. Our refined dataset contains **1182** non-Ponzi and **79** Ponzi applications. The Ponzi types statistics are displayed in Table 1.

Transaction-Based Features Extraction. We classify transaction-based features into two types: *account features* and *time-series features*. Transaction-based detection models proposed so far in the literature only used account features [7], which capture general statistics of the transactions associated with the application, e.g. the total/average investment amount, the final balance of the contract, or the maximum number of payments to an investor. As mentioned in our full paper [16, Section 3.2], using only account features led to rather poor prediction performance. To improve transaction-based Ponzi detection models, it is essential to employ both account features and time-series features. We discuss in detail below how to extract these features.

Account Features: This type of feature captures general information about the contract of interest and has been widely used in previous studies [7,8,18,22]. More specifically, general statistic metrics can be extracted from the set of all relevant transactions to aggregate account features. Although account features are insufficient to capture all behaviours of the Ponzi scheme, they are still very useful in revealing Ponzi's working logic. Therefore, we still include in our list 29 account features [16, Appendix B] introduced earlier in [7,8,18,22].

Time-Series Features: As discussed earlier, time-series features play an important role in identifying Ponzi applications. Unlike account features, they capture the behaviours and activities throughout the application's lifetime. To aggregate time-series features, we *first* partitioned our transactions into several *time intervals* (with interval length of either 12, 24, or 48 h) and built 43 *time series* (see [16, Appendix C]), which measure various aspects of the transactions. These times series form three dimensions, namely, the contract address, the interval, and the data value for that contract in that interval (e.g. account balance). We then use a dimensionality-reduction technique to capture various characteristics (e.g., mean, entropy, spikiness) of aggregated time-series and map the 3-D data into the 2-D space to produce the final time-series features. The creation steps of time series are depicted clearly in [16, Section 3.3].

4 Experiments

4.1 Machine Learning Models and Experiment Settings

Machine Learning Models. To measure the effectiveness of our proposed set of features (account and time-series features), we reused classification methods employed in the previous studies [7,18], namely, Random Forest (RF) [21] and XGBoost (XGB) [6]. In addition, other well-known classification methods such as K-nearest neighbour (KNN) [11], Support vector machine (SVM) [15], and LightGBM (LGBM) [19] were also included in our experiments in order to find the most suitable classification model for the problem.

Evaluation Metrics and Experiment Setting. After account features and time-series features were produced, these two feature groups were used individually and as a combination in different models. To evaluate the performance of our models, we use standard prediction metrics, including Accuracy, Precision, Recall, and F1-score. In our detection experiments, the dataset and their feature groups were split into a training set (80%) and a test set (20%). The former is used for training a detection model, while the latter is used to evaluate the trained model. Moreover, the Ponzi applications in our dataset only occupy 6% of total applications. Therefore, we adopted the well-known oversampling method SMOTE [14] to generate new Ponzi instances that have more than half of the K nearest neighbours being non-Ponzi applications. That helps to enhance the existence of Ponzi applications that are more likely to be misclassified as they are located near the border of the two classes. A classifier then is trained by applying the K-fold cross-validation method with $K = 5$. Finally, a trained model was used to classify the applications in the unseen test dataset. We repeated our experiment process 50 times, and the result was obtained by taking the average.

Table 1. Ponzi types statistics for our refined dataset.

Ponzi type	Number of applications	Percentage
Chain-shaped	68	86%
Tree-shaped	1	1.3%
Handover	1	1.3%
Waterfall	4	5%
Other	5	6.4%

4.2 Experimental Results

Experiment 1 (Feature Sets and Detection Models Evaluation). In this experiment, we aimed to evaluate the effectiveness of our proposed feature list while applying it across diverse machine learning models. As already mentioned, most of the previous studies used either opcode features or both opcode features and account features to build their detection models. Only a few works attempted a transaction-based approach (without using opcode features) separately [7,18]. To show advantages over previous studies, we rerun their approaches on our dataset as the baselines. However, their codes and feature data have not been released to the community, so we re-implemented those models based on the descriptions in their papers, including feature lists and machine learning models. In this experiment, we first evaluated our feature sets corresponding to different time intervals (T = 12, 24, 48 h). We also tested with three feature sets: ACC consists of account features only, TS consists of time-series features only, and ACC-TS consists of both. A comparison of various metrics between our feature sets and the baselines including the feature set from Chen *et al.* [7] and from Jung *et al.* [18] (for more details, see [16, Appendix B]) is provided in Table 2. Finally, we evaluated the detection performance of different machine learning models using our ACC-TS feature sets (see Table 3).

As shown in Table 2, the detection models using our ACC-TS 24 Hrs feature set improved the `F1-score` of the models by Jung *et al.* [18] and Chen *et al.* [7] by 5.7% and 30.3%, respectively. It is also clear that using both account and time-series feature lead to better `Accuracy`, `Precision`, `Recall`, and `F1-score` compared to using individual types of features. Note that when using time-series features (TS) alone, these models already yielded higher `F1-scores` than the baselines. From Table 3, we observed that tree-based classifiers were more efficient in Ponzi detection than other algorithms. More specifically, RF, XGB, and LGBM achieved better `Accuracy`, `Precision`, and `F1-score` values than other classifiers across different ACC-TS feature sets. Among tree-based models, LGBM with the ACC-TS 12 Hrs features achieved the best `F1-score`, `Accuracy`, and `Precision`. Last but not least, our models achieved 11% higher F1-score for RF compared to [18] and 30% higher F1-score for XGB compared to [7].

Table 2. Effectiveness of the new feature set. The asterisk '*' indicates that our feature list outperforms both baselines [7,18].

Features Set	Number of Features	Model	Accuracy	Precision	Recall	**F1**
Jung *et al.* [18]	18	RF	0.966	**0.837**	0.604	0.694
Chen *et al.* [7]	7	XGB	0.942	0.587	0.456	0.499
ACC	29	RF	0.961	0.670	0.823*	0.733*
		XGB	0.965	0.700	0.835*	0.756*
TS	516	RF	0.957	0.638	0.813*	0.710*
		XGB	0.962	0.681	0.830*	0.743*
ACC-TS 12 Hrs	545	RF	0.965	0.706	0.826*	0.755*
		XGB	0.972*	0.752	0.856*	0.797*
ACC-TS 24 Hrs	545	RF	0.967*	0.691	0.840*	0.751*
		XGB	**0.974***	0.743	**0.887***	**0.802***
ACC-TS 48 Hrs	545	RF	0.969*	0.704	0.816*	0.748*
		XGB	0.973*	0.733	0.854*	0.782*

Table 3. Performance comparison among different models and feature sets.

Features Set	Number of Features	Model	Accuracy	Precision	Recall	F1
ACC	29	SVM	0.894	0.378	0.829	0.510
		KNN	0.898	0.388	0.875	0.532
		RF	0.961	0.670	0.823	0.733
		XGB	0.965	0.700	0.835	0.756
		LGBM	0.967	0.717	0.823	0.760
ACC-TS 12 Hrs	545	SVM	0.828	0.282	0.964	0.432
		KNN	0.899	0.392	0.928	0.547
		RF	0.965	0.706	0.826	0.755
		XGB	0.972	0.752	0.856	0.797
		LGBM	**0.975**	**0.779**	0.867	**0.817**
ACC-TS 24 Hrs	545	SVM	0.845	0.281	**0.973**	0.433
		KNN	0.898	0.368	0.918	0.521
		RF	0.967	0.691	0.840	0.751
		XGB	0.974	0.743	0.887	0.802
		LGBM	**0.975**	0.768	0.878	0.812
ACC-TS 48 Hrs	545	SVM	0.824	0.242	0.950	0.380
		KNN	0.886	0.326	0.922	0.476
		RF	0.969	0.704	0.816	0.748
		XGB	0.973	0.733	0.854	0.782
		LGBM	0.974	0.737	0.854	0.784

Experiment 2 (Contribution of Time-Series Features). Next, we investigate how much the newly proposed time-series features have contributed to LGBM's performance, which was the best-performing model. To do this, we first retrieve the list of feature importance from LGBM in the previous experiment. The *importance* of a feature in the LGBM model is defined to be the number of times this feature is used to split the data across all decision trees. In LGBM, an effective feature selection technique, namely Exclusive Feature Bundling (EFB), has been adopted to reduce the number of features without affecting the model's performance. We find that only 205/545 features (516 time-series features and 29 account features) had been used at least once to build a tree in the LGBM detection model. More specifically, these 205 important features consist of 176 time-series features and 29 account features. We sorted these 205 features in descending order of importance. After that, we conducted a detection with the LGBM model using only the $5, 10, 15, \ldots, 205$ most important features among the 205. The experimental results shown in Fig. 1 demonstrate how the `F1-score` values of the prediction were increased as more time-series features were added in the model. We can also observe in the bottom sub-figure that from the top 5

onward, time-series features start to appear. For example, the top 30 contains 15 account features and 15 time-series features.

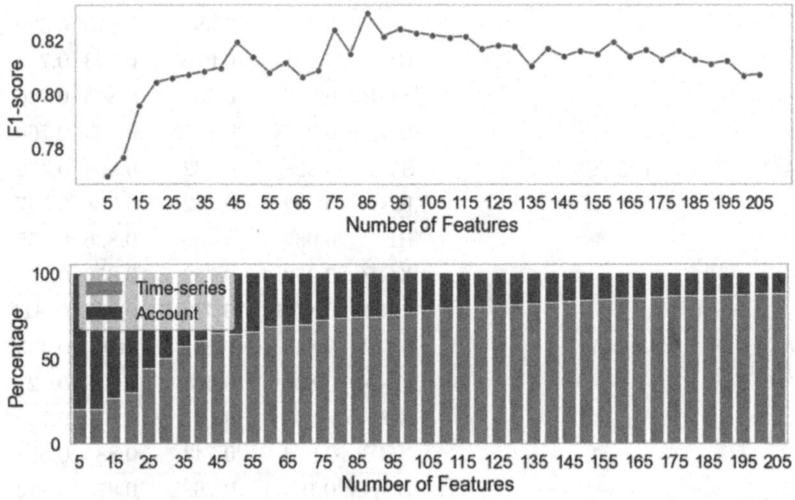

Fig. 1. LGBM's performance when using the most important features (top sub-figure) and the percentages of time-series features among top features (bottom sub-figure).

As can be seen from Fig. 1, the `F1-score` sharply increases when we increase the number of features, especially at the beginning. According to the F1-score in Fig. 1, the value exceeds 0.8 when at least 20 features out of 205 most important features are used, reaching a peak at 0.83 with the top 85 features, which consist of 63 time-series features and 22 account features. Then, the `F1-score` values fluctuate around 0.81 as the number of features further increases. As shown in the bottom sub-figure of Fig. 1, the percentage of time-series features in the important feature list increases in the same direction as `F1-score`. It proves that our proposed time-series features have significantly contributed to the best-performing model (LGBM) in Experiment 1.

According to the above experiment, we refined the ACC-TS 12 Hrs feature set by selecting the top 85 important features of the best model (see [16, Appendix E]), labelled as RF-ACC-TS 12 Hrs. To improve the detection performance, we ran all detection models with selected features instead of the full set of features. Table 4 shows the detection performance results between models that use ACC-TS 12 Hrs and RF-ACC-TS 12 Hrs feature sets. Remarkably, the models using RF-ACC-TS 12 Hrs features show an average improvement of 2.1%, 5.5%, 1.6%, 5.3% for `Accuracy`, `Precision`, `Recall`, and `F1-score`, respectively.

Experiment 3 (Detecting a New Type of Ponzi). To verify whether our classification model using the proposed feature list can detect a new Ponzi type, we conducted the third experiment using the LGBM model as follows. The key idea is to train our model on some types of Ponzi schemes and test it on other types of Ponzi schemes to see if it can still accurately detect these schemes.

Table 4. Our new list of 85 features (RF-ACC-TS) completely outperformed the list of originally proposed 545 features (ACC-TS) for all metrics.

Features Set	NoF	Model	Accuracy	Precision	Recall	F1	Time (Seconds)
ACC-TS 12 h	545	SVM	0.828	0.282	0.964	0.432	0.359
		KNN	0.899	0.392	0.928	0.547	0.094
		RF	0.964	0.696	0.822	0.749	1.439
		XGB	0.972	0.752	0.856	0.797	2.437
		LGBM	0.975	0.779	0.867	0.817	6.493
RF-ACC-TS 12 h	85	SVM	**0.910**	**0.425**	**0.967**	**0.586**	**0.111**
		KNN	**0.909**	**0.422**	**0.963**	**0.582**	**0.063**
		RF	**0.973**	**0.767**	**0.855**	**0.804**	**0.849**
		XGB	**0.973**	**0.770**	**0.857**	**0.803**	**0.715**
		LGBM	**0.977**	**0.795**	**0.876**	**0.830**	**3.076**

We first removed all applications for each known type of Ponzi scheme mentioned in Sect. 3 from our training set. The removed applications were then used in a test set for testing the trained model's new Ponzi detection ability. However, we only removed each of the three Ponzi types (waterfall schemes, tree-shaped schemes, and handover schemes) or all three and not the chain-shaped schemes, which account for 86% of all the Ponzi schemes in the dataset. If we remove all chain-shaped schemes, the number of Ponzi samples becomes too small to learn the scam's behaviours. Furthermore, various test sets with different scam rates were used to test our model in different situations, e.g., with a full-scam test set (100% scams), a balance test set (50% scams), and a few-scam test set (6% scams, similar to our entire dataset's scam rate). Due to the lack of Ponzi (P) applications, we can only decrease the scam rate by increasing the number of non-Ponzi (non-P) applications in test sets.

Table 5. The outcomes of Experiment 3 (Detecting a new type of Ponzi).

Test scheme	Scam rate	#P	#non-P	Accuracy	Precision	Recall	F1-score
Waterfall	100%	4	0	0.91	1.0	0.91	0.94
	50%	4	4	0.94	0.98	0.89	0.93
	6%	4	62	0.97	0.79	0.89	0.83
Tree-shaped	100%	1	0	1.0	1.0	1.0	1.0
	50%	1	1	0.99	0.99	1.0	0.99
	6%	1	15	0.98	0.87	1.0	0.91
Handover	100%	1	0	0.97	0.97	0.97	0.97
	50%	1	1	0.97	0.94	0.95	0.94
	6%	1	15	0.98	0.80	0.94	0.85
All of above	100%	6	0	0.92	1.0	0.92	0.95
	50%	6	6	0.94	0.98	0.91	0.93
	6%	6	94	0.98	0.80	0.91	0.84

The results demonstrated in Table 5, indicate that the detection model can detect over 89% of actual new Ponzi applications in a given test set (greater than 89% of `Recall` value in most cases). Moreover, the `Precision` value is approximately 80% even in test sets with very few scams, and the model also achieved `F1-score` at least 90% in all cases. Analysing the top 30 important features exported from the trained model, we notice that more than 80% of features in the list are aggregated from *transaction volume*, *investment and payment activities*, and *application balance* with 50% of them being time-series features. It is not surprising since those features help discriminate between Ponzi and non-Ponzi applications, as clearly shown in [16, Section 3.2]. That confirms the ability of the transaction-based approach to detect a new Ponzi and the importance of the time factor. Although the dataset we use (from [9]) is not ideal in the sense that there are very few Ponzi applications of types other than the chain-shaped, which may affect the reliability of our third experiment, the outcome still gives strong evidence that a completely new Ponzi type can be detected.

Acknowledgements. This work was funded by the Australia Research Council Discovery Project Grant DP200100731.

References

1. How blockchain technologies impact your business model: Bus. Horiz. **62**(3), 295–306 (2019). https://doi.org/10.1016/j.bushor.2019.01.009
2. Bartoletti, M., Carta, S., Cimoli, T., Saia, R.: Dissecting Ponzi schemes on ethereum: identification, analysis, and impact. Futur. Gener. Comput. Syst. **102**, 259–277 (2020)
3. BiAn: a source code level code obfuscation tool developed for solidity smart contract (2022). https://github.com/xf97/BiAn
4. Chainalysis: Crypto Crime Series: Decoding Ethereum Scams (2019). https://blog.chainalysis.com/reports/ethereum-scams/

5. Chainalysis: The Chainalysis 2021 Crypto Crime Report (2021). https://go.chainalysis.com/2021-Crypto-Crime-Report.html
6. Chen, T., Guestrin, C.: XGBoost: a scalable tree boosting system. In: Proceedings of the 22nd ACM SIGKDD International Conference on Knowledge Discovery and Data Mining, pp. 785–794 (2016)
7. Chen, W., Zheng, Z., Cui, J., Ngai, E., Zheng, P., Zhou, Y.: Detecting Ponzi schemes on ethereum: towards healthier blockchain technology. In: Proceedings of the 2018 World Wide Web Conference, pp. 1409–1418 (2018)
8. Chen, W., Zheng, Z., Ngai, E.C.H., Zheng, P., Zhou, Y.: Exploiting blockchain data to detect smart Ponzi schemes on ethereum. IEEE Access **7**, 37575–37586 (2019)
9. Chen, W., et al.: SADPonzi: detecting and characterizing Ponzi schemes in Ethereum smart contracts. In: Proceedings of the ACM on Measurement and Analysis of Computing Systems, vol. 5, no. 2, pp. 1–30 (2021)
10. Coinmarketcap: Market Cap (2023). https://coinmarketcap.com/charts/
11. Cover, T., Hart, P.: Nearest neighbor pattern classification. IEEE Trans. Inf. Theory **13**(1), 21–27 (1967)
12. Etherscan: Transaction fee (2022). https://etherscan.io/chart/avg-txfee-usd
13. Fan, S., Fu, S., Xu, H., Zhu, C.: Expose your mask: smart Ponzi schemes detection on blockchain. In: 2020 International Joint Conference on Neural Networks (IJCNN), pp. 1–7. IEEE (2020)
14. Han, H., Wang, W.Y., Mao, B.H.: Borderline-SMOTE: a new over-sampling method in imbalanced data sets learning. In: International Conference on Intelligent Computing, pp. 878–887. Springer (2005)
15. Hearst, M.A., Dumais, S.T., Osuna, E., Platt, J., Scholkopf, B.: Support vector machines. IEEE Intell. Syst. Appl. **13**(4), 18–28 (1998)
16. Huynh, P.D., Dau, S.H., Li, X., Luong, P., Viterbo, E.: Improving the accuracy of transaction-based ponzi detection on ethereum. arXiv:2308.16391 (2023)
17. Ibba, G., Pierro, G.A., Di Francesco, M.: Evaluating machine-learning techniques for detecting smart Ponzi schemes. In: 2021 IEEE/ACM 4th International Workshop on Emerging Trends in Software Engineering for Blockchain (WETSEB), pp. 34–40. IEEE (2021)
18. Jung, E., Le Tilly, M., Gehani, A., Ge, Y.: Data mining-based ethereum fraud detection. In: 2019 IEEE International Conference on Blockchain (Blockchain), pp. 266–273. IEEE (2019)
19. Ke, G., et al.: LightGBM: a highly efficient gradient boosting decision tree. In: Advances in Neural Information Processing Systems, vol. 30 (2017)
20. Sun, W., Xu, G., Yang, Z., Chen, Z.: Early detection of smart Ponzi scheme contracts based on behavior forest similarity. In: 2020 IEEE 20th International Conference on Software Quality, Reliability and Security, pp. 297–309. IEEE (2020)
21. Svetnik, V., Liaw, A., Tong, C., Culberson, J.C., Sheridan, R.P., Feuston, B.P.: Random forest: a classification and regression tool for compound classification and QSAR modeling. J. Chem. Inf. Comput. Sci. **43**(6), 1947–1958 (2003)
22. Wang, L., Cheng, H., Zheng, Z., Yang, A., Zhu, X.: Ponzi scheme detection via oversampling-based long short-term memory for smart contracts. Knowl.-Based Syst. **228**, 107312 (2021)
23. XBlock: XBlock: Ethereum On-chain Data (2022). https://xblock.pro/xblock-eth.html
24. Zhou, Y., Kumar, D., Bakshi, S., Mason, J., Miller, A., Bailey, M.: Erays: reverse engineering ethereum's opaque smart contracts. In: 27th USENIX Security Symposium (USENIX Security 2018), pp. 1371–1385 (2018)

A2V: Anonymous and Accountable Voting Framework via Blockchain

Zhimei Sui[1(✉)] and Liangrong Zhao[2]

[1] Shanghai University, Shanghai, China
zmsui@shu.edu.cn
[2] Monash University, Clayton, Australia
Liangrong.zhao@monash.edu

Abstract. This paper introduces, **A2V**, a decentralized e-voting framework utilizing blockchain and Public Key Infrastructure (PKI) for anonymous voting and vote auditing. **A2V** employs a (t, n)-threshold secret sharing scheme to distribute voter identities among an auditing committee, enhancing security and reducing the risk of fraud voting. Votes are encrypted and recorded on an immutable blockchain, with continuous monitoring for anomalies like double voting. If a fraud vote is suspected, the system reconstructs identities from shares to verify voters and address cheaters. We provide necessary pseudocode, smart contract functions, and an illustrative diagram to demonstrate the system's implementation and flow. We also discuss its security and performance to demonstrate that **A2V** can be implemented securely.

Keywords: E-Voting System · Blockchain · Privacy · Accountability

1 Introduction

The e-voting system [2,9,10,15,18,25], introduced decades ago, aims to improve the efficiency, accuracy, and security, reducing human error and fraud while expediting vote tallying. While ensuring voter privacy [10,14] has been a priority to protect individuals from coercion, it often comes at the expense of accountability. This focus can lead to challenges, such as limited verifiability and public skepticism if results differ from expectations. Kohno et al. [2] suggest that a voter-verifiable audit trail is the best solution to these issues, as insufficient accountability measures can increase the risk of fraud without a robust mechanism to detect and address irregularities.

Designed to be both anonymous and accountable, the voting process ensures fairness and credibility. Recent works [11,12,26] utilize blockchain for votes verification and storage, enhancing transparency, security, and trust. Blockchain's decentralized, immutable ledger allows for auditing without compromising voter anonymity. Compared to traditional systems, blockchain-based voting offers greater decentralization, transparency, and robustness, ensuring more fairness and accessibility. Traditional systems rely on central authorities, which can lack transparency and be vulnerable to manipulation.

J. K. Liu et al. (Eds.): ProvSec 2024, LNCS 14904, pp. 288–297, 2025.
https://doi.org/10.1007/978-981-96-0957-4_18

Related Works. Blockchain [1,17] offers a decentralized and tamper-proof ledger, which has been recognized for its potential to transform the voting landscape. It ensures that votes are recorded immutably and transparently, thereby increasing trust in the electoral process. Electronic voting systems based on blockchain [5,11,12,16,19,20,22,26] have undergone significant reorganization to address various challenges and capitalize on the benefits offered by this innovative technology. These protocols [5,11,16,19,22] leverage blockchain's distributed ledger to facilitate secure, transparent, and verifiable voting. They also utilize cryptographic techniques to ensure voter anonymity while enabling transparent tallying and auditing of votes. They use smart contracts play a crucial role in automating voting processes, including voter registration, ballot casting, and result tabulation. Operating on blockchain platforms, these contracts provide tamper-resistant and auditable voting mechanisms. Maintaining voter privacy without compromising the transparency of the election outcome is a primary concern. There are technologies employed for the privacy property, such as zero-knowledge proofs, ring signatures, and homomorphic encryption are explored to strike this delicate balance. While these blockchain-based e-voting protocols ensure privacy and verifiability, our work emphasizes auditing the entire voting process.

This work aims to overcome the limitations of traditional voting methods by using blockchain-based electronic voting systems, leveraging blockchain's unique capabilities to create secure, transparent, and inclusive voting solutions.

Contributions. We summarize our contributions as follows:

1) We propose an innovative e-voting framework, **A2V**, that leverages blockchain to ensure both voter anonymity and accountability. By harnessing the capabilities of blockchain, **A2V** offers a robust and transparent voting solution that addresses the inherent challenges of traditional voting system.
2) We conduct a thorough examination of the security and performance aspects of **A2V**. Through comprehensive analysis and evaluation, we demonstrate the effectiveness of our proposed scheme in safeguarding against potential threats while maintaining efficient voting operations.
3) We acknowledge the limitations of **A2V** and provide the further direction of improvement. By identifying these shortcomings, we pave the way for future research and development effort aimed at enhancing the effectiveness and usability of electronic voting systems based on blockchain technology.

2 Preliminary

This section outlines the essential components of this work.

E-Voting System. We utilize the e-voting system described in the work by Halmarsson et al. [11]. To ensure a secure, transparent, and trustworthy e-voting system, there are several essential requirements should be met: 1) **Prevent Coerced Voting**. The system should ensure that voters are not forced or coerced into voting in a certain way. 2) **Maintain Anonymity**. The system should prevent the traceability of votes to voters' identifying credentials. 3) **Verify Vote Integrity**. The system should ensure and prove to voters that their votes were counted and counted correctly. 4) **Prevent Tampering**. The system should prevent any third party from tampering with votes. 5) **Distributed Control**. The system should not allow a single entity to control the tallying of votes or the determination of election results. 6) **Eligibility Verification**. The system should ensure that only eligible individuals are allowed to vote.

Blockchain. Blockchain is a distributed ledger that records transactions immutably. It supports smart contracts that are automatically executed, eliminating intermediaries and enhancing trust through transparency and verifiability.

Public Key Encryption. Public key encryption [4,24] ensures secure message transmission, with only the private key holder able to decrypt the original message. A public key encryption scheme typically consists of three algorithms:

- $(pk, sk) \leftarrow \text{ENC.GEN}(1^\lambda)$: This algorithm generates a public/private key pair based on the security parameter λ. The public key pk is used for encryption, while the private key sk is used for decryption.
- $c \leftarrow \text{ENC}(pk, m)$: Given the public key pk and a plaintext message m, this algorithm encrypts the message, producing a ciphertext c.
- $m \leftarrow \text{DEC}(sk, c)$: Given the private key sk and a ciphertext c, this algorithm decrypts the ciphertext to recover the original plaintext message m.

Digital Signature. A signature scheme [13,21] allows a signer to authenticate messages, proving their origin and ensuring integrity and non-repudiation. A digital signature scheme consists of three algorithms:

- $(pk, sk) \leftarrow \text{SIG.GEN}(1^\lambda)$: It takes a security parameter λ as input and outputs a key pair (pk, sk).
- $\sigma \leftarrow \text{SIGN}(sk, m)$: It takes the private key sk and a message m as inputs, and outputs a signature σ.
- $0/1 \leftarrow \text{VRFY}(\sigma, pk, m)$: It takes the signature σ, the public key pk, and the message m as inputs, and outputs 1 for accept σ and 0 for rejection.

Secret Sharing. A secret-sharing scheme [3,6,27], distributes a secret among participants, each holding a share. The secret is only reconstructed when enough shares are combined. In a (t, n)-threshold scheme, the secret is divided into n shares, with any t or more shares able to reconstruct it, while fewer than t shares reveal no information, balancing accessibility and security. For example, in Shamir's Secret Sharing scheme [23], to distribute a secret s:

Polynomial Generation: Generate a random polynomial $P(x)$ of degree $t-1$ such that $P(0) = s$.

Share Distribution: Generate n shares $\{(i, P(i))\}$, where i is each participant's identifier.

Share Reconstruction: Executing polynomial interpolation algorithm (e.g., Lagrange interpolation) with at least t shares to find the value of $P(0)$, which is the secret s.

3 Overview

We demonstrate **A2V**, a blockchain-based voting system, in Fig. 1.

In the **initialization phase**, voters require their key pair and register the public key as their real identity on-chain, respectively. Voter registration involves securely registering each voter's identity and distributing the identity to the auditing committee. These shares are encrypted and stored on the blockchain, accessible only to members of a decentralized auditing committee. A voter uses a one-time identity for each voting which is produced from the real identity.

The **voting process** allows voters to cast their votes using their one-time identity, respectively. Each vote will be recorded on the blockchain.

The auditing committee continuously monitors voting transactions on-chain in **the auditing phase**. Automated scripts and smart contracts identify multiple votes cast by the same voter ID, flagging these transactions for further investigation. Upon detection of fraud voting, the auditing committee initiates a review process. If a predefined threshold of committee members (at least t members) agrees that a double voting has occurred, they proceed to disclose their shares of the voter's identity. This disclosure is facilitated by smart contracts that securely collect and combine the shares.

The cheater's identity will be reconstructed and verified against registered identities with at least t valid shares, and then be disclosed to the relevant authorization (same as auditing committee in the diagram). Appropriate actions, such as legal penalties or disqualification, are taken against the cheater.

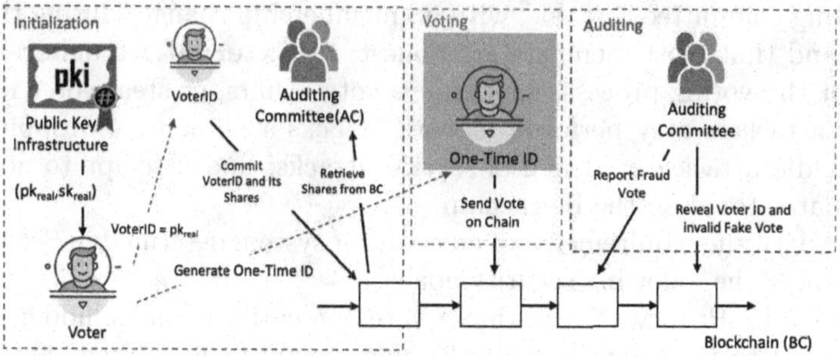

Fig. 1. Diagram of **A2V**

4 Protocol

This section provides a detailed formalization of **A2V**.

4.1 System Model

Components. A2V consists some necessary components listed below:

Blockchain. A decentralized ledger that records votes and related data transparently and immutably. **Smart Contract** is automated programs on the blockchain that enforce voting rules and facilitate auditing.

Auditing Committee. A group of parties that holds shares of voter identities, counts votes, and monitors misbehavior during the voting process. Let PK_{ac} be the public key of the auditing committee, enabling each member to decrypt ciphertexts encrypted under PK_{ac}. This encryption scheme ensures the auditing committee to decrypt ciphertexts only after the voting process, preventing them from biasing the results. This delay decryption feature could be realized by using a timed-release encryption scheme [7] or timed-lock puzzles scheme [8]. Let $\langle acpk_1, \ldots, acpk_n \rangle$ be the public key set of the auditing committee. The public key PK_{ac} and public key set $\langle acpk_1, \ldots, acpk_n \rangle$ are two different public key systems.

Security Model. We then provide the potential threats in the **A2V** system as follows: 1) **Voters** may attempt to cast multiple conflicting votes (e.g., double voting) or collude with others to undermine the voting process. They can attempt to vote more than once or share their voting keys with others; 2) **Auditing Committee Members** may be dishonest and attempt to reveal voters' identities or manipulate the audit process. They can collude with other committee members or external parties. Since they can access to shares of $\mathsf{VoterID}$ and may try to reconstruct $\mathsf{VoterID}$ without meeting the threshold. We assume that the auditing committee is stable, with no membership changes during the voting process, and that most members are honest; 3) **External Attackers** may try to disrupt the voting process, manipulate vote counts, or steal voter identities. External attackers may perform network attacks such as eavesdropping, man-in-the-middle attacks, or denial-of-service attacks, and attempt to access and decrypt data stored on the blockchain.

In line with the requirements of an e-voting system described in Sect. 2, **A2V** needs to meet the following security goals:

1) The Voter Privacy ensures that a voter's identity remains hidden and cannot be linked to their specific vote; 2) The Integrity ensures that all votes are accurately recorded and counted as intended by the voters. This includes but not limited to any honest votes alteration, deletion, or addition; 3) The Accountability requires the voting system to detect and flag any voting irregularities or misbehaviors, and also provide a transparent and verifiable process for auditing votes and identifying misbehavior.

4.2 A2V

A2V consists of three parts: Initialisation, Voting Process, and Auditing Process.

Initialisation. Assuming that there is a trusted Public Key Infrastructure (PKI) for the generation of a pair of secret and public keys $(\mathsf{SK}, \mathsf{PK})$ for all participants. The Initialisation phase initializes the anonymous registration of all potential voters:

1) Each voter interactive with the PKI to generate a pair of secret and public keys ($\mathsf{SK}_{\text{real}}, \mathsf{PK}_{\text{real}}$) for their real identity, and also the corresponding commitment of the $\mathsf{PK}_{\text{real}}$. We use $\mathsf{PK}_{\text{real}}$ as the voter's unique identity VoterID, and denote CVoID the commitment of VoterID.
2) The voter then splits his VoterID into n shares using a (t, n)-threshold secret sharing scheme, where t is the threshold required to reconstruct the VoterID. The vote also encrypts these VoterID shares using the public key of the auditing committee $acpk_i$, respectively.
3) The voter stores the vote $\langle \mathsf{CVoterID}, \mathsf{EVIDshare}_1 \ldots, \mathsf{EVIDshare}_n \rangle$ on Blockchain, by calling the RegisterVoter function, where $\mathsf{EVIDshare}_i$ denotes the ciphertext of i-th Voter ID share $\mathsf{VIDshare}_i$ by using public key $acpk_i$.

Voting Process. Let VoteID denote the unique ID of a voting procedure. The voting process describes how voters cast their votes for VoteID:

1) The voting committee releases the voter list $\langle \mathsf{CVoID}_1, \ldots, \mathsf{CVoID}_m \rangle$, which are selected from the registered voters in the Initialisation phase;
2) Each selected voter generates a one-time voting key-pair ($\mathsf{PK}_{\text{vote}}, \mathsf{SK}_{\text{vote}}$) from his real key pair and the current vote id VoteID. The public one-time key pair is also his one-time vote id, denoted as OTVoID. Each one-time voting ID is linkable to the shares held by the auditing committee. Therefore, if the OTVoID behaves dishonestly, the auditing committee can reveal the corresponding shares to reconstruct the voter's real identity.
3) The voter casts their vote with the corresponding signature σ by using the voting secret key $\mathsf{SK}_{\text{vote}}$. The vote is formed as $\langle \mathsf{OTVoID}, \sigma, \mathsf{EVD} \rangle$, where EVD is the ciphertext of this vote, encrypted using PK_{ac}.
4) The function *CastVote* checks the vote validation by using $\mathsf{PK}_{\text{vote}}$.
5) If fraud voting is detected, the transaction is reverted. Otherwise, the vote is recorded on the blockchain.

Since the vote description is encrypted, the blockchain maintainers only check whether the one-time VoteID has been used, but not the vote's correctness.

Auditing Process. The Auditing Process ensures the integrity of the voting system through continuous **monitoring** and **auditing**. The auditing committee monitors all on-chain votes. If fraud votes, such as double votes, are detected, all honest members of the auditing committee initiate the **report process**.

Monitoring: 1) After the voting process, the auditing committee continuously scans and decrypts on-chain votes; 2) If an anomaly is detected (such as double voting), the vote is flagged, and the InitiateAudit process is triggered.

Auditing: 1) Any of the honest auditing committee can trigger the *InitiateAudit* function to request the shares of the voter's VoterID from the auditing committee; 2) Honest members in the auditing committee sends their shares of the cheated voter to the authority; 3) The voter's VoterID can be reconstructed by the authority using the *CombineShares* function with at least t shares. 4) The real identity associated with the VoterID is verified; 5) If the identity is valid and fraud voting is confirmed, the *ReportCheater* function is called.

Reporting: 1) The *ReportCheater* function invalidates votes cast by the identified cheater; 2) The incident is recorded, and authority closes the audit.

We present the pseudocode of **A2V** in Algorithm 1, and the required smart contracts in Algorithm 2 with the following functions:

RegVoter(VoterID,EVIDshares): Stores the VoterID and its shares EVIDshares on the blockchain.

CastVote(VoterID, Vote): Checks for double votes and records the encrypted vote on the blockchain.

MonitorVotes(VoteList[]): Continuously monitors for new votes and detects anomalies.

InitiateAudit($PK_{\mathbf{vote}}$): Initiates the audit process if an anomaly is detected, requesting and combining shares to reconstruct the VoterID.

CombineShares(Shares[]): Reconstructs the VoterID from the share set Shares[].

ReportCheater(VoterID): Invalidates the cheater's votes, records the incident on the blockchain, and closes this auditing.

Algorithm 1. Voting Process Algorithm

```
Initialisation
(SK_real, PK_real) ← PKI.GENERATE(1^λ)
CVoID ← COMMIT(PK_real)
VIDshares ← SPLTSECRET(VoterID, t, n)
for i ∈ 1...n do
    EVIDshare_i ← ENC(acpk_i, VIDshare_i)
end for
Call RegVoter(⟨CVoID, EVIDshare_1, ..., EVIDshare_n⟩)
Voting Process
VoterList ← GETCONFIRMEDVOTERS()
for each CVoID_i ∈ VoterList do
    (PK_vote, SK_vote) ← GENOTKEYPAIR(PK_real, SK_real)
    OTVoID ← PK_vote
    σ ← SIGN(SK_vote, VoteID)
    EVD ← ENC(PK_ac, VoteDescription)
    Call CastVote(⟨OTVoID, σ, EVD⟩)
end for
Auditing Process
for each new vote Vote_i on the blockchain: do
    VoteList[i] = Vote_i
end for
Once the Voting process end:
    Call IsCheat = MonitorVotes(VoteList[])
if IsCheat!=⊥: then
    Call CombineShares(Shares[])
end if
```

5 Security Discussion

This section provides a security discussion on the following properties.

Voter Privacy ensures that voters cannot be linked to their votes, preventing coercion and vote buying. In **A2V**, each voter's real identity is securely shared to

---

Algorithm 2. Smart Contract

1: function **RegVoter**(CVoID, EVIDshares):
2: Store CVoID and EVIDshares on the blockchain

3: function **CastVote**(OTVoID, σ, VD):
4: if HASVOTED(OTVoID) then
5:     Revert transaction
6: else
7:     Validate σ with PK_{vote}
8:     if ISVALID(σ) then
9:         Store $\langle$OTVoID, σ, EVD$\rangle$ on the blockchain
10:     else
11:         Revert transaction
12:     end if
13: end if

14: function **MonitorVotes**(VoteList[]):
15: for each vote in VoteList[i] do
16:     VD $\leftarrow$ DECRYPT(SK_{ac}, EVD)
17:     if CHECKDUPLICATECANDIDATES(VD) then
18:         Call InitiateAudit(OTVoID)
19:         Obtain Shares[]

20:         Return Shares[]
21:     end if
22: end for
23: Return $\perp$

24: function **InitiateAudit**(OTVoID):
25: Request shares of VoterID
26: Return Shares[]

27: function **CombineShares**(SHARES[]):
28: VoterID $\leftarrow$ RECONSTRUCT(SHARES[])
29: Verify real identity associated with VoterID
30: if identity is valid and fraud voting is confirmed
    then
31:     Call ReportCheater(VoterID)
32: end if

33: function **ReportCheater**(VoterID):
34: Invalidate all votes cast by the cheater
35: Record the incident on the blockchain
36: Close the auditing process

---

the auditing committee and committed on blockchain. The real identity is used only to generate the voting key pair. A commitment scheme securely hides the committed messages, requiring at least t shares to reconstruct the original secret. This prevents malicious parties from inferring information about the committed identity or encrypted shares. A voter's real identity remains unlinked to their vote on the blockchain.

Integrity ensures that all votes are accurately recorded and counted. Since **A2V** uses Blockchain to record all votes, Blockchain's immutable nature guarantees that once votes are recorded, they cannot be altered or deleted. **A2V** prevents abnormal votes, such as double votes, by checking if a voter has cast a vote without following the voting rules using their unique voting public key.

Accountability is maintained by identifying misbehaving voters while preserving the anonymity of compliant ones. If anomalies like double voting are detected, the auditing committee can reconstruct the VoterID from shares on the blockchain. This detection and auditing process is transparent and verifiable by all participants, ensuring system trust.

6   Performance

This section provides the performance discussion of **A2V**.

Computational Overhead. The generation of key pairs and casting a vote involve standard cryptographic operation (e.g., asymmetric encryption), which are computationally feasible within the modern hardware. The use of Shamir's Secret Sharing introduces additional computational steps for splitting and reconstructing VoterID. These operations are efficient and can be performed quickly.

Storage Overhead. Blockchain Storage: Each vote, along with the necessary metadata, is stored on the blockchain. The storage requirements increase linearly with the number of voters and votes. Share Storage: Storing VoterID shares also adds to the storage requirements. However, since each share is small and the number of shares is fixed, this overhead is manageable.

Network Latency. In the voting process, the network latency is introduced during the submission and confirmation of the votes on the blockchain. This latency is inherent to blockchain systems and depends on the network's consensus mechanism. In the auditing process, the latency occurs when the auditing committee retrieves shares from the blockchain, which introduces additional latency. The impact is minimized by the efficient retrieval and reconstruction protocol.

Scalability. **A2V**'s scalability depends on the underlying blockchain platform. High throughput and fast consensus mechanism improve scalability. The use of a decentralized auditing committee allows for parallel processing of audits, enhancing the system ability to handle large-scale elections.

7 Limitations and Future Direction

Limitations. The voter privacy and accountability of **A2V** are based on the assumption that the majority of auditing committee members are honest and will diligently monitor and scan votes on the blockchain, reporting any abnormal votes. Ensuring that this "honest majority" assumption is maintained remains an open challenge and a potential vulnerability in the system.

Future Directions. The reputation system could be used to track behavior and penalize misbehavior for both voters and the auditing committee to incentivize honesty and improve system integrity. Additionally, interdisciplinary collaboration among researchers, policymakers, technologists, and stakeholders is essential for addressing challenges and refining electronic voting systems.

In addition, **A2V** provides a framework for an anonymous and auditable voting system over blockchain. Some internal algorithms, such as GenOTKeyPair$(\cdot,\cdot)$, GetConfirmedVoters(), etc., must be carefully initialized before use. The development of feasible algorithms to enable the implementation of **A2V** is an open question and requires futher research.

References

1. Ethereum. https://ethereum.org/en/
2. Analysis of an electronic voting system. In: 2004 Proceedings of the IEEE Symposium on Security and Privacy, pp. 27–40. IEEE (2004)
3. Beimel, A.: Secret-sharing schemes: a survey. In: International Conference on Coding and Cryptology, pp. 11–46. Springer (2011)
4. Bellare, M., Boldyreva, A., Micali, S.: Public-key encryption in a multi-user setting: security proofs and improvements. In: Advances in Cryptology-EUROCRYPT 2000: International Conference on the Theory and Application of Cryptographic Techniques, Bruges, Belgium, 14–18 May 2000, pp. 259–274. Springer (2000)

5. Benabdallah, A., Audras, A., Coudert, L., El Madhoun, N., Badra, M.: Analysis of blockchain solutions for e-voting: a systematic literature review. IEEE Access **10**, 70746–70759 (2022)
6. Chattopadhyay, A.K., Saha, S., Nag, A., Nandi, S.: Secret sharing: a comprehensive survey, taxonomy and applications. Comput. Sci. Rev. **51**, 100608 (2024)
7. Choi, G., Vaudenay, S.: Timed-release encryption with master time bound key. In: You, I. (ed.) Information Security Applications, pp. 167–179. Springer, Cham (2020)
8. Dujmovic, J., Garg, R., Malavolta, G.: Time-lock puzzles with efficient batch solving. Cryptology ePrint Archive, Paper 2023/1582 (2023). https://eprint.iacr.org/2023/1582
9. Gritzalis, D.A.: Principles and requirements for a secure e-voting system. Comput. Secur. **21**(6), 539–556 (2002)
10. Hanifatunnisa, R., Rahardjo, B.: Blockchain based e-voting recording system design. In: 2017 11th International Conference on Telecommunication Systems Services and Applications (TSSA), pp. 1–6. IEEE (2017)
11. Hjálmarsson, F.Þ., Hreiðarsson, G.K., Hamdaqa, M., Hjálmtỳsson, G.: Blockchain-based e-voting system. In: 2018 IEEE 11th International Conference on Cloud Computing (CLOUD), pp. 983–986. IEEE (2018)
12. Jafar, U., Aziz, M.J.A., Shukur, Z.: Blockchain for electronic voting system-review and open research challenges. Sensors **21**(17), 5874 (2021)
13. Katz, J.: Digital Signatures, vol. 1. Springer, Heidelberg (2010)
14. Kiayias, A., Korman, M., Walluck, D.: An internet voting system supporting user privacy. In: 2006 22nd Annual Computer Security Applications Conference (ACSAC 2006), pp. 165–174. IEEE (2006)
15. Kumar, S., Walia, E.: Analysis of electronic voting system in various countries. Int. J. Comput. Sci. Eng. **3**(5), 1825–1830 (2011)
16. Mookherji, S., Vanga, O., Prasath, R.: Blockchain-based e-voting protocols. In: Blockchain Technology for Emerging Applications, pp. 239–266. Elsevier (2022)
17. Nakamoto, S.: Bitcoin: a peer-to-peer electronic cash system (2008)
18. Ofori-Dwumfuo, G., Paatey, E.: The design of an electronic voting system. Res. J. Inf. Technol. **3**(2), 91–98 (2011)
19. Pandey, A., Bhasi, M., Chandrasekaran, K.: VoteChain: a blockchain based e-voting system. In: 2019 Global Conference for Advancement in Technology (GCAT), pp. 1–4. IEEE (2019)
20. Pawlak, M., Poniszewska-Marańda, A.: Trends in blockchain-based electronic voting systems. Inf. Process. Manage. **58**(4), 102595 (2021)
21. PUB, F.: Digital signature standard (DSS). Fips pub, pp. 186–192 (2000)
22. Sallal, M., de Fréin, R., Malik, A.: PVPBC: privacy and verifiability preserving e-voting based on permissioned blockchain. Future Internet **15**(4) (2023). https://doi.org/10.3390/fi15040121, https://www.mdpi.com/1999-5903/15/4/121
23. Shamir, A.: How to share a secret. Commun. ACM **22**(11), 612–613 (1979). https://doi.org/10.1145/359168.359176
24. Shoup, V.: A proposal for an ISO standard for public key encryption. Cryptology ePrint Archive (2001)
25. Taban, H., Konde, S., Sebwato, N.: Design and implementation of electronic voting system (2017)
26. Taş, R., Tanrıöver, Ö.Ö.: A systematic review of challenges and opportunities of blockchain for e-voting. Symmetry **12**(8), 1328 (2020)
27. Yang, C.C., Chang, T.Y., Hwang, M.S.: A (t, n) multi-secret sharing scheme. Appl. Math. Comput. **151**(2), 483–490 (2004)

Quantum Safe Computation-Friendly Identity-Binding Password Authenticated Key Exchange

Pratima Jana[1(✉)], Ratna Dutta[1], and Cong Zuo[2]

[1] Department of Mathematics, Indian Institute of Technology Kharagpur, Kharagpur 721302, India
pratimajanahatiary@kgpian.iitkgp.ac.in, ratna@maths.iitkgp.ac.in
[2] School of Cyberspace Science and Technology, Beijing Institute of Technology, Beijing 100081, China

Abstract. *Password Authenticated Key Exchange* (PAKE) protocols are of paramount importance in applications like the Internet of Things (IoT) and wireless networking ensures the security of communication systems by enabling two parties to establish a shared secret key using only a low-entropy password. Recent advances in PAKE protocols have aimed to provide stronger security assurances including resilience against offline dictionary attacks, replay attacks, compromise attacks for both parties (client and server), pre-computation attacks, mutual authentication and perfect forward secrecy. Despite several improvements, challenges persist in both security and efficiency for existing PAKE proposals. To address these challenges, Cremers et al. (Crypto '22) introduced the concept of identity-binding PAKE. None of the existing identity-binding PAKE is post-quantum secure. In response to these challenges, our contribution aims to bridge the gap in practical and secure post-quantum identity-binding PAKE. Our work proposes a post-quantum secure identity-binding PAKE protocols, LPAKE with enhanced security. Our lattice-based protocol LPAKE is secure based on the *Module Pairing with Errors* (MPWE) assumption and the *Decision Module Learning with Errors* (DMLWE) assumption. We present comprehensive security proof in a conventional game-based indistinguishability security model. Through rigorous performance evaluations, the paper demonstrates that the proposed PAKE scheme exhibits notable advantages in terms of total computation cost with enhanced security properties compared to existing identity-binding PAKE protocols.

Keywords: Post-quantum Cryptography · Authenticated Key Exchange · Lattice-based Cryptography · Internet of Things

1 Introduction

Passwords are extensively employed as a primary method for authentication across a diverse range of applications. They serve as the means for logging into

J. K. Liu et al. (Eds.): ProvSec 2024, LNCS 14904, pp. 298–309, 2025.
https://doi.org/10.1007/978-981-96-0957-4_19

websites, facilitating secure file transfers, accessing WiFi networks, connecting to mesh networks, safeguarding encrypted backups and remotely logging into servers. However, this widespread reliance on passwords also presents significant security challenges. A prominent issue is the prevalence of weak or easily guessable passwords, as it is vulnerable to brute force or dictionary attacks. To address this issue, Bellovin and Merritt [5] introduced *Password Authenticated Key Exchange* (PAKE) protocols in 1992. A PAKE protocol enables two parties to authenticate each other over an insecure channel and establish a shared high entropy session key from a shared low entropy secret or password that they can agree on over a phone or in a physical meeting.

Over the past three decades, numerous PAKE proposals have been introduced following the first work of Bellovin and Merritt [5]. In traditional PAKE, both parties store passwords directly on their devices, which poses security risks if either party's storage is compromised. To mitigate the risks inherent in traditional PAKE, in 1993 the concept of asymmetric PAKE (aPAKE) was put forward by Bellovin and Merritt to safeguard servers from compromise. However, aPAKE is vulnerable to pre-computation attacks, where an attacker pre-computes a table of possible passwords and their corresponding intermediate values, enabling quick password derivation if the server is compromised. Jarecki et al. [7] highlighted vulnerabilities against pre-computation attacks in aPAKE and introduced *strong asymmetric* PAKE (saPAKE) in 2018 which serves as a remedy for this vulnerability. Nonetheless, it is important to note that only the server is safeguarded against pre-computation attacks in a saPAKE protocol. This asymmetry is not universally applicable as some use cases explicitly require symmetric settings. Prime examples of such symmetric settings are found in wireless networking and the *Internet of Things* (IoT). In an IoT environment, the information stored on the client device is at risk of compromise, which leaves the client side vulnerable. Consequently, achieving the privacy of both parties' passwords is a critical issue that can't be ignored. Another issue is that PAKE protocols permit an attacker who corrupts a party to learn a password and subsequently impersonate any party using the same password. In a setting where multiple devices share the same password, this results in catastrophic impersonation following the compromise of even a single device. To address this, Cremers et al. [13] proposed the notion of identity-binding PAKE (iPAKE) in 2022. However, the protocol requires a large number of pairing operations and hashing onto groups, which results in significant computing costs. Moreover, identity privacy is lacking in this scheme. Recognizing these limitations, Lian et al. [12] proposed an identity-binding PAKE solution that relies on the *Discrete Logarithm problem* (DLP). However, this poses security concerns with the development of quantum computing techniques. Nowadays, there has been a rapid race for quantum technology in academia and industry due to the advancement of quantum computers.

PAKE in the Post-quantum World. A limited number of PAKE schemes are designed to be secure in a post-quantum setting. In 2009, Katz and Vaikuntanathan [9] proposed the first quantum secures PAKE in the lattice-based setting. There were subsequent works [11] based on lattice using smooth projective hashing. In 2017, Ding et al. [6] proposed RLWE based PAKE schemes and Ren and Gu [14] extended this work in the field of module lattice. In 2019, Terada and Yoneyama [15] introduced two PAKE protocols based on isogeny-based cryptography. However, subsequent analysis by Azarderakhsh et al. [3] in 2020 revealed vulnerabilities in the proposed protocols [15], specifically susceptibility to offline dictionary attacks. In 2022, Abdalla et al. [1] presented two isogeny-based provably secure PAKE. These protocols are proven to be secure in the *Random Oracle Model* (ROM) and rely on commutative group action for their security guarantees. None of the existing post-quantum secure PAKE schemes are identity-binding PAKE and pre-computation attack resistant.

Contribution. Computational efficiency makes a PAKE a highly suitable cryptographic tool for securing the IoT ecosystem. A PAKE should typically include several key security features to ensure comprehensive security. Offline dictionary attack resilience defends against exhaustive password searches, while replay attack resilience prevents interception and re-transmission of valid authenticated messages. Compromise resilience protects if one party's password is compromised. Mutual authentication guarantees that both parties securely confirm each other's identities during the authentication process. Perfect forward secrecy secures past session keys despite compromising the password file. Pre-computation attack resilience prevents an attacker from pre-creating tables for faster password guessing. Identity privacy ensures the privacy of user identities during the authentication process. Post-quantum cryptography offers robust resistance against quantum threats and guarantees the reliability of communication and integrity with the advancement of quantum computing capability. The somewhat unsatisfactory state of the art motivates our search for a post-quantum secure identity-binding PAKE with compact storage size and low computation cost providing enhanced security guarantees. The key contributions to this work are specifically listed below.

- We propose a lattice-based identity-binding PAKE schemes, LPAKE. It comprises an offline registration phase and an interactive online phase.
- LPAKE is secure based on the *Module Pairing with Errors* (MPWE) assumption and *Decision Module Ring Learning with Errors* (DMLWE) assumption. We present a thorough security analysis in a standard security framework for our scheme LPAKE following the security model of [12] that addresses offline dictionary attacks, replay attacks, compromise attacks for both parties (client and server) and perfect forward secrecy. Additionally, our construction satisfies mutual authentication, resistance to pre-computation attacks and identity privacy.
- In Table 1, we compare the computation, communication and storage cost of LPAKE with existing identity-binding PAKE. During the offline password file derivation phase, our PAKE protocol and that of [12] necessitate only two hash value calculations while [13] requires three additional exponentiation, making it significantly more expensive. The PAKE protocols in [12,13] require a minimum of six exponentiations during the online key exchange while LPAKE requires twenty multiplications over R_q. Thus, LPAKE outperforms compared

to existing PAKE protocols in Table 1 in terms of computational complexity. The communication and storage cost of our scheme is similar to those of [12,13]. However, the PAKE of [12,13] do not exhibit post-quantum security, whereas LPAKE can resist quantum computer threats.

- All the schemes presented in the table satisfy offline dictionary attacks, replay attacks, compromise attacks for both parties (client and server) and pre-computation. The PAKE proposed in [13] lacks mutual authentication, identity privacy, perfect forward secrecy and post-quantum security. The PAKE proposed in [12] exhibits resilience against pre-computation, mutual authentication, identity privacy and perfect forward secrecy, but it is not post-quantum secure. Our protocol fulfill all the properties and demonstrate superiority over other related protocols in terms of security.

Table 1. Comparison of the computation, communication and storage cost of the existing identity-binding PAKE.

Scheme	Offline Phase	Online Phase			Communication Cost	Storage Cost	Security Assumption
		Sender	Receiver	Total			
[13]	3E + 2H	3E + 1H + 3P	3E + 1H + 3P	6E + 2H + 6P	$2\|R_H\| + 4\|G\|$	$3\|G\| + 1\|\Lambda\|$	GGM
[12]	2H	3E + 7H	3E + 7H	6E + 14H	$4\|G\| + 2\|\mathcal{C}\| + 2\|T\|$	$1\|\mathbb{Z}_q\| + 1\|\Lambda\|$	CDH, DL
LPAKE	2H	10M + 7H	10M + 7H	20M + 14H	$4\|R_q\| + 2\|\mathcal{C}\| + 1\|T\| + 1\|\mathbb{Z}_g^n\|$	$1\|R_q\| + 1\|\Lambda\|$	MPWE, DMLWE

H denotes the number of hash operations, E denotes the number of modular exponentiation in the group G, P denotes the number of bilinear pairing operation, M denotes the number of multiplication of elements within the set $R_q = \frac{\mathbb{Z}_q[x]}{(x^n+1)}$ where n and q are integers. GGM: Generic Group Model, CDH: Computational Diffie-Hellman assumption, DL: Discrete Logarithmic problem, MPWE: Module Pairing with Errors assumption, DMLWE: Decision Module Learning with Errors assumption

2 Preliminary

Notations. Let λ represent the security parameter. We denote $a \xleftarrow{\$} A$ to address a is uniformly sampling from the set A and the sampling from the distribution χ is denoted by $a \leftarrow \chi$. When $y \leftarrow \mathcal{A}$, it signifies that y is an output of algorithm $\mathcal{A}$. We use the usual notation $\mathbb{Z}$ and $\mathbb{R}$ to denote the set of integers and real numbers respectively. $\mathbb{Z}[x]$ and $\mathbb{Z}_q[x]$ symbolize the ring of polynomials over $\mathbb{Z}$ and $\mathbb{Z}_q$ respectively. R and R_q represent the ring $\frac{\mathbb{Z}[x]}{(x^n+1)}$ and $\frac{\mathbb{Z}_q[x]}{(x^n+1)}$ respectively. We consider all vectors $\overrightarrow{\mathbf{s}} \in R_q^d$ as a $d \times 1$ column vector throughout this paper. The modulus of integer $e \in \mathbb{Z}$ is represented by $|e|$. For any real number x, $\lfloor x \rfloor$ denotes the largest integer that is less than or equal to x and $\lfloor x \rceil = \lfloor x + \frac{1}{2} \rfloor$. The Euclidean norm for $\boldsymbol{a} = \sum_{i=0}^{n-1} a_i x^i = (a_0, \ldots, a_{n-1}) \in R_q$ is denoted by $||\boldsymbol{a}|| = \sqrt{a_0^2 + \ldots + a_{n-1}^2}$ and $||\mathbf{a}||_\infty = \max\{|a_0|, \ldots, |a_{n-1}|\}$. We consider the notation $s_1||s_2$ to denote the concatenation of two strings s_1 and s_2. For $\boldsymbol{a} = \sum_{i=0}^{n-1} a_i x^i = (a_0, \ldots, a_{n-1})$, $\boldsymbol{b} = \sum_{i=0}^{n-1} b_i x^i = (b_0, \ldots, b_{n-1}) \in R_q$. We define $\boldsymbol{a} \cdot \boldsymbol{b} = (\sum_{i=0}^{n-1} a_i x^i)(\sum_{i=0}^{n-1} b_i x^i) \pmod{x^n + 1} \in R_q$. The distance between two elements $a, b \in \mathbb{Z}_q$ is defined as $|a-b|_q = \min\{(a-b) \pmod q, (b-a) \pmod q\}$. The distance between $\mathbf{w} = \sum_{i=0}^{n-1} w_i x^i = (w_0, \ldots, w_{n-1}) \in R_q$, $\mathbf{v} = \sum_{i=0}^{n-1} v_i x^i = (v_0, \ldots, v_{n-1}) \in R_q$ is defined as $|\mathbf{w} - \mathbf{v}|_q = \max\{|w_1 - v_1|_q, |w_2 - v_2|_q, \cdots, |w_{n-1} - v_{n-1}|_q\}$.

2.1 Key Consensus with Noise

A Key Consensus with Noise (KCN) scheme KCN = (Setup, Con, Rec) consists of three polynomial time algorithms designed to enable two users (denoted as U_A and U_B) to compute a common secret. Specifically, if the user U_B computes secret $\mathbf{k}$ by using Con with an input $\boldsymbol{\sigma}_B \in R_q$ then the U_B can calculate the same secret $\mathbf{k}$ by using Rec on the input of $\boldsymbol{\sigma}_A \in R_q$ under the condition $|\boldsymbol{\sigma}_A - \boldsymbol{\sigma}_B|_q \leq \ell$. In the following, we extend the KCN scheme over $\mathbb{Z}_q$ presented by Jin et al. [8] to KCN scheme over $\mathbb{Z}_q^n$.

Construction of Optimally-Balanced Key Consensus with Noise (OKCN):

- $\mathsf{Setup}(1^\lambda) \to$ params: A trusted authority selects the positive integers q, m, g, ℓ satisfying $2 \leq m, g \leq q$ and $0 \leq \ell \leq \lfloor \frac{q}{2} \rfloor$, computes $q' = \mathsf{lcm}(q, m)$, $\alpha = \frac{q'}{q}$, $\beta = \frac{q'}{m}$, sets aux $=(q', \alpha, \beta)$ and the public parameter params $= (q, m, g, \ell,$ aux) publishes.
- Con(params, $\boldsymbol{\sigma}_B = (\sigma_0^B, \ldots, \sigma_{n-1}^B)) \to (\mathbf{k}_B, \boldsymbol{v})$: On input of $\boldsymbol{\sigma}_B = (\sigma_0^B, \cdots, \sigma_{n-1}^B) \in \mathbb{Z}_q^n$ and the public parameter params $= (q, m, g, \ell,$ aux $=(q', \alpha, \beta))$, the user U_B runs the probabilistic polynomial time (PPT) conciliation algorithm Con performs the following steps:
  - *i.* Uniformly samples e_i from $[-\lfloor \frac{\alpha-1}{2} \rfloor, \lfloor \frac{\alpha}{2} \rfloor]$ and computes $\sigma_i = (\alpha\sigma_i^B + e_i) \pmod{q'}$ and $v_i' = \sigma_i \pmod \beta$ for $i = 0, \ldots, n-1$.
  - *ii.* Sets $\mathbf{k}_B = (k_0^B, \ldots, k_{n-1}^B)$ and $\boldsymbol{v} = (v_0^B, \ldots, v_{n-1}^B)$ where $k_i^B = \lfloor \frac{\sigma_i}{\beta} \rfloor \in \mathbb{Z}_m$ and $v_i = \lfloor \frac{v_i' g}{\beta} \rfloor \in \mathbb{Z}_g$ for $i = 0, \ldots, n-1$ by extracting q', α, β from aux.
  - *iii.* The user U_B publishes $\boldsymbol{v}$ and keeps $\mathbf{k}_B$ to itself.
- Rec(params, $\boldsymbol{\sigma}_A = (\sigma_0^A, \ldots, \sigma_{n-1}^A), \boldsymbol{v} = (v_0, \ldots, v_{n-1})) \to \mathbf{k}_A$: The user U_A takes as input the public parameter params $= (q, m, g, \ell,$ aux $=(q', \alpha, \beta))$, two vectors $\boldsymbol{\sigma}_A = (\sigma_0^A, \ldots, \sigma_{n-1}^A) \in \mathbb{Z}_q^n$ and $\boldsymbol{v} = (v_0, \ldots, v_{n-1}) \in \mathbb{Z}_g^n$ and executes the following steps:
  - *i.* Sets $\mathbf{k}_A = (k_0^A, \ldots, k_{n-1}^A)$ by computing $k_i^A = \lfloor \frac{\alpha\sigma_i^A}{\beta} - \frac{v_i + \frac{1}{2}}{g} \rceil \pmod m$ for $i = 0, \ldots, n-1$..
  - *ii.* The user U_A keeps $\mathbf{k}_A \in \mathbb{Z}_m^n$ secret to itself.

Definition 2.1 (Correctness). *A* KCN *scheme is correct if it holds* $\mathbf{k}_A = \mathbf{k}_B$ *for any* $\boldsymbol{\sigma}_A, \boldsymbol{\sigma}_B \in \mathbb{Z}_q^n$ *such that* $|\boldsymbol{\sigma}_A - \boldsymbol{\sigma}_B|_q \leq \ell$.

Definition 2.2 (Security [8]**).** *A* KCN *scheme is secure if* $\mathbf{k}_B$ *and* $\boldsymbol{v}$ *are independent and* $\mathbf{k}_B$ *is uniformly distributed over* $\mathbb{Z}_m^n$, *whenever* $\boldsymbol{\sigma}_B \xleftarrow{\$} \mathbb{Z}_q^n$.

Lemma 2.1 ([8]). *For any $x, y, q, \ell \in \mathbb{Z}$ where $q \geq 1$ and $\ell \geq 0$, if $|x-y|_q \leq \ell$, then there exists $\theta \in \mathbb{Z}$ and $\delta \in [-\ell, \ell]$ such that $x = y + \theta q + \delta$.*

Theorem 2.2 ([8]). *If $|\boldsymbol{\sigma}_A - \boldsymbol{\sigma}_B| < \ell$ and the system parameters satisfy $(2\ell+1)m < p(1-\frac{1}{g})$ where $m \geq 2$ and $g \geq 2$. Then, the* OKCN *scheme is the correct meaning $\mathbf{k}_A = \mathbf{k}_B$.*

Theorem 2.3 ([8]). OKCN *is secure, i.e. if $\boldsymbol{\sigma}_B \xleftarrow{\$} \mathbb{Z}_q^n$ then $\mathbf{k}_B$ and $\mathbf{v} \in \mathbb{Z}_g^n$ are independent and $\mathbf{k}_B$ is uniform over $\mathbb{Z}_m^n$, where the probability is taken over the sampling of $\boldsymbol{\sigma}_B$ and the random coins used by* Con.

2.2 Module Lattice-Based Hard Problem

Definition 2.3 (Centered Binomial Distribution [2]**).** *For each positive integer η, the centered binomial distribution B_η of width η has support $\{-\eta, -\eta+1, \ldots, -1, 0, 1, \ldots, \eta-1, \eta\}$ and defined as $B_\eta(k) = \binom{2\eta}{\eta+k}2^{-2\eta}$ for $k \in [-\eta, \eta] \cap \mathbb{Z}$.*

The distribution B_η is symmetric around zero with mean zero and the variance $\mathsf{var}(B_\eta) = \frac{\eta}{2}$. Sampling from B_η can be done [2] by computing $\sum_{i=0}^{\eta-1}(b_i - b_i')$ where the bits $b_i, b_i' \in \{0,1\}$ are uniform independent. If v is an element of R, we write $v \leftarrow B_\eta$ to mean that $v \in R$ is generated from a distribution where each of its coefficients is generated according to B_η. For a fixed $\overrightarrow{\mathbf{s}} \leftarrow B_\eta^d$, let $D_{\mathbf{s}, B_\eta^d}$ be the distribution over the pairs $(\mathbf{A}, \mathbf{A}\overrightarrow{\mathbf{s}} + \overrightarrow{\mathbf{e}}) \in R_q^{d \times d} \times R_q^d$, where $\mathbf{A} \xleftarrow{\$} R_q^{d \times d}$ is chosen uniformly at random and $\overrightarrow{\mathbf{e}} \leftarrow B_\eta^d$ is independent of $\mathbf{A}$.

Lemma 2.4 ([6]). *If $\mathbf{u}$ and $\mathbf{v} \in R_q = \frac{\mathbb{Z}_q[x]}{(x^n+1)}$ then $||\mathbf{u} \cdot \mathbf{v}|| \leq \sqrt{n} \cdot ||\mathbf{u}|| \cdot ||\mathbf{v}||$ and $||\mathbf{u} \cdot \mathbf{v}||_\infty \leq n \cdot ||\mathbf{u}||_\infty \cdot ||\mathbf{v}||_\infty$.*

Definition 2.4 (The Decision Module Learning with Errors (DMLWE**) Assumption** [14]**).** *The* DMLWE *problem is to distinguish between polynomial independent samples from $D_{\mathbf{s}, B_\eta^d}$ and the same number of independent samples from an oracle $\mathcal{U}$ that returns uniform random samples from $R_q^{d \times d} \times R_q^d$.*

Definition 2.5 Module Pairing with Errors (MPWE**) Assumption** [14]**).** *Let $\mathcal{A}$ be a PPT adversary and $\mathbf{A} \xleftarrow{\$} R_q^{d \times d}$, $\overrightarrow{\boldsymbol{x}} \xleftarrow{\$} R_q^d$, $\overrightarrow{\mathbf{s}}, \overrightarrow{\mathbf{e}} \leftarrow B_\eta^d$, $\mathbf{e}_\sigma \leftarrow B_\eta$. The goal of the adversary $\mathcal{A}$ is to find a value $\mathbf{k} \in \mathbb{Z}_m^n$ by taking inputs of the form $(\mathbf{A}, \overrightarrow{\boldsymbol{x}}, \overrightarrow{\boldsymbol{y}}, \mathbf{v}) \in R_q^{d \times d} \times R_q^d \times R_q^d \times \mathbb{Z}_g^n$ which satisfies* $\mathsf{Con}(\mathsf{params}, \overrightarrow{\boldsymbol{x}}^T\overrightarrow{\mathbf{s}} + \mathbf{e}_\sigma) = (\mathbf{k}, \mathbf{v}) \in \mathbb{Z}_m^n \times \mathbb{Z}_g^n$ *and $\overrightarrow{\boldsymbol{y}} = \mathbf{A}^T\overrightarrow{\mathbf{s}} + \overrightarrow{\mathbf{e}}$ where* $\mathsf{params} = (q, m, g, \ell, \mathsf{aux} = (q', \alpha, \beta))$ *is defined in Sect. 2.1. We define the advantage of $\mathcal{A}$ as $\mathsf{Adv}_{R_q,\mathcal{A}}^{\mathsf{MPWE}}(1^\lambda) = Pr[\mathbf{k} \leftarrow \mathcal{A}(\mathbf{A}, \overrightarrow{\boldsymbol{x}}, \overrightarrow{\boldsymbol{y}}, \mathbf{v})]$. Let $\mathsf{Adv}_{R_q}^{\mathsf{MPWE}}(t, N) = \max_{\mathcal{A}}\{\mathsf{Adv}_{R_q,\mathcal{A}}^{\mathsf{MPWE}}(1^\lambda)\}$ where the maximum is taken over all adversaries of time complexity at most t that output a list containing at most N elements of $\{0,1\}^n$. The* MPWE *assumption states that, $\mathsf{Adv}_{R_q}^{\mathsf{MPWE}}(t, N)$ is negligible in λ.*

2.3 Hash Function

Definition 2.6 *A collection of functions is called a (m, n)- family of hash functions $\mathcal{H}$ if all of its functions take binary strings of length m as input and return binary strings of length n as output.*

Definition 2.7 *A family of hash functions $\mathcal{H}$ is collision resistant* (CR) *if for all PPT adversaries $\mathcal{A}$, there is a negligible function $\epsilon(\lambda)$ such that $Pr[\mathsf{Exp}^{\mathsf{CR}}_{\mathcal{H},\mathcal{A}}(\lambda) = 1] \le \epsilon(\lambda)$ where the experiment $\mathsf{Exp}^{\mathsf{CR}}_{H,\mathcal{A}}(\lambda)$ between the adversary $\mathcal{A}$ and the challenger $\mathcal{C}$ is described in Fig. 1.*

Setup: The challenger $\mathcal{C}$ samples a hash function H uniformly sampled from $\mathcal{H}$.
Guess: The adversary $\mathcal{A}$ outputs u, v.
End: The challenger $\mathcal{C}$ outputs 1 if ($u \neq v$ and $H(u) = H(v)$) ; otherwise, it returns 0.

Fig. 1. CR security experiment $\mathsf{Exp}^{\mathsf{CR}}_{\Pi,\mathcal{A}}(\lambda)$ of hash function $H \in \mathcal{H}$

Definition 2.8 ([10]). *An (m, n)-family of hash functions $\mathcal{H}$ is $\oplus$-linear if for all $M, M' \in \{0,1\}^m$, it holds that $H(M \oplus M') = H(M) \oplus H(M')$ for all $H \in \mathcal{H}$.*

2.4 Security Model of Identity-Binding PAKE

We describe below the security model for the Identity-binding PAKE protocol following Lian et al. [12] which is an adaptation of the originally proposed model by Bellare, Pointcheval and Rogaway [4]. We employ the following symbols and conventions to describe the security model. Let U^i_A represent i-th instance of user U_A. Also assume that sk^i_A denotes the session key, sid^i_A signifies the session identity, pid^i_A refers to the partner identity and acc^i_A denotes a binary variable taking values 0 or 1, indicating whether the session terminated normally (set to 1) or not (set to 0) of user U_A for instance U^i_A after execution of the protocol.

Definition 2.9 *[Partnering] Two instances U^i_A and U^j_B are considered partners if they are in the accepted state i.e. $\mathsf{acc}^i_A = 1$ and $\mathsf{acc}^i_B = 1$, $\mathsf{pid}^i_A = U^j_B$ and $\mathsf{pid}^j_B = U^i_A$, $\mathsf{sid}^i_A = \mathsf{sid}^j_B = \mathsf{sid}$ and this value is not empty and no other instance accepts with a session identity* sid.

Definition 2.10 *[Freshness] We refer to an instance U^i_A as fresh if i) $\mathsf{acc}^i_A = 1$ and the adversary did not make $\mathsf{Reveal}(U^i_A)$ query to U^i_A, ii) if $\mathsf{pid}^i_A = U^j_B$ then the adversary did not make the query $\mathsf{Reveal}(U^j_B)$ to U^j_B.*

Security game: This security is modeled as a game played between a challenger $\mathcal{C}$ and a PPT adversary $\mathcal{A}$ described below. During the game, a user can associate with an unlimited number of user instances U^i_A where i is a positive integer.

Setup: The challenger $\mathcal{C}$ takes on the role of running the protocol on behalf of honest users, effectively generating network traffic for the adversary $\mathcal{A}$. When an instance U_A^i is in an acceptance state ($\mathsf{acc}_A^i = 1$) possesses a partner identity pid_A^i, a session identity sid_A^i and a session key sk_A^i.
Oracle access: We suppose the adversary $\mathcal{A}$ regulates all network communications. $\mathcal{A}$ is permitted to simultaneously and in any sequence query the following oracles, enabling it to observe, intercept and manipulate all messages.

- $\mathsf{Send}(U_A^i, M)$: This query enables the adversary to transmit a message M to the entity U_A^i and subsequently receive the response from U_A^i. This query simulates an active attack.
- $\mathsf{Execute}(U_A^i, U_B^j)$: This oracle query provides a record of all messages transmitted between two specific instances, denoted as U_A^i and U_B^j, during the execution of a protocol. The adversary can observe and record all messages exchanged between two unused instances U_A^i and U_B^j during the protocol execution. This scenario simulates passive attacks.
- $\mathsf{Reveal}(U_A^i)$: This oracle allows the adversary to obtain the session key sk_A^i of an instances U_A^i. It models an adversary's ability to access session keys.
- $\mathsf{Corrupt}(U_A^i)$: This oracle simulates the ability of the adversary to corrupt client U_A^i. The adversary receives the password file of instance U_A^i containing values related to the password and identity. However, it cannot access any other internal state of U_A^i. This query ensures perfect forward secrecy.
- $\mathsf{Test}(U_A^i)$: This oracle query is allowed only once to query a fresh instance. At the onset, it randomly selects a bit $b \in \{0, 1\}$. If the session key hasn't been set or if the instance U_A^i (or its partner) is not fresh according to a specific Definition 2.10, then the oracle returns $\perp$ indicating failure. Otherwise, it returns a randomly chosen key if $b = 0$ and the actual session key if $b = 1$.

Ending the game: The adversary $\mathcal{A}$ terminates the game by outputting a single guess bit b' for b.

Definition 2.11 *[*PAKE *Security] If $b' = b$ then the experiment* $\mathsf{Exp}_{\mathcal{A}}^{\mathsf{PAKE}}(\lambda)$ *outputs 1; otherwise 0. The advantage of an adversary in breaking the semantic security of a* PAKE *protocol, denoted by* $\mathsf{Adv}_{\mathcal{A}}(\lambda)$, *is defined as* $\mathsf{Adv}_{\mathcal{A}}(\lambda) = Pr[\mathsf{Exp}_{\mathcal{A}}^{\mathsf{PAKE}}(\lambda) = 1]$. *A* PAKE *protocol is said to be secure if* $\mathsf{Adv}_{\mathcal{A}}(\lambda)$ *is negligible.*

Definition 2.12 *[Identity Privacy] A* PAKE *protocol is said to achieve identity privacy if the transmission data and password file do not leak any identity information of the participants.*

3 LPAKE: Lattice-Based Identity-Binding PAKE

3.1 Protocol Description

System parameter generation. Let λ be a security parameter and user identity $\mathsf{id} \in \{0,1\}^\lambda$. A third party runs the setup algorithm $\mathsf{Setup}(1^\lambda)$ of ONKC defined in Sect. 2.1 and generates $\mathsf{params} = (q, m, g, \ell, \mathsf{aux} = \{q', \alpha, \beta\})$ where $q, m, g, \ell, q', \alpha$ and β are defined in Sect. 2.1. Let $\mathbf{A}$ be a matrix chosen uniformly at random from $R_q^{d\times d}$ and given to all users. We consider the centered binomial distribution B_η of width η for a positive integer η. Let $\Pi_{\mathrm{E}} = (\mathsf{KGen}, \mathsf{Enc}, \mathsf{Dec})$ be a private key encryption scheme with key space $\mathcal{K} = \{0,1\}^\lambda$, message space $\mathcal{M} = T \times R_q \times B_\eta^d \times B_\eta^d$ and ciphertext space $\mathcal{B}$ where T is the set of timestamps. A timestamp is a combination of date and time with date first. We consider two cryptographic hash functions $H : \{0,1\}^* \to \{0,1\}^{p(\lambda)}$ and $H_1 : \{0,1\}^* \to R_q$ modeled as random oracles where $p(\lambda)$ is the length of the session key which is a polynomial in λ and $H_2 : R_q \to \{0,1\}^\lambda$ be $\oplus$-linear hash function (see Definition 2.8). Let $\mathsf{crs} = (\lambda, \eta, q, \mathbf{A}, H, H_1, H_2, \mathsf{params})$ be the system parameter and is made public to all users.

- **Offline phase (Password file derivation):** In this phase, the user performs pre-computation to obtain a password file on input password pw_A, its identity id_A and a random salt $\mathbf{s}_A$.
  - Registration of U_A: The user U_A with its password $\mathsf{pw}_A \in \mathcal{D}$ and identity $\mathsf{id}_A \in \{0,1\}^\lambda$ randomly selects a salt $\mathbf{s}_A$ from $R_q = \frac{\mathbb{Z}_q[x]}{(x^n+1)}$, computes $\mathsf{sw}_A = H_1(\mathsf{pw}_A) \oplus \mathbf{s}_A \in R_q$ and $\mathsf{sd}_A = H_2(\mathbf{s}_A) \oplus \mathsf{id}_A \in \{0,1\}^\lambda$ and sets the password file $\mathsf{File}_A = \langle(\mathsf{sw}_A, \mathsf{sd}_A)\rangle$.
- **Online phase (Authenticated key exchange):** This is an online phase. It executes between i-th instance of user U_A and j-th instance of user U_B to achieve mutual authentication and generate a shared session key using the public parameter $\mathsf{crs} = (\lambda, \eta, q, \mathbf{A}, H, H_1, H_2, \mathsf{params})$.
  - Initiated: The i-th instance of user U_A with timestamp $t_A \in T$ and partner U_B in the current session retrieves its password file $\mathsf{File}_A = \langle(\mathsf{sw}_A, \mathsf{sd}_A)\rangle$, randomly selects $\overrightarrow{\mathbf{r}_A} \leftarrow B_\eta^d$ and $\overrightarrow{\mathbf{e}_A} \leftarrow B_\eta^d$, computes $\overrightarrow{\mathbf{y}_A} = \mathbf{A}\overrightarrow{\mathbf{r}_A} + \overrightarrow{\mathbf{e}_A} \in R_q^d$ and $\mathbf{x}_A = H_2(\mathsf{sw}_A) \oplus H_2(H_1(\overrightarrow{\mathbf{r}_A} \| \overrightarrow{\mathbf{e}_A})) \in \{0,1\}^\lambda$ and sends $(\mathbf{x}_A, \overrightarrow{\mathbf{y}_A}, t_A)$ to U_B.
  - Response: On receiving $(\mathbf{x}_A, \overrightarrow{\mathbf{y}_A}, t_A)$ from U_A, the user U_B aborts if the timestamp $t_A \in T$ is not fresh. Otherwise, retrieves its password file $\mathsf{File}_B = \langle(\mathsf{sw}_B, \mathsf{sd}_B)\rangle$ and executes the following steps:
    i. Randomly selects $\overrightarrow{\mathbf{r}_B} \leftarrow B_\eta^d$ and $\overrightarrow{\mathbf{e}_B} \leftarrow B_\eta^d$ and computes $\overrightarrow{\mathbf{y}_B} = \mathbf{A}^T\overrightarrow{\mathbf{r}_B} + \overrightarrow{\mathbf{e}_B} \in R_q^d$, $\mathbf{x}_B = H_2(\mathsf{sw}_B) \oplus H_2(H_1(\overrightarrow{\mathbf{r}_B} \| \overrightarrow{\mathbf{e}_B})) \in \{0,1\}^\lambda$.
    ii. It then selects $\mathbf{e}_\sigma \leftarrow B_\eta$ and calculates $\boldsymbol{\sigma}_B = \overrightarrow{\mathbf{y}_A}^T\overrightarrow{\mathbf{r}_B} + \mathbf{e}_\sigma \in R_q$ and $\mathsf{ONKC.Con}(\mathsf{params}, \boldsymbol{\sigma}_B) = (\mathbf{k}_B, \boldsymbol{v}) \in \mathbb{Z}_m^n \times \mathbb{Z}_g^n$.
    iii. Finally, it sets $\mathsf{tk}_B = \mathbf{x}_A \oplus \mathsf{sd}_B \oplus \mathsf{id}_B \oplus H_2(H_1(\overrightarrow{\mathbf{r}_B} \| \overrightarrow{\mathbf{e}_B})) \oplus H_2(H_1(\mathbf{k}_B)) \in \{0,1\}^\lambda$, computes a ciphertext $\Pi_{\mathrm{E}}.\mathsf{Enc}(\mathsf{tk}_B, (t_B, \mathsf{sw}_B, \overrightarrow{\mathbf{r}_B}, \overrightarrow{\mathbf{e}_B})) \to C_B \in \mathcal{B}$ and sends $(\mathbf{x}_B, \overrightarrow{\mathbf{y}_B}, C_B, \boldsymbol{v})$ to U_A.

– Initiator finish: On receiving $(\mathbf{x}_B, \overrightarrow{\mathbf{y}_B}, C_B, \boldsymbol{v})$ from U_B, the i-th instance of the user U_A computes $\boldsymbol{\sigma}_A = \overrightarrow{\mathbf{r}_A}^T \overrightarrow{\mathbf{y}_B} \in R_q$ and $\mathbf{k}_A = \mathsf{ONKC.Rec}(\mathsf{params}, \boldsymbol{\sigma}_A, \boldsymbol{v}) \in \mathbb{Z}_g^n$, sets $\mathsf{tk}_A = \mathbf{x}_B \oplus \mathsf{sd}_A \oplus \mathsf{id}_A \oplus H_2(H_1(\overrightarrow{\mathbf{r}_A} || \overrightarrow{\mathbf{e}_A})) \oplus H_2(H_1(\mathbf{k}_A)) \in \{0,1\}^\lambda$, proceeds to decrypt the received ciphertext C_B by running $\Pi_{\mathrm{E}}.\mathsf{Dec}(\mathsf{tk}_A, C_B) \rightarrow (\widehat{t_B}, \widehat{\mathsf{sw}_B}, \overrightarrow{\rho_B}, \overrightarrow{\xi_B})$ and aborts if $\widehat{t_B}$ is not fresh. Otherwise, U_A verifies whether $\overrightarrow{\mathbf{y}_B} = \mathbf{A}^T \overrightarrow{\rho_B} + \overrightarrow{\xi_B} \in R_q$ and $\mathbf{x}_B = H_2(\widehat{\mathsf{sw}_B}) \oplus H_2(H_1(\overrightarrow{\rho_B} || \overrightarrow{\xi_B})) \in \{0,1\}^\lambda$. If the verification fails then aborts. Otherwise, it computes ciphertext $\Pi_{\mathrm{E}}.\mathsf{Enc}(\mathsf{tk}_A, (t_A, \mathsf{sw}_A, \overrightarrow{\mathbf{r}_A}, \overrightarrow{\mathbf{e}_A})) \rightarrow C_A$ and sends it to U_B. Finally, it sets the session identity $\mathsf{sid}_A^i = \mathbf{x}_A || \overrightarrow{\mathbf{y}_A} || \mathbf{x}_B || \overrightarrow{\mathbf{y}_B}$ and computes session key $\mathsf{sk}_A^i = H(\mathsf{tk}_A || \mathsf{sid}_A^i) \in \{0,1\}^{p(\lambda)}$.
– Responder finish: Upon receiving C_A from U_A the device U_B decrypts the ciphertext C_A by running $\Pi_{\mathrm{E}}.\mathsf{Dec}(\mathsf{tk}_B, C_A) \rightarrow (\widehat{t_A}, \widehat{\mathsf{sw}_A}, \overrightarrow{\rho_A}, \overrightarrow{\xi_A})$. If $t_A = \widehat{t_A}$ then U_B proceeds to verify the conditions $\overrightarrow{\mathbf{y}_A} = \mathbf{A}\overrightarrow{\rho_A} + \overrightarrow{\xi_A} \in R_q$ and $\mathbf{x}_A = H_2(\widehat{\mathsf{sw}_A}) \oplus H_2(H_1(\overrightarrow{\rho_A} || \overrightarrow{\xi_A})) \in \{0,1\}^\lambda$. If the verification fails then it aborts. Otherwise, it sets the session identity $\mathsf{sid}_B^j = \mathbf{x}_A || \overrightarrow{\mathbf{y}_A} || \mathbf{x}_B || \overrightarrow{\mathbf{y}_B}$ and the session key $\mathsf{sk}_B^j = H(\mathsf{tk}_B || \mathsf{sid}_B^j) \in \{0,1\}^{p(\lambda)}$.

3.2 Correctness and Security

Lemma 3.1. *If $\overrightarrow{\mathbf{e}}$ and $\overrightarrow{\mathbf{r}}$ in B_η^d then $|\overrightarrow{\mathbf{e}}^T \overrightarrow{\mathbf{r}}|_q \leq nd\eta^2$.*

Proof. Let $\overrightarrow{\mathbf{e}}^T = (\mathbf{e}_1, \ldots, \mathbf{e}_d)$ and $\overrightarrow{\mathbf{r}}^T = (\mathbf{r}_1, \ldots, \mathbf{r}_d)$ where $\mathbf{e}_i, \mathbf{r}_i \in R_q$ for $i = 1, \ldots, d$. So, $\overrightarrow{\mathbf{e}}^T \overrightarrow{\mathbf{r}} = \sum_{i=1}^d \mathbf{r}_i \cdot \mathbf{e}_i \in R_q$. Observe that, $|\overrightarrow{\mathbf{e}}^T \overrightarrow{\mathbf{r}}|_q \leq ||\overrightarrow{\mathbf{e}}^T \overrightarrow{\mathbf{r}}||_\infty$ and $||\overrightarrow{\mathbf{e}}^T \overrightarrow{\mathbf{r}}||_\infty \leq d\, ||\mathbf{r}_i \cdot \mathbf{e}_i||_\infty$. By using Lemma 2.4 we get $||\mathbf{r}_i \cdot \mathbf{e}_i||_\infty \leq n ||\mathbf{r}_i||_\infty \cdot ||\mathbf{e}_i||_\infty$. By combining all, $|\overrightarrow{\mathbf{e}}^T \overrightarrow{\mathbf{r}}|_q \leq dn ||\mathbf{r}_i||_\infty \cdot ||\mathbf{e}_i||_\infty$ which in turn, $|\overrightarrow{\mathbf{e}}^T \mathbf{r}|_q \leq nd\eta^2$ since $||\mathbf{r}_i||_\infty \leq \eta, ||\mathbf{e}_i||_\infty \leq \eta$ as $\overrightarrow{\mathbf{e}}$ and $\overrightarrow{\mathbf{r}}$ are in B_η^d.

Theorem 3.2. *Let q be an odd prime and m, g, ℓ are positive integers satisfying $2 \leq m, g \leq q, 0 \leq \ell \leq \lfloor \frac{q}{2} \rfloor$ and $2nd\eta^2 + \eta \leq \ell < \frac{q(1-1/g)-m}{2m}$. Let two parties U_A and U_B have the same shared password $\mathsf{pw}_A = \mathsf{pw}_B$ and they establish a session key by honestly following the lattice-based* PAKE *protocol* (LPAKE). *Then they will share a common session key and session identity at the end of the protocol with overwhelming probability, i.e.* $\mathsf{sk}_A^i = \mathsf{sk}_B^j$ *and* $\mathsf{sid}_A^i = \mathsf{sid}_B^j$.

Proof. The proof of the Theorem 3.2 is omitted due to page restrictions and will appear in the full version of the paper.

Theorem 3.3. *The Lattice-based identity-binding* PAKE *protocol* LPAKE *is secure as per the security model presented in Sect. 2.4 provided the authenticated encryption Π_{E} =* (KGen, Enc, Dec) *is* CCA *secure and unforgeable, the* DMLWE *assumption (in Definition 2.4), the* MPWE *assumption (in Definition 2.5) holds, the hash function H_2 is a $\oplus$-linear collision-resistance hash function (see Sect. 2.3) and the hash functions H and H_1 are modeled as random oracles.*

Proof. The proof of the Theorem 3.3 will appear in the full version of the paper.

Theorem 3.4. *The* LPAKE *protocol does not leak the identity* (id_A *or* id_A) *of the participants during the online or offline phase and it also satisfies mutual authentication and resistance to pre-computation attacks.*

Proof. The proof of the Theorem 3.4 will appear in the full version of the paper.

Acknowledgements. This work is supported in part by the National Natural Science Foundation of China (62372040) and the National Key Research and Development Program of China (2023YFB2704000).

References

1. Abdalla, M., Eisenhofer, T., Kiltz, E., Kunzweiler, S., Riepel, D.: Password-authenticated key exchange from group actions. In: Annual International Cryptology Conference, pp. 699–728. Springer (2022)
2. Alkim, E., Ducas, L., Pöppelmann, T., Schwabe, P.: Post-quantum key {Exchange-A} new hope. In: 25th USENIX Security Symposium (USENIX Security 2016), pp. 327–343 (2016)
3. Azarderakhsh, R., Jao, D., Koziel, B., LeGrow, J.T., Soukharev, V., Taraskin, O.: How not to create an isogeny-based PAKE. In: Applied Cryptography and Network Security: 18th International Conference, ACNS 2020, Part I, Rome, Italy, 19–22 October 2020, pp. 169–186. Springer (2020)
4. Bellare, M., Pointcheval, D., Rogaway, P.: Authenticated key exchange secure against dictionary attacks. In: International Conference on the Theory and Applications of Cryptographic Techniques, pp. 139–155. Springer (2000)
5. Bellovin,S.M., Merritt, M.: Encrypted key exchange: password-based protocols secure against dictionary attacks (1992)
6. Ding, J., Alsayigh, S., Lancrenon, J., Rv, S., Snook, M.: Provably secure password authenticated key exchange based on RLWE for the post-quantum world. In: Cryptographers' Track at the RSA conference, pp. 183–204. Springer (2017)
7. Jarecki, S., Krawczyk, H., Xu,J.: OPAQUE: an asymmetric PAKE protocol secure against pre-computation attacks. In: Advances in Cryptology–EUROCRYPT 2018: 37th Annual International Conference on the Theory and Applications of Cryptographic Techniques, Part III, Tel Aviv, Israel, 29 April–3 May 2018, pp. 456–486. Springer (2018)
8. Jin, Z., Zhao,Y.: Optimal key consensus in presence of noise. arXiv preprint arXiv:1611.06150 (2016)
9. Katz, J., Vaikuntanathan,V.: Smooth projective hashing and password-based authenticated key exchange from lattices. In: International Conference on the Theory and Application of Cryptology and Information Security, pp. 636–652. Springer (2009)
10. Krawczyk, H.: LFSR-based hashing and authentication. In: Annual International Cryptology Conference, pp. 129–139. Springer (1994)
11. Li, Z., Wang, D.: Achieving one-round password-based authenticated key exchange over lattices. IEEE Trans. Serv. Comput. **15**(1), 308–321 (2019)
12. Lian, H., Yang, Y., Zhao, Y.: Efficient and strong symmetric password authenticated key exchange with identity privacy for IoT. IEEE Internet Things J. **10**(6), 4725–4734 (2022)

13. Naor, M., Paz, S., Ronen, E.: CRISP: compromise resilient identity-based symmetric PAKE. IACR Cryptol. ePrint Arch. **2020**, 529 (2020)
14. Ren,P., Gu, X.: Practical post-quantum password-authenticated key exchange based-on module-lattice. In: International Conference on Information Security and Cryptology, pp. 137–156. Springer (2021)
15. Terada, S., Yoneyama, K.: Password-based authenticated key exchange from standard isogeny assumptions. In: Provable Security: 13th International Conference, ProvSec 2019, Cairns, QLD, Australia, 1–4 October 2019, pp. 41–56. Springer (2019)

Author Index

J. K. Liu et al. (Eds.): ProvSec 2024, LNCS 14904, pp. 311–312, 2025.
https://doi.org/10.1007/978-981-96-0957-4

Printed in the United States
by Baker & Taylor Publisher Services

Printed in the United States
by Baker & Taylor Publisher Services